AUDITING A Risk Analysis Approach

The Robert N. Anthony/Willard J. Graham Series in Accounting

AUDITING A Risk Analysis Approach

Michael Grobstein, CPA

Vice Chairman—Accounting and Auditing Services
Ernst & Whinney

Stephen E. Loeb, Ph.D., CPA

Professor of Accounting
Ernst & Whinney Alumni Research Fellow
The University of Maryland

Robert D. Neary, CPA

Co-Chairman—Professional Services
Ernst & Whinney

1985

RICHARD D. IRWIN, INC. Homewood, Illinois 60430

ISBN 0-256-02791-9

Library of Congress Catalog Card No. 84–80814

Printed in the United States of America

1 2 3 4 5 6 7 8 9 0 K 2 1 0 9 8 7 6 5

PREFACE

Auditing: A Risk Analysis Approach is a "state-of-the-art" approach to financial auditing with a student-oriented pedagogy. The approach of the book is risk analysis, which operationalizes *Statement on Auditing Standards No. 47*, "Audit Risk and Materiality in Conducting an Audit." We feel that this orientation, which was pioneered by Ernst & Whinney, reflects the direction that financial auditing will take in the foreseeable future. The book is a blend of practice and theory with much of the content taken from Ernst & Whinney training manuals and other Ernst & Whinney publications.

The risk analysis approach to auditing is a "custom-design" approach to auditing, i.e., it is an approach that is tailored to fit the characteristics of each audit client. The thought process that underlies this approach is called "risk analysis." A set of specialized planning working papers is used to develop a formal risk analysis that focuses on the combined impact of a client's operating environment, financial and operating results, and system of internal controls for each important account in the financial statements.

KEY FEATURES OF THE RISK ANALYSIS APPROACH

The risk analysis approach is based on a thorough, up-to-date understanding of an entity's business and industry. Key features of the approach include:

A systematic approach to planning is used in which the independent auditor acquires an overall understanding of a company's business.

An evaluation of internal control is made from a business perspective. The approach focuses on what the accounting system is designed to do in each operating component of the business and then considers how well the controls function. This approach enables the independent auditor to minimize audit time in areas where controls are effective and concentrate on areas with higher potential for error.

Analytical review procedures are applied in all phases of an audit, to see that financial and operating trends and relationships make sense. This increases the effectiveness of planning and minimizes detail testing.

Comparison to Other Approaches

The risk analysis approach provides a broader perspective than the traditional "balance sheet" approach, which emphasizes the details of year-end financial statement balances, or the "transaction cycle" approach, which focuses on whether controls are in place at various points in a company's transaction flow. The matrix presented below contrasts the three approaches to auditing:

	Balance Sheet Approach	*Transaction Cycle Approach*	*New Risk Analysis Approach*
Overall Framework	Financial statement balances	Major transaction flows (e.g., sales, receipts)	Business operating components (e.g., sales, production, finance, administration
Approach to Evaluating Internal Control	One series of standard control objectives or questionnaire related to financial statement captions	Standard control objectives or questionnaire based on transaction cycles	Customized control objectives derived from operating components and related to specific accounts
Approach to Risk Analysis and Audit Program	Standard procedures related to specific financial statement balances	Detail analysis of risks in accounting system and correlation to related tests; general risk analysis of other factors without direct correlation to audit program	Formalized analysis and direct correlation of environmental factors, operating and financial data, and system evaluation to audit program for specific aspects of important accounts

ORGANIZATION

The book may be thought of as consisting of seven parts.

Part I (Chapters 1 and 2) discusses the auditing environment. Chapter 1 is an introduction to both auditing and the public accounting profession.

Coverage includes the nature of auditing, the public accounting profession, corporate audit committees, the AICPA, the FASB, auditing standards, and the auditor's report. Chapter 2 provides an overview of the audit process, introduces the concept of risk analysis, and also discusses audit evidence and audit working papers.

Part II (Chapters 3–7) covers the components of the "initial planning" and "program development" phases of the audit process. Chapter 3 discusses planning and environmental considerations. Chapter 4 discusses the evaluation of accounting systems. Included in this chapter are discussions of internal control, the documentation of accounting systems, and the updating of systems evaluations. Chapter 4 contains two appendices—the first is an example of a Control Environment Questionnaire and the second is a discussion of flowcharting.

Chapter 5 discusses the evaluation of a computerized accounting system. The chapter also contains a unique appendix on computer fraud. Chapter 6 contains a detailed discussion of analytical review, and Chapter 7 discusses the preparation of the audit program.

Part III covers statistical sampling and includes chapters 8 and 9. Chapter 8 provides an introduction to statistical sampling including attribute sampling. Chapter 9 discusses probability proportional to size and variables estimation sampling.

Part IV (Chapters 10–15) considers the detailed audit procedures. Chapter 10 discusses the audit of the sales component and covers sales, receivables, and cash receipts. Chapter 11 discusses the materials, labor, and overhead portions of the production or service component. Chapter 12 covers the audit of inventory and property, plant, and equipment portions of the production or service component audit. Chapter 13 discusses the audit of the finance component. Included are discussions of the audit of cash balances, notes receivable, marketable securities, debt and lease obligations, and shareholders' equity. Chapter 14 includes consideration of the audit of the administrative component—general and administrative expenses, prepaid and deferred items, other assets, income taxes, and accrued liabilities. Also covered in this chapter are the audit aspects relating to commitments and contingencies, related party transactions, illegal acts by clients, corporate minutes, subsequent events, letters of representation, use of internal auditors, outside specialists, segment information, and interim financial information.

Chapter 15 covers the application of the risk analysis approach to small businesses. This chapter presents a modified version of the risk analysis approach that considers the effectiveness of owner/management involvement in minimizing the likelihood of material error in small privately owned businesses even though formal control or adequate segregation of duties may not be present.

Part V (Chapters 16–18) considers the communications of independent auditors. Chapter 16 discusses the auditor's report, while Chapter 17 covers special reports and unaudited financial statements.

Chapter 18 includes an extended discussion of management letters, along with numerous examples. This often neglected area is of vital importance in today's public accounting environment.

Part VI (Chapters 19 and 20) contains a discussion of social control and the public accounting profession. Chapter 19 considers professional ethics and accountants' legal liability. Chapter 20 discusses the SEC and the independent auditor.

Part VII consists of the three appendices at the end of the text which are key aspects of understanding and using the risk analysis approach. The appendices provide lists of (1) environmental factors to consider, (2) key attributes that may exist in a system of internal accounting control, and (3) analytical data that may be useful.

There are numerous questions and problems at the end of each chapter. Some of these questions and problems have been taken or adapted from CPA examinations. Others are based on material developed by Ernst & Whinney.

The material is current, reflecting professional pronouncements through June 1984.

ACKNOWLEDGMENTS

A number of individuals made contributions to the writing of this book. A special acknowledgment is due to Professor Roger H. Hermanson, Ernst & Whinney Alumni Professor and Research Professor of Accounting, Georgia State University, and Professor Robert H. Strawser, the Arthur Andersen & Co. Former Students Professor of Accounting, Texas A & M University, both of whom collaborated with us on this project.

We are indebted to a number of present and former Ernst & Whinney executives and staff for their contributions that helped in the development of this book. John M. Saada played a major role in the initiation and development of this present book. Matthew D. Shedd had a major role in the development of the Ernst & Whinney audit approach, on which this book is based. Two individuals—Paul W. Craig and Mark J. MacGuidwin—participated in the development and writing of a number of chapters, appendices, and questions and problems and their related solutions. Special thanks are also due John G. Baab, David A. Brown, Harry Brown, Richard D. Hissam, Michael J. Jett, William H. Marquard, Daniel D. Montgomery, David H. Morton, Steven M. Paroby, and William G. Roost.

Finally, we acknowledge the many other individuals at Ernst & Whinney who played a part in the development of the book by doing typing, proofing, editing, and so on.

A number of academics provided useful guidance to the authors in the development of the manuscript. These individuals include Richard Asebrook (University of Massachusetts, Amherst), Virginia Bakay (University of Nevada, Las Vegas), Donald Berquist (University of Akron), S. Michael Groomer (Indiana University), Allen W. McConnell (University of Northern Colorado), Frederick L. Neumann (University of Illinois), Blaine Ritts (Bowling Green State University), and Carl Warren (University of Georgia).

Part of the material on legal liability in Chapter 19 was written from material originally developed by Professor Arthur J. Francia of the University of Houston.

We appreciate the permission given by copyright holders for the use of material. Our special thanks go to the American Institute of Certified Public Accountants for granting permission to use material from their various publications (including CPA examinations).

A brief article drawn from this text appeared in Volume 3, Number 2 (Spring 1984) of *Auditing: A Journal of Practice and Theory*. That article was authored by Michael Grobstein and Paul W. Craig and is entitled "A Risk Analysis Approach to Auditing."

Finally, we accept responsibility for any shortcomings in the book. If you have suggestions for improvement, please contact us.

Michael Grobstein
Stephen E. Loeb
Robert D. Neary

CONTENTS

AUDITING A Risk Analysis Approach

INTRODUCTION TO AUDITING AND THE PUBLIC ACCOUNTING PROFESSION

The environment in which businesses operate has become increasingly complex. For companies to survive in this environment, management must (1) identify and deal with business risks, (2) control costs, (3) manage liquidity, and (4) gain a competitive advantage—all under intense scrutiny from shareholders, creditors, and regulators. The result is that management's attention is focused on planning and setting company objectives, designing systems that contribute to operating efficiency, and obtaining reliable operating and financial information to be able to effectively monitor and evaluate results. Various types of auditors, both internal and external to the firm, assist management in achieving the company's objectives; dealing with business risks; and reporting results to shareholders, creditors, and regulators.

The principal focus of this textbook is on audits of financial statements performed by independent certified public accountants (CPAs). The authors take a risk analysis approach to auditing that emphasizes a formalized methodology for analyzing the risks associated with each audit. The systematic way in which the various risk factors are analyzed and integrated provides a practical and theoretically sound framework for the auditor's thought process. The focus of the risk analysis approach is on a typical commercial or industrial company's basic operating components—sales, production or service, finance, and administration.

The risk analysis approach (which is introduced in Chapter 2) differs from the "transaction cycle" and "balance sheet" perspectives traditionally used by auditors. The auditor using the risk analysis approach plans and executes the audit using the same perspective that management uses to operate the business.

This chapter defines auditing in general terms and describes some of the more common types of audits and auditors. Further, the chapter provides an introduction to the public accounting profession—specifically the qualifications of CPAs, the services they perform, their relationship to corporate audit committees, and the organizations and standards that govern their work.

1

NATURE OF AUDITING

The American Accounting Association's Committee on Basic Auditing Concepts has broadly defined auditing as:

> . . . a systematic process of objectively obtaining and evaluating evidence regarding assertions about economic actions and events to ascertain the degree of correspondence between those assertions and established criteria and communicating the results to interested users.[1]

The auditor develops the basis for the audit opinion by examining the relevant population and evaluating whether the results of the examination are consistent with the applicable criteria. Because the cost of the audit process should be commensurate with the benefit to be derived from it, the auditor generally cannot examine an entire population. Instead, the audit is restricted to examination of sample items from the population. The results of those tests enable the auditor to form an opinion on the entire population.

Financial Statement Audits

Shareholders, creditors, and regulators need a basis for assessing a company's past and present operating results and the outlook for its future. Financial statements prepared in accordance with generally accepted accounting principles (GAAP) provide the necessary information. But that information also must have credibility if it is to be accepted by third parties. Thus, the need for an independent financial statement audit arises.[2] A financial statement audit is an examination of accounting records and underlying internal controls of a business enterprise, typically performed by an indepen-

---

[1] Joseph A. Silvoso et al., "Report of the Committee on Basic Auditing Concepts," Supplement to Volume 47 of *The Accounting Review,* 1972, p. 18.

[2] See ibid., pp. 26–29.

dent CPA. Independent auditors are engaged by the shareholders, board of directors (or its audit committee), or management of a company. The objective of the independent auditor's examination is to assure that the financial statements present fairly the enterprise's financial position (balance sheet), results of operations (income statement), and changes in financial position (statement of changes in financial position) for the period under audit [See *SAS No. 1*, (AU 110.01)].

The independent auditor expresses an opinion on the financial statements in an *audit report*. This process is called attestation, and the auditor's role is referred to as the *attest function*. The American Accounting Association's Committee on Basic Auditing Concepts defines attestation as:

> . . . a communicated statement of opinion (judgment), based upon convincing evidence, by an independent, competent, authoritative person, concerning the degree of correspondence in all material respects of accounting information communicated by an entity (individual, firm, or governmental unit) with established criteria.[3]

Users of accounting information are concerned with both the information content of the subject matter and the quality of the information received. Auditing assists users in evaluating the quality of the accounting information communicated to them.[4] The auditor's report is relied on by various users of the financial statements. It is the final product of a thorough examination of the data supporting the financial statements, the steps of which are discussed in the remaining chapters.

It is important to distinguish between financial accounting and financial statement auditing. R. K. Mautz and Hussein A. Sharaf make the following distinction:

> Accounting includes the collection, classification, summarization, and communication of financial data; it involves the measurement and communication of business events and conditions as they affect and represent a given enterprise or other entity. The task of accounting is to reduce a tremendous mass of detailed information to manageable and understandable proportions. . . . Auditing must consider business events and conditions too, but it does not have the task of measuring or communicating them. Its task is to review the measurements and communications of accounting for propriety. Auditing is analytical, not constructive; it is critical, investigative, concerned with the basis for accounting measurements and assertions.[5]

To illustrate the relationship of accounting and auditing, Mautz and Sharaf draw an analogy to the relationship between an author and an editor. They point out that an author achieves his or her objective of communicating

---

[3] Ibid., p. 22.

[4] Ibid., p. 25.

[5] R. K. Mautz and Hussein A. Sharaf, *The Philosophy of Auditing* (American Accounting Association, 1961), p. 14.

to a reader by putting ideas, experiences, or results of research into writing in an organized fashion, and then submitting it to an editor. The editor has the same goal—to communicate to a reader, but his or her approach is different. The editor does not construct the document but instead challenges whether it is understandable, accurate, and consistent with the author's objective. Mautz and Sharaf conclude that writing and editing complement one another—as do accounting and auditing.[6]

CPAs are bound by a code of ethics, which will be discussed in Chapter 19. The code requires CPAs to be independent in matters relating to an audit. The code does not define independence precisely. Thus, an auditor must consider whether a reasonable person, with knowledge of all the facts, would conclude that his or her independence is impaired by a relationship with the client. For example, to be recognized as independent, an auditor should not have a financial interest in a client or a close relative in an important position with the client. It is the auditor's opinion that provides credibility to the financial information presented to shareholders, creditors, and regulators. The auditor's independence lends credibility to the opinion.

After the stock market crash of 1929, Congress enacted the Securities Act of 1933 and the Securities Exchange Act of 1934, and established the Securities and Exchange Commission (SEC). The 1933 act requires companies registering securities for public sale to provide prospective investors with certain information about the company, including audited financial statements and other financial information. The 1934 act requires SEC-registered companies to include audited financial statements in their annual reports to shareholders and provide other financial information in an annual filing to the SEC. The SEC requires that the other financial information in those reports also be examined by independent auditors. Independent auditors also examine financial information included in reports to various other governmental agencies (e.g., reports of employee benefit plans filed with the Department of Labor).

Operational Audits

Operational audits, also known as performance, management, or value-added audits, evaluate the economy (cost), efficiency, and effectiveness of an organization's operations. A 1982 report by the American Institute of Certified Public Accountants (AICPA) Special Committee on Operational and Management Auditing, entitled *Operational Audit Engagements,* states that an operational audit ". . . involves a systematic review of an organization's activities, or of a stipulated segment of them, in relation to specified objectives. The purposes of the engagement may be *(a)* to assess performance, *(b)* to identify opportunities for improvement, and *(c)* to develop recommen-

---

[6] Ibid.

dations for improvement or further action."[7] The report also discusses many of the factors to be considered in an operational audit engagement.

Compliance Audits

Compliance audits evaluate whether the company or a particular division or department is in conformity with certain rules or procedures set forth by either the company or a third party. Some examples include a company's compliance with:

Prescribed purchasing and cash disbursement procedures.

Restrictive covenants imposed by a bank in a loan agreement.

Regulatory requirements for a company in a specialized industry (e.g., compliance with the Investment Company Act of 1940 by a regulated investment company).

Fair-hiring practices in connection with a contract for the federal government.

Types of Auditors

The role of CPAs as independent auditors was described earlier. Their qualifications and other services performed will be discussed in the next section. Various other types of auditors are considered below.

Companies often employ *internal auditors* to perform audits of various accounting and operating functions within their organizations. Internal auditors normally report to a member of senior management. Internal audit staffs vary in size, as well as in the auditors' backgrounds and experience. Their principal role also varies. They often perform operational audits and typically participate in designing a company's system of internal control and monitor compliance with the system once it is in place. By performing periodic tests or reconciliations of accounting records, internal auditors may function as part of the system of internal control. In addition, they may assist the independent auditors in the conduct of the annual financial statement audit (this is discussed further in Chapter 14).

Various departments of the federal government also employ auditors. For example, the U.S. General Accounting Office (GAO) is responsible to the Congress and performs the audit function for it. *GAO auditors* audit the revenues and expenditures of various agencies of the federal government, perform operational audits of agencies, and review agency transactions for compliance with applicable laws and regulations. *Internal Revenue agents* perform a specialized type of compliance audit. They are employed by the

---

[7] AICPA Special Committee on Operational and Management Auditing, *Operational Audit Engagements*, American Institute of Certified Public Accountants, 1982, p. 2.

Internal Revenue Service (IRS), a branch of the U.S. Department of the Treasury, to audit income tax returns. Their objective is to assure that the returns have been prepared in accordance with the tax laws. Examples of other federal government departments that employ auditors are the Department of Housing and Urban Development (expenditures of grant funds) and the Department of Defense (defense contracts).

THE PUBLIC ACCOUNTING PROFESSION

Certified Public Accountants (CPAs)

CPAs are recognized as experts in accounting and auditing. An individual becomes a CPA by first passing a national uniform examination in accounting theory and practice, business law, and auditing. The examination is prepared and graded by the AICPA but administered by each jurisdiction (state, U.S. territory, or the District of Columbia). In addition to the examination, some jurisdictions require an individual to have accounting work experience (e.g., two years) before being permitted to practice as a CPA.

In 1896, the New York legislature passed the first accountancy law, legally recognizing the public accounting profession. Other states soon followed. Today, each jurisdiction has enacted public accounting legislation that is administered by a board of accountancy. It is the responsibility of each board to determine, within the standards set by law, who is qualified to sit for the CPA examination. The results of the CPA examination are communicated to the boards of accountancy, which award the CPA certificate to successful candidates.

CPAs' Services

In addition to performing independent audits of an entity's financial statements, CPAs can perform other services—as long as the services do not impair their independence. These services include reports for government agencies, compliance audits, and operational audits (discussed earlier); tax services; management advisory services; litigation support services; compilations and reviews of unaudited statements; and bookkeeping services.

Tax Services.   The basic objectives of tax services are to help clients comply with the tax law and minimize their taxes. To this end, the CPA advises on tax-saving measures, prepares and reviews tax returns, and, if necessary, accompanies the client to meetings with the IRS or to court proceedings.

Management Advisory Services.   The auditors' role as knowledgeable, independent observers provides a unique opportunity to advise clients on many matters beyond auditing and tax services. Management advisory services (MAS), also referred to as management consulting services (MCS), are important in the practices of most accounting firms, many of which have separate MAS departments. The range of services offered includes such diverse activities as accounting, cost, and budgeting systems; production planning, scheduling, and control; financial forecasts and feasibility studies; financial planning and analysis using computer modeling; pricing or rate studies (e.g., for public utilities); organizational and personnel planning; compensation program evaluations; and data systems hardware evaluation and installation and security reviews.

Litigation Support Services.   Litigating attorneys frequently must organize and analyze large quantities of financial and technical evidence, testimony, and documentation—usually under tight time constraints. In many instances, they retain the financial, accounting, and technical expertise of CPAs to assist them in analyzing and interpreting the material or to provide expert testimony.

Compilation and Review Services.   Clients frequently ask CPAs to prepare or assist in preparing financial statements that are not audited. Also, when a company does not have its interim or annual financial statements audited, it may ask independent CPAs to review and then comment on those statements.

In a *compilation* of financial statements, a CPA presents management-supplied information of a nonpublic entity in the form of financial statements without any assurance of fair presentation. In a *review* of financial statements, a CPA makes certain inquiries and performs an overall analysis of financial position and results of operations. These review procedures provide a basis for expressing limited assurances on the financial statements. Compilations and reviews are discussed in detail in Chapters 15 and 17.

Bookkeeping Services.   Some small businesses do not have their own internal accountants. Instead they rely on a CPA to periodically do some or all of their bookkeeping. The amount of this bookkeeping will depend on the accounting expertise of the businesses' owners or employees. Sometimes the accounting services are limited to preparing closing and adjusting entries and advising about unusual transactions. Bookkeeping services often are referred to as *write-up work*.

Organization of CPA Firms

CPAs practice either individually or in firms. CPA firms in the United States fall into three general categories: national firms, regional firms, and local firms. The national firms typically have offices in most major cities of the United States and, in many instances, in cities around the world.

vices (MAS), also referred to as management consulting services (MCS), are important in the practices of most accounting firms, many of which have separate MAS departments. The range of services offered includes such diverse activities as accounting, cost, and budgeting systems; production planning, scheduling, and control; financial forecasts and feasibility studies; financial planning and analysis using computer modeling; pricing or rate studies (e.g., for public utilities); organizational and personnel planning; compensation program evaluations; and data systems hardware evaluation and installation and security reviews.

Litigation Support Services. Litigating attorneys frequently must organize and analyze large quantities of financial and technical evidence, testimony, and documentation—usually under tight time constraints. In many instances, they retain the financial, accounting, and technical expertise of CPAs to assist them in analyzing and interpreting the material or to provide expert testimony.

Compilation and Review Services. Clients frequently ask CPAs to prepare or assist in preparing financial statements that are not audited. Also, when a company does not have its interim or annual financial statements audited, it may ask independent CPAs to review and then comment on those statements.

In a *compilation* of financial statements, a CPA presents management-supplied information of a nonpublic entity in the form of financial statements without any assurance of fair presentation. In a *review* of financial statements, a CPA makes certain inquiries and performs an overall analysis of financial position and results of operations. These review procedures provide a basis for expressing limited assurances on the financial statements. Compilations and reviews are discussed in detail in Chapters 15 and 17.

Bookkeeping Services. Some small businesses do not have their own internal accountants. Instead they rely on a CPA to periodically do some or all of their bookkeeping. The amount of this bookkeeping will depend on the accounting expertise of the businesses' owners or employees. Sometimes the accounting services are limited to preparing closing and adjusting entries and advising about unusual transactions. Bookkeeping services often are referred to as *write-up work*.

Organization of CPA Firms

CPAs practice either individually or in firms. CPA firms in the United States fall into three general categories: national firms, regional firms, and local firms. The national firms typically have offices in most major cities of the United States and, in many instances, in cities around the world.

to a reader by putting ideas, experiences, or results of research into writing in an organized fashion, and then submitting it to an editor. The editor has the same goal—to communicate to a reader, but his or her approach is different. The editor does not construct the document but instead challenges whether it is understandable, accurate, and consistent with the author's objective. Mautz and Sharaf conclude that writing and editing complement one another—as do accounting and auditing.[6]

CPAs are bound by a code of ethics, which will be discussed in Chapter 19. The code requires CPAs to be independent in matters relating to an audit. The code does not define independence precisely. Thus, an auditor must consider whether a reasonable person, with knowledge of all the facts, would conclude that his or her independence is impaired by a relationship with the client. For example, to be recognized as independent, an auditor should not have a financial interest in a client or a close relative in an important position with the client. It is the auditor's opinion that provides credibility to the financial information presented to shareholders, creditors, and regulators. The auditor's independence lends credibility to the opinion.

After the stock market crash of 1929, Congress enacted the Securities Act of 1933 and the Securities Exchange Act of 1934, and established the Securities and Exchange Commission (SEC). The 1933 act requires companies registering securities for public sale to provide prospective investors with certain information about the company, including audited financial statements and other financial information. The 1934 act requires SEC-registered companies to include audited financial statements in their annual reports to shareholders and provide other financial information in an annual filing to the SEC. The SEC requires that the other financial information in those reports also be examined by independent auditors. Independent auditors also examine financial information included in reports to various other governmental agencies (e.g., reports of employee benefit plans filed with the Department of Labor).

Operational Audits

Operational audits, also known as performance, management, or value-added audits, evaluate the economy (cost), efficiency, and effectiveness of an organization's operations. A 1982 report by the American Institute of Certified Public Accountants (AICPA) Special Committee on Operational and Management Auditing, entitled *Operational Audit Engagements,* states that an operational audit ". . . involves a systematic review of an organization's activities, or of a stipulated segment of them, in relation to specified objectives. The purposes of the engagement may be *(a)* to assess performance, *(b)* to identify opportunities for improvement, and *(c)* to develop recommen-

---

[6] Ibid.

dations for improvement or further action."[7] The report also discusses many of the factors to be considered in an operational audit engagement.

Compliance Audits

Compliance audits evaluate whether the company or a particular division or department is in conformity with certain rules or procedures set forth by either the company or a third party. Some examples include a company's compliance with:

Prescribed purchasing and cash disbursement procedures.

Restrictive covenants imposed by a bank in a loan agreement.

Regulatory requirements for a company in a specialized industry (e.g., compliance with the Investment Company Act of 1940 by a regulated investment company).

Fair-hiring practices in connection with a contract for the federal government.

Types of Auditors

The role of CPAs as independent auditors was described earlier. Their qualifications and other services performed will be discussed in the next section. Various other types of auditors are considered below.

Companies often employ *internal auditors* to perform audits of various accounting and operating functions within their organizations. Internal auditors normally report to a member of senior management. Internal audit staffs vary in size, as well as in the auditors' backgrounds and experience. Their principal role also varies. They often perform operational audits and typically participate in designing a company's system of internal control and monitor compliance with the system once it is in place. By performing periodic tests or reconciliations of accounting records, internal auditors may function as part of the system of internal control. In addition, they may assist the independent auditors in the conduct of the annual financial statement audit (this is discussed further in Chapter 14).

Various departments of the federal government also employ auditors. For example, the U.S. General Accounting Office (GAO) is responsible to the Congress and performs the audit function for it. *GAO auditors* audit the revenues and expenditures of various agencies of the federal government, perform operational audits of agencies, and review agency transactions for compliance with applicable laws and regulations. *Internal Revenue agents* perform a specialized type of compliance audit. They are employed by the

---

[7] AICPA Special Committee on Operational and Management Auditing, *Operational Audit Engagements,* American Institute of Certified Public Accountants, 1982, p. 2.

Internal Revenue Service (IRS), a branch of the U.S. Department of the Treasury, to audit income tax returns. Their objective is to assure that the returns have been prepared in accordance with the tax laws. Examples of other federal government departments that employ auditors are the Department of Housing and Urban Development (expenditures of grant funds) and the Department of Defense (defense contracts).

THE PUBLIC ACCOUNTING PROFESSION

Certified Public Accountants (CPAs)

CPAs are recognized as experts in accounting and auditing. An individual becomes a CPA by first passing a national uniform examination in accounting theory and practice, business law, and auditing. The examination is prepared and graded by the AICPA but administered by each jurisdiction (state, U.S. territory, or the District of Columbia). In addition to the examination, some jurisdictions require an individual to have accounting work experience (e.g., two years) before being permitted to practice as a CPA.

In 1896, the New York legislature passed the first accountancy law, legally recognizing the public accounting profession. Other states soon followed. Today, each jurisdiction has enacted public accounting legislation that is administered by a board of accountancy. It is the responsibility of each board to determine, within the standards set by law, who is qualified to sit for the CPA examination. The results of the CPA examination are communicated to the boards of accountancy, which award the CPA certificate to successful candidates.

CPAs' Services

In addition to performing independent audits of an entity's financial statements, CPAs can perform other services—as long as the services do not impair their independence. These services include reports for government agencies, compliance audits, and operational audits (discussed earlier); tax services; management advisory services; litigation support services; compilations and reviews of unaudited statements; and bookkeeping services.

Tax Services. The basic objectives of tax services are to help clients comply with the tax law and minimize their taxes. To this end, the CPA advises on tax-saving measures, prepares and reviews tax returns, and, if necessary, accompanies the client to meetings with the IRS or to court proceedings.

Management Advisory Services. The auditors' role as knowledgeable, independent observers provides a unique opportunity to advise clients on many matters beyond auditing and tax services. Management advisory ser-

The "Big Eight" national firms are Arthur Andersen & Co.; Arthur Young & Company; Coopers & Lybrand; Deloitte Haskins & Sells; Ernst & Whinney; Peat, Marwick, Mitchell & Co.; Price Waterhouse & Co.; and Touche Ross & Co. Other national firms include Alexander Grant & Co., *Grant + Thornton + Co* Laventhol & Horwath, and KMG Main Hurdman. Regional firms usually have offices in one or two geographic regions. Local firms usually practice in only one city or town.

CPA firms are organized as either partnerships or professional corporations. In a typical partnership, the professional staff consists of partners, managers, supervisors, seniors, and staff accountants. The exact titles and levels vary from firm to firm.

Partners.   In a firm organized as a partnership, the partners own and administer their firm. Thus, only a partner may sign the auditors' report that results from an audit engagement. The partners' major audit responsibilities include planning the engagement; performing the final review of the working papers and financial statements for appropriateness and completeness; meeting with the client's management, board of directors, and audit committee to discuss audit plans, financial statements, emerging issues, and the evaluation of the system of internal control; billing and collecting the fees for services; and pursuing new business. The audit partner typically provides business advice to management on various matters, ranging from how to account for complex transactions to assistance on organizational and operating matters.

Managers and Supervisors.   Managers and supervisors administer the entire scope and direct the field work of several engagements at the same time. Managers' and supervisors' responsibilities generally include planning the engagement, reviewing the work of staff, preparing or reviewing drafts of the financial statements, maintaining contact with the client, assisting with the billing and collecting of fees, participating in client meetings, and preparing and reviewing various client communications and reports.

Senior Accountants.   Senior accountants are responsible for the day-to-day field work of the audit. Also, the senior generally performs the work in audit areas requiring a significant amount of judgment based on experience, such as evaluating collectibility of accounts receivable, liabilities for product warranty, or obsolescence of inventory.

The responsibilities of running the day-to-day field work of the engagement are considerable. As part of these responsibilities, the senior assists the manager and supervisor in evaluating the system of internal control and planning the engagement; plans and supervises the work of the staff assigned to the engagement; coordinates and monitors assistance to be provided by the client; develops an overall timetable for the audit; coordinates completion of the engagement with the partner, manager, and supervisor; and assists in drafting or reviewing the financial statements and other client reports.

Staff Accountants. Staff accountants participate in audit engagements under the supervision of more experienced personnel. They perform specific procedures to test a client's system of internal control, as well as the reasonableness of recorded assets, liabilities, and results of operations. For example, they test the functioning of key attributes of the internal control system, evaluate the validity of accounts receivable, search for unrecorded liabilities, and analyze or test the reasonableness of revenue and expense amounts. Staff accountants also gather information for reports (e.g., audit or SEC), tax returns, and suggested improvements in procedures and controls. As staff accountants gain experience on successive assignments, they develop auditing skills that allow them to take on increased responsibilities.

CORPORATE AUDIT COMMITTEES

Many corporations appoint audit committees, composed of members of the board of directors, to interact directly with both internal and independent auditors. Generally, a majority of the committee members are "outside directors" (directors who are not members of management). The establishment of audit committees by boards of directors of public companies has been recommended by the AICPA, the SEC, and other organizations concerned with financial reporting and fiduciary duties of directors. Since 1978, audit committees composed entirely of outside directors have been required as a condition of listing by the New York Stock Exchange.[8]

During the 1970s, strong support for audit committees developed. For example, in 1974, the SEC required that corporations disclose to shareholders whether they had an audit committee.[9] Later, as a result of formal proceedings regarding certain reporting violations, the SEC required the corporations involved to establish audit committees with specified responsibilities.

In the late 1970s, the AICPA's Special Committee on Audit Committees *encouraged* companies to establish audit committees, and it suggested the following general duties for audit committees:

1. Approve the selection of the independent auditor.
2. Review the arrangements and scope of the audit.
3. Consider the comments from the independent auditor with respect to weaknesses in internal accounting control and the consideration given or corrective action taken by management.

---

[8] *Report of the Special Committee on Audit Committees,* American Institute of Certified Public Accountants, 1979, p. 1.

[9] Securities and Exchange Commission, *Accounting Series Release No. 165.*

4. Discuss matters of concern to the audit committee, the auditor, or management relating to the company's financial statements or other results of the audit.
5. Review internal accounting controls with the company's financial and accounting staff.
6. Review the activities and recommendations of the company's internal auditors.[10]

The Committee also stated that "it may also be appropriate for the audit committee to perform additional duties as assigned by the board of directors. Such duties might include review of financial statements and other financial information distributed by the company to the public, review of changes in accounting principles or methods of applying them, review of nonaudit services performed by the independent auditor, establishment and monitoring of policies to prohibit unethical, questionable, or illegal activities by company employees, or review of executive perquisites."[11]

The importance of the relationship between the audit committee and the independent auditor is clear from the nature and extent of duties ascribed to audit committees. The audit committee recommends selection of the independent auditor and reviews the scope of the audit. Further, the audit committee relies heavily on the results of the independent auditors' work to carry out its responsibilities.

ROLES OF THE AICPA AND FASB

The AICPA, headquartered in New York City, is the principal professional association of CPAs. Since membership in the AICPA is voluntary, not all CPAs are members.

Through its full-time staff and various committees composed of members, the AICPA—

1. Promulgates standards for auditing, review, taxation, and management advisory services; professional ethics; and quality control.
2. Publishes statements of position on accounting issues.
3. Performs research and provides members with advice on technical issues.
4. Publishes various materials and sponsors educational courses related to accounting and auditing.
5. Provides a national political lobby for the public accounting profession.

The AICPA's initial concerns were to establish generally accepted accounting principles (GAAP), standards for performing audit procedures, and ethical guidance for an auditor's conduct. Thus, the AICPA began and continues

---

[10] *Report of the Special Committee on Audit Committees,* American Institute of Certified Public Accountants, 1979, p. 9.

[11] Ibid.

today to be part of the standard-setting process. Further, the AICPA's *Code of Professional Ethics* requires compliance with GAAP and auditing standards.

In addition to the AICPA, CPAs in various states have organized CPA societies. These state societies are voluntary associations that provide various informational, professional development, and administrative services to members. Like the AICPA, much of their work is accomplished through committees composed of members. Societies also act as a lobbying force to their state legislatures. While state societies have no direct affiliation with the AICPA, the organizations cooperate on various matters.

Since 1973, the Financial Accounting Standards Board (FASB) has been responsible for establishing standards of financial accounting and reporting. These standards govern the preparation of financial reports and are recognized as authoritative by the SEC. Unlike its predecessors, the FASB, headquartered in Stamford, Connecticut, is not part of the AICPA. It is an autonomous body, composed of seven full-time Board members from various backgrounds, including public accounting, private industry, government, and academe.

Generally Accepted Accounting Principles (GAAP)

On each audit, the independent accountant is responsible for determining ". . . whether the financial statements are presented in accordance with generally accepted accounting principles . . ." (see page 17) and must include a statement to that effect in the auditors' report. Any material deviations from GAAP must be explained.

GAAP are not precisely defined and are subject to continued review and change as the information needs of the users of financial statements change. However, GAAP have been described by the AICPA Special Committee on Opinions of the Accounting Principles Board as principles "having substantial authoritative support."[12] This support is found in the following pronouncements issued by the AICPA[13] and the FASB:

1. *Accounting Research Bulletins (ARBs).* These were published by the AICPA's Committee on Accounting Procedure beginning in 1939. The first 42 *ARBs* were combined and reissued as *ARB No. 43. ARB No. 43* and *ARB Nos. 44 to 51* (the last one issued in 1959) were adopted by the Committee's successor, the Accounting Principles Board (APB), and remain in effect except where superseded by later pronouncements.
2. *Accounting Principles Board (APB) Opinions.* Before its dissolution in 1973

---

[12] As quoted in *APB Statement No. 4,* "Basic Concepts and Accounting Principles Underlying Financial Statements of Business Enterprises," American Institute of Certified Public Accountants, 1970, chap. 6, par. 137, fn. 38.

[13] See *Statement on Auditing Standards No. 5,* as amended by *Statement on Auditing Standards No. 43.*

on the formation of the FASB, the APB issued 31 *Opinions.* Except as superseded by later pronouncements, *APB Opinions* continue to represent GAAP.

3. *FASB Statements and Interpretations.*   The Board issues *Statements of Financial Accounting Standards, Statements of Concepts,* and *Interpretations. Statements of Financial Accounting Standards* establish new accounting standards or supersede or amend previous pronouncements. In contrast, *Statements of Concepts* do not establish new standards or revise existing principles. Instead, these *Concepts* act to provide guidance to the FASB in solving problems and to financial information users so that they may better understand the context in which standards have been formulated. *Interpretations* are issued by the Board to clarify, explain, and/or elaborate on existing accounting standards.

In addition to the above sources of "substantial authoritative support" for GAAP, the following pronouncements also should be considered:

1. *Statements of Position.*   At about the time the FASB was established, the Accounting Standards Executive Committee (AcSEC) was formed by the AICPA. AcSEC sets the AICPA's policies on financial accounting and reporting standards and issues *Statements of Position (SOPs),* which deal with current accounting topics. While SOPs do not necessarily constitute GAAP and are thus not binding on CPAs in the same manner as FASB *Statements,* they do provide useful guidance in areas not covered by *ARBs,* APB *Opinions,* and FASB *Statements* or *Interpretations.*

2. *Industry Audit Guides.*   Because of the unique aspects of accounting and financial reporting in a number of specialized industries, several AICPA industry committees have been established. Many of these committees have published "Industry Audit Guides," setting forth recommended accounting and reporting practices for specific industries. Examples of industries for which Guides have been issued are banks, stock life insurance companies, hospitals, state and local government units, colleges and universities; and savings and loan institutions. Independent accountants can be required to justify departures from these Guides.

3. *Technical Bulletins.*   These are issued by the FASB staff without formal Board approval to provide supplemental guidance on certain financial accounting and reporting problems on a timely basis. They are of a purely interpretative nature and are consistent with the intent of the original pronouncement.

Statements on Auditing Standards

In the early history of public accounting, the quality of audit examinations often varied widely depending on the skill, understanding, and judgment of each individual auditor. In 1939, the AICPA Committee on Auditing Procedures began issuing *Statements on Auditing Procedures (SAPs),* the first authoritative statements on auditing matters. The *SAPs* were designed to guide the independent auditor in using judgment in the application of audit procedures.

In 1972, the Committee on Auditing Procedures was replaced by the Auditing Standards Executive Committee (AudSEC), which in 1973 issued *Statement on Auditing Standards (SAS) No. 1,* a codification of all previous *SAPs. SAS No. 1* identified the 10 generally accepted auditing standards (GAAS) from the *SAPs,* which are discussed later in this chapter. AudSEC continued to issue additional *SASs* on various topics. *SASs* are regarded as interpretations of generally accepted auditing standards, and as noted earlier, adherence to *SASs* is required by the AICPA *Code of Professional Ethics.*

In 1978, AudSEC was restructured and renamed the Auditing Standards Board (ASB). Today, the ASB is responsible for establishing all auditing standards. It also establishes standards for auditors' association with unaudited financial statements of publicly held companies.

Statements on Standards for Accounting and Review Services

For many years, companies could not obtain any assurance from CPAs regarding their financial statements unless a full audit was performed. This limited the usefulness of companies' unaudited financial statements to outsiders (e.g., lenders). This was particularly a problem for small, privately owned companies. As a result, the AICPA formed the Accounting and Review Services Committee (ARSC). In 1979, the ARSC issued the first *Statements on Standards for Accounting and Review Services (SSARS)*. These standards cover unaudited financial statements and other accounting services (e.g. compilations and reviews) for nonpublic entities. The *SSARS* are discussed further in Chapters 15 and 17.

Code of Professional Ethics

The AICPA has had a code of ethics for many years. Members who breach any of the rules specified in the *Code of Professional Ethics* may be warned, censured, suspended, or expelled. The Code is discussed in detail in Chapter 19.

Quality Control

SAS No. 25, "The Relationship of Generally Accepted Auditing Standards to Quality Control Standards" (AU 161.02), states that an accounting firm:

. . . should establish quality control policies and procedures to provide it with reasonable assurance of conforming with generally accepted auditing standards in its audit engagements. The nature and extent [of such policies and procedures utilized by an accounting firm] . . . depend on factors such as its size, the degree of operating autonomy allowed its personnel and its practice offices, the nature of its practice, its organization, and appropriate cost-benefit consider-ations.

In 1978, the AICPA established the Quality Control Standards Committee. In *Statement on Quality Control Standards No. 1 (SQCS No. 1)*, it identified nine elements of quality control: (1) "independence," (2) "assigning personnel to engagements," (3) "consultation," (4) "supervision," (5) "hiring," (6) "professional development," (7) "advancement," (8) "acceptance and continuance of clients," and (9) "inspection." In 1983, the AICPA decided that the issuance of further pronouncements relating to quality control standards are to be the responsibility of the Auditing Standards Board; consequently, the Quality Control Standards Committee was dissolved.

Accounting firms employ various quality control measures, depending on their size. First is the establishment of specific responsibilities for review and approval of audit working papers. In addition, large firms with more than one office typically have a program of interoffice review. Under these programs, representatives of one office periodically review the working papers and related documents of selected audit engagements of another office for compliance with firm policy and professional standards. Many firms also engage other CPA firms to perform a similar quality control review, called a peer review.

AICPA Division for CPA Firms[14]

The AICPA established the division for CPA firms in 1977 and for the first time is able to regulate CPA firms as well as individual CPAs. The division for firms was created to demonstrate the profession's commitment to self-regulation.

The division for CPA firms consists of the SEC Practice Section and the Private Companies Practice Section. Membership in each section is voluntary. The overall objectives of the division, as established by the AICPA, are:

1. To improve the quality of CPA services by setting practice requirements.
2. To self-regulate member firms through mandatory peer reviews, quality controls, and sanctions when necessary.
3. To provide a vehicle for member firms to exchange technical information.

Each section has an Executive Committee and a Peer Review Committee.

---

[14] This section is based in part on: *Division for CPA Firms SEC Practice Section: Peer Review Manual,* Revised Edition 1981 (as amended), American Institute of Certified Public Accountants, 1981; and *Division for CPA Firms Private Companies Practice Section: Peer Review Manual,* Review Edition 1981, American Institute of Certified Public Accountants, 1981.

Among other things, member firms of the SEC Practice Section are required to:

1. Follow certain quality control standards and have a peer review, usually every three years.
2. Have all professional staff residing in the United States comply with the Section's continuing professional education (CPE) requirements of 120 hours of continuing education over a three-year period, with a minimum of 20 hours per year.
3. Maintain certain minimum amounts and types of liability insurance.
4. File certain organizational information with the Section.
5. Rotate audit partners in charge of SEC engagements every seven years.
6. Have a second partner review the audit report of every SEC engagement.
7. Adhere to certain restrictions on nonaudit services.

Member firms of the Private Companies Practice Section are subject to the requirements in items 1 through 4 above.

The SEC Practice Section also has a Public Oversight Board whose main responsibility is to monitor and evaluate the Section's self-regulatory program. Its five members are appointed from various fields, such as business, education, banking, law, economics, and government.

AUDITING STANDARDS

A clear distinction should be made between *auditing standards* and *auditing procedures*. Auditing *standards* define the broad objectives for every independent audit, provide a gauge for judging the quality of an auditor's performance, and are recognized throughout the business and legal world as standards of the profession. On the other hand, auditing *procedures* are the methods and techniques used by the auditor during the examination to meet the requirements of generally accepted auditing standards. The procedures used will vary according to the circumstances of the particular audit examination.

SAS No. 1 (AU 150.02) divides the 10 generally accepted auditing standards into three broad categories: *general standards, standards of field work,* and *standards of reporting.* They are:

General Standards

1. The examination is to be performed by a person or persons having adequate technical training and proficiency as an auditor.
2. In all matters relating to the assignment, an independence in mental attitude is to be maintained by the auditor or auditors.
3. Due professional care is to be exercised in the performance of the examination and the preparation of the report.

Standards of Field Work

1. The work is to be adequately planned and assistants, if any, are to be properly supervised.

2. There is to be a proper study and evaluation of the existing internal controls as a basis for reliance thereon and for the determination of the resultant extent of the tests to which auditing procedures are to be restricted.
3. Sufficient competent evidential matter is to be obtained through inspection, observation, inquiries, and confirmations to afford a reasonable basis for an opinion regarding the financial statements under examination.

Standards of Reporting

1. The report shall state whether the financial statements are presented in accordance with generally accepted accounting principles.
2. The report shall state whether such principles have been consistently observed in the current period in relation to the preceding period.
3. Informative disclosures in the financial statements are to be regarded as reasonably adequate unless otherwise stated in the report.
4. The report shall either contain an expression of opinion regarding the financial statements, taken as a whole, or an assertion to the effect that an opinion cannot be expressed. When an overall opinion cannot be expressed, the reasons therefore should be stated. In all cases where an auditor's name is associated with financial statements the report should contain a clear-cut indication of the character of the auditor's examination, if any, and the degree of responsibility he is taking.

Auditing standards require an accountant to make sound judgments in a variety of circumstances, a skill that is mastered only with experience. Each standard and its implications to the auditor is discussed below. The remaining chapters of this textbook will describe how auditors specifically meet those standards.

General Standards

1. The examination is to be performed by a person or persons having adequate technical training and proficiency as an auditor.

Auditors are expected to have adequate academic training in accounting, taxation, auditing, and other areas that relate to their profession. In addition, they should receive further training, both formal and informal, throughout their careers. This standard has several long-range implications for accountants who wish to grow within the profession. They should pass the CPA examination and keep up with current developments in accounting, auditing, and tax matters. In fact, an increasing number of jurisdictions now require CPAs to participate in continuing professional education to maintain their license to practice. Also, as stated earlier, firms that join the AICPA's division for CPA firms are required to provide their professional staff with a certain amount of continuing education. Further, the CPA should be willing to acquire technical knowledge in new subject areas. To become proficient, auditors need a combination of practical experience and academic training. Auditors must understand the accounting and auditing problems involved in every assignment they undertake.

SQCS No. 1 suggests that CPA firms should establish other policies to assure that the audit work is performed by qualified people. These policies (described in *SQCS No. 1*) relate to:

(a) *Assignments.* It is suggested that individuals assigned to an engagement should have proper training. This requires careful planning.

(b) *Consultation.* It is suggested that individuals assigned to an engagement should seek appropriate assistance when they are confronted with a problem beyond their expertise.

(c) *Hiring.* It is suggested that firms should establish policies for their hiring practices.

(d) *Advancement.* It is suggested that there should be definite assurance that individuals promoted are qualified for their new responsibilities.

2. In all matters relating to the assignment, an independence in mental attitude is to be maintained by the auditor or auditors.

The *Code of Professional Ethics* (ET 101.01) states that a CPA ". . . shall not express an opinion on financial statements of an enterprise unless he and his firm are independent with respect to such enterprise. . . ."

Auditors must be independent in both fact and appearance. Since it is impossible to provide rules for every situation in which independence may be an issue, auditors are expected to use common sense at all times. *SQCS No. 1* suggests that CPA firms establish policies and procedures to help ensure that all firm personnel are independent. Audit independence is discussed further in Chapter 19.

3. Due professional care is to be exercised in the performance of the examination and the preparation of the report.

"Due care" imposes several important requirements on auditors. First, and most obvious, auditors should understand what they are doing and why they are doing it. If they are uncertain about any phase of the assignment, it is their responsibility to seek the guidance of their superiors. Second, because the typical audit involves the use of tests and samples, due care means that each item selected for testing must be carefully examined. Finally, due care requires auditors to prepare working papers that are both accurate and complete. If working papers are carelessly prepared or incomplete, the quality of the evidential matter gathered by the auditor may be questioned.

Standards of Field Work

1. The work is to be adequately planned and assistants, if any, are to be properly supervised.

Adequate planning of the audit field work is key to performing the examination efficiently and controlling the quality of the work. However, since the audit plans for field work are subject to modification as the examination progresses, the auditors' work often leads to changes in the initial plans. Also, auditors may find that not all of their instructions are completely detailed; often they must use judgment in planning the details of specific tasks within the framework of the general plan. For example, an instruction may require the auditor to observe and test the taking of a physical inventory at a plant. It may be the auditor's responsibility to decide such matters as how extensive the observation in each department should be and how the performance of the client personnel taking the inventory should be checked.

SAS No. 22, "Planning and Supervision" (AU 311.09), states that "supervision involves directing the efforts of assistants who are involved in accomplishing the objectives of the examination and determining whether those objectives were accomplished. . . . The extent of supervision appropriate in a given instance depends on many factors, including the complexity of the subject matter and the qualifications of persons performing the work." Some of the factors that *SAS No. 22* suggests are related to proper supervision of staff include:

(a) Informing staff of their responsibilities and the objectives of the audit procedures they will be performing.

(b) Informing staff of their responsibility to bring to their supervisor's attention any important questions raised during their work.

(c) Reviewing the work of staff.

(d) Establishing a system under which staff may document any disagreement they may have with the final conclusions of the examination.

2. **There is to be a proper study and evaluation of the existing internal control as a basis for reliance thereon and for the determination of the resultant extent of the tests to which auditing procedures are to be restricted.**

Internal control will be discussed in Chapters 4 and 5. Briefly, from the perspective of the auditor, internal control is embodied in the plans and procedures used by a business entity to ensure that transactions are recorded accurately and the assets are safeguarded. Internal control also includes administrative control—the decision process that leads to the authorization of a transaction. As will be explained in later chapters the auditor's evaluation of internal control affects the audit procedures used.

3. **Sufficient competent evidential matter is to be obtained through inspection, observation, inquiries, and confirmations to afford a reasonable basis for an opinion regarding the financial statements under examination.**

To comply with this standard, the auditor should: (1) understand the assignment completely and follow instructions; and (2) prepare complete and self-explanatory working papers that document observations, errors and unusual or questionable items noted, and any important judgments. Evidence and working papers are discussed in Chapter 2.

Standards of Reporting

Accountants who prepare auditors' reports need to understand the meaning and implications of the reporting standards and draw on their knowledge of GAAP. The following section provides background for understanding the reporting standards.

THE AUDITORS' STANDARD REPORT

The financial statements of an entity belong to and are the responsibility of its management. The independent auditor who evaluates the statements is responsible for rendering a professional opinion on the fairness of the statements. This opinion is expressed in what is known as an auditor's report. Figure 1–1 shows how the auditors' standard report summarizes the results of the examination in accordance with general accepted auditing standards.

The auditors' report is addressed to the group or individuals that engaged them—e.g., the stockholders or the board of directors. In their report, the auditors discuss the scope of their examination (usually referred to as the scope paragraph—the first paragraph) and their opinion on the fair presentation of the financial statements (usually referred to as the opinion paragraph—the second paragraph). The report is signed by a partner of the CPA firm. It is dated as of the date the audit field work was completed, so the reader will know at what point the auditor was in a position to render an opinion. Five key phrases in the report relate to auditing standards. Two are included in the scope paragraph and three in the opinion paragraph.

Scope Paragraph

Generally Accepted Auditing Standards (GAAS). In the scope paragraph, the statement, "Our examination was made in accordance with generally accepted auditing standards" relates to both the general standards and the standards of field work. In the area of general standards, this statement implies that the examination was performed by adequately trained, proficient auditors who maintained an independent attitude and used due professional care. As to field standards, the statement implies that the work was properly planned; that assistants, if any, were properly supervised; that a proper study and evaluation of internal control was made; and that sufficient competent evidential matter was obtained.

Tests of the Accounting Records. The scope paragraph also states that the examination ". . . included such tests of the accounting records and

FIGURE 1-1 The Auditors' Standard Report

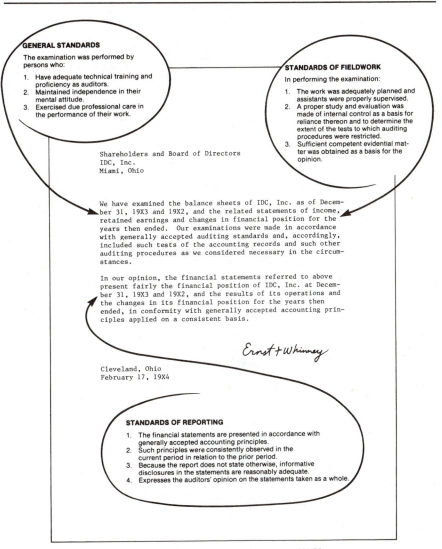

GENERAL STANDARDS

The examination was performed by persons who:

1. Have adequate technical training and proficiency as auditors.
2. Maintained independence in their mental attitude.
3. Exercised due professional care in the performance of their work.

STANDARDS OF FIELDWORK

In performing the examination:

1. The work was adequately planned and assistants were properly supervised.
2. A proper study and evaluation was made of internal control as a basis for reliance thereon and to determine the extent of the tests to which auditing procedures were restricted.
3. Sufficient competent evidential matter was obtained as a basis for the opinion.

Shareholders and Board of Directors
IDC, Inc.
Miami, Ohio

We have examined the balance sheets of IDC, Inc. as of December 31, 19X3 and 19X2, and the related statements of income, retained earnings and changes in financial position for the years then ended. Our examinations were made in accordance with generally accepted auditing standards and, accordingly, included such tests of the accounting records and such other auditing procedures as we considered necessary in the circumstances.

In our opinion, the financial statements referred to above present fairly the financial position of IDC, Inc. at December 31, 19X3 and 19X2, and the results of its operations and the changes in its financial position for the years then ended, in conformity with generally accepted accounting principles applied on a consistent basis.

Ernst + Whinney

Cleveland, Ohio
February 17, 19X4

STANDARDS OF REPORTING

1. The financial statements are presented in accordance with generally accepted accounting principles.
2. Such principles were consistently observed in the current period in relation to the prior period.
3. Because the report does not state otherwise, informative disclosures in the statements are reasonably adequate.
4. Expresses the auditors' opinion on the statements taken as a whole.

Source: *AICPA Professional Standards, Vol. 1,* AU 150.02 and AU 505.03.

such other auditing procedures as we considered necessary in the circumstances." This statement relates to the second and third standards of field work. Sufficient competent evidential matter must be obtained to justify an opinion on the financial statements (Chapter 2). In addition, the auditor's tests must be based on a proper study and evaluation of the client's system of internal control (Chapters 4 and 5).

Opinion Paragraph

Generally Accepted Accounting Principles (GAAP). The phrase ". . . in conformity with generally accepted accounting principles . . ." complies with the first reporting standard. *SAS No. 5*, "The Meaning of 'Present Fairly in Conformity with Generally Accepted Accounting Principles' in the Independent Auditor's Report" (AU 411.03), states that ". . . 'fairness' of the overall presentation of financial statements should be applied within the framework of generally accepted accounting principles." It (AU 411.04) also notes that the auditor's opinion should be based on his or her judgment of whether the accounting principles applied in the circumstances are generally accepted and are considered appropriate, and whether the statements (including any related notes) contain adequate disclosures of all important matters.

Consistency. The phrase ". . . applied on a basis consistent . . ." relates to the second reporting standard. *SAS No. 1* (AU 420.02) states that:

The objective of the consistency standard is:

(a) to give assurance that the comparability of financial statements between periods has not been materially affected by changes in the accounting principles, which include not only accounting principles and practices, but also methods of applying them, or

(b) if comparability has been materially affected by such changes, to require appropriate reporting by the independent auditor regarding such changes. It is implicit in the objective that such principles have been consistently observed within each period.

Adequate Disclosure. The phrase ". . . the financial statements referred to above present fairly . . ." relates to the third reporting standard, which notes that informative disclosures in the financial statements are to be considered reasonably adequate unless the report includes a statement to the contrary. This standard emphasizes the auditor's responsibility for determining that adequate disclosure has in fact been made in the financial statements. It requires the auditor to report any important fact needed to ensure that the financial statements are not misleading. The auditor must use professional judgment in determining which matters require disclosure.

Expression of Opinion. The fourth reporting standard requires the auditors to express an opinion on audited financial statements, or if they cannot express an opinion, to indicate so and clearly state why.

The auditors' *unqualified* or "clean" opinion signifies that the examination was made in accordance with generally accepted auditing standards and that the financial statements (1) are presented fairly in conformity with GAAP applied on a consistent basis and (2) include all necessary disclosures. Otherwise the auditors must give a qualified opinion, an adverse opinion, or a disclaimer of opinion.

In a *qualified opinion,* the auditors express certain reservations in their report concerning either the scope of the audit and/or the financial statements. In an *adverse opinion,* the auditors state that the financial statements *do not* present fairly the financial position of the company, the results of its operations, or the changes in its financial position. In a *disclaimer of opinion,* the auditors state that they cannot give an opinion because of a scope limitation or some other reason (e.g., the auditors are not independent). The auditors' report in Figure 1–1 is an *unqualified opinion.*

It is important to understand that while CPAs are responsible for their auditors' report, management—not the auditor—is responsible for both the accuracy and adequacy of the financial statements. Although the CPA may assist in preparing the statements or suggest changes in form, they are still management's responsibility.

QUESTIONS AND PROBLEMS

1–1. Define auditing.

1–2. Define a financial statement audit.

1–3. What is the objective of a financial statement audit?

1–4. Why are financial statement audits necessary?

1–5. Define attestation.

1–6. Discuss the difference between accounting and auditing.

1–7. What is meant by an auditor's independence?

1–8. Describe the Securities Act of 1933 and the Securities Exchange Act of 1934.

1–9. Define an operational audit.

1–10. Define a compliance audit.

1–11. What functions do internal auditors perform?

1–12. What are the major services usually performed by CPAs?

1–13. Discuss an audit committee's relationship with its independent accountants.

1–14. What are the differences between the FASB and ASB?

1–15. Describe the AICPA division for CPA firms.

1–16. What is the difference between auditing standards and auditing procedures?

1–17. List and discuss the general standards.

1–18. List and discuss the standards of field work.

1–19. Discuss the elements that are needed in properly supervising staff.

1–20. List and discuss the reporting standards.

1–21. What is the objective of the consistency standard?

1–22. Write the auditors' standard report.

1–23. Select the *best* answer for each of the following items.
   a. Independent auditing can be described as:
   (1) A branch of accounting.
   (2) A discipline that attests to the results of accounting and other functional operations and data.
   (3) A professional activity that measures and communicates financial business data.
   (4) A regulatory function that prevents the issuance of improper financial information.

   b. Auditing standards differ from auditing procedures in that procedures relate to:
   (1) Measures of performance.
   (2) Audit principles.
   (3) Acts to be performed.
   (4) Audit judgments.

   c. The primary reason why a CPA firm establishes quality control policies and procedures for continuing education of professional staff is to:
   (1) Comply with the continuing education requirements imposed by various states for all professional staff in CPA firms.
   (2) Establish, in fact as well as in appearance, that professional staff are increasing their knowledge of accounting and auditing matters.
   (3) Provide a forum for professional staff to exchange their experiences and views concerning firm policies and procedures.
   (4) Provide reasonable assurance that professional staff will have the knowledge required to enable them to fulfill their responsibilities.

   d. The first general standard, which states that the examination is to be performed by a person or persons having adequate technical training, requires that an auditor have:
   (1) Education and experience in the field of auditing.
   (2) Ability in the planning and supervision of the audit work.
   (3) Proficiency in business and financial matters.
   (4) Knowledge in the areas of financial accounting.

   e. The third general standard states that due care is to be exercised in the performance of the examination. This standard should be interpreted to mean that a CPA who undertakes an engagement assumes a duty to perform—
   (1) With reasonable diligence and without fault or error.
   (2) As a professional who will assume responsibility for losses consequent upon an error of judgment.
   (3) To the satisfaction of the client and third parties who may rely upon it.
   (4) As a professional possessing the degree of skill commonly possessed by others in the field.

   f. The first standard of field work, which states that the work is to be adequately planned, and assistants, if any, are to be properly supervised, recognizes that:

(1) Early appointment of the auditor is advantageous to the auditor and the client.

(2) Acceptance of the audit engagement after the close of the client's fiscal year is generally *not* permissible.

(3) Appointment of the auditor subsequent to the physical count of inventories requires a disclaimer of opinion.

(4) Performance of substantial parts of the examination is necessary at interim dates.   (AICPA, adapted)

1–24. In April, you are told that your next assignment will start May 15. This is a new client engaged in manufacturing work clothing. You are advised that the client has a standard cost system and prices a portion of inventory on the last-in, first-out (LIFO) method. You have had no practical experience with either standard costs or LIFO inventories. Should you request another assignment since you lack experience in these matters? Alternatively, what might you do to prepare yourself for this assignment?

1–25. As a staff accountant, you ask the client's treasurer for copies of bank reconciliations and canceled checks for several months of the year under examination. The treasurer says he will get them for you. After several days you ask again, and he informs you that the reconciliations and checks have been accidentally lost and suggests that you do your work for different months. What would you tell the treasurer? What other things might you do?

1–26. During the course of an audit, the independently wealthy president of the company poses certain involved questions about estate and inheritance taxes. It appears to you that the president has explored the area thoroughly but is in need of specific answers to a few questions that bear directly on her own personal situation. How should you handle this matter?

1–27. How would you reply to the following questions?
a. Since responsible financial reporting seems to be directed principally toward outside stockholders and creditors, to what extent do you suppose generally accepted auditing standards can be relaxed in the case of:
(1) A small corporation that has no creditors and is wholly owned by the chairman of the board who asks for an audit?
(2) A sole proprietorship with no creditors?
b. Since the accountants' report is sometimes referred to as a "certificate," what do you think about changing the wording to: "We hereby certify that the . . . (financial statements) . . . are accurate . . . etc."?
c. Generally accepted auditing standards state that the auditor must disclose any exceptions that are taken to the financial statements. Rather than qualify the opinion, why doesn't the auditor simply change the statements to reflect an acceptable treatment?

1–28. "An audit by a CPA is essentially negative and contributes to neither the gross national product nor the general well-being of society. The auditor does not create; he or she merely checks what someone else has done." Comment on the statement.
                                                                        (AICPA, adapted)

1–29. The following statement is representative of attitudes and opinions sometimes encountered by CPAs in their professional practices:

> It is important to read the footnotes to financial statements, even though they often are presented in technical language and are incomprehensible. The auditor may reduce his exposure to third-party liability by stating something in the footnotes that contradicts completely what he has presented in the balance sheet or income statement.

Required:

Evaluate the above statement and indicate:

a. Areas of agreement with the statement, if any.
b. Areas of misconception, incompleteness, or fallacious reasoning included in the statement, if any. (AICPA, adapted)

1–30. CPA X was faced with the following situations during the past year:
a. During the year ended December 31, 1985, Jolly Corporation (a client of CPA X) had its fixed assets appraised and found that they had substantially appreciated in value since the date of their purchase. The appraised values have been reported in the balance sheet as of December 31, 1985; the total appraisal increment has been included as an extraordinary item in the income statement for the year then ended; and the appraisal adjustment has been fully disclosed in the footnotes. CPA X believes that the values are reasonable. What type of opinion should he issue?
b. CPA X accepted the audit engagement of Sad Mfg. Inc. During the audit, X became aware of the fact that he did not have the competence required for the engagement. What should X have done? (AICPA, adapted)

1–31. Student A says that the primary responsibility for the adequacy of disclosure in the financial statements and footnotes rests with the auditor in charge of the audit field work. Student B says that the partner in charge of the engagement has the primary responsibility. Student C says that the staff person who drafts the statements and footnotes has the primary responsibility. Student D contends that it is the client's responsibility. Which student is correct? (AICPA, adapted)

1–32. Feiler, the sole owner of a small hardware business, has been told that the business should have financial statements reported on by an independent CPA. Feiler, having some bookkeeping experience, has personally prepared the company's financial statements and does not understand why such statements should be examined by a CPA. Feiler discussed the matter with Farber, a CPA, and asked Farber to explain why an audit is considered important.

Required:

a. Describe the objectives of an independent audit.
b. Identify 10 ways in which an independent audit may be beneficial to Feiler.
(AICPA)

1–33. Ray, the owner of a small company, asked Holmes, CPA, to conduct an audit of the company's records. Ray told Holmes that the audit must be completed in time to submit audited financial statements to a bank as part of a loan application. Holmes immediately accepted the engagement and agreed to provide an auditor's report within three weeks. Ray agreed to pay Holmes a fixed fee plus a bonus if the loan was granted.

Holmes hired two accounting students to conduct the audit and spent several hours telling them exactly what to do. Holmes told the students not to spend time reviewing the controls but instead to concentrate on proving the mathematical accuracy of the ledger accounts and summarizing the data in the accounting records that support Ray's financial statements. The students followed Holmes's instructions, and after two weeks gave Holmes the financial statements and prepared an unqualified auditor's report. The report, however, did not refer to GAAP or to the year-to-year application of such principles.

Required:

Briefly describe each of the generally accepted auditing standards and indicate how the action(s) of Holmes resulted in a failure to comply with each standard.

(AICPA, adapted)

OVERVIEW OF THE AUDIT PROCESS, EVIDENCE, AND WORKING PAPERS

2

The objective of an audit is to determine whether an entity's financial statements are fairly presented in accordance with generally accepted accounting principles (GAAP), applied on a consistent basis. In pursuing this objective, all CPA firms must consider the likelihood of errors in the financial statements—a risk that is affected largely by the nature of the client's business activities and the extent of control exercised over them.

CPA firms achieve this audit objective in different ways. Some build their strategy around a standard audit program that varies little from one client to another. Others, in varying degrees, tailor their approach to fit each client's individual characteristics.

This chapter provides an overview of an audit approach that is based on the custom-design concept. The underlying thought process of the approach is referred to as risk analysis—shown in Figure 2–1. A set of specialized planning working papers is used to develop a formal risk analysis that focuses on the combined impact of a client's operating environment, financial and operating results, and system of internal controls on each important account in the financial statements. The result is an audit strategy based on each client's unique characteristics.

Working papers, along with the auditor's conclusions, are documentary evidence of the auditor's work. This chapter also discusses the nature of audit evidence and working papers.

OVERVIEW OF THE AUDIT PROCESS

The first three phases of an audit—initial planning, program development, and program execution—comprise the audit process. It is diagrammed in Figure 2–2. The fourth step, reporting the findings, is discussed briefly in this chapter and in more detail in Chapter 16.

On paper, each phase—and each step within it—appears as a separate activity. However, in practice, the phases and steps are closely interrelated and should not be regarded as distinct steps that are set aside when done. The risk analysis process in Figure 2–1 is completed during the initial planning and program development phases. Throughout an audit, the auditor should be alert for new developments that may affect the client's business or industry, and should continue to challenge the effectiveness and efficiency of audit procedures, and modify them if necessary.

SAS No. 47, "Audit Risk and Materiality in Conducting an Audit," describes the concept of *audit risk* in detail. To summarize, *SAS No. 47* (AU 312.20) suggests that audit risk related to an individual account or class of transactions on the financial statements is the product of the risks that (1) environmental factors, before considering the functioning of internal controls, will lead to a material error—*inherent risk;* (2) the system of internal control will not prevent a material error or detect it on a timely basis—*control risk;* and (3) the auditor's procedures will fail to detect a material error not detected by the system of internal control—*detection risk.* This concept of audit risk underlies the risk analysis approach described in this textbook.

The risk analysis audit approach is based upon the auditor having an up-to-date understanding of a client's business and industry. This understanding is obtained through a comprehensive analysis of both the external and internal environments in which the client operates. It enables the auditor to design an audit program that includes the most effective and efficient combination of tests responsive to each client's unique circumstances. It also provides a uniform method for developing and documenting the basis for the audit program.

This audit approach enables the auditor to plan his or her efforts to be proportionate to the risk of material error in specific accounts and transactions. As a result, the auditor can avoid both overauditing and underauditing and can distribute audit work more evenly throughout the year. The analysis

FIGURE 2-1 Risk Analysis

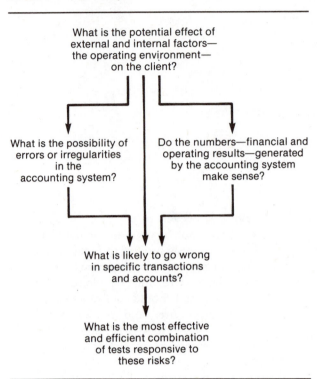

of risk for each client is based upon the auditor's knowledge and analysis of:

The conditions surrounding the business and industry. This is discussed in detail in Chapter 3.

The effectiveness of the client's accounting system. This is covered in Chapters 4 and 5.

Trends and relationships in significant financial and operating data. These are discussed in Chapter 6.

Initial Planning

Initial planning is important in meeting the first standard of field work. It involves the following three elements:

1. Obtaining an understanding of the client's business and industry.
2. Reviewing current developments and performing an overall analytical review.

FIGURE 2–2   The Audit Process

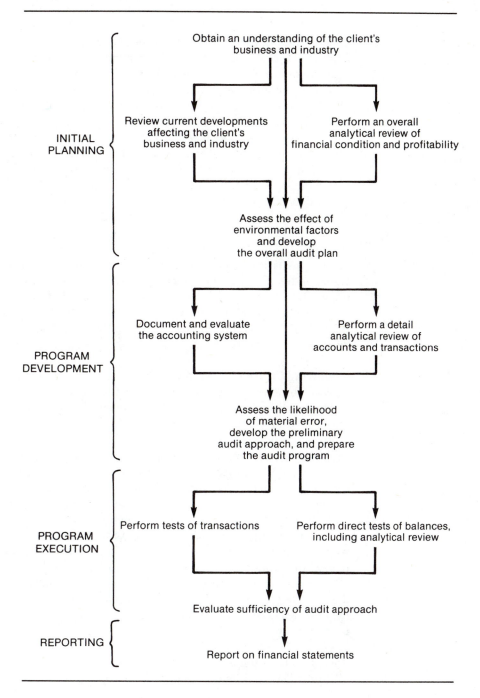

3. Assessing the effects of environmental factors and developing the overall audit plan.

Understanding the Client's Business and Industry. In order to effectively analyze the risks associated with an audit and develop an audit program, it is essential for the auditor to be familiar with the client's business and industry. Initially this means the auditor should obtain an overall understanding of the client's operations. For example, if the client is a manufacturer, the auditor should first obtain a general understanding of the manufacturing process (e.g., principal raw materials used and where they are obtained, relative amounts of materials and labor converted into the product, and capital equipment used in the production process). Understanding the market for the product is another important consideration. For example, is the product widely distributed or is there a limited number of customers? Is the product standardized or can it be custom designed?

During initial planning, the auditor should develop an understanding of the business by focusing on specific factors in the external and internal environments in which the client operates. The external environment includes industry conditions, regulatory requirements, and reporting obligations. The internal environment includes ownership influences and management, financial, and operating characteristics. Chapter 3 and Appendix I at the end of this textbook discuss how to gather information about the client's business and industry, along with environmental factors to consider.

Reviewing Current Developments and Performing Overall Analytical Review. The auditor expands his or her understanding of the client's business and industry and identifies potential problems by reviewing current developments or changes in the environment. Developments or changes that may cause auditing, accounting, or reporting problems include changes in key personnel, procedures, or systems; new contracts, products, or contingencies; and acquisitions or discontinued operations. Of course, changes in the environment also may *reduce* the likelihood of audit problems.

The auditor identifies current developments and changes in the environment through discussions with key members of the client's management and staff and by referring to various other information sources. Another way to identify changes in conditions is to perform an overall analytical review (described later) of interim operating results. This might uncover (1) changes in profitability trends; (2) losses on certain operations or product lines; (3) deterioration in liquidity or capital adequacy; or (4) unusual changes in key financial statement classifications, such as an unexpected large increase in inventory.

Assessing the Effects of Environmental Factors and Developing the Overall Audit Plan. Based on an understanding of the client's business, external and internal environment, current developments and changes in the environment, and results of the overall analytical review, the auditor should assess the potential for audit problems. In making the assessment, the auditor should consider the likelihood of material errors and irregularities and the degree of difficulty in gathering sufficient audit evidence. This leads to an overall audit plan that is documented in planning working papers and summarized in a planning memorandum.

Program Development

After the initial planning phase, the auditor begins the preparation of the audit program—the written plan for the engagement. To properly develop a program, the auditor should consider the environmental factors and materiality considerations noted in initial planning along with the observations from detail analytical review and an evaluation of the accounting system. The auditor considers these factors by performing a risk analysis, which provides the basis for determining the nature, timing, and extent of audit procedures.

In preparing an audit program that is both effective and efficient, the auditor's aim should be to:

1. Audit all important financial statement amounts.
2. Avoid redundant audit procedures.
3. Use procedures that accomplish more than one purpose.
4. Provide for tests of balances prior to year-end when justified by the accounting system and environmental factors.
5. Maximize use of efficient analytical review procedures.

Identify Environmental Factors that Directly Affect the Audit Program. The auditor's assessment of the effects of certain environmental factors may influence the analysis of the inherent risks associated with specific accounts or transactions. The auditor should identify those specific environmental factors as the first step in the risk analysis.

Perform a Detail Analytical Review. Along with the auditor's evaluation of the accounting system, the detail analytical review (discussed in Chapter 6) should confirm or challenge the auditor's understanding of the client's business and industry. It also helps identify (1) areas in which the auditor's procedures may be restricted because of the reasonableness of amounts or (2) significant fluctuations or transactions that require further investigation.

The detail analytical review is more comprehensive than the overall analytical review. It focuses on comparisons of details comprising financial statement amounts, and on operating and financial ratios related to specific accounts and transactions. In addition to comparing current period financial data to budgeted, prior period, and available competitor or industry data, the detail analytical review also might include similar comparisons of operating data, such as units produced, units sold, number of employees, or number of hours worked. The data available for analytical review varies greatly among companies, so it is impractical to specify procedures for all engagements. However, the review ordinarily includes:

1. Comparison of current levels of activity to prior periods and budgets.
2. Analysis of key financial statement relationships, such as inventory turnover and days' sales in receivables.
3. Review of management analyses, such as agings of accounts receivable and schedules of product-line profitability in an industrial company.

Document and Evaluate the Accounting System. The second standard of field work requires the auditor to make a proper study and evaluation of internal control. The auditor's evaluation focuses on whether or not there is reasonable assurance that the accounting system achieves certain specific control objectives. If it does, the auditor assesses control risk as low. Thus, the auditor can plan to test the internal control procedures in the system that support that conclusion and limit the overall extent of testing at interim dates and year-end. However, if the auditor concludes that the accounting system does not achieve the objectives and thus assesses control risk as high, audit efforts should be directed to detecting errors or irregularities and estimating their impact on the accounts affected.

There are five general control objectives that an accounting system should be expected to achieve. The first three—authorization, recording, and safeguarding—relate to establishing the system of accountability and provide for the prevention of errors and irregularities. The fourth objective—reconciliation—ties together the system of accountability established by the first three and, along with the fifth objective—valuation—provides for the detection of errors and irregularities.

How each of these general control objectives applies depends on the nature of the transactions or accounts covered by the system. To facilitate the evaluation of an accounting system, the general objectives have been translated into specific control objectives related to the various operating activities of a business. For example, authorization of cash disbursement transactions and safeguarding of cash are translated into this specific control objective: "Cash disbursements are for goods or services authorized and received."

Chapter 4 and Appendix II at the end of this textbook cover the concept of control objectives, explain how to evaluate accounting systems, and show the relationship between system controls and the audit program.

The auditor's evaluation of environmental considerations, along with the detail analytical review, may indicate that it is unnecessary to document, evaluate, and test the related accounting system. For example, direct tests might be the most effective and efficient approach. In general however, the auditor will place some reliance on the client's accounting system.

Assess the Likelihood of Material Error and Develop the Preliminary Audit Approach. The auditor summarizes the three inputs—environmental considerations, observations from detail analytical review, and systems evaluation—on the risk analysis working paper. Because specific control objectives provide convenient points of reference, they are used as focal points for the risk analysis. Based on the interaction of these three inputs to the risk analysis, the auditor assesses the likelihood of material error in the accounts affected by each specific control objective. The preliminary audit approach that results should focus on the specific risks that have been identified, and should be the minimum effort necessary based on the likelihood of material error that arises from those risks. *SAS No. 47* indicates that inherent risk and control risk are inversely related to detection risk. By this, *SAS No. 47* suggests that the less inherent risk and control risk the auditor believes exist, the greater the detection risk that can be accepted. This means the auditor avoids wasting effort on audit procedures that relate to areas for which little or no inherent risk or control risk has been identified.

The auditor's overall goal is to obtain sufficient evidence to be able to render an opinion on the fair presentation of the financial statements. The assessment of the likelihood of material error determines how persuasive the evidence should be in order to meet that goal. It is the basis for determining the audit procedures that most effectively and efficiently satisfy the auditor that the accounts and transactions affected by each specific control objective are free of material error. In deciding on procedures, the auditor should consider the alternatives and decide which would be the most responsive in light of the risks. As a general rule, the higher the likelihood of material error, the more persuasive the evidence should be. As a practical matter, in some cases, the client may ask the auditor to perform additional work not called for by the risk analysis. For example, the auditor may be asked to confirm all customer accounts receivable where the auditor would have confirmed only a sample. (In such a confirmation the auditor asks the debtor whether the debtor's balance per the client's records is correct.)

The risk analysis is not limited to routine transactions such as sales, receipts, or disbursements. Periodic or infrequently occurring transactions, such as those involving income taxes and loss contingencies, also should be considered. Ordinarily, the system evaluation will not influence the risk analysis for these transactions as much as it will for routine transactions. For periodic or infrequently occurring transactions, the environmental considerations and observations from the detail analytical review often will be the principal components of the risk analysis.

How a completed risk analysis working paper might look is illustrated in Figure 2–3 with an example that covers two specific control objectives

FIGURE 2-3   Example of a Risk Analysis Working Paper

Risk Analysis Prepared By/Date ___ PWC 7-31 ___
PAA* Prepared By/Date ___ RDH 8-15 ___
Reviewed By/Date ___ MG 8-20 ___

Sales

S-1 Customer Orders Require Approval of Credit and Terms Before Acceptance
S-2 Uncollectible Amounts Are Promptly Identified and Provided For

Risk Analysis

Environmental Considerations Company sells construction materials to large commercial and residential contractors. Bad debts have been minor in the past. Commercial construction backlog is substantial. But high interest rates caused residential housing starts to decline dramatically in the last two quarters, adversely affecting residential contractors. Approximately 30% of the sales are to residential contractors.

Observations from Detail Analytical Review Accounts receivable have increased $570,000 (13%) over prior year. Days' sales in receivables at 6/30/X9 were 70 days (58 days at 12/31/X8). Over 60-day aging category increased $700,000, substantially all from residential contractors (including 20 accounts over $25,000). Only 2 commercial accounts were over 60 days old, both over $150,000. Allowance for doubtful accounts is $125,000 at 6/30/X9 ($100,000 at 12/31/X8). Write-offs through 6/30/X9 total $45,000 vs. $60,000 during all of 19X8.

System Evaluation

System Design Provides Reasonable Assurance Objective Being Achieved

	Yes	No		Yes	No
S-1	☑	☐	S-2	☑	☐

	Reference	
Key Attributes (Deficiencies) Supporting Evaluation	System Documentation A/R Flow	PAA*
S-1 Credit limits based on outside agencies' ratings (e.g., D&B), audited financials, etc. Credit Dept. (independent of Sales and A/R Depts.) reviews all orders based on credit limit and outstanding balance, and notes approval or disapproval.	Chart-1,2	1,2
S-2 Credit Dept. handles collection effort based on monthly review of A/R aging and prepares journal entries for writing off bad debts (independent of A/R Dept. and cash receipts).	A/R Flow Chart-3,4	3

Likelihood of Material Error in Accounts Affected (Conclusion based on Risk Analysis. Explain if not obvious.) System appears to achieve specific control objectives (as supported by higher allowance and year-to-date write-offs), but decline in housing starts and deterioration in aging indicate possible problems in collections from residential contractors.

☐ High
☑ Moderate
☐ Low

Preliminary Audit Approach Responsive to Risk Analysis

Audit Program Reference

1. Randomly select 25 sales invoices through August. Test for credit approval and review for current documentation used to set customer credit limit. — S-1
2. Use software package to compare customer credit limits with balances at October 31 and to test the accuracy of A/R aging. — S-2
3. Examine Credit Dept. copies of monthly agings through August 31 for evidence of review. — S-3
4. At October 31, review collectibility of accounts over 60 days old exceeding $25,000 for residential and $150,000 for commercial. Examine subsequent receipts or discuss collectibility with credit manager. — S-4
5. At year-end, update collectibility review for residential contractors. Limit review of commercial accounts to general inquiry of credit manager. — S-5

(S-1, S-2)

*Authors' Note: PAA is preliminary audit approach.

relating to sales, accounts receivable, and the allowance for doubtful accounts. Each specific control objective relates to several accounts, and most accounts are affected by several objectives. The nature, timing, and extent of procedures comprising the program in an audit area are based on the risk analyses for all the control objectives that affect it. *The result is that the auditor knows why each audit procedure is being performed.* Appendix II at the end of this textbook lists the financial statement classifications typically affected by each specific control objective; and figures included in Chapters 10, 11, 13, and 14 show the relationship of specific control objectives to the debits or credits for each financial statement classification.

Preparing the Audit Program.   After the preliminary audit approaches for the specific control objectives are developed on the risk analysis working papers, they are combined to prepare the formal audit program for execution.

Program Execution

This phase consists of performing the audit procedures outlined in the audit program and reviewing the results. The audit procedures must be performed by the auditor before an opinion may be expressed on the financial statements. Due care is essential in performing audit procedures and reviewing the results. Audit procedures may be performed (1) at one time, near year-end; (2) in several stages, including some work at a time prior to the company's year-end (referred to as "preliminary," "interim," or "bring-up" work); or (3) on a continuous basis throughout the year. As a matter of good practice, auditors normally attempt to transfer as much audit work as possible from the busy year-end to an interim period. This transfer permits auditors to study internal controls at an earlier date, enables them to consider in advance the nature of any changes in the company's business or accounting procedures that may require modification in the audit program, and may make it possible for them to issue their report earlier.

A review of the work performed is made to check that the (1) audit procedures have been properly applied, (2) work of the staff is satisfactory, (3) working papers are complete and adequate, and (4) procedures necessary to form an opinion have been completed. The review normally is conducted by the more senior personnel of the independent auditing firm.

Types of Audit Tests.   Audit tests can be categorized into two major types—*compliance tests* and *substantive tests*. Compliance tests are tests made by the auditor to test the extent to which established procedures and controls are functioning *as intended*. Substantive tests are performed to test or support the validity and propriety of specific transactions or account balances, and thus provide the evidence required by the third standard of field work. [*SAS No. 1,* as amended (AU 320.59 and .74)] *SAS No. 1* (as amended by *SAS No. 23*) (AU 320.74) states that substantive tests consist of the following two general classes of auditing procedures: ". . . *(a)* tests of details of transactions and balances and *(b)* analytical review procedures applied to financial information."

Conceptually, the difference between compliance tests and substantive tests may be an important distinction; however, in practice, the results of either type of test contribute toward the purpose of the other. Errors having an impact on the financial statements may be discovered when conducting compliance tests, and compliance exceptions may be discovered when conducting substantive tests. Further, substantive tests can confirm or challenge the evaluation of the effectiveness of the accounting system, which is usually the task of compliance tests. Although a test may have a primary purpose (compliance or substantive), the same sample of transactions or balances often is used to obtain both types of evidence. By integrating compliance tests with substantive tests, it is possible to maximize the benefits provided by all audit procedures. These integrated procedures are referred to as "dual-purpose tests."

Performing Tests of Transactions. The testing of the details of specific transactions (e.g., authorization of purchases of inventories) is referred to as tests of transactions. Such tests, as suggested above, can include both compliance and substantive aspects. Consequently, they may function as dual-purpose tests.

The auditor's interim tests of transactions should provide evidence that the accounting system is functioning as documented and the audit program is appropriate. If not, the auditor should reconsider the planned reliance on the system of internal control and revise the audit program accordingly. By substantively testing significant transactions at an interim date, the auditor also can obtain evidence that material errors or irregularities have not occurred and account balances are proper.

Performing Direct Tests of Balances. Direct tests of balances are a type of substantive test in which the auditor tests the validity and propriety of account balances (e.g., cash, accounts receivable, sales). The auditor may perform certain direct tests of balances at an interim date. Then close to year-end, the auditor returns to the client for further direct tests of balances. The procedures applied at that time will have been planned to anticipate significant audit problems. Direct tests of balances should include year-end analytical review procedures to confirm that the elements of the system the auditor planned to rely on have produced the expected amounts (i.e., the numbers make sense) and to identify specific transactions or accounts that may require additional audit effort.

Evaluate Sufficiency of Audit Approach. The sufficiency of the auditor's planned approach can be determined only after evaluating the results of the audit procedures. As the auditor performs tests of transactions and direct tests of balances, the audit program should be challenged in view of the findings. The auditor should compare the findings with what was expected and consider the effects on the audit program. Finding errors of any size when none were expected is more significant than finding errors that were expected. Finding unexpected errors requires action—the auditor should change the audit program if the planned procedures are no longer appropriate.

Reporting

Reporting on the financial statements is the ultimate goal of an audit and represents the fourth step in the audit process. This step involves management preparation of the financial statements and auditor preparation of the auditor's report. Remember that the financial statements, including footnotes, are the representations and primary responsibility of the management of the business entity, not the auditor—even though the auditor sometimes assists in or supervises the preparation of the statements. On the other hand, the auditor is entirely responsible for the scope of the examination and the opinion expressed.

Each time a CPA signs an auditor's report, it should be done with a keen awareness of the professional and legal responsibilities involved. Each audit examination presents the auditor with a new set of circumstances and findings. Before signing the report, the auditor must be fully satisfied that the work of everyone involved in the engagement conforms to generally accepted auditing standards.

Operating Components

To provide a framework for performing the risk analysis, a typical commercial or industrial company has been divided into four basic operating components. Figure 2–4 outlines these components and identifies the principal activities normally associated with them.

The operating components are used as the basic framework for performing the risk analysis. Gaining an understanding of a business and its systems from an operating perspective allows the auditor to view the business in much the same way as management does. The focus on operating components facilitates the auditor's communications with management. Under this approach, the risk analysis working papers, the audit program, and the audit working papers are all organized by operating component.

The risk analysis approach differs from the transaction cycle approach that traditionally has been used by most auditors. The transaction cycle approach focuses on whether control procedures are in place at key points in a company's flow of transactions. And the auditor's tests are directed toward the major cycles (e.g., sales, receivables, cash receipts) that cover those transaction flows. On the other hand, under the risk analysis approach, the focus on operating components provides the auditor with a business perspective that is more consistent with that of the entity's management

FIGURE 2–4 Operating Components of a Typical Commercial or Industrial Business

Administration
(Control and support of operating activities)
Plan of organization
Policies and procedures
Information systems and financial reporting
Budgets
Reconciliation of detail records to
   control accounts and physical
   assets to accounting records
Internal audit
Tax administration
Legal
Risk management (Insurance)

Sales
(Marketing, distribution, billing,
   and collection)
Advertising and promotion
Selling and distribution
Order acceptance
Order entry
Shipping/Service
Billing
Recording
Collection efforts
Adjustment and credits

Production or Service
(Acquisition and conversion of
   resources into products or services)
Materials and Overhead
   Requisition
   Purchasing
   Receiving
   Recording
Labor
   Hiring and termination
   Wage and salary administration
   Fringe benefits
   Timekeeping
   Payroll preparation
   Recording
Property, Plant, and Equipment
   Authorization
   Purchasing
   Receiving
   Recording
   Depreciation
   Disposals
   Repairs and maintenance
Accountability and Physical Safeguards
   Cost accounting system
   Reporting usage and production
   Overstock and obsolescence
   Valuation
   Security

Finance
(Management of financial
   resources)
Cash
   Receipts
   Disbursements
Debt and Leases
   Authorization
   Recording
   Compliance
Equity
   Authorization
   Issuance
   Recording
Investments
   Authorization
   Execution
   Income
   Recording
   Valuation
   Safeguarding

and therefore provides a more meaningful framework for performing the risk analysis.

The risk analysis approach also differs from the so-called balance sheet approach, where auditors direct emphasis toward the details of year-end balance sheet accounts, with less emphasis on interim transactions or internal controls.

Specific Control Objectives

A key element in the audit approach is the relationship of specific control objectives to transactions and accounts. Specific control objectives relate to the activities in each operating component that originate and process transactions. Each type of transaction results in either debits or credits to various accounts. Thus, control objectives provide convenient points of reference for considering environmental factors, performing detail analytical review procedures, and evaluating the accounting system and then relating these inputs to the likelihood of understatements or overstatements in specific transactions and accounts.

The following specific control objectives have been defined for a typical commercial or industrial business. The reference numbers will be used for ease of reference throughout the textbook.

Reference
No.

SALES

S–1 Customer orders require approval of credit and terms before acceptance
S–2 Uncollectible amounts are promptly identified and provided for
S–3 Products shipped or services rendered are billed
S–4 Billings are for the correct amount
S–5 Revenues are recorded correctly as to account, amount, and period
S–6 Recorded billings are for valid transactions
S–7 Customer returns and other allowances are approved and recorded correctly as to account, amount, and period

PRODUCTION OR SERVICE—MATERIALS AND OVERHEAD

P–1 Goods or services are purchased only with proper authorization
P–2 Goods or services received are recorded correctly as to account, amount, and period

PRODUCTION OR SERVICE—LABOR

P–3 Salary, wage, and benefit expenses are incurred only for work authorized and performed
P–4 Salaries, wages, and benefits are calculated at the proper rate
P–5 Salaries, wages, benefits, and related liabilities are recorded correctly as to account (department, activity, cost center, etc.), amount, and period

PRODUCTION OR SERVICE—INVENTORY ACCOUNTABILITY
AND PHYSICAL SAFEGUARDS

P–6 Costs are assigned to inventory in accordance with the stated valuation method
P–7 Usage and movement of inventory is recorded correctly as to account, amount (quantities and dollars), and period

Reference
No.

P–8   Physical loss of inventory is prevented or promptly detected

P–9   Obsolete, slow-moving, and overstock inventory is prevented or promptly detected and provided for

P–10   Inventory is carried at the lower of cost or market

PRODUCTION OR SERVICE—PROPERTY, PLANT, AND EQUIPMENT

P–11   Property, plant, and equipment are purchased only with proper authorization

P–12   Property, plant, and equipment purchases are recorded correctly as to account, amount, and period

P–13   Disposals, retirements, trade-ins, idle plant and equipment, and other losses are identified and recorded correctly as to account, amount, and period

P–14   Physical loss of property, plant, and equipment is prevented

P–15   Depreciation is calculated using proper lives and methods

FINANCE

F–1   Cash receipts are recorded correctly as to account, amount, and period and are deposited

F–2   Cash receipts are properly applied to customer balances

F–3   Cash disbursements are for goods or services authorized and received

F–4   Cash disbursements are recorded correctly as to account, amount, and period

F–5   Debt and lease obligations and related expenses are authorized and recorded correctly as to account, amount, and period

F–6   Equity transactions are authorized and recorded correctly as to account, amount, and period

F–7   Investments in and advances to/from subsidiaries and other affiliates are authorized and recorded correctly as to account, amount, and period

F–8   Investment transactions are authorized and recorded correctly as to account, amount, and period

F–9   Income earned on investments is recorded correctly as to account, amount, and period

F–10   Loss in value of investments is promptly detected and provided for

F–11   Physical loss of investments is prevented or promptly detected

ADMINISTRATION

A–1   Expenses are incurred only with proper authorization

A–2   Expenses and related liabilities are recorded correctly as to account, amount, and period

A–3   Salary, wage, and benefit expenses are incurred only for work authorized and performed

A–4   Salaries, wages, and benefits are calculated at the proper rate

A–5   Salaries, wages, benefits, and related liabilities are recorded correctly as to account (department, activity, etc.), amount, and period

A–6   Amortization or loss in value of intangibles is recorded correctly as to account, amount, and period

A–7   Provisions for income taxes and related liabilities and deferrals are recorded correctly as to account, amount, and period

A–8   Commitments and contingencies are identified, monitored, and, if appropriate, recorded or disclosed

Risk Analysis Working Paper

Under the risk analysis approach, on each audit engagement the auditor completes risk analysis working papers for all specific control objectives related to important financial statement classifications. Control objectives for any significant unique activities should be defined, and additional pages completed. Figure 2–5 describes how to complete a risk analysis working paper.

AUDIT EVIDENCE

The third standard of field work requires the auditor to obtain sufficient competent evidential matter before issuing an opinion as to the fair presentation of the client's statements. *SAS No. 31*, "Evidential Matter" (AU 326.02) suggests that the auditor should exercise professional judgment to assess the validity of the evidence.

Nature of Audit Evidence

SAS No. 31 (AU 326.14) states that "evidential matter supporting the financial statements consists of the underlying accounting data and all corroborating information available to the auditor." Furthermore, *SAS No. 31* suggests that the data generated by the accounting system alone (e.g., journals, ledgers, manuals, worksheets) are not sufficient evidence on which to base an opinion. The accounting system might be producing inaccurate or incomplete financial information. Consequently, the independent auditor also gathers other information. The degree to which the auditor can rely on the evidence depends upon its source and form. Since the auditor's *evaluation* of the fairness of the presentation of the financial statements is heavily dependent upon the *evidence* of their fairness, care must be taken to obtain as much evidence as is needed to make a proper evaluation.

The financial statements of an entity consist of many different accounts. In attempting to evaluate the fairness of the amounts in each account, the auditor must consider the basic nature of each account. For example, the nature of cash is very different from that of plant and equipment. Both are assets, but the risks of errors and irregularities in each differ. Cash is generally much more susceptible to manipulation and theft. The auditor must decide what is the best evidence of the fairness of each account under the circumstances.

Sufficiency and Competence of Evidence

Sufficiency of Evidence.   Sufficiency is concerned with having enough evidence. It relates to the *quantity of* evidence that the auditor needs in a particular circumstance.

FIGURE 2-5 How to Complete the Risk Analysis Working Paper

Risk Analysis Prepared By/Date _____

PAA Prepared By/Date _____

Reviewed By/Date _____

Production or Service—Materials and Overhead

P-1 Goods or Services Are Purchased Only with Proper Authorization

P-2 Goods or Services Received Are Recorded Correctly as to Account, Amount, and Period

Risk Analysis

Environmental Considerations _____

_____

_____

_____

_____

Observations from Detail Analytical Review _____

_____

_____

_____

_____

System Evaluation

   System Design Provides Reasonable Assurance Objective Being Achieved

P-1   Yes No   P-2   Yes No   P-2   Yes No   P-2   Yes No

     ☐ ☐   Account ☐ ☐   Amount ☐ ☐   Period ☐ ☐

Reference

System

Key Attributes (Deficiencies) Supporting Evaluation   Documentation   PAA

_____ _____ _____

_____ _____ _____

_____ _____ _____

_____ _____ _____

_____ _____ _____

_____ _____ _____

Likelihood of Material Error in Accounts Affected (Conclusion based on Risk Analysis.

Explain if not obvious.) _____ ☐ High

_____ ☐ Moderate

_____ ☐ Low

_____

_____

Audit

Program

Preliminary Audit Approach Responsive to Risk Analysis   Reference

_____ _____

_____ _____

_____ _____

_____ _____

_____ _____

_____ _____

_____ _____

_____ _____

_____ _____

(P-1, P-2)

1. Summarize the external and internal factors and their potential impact on accounts or transactions affected by the control objectives. These factors may increase or decrease the likelihood of material error and lead the auditor to emphasize specific audit areas or help justify minimum audit effort.

2. Summarize pertinent information obtained from analytical review of interim financial and operating data. Quantify changes in conditions and circumstances and cover important trends and relationships that confirm or challenge the auditor's understanding of the environment or accounting system. Indicate specific amounts and percentages relating to accounts and transactions affected by the control objectives.

3. Indicate "yes" or "no" conclusion based on review of system design.

4. Summarize key attributes or deficiencies that support the auditor's conclusion. Cross-reference to (a) flowcharts, narratives, or other working papers and (b) related audit procedures in the preliminary audit approach.

5. Assess the likelihood of material error occurring in the accounts affected by the control objectives, based on the interaction of the inputs to the risk analysis. When there is a conflict among the inputs, or the conclusion is otherwise unclear, include an explanation.

6. Develop a preliminary audit approach for the transactions and accounts affected by each control objective. The preliminary audit approach should be responsive to the risks identified and include both interim and year-end procedures—tests of transactions and direct tests of balances. Cross-reference the preliminary audit approach to steps in the audit program.

Competence of Evidence.   Competence is concerned with the *qualitative* aspects of evidence. It relates to the persuasiveness of the evidence to be used in the audit.

SAS No. 31 (AU 326.18) suggests that competent evidence is both valid and relevant. While validity may vary with the circumstances, *SAS No. 31* (AU 326.18) makes the following presumptions concerning the validity of evidence:

a.   When evidential matter can be obtained from independent sources outside an entity, it provides greater assurance of reliability for the purposes of an independent audit than that secured solely within the entity.

b.   When accounting data and financial statements are developed under satisfactory conditions of internal accounting control, there is more assurance about their reliability than when they are developed under unsatisfactory conditions of internal accounting control.

c. The independent auditor's direct personal knowledge obtained through physical examination, observation, computation, and inspection is more persuasive than information obtained indirectly.

Factors Affecting the Evidence to Be Gathered

SAS No. 31 (AU 326.19) suggests that the amount and kind of evidence required for the auditor to issue an opinion on financial statements is dependent upon the professional judgment of the auditor. Obtaining large amounts of evidence is usually expensive. Consequently, in determining the quantity of evidence needed in a particular circumstance, the auditor must consider the cost of gathering it. *SAS No. 31* (AU 326.21) states that "as a guiding rule, there should be a rational relationship between the cost of obtaining evidence and the usefulness of the information obtained. In determining the usefulness of evidence, relative risk may be properly given consideration. The matter of difficulty and expense involved in testing a particular item is not itself a valid basis for omitting the test."

The client may need to publish the audited statements within some reasonable time after the end of the year. Thus, an audit cannot continue indefinitely (*SAS No. 31,* AU 326.20). But the auditor must not let a time constraint result in substandard work. Consequently, the auditor must take sufficient time to gather the amount and kind of evidence necessary to issue an informed opinion.

SAS No. 31 (AU 326.11) suggests that the amount and kind of evidence gathered also is related to the materiality or significance of the account under consideration and the materiality of potential errors and irregularities. An item is "material" if its omission or misstatement would affect the decision of a knowledgeable user. What a material item is in a given circumstance is a matter of professional judgment. Items of limited materiality require less consideration than do very material accounts. Furthermore, Mautz and Sharaf note that if ". . . some evidence is much more compelling or strong than other evidence, we are led to a conclusion that more compelling evidence is required for material assertions than for assertions that are not material. Note that the important point is not, the quantity of evidence but rather the quality of evidence."[1]

Types of Evidence

There are various types of evidence discussed in detail in this section.

[1] R. K. Mautz and Hussein A. Sharaf, *The Philosophy of Auditing* (American Accounting Association, 1961), p. 104.

Internally Generated Data.   The data generated by an accounting system is a form of evidence. The extent to which the auditor can rely on internally generated accounting data generally depends on the quality of the system of internal control that is present and operating in the entity being examined. If the system of internal control is strong, the auditor may rely to some extent on internally generated data. Thus, there is less need for large amounts of other kinds of evidence.

Physical Evidence.   The actual physical inspection of many assets is the best evidence of their existence. However, while inspection may prove existence, ordinarily it does not tell the auditor very much about the ownership (who has title), quality, or value of the asset. These matters also must be investigated by the auditor.

Documents Created Outside the Organization.   There are two major types of documentary evidence created outside an organization: (1) evidence sent directly to the auditor and (2) evidence retained by the client. Documents created by outside entities and sent directly to the auditor are perhaps the best type of documentary evidence. There is little possibility that client personnel have altered these documents. An example of such evidence is a confirmation of accounts receivable received directly by the auditor.

Documents created externally but held by the client generally are not as valid a type of evidence as those created externally and sent directly to the auditor. However, often they must be used. The degree of validity of such evidence depends on the ease with which client personnel could either alter or create the documents and on their motivation and inclination to do so under the circumstances. Insurance policies, deeds, brokers' advices, and bank debit memos are examples.

Documents Internally Generated.   Documents created within a client's organization are generally considered to be evidence of a lower quality than those created outside the organization. The degree of reliance that an auditor can place on internally generated documents depends in large measure on the quality of the system of internal control that is present and operating in the entity. For example, if no single individual handles payroll transactions from start to finish, more reliance may be placed on payroll documents than in a system in which one individual performs all the payroll work. Generally, if a document is reviewed by one or more employees other than the preparer of the document, there is less chance that the preparer has altered or falsified the document.

Internally generated documents, such as canceled checks that circulate outside the client's organization, are reviewed by outside agencies, and are then returned to the client, have an added degree of reliability. A canceled check has been reviewed by the payee who endorsed it, as well as by various bank employees.

Comparisons, Ratios, and Computations.   Comparisons and ratios are analytical review procedures that provide another form of evidence that an auditor may use. For example, when comparing account balances between and within periods, the auditor looks for unusual changes that reveal something concerning the account in question. Comparison of actual amounts to budgets or industry data also may reveal useful information. Identifying changes or trends in financial ratios over time also may reveal changes that should be investigated (see *SAS No. 23* "Analytical Review Procedures").

The auditor often will perform independent calculations as a step in the process of verifying an account balance. These calculations may take the form of proving the totals on an invoice or independently calculating a payroll accrual.

Inquiry.   A somewhat weak but useful type of evidence is information supplied by client personnel. An auditor frequently asks client personnel questions that are related to the various accounts under review. The responses to these questions can be very helpful, but as evidence they are not sufficient. When possible, inquiry should be confirmed by other types of evidence. Often the auditor can verify the client's statements by reference to internal and/or external documents.

Written Representations.[2]   Written representations, covered by *SAS No. 19*, "Client Representations" (AU 333), are addressed to the auditor and signed by the client (although often prepared by the auditor). The representations are made by the company officials to supplement information that the auditor has obtained from the books and records of the company, or to confirm information given to the auditor orally. Written representations become an integral part of the working papers. Matters addressed in written representations include absence of errors or unrecorded transactions in the financial statements, subsequent events, related party transactions, losses from purchase or sale commitments, and contingencies. The written representations provide the company's officials an opportunity to consider whether all important matters have been disclosed to the auditor, and also act as a reminder to management of its primary responsibility for the fairness of presentation of the financial statements. However, the representations are not substitutes for other tests by the auditor. Chapter 14 further describes the purpose and contents of written representations.

---

[2] This section is based on *Statement on Auditing Procedures No. 19* "Client Representations," American Institute of Certified Public Accountants, 1977.

WORKING PAPERS

Auditors use working papers to document the audit procedures performed and conclusions reached. Working papers should provide the necessary information (evidence) to support the evaluation of the adequacy of the audit scope and opinion as to whether the financial statements being examined are fairly presented.

The importance of a complete, concise, and logically arranged set of working papers cannot be overemphasized. An audit program step is not completed until the work performed (procedures) and an evaluation of the results (conclusions) are *explicitly documented.* The audit reviewer should not have to make inferences from the working papers to determine whether procedures have been performed. The reviewer also should be able to readily determine the preparer's conclusions. In this way, the reviewer can correlate the conclusions of all the members of the audit team to ensure that the auditors' report is supported by the findings.

In addition to serving as documentation for the audit procedures performed, working papers may be a source of information for other aspects of an engagement. For example, schedules filed with income tax returns or reports to the Securities and Exchange Commission (SEC) are often prepared from audit working papers.

Each working paper is a formal and permanent document describing precisely the work performed and a conclusion as to the results. Working papers may be reviewed, often years after the fact, by third parties. The following are examples of situations in which such third-party reviews are possible:

1. Other independent auditors may review working papers when clients merge, sell, or change auditors.
2. Other independent auditors who have been engaged to perform a peer review may review working papers. The purpose of the peer review is to constructively criticize the firm being reviewed and make recommendations that may be used by the reviewed firm to assist in the performance of their future work.
3. Parties to a legal action may subpoena working papers to be used as evidence.
4. IRS field agents may review selected schedules when making a tax examination.
5. The SEC may review working papers during an investigation.

Communications between independent auditors and their clients are *not* "privileged," as are certain communications between lawyers and their clients. The auditor can be required to produce audit and tax return working papers in a court of law. Although subsequent legal action against either the auditor or client generally is not anticipated during the audit, there is always that possibility. Thus, it is important that the working papers evidencing the examination be accurate and objective and contain no careless, ambiguous, or irrelevant comments that could be interpreted to the detriment of the auditor or client.

What Constitutes Working Papers

Working papers include all documentation that is created or obtained from the client or others that demonstrates compliance with auditing standards and documents the audit procedures performed. This includes flowcharts, risk analysis working papers, trial balances, summary schedules, adjusting journal entries, account analyses, audit memoranda, confirmations, computer listings, correspondence, adding machine tapes, and catalogs. In essence, just about any kind of material can become an "audit working paper." To illustrate, for an audit of a construction contractor, photographs of job sites are considered audit working papers.

SAS No. 41, "Working Papers" (AU 339.04), provides the following guidelines:

> Factors affecting the auditor's judgment about the quantity, type, and content of the working papers for a particular engagement include the *(a)* nature of the engagement, *(b)* nature of the auditor's report, *(c)* nature of the financial statements, schedules, or other information on which the auditor is reporting, *(d)* nature and condition of the client's records, *(e)* degree of reliance on internal accounting control, and *(f)* needs in the particular circumstances for supervision and review of the work.

SAS No. 41 (AU 339.05) goes on to state:

> The quantity, type, and content of working papers vary with the circumstances . . . , but the papers should be sufficient to show that the accounting records agree or reconcile with the financial statements or other information reported on, and that the applicable standards of field work have been observed. Working papers ordinarily should include documentation showing that—
>
> a. The work has been adequately planned and supervised, indicating observance of the first standard of field work.
> b. The system of internal accounting control has been studied and evaluated to the degree necessary to determine whether, and to what extent, other auditing procedures are to be restricted, indicating observance of the second standard of field work.
> c. The audit evidence obtained, the auditing procedures applied, and the testing performed have provided sufficient competent evidential matter to afford a reasonable basis for an opinion, indicating observance of the third standard of field work.

Headings of Audit Working Papers

Generally, the heading of each audit working paper should include the name of the client, the audit period or balance sheet date, a title or description of the working paper, and the names of the auditors who prepare and/or review the working papers along with the date completed. When using client-prepared working papers, the auditor should indicate so in the heading.

Planning Each Audit Working Paper

Whether preparing an account analysis or a memorandum, the goal is the same—to prepare a clear, concise, and well-organized record of audit procedures performed. To do this efficiently, the organization of each working paper should be planned. Time spent in planning generally saves at least as much or more time in documenting audit procedures.

Whenever possible, the auditor should request clients to prepare selected working papers (e.g., trial balances or account analyses). This requires additional audit planning; however, it helps control the cost of audits. The format and content of each working paper, along with the dates when they will be needed, should be carefully specified and reviewed with the client. Obviously, client-prepared working papers should not be accepted until they meet the auditor's specifications. When using client-prepared working papers, the auditor should clearly distinguish between comments or notations made by the client and those made by the auditor.

Types of Working Papers

Trial Balance. A trial balance consists of a list of a client's general ledger account balances organized in the sequence they appear in the general ledger. It is common for the client to prepare the trial balance. A trial balance provides a bridge between the financial statements and the audit working papers. Totals on other audit working papers should agree with related amounts on the trial balance. The trial balance is used to (1) determine that the general ledger is in balance, (2) cross-reference accounts to related audit working papers, (3) comment on the reasonableness of certain account balances (e.g., immaterial balances or income and expense totals explained by analytical review for which no detail analysis is needed), (4) determine that the financial statements agree with the accounting records, (5) make combinations of accounts comprising financial statement captions, and (6) adjust preliminary account balances to final amounts if necessary. Figure 2–6 is an example of a trial balance.

Audit procedures performed on trial balances normally include testing clerical accuracy and tracing the prior year final and current year preliminary account balances to the general ledger.

FIGURE 2-6 Example of a Trial Balance

TRIAL BALANCE
Client Name Simon Industries
Audit Date December 31, 19X1

Prepared by Greenman 2/1/X2
Reviewed by Hill   2/15/X2

Account Number	Account Title	Working Paper Reference	Prior Year Balances Dr. (Cr.)	Preliminary Balances Debits	Preliminary Balances Credits	Adjustments Debits	Adjustments Credits	Final Balances Debits	Final Balances Credits	Comments
100	Petty cash		100.00	100.00				100.00		
101	Cash—general account	FA-1.1	273,338.18	220,585.18				220,585.18		
102	Cash—salary payroll	FA-2.1	1,000.00	1,000.00				1,000.00	2,046,336.93	
103	Cash—hourly payroll	FA-3.1	1,000.00	1,000.00				1,000.00	AFS	
110	Certificates of deposit	FA-4.1	2,300,230.00	1,815,000.00				1,815,000.00		
111	Accrued interest receivable	FA-4.2	36,227.50	8,651.75				8,651.75		
120	Trade accounts receivable	SA-1	4,098,268.78	9,556,373.22		27,658.20		9,584,031.42		
121	Trade notes receivable		22,459.26	26,685.77				26,685.77		Change due to new $6,000 note less repayments. None past due.
125	Allowance for uncollectible accounts	SB-5	(60,000.00)		125,000.00		3,000.00		128,000.00	

Note: The auditor may not always find it necessary to prepare an audit schedule for each account balance. In the above example, the procedures regarding the immaterial balance of Trade Notes Receivable are documented by analytical review comments in the comments section of the trial balance. This technique may be used to save time in areas where preparing a separate working paper would not result in significant additional data for the working papers.

Summary Schedules. Summary or lead schedules are comparable to trial balances and may be used instead of a trial balance. One lead schedule would be prepared for each financial statement caption and contain the detailed accounts from the general ledger that make up the caption total.

Adjusting Journal Entries. In analyzing the various accounts, the auditor may find items that require adjustment. This may be due to either an error or a difference of opinion regarding the accounting treatment for a particular item.

Although the auditor normally prepares the adjusting journal entries, they should be reviewed with and approved by client management, as they have the primary responsibility for the financial statements. Each proposed adjustment should be completely documented in the working papers.

The determining factor in deciding whether a proposed adjustment should be made is materiality. However, the auditor also needs to evaluate the cumulative effect of those adjustments that were not made because in total they may be material. To make this evaluation, auditors normally prepare a working paper summarizing the adjusting journal entries not made.

Account Analyses. Account analyses are columnar worksheets that provide narrative and numerical information about account balances or classes of transactions. They are sometimes called *audit schedules.* Since most numerical data in the schedules represent dollar amounts, dollar signs are usually omitted; however, the meaning of all other numbers (e.g., dates, percents, pieces, feet) should either be identified or be self-evident. Captions should be sufficiently descriptive and specific to enable the reviewer to understand the data.

Audit schedules may relate to (1) a moment in time, (2) a period of time, or (3) a combination of both. A moment-in-time audit schedule analyzes an account balance as of a specific date (examples are an accounts receivable aging schedule, unexpired insurance analysis, and inventory price test). A period-of-time analysis summarizes transactions in an account or group of accounts for the period under examination (examples are income and expense analyses). It is also possible for the auditor to use a *combination* of these analyses by summarizing transactions during the year, together with year-end detail.

Designing audit schedules to achieve the objectives of audit procedures requires a clear understanding of the objectives. For example, an audit procedure might require the auditor to analyze and support the professional fees account. The primary reason for performing this procedure is to identify matters that may be important to the auditor (e.g., existence of major litigation). Review the schedule of professional fees illustrated in Figure 2–7. Although the auditor examined supporting invoices for each professional fee, this schedule fails to meet the audit objectives because it does not tell

FIGURE 2–7   Schedule that Does Not Satisfy Audit Objective

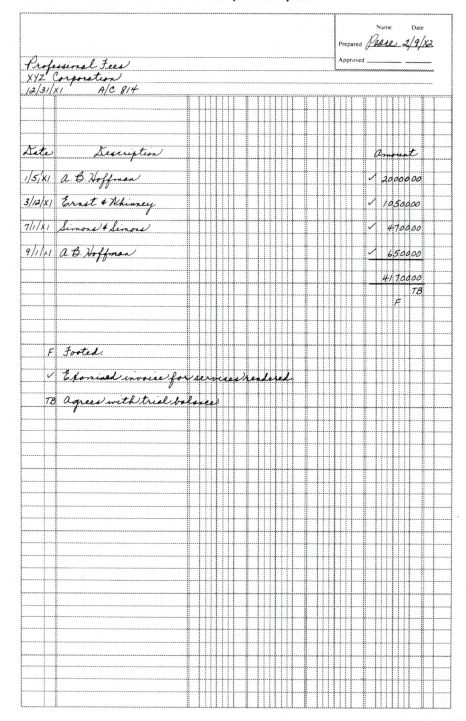

whether these fees relate to major litigation. The reviewer should not have to assume that the preparer would have recorded information related to any major litigation he or she noted when reviewing the supporting invoices. Rather, the preparer should provide enough information for the reviewer to agree with the preparer's conclusion regarding the facts.

On the schedule illustrated in Figure 2–8, the auditor noted agreement of account, amount, and period, *and described the nature of the services.* It enables the primary audit objective to be accomplished—to determine that professional fees do not relate to major litigation or other important matters.

Symbols, commonly called *tick marks,* are used to describe the audit procedures performed on data in the working papers. Tick mark explanations should be clear and concise, and should specifically describe the work performed. Tick mark explanations normally include a description of:

Evidence examined, findings, and results;

Unusual items noted in a test and how they were resolved; and/or

Clerical accuracy tests.

Some sample tick mark explanations are included in Figure 2–8.

Other comments on audit schedules might include (1) a brief summary of discussions with client personnel, (2) data needed for notes to the financial statements, (3) a description of an account when it is not evident from the title, and (4) working paper conclusion statements.

Audit Memoranda. Audit memoranda are efficient means of documenting the auditor's consideration of important accounting and auditing issues and the performance of certain audit procedures (e.g., observation or inquiry procedures not otherwise evidenced in the working papers). In certain situations, audit memoranda also are useful to document the auditor's conclusions in audit areas. However, it is not necessary to prepare an audit memorandum for each financial statement caption or account. Further, memoranda can be used to supplement accounting systems documentation, and to document meetings with client personnel.

Other Items. Other items may be included in the working papers. These include various questionnaires, flowcharts, the audit program, and documents created by others. Examples of the latter may include letters of representation, letters from attorneys, other correspondence, copies of selected client documents, corporate minutes, a copy of the bylaws, and a copy of the articles of incorporation.

Documenting Audit Conclusions

It is important for each auditor to accept responsibility for having performed the work called for by the audit program and express a conclusion

FIGURE 2–8 Schedule that Satisfies Audit Objective

	Name	Date
Prepared	Good	2/9/X2
Approved		

Professional Fees
XYZ Corporation
12/31/X1 A/C 814

Date		Description of Services		Amount
1/5/X1	A.B. Hoffman	Annual retainer (for services performed in connection with maintaining minutes of directors meetings, preparation of 10-K, and general consultation) for corporate counsel—covering the period from 1/1/X1–12/31/X1.	✓	20000.00
3/12/X1	Ernst & Whinney	Fees for annual audit year ended 12/31/X0.	✓	10500.00
7/1/X1	Simons & Simons	Fees for patent for new super widget first marketed in April of 19X1. (See copy of patent rights in permanent file working papers PF-A)	(A)	4700.00
9/1/X1	A.B. Hoffman	Fees in addition to annual retainer for work performed in negotiation of new union contract. (Copy of the new contract is included in the permanent file working papers PF-P.)	✓	6500.00
		Balance at 12/31/X1		41700.00 TB F
		Balance at 12/31/X0		34100.00 TB

F Footed.

✓ Examined invoice noting agreement of account, amount, period, and description of services set forth above.

(A) The company's policy is to expense costs of acquiring patents in the year incurred.

TB Agrees with trial balance

I have analyzed professional fees in accordance with the audit program and found no indication of major litigation or other important matters which should be recorded or disclosed in the financial statements.

based on the audit evidence examined. As previously discussed, audit memoranda are useful in certain situations to document audit conclusions. However, this can usually be accomplished more efficiently and effectively on individual audit schedules with conclusion statements such as:

Test of key attributes. I have tested the operation of the key attributes relating to the processing of sales, receivables, and cash receipts in accordance with the audit program. In my opinion, the key attributes are functioning as designed and related transactions are properly recorded.

Direct tests of balances of transactions. I have examined the trade accounts receivable balances in accordance with the audit program. In my opinion, these balances are free of material error.

Ownership, Custody, and Confidentiality of Working Papers

Working papers prepared for an engagement are owned by the auditor. This includes those prepared by the client. Once an engagement is completed, the auditor should retain custody of the working papers for future reference and to satisfy any legal requirements.

The auditor is under no obligation to allow *any* party (client or otherwise) to examine the engagement working papers unless under a legal subpoena. However, independent auditors frequently allow internal auditors to review their working papers to assist them in their work; and they may allow client accounting personnel to review selected working papers if appropriate (e.g., the documentation of important computations). The working papers also can be provided to third parties, but *only* with client permission.

Rule 301 of the *Code of Professional Ethics* addresses the auditor's responsibilities relating to confidential client information. As noted previously, communications between accountants and their clients are not privileged but the information is confidential. Confidential information obtained in the course of an engagement can be discussed if the auditor has the client's consent.

Permanent Audit Files

In addition to compiling a set of working papers for each year examined, auditors also maintain working papers in permanent files. Permanent files normally contain information that will be used on the engagement in future years. The information that may be included in the permanent file varies, but usually it includes the following:

1. Copy of articles of incorporation and bylaws, or excerpts therefrom.
2. Information about the client's ownership, organization and personnel practices, monitoring procedures, and internal audit activities.

3. Information about the client's business and industry.
4. List of related parties.
5. Copies of currently significant agreements (e.g., loans, leases, or contracts), with notations as to sections pertinent to the financial statements.
6. Excerpts of minutes of meetings of directors, shareholders, or committees that related to matters of continuing significance (e.g., authorizations for continuing or future actions).
7. Pertinent portions of filings or correspondence with regulatory agencies (e.g., registration statements or stock exchange listing applications).
8. Management letters (e.g., previous recommendations not implemented).
9. Details of standard consolidating adjustments.
10. History of rotation of visits to accounting units and related scope designations.
11. Memoranda (and related support) on decisions regarding particular accounting treatments adopted (those that have continuing impact) and the rationale behind them.
12. Accounting systems documentation.
13. Computations of retained earnings restrictions under loan agreements.
14. Analyses of capital and retained earnings accounts.
15. Data relating to employee benefit plans (e.g., bonus, pension, or stock option plans).
16. Data relating to income tax matters of continuing significance (e.g., tax basis of assets, especially goodwill; summaries of tax examinations; and open years).
17. Information regarding investments (e.g., investments in subsidiaries and other affiliates and cost allocation details).

Working Paper Review

Working papers are the primary evidence of the auditor's work. They must contain evidence supporting the audit report. A planned series of reviews by more experienced auditors qualified to determine the adequacy of the work helps ensure high-quality working papers and audit reports.

The review function is an important step in satisfying the first field standard, "the work is to be adequately planned and assistants, if any, are to be properly supervised." The review process is not simply a repeat of the preparer's work. It should add something to the original preparation. The reviewer has an advantage compared to the preparer in that information relevant to the specific audit procedure performed has been gathered, analyzed, and presented in what should be an interpretative format. Without devoting substantial effort to preparation, the reviewer can concentrate on matters that the preparer might have missed and challenge the adequacy of the preparer's work and resulting conclusions, as evidenced by the working papers.

QUESTIONS AND PROBLEMS

2–1.   Do all CPA firms go about achieving their audit objective in the same way?

2–2.   List the first three phases of an audit. How are the phases related?

2–3.   An auditor's risk analysis is based on the interaction of three inputs. Identify these inputs.

2–4.   What are the three elements of initial planning?

2–5.   What are the auditor's aims in preparing the audit program?

2–6.   Describe the program execution phase of an audit.

2–7.   When are audit procedures performed?

2–8.   Define compliance test and substantive test.

2–9.   List the four operating components of a typical commercial or industrial company.

2–10. Discuss the advantages to the auditor of the use of ratios as overall checks in an audit.   (AICPA, adapted)

2–11. Why is the independent auditor interested in evidence?

2–12. The source of the accounting evidence is of primary importance in the CPA's evaluation of its quality. Accounting evidence may be classified according to source. List the classifications of accounting evidence according to source, briefly discussing the effect of the source on the reliability of the evidence.   (AICPA, adapted)

2–13. In evaluating the quality of the accounting evidence, the CPA also considers factors other than the sources of evidence. List these other factors.   (AICPA, adapted)

2–14. Compare and contrast the competence of the following in terms of their use as evidence:
 a. Purchase order.
 b. Canceled check.
 c. Confirmation sent directly to the auditor.

2–15. Student B makes the following statement: "An independent auditor should spare no expense in obtaining evidence. Cost should never be a consideration." Comment on Student B's remark.

2–16. What are written representations?

2–17. Select the best answer for each of the following items:
 a. To be competent, evidence must be both:
   (1) Timely and substantial.
   (2) Reliable and documented.
   (3) Valid and relevant.
   (4) Useful and objective.
 b. The following four statements were made in a discussion of audit evidence between two CPAs. Which statement is *not* valid concerning evidential matter?
   (1) "I am seldom convinced beyond all doubt with respect to all aspects of the statements being examined."

      (2) "I would not undertake the procedure because at best the results would only be persuasive and I'm looking for convincing evidence."

      (3) "I evaluate the degree of risk involved in deciding the kind of evidence I will gather."

      (4) "I evaluate the usefulness of the evidence I can obtain against the cost to obtain it."

   c. Evidential matter supporting the financial statements consists of the underlying accounting data and all corroborating information available to the auditor. Which of the following is an example of corroborating information?

      (1) Minutes of meetings.

      (2) General and subsidiary ledgers.

      (3) Accounting manuals.

      (4) Worksheets supporting cost allocations.

   d. From which of the following evidence-gathering audit procedures would an auditor obtain most assurance concerning the existence of inventories?

      (1) Observation of physical inventory counts.

      (2) Written inventory representations from management.

      (3) Confirmation of inventories in a public warehouse.

      (4) Auditor's recomputation of inventory extensions.

   e. During the course of an audit, an auditor required additional research and consultation with others. This additional research and consultation is considered to be:

      (1) An appropriate part of the professional conduct of the engagement.

      (2) A responsibility of the management, not the auditor.

      (3) A failure on the part of the CPA to comply with generally accepted auditing standards because of a lack of competence.

      (4) An unusual practice that indicates that the CPA should not have accepted the engagement.   (AICPA, adapted)

2–18. What is the significance of the auditor's working papers?

2–19. What are the general contents of working papers?

2–20. List the forms or types of working papers that you would expect to find in an ordinary annual audit.

2–21. An auditor obtains data from several sources in the course of making an audit. These data and other details are incorporated in the working papers. List six general classifications of the content of working papers that are usually prepared in connection with an annual audit, and give an example of each classification. In classifying the content, consider the source of evidence and the auditor's activities.

                                                       (AICPA, adapted)

2–22. "Independent auditors should always prepare their own working papers. Client personnel should never be allowed to participate in the preparation of working papers." Comment on these statements.

2–23. What are permanent audit files?

2–24. What is the purpose of reviewing working papers?

2–25. I. M. Young is a new staff accountant with Big and Small, a public accounting firm. Young is assigned to his first task—auditing the Cash account of a large client. After spending two hours on the task, Young shows the working papers to the senior in charge of the job. The senior finds that Young made some mistakes and consequently has to start over again. Young asks the senior what should be done with the working papers that reflect the incorrect work. The senior says: "They are of no value; however, you might as well include them in the working papers so that someone does not make the same mistake next year."

Required:

Comment on the senior's statement.

2–26. Janice Smith, CPA, has performed the annual audit of Mean, Inc., for a number of years. In January of 1984, the board of directors of Mean, Inc., decided to change auditors. The president of Mean, Inc., asked Smith for all of her working papers for the Mean, Inc., audits. The president asserts that the working papers belong to Mean and he wants to give them to the new auditors.

Required:

a. Comment on the president's assertion that the working papers belong to Mean, Inc.

b. Comment on how the new auditor may gain access to the working papers.

2–27. CPA X is ordered by a federal court to submit to the court all of her working papers related to her client, The Small Company. CPA X declines to do so, claiming that the working papers are confidential. Comment.

2–28. An important part of every examination of financial statements is the preparation of audit working papers.

Required:

a. Discuss the relationship of audit working papers to each of the standards of field work.

b. You are instructing an inexperienced staff person on her first auditing assignment. She is to examine an account. An analysis of the account has been prepared by the client for inclusion in the audit working papers. Prepare a list of the comments, commentaries, and notations that the staff person should make or have made on the account analysis to provide an adequate working paper as evidence of her examination. (Do not include a description of auditing procedures applicable to the account.)   (AICPA, adapted)

2–29. The preparation of working papers is an integral part of the CPA's examination of financial statements. On a recurring engagement, a CPA reviews the audit programs and working papers from the prior examination while planning the current examination to determine their usefulness for the current engagement.

Required:

a. (1) What are the purposes or functions of audit working papers?

   (2) What records may be included in audit working papers?

b. What factors affect the CPA's judgment of the type and content of the working papers for a particular engagement?

c. To comply with generally accepted auditing standards, a CPA includes certain evidence in the working papers—for example, "evidence that the engagement was planned and work of assistants was supervised and reviewed." What other evidence should a CPA include in audit working papers to comply with generally accepted auditing standards? (AICPA, adapted)

2–30. You have been assigned by your firm to complete the examination of the 1983 financial statements of Carter Manufacturing Corporation because the senior accountant and his inexperienced assistant who began the engagement were hospitalized after an accident. The engagement is about half completed. Your auditor's report must be delivered in three weeks as agreed when your firm accepted the engagement. You estimate that by utilizing the client's staff to the greatest possible extent you can complete the engagement in five weeks. Your firm cannot assign an assistant to you. The working papers show the status of work on the examination as follows:

a. Completed: cash, fixed assets, depreciation, mortgage payable, and stockholders' equity.

b. Completed except as noted later: inventories, accounts payable, tests of purchase transactions, and payrolls.

c. Nothing done: trade accounts receivable, inventory receiving cutoff and price testing, accrued expenses payable, unrecorded liability test, tests of sales transactions, payroll deductions test and observation or payroll check distribution, other expenses, analytical review of operations, vouching of December purchase transactions, auditor's report, internal control investigation, internal control letter, minutes, preparation of tax returns, procedural recommendations for management, subsequent events, supervision, and review.

Your review discloses that the assistant's working papers are incomplete and were not reviewed by the senior accountant. For example, the inventory working papers present incomplete notations, incomplete explanations, and no cross-referencing.

Required:

a. What standards of field work have been violated by the senior accountant who preceded you on this assignment? Explain why you feel the standards you list have been violated.

b. In planning your work to complete this engagement, you should scan working papers and schedule certain work as soon as possible and also identify work that may be postponed until after the report is rendered to the client.

 (1) List the areas on which you should plan to work first, say, in your first week of work; and for each item explain why it deserves early attention.

 (2) State which work you believe could be postponed until after the report is rendered to the client and give reasons why the work may be postponed.

(AICPA, adapted)

2–31. In examining financial statements, an auditor must judge the validity of the audit evidence obtained.

Required:

 Assume that you have evaluated internal control and found it satisfactory.

a. In the course of the examination, the auditor asks many questions of client officers and employees.

 (1) Describe the factors that the auditor should consider in evaluating oral evidence provided by client officers and employees.

(2) Discuss the validity and limitations of inquiry.

b. An auditor's examination may include computation of various balance sheet and operating ratios for comparison to prior years and industry averages. Discuss the validity and limitations of ratio analysis.

c. In connection with the examination of the financial statements of a manufacturing company, an auditor is observing the physical inventory of finished goods, which consists of expensive, highly complex electronic equipment. Discuss the validity and limitations of the audit evidence provided by this procedure.

(AICPA, adapted)

PLANNING AND ENVIRONMENTAL CONSIDERATIONS

Chapter 2 presented an overview of the various phases of an audit—initial planning, program development, program execution, and reporting. This chapter provides an in-depth discussion of the planning process including the factors to consider in acquiring an understanding of the client's business and industry. Also, this chapter addresses how to relate the understanding of the client's business and industry to the risk analysis.

Effective and timely planning is essential to the performance of efficient audits. This provides for considered development of the overall audit plan and effective utilization of a CPA firm's resources. It should help to achieve:

Early communication between the auditor and the client regarding the auditor's requirements and the client's expectations concerning the audit.

Minimization of time pressures through early identification of areas requiring audit emphasis.

Assignment of personnel with appropriate experience and specialized skills.

Efficient scheduling.

The initial planning effort should lead to an overall audit plan based on an up-to-date understanding of the client's business and industry and an initial assessment of the overall potential for audit problems. The plan should specify:

Overall allocation of audit effort, including locations to be visited and areas requiring audit emphasis.

Environmental considerations that may affect the audit plan.

Detail analytical review procedures to be performed.

Accounting systems to be documented and evaluated after giving consideration to the effectiveness of the control environment and the extent of computer involvement in the accounting process.

3

Timing and staffing requirements.

THE CLIENT'S BUSINESS AND INDUSTRY

The personnel assigned to an audit engagement should understand the client's business and industry to effectively assess the risks associated with the engagement. The level of understanding will depend on the experience and training of the audit personnel. The auditor cannot be expected to achieve the same level of understanding as management. Nevertheless, the auditor should gain sufficient knowledge of significant economic, operational, and organizational factors that affect the client's business to effectively perform the audit. Such knowledge is important to the auditor's evaluation of the reasonableness of various management estimates including, for example, allowances for loan losses for a bank, obsolescence of inventories for a manufacturer, overstock for a retailer, or claim reserves for an insurance company.

Understanding the client's business and industry also helps the auditor communicate effectively with the client management, evaluate the overall reasonableness of the financial statements, and identify additional client needs. Gaining an understanding of the client's business and industry is a continuing educational process for both new and recurring engagements.

New Engagements

For new engagements (audits being conducted by the CPA firm for the first time) or in situations where an existing client acquires a new business, an understanding of the business and industry can be gained through:

1. Reference to various publications, including AICPA Industry Audit and Accounting Guides, trade journals, and other periodicals.

2. Review of annual reports and SEC filings of the client and of other companies in the same industry.
3. Review of investment advisory, brokerage firm, or credit rating agency reports on the company or the industry.
4. Discussions with management regarding the factors that are important or unique to their business.
5. Visits to client plant or service facilities.

On continuing engagements, an auditor involved in planning the engagement for the first time also should follow the above procedures and confer with other auditors who are familiar with the engagement.

Special Audit Procedures for New Engagements. In addition to obtaining an understanding of the business, the auditor should:

1. Review the articles of incorporation (or partnership agreements) and minutes of meetings of shareholders and directors (from inception, if practicable).
2. Prepare or obtain a summary of shareholders' equity/proprietary accounts (from inception, if practicable), with particular attention to prior reorganizations, revaluations of assets, issuances of stock for other than cash, and other unusual equity transactions.
3. Obtain and review any prior auditors' reports and arrange to review selected prior audit working papers.
4. Establish the reasonableness of beginning balances for significant balance sheet accounts. For example, the auditor should determine the basis of the property accounts (book and tax) and examine evidence of title to at least the principal real estate. The auditor also should determine the propriety of the classifications used, the reasonableness of the accumulated allowances for depreciation and amortization, and whether any significant amounts of properties are not used in operations.
5. Determine the origin of other continuing accounts, such as intangibles and deferrals.
6. Review income tax returns and revenue agents' reports for several years to determine the adequacy of the recorded liability for taxes.

Recurring Engagements

For recurring engagements, the auditor's experience with the client serves as a basis for design of the overall audit plan. The auditor should be alert to conditions that would increase or decrease the likelihood of problems based on prior experience. The auditor should consider previous knowledge of:

1. Adequacy and timeliness of financial information provided by the accounting system.

2. Management's ability to make accurate estimates (e.g., percentage of completion or warranty liabilities).
3. Likelihood that management will exert undue pressure to achieve forecasted operating results.
4. Need for significant audit adjustments.
5. Likelihood of:
   Obsolete, slow-moving, or overstock inventory.
   Significant book-to-physical adjustments.
   Uncollectible accounts receivable.
   Reduction in future selling prices of products.
   Underaccrued liabilities.

Certain working papers from the prior year may be helpful in identifying important accounting and auditing issues for the current year. The auditor should review the prior year's planning memorandum, any summary memoranda on the results of the audit, closing conference and audit committee meeting memoranda, list of audit adjustments, and management letter comments and client responses. In addition, memoranda relating to any timely interim reviews of quarterly financial statements should be reviewed.

Early discussions with key operating and financial executives will help identify current developments as well as other matters that are of concern to management. Reference to the following may assist in identifying current developments that affect the audit:

1. Quarterly reports to shareholders.
2. Current filings with the SEC.
3. Proxy statements for the prior year.
4. Minutes of current-year meetings of board of directors, board committees, or other policy-making groups.
5. Revenue agents' examination reports.
6. Regulatory agency examination reports.
7. Internal audit reports.
8. Reports on special studies conducted by the company or other consultants, such as management consultants or tax specialists.
9. Client's year-end closing instructions to operating units.

Overall Analytical Review

An overall analytical review of interim financial statement amounts and relationships helps update and enhance the auditor's understanding of the client's business. These review procedures might include comparison of (1) current operating results and financial condition to prior periods, (2) actual results to budget, and (3) key financial and operating ratios to industry data.

Overall analytical review procedures might highlight (1) unexpected changes or the absence of expected changes in key financial statement balances, (2) changes in profitability trends, (3) indications of losses for certain operations, or (4) deterioration in liquidity or capital adequacy. The auditor's overall analytical review should focus attention on significant events (e.g., government regulations causing major product redesign and retooling), shifts in corporate strategy (e.g., planned phasing out of a significant operation), and management operating objectives (e.g., expectations of sales and income). Financial relationships that may be used in the overall analytical review are described in Chapter 6.

For clients that operate in several industry segments and issue consolidated financial statements, the auditor should apply overall analytical review procedures to segment-level data in order to identify the varying influences of each segment on the consolidated financial statements. For multilocation clients, the overall analytical review should be directed to the financial information for the separate operating units.

When performing overall analytical review procedures, the use of carry-forward schedules to summarize financial statement amounts and relationships is normally the most efficient approach. It will allow for effective comparison of historical information covering a number of years.

EFFECT OF ENVIRONMENTAL CONSIDERATIONS

The environment in which an auditor's client operates includes (1) external factors—industry conditions, regulatory requirements, and reporting obligations; and (2) internal factors—ownership influences and management, financial, and operating characteristics. An understanding of these factors allows the auditor to determine (1) the overall potential for material errors or irregularities and (2) the degree of difficulty the auditor may encounter in gathering sufficient audit evidence. An assessment of the inherent risk related to these factors will help the auditor establish an overall audit plan responsive to the unique characteristics of each client.

Some environmental factors have a pervasive impact on the audit, and thus affect the degree of professional skepticism required for the engagement. An auditor always should maintain an attitude of "healthy skepticism"; however, some of those factors (particularly those related to reporting obligations, ownership influences, and management and financial characteristics described below under "External Environmental Considerations" and "Internal Environmental Considerations") cause an increase in the degree of this skepticism. Increased professional skepticism should result in greater challenge of management representations. This may lead the auditor to request confirmation of management representations from sources outside of the client, increase sample sizes, or otherwise obtain additional audit evidence to support transactions and accounts.

Some environmental factors also may affect the risk analysis associated with specific transactions and accounts. The auditor should identify those factors in the "Environmental Considerations" section of the applicable risk analysis working paper.

Changes in the environment may be sudden and obvious, or they may be subtle and occur over a long period of time. Changes may create potential audit problems and result in increased likelihood of material error; or they may alleviate audit problems encountered in previous years and signal a reduction of risk. It is important to identify favorable as well as unfavorable changes and give effect to both in developing the overall audit plan and audit program.

The discussion of "External Environmental Considerations" and "Internal Environmental Considerations" on the following pages includes questions that may be useful in developing an understanding of a client's business and industry. Figure 3–1 provides examples of environmental factors related to some specific control objectives. These are the types of factors that can help the auditor understand the client's business and industry and properly assess audit risk.

FIGURE 3–1   Examples of Environmental Factors Related to Specific Control Objectives

Specific Control Objective	*Factors to Consider*
1. Physical loss of inventory is prevented or promptly detected	Nature of product (e.g., susceptibility to pilferage) Method of distribution Causes of book-to-physical adjustments Nature, quantity, and market value of scrap generated Number and geographic dispersion of inventory locations
2. Depreciation is calculated using proper lives and methods	Industry practices Condition of property ledger/lapse schedules Extent to which technological factors may affect useful lives Differences in lives and methods for financial and tax reporting Extent of property additions or disposals
3. Debt and lease obligations and related expenses are authorized and recorded correctly as to account, amount, and period	Nature of obligations (term loan, revolving line of credit, etc.) Significant terms and restrictions

Appendix I at the end of this textbook provides examples of environmental considerations for each specific control objective.

EXTERNAL ENVIRONMENTAL CONSIDERATIONS

The external environment is broadly defined as conditions, circumstances, and influences that affect operations but are beyond management's direct control. The external environment encompasses the following factors:

Industry Conditions	Regulatory Requirements	Reporting Obligations
Economic	Federal	Owners
Competitive	State	Creditors
Accounting practices	Local	Insurers
	Foreign	Regulators
		Taxing authorities

Industry Conditions

Economic. The auditor should identify the economic factors that have influenced the industry in the past and those that are currently doing so. This knowledge enables the author to explain current industry behavior and anticipate likely future trends and to better understand the client's position in the industry. Economic conditions may explain changes in the client's activities or results of operations or identify specific problems (e.g., a recession might indicate potential collectibility problems, or technological changes might cause possible inventory obsolescence). In reviewing economic conditions, the auditor might consider the following:

1. Are there any significant growth trends within the industry (e.g., growing, stable, or declining)? Are there local, national, or international economic indicators that could be used to predict or explain industry behavior?
2. How do the client's growth and financial results compare with those of the industry? What are the reasons for significant variances?
3. Is the industry subject to cyclical or seasonal fluctuations? Is the client typical of the industry? What is the client doing to minimize its vulnerability to these fluctuations?
4. Is the industry subject to frequent or significant litigation?
5. Is demand for the client's products relatively elastic or inelastic (i.e., do customers respond to price changes)?
6. Is the industry labor-intensive? Have there been any unusual labor problems or shortages? Does the client have good relations with labor? What is the degree of unionization within the labor force of the client and the industry?

7. Is new capital investment necessary as a result of technological change, replacement, or new capacity requirements? Could new products create obsolescence problems?

Competitive. The auditor should gather facts about the client's principal competitors—not only in the same industry, but in related industries as well (e.g., a bank's competitors include money market funds and savings and loan associations as well as other banks). Knowledge of competitors and significant developments relating to their operations might help the auditor anticipate potential audit problems. Consideration of competitive factors might include the following:

1. Who are the client's principal competitors? What share of the market does each maintain? Has there been any significant shift in market penetration?
2. Is competition by foreign companies growing? Do foreign competitors have any significant advantages domestically or internationally?
3. Is there differentiation between the client's and competitors' products or services? Do the client's sales depend on price, or do other factors (e.g., customer service or warranties) influence consumer demand?
4. Are any competitors experiencing financial or operating problems? Could the client be subject to the same problems?
5. Are technological, marketing, or manufacturing advancements being made by competitors? What is the client's reaction or planned reaction? What companies historically lead the industry in these advancements?

Accounting Practices. The auditor should be aware of accounting practices unique to the industry and the acceptable alternatives. This will help determine the appropriateness of the client's accounting practices and the comparability of the client's financial data to its competitors. Considerations should include the following:

1. What are the significant industry accounting practices? Are any practices predominantly followed? Does the client follow any practices that are not predominant?
2. Do any new accounting or reporting pronouncements (such as those by the FASB, AICPA, and SEC) affect the client?
3. Are any of the significant accounting practices under review by the profession or regulatory agencies? What is the likelihood that the client's practices will require change? How will this affect financial results?
4. What significant accounting estimates are required in the financial statements? How accurate have these estimates been in the past?

Regulatory Requirements

Government involvement in business operations has resulted in significant regulatory legislation, especially in the following areas:

1. *Employee protection*—Fair Employment Practices Act, Equal Opportunity Act, Employee Retirement Income Security Act, Occupational Safety and Health Act, and Age Discrimination in Employment Act.
2. *Environment protection*—Air Pollution Control Act, Federal Water Pollution Control Act, Noise Pollution and Control Act, and Safe Drinking Water Act.
3. *Consumer protection*—Consumer Credit Protection Act, Interstate Land Sales Full Disclosure Act, Public Health Smoking Act, and Consumer Product Safety Act.

The auditor should be aware of the impact of these and other federal laws, as well as state and local regulatory laws, on the client's operations. Also, the auditor should consider the effects of foreign regulatory laws on clients with operations in other countries. In reviewing regulatory requirements, the auditor might consider the following:

1. Is the industry subject to extensive regulation? How has regulation or the threat of regulation affected the economic development of the industry?
2. Is there government control over prices or wages? Has this created any significant financial problems in the industry?
3. What is the extent of government regulation over the quality of the goods or services produced? Is the industry or client subject to unusual warranty or product liability claims?
4. What has the client done to demonstrate compliance with the Foreign Corrupt Practices Act? (See discussion of the act in Chapter 14.)
5. What laws have had or are expected to have a significant impact on the industry or on the client's products or services? Do any laws put the industry at a competitive advantage or disadvantage with foreign companies?

Reporting Obligations

Some reporting obligations, such as IRS and SEC filings, are familiar because they affect so many clients. But others may be unique to the industry— e.g., special reporting requirements for insurance companies and hospitals. Still others may be unique to the client—e.g., a reporting requirement for a loan covenant. The latter is an example of a reporting requirement that might influence management's decisions (e.g., to overstate working capital) or cause audit problems if not satisfied (e.g., failure to satisfy a covenant could accelerate the due date and create liquidity and financial statement classification problems). The auditor should be familiar with the client's reporting obligations to owners, creditors, insurers, regulators, and taxing authorities, and determine how the client is complying. Some questions to ask are:

1.   What are the client's reporting obligations? Do they contain any restrictions affecting operations? Is the auditor required to report on compliance? Are separate reports required for the parent company or certain subsidiaries?

2.   What underlying accounting principles or practices are followed for purposes of complying with reporting obligations other than to owners or the SEC? How do these differ from generally accepted accounting principles (GAAP)?

INTERNAL ENVIRONMENTAL CONSIDERATIONS

The internal environment is broadly defined as conditions, circumstances, and influences within the client's business that affect or determine the course of operations. It involves the following:

Ownership influences.

Management characteristics.

Financial characteristics.

Operating characteristics.

The auditor should identify unique characteristics of the client, including changes and new developments that create potential audit problems or alleviate problems experienced in prior years.

Ownership Influences

The nature and extent of owner involvement in operations varies significantly among organizations. The role that the owners play in an organization where management is independent of the owners most likely will differ from an organization where management has a significant ownership interest. Specific authorizations may be retained by the owners, while others may be assigned to management. The degree of specific authorization retained and the extent of involvement in internal affairs by owners are important factors in assessing ownership influences on operations. The auditor's considerations might include the following:

1.   Is there a concentration of ownership in one or a few significant shareholders? Are shares actively traded? What degree of ownership is held by management? Is the client vulnerable to acquisition?

2. Who serves on the board of directors? Are there members of the board who are independent of management? What are the relationships of board members to the organization? Are there representatives of the client's bank, outside counsel, or major suppliers on the board? What are the business reputation, relevant experience, and other affiliations (including other directorships) of each director? Are close relatives of management on the board? How many years has each director served?

3. What duties have been assumed by the board of directors, the audit committee, and other committees of the board? Does the board of directors or audit committee consider the effectiveness of internal controls? What specific authorizations are retained by the board or its committees?

For publicly held companies most of this information is available in proxy statements.

Management Characteristics

Management is responsible for directing and controlling operations and for establishing, communicating, and monitoring policies and procedures. The ability of management to achieve the company's goals is a significant factor in the internal environment. *SAS No. 16*, "The Independent Auditor's Responsibility for the Detection of Errors and Irregularities" (AU 327.09), states:

> . . . the auditor should be aware of the importance of management's integrity to the effective operation of internal accounting control procedures and should consider whether there are circumstances that might predispose management to misstate financial statements.

Because it is subjective in nature, the auditor's consideration of management characteristics can be difficult. However, the auditor should be familiar with the business reputations, relevant experience, and history of prior successes or failures of key members of management. The auditor should be alert to any conditions that might indicate management's motivations and intentions, for example:

1. Undue emphasis placed on achieved earnings per share forecasts or on maintaining market value of capital stock.
2. Unexpected reorganization or replacement of management, or high turnover among key executives.
3. Undue pressure on new management to outperform predecessor results.
4. Overly optimistic news releases or shareholder communications.
5. Pattern of financial estimates that are later found to be significantly wrong.
6. Significant incentive compensation arrangements based on financial results.

7. Key operating positions understaffed, resulting in constant crisis.
8. History of completing significant or unusual transactions around year-end.

The management of the client's accounting and finance functions is of particular concern to the auditor. The auditor should evaluate whether the likelihood of errors or irregularities is increased by the presence of such deficiencies as:

1. Understaffed accounting department or poorly trained or inexperienced accounting personnel.
2. Lack of coordination between accounting and EDP departments, resulting in incomplete reports and delayed closings.
3. Dependence on a few individuals, resulting in a state of constant crisis and loss of accounting control.
4. Erroneous or tardy financial reports.
5. Lack of concern with, or inability or refusal to correct, important weaknesses in the system of internal control.

Consideration of management characteristics is particularly significant to the audit of transactions or accounts that require subjective determinations by management. Examples include inventory valuation adjustments, allowances for doubtful accounts, percentage-of-completion estimates on long-term contracts, write-downs for permanent impairment in value of investments, self-insurance liabilities, warranty liabilities, expense deferrals, and estimates related to existing or potential litigation. These areas generally are difficult to audit because of the inherent degree of subjectivity and the lack of conclusive evidence to confirm or challenge management's judgment.

The auditor should be alert to situations that might lead a member of management to commit fraud either against or on behalf of the company. For example, personal or economic pressures may result in an individual misappropriating company assets. Job-related pressures may lead an individual to commit fraud to "help" the business report continued growth or avoid showing a loss.

If events or circumstances raise doubts about management (e.g., competence, credibility, sufficiency, philosophy, or motivation) that might affect particular audit areas, the circumstances should be summarized or referred to in the working papers. To be helpful, the working papers should describe specific circumstances that raise concern and should avoid generalizations about management's competence or integrity.

Financial Characteristics

The auditor should understand the client's current and prospective financial condition. This involves a review of (1) profitability—the current and prospective trend in earnings, (2) liquidity—ability to meet short-term obligations, and (3) capital adequacy—ability to meet long-term obligations and obtain financing for growth. Such a review might consider the following:

1. How do the client's earnings compare to industry trends? What have been the reasons for significant variations between years?
2. What has been the trend of cash generated from operations? What are the reasons for significant differences between cash flow generated and net income (e.g., income recognized in advance of cash collections or cash disbursed in advance of expense recognition)?
3. Does the client forecast cash flow from operations and cash requirements? Are current liquidity needs expected to be satisfied from operations? How are short-term cash needs financed?
4. Does the client forecast long-term cash requirements? Do the forecasts reflect major capital expenditures? Is there a need to obtain additional financing to repay scheduled maturities?
5. Is the client able to obtain financing at terms and rates comparable to its competitors? If not, why?

Operating Characteristics

As discussed in Chapter 2, four operating components provide a framework for understanding a typical client's operations in the light of environmental factors. They are:

Administration—control and support of operating activities.

Sales—marketing, distribution, billing, and collection.

Production or service—acquisition of resources and conversion into products or services.

Finance—management of financial resources.

Administration.　Administration activities provide the control and support needed to operate a business. Together with ownership influences and management characteristics, they establish the level of "control consciousness." This is the basis for the control environment, the framework in which the accounting system operates. Organization charts, detailed position descriptions, a conflict-of-interest policy, and regularly scheduled training programs do not in themselves guarantee adequate internal control. But they do contribute to a disciplined control environment. In reviewing the organization and personnel practices of a company, the auditor might ask:

1. Are there up-to-date organization charts? Do they reflect the corporate structure, areas of responsibility, and lines of reporting?
2. Are there formal position descriptions for administrative and financial personnel? Do they clearly set out duties and responsibilities?

3. Are backgrounds and references of applicants for administrative and financial positions investigated?

4. Are personnel policies and employee benefits documented and communicated to employees?

5. Is there a formal conflict of interest policy or code of conduct in effect? If so, does it require periodic declarations by officers, directors, and key employees? Is there a system to monitor compliance?

6. Are employees who handle cash, securities, and other valuable assets bonded?

7. Do related employees, if any, have job assignments that minimize opportunities for collusion? Is rotation of duties enforced by mandatory vacations?

8. Is job performance periodically evaluated and reviewed with each employee?

9. Are there training programs for administrative and financial personnel?

Monitoring procedures include management's use of financial statements, operating analyses, and budgets in controlling operations. The information in these should be up-to-date and sufficiently detailed to provide a sound basis for decision making. In this area, the auditor might ask:

1. Are financial statements submitted at regular intervals to operating management? Are they submitted to the board of directors or to the audit committee?

2. Are financial statements accompanied by analytical comments? Do they show comparisons with prior periods, budgets, and forecasts?

3. What major operating analyses (e.g., agings of receivables, schedules of product line profitability) are prepared and provided to management on a regular basis?

4. Are the same accounting and closing practices followed at interim dates as at year-end?

5. Who reviews and approves financial information for public distribution (e.g., press releases, filings with regulatory bodies, and shareholders' reports)?

6. Does the company maintain up-to-date accounting policies and procedural manuals? Is a chart of accounts maintained? Does it describe the nature of each account?

7. Are all general journal entries other than standard entries required to be approved by a responsible official not involved with their origination? Are the entries supported by explanation and/or documentation?

8. What are the qualifications of the employees who prepare the financial statements?

9. Is access to accounting and financial records restricted to authorized personnel?

10. Is there a formal system of budgeting in use? Do budgeting procedures cover all divisions and departments?

11. Do budgets and forecasts cover revenues, costs and expenses, capital expenditures, and cash flows?

12. Are budgets and forecasts submitted to management on an established timetable? Are forecasts updated on a regular basis during the year? Are budget variances reported and analyzed?

13. Are assets such as cash, inventories, and investments reconciled with accounting records? Are differences investigated and reported to appropriate personnel? Are control and subsidiary accounts reconciled regularly and discrepancies reported to appropriate personnel? Are changes between beginning and ending balances accounted for as to property, depreciation, long-term debt, deferred taxes, and similar items?

If the client has an internal audit staff, the auditor should assess its competence and objectivity. This is discussed in more detail in Chapter 14.

Sales, Production or Service, and Finance. The following questions might be considered in the areas of sales, production or service, and finance:

Sales

1. What are the major types of customers (e.g., manufacturers, distributors, consumers)? Who are the major customers? Is the client dependent on one or a few customers? What is the client doing to minimize its dependence? Does the client do a significant amount of business with entities that lack financial strength?

2. What percentage of sales is derived from foreign sources? Are there any unusual business practices related to these sales?

3. What methods are used to advertise, sell, and distribute the client's products or services? Are salesmen on a commission basis?

4. What is the turnaround time between order acceptance and delivery to the customer?

5. What is the trend in backlog?

Production or Service

1. What are the principal product lines or services (including relative volume and mix, extent of custom manufacturing versus production for stock)?

2. What are the stages in the client's production cycle? What is the basis for planning production (e.g., individual sales orders, projected annual sales volume, projected seasonal demand)? Has the client experienced any significant production overruns? Is a significant quantity of scrap produced?

3. What are the principal materials and services purchased? Who are the principal suppliers? Do alternative sources of supply exist? Does the client finance any of its supplier's activities?

4. How stable is the work force? Are there any significant union contracts expiring?

5. What are the key features and the funding policy of the employee benefit plans? What is the likelihood of complete or partial termination of any plan?

6. Where are the client's plant and equipment located? Have there been any labor or power shortages in these areas? What is the general condition of the facilities?

7. At what level of production capacity is the client operating? Have there been any labor or material shortages?

8. Have the client's operations been adversely affected by technological advances? What is the nature and extent of the client's research and development effort?

9. What expressed or implied warranties are associated with the product? Does the client maintain historical accounting records identifying these costs? Has the client been subject to product liability suits?

Finance

1. Is there centralized handling of cash? Is excess cash invested in short-term investments? Are the number, type, and location of bank accounts adequate for the client's operating needs?

2. Does the client manage cash flow?

3. Are asset additions financed through lease arrangements?

4. Are there significant commitments under operating leases?

5. Are there stock options, outstanding warrants, convertible debt, stock purchase agreements, or pending or existing commitments to issue stock in merger or acquisition agreements? Are there plans relating to issuance, purchase, conversion, or retirement of preferred or common stock?

6. To what extent is the client self-insured?

DOCUMENTING THE EFFECT OF ENVIRONMENTAL CONSIDERATIONS

The auditor should summarize external and internal environmental factors that affect specific accounts or transactions on the applicable risk analysis working paper. Focusing on *how* environmental factors might affect specific accounts or transactions helps determine the appropriate risk analysis working paper and helps design audit procedures that are responsive to the likelihood of problems. For example, a downturn in the business of a client's customers that increases the likelihood of uncollectible receivables (specific control objective S–2) and customer returns (S–7) would lead to increased audit effort in these areas. Or an improvement in quality control practices that reduces the likelihood of customer returns (S–7) and defective inventory (P–8) would minimize audit effort in these areas.

Pervasive environmental factors (e.g., a conservative management) should not be repeated throughout the risk analysis working papers. They should be included only when they are particularly relevant to the likelihood of material error, or when they may affect the audit procedures for a specific account. The auditor should avoid generalities because the more general the items are, the less useful they are in analyzing audit risks and developing the preliminary audit approach. Following are some examples of pervasive environmental factors and how an auditor might address them:

An economic recession or industry downturn might only affect the allowance for doubtful accounts and overstock inventory. These factors would then be included on the applicable risk analysis working papers.

The presence or absence of competent client personnel may be a factor in a technical area (e.g., LIFO or income taxes). The auditor's risk analysis should describe experience from previous audits (e.g., "no errors noted" or "significant adjustments required" in prior years) and the training and background of the individuals.

Management's philosophy (e.g., conservative) may be applicable in an area where management makes subjective determinations and estimates (e.g., warranty reserve).

Pervasive environmental factors should be documented in an audit planning memorandum or a separate memorandum organized by operating component (i.e., grouped on the basis of their effect on sales, production, finance, and administration). If the factors have ongoing relevance, the memorandum can be included in the carry-forward working papers.

The following example illustrates how information about a client's environment impacts the risk analysis and audit program. Assume that the auditor learns the following information about a client that manufactures recreational vehicles:

External Environment

Economic. Overcapacity in the industry has caused intense competition in the past. This situation is now worsened because of fuel shortages and rising prices. The result is decreased demand.

Competitive. The client and its competitors continuously search for dealers to sell recreational vehicles. Dealers consider product differentiation to be minimal and frequently switch brands.

Internal Environment

Sales. Dealer turnover was 40 percent during the first half of the year, compared with 25 percent in the prior year. An annual turnover of 25–40 percent is typical of the industry.

Administration. Effective April 1, the client began using a new computerized accounting system designed to identify possible obsolete, slow-moving, or overstock inventory of raw materials or finished goods.

Those environmental considerations could be described in the risk analysis working papers as shown in Figure 3–2.

FIGURE 3–2 Environmental Considerations Recorded on Risk Analysis Working Papers

---

Risk Analysis Prepared By/Date ____ PWC 7–31

PAA Prepared By/Date ____ RDH 8–15

Reviewed By/Date ____ MG 8–20

Sales

S–1 Customer Orders Require Approval of Credit and Terms Before Acceptance

S–2 Uncollectible Amounts Are Promptly Identified and Provided For

Risk Analysis

Environmental Considerations There is an increased rate of turnover of the client's major customers. In the past, high turnover has resulted in orders being accepted from dealers who are poor credit risks. Potential for uncollectible amounts also may be increased because there are dealers who have dropped client's line and others who may no longer be profitable as a result of the drop in demand caused by higher fuel prices.

Risk Analysis Prepared By/Date ____ PWC 7–31

PAA Prepared By/Date ____ RDH 8–15

Reviewed By/Date ____ MG 8–20

Sales

S–7 Customer Returns and Other Allowances Are Approved and Recorded Correctly as to Account, Amount, and Period

Risk Analysis

Environmental Considerations In the past, many dealers dropped client's line and returned merchandise instead of paying their balance. This means an increased likelihood that returns will not be adequately provided for in the accounts at year-end.

Risk Analysis Prepared By/Date ____ PWC 7–31

PAA Prepared By/Date ____ RDH 8–15

Reviewed By/Date ____ MG 8–20

Production or Service—Inventory Accountability and Physical Safeguards

P–9 Obsolete, Slow-Moving, and Overstock Inventory Is Prevented or Promptly Detected and Provided For

Risk Analysis

Environmental Considerations There is an increased risk of overstock and obsolete inventory because it is becoming more common for dealers to (1) return merchandise instead of paying their balance or (2) cancel orders for items that are being custom built. Effective April 1, the client began using a new computerized accounting system designed to identify possible obsolete, slow-moving, or overstock inventory.

The environmental considerations identified in S–1, S–2, and S–7 lead the auditor to consider extensive procedures for reviewing collectibility and customer returns at or near year-end. However, the other inputs to these risk analyses (e.g., system evaluation and detail analytical review) may mitigate the effect of these environmental factors and result in a plan to limit the extent of audit procedures. For example, the auditor might find that the accounting system includes procedures that reasonably assure that uncollectible amounts are promptly identified and provided for. Or the detail analytical review might indicate that management has given recognition to the problem by increasing the provision for bad debts compared to the prior year. In light of these factors, the need for extending audit procedures or performing them at or near year-end would be lessened.

The environmental considerations identified in P–9 indicate that there is increased risk of overstock or obsolete inventory. But a new system was installed to reduce that risk. The new system should help management detect, and thus either prevent obsolete, slow-moving, or overstock inventory (e.g., by promptly curtailing production and reducing prices) or provide for appropriate losses.

The audit impact of the reduction of risk in P–9 (assuming no adverse indications from the system evaluation or observations from detail analytical review) is that the auditor may limit procedures in the area affected (e.g., limit obsolescence review to significant overstock inventory), and the procedures can be performed at an interim date. The auditor also should test the reliability of the accounting system and use analytical review procedures as direct tests of year-end balances.

PLANNING THE DETAIL ANALYTICAL REVIEW

The auditor's understanding of the client's business and industry and knowledge of current developments should lead to the expectation of certain relationships and trends in the financial data. These expectations should be confirmed or challenged by the results of detail analytical review procedures to be performed during the program development phase.

The auditor's expectations about the relationships and trends in financial data help develop useful detail analytical review procedures. Discussions with operating and financial executives should help identify reports and relationships, as well as general economic and industry statistics, that management uses in monitoring and evaluating operations. As part of initial planning, the auditor should decide the scope of the detail analytical review by identifying important financial data and relationships that he or she will want to gather or compute for each relevant risk analysis working paper. Chapter 6 discusses the use of detail analytical review procedures in the risk analysis.

PLANNING THE SYSTEM EVALUATION

Understanding the client's business and industry will help the auditor identify the important accounting systems on which to rely. These are the systems that require documentation and evaluation. During initial planning, the auditor should consider the effectiveness of the control environment and the extent of computer involvement in the accounting process. In addition, the auditor should consider changes made since the last audit and planned changes in accounting systems and procedures, including those in computer equipment or applications. Then system documentation priorities can be set—i.e., to what extent the auditor's existing documentation or client documentation can be used, which systems require flowcharting, and what the auditor can expect the client to do.

The Control Environment

An effective control environment provides a basis for expecting that accounting systems tested at an interim date will continue to function during the entire year. Therefore, the effectiveness of the control environment is one of the factors to consider in determining how early in the year the auditor can perform these tests. An assessment of the overall control environment and how it affects the auditor's expectations regarding the reliability of the client's accounting information should be made for all audits and documented in a planning memorandum.

Computerized Accounting Systems

During initial planning, the auditor should obtain information about both the computer installation and any accounting applications processed by the computer. This information should enable the auditor to assess the (1) size and complexity of the computer system; (2) extent of computer involvement in the accounting process, i.e., the principal accounting applications and the specific control objectives affected; and (3) need for assistance from someone knowledgeable in evaluating computer-based systems. When the computer is used to process or maintain transactions or balances that are material to the financial statements, the auditor should plan a general controls review (discussed in Chapter 5).

OTHER INITIAL PLANNING ACTIVITIES

Timing and Staffing

Planning should be performed as early as possible. For large or complex engagements, the planning process normally will be accomplished in phases, which may occur over an extended period of time. In these cases, the planning effort should start as early in the year as is practicable. After the initial planning effort is completed, however, new developments or unexpected results of audit procedures may cause the auditor to revise the plans. Thus, various forms of planning will take place throughout the conduct of the audit. For small engagements, the initial planning and program development activities may occur at the same time.

Early in the planning process, the auditor should establish the timing of significant phases of the audit and set tentative deadlines for their completion. Significant audit dates might include dates for physical inventories, accounts receivable confirmation, commencement and completion of interim work (including any timely interim reviews yet to be performed during the current year), year-end work, meetings with the board of directors or audit committee, issuance of the audit report and other reports, such as the management letter and preparation or review of reports to the SEC.

In addition, it is desirable to reach early agreement regarding the timing of any special services to be performed for the current year, such as separate reports for subsidiaries, audits of pension plans, and preparation of federal and state tax returns.

Overall time estimates for the audit should be developed on the basis of the overall audit plan. Appropriate consideration should be given to anticipated internal audit and other client assistance and the effect of potential auditing, accounting, and reporting problems. Then a general staffing plan should be developed. Auditors with adequate experience and industry knowledge should be among those assigned to the engagement.

Audit Planning Meeting

An effective planning meeting is especially important to initial planning and will result in time savings on the audit. The key members of the client service team should attend. The auditor should consider the following in conducting a meeting:

1. Use the risk analysis working paper as a framework for the discussion. For each relevant area discuss (a) matters to consider in the risk analysis, such as current developments, analytical review data to be gathered, and whether a system evaluation is necessary; (b) likelihood of problems; and (c) alternative audit procedures.
2. Discuss ideas for audit efficiency (e.g., use analytical review procedures as substantive tests or confirm specific sales invoices instead of accounts receivable balances).
3. Review last year's time budget and consider how overruns might be avoided this year. Challenge prior time allocations in view of current audit risks.

4. Assign program development responsibilities to specific members of the team.
5. Discuss the approach for resolving significant accounting and auditing issues.

Communicating with the Client

Client Management. Timely communication of planning considerations to the client's management and staff, particularly those from whom the auditor will be requesting information and assistance, results in better client relations and timely cooperation. The auditor should provide the client's management with a formal timetable for the audit.

The extent of client assistance to be provided during the audit should be determined as early as possible. Prior to the program execution phase, a list of schedules and analyses to be provided by the client should be prepared. The auditor should review the list with the client and agree on the dates they are to be completed. To assure that the necessary information (e.g., account activity for the year or details of year-end balance) is obtained, the auditor might provide formats for the schedules and analyses and written instructions for preparation.

Internal Auditors. In developing the overall audit plan, the auditor should discuss with the internal auditors the scope and findings of their work, their plans for the remainder of the year, and—if satisfied with their competence and objectivity—whether they can provide direct assistance in the audit. Chapter 14 discusses how internal auditors may affect the audit.

Audit Committees. The auditor should discuss the overall audit plan with the audit committee before beginning program execution. While the allocation of audit effort is primarily the auditor's responsibility, experience has shown that audit committees are interested and frequently request auditors to increase effort in certain areas or to perform additional audit procedures. Even though the audit committee may not make such requests, it is nonetheless important that they understand the overall audit plan.

DOCUMENTING INITIAL PLANNING

The auditor's overall audit plan and assessment of the likelihood of problems in significant audit areas should be supported by underlying documentation. Information about the client's business and industry should be carried forward from the prior year and updated by reviewing current developments in the client's organization and operations and performing overall analytical review procedures. The auditor's findings should be documented in the working papers and summarized in a planning memorandum.

Planning Memorandum

A planning memorandum summarizing the overall audit plan usually is prepared for audit engagements. It includes (but is not necessarily limited to):

1. Significant economic or other external factors affecting the client's business and industry.
2. Major changes in client ownership, operations, personnel, and accounting procedures.
3. Significant changes in other external and internal environmental factors.
4. Assessment of the control environment.
5. Identification of potential auditing, accounting, and reporting problems.
6. The overall audit plan, including the general audit effort required at subsidiary and divisional locations.
7. Identification of accounting systems to be documented and evaluated.
8. Timing of significant phases of the audit, as well as tentative deadlines for completion of these phases.
9. Staffing requirements in general.
10. Significant planning activities, such as meetings with the client, including dates, who attended, and the subjects discussed.

The length of the memorandum will depend on the size and complexity of the engagement. For example, it normally would be sufficient to summarize the overall audit plan, including comments on significant changes from the preceding year and the reasons for emphasizing certain areas, without repeating details of the significant financial statement items by location or other information contained in the planning working papers.

Near completion of the examination, the auditor may want to reread the memorandum to be sure that all matters indicated had been considered during the course of the audit. To the extent there have been major changes in the audit plan (e.g., changes resulting from significant acquisitions or dispositions), an addendum to the memorandum commenting on these matters and how they have been resolved would be appropriate.

Planning Working Papers

To provide for organized documentation of the initial planning effort, all planning working papers should be included in a separate section of the working papers. Examples of initial planning documentation include:

1. Planning memorandum.
2. Environmental considerations working papers (e.g., memoranda of discussions with operating and financial executives).
3. Financial information (including overall analytical review working papers) used to develop the overall audit plan.

4. Agenda and memoranda of planning meetings with client personnel and the audit staff assigned to the engagement.
5. Overall time estimates, staffing plan, and work schedules.
6. Reports to the audit committee outlining the overall audit plan and related memoranda of meetings with the committee.

In addition, it may be appropriate to cross-reference certain matters in the planning working papers to other sections of the working papers that include materials used to identify significant developments.

QUESTIONS AND PROBLEMS

3–1. What should be the result of effective and timely planning by the auditor?

3–2. What should be included in the auditor's overall audit plan?

3–3. When does the audit planning process usually occur?

3–4. How can an auditor on a new engagement obtain an understanding of the client's business and industry?

3–5. What documents should an auditor examine on recurring engagements to assist in identifying current developments?

3–6. What might be included in an overall analytical review of a client's interim financial statements?

3–7. What information might be highlighted by an overall analytical review of interim financial statements?

3–8. How should overall analytical review procedures be applied to consolidated financial data of clients with several industry segments?

3–9. *a.* The environment in which an auditor's client operates includes both external and internal factors. Identify these factors.
   b. What will an understanding of these factors help an auditor determine?

3–10. In studying industry conditions, what factors should an auditor consider?

3–11. Why is it important for an auditor to identify and understand both the economic factors that have influenced the client's industry in the past and those that are doing so today?

3–12. Why should an auditor gather facts about the client's principal competitors?

3–13. In studying regulatory requirements that may affect a client, what governmental entities should an auditor consider?

3–14. Discuss the importance of ownership influences in the auditor's study of the client's internal environment.

3–15. What factors should an auditor review to gain an understanding of a client's current and prospective financial condition?

3–16. List some items that might be included in an audit planning memorandum.

3–17. Where should the auditor place documentation relating to the initial planning effort?

3–18. How does an auditor's understanding of a client's business and industry and knowledge of current developments relate to the detail analytical review?

3–19. Listed below are two specific control objectives. Identify some environmental factors related to these objectives.
   a. Customer returns and other allowances are approved and recorded correctly as to account, amount, and period.
   b. Amortization of loss in value of intangibles is recorded correctly as to account, amount, and period.

3–20. Identify the specific control objectives affected by the following situations and discuss the environmental factors and the effect they have on the related accounts and transactions.
   a. Your client, Energy Corporation, a natural gas producer, has used excess cash to speculate in precious metals for the past two years. Six months prior to year-end the company liquidated its holdings and reinvested the proceeds in large denomination short-term certificates of deposit.
   b. Your client, Armor Plating, Inc., recently negotiated a new contract with the labor union, which brought to an end the longest strike in the company's history. The new contract calls for retroactive cost-of-living adjustments and significant future increases in wages and benefits.

3–21. In June 1984, the CPA firm of Very, Many, and Associates was engaged by Boslem, Inc., to perform the annual audit for the year ended December 31, 1984. Allan Very is to be the partner in charge of the engagement. Mr. Very views himself as a "shirt-sleeve" manager—a "doer." He does not like to "waste valuable time" planning.
   a. Explain to Mr. Very the advantages of early audit planning.
   b. Explain to Mr. Very how he can acquire an understanding of the client's business and industry.

3–22. Identify the primary specific control objective affected in each of the following situations:
   a. Management closely monitors the shipping and billing processes since there are numerous large orders and salesmen are paid on a commission basis. Actual sales are compared to forecasts, and variances are pursued.
   b. Finished goods are cycle counted so that each item in finished goods inventory is counted quarterly. No large unexplained adjustments to the perpetual records resulting from these cycle counts have occurred in the past.
   c. During the past year, the company acquired a company in an unrelated industry.

3–23. Compare the following two situations taken from the environmental considerations section of a risk analysis working paper.
   1. Raw materials consist mainly of steel wire and other steel products. These products are purchased from approximately 100 different companies since one supplier can't meet all of the company's different needs and the company does not want to be dependent on only one or a few suppliers.

2. Assume the same facts as in situation 1 above, except that the environmental section states that the company purchases approximately 90 percent of its raw materials from five suppliers. These are the only suppliers from which the company can purchase certain of its needed materials.

Required:

Based on these facts:

a. Identify the specific control objective(s) for which the risk analysis working paper was prepared.

b. Which situation is more favorable to the company? To the auditor? Explain.

3–24. Complete the environmental considerations section of the risk analysis working papers for specific control objectives S–1, S–2 (combined) and S–4, S–5, S–6 (combined), using the following information:

Core Corporation manufactures many different types of fasteners and other components used primarily by automobile manufacturers or part distributors. The big three auto makers account for approximately 40 percent of sales. The remaining sales are made to approximately 2,500 parts distributors. Customers are billed based on established guidelines per standard price lists. The standard price lists provide salespeople with some flexibility in establishing customers' billings. This flexibility is considered critical by management since the market conditions are extremely competitive.

The auto industry has been in a slump for the last several years, which has directly affected the company's sales. This year's auto industry sales are up slightly. However, many of the company's customers are still experiencing cash flow problems resulting in a deterioration in the customer agings. One customer that accounts for 15 percent of sales, the Large Corporation, is in financial difficulty but continues to operate through loans guaranteed by foreign bankers.

Our experience has been that the big three auto makers will not confirm account balances. However, they will confirm individual invoice amounts. In addition, our experience in confirming account balances with the other customers has uncovered few problems. Prior year bad debt write-offs have been minimal.

3–25. Identify the specific control objective, if any, that would be directly affected by the following environmental considerations:

a. Most equipment additions have been to replace older equipment.

b. The electrical safety standards of most localities are so strict that they require public facilities to use the uninterruptible power systems manufactured by our client.

c. Three significant leases were entered into during the last year: two related to warehouses and one related to data processing equipment.

d. Some older equipment (still on the books) has not been used for the last several years.

3–26. Using the following information excerpted from the planning working papers, draft the environmental considerations section of specific control objective working paper A–8, "Commitments and contingencies are identified, monitored, and, if appropriate, recorded or disclosed."

The company is a leader in its industry and believes it will continue to be so because of its marketplace position. Management attributes the company's success to the quality of its products and personnel. However, the industry's market conditions are influenced by aggressive competition throughout.

One reason why the company is successful is because of its one-year warranty—unparalleled in the industry. The reserve for estimated future warranty expense is adjusted quarterly.

Management has stated that there are no lawsuits currently pending. Any lawsuits are referred to outside counsel.

Cash flow historically has been sufficient to finance normal operations. However, the company borrowed $5 million earlier in the year in anticipation of the slowdown in the collections of accounts receivable.

As do other companies in the industry, the company must follow OSHA and EPA regulations. The last serious deficiency resulting from inspections by those agencies occurred 20 years ago.

3–27. Assume that Wester, Inc., has expanded its operations to include the lucrative foreign market. Foreign customers must remit payments directly to Wester's offices. Wester's bank, which handles domestic cash receipts through a lock box arrangement, will not handle foreign remittances. Foreign sales for the year will approximate 25 percent of total sales. In general terms, what impact will this change in the company's environment have on the audit?

EVALUATING ACCOUNTING SYSTEMS

This chapter discusses internal control and how the auditor documents and evaluates accounting systems. Control objectives are used as a point of reference. The considerations unique to evaluating computerized accounting systems are covered in Chapter 5. Chapter 7 describes how to relate the evaluation of the accounting system to the audit program.

INTERNAL CONTROL

Management and corporate directors depend on internal control to provide reliable and timely financial information and to fulfill their responsibility for safeguarding assets. Internal controls are fundamental to the accurate recording of transactions and the preparation of reliable financial reports. Many business activities involve a high volume of transactions each day. Without adequate controls to assure the proper recording of transactions, the resulting financial data become unreliable and undermine management's ability to make decisions and effectively serve the company's customers.

Management and directors are not the only ones who look to the system of internal control for assurance as to the reliability of information. Auditors also rely on the system of internal control in determining the nature, timing, and extent of their audit procedures.

As will be explained in later chapters, auditors usually do not verify every transaction that occurs during the year, since doing so would be both unnecessary and uneconomical. Auditing standards require only that the auditor obtain "sufficient competent evidential matter . . ." on which to base an opinion. Much of this evidence is obtained by testing—examining less than all of the items comprising an account balance or class of transactions. The extent of testing that is required in a particular circumstance largely depends on the auditor's evaluation of the effectiveness of the client's system of internal control.

The second standard of field work requires ". . . a proper study and

4

evaluation of the existing internal control as a basis for reliance thereon and for the determination of the resultant extent of the tests to which auditing procedures are to be restricted." Generally, the more effective the controls, the smaller the sample that will be required to obtain satisfactory audit evidence of the fairness of a year-end account balance.

Nature of Internal Control

SAS No. 1 (AU 320.20) states that "transactions are the basic components of business operations and, therefore, are the primary subject matter of internal control. . . . The primary functions involved in the flow of transactions and related assets include the authorization, execution, and recording of transactions and the accountability for resulting assets."

In discussing internal control, *SAS No. 1* differentiates accounting control and administrative control. Accounting control is defined as (AU 320.28):

> . . . the plan of organization and the procedures and records that are concerned with the safeguarding of assets and the reliability of financial records, and consequently are designed to provide reasonable assurance that:
>
> a. Transactions are executed in accordance with management's general or specific authorization.
> b. Transactions are recorded as necessary (1) to permit preparation of financial statements in conformity with generally accepted accounting principles or any other criteria applicable to such statements and (2) to maintain accountability for assets.
> c. Access to assets is permitted only in accordance with management's authorization.
> d. The recorded accountability for assets is compared with the existing assets at reasonable intervals and appropriate action is taken with respect to any differences.

Administrative control is defined as (AU 320.27) including but not limited to:

> . . . the plan of organization and the procedures and records that are concerned with the decision processes leading to management's authorization of transactions. . . . Such authorization is a management function directly associated with the responsibility for achieving the objectives of the organization and is the starting point for establishing accounting control of transactions.

SAS No. 1 (AU 320.29) further states that these definitions of accounting and administrative controls ". . . are not necessarily mutually exclusive because some of the procedures and records comprehended in accounting control may also be involved in administrative control."

SAS No. 1 (AU 320.31) notes that the responsibility for the establishment and maintenance of internal control rests solely with management. Management should review the system on an ongoing basis and initiate necessary changes and improvements. The auditor evaluates internal control in connection with the audit and in many cases will assist management in design, installation, and modification of the system.

Reasonable Assurance

SAS No. 1 (AU 320.32) recognizes that "the definition of accounting control comprehends reasonable, but not absolute, assurance that the objectives expressed in it will be accomplished by the system. The concept of reasonable assurance recognizes that the cost of internal control should not exceed the benefits expected to be derived." *SAS No. 1* notes further that this cost-benefit relationship should be recognized by management and taken into consideration when designing a system of internal control.

Limitations of Internal Control

No system of internal control is perfect. There are always inherent limitations. *SAS No. 1* (AU 320.34) suggests that limitations may be due to such factors as (1) misunderstanding of instructions, (2) errors in judgment, (3) carelessness, (4) distraction or fatigue, and (5) collusion. In addition, *SAS No. 1* suggests that management may deliberately override effective controls.

Errors versus Irregularities

The impact of an error or an irregularity on the financial statements is, for all practical purposes, the same. However, for purposes of evaluating an accounting system (and designing an audit program), it is important to understand the distinction.

SAS No. 16, (AU 327.02–.03), differentiates *errors* from *irregularities.* Errors are defined as:

> . . . unintentional mistakes in financial statements and include mathematical or clerical mistakes in the underlying records and accounting data from which the financial statements were prepared, mistakes in the application of accounting principles, and oversight or misinterpretation of facts that existed at the time the financial statements were prepared.

In contrast, this SAS defines irregularities as:

> . . . intentional distortions of financial statements such as deliberate misrepresentations by management, sometimes referred to as management fraud, or misappropriations of assets sometimes referred to as defalcations. . . .

Inherent Limitations of an Audit

SAS No. 16 (AU 327.11–.13) points out that independent audits are subject to certain inherent limitations. These include:

1. The fact that an audit is a testing process (see Chapters 8 and 9 for discussion of sampling) means there is always the possibility that material errors or irregularities may not be detected.
2. The risk that ". . . management's override of internal controls, collusion, forgery, or unrecorded transactions. . . ." (AU 327.12) may result in material errors or irregularities being missed. *SAS No. 16* (AU 327.12) takes the position that "unless the auditor's examination reveals evidential matter to the contrary, his reliance on the truthfulness of certain representations [e.g., representations of management concerning the entity's records, confirmations and documents received from third parties] and on the genuineness of records and documents obtained during his examination is reasonable." The independent auditor is not obligated to extend procedures to look for unrecorded transactions unless there is evidence that such transactions may exist.

SAS No. 16 (AU 327.13) concludes that "the auditor is not an insurer or guarantor; if his examination was made in accordance with generally accepted auditing standards, he has fulfilled his professional responsibility."

EVALUATING ACCOUNTING SYSTEMS

As was pointed out in Chapter 2, the audit program should not be based on the system evaluation alone. Rather, the determination of the appropriate nature, timing, and extent of audit tests requires an assessment of the likelihood of material errors in important financial statement areas by reviewing the *three* inputs to the risk analysis: (1) environmental considerations, (2) observations from detail analytical review, and (3) system evaluation. The following discussion is concerned with the system evaluation—the process of determining whether there is reasonable assurance that specific control objectives are being achieved by the accounting system, thus minimizing control risk. The auditor should identify and record either (1) system attributes that provide reasonable assurance that these control objectives are being achieved or (2) system deficiencies that result in the objectives not being achieved.

Each specific control objective relates to certain transactions and accounts and to the prevention or detection of errors and irregularities. Key attributes or system deficiencies related to each specific control objective are summarized on the risk analysis working paper along with the other inputs to the risk analysis.

General Control Objectives

An accounting system is composed of related procedures designed to accomplish specific purposes. For example, a system may be established for billing shipments to customers and summarizing these transactions for recording in the general ledger. There are five general control objectives—authorization, recording, safeguarding, reconciliation, and valuation—that an accounting system should be expected to achieve to provide reasonable assurance that financial information is accurate and complete and that the assets are safeguarded. These general control objectives, which are discussed below, have been derived from the definitions of accounting and administrative controls in *SAS No. 1.*

Authorization. Transactions should be executed in conformity with management's intentions. Authorizations may be general and apply to a large number of similar transactions, or they may be specific. General authorizations are granted by establishing policies such as standard price lists, customer credit limits, or inventory reorder points. Specific authorizations may be required over and above the general authority given by management. For example, management may require specific authorization of individual purchases of plant assets in excess of a certain dollar amount.

Frequently, specific authorization is given by an approval process occurring after a transaction is initiated but before it is completed. Approval of a transaction is distinguished from authorization in that approval is an indication that conditions required for authorization have been met. Authorizations generally serve to prevent transactions not in accordance with management's intentions, while approvals generally serve to detect such transactions.

Recording. All authorized transactions should be recorded at the correct amount, in the accounting period they were executed, and in the appropriate account (including amounts and/or quantities in subsidiary records). No fictitious transactions should be recorded.

The physical evidence of recording includes documents (e.g., sales invoices, purchase orders, timecards) and records (e.g., subsidiary ledgers, sales journals, general ledger) in which the transactions are entered and summarized. Documents and records should be designed to limit the possibility that a transaction will be recorded incorrectly, recorded more than once, or omitted from the records. For example, a document might include preprinted numbers, instructions for proper routing, and spaces for authorizations and approvals.

Safeguarding. Responsibility for physical custody of assets should be assigned to specific personnel who are independent of related recordkeeping functions. Both direct (physical) and indirect (paperwork) access to assets should be limited to those who are properly authorized. Safeguarding also is achieved through physical precautions (e.g., locked storerooms for inventory and fireproof vaults for the protection of currency and securities).

Reconciliation. Records should be compared with related assets, documents, records, or control accounts (e.g., periodic bank reconciliations and reconciliation of investment securities to detail records and control accounts). The nature and amount of any differences should be determined and appropriate adjustments recorded. Reconciliation procedures help provide assurance that other general control objectives have been achieved.

Valuation. Recorded amounts should be reviewed for impairment in value. Direct write-down, allowance, or other adjustment should be recorded as appropriate to conform with GAAP (e.g., allowance for uncollectible loans or receivables and adjustment of inventory to market, if lower than cost).

The first three general objectives—authorization, recording, and safeguarding—relate to establishing the system of accountability and provide for the *prevention* of errors and irregularities. The fourth objective—reconciliation—ties together the system of accountability established by the first three objectives and along with the fifth objective—valuation—provides for the *detection* of errors and irregularities. The applicability of each of the general control objectives depends on the nature of the transactions or accounts.

Specific Control Objectives

The five general control objectives provide a common basis for evaluating any system. However, to effectively make this evaluation, it is necessary to relate the control objectives to the purposes of a particular system. To do this, it is necessary to translate the general control objectives to specific control objectives for each aspect of the system. Examples of this relationship and the transactions and accounts that are directly affected are:

General Control Objectives	Specific Control Objectives	Transactions and Accounts
Authorization	Salary, wage, and benefit expenses are incurred only for work authorized and performed	Payroll, accrued liabilities
Recording, safeguarding	Cash receipts are recorded correctly as to account, amount, and period and are deposited	Cash receipts, cash, receivables

A list of specific control objectives for a typical commercial or industrial business is included in Chapter 2. Some of these objectives may not be applicable to a particular client's operations and activities and need not be evaluated. Also, there may be unique activities for which additional specific control objectives will require definition and inclusion in the working papers.

An understanding of the concept of general control objectives is necessary for the evaluation of systems that relate to unique activities. For example, if a client has a large number of repossessions from merchandise sold under installment credit arrangements, a customized specific control objective such as the following may be necessary to address authorization, recording, and valuation:

Repossessions are authorized and recorded correctly as to account, amount (net realizable value), and period.

Some specific control objectives contain two or more parts. For example, those involving recording as to account, amount, and period may be considered three separate objectives. The auditor's system evaluation should address each specific control objective and each part of a multipart objective separately.

Operating Components

To provide a framework for evaluating internal accounting control, the specific control objectives have been organized along the lines of the basic operating components of a typical business entity as described in Chapter

2. These components are administration, sales, production or service, and finance.

Control objectives relate to the prevention or detection of errors and irregularities in specific transactions and accounts. Because most transactions originate in one of the four basic operating components and are completed in another, they are subject to differing controls at differing times. For example, purchases of office supplies usually originate in and are subject to controls of the administration component. Inventory purchases originate in the production or service component and are subject to different controls. However, when the related invoices are received for payment, these transactions generally are entered into the accounts payable/cash disbursements system under the same controls. While the evaluation of the system should follow the organization of the operating components, testing procedures will cover transaction cycles and therefore cross component lines.

In the administration component, most of the specific control objectives relate to the authorization and recording of the costs associated with the related control and support activities (e.g., administrative expenses including related payroll). For purposes of system evaluation, these costs are combined with the costs associated with marketing and distribution because they typically are subject to similar procedures and controls.

Separate evaluations should be completed if different systems are used to process similar types of transactions (e.g., standard product and custom order sales or computerized and manual cash disbursements). In some circumstances, the auditor may conclude that only one system should be evaluated because the other transactions are not material.

Before performing any audit tests, the auditor, based on his or her understanding of the client's system, should identify the system attributes that provide reasonable assurance the specific control objective is being achieved. Alternatively, the auditor should identify system deficiencies that indicate the control objective is not being achieved.

In making such an evaluation, the auditor is not concerned with all of a system's attributes. Rather, the auditor is concerned with the *minimum number* that provide reasonable assurance that the specific control objective is being achieved. These are the *key attributes*. Determining whether there is "reasonable assurance" is a matter of judgment. The auditor should evaluate whether system attributes make it unlikely that material errors or irregularities could occur, or go undetected if they did occur.

Identifying Key Attributes

An important characteristic of many key attributes is that they function as checks on other procedures. When the auditor analyzes the flow of transactions through an accounting system, he or she should distinguish between *processing procedures* and *control procedures.* Processing procedures are necessary to identify, calculate, summarize, classify, and report transactions. Control procedures are necessary to assure that transactions being processed are accurate and complete. Specifically, they help assure that all transactions are authorized and recorded correctly, assets are safeguarded, and any errors that arise from processing procedures are promptly detected and corrected. *The minimum number of control procedures that provide reasonable assurance are the key attributes.* There are several ways to identify key attributes:

1. Review documentation of the system.
2. Inquire of accounting or operating personnel.
3. Refer to Appendix II at the end of this textbook which provides helpful lists of system attributes to consider and what can go wrong (errors or irregularities) for each specific control objective.

Figure 4–1 indicates the types of system attributes that often are key to achieving specific control objectives.

Review Documentation.   In some cases, it will be very clear from the system documentation how certain procedures provide reasonable assurance that a control objective is being achieved. For example, the use of a lock box system provides reasonable assurance that cash receipts are deposited. However, more often, a subjective evaluation will be required to determine how various prevention and detection procedures combine to provide reasonable assurance. For example, reasonable assurance that cash receipts are prop-

FIGURE 4–1   Types of Key Attributes

Types of Key Attributes	*Examples*
Independent checks, reviews, approvals	Controller's review of support for disbursement
Matching documents	Matching receiving reports to vendor invoices
Prenumbering and sequence checking	Accounting for numerical sequence of prenumbered shipping documents
Recalculations	Recalculating extensions and footings on vendor invoices
Reconciliation to control totals	Postings to receivable records reconciled to total cash received
Reconciliation to outside information	Reconciliation of trade accounts payable to vendor statements
Access restrictions	Locked storage facility, or cashiers denied access to accounts receivable records

erly applied to customer accounts may be achieved by several related attributes, such as posting to customers' receivable accounts by an individual independent of cash receipts, regular mailing of statements, and independent follow-up of customer inquiries.

Make Inquiries.   In some cases, it may be helpful to ask employees involved with the related aspects of the accounting system what procedures they think provide reasonable assurance that the objective is being achieved. For example, the auditor might ask the billing supervisor what aspects of the system provide reasonable assurance that all shipments are billed.

Use Examples of System Attributes.   The Reference Lists for System Evaluation and Preliminary Audit Approach in Appendix II include examples of system attributes that may contribute to the achievement of each specific control objective. These lists are simply examples and are not all-inclusive. The presence of most or even all of the items listed does not necessarily mean that a control objective is being achieved. In some cases, the presence of just one procedure, such as the supervision and review by the owner/ manager of a small business, may be the only means by which a control objective is achieved.

Use Examples of What Can Go Wrong.   The Reference Lists also include examples of what can go wrong if the specific control objectives are not being achieved. Consideration of the types of errors or irregularities that could occur in specific accounts should help assure that the auditor's evaluation has focused on the system's key attributes. The possible ways of making errors or committing irregularities are virtually limitless. These examples are presented solely to stimulate thought.

Segregation of Duties

Ordinarily, the achievement of control objectives requires segregation of duties. This segregation of duties means that different people should be responsible for the authorization of transactions, recording of transactions, and the physical custody of assets. Segregation is adequate when no one person can misappropriate assets or improperly record or account for transactions without reasonable assurance of detection by another person. Of course, transactions may be recorded and reported correctly without appropriate segregation of duties; however, the system would not provide reasonable assurance that this is the case.

Reconciliations

Effective reconciliation procedures tie together the system of accountability and help provide reasonable assurance that control objectives are being achieved. The auditor should determine whether the client has reconciliation procedures designed to discover and report errors and differences.

Assets should be compared periodically with accounting records, and control and subsidiary accounts should be reconciled on a regular basis. Changes between beginning and ending balances also should be accounted for. Any discrepancies should be investigated and reported to the appropriate personnel for ultimate resolution.

Summarizing the System Evaluation

The auditor should summarize in the risk analysis working papers those key attributes that support the evaluation. These are the system attributes that are to be tested and relied upon in determining the nature, timing, and extent of other audit tests. If the accounting system does not have attributes that provide for achieving the control objective, the auditor should identify the deficiencies in the risk analysis working papers.

System attributes may provide reasonable assurance except at a particular point in the processing of a transaction. Although transactions may successfully pass the point with reasonable assurance that errors or irregularities are not occurring, the auditor should conclude that there is not reasonable assurance that the control objective is being achieved. In these instances, the auditor should recognize that the likelihood of errors or irregularities is greatest at the point in question and should plan audit tests directed at error detection (or estimation) at that point. However, the audit program may be designed to establish reliance on the other aspects of the system by planning tests of the applicable key attributes that provide assurance up to that point.

In most cases, the effect of a system deficiency will be apparent. For example, if unmatched receiving reports are not controlled, goods received may not be recorded in the correct period. However, if it is not apparent, the auditor should document how the deficiency might affect the accounts related to the specific control objective so that appropriate audit tests can be planned. For example, if a company has some cost-plus contracts and others that are fixed fee, the lack of procedures to provide reasonable assurance that labor-hours are charged to the proper job in process could result in lost revenue to the company.

If the auditor believes there is not reasonable assurance that a specific control objective is being achieved, the auditor should discuss the situation promptly with the client. It may be that:

1. There are compensating controls of which the auditor is unaware.
2. The client has time to plan and implement corrective action that might mitigate the need to perform extended audit tests.

Negative evaluations may indicate that there is a material weakness[1] that should be communicated to senior management and the board of directors or its audit committee.

Effect of the Control Environment

Chapter 3 describes the internal environmental factors that provide the framework, or control environment, in which the accounting systems function. Factors such as the plan of organization and the establishment, communication, and monitoring of policies and procedures all contribute to the likelihood that control objectives are being achieved throughout the period.

In some cases, the auditor's documentation of the system may not identify any key attribute that provides reasonable assurance that a specific control objective is being achieved; in fact a deficiency may be identified. The auditor's initial reaction may be that the specific control objective is not being achieved. However, the auditor may be able to identify monitoring procedures within the control environment that provide for the detection of material errors in the specific accounts affected. Practices such as the following may allow the auditor to conclude that it is unlikely that a material error could occur in the accounts affected by the specific control objective without being detected:

1. Careful review of financial statements by management, including budgetary analysis.
2. Effective internal audit activities.

These monitoring procedures may help the auditor conclude that the specific control objective is being achieved, and they should be documented in the risk analysis working papers. For example, management's detail comparison of monthly expenses by department to budgeted amounts and analysis of fluctuations might help provide reasonable assurance that all expenses are authorized and recorded correctly as to account, amount, and period.

For small, privately held companies or nonprofit organizations with a limited number of accounting personnel (e.g., one bookkeeper or office manager), the lack of segregation of duties often is offset by close supervision and review by management.

A questionnaire, such as the one in Appendix 4A to this chapter, may be helpful in identifying and documenting practices that contribute to an

---

[1] A material weakness is defined in *SAS No. 20* (AU 323), as amended by *SAS No. 30* (AU 642), as:

"... a condition in which the specific control procedures or the degree of compliance with them do not reduce to a relatively low level the risk that errors or irregularities in amounts that would be material in relation to the financial statements being audited may occur and not be detected within a timely period by employees in the normal course of performing their assigned functions."

effective control environment. Included are sections covering ownership influences, organization and personnel practices, monitoring procedures (including financial reporting, budgets, and reconciliations), and internal audit activities.

Suspicion of Errors or Irregularities

Material Items. *SAS No. 16* (AU 327.14) suggests that if an independent auditor suspects errors or irregularities, he or she must decide whether the effect would be so material as to alter the opinion on the financial statements. In the case of a possible material error or irregularity, this SAS (AU 327.14) suggests the following:

1. First discuss the matter with an appropriate member of the client's management who is at least one level higher in the organization than the individuals who may be involved in the error or irregularity.
2. If after this discussion the auditor still believes that errors or irregularities may exist, then the auditor should make sure that the board of directors or the audit committee is aware of the circumstances.
3. Also the auditor should gather evidence as to the existence and effect of suspected errors or irregularities. This might include discussion with the client's legal counsel.

SAS No. 16 (AU 327.14) also states that in some cases the auditor may believe that irregularities or errors are present, but may find it:

> . . . impractical or impossible to obtain sufficient evidential matter to determine the existence, or related effect, of material errors or possible irregularities, or management may impose a limitation on the scope of the auditor's search for the evidential matter. . . . [In those instances, when] the auditor remains uncertain about whether these errors or possible irregularities may materially affect the financial statements, he should qualify his opinion or disclaim an opinion on the financial statements and, depending on the circumstances, consider withdrawing from the engagement, indicating his reasons and findings in writing to the board of directors. . . .

Immaterial Items. *SAS No. 16* (AU 327.15) suggests that if an independent auditor finds errors or irregularities during the examination but concludes that the errors or irregularities are not material enough to affect the opinion, the auditor should simply refer the matter to an appropriate member of the client's management who is at least one level higher than the individuals involved.

Service Organizations

Many companies use service organizations to meet some or all of their accounting, investment, or data processing needs. Examples include payroll services performed by a bank or other organization, investment transactions managed by a bank trust department, and data processing performed by a computer service bureau. The use of a service organization does not change the approach to evaluating accounting systems. The auditor still must evaluate whether specific control objectives are achieved, but may obtain information and document controls differently. This is due to the practical considerations involved in evaluating controls at a remote location not under the control of the company, and because other auditors may evaluate and report on the controls maintained by the service organization. The auditor's responsibilities with respect to client accounting records maintained by a service organization are discussed in Chapter 5, particularly in the context of a computer service bureau.

DOCUMENTING ACCOUNTING SYSTEMS

Audit working papers should contain descriptions of the accounting systems that affect accounts or transactions *important* to the financial statements. To gather the necessary data, the auditor should interview appropriate client personnel, read available client documentation, and observe operating procedures and physical safeguards. The resulting system documentation should support the evaluation of the system and provide each working paper reviewer with a basic understanding of the system.

Form of Documentation

System documentation can be in the form of flowcharts, questionnaires (see Appendix 4A), or narratives. The documentation of most accounting systems will include a combination of these forms.

Flowcharting often is the clearest way to document significant aspects of an accounting system. Flowcharts indicate the flow of documents and information from their sources to final disposition using easily recognized symbols and a minimum of narrative description—although brief supplemental narratives often will be required to clarify or expand the description of information depicted in a flowchart. Flowcharts assist in identifying all significant accounting procedures and processes. Appendix 4B contains a discussion of flowcharting.

System documentation should depict the procedures that are supposed to be functioning. Documentation should indicate the source of the information (e.g., the department supervisor, client policy manual). If the auditor obtains client-prepared documentation, the auditor should be sure that it has been approved by appropriate supervisory personnel.

In the process of preparing the documentation, it may be desirable to trace one or two of each type of transaction through the system from inception to completion. This procedure is known as a transaction walk-through. Transaction walk-throughs always should be performed on system documentation prepared by clients. The walk-through should be performed to formulate or confirm an understanding of a system before the auditor designs audit tests. A walk-through is not performed to test key attributes or substantiate balances.

As part of the documentation and evaluation process, the auditor should inquire as to whether a system is ever overridden by someone in a supervisory or management position. If it is, the auditor should determine the circumstances and evaluate whether or not the key attributes that have been identified can be relied upon.

The size of a company does not affect the importance of control objectives. For example, it is just as important to a small company as it is to a large company that all shipments are billed and that wages are paid only for work authorized and performed. However, procedures and controls used to achieve these objectives in a small business may be substantially less sophisticated. In many instances, the primary controls may be a competent bookkeeper and close supervision by the owner/manager (e.g., by signing checks after reviewing supporting documents, approving credit arrangements and bad debt write-offs, and comparing actual costs and expenses to budgets).

Although the importance of adequate system documentation is not affected by the size of a company, the form of such documentation will vary depending on the complexity of the system. For example, because it often is difficult to segregate duties in small companies, it may be appropriate to prepare a working paper summarizing the duties of each person involved in the accounting function. Figure 4–2 is an example of such a working paper. This type of analysis may help to focus on existing control procedures and may lead to recommendations to management about improving segregation of duties without impairing efficiency.

Extent of Documentation

In the initial planning phase, it is essential that the auditor determine priorities for documenting the client's accounting systems. Identifying all important accounting systems and determining the adequacy of existing documentation is the first step. No new documentation needs to be prepared if existing documentation enables the auditors to (1) understand the flow of transactions and documents and (2) identify key attributes that support achievement of specific control objectives (or deficiencies that prevent achievement). The auditor's review of existing documentation should lead to a plan for needed revisions and/or preparation of new documentation.

Time spent documenting a client's systems will depend upon the size and complexity of the engagement, as well as the client's involvement in documenting existing systems. When a client intends to make major changes to an existing system in the near future, it is usually not necessary to prepare flowcharts or detail narratives to document that system. However, at a minimum, system documentation should provide information as to who performs

FIGURE 4-2 Working Paper that Documents Accounting Function in a Small Company

Duties	General Ledger Bookkeeper	President's Secretary	Billing Clerk	Purchase Agent	Vice President
Sales, Accounts Receivable, & Cash Receipts					
Approves shipper					X
Prepares customer invoice			X		
Accounts for numerical sequence of shipper			X		
Reconciles products shipped to products billed			X		
Prepares customer credit memo	X				
Approves goods returned by customer					X
Posts accounts receivable ledger	X				
Posts sales records	X				
Deposits receipts on sales	X				
Reconciles bank accounts	X				
Accounts Payable & Cash Disbursements					
Approves administrative expenses	X				
Approves purchase orders for materials				X	
Matches receiver to vendor invoice	X				
Prepares disbursement checks	X				
Signs disbursement checks	X				
Records disbursements & payables	X				
Prepares monthly financial statements	X				
Determines account distribution	X				
Payroll					
Approves timecards	X				X
Prepares payroll checks	X				
Updates employee payroll records		X			
Records payroll expense	X				
Signs payroll checks	X				
Distributes payroll checks	X				X
Holds undistributed payroll checks	X				X

In this example, the auditor might recommend the following changes in responsibilities that could improve internal controls without impairing the efficiency of the small staff of the company:

1. The president's secretary should open the mail, list the cash receipts before forwarding the receipts to the bookkeeper for posting to customer accounts, and forward the list to the billing clerk. The billing clerk should reconcile the list to the deposit slip and take the deposits to the bank.
2. Someone other than the bookkeeper (e.g., president's secretary) should reconcile the bank accounts.
3. Someone other than the bookkeeper (e.g., vice president) should review supporting documentation and sign the regular and payroll checks.

important procedures, what documents and records are available, and where the records are located for each significant class of transaction. This information, which is necessary even when the auditor is not going to rely on a system, should facilitate the design of specific audit tests.

UPDATING THE SYSTEM EVALUATION TO END OF PERIOD

Generally, the evaluation of accounting systems is performed prior to the end of the period under audit. However, because accounting systems can change, it is necessary to determine the appropriateness of the system evaluation through the end of the period. The primary purpose of updating the system evaluation is to identify changes that indicate a need to modify the nature, timing, or extent of planned audit procedures.

Whenever the tests of key attributes do not include the entire period under audit, the auditor should (1) inquire of appropriate client personnel and observe procedures to identify significant changes in the accounting systems, (2) determine whether additional tests may be desirable, and (3) prepare a memorandum for the working papers stating conclusions about the need for additional tests and the reasons for that conclusion.

Identifying Changes in the Systems

The auditor should attempt to identify changes in the accounting systems through observation and inquiry. More specifically, the auditor should seek information from appropriate officers and employees and look for evidence of reassignment of duties, changes in key personnel, introduction of new equipment or procedures, and any other changes that, in the circumstances, may affect conclusions about whether specific control objectives continue to be achieved. The auditor's inquiries and observations should be directed to each aspect of a system covered by a specific control objective, rather than to the system as a whole. Effective controls in one part of a system cannot compensate for deficiencies in another.

Desirability of Additional Tests

In assessing the need for additional tests of key attributes, the following factors should be considered:

1. *Changes identified as a result of inquiries and observations.* To the extent that any significant changes in the accounting systems have occurred, the previous tests of key attributes may no longer be relevant, so new tests may be needed. Changes should be viewed as significant only if they affect the continued functioning and effectiveness of the key attributes on which the auditor is relying to design the nature, timing, or extent of other audit tests.
2. *Length of the remaining period.* Only if the auditor believes that the period covered by the tests of key attributes is not representative of the full year will the length of the remaining period, by itself, make additional tests of key attributes necessary.

3. *Evidence of compliance provided by other tests.* Direct tests of balances often provide evidence about the continued functioning of key attributes. For example, when the auditor examines vendors' invoices in support of year-end asset or expense account balances, a determination can be made as to whether key attributes relating to authorization and recording of these transactions continue to function. To the extent that other audit tests provide evidence of compliance from the date of tests of key attributes to the end of the period under audit, additional tests that otherwise may have been necessary can be reduced.

4. *Changes in the control environment.* An effective control environment allows the auditor to limit tests of key attributes to a period through an interim date. If the auditor becomes aware of changes in the control environment, such as loss of employees causing an understaffed condition, the auditor might decide that additional tests of key attributes are necessary.

In most cases, companies will not have made significant changes in their accounting systems between completion of the auditor's tests of key attributes and year-end. If this is the case and there is an effective control environment, the auditor can become satisfied that key attributes continue to function by inquiry and observation without the need for additional tests.

Figure 4–3 provides an example of a form used for updating the system evaluation.

RECURRING ENGAGEMENTS

A systems evaluation should be performed each year as part of the risk analysis and development of the preliminary audit approach. Of the three inputs to the risk analysis, the auditor would expect the systems evaluation to change the least from year to year. Nevertheless, as part of the initial planning for recurring engagements, the auditor should inquire about significant systems changes. If no changes have occurred, there is no need to prepare new systems documentation. However, because systems changes may be initiated by an employee without management's knowledge and the impact on controls of even a small change can be important, it is desirable to perform a walk-through each year to verify that the existing systems and the working paper documentation are in agreement. Whether or not there have been changes in the systems, the auditor should challenge prior year evaluations and related programs.

EFFECT OF SYSTEMS EVALUATION ON THE PRELIMINARY AUDIT APPROACH

The systems evaluation is one of three inputs to the auditor's analysis of the likelihood of material error in accounts and transactions affected by

FIGURE 4-3   Examples of System Evaluation Update Form

	Name	Date
Prepared	_____	_____
Approved	_____	_____

Update of System Evaluation

Client _____

Audit Date _____

If tests of key attributes do not include the entire period under audit, indicate below the related specific control objectives and the period covered (e.g., S–4/5/6, 1/1 to 9/30).

Sales _____   Finance _____

Production/Service _____   Administration _____

Make inquiries and observations as to the following matters relating to changes in the accounting system subsequent to the date through which key attributes were tested. Inquiry made of (names and positions): _____

	Sales		Production/ Service		Finance		Administration	
	Yes	No	Yes	No	Yes	No	Yes	No
a. Changes in key personnel	___	___	___	___	___	___	___	___
b. Reassignment of duties	___	___	___	___	___	___	___	___
c. New EDP or other processing equipment or EDP software	___	___	___	___	___	___	___	___
d. New procedures	___	___	___	___	___	___	___	___
e. Changes in control environment	___	___	___	___	___	___	___	___
f. Other changes	___	___	___	___	___	___	___	___

If any of the above are answered "Yes," describe the changes.

_____
_____
_____
_____
_____
_____
_____
_____

Conclusion: Audit program requires revision   Yes ___   No ___

If any changes were noted, explain the reason for conclusion, describe any revisions to the audit approach, and cross-reference to the audit program.

_____
_____
_____
_____
_____
_____
_____

each specific control objective. Because effective systems can reduce the likelihood of material error in accounts and transactions, relying on the systems can reduce the extent and/or change the timing and nature of other audit tests in the preliminary audit approach.

It is important to keep in mind that, at the time the preliminary audit approach is developed, no tests of key attributes have been performed. The evaluation of whether a control objective is being achieved is based on the auditor's understanding of the system as documented in working papers. The preliminary audit approach should be designed to test whether the key attributes on which the auditor intends to rely are operating effectively.

By recognizing how a transaction affects various accounts, the auditor can design a combination of tests to achieve the maximum benefit. Satisfactory results of tests of key attributes can limit direct tests of balances needed to arrive at an audit conclusion. The Reference Lists in Appendix II at the end of this textbook indicate the account classifications typically affected by each specific control objective. Figures included in Chapters 10, 11, 13, and 14 show the relationship of specific control objectives to the debits or credits for each financial statement classification.

Appendix II also includes the principal audit tests to consider for the aspects of the accounts affected by each specific control objective if (1) the objective is achieved and (2) it is not achieved. These audit tests are not all inclusive but are included to illustrate the possible effects of the system evaluation on the preliminary audit approach. However, the other inputs to the risk analysis—environmental considerations and the observations from detail analytical review—also affect the likelihood of material error and, ultimately, the preliminary audit approach.

APPENDIX 4A

**AN EXAMPLE OF A CONTROL
ENVIRONMENT QUESTIONNAIRE**

Control Environment Questionnaire

Company _____ Powertronics, Inc. _____

Subsidiary or Division _____

Prepared or Updated by	Date	Approved by	Date
M. J. Mann	7–17–X5	R. D. Hunt	7–31–X5
		M. Grimm	8–2–X5

This Questionnaire should assist in assessing the overall effectiveness of the control environment. It focuses on ownership influences, organization and personnel practices, monitoring procedures (including financial reporting, budgets, and reconciliations), and internal audit activities. A "No" response does not necessarily indicate a deficiency in the control environment; the combined effect of the various factors should be considered in arriving at an overall assessment.

I. OWNERSHIP INFLUENCES

Yes   No

A. Concentration of Ownership

In a separate memorandum, describe the concentration of ownership, including approximate number of shareholders, any significant shareholders, whether shares are actively traded, extent of management's ownership interest.   *

B. Board of Directors

In a separate memorandum, describe the makeup of the board of directors, including number of directors, affiliations of outside directors, relationship of each director to the organization, and number of years as a director.   *

C. Is there an audit committee? (Company plans to form one)   ____   X
How many members serve on the committee? ____N/A____
How many are outside directors? _____N/A_____
How often does the committee meet? _____N/A_____

Are minutes of meetings prepared and retained?   N/A ____

D. Duties of the Board and Its Committees

Excerpt from articles of incorporation and bylaws a description of the duties assigned and performed by the board of directors, its audit committee, and any other committees of the board. Include description of any specific authorizations retained by the board or its committees.   *

Comment on ownership influences:

Ownership is spread among many small shareholders except for Jenks, CEO, who owns 5%. No undue pressures to achieve particular results. Present lack of audit committee is not considered a problem, because there are three outside directors—they appear to have an independent influence on the Board.

II. ORGANIZATION AND PERSONNEL PRACTICES

Yes   No

Organization

A. Does documentation include up-to-date:

   Corporate structure chart?   X ____

   Personnel organization chart?   X ____

Obtain copies. If none, prepare charts for working papers. (In permanent file)

B. Do the charts clearly reflect areas of responsibility and lines of reporting and communication?   X ____

*Memorandum is not necessary to obtain a general understanding of this questionnaire and is therefore omitted from this example.

	Yes	No

C. Are there formal position descriptions for administrative and financial personnel?   X ___

Do they clearly set out duties and responsibilities?   X ___

Comment on organization practices:

Organization provides for separation of incompatible duties. No discernible gaps or overlaps in assignment of responsibility. Company always has been effectively supervised by upper management; good monitoring of overall activities.

Personnel

D. Does the recruitment and selection process for new employees in the administrative and financial areas require investigation of background and references?   X ___

E. Are personnel policies and employee benefits documented and communicated to employees?   X ___

F. Is there a formal conflict of interest policy or code of conduct in effect? Obtain copies.   ___ X

Does it require periodic declarations by officers, directors, and key employees?   N/A ___

Are there established procedures by which employees may confidentially report violations of the company's code of conduct or other standards?   N/A ___

In a separate memorandum, describe the system used to monitor compliance with the conflict of interest policy and/or code of conduct.   See Note

G. Are employees who handle cash, securities, and other valuable assets bonded?   X ___

H. Do related employees, if any, have job assignments that minimize opportunities for collusion?   X ___

I. Is rotation of duties enforced by mandatory vacations?   X ___

J. Is job performance periodically evaluated and reviewed with each employee?   X ___

K. Are there training programs for administrative and financial personnel?   X ___

In a separate memorandum, describe the training programs.   See Note

Comment on personnel practices:

Company has effective policies and procedures for hiring, evaluation, compensation, promotion, etc. The Company puts emphasis on recruiting and employing college graduates.

(Item F.) Client is drafting a conflict of interest policy and code of conduct, which will be reviewed by E&W prior to being implemented, probably 4th quarter 19X5.

(Item K.) Marketing Training Program—Newly recruited salesmen get four weeks intensive training. This is a significant element in control over the level of returns.

III. MONITORING PROCEDURES

	Yes	No

Financial Reporting

	Yes	No
A. Are financial statements submitted at regular intervals to operating management?	X	___
To the board of directors?	X	___
To the audit committee?	N/A	___
Are they accompanied by analytical comments?	X	___
Do they show comparisons with:		
Prior periods?	X	___
Budgets?	X	___
Forecasts?	X	___
B. Operating Analyses		
In a separate schedule, list the principal operating analyses used. Describe contents and indicate frequency of preparation. Samples may be attached in lieu of schedule.	See Note	
C. Are the same accounting and closing practices followed at interim dates as at year-end?	X	___
D. Is prior review and approval by a responsible official required for financial information for public distribution (e.g., press releases, filings with regulatory bodies, and shareholders' reports)?	X	___
E. Does documentation include up-to-date:		
Accounting policies and procedures?	X	___
Chart of accounts describing nature of each account?	X	___
Obtain copies.		
F. Are all general journal entries other than standard entries required to be authorized by a responsible official not involved with the origination of entries?	X	___
Are the entries supported by explanation and/or documentation?	X	___
G. In a separate memorandum, summarize the qualifications of the key employees responsible for preparation and issuance of financial statements. Include names, titles, job responsibilities, background, and number of years in present position.	*	
H. Is access to accounting and financial records restricted to authorized personnel?	X	___

* Memorandum is not necessary to obtain a general understanding of this questionnaire and is therefore omitted from this example.

116

Comment on financial reporting practices:

Financial reports are sufficiently detailed to permit
identification of significant operating and financial changes.
Treasurer-Controller, Executive V.P., and President meet with
operating managers quarterly to review results to date and
current forecasts.

(Item B.) Monthly agings of receivables, and sales and earnings
breakdowns by division are submitted to Treasurer-Controller
and Executive V.P.

Budgets

		Yes	No
I.	Is there a budgetary system?	X	
	Do budgeting procedures cover all divisions and departments?	X	
	Do budgets and forecasts cover:		
	Revenues?	X	
	Costs and expenses?	X	
	Capital expenditures?	X	
	Cash flow?	X	
	Are budgets and forecasts submitted to management on an established timetable?	X	
	Are forecasts updated on a regular basis during the year?	X	
	Are budget variances reported and analyzed?	X	

Comment on budget practices:

Budget preparation is on a detail item basis (i.e., specific
items and expense amounts) and management meets quarterly to
review and analyze status vs. plan. Responsibility for
achieving forecasts and adhering to budgets parallels plan of
organization. Budgets have been effective for evaluating
performance, helping ensure that transactions are executed
in accordance with management's authorization, enforcing
accountability at all levels. Budget consciousness pervades
the Company.

Reconciliations

These questions should be considered when evaluating the specific control
objectives referenced parenthetically.

		Yes	No	Frequency	Performed By
J.	Are the following assets reconciled with accounting records:				
	Cash (F–1, F–4)?	X		Monthly	E. Hampton
	Inventory (P–2, P–6, P–7, P–8)?	X		*	M. Reynolds
	Property, plant, and equipment (P–12, P–13, P–14)?		X		
	Investments (F–8, F–11)?	X		Monthly	M. Reynolds

* Cycle counts throughout year; annual physical count at 10/31.

	Yes	No	Frequency	Performed By
K. Are detail and control accounts kept in balance as to:				
Accounts receivable (S–5, F–2)?	X	___	Monthly	D. Stevens
Notes receivable (S–5, F–2)?	N/A	___	_____	_____
Inventory (P–7, P–8)?	N/A	___	_____	_____
Property, plant, and equipment (P–12, F–4)?	X	___	At least annually	B. Dillon
Investments (F–8)?	X	___	Monthly	M. Reynolds
Accounts payable (A–2, P–2, P–12, F–4)?	X	___	Monthly	D. Patterson
Debt (F–4, F–5)?	X	___	Monthly	M. Reynolds
Capital stock (F–6)?	X	___	Quarterly	M. Reynolds
L. Are changes between beginning and ending balances accounted for as to:				
Property, plant, and equipment (P–11, P–12, P–13, P–14)?	X	___	At least annually	M. Reynolds
Allowances for depreciation (P–13, P–15)?	X	___	At least annually	M. Reynolds
Long-term debt (F–4, F–5)?	X	___	At least annually	M. Reynolds
Deferred income taxes A–7)?	X	___	At least annually	M. Reynolds
Capital stock (F–6)?	X	___	At least annually	M. Reynolds

Comment on reconciliation practices:

Reconciliations are effective for identifying and reporting errors, differences, and deviations from expected results. Duties are segregated as to physical custody of assets and related reconciliations. Discrepancies are reported to appropriate personnel. Emphasis on timely resolution of any out-of-balance conditions.

IV. INTERNAL AUDIT ACTIVITIES

	Yes	No
A. Is the scope of internal audit activities planned in advance with:		
	See Note	
Senior management?	N/A	___
Board of directors or audit committee?	N/A	___
Independent auditors?	N/A	___

	Yes	No

B. Are the results of the internal audit activities reported to:

Senior management? — N/A ____

Board of directors or audit committee? — N/A ____

Independent auditors? — N/A ____

C. Do internal auditors have direct access to senior management and the board of directors or audit committee? — N/A ____

D. Do internal auditors prepare and follow written audit programs? — N/A ____

E. Do internal audit working papers include system documentation? — N/A ____

F. Are internal audit reports prepared and issued on a timely basis for all assignments? — N/A ____

Are the reports issued to appropriate executives? — N/A ____

Are responses to recommendations documented? — N/A ____

Is implementation of internal audit recommendations monitored? — N/A ____

G. Are there training programs for internal auditors? — N/A ____

In the memorandum in I, describe the training programs (e.g., training to review computer systems), including any established continuing education requirements.

H. Are any internal auditors or members of their families related to other employees? (Describe in the memorandum in I.) — N/A ____

I. In a separate memorandum, describe the normal duties of the internal auditors (including extent of financial audits and operational audits) and an evaluation of their competence and objectivity. Consider responses in questions A through H above and the following:

Size and organization of the staff (including ratio of supervisors to staff)

Prior experience of staff members

Number of CPAs and CIAs

Extent of supervision of less experienced staff

Specificity of audit programs

Administrative reporting responsibility

Scope restrictions

Perceptions of internal audit management and operating and financial managers as to their influence on audit assignments, procedures, and reports.

Note: The Internal Auditor, Mr. White, has twelve years of experience in public accounting and private industry and is a CPA. However, since his employment in 19X4, he has been working on special projects for the President and, thus, has performed no significant internal auditing procedures. His work has had no effect on our audit.

APPENDIX 4B

FLOWCHARTING

A flowchart is a pictorial description of how accounting transactions flow through a system. Flowcharting helps depict all important aspects of an accounting system and identify important system control points. Flowcharts conveniently describe complex relationships because they reduce narrative explanations to a picture of the system. They visually communicate system processing and control procedures and the sequence in which they occur.

The primary purpose of the approach to flowcharting used in this textbook is to identify key attributes—system attributes that achieve control objectives. The approach helps identify key attributes or deficiencies in a system that lead to an evaluation as to whether or not control objectives are being achieved.

This textbook's approach to flowcharting emphasizes the procedures applied to both documents and information as they flow through an accounting system. Specifically, the following characteristics of the approach set it apart from other flowcharting methods:

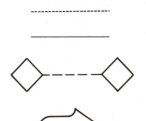

A broken line represents the flow of information.

A solid line represents document flow.

Small diamonds combined with a broken line represent the comparison of information among various documents. Such comparisons can represent significant key attributes.

A reference point symbol identifies the existence of key attributes or deficiencies in the system.

Different symbols for manual and EDP documents help determine the extent of EDP involvement in an accounting system.

Only a few symbols are necessary to describe procedures.

These characteristics result in an approach that is easy for both the preparer and the reviewer to use. Neither person needs extensive flowcharting experience.

Symbols and Flow Lines

This approach to flowcharting uses 12 basic symbols and two types of flow lines. The basic symbols are of four types: document, file, processing, and reference. Annotations are used inside the symbols to add flexibility and additional meaning.

Flow lines map the flow of documents and information through the system.

The flow of accounting documents from one process to another.

Document Flow

The flow of accounting information from one document to another document or process.

Information Flow

There are two document symbols—manual and EDP.

Manual Document

Any document not prepared by the computer, such as an invoice, check, purchase order, etc.

EDP Document

Any document prepared by the computer, such as an invoice, check, purchase order, etc.

The name of the document is always written inside the symbol.

Whenever the document is a journal or ledger, the document symbol is drawn with a vertical line down the left side.

GENERAL
LEDGER

A manually prepared general ledger.

SALES
JOURNAL

An EDP prepared sales journal.

There are other annotations that should be used in this approach to flow-charting. A number sign (#) indicates that a document is serially numbered. Documents with multiple copies should show the copy number in the upper right-hand corner and the copy name on the bottom edge of the symbol.

Accounting documents may be stored in manual or EDP files.

Manual File

Storage of accounting documents or data in non-EDP files.

EDP File

Storage of accounting information in EDP files (e.g., magnetic tape, disk, or punched card).

The manual file symbol is generally annotated to show how the documents are filed (e.g., month, date, customer number, part number, etc.) and for how long they are retained. The EDP file symbol should always indicate what type of file is being used (e.g., magnetic tape, disk, or punched card).

Processing symbols are used to describe the procedures applied to documents and information as they flow through the accounting system.

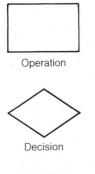

Operation

An operation or group of operations (including EDP applications) applied to documents or information (e.g, approval, restrictive endorsement, open mail, or invoicing).

Decision

A point in the system where there is a choice as to the flow of the document or information (e.g., credit approved?, balance past due?).

Data Transmission

The transmission of data directly into or out of EDP via online devices.

Comparison

Used with a broken line to indicate the comparison of information on one document with information on one or more other documents.

The nature of the processing is described within the operation, decision, and data transmission symbols. A decision symbol is not necessary if the choice is either processing the document further or resubmitting it. For example, if an operation symbol describes a review for proper approval and documents are returned to the originating department if that approval is missing, then a decision symbol is not necessary. On the other hand, if the decision is between alternative sets of procedures that have not been applied previously (e.g., the approval procedures for orders requesting special prices versus the procedures for orders involving standard prices), then a decision symbol would be used to illustrate the choice of procedures.

Comparison symbols always are joined with a broken line to indicate the comparison of information. Whenever there is a comparison of information on documents located in different departments, one comparison symbol is shaded to indicate the department that performs the comparison. This type of comparison is shown in the illustrative flowchart.

Four other symbols are used in preparing the flowchart. These symbols indicate the entry or exit of documents, connect the flow of documents, and reference key attributes or deficiencies in the system.

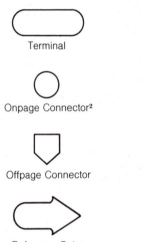

The entry or exit of accounting documents or information into or from the system.

Cross-reference within the same page of the flowchart.[2]

Cross-reference to another page of the flowchart.

Used to identify key attributes, system deficiencies, and supplemental narrative comments.

The source or disposition (e.g., from customer to sales department) of documents should be described inside the terminal symbol. Numbers and letters are commonly used inside the connector symbols. Each onpage connector should have a unique number or letter. Number-letter combinations or other abbreviations may be used for offpage connectors.

Reference points should be labeled with a unique number or letter so that each may be referred to in marginal comments supplementing the flowchart or in the working papers documenting an evaluation of control objectives. Reference points that support the evaluation of a specific control objective also should be labeled with the letter-number combination assigned to that objective (e.g., S–3 for "Products Shipped or Services Rendered Are Billed"). Guidelines concerning the use of the reference point are given in the section on drawing the flowchart.

Other systems of flowcharting use symbols in addition to, or slightly different from, the flowcharting systems presented in this appendix. These include the following:

[2] Reprinted by permission from IBM flowcharting template. © by International Business Machines Corporation. Courtesy of International Business Machines Corporation.

Basic Symbols

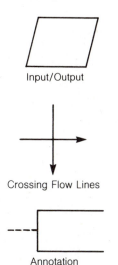

Input/Output

Indicates the input or output of information. Can be used in place of the document symbol when a document first enters the system for processing (e.g., sales order from customer, customer remittance, invoice).

Crossing Flow Lines

If flow lines cross, they are not interrelated.

Annotation

For the addition of comments. May be connected to a symbol or a flow line.

Input/Output Symbols

The following specialized symbols may indicate an input/output function as well as the medium for recording or the means of handling information. When appropriate specialized symbols exist, they are used instead of the basic symbols.

Punched Card

Using any kind of punched card in an input/output function.

Card Deck

A deck of punched cards.

Online Storage

Using some sort of online storage (e.g., payroll transaction tape loaded on a tape drive under the control of a central processing unit) in an input/output function.

Offline Storage

Storage of information or documents. The method of storage may be indicated inside the symbol (e.g., date, number).

Magnetic Tape

Using magnetic tape in an input/output function.

Magnetic Disc

Using magnetic disc in an input/output function.

Punched Tape

Using punched paper tape in an input/output function.

Document

For example, sales invoice, purchase order, check, remittance advice.

Transmittal Tape[3]

Adding machine tape proof, or similar batch control information.[3]

Processing Symbols

Manual Operation

The processing of data in a system by manual techniques.

Auxiliary Operation

An operation done on equipment that is not controlled by a computer (e.g., card file sort by customer number).

[3] Ibid.

Preparing Flowcharts

Preparing the flowchart consists of three steps:

1. Obtain information about a system.
2. Drawing the flowchart.
3. Checking the flowchart for clarity and accuracy.

Obtaining information about a system is the most important step in preparing a flowchart. Failure to completely understand the system will result in a flowchart that is erroneous or ambiguous.

Before attempting to obtain information, the auditor should define the system that is to be flowcharted and consider whether or not the system consists of several subsystems for different types of similar transactions. For example, the payroll accounting system may contain subsystems for salaried and nonsalaried employees. Because it is difficult to prepare one flowchart for a system containing several subsystems, it is usually better to prepare separate flowcharts for each subsystem.

Remember that the primary purpose of preparing a flowchart is to identify key attributes—those system attributes that achieve control objectives. In order to accomplish this, it is necessary to identify:

1. Significant documents or information used in the system.
2. Procedures used in the system and who performs them.
3. Sequence in which the procedures are performed.

This information may be obtained by making inquiries, reading written system descriptions, examining documents used in the system, and observing the procedures in operation.

Try to visualize the flowchart when obtaining information. It is best to take notes, either in narrative or rough flowchart form, and refrain from drawing the final flowchart until all information is gathered. After gathering the information, the preparer should have an understanding of the system and a mental picture of how the flowchart will look.

Drawing a flowchart is simply drawing a picture of how accounting documents and information flow through a system. An objective in drawing the flowchart is to communicate with clarity and simplicity. Therefore, the first step is to properly organize the flowchart layout.

There are essentially three variables in any flowchart: documents or information, procedures, and the organizational units that perform the procedures. Organizing the flowchart layout consists of dividing the system into organizational units. An organizational unit can be a department (sales or accounts receivable), a person (treasurer or cashier), or activity (billing or receiving). Double lines should be used to divide the working paper into organizational units (see the illustrative flowchart). Each organizational unit should be labeled and should contain at least one flowcharting symbol. Whether an organizational unit is a department, person, or activity depends upon the system, but each should identify a distinct area of responsibility. Dividing the flowchart into organizational units highlights segregation of duties within the system being flowcharted.

The next step is to map the flow of documents and information through the organizational unit and indicate which procedures are applied to the documents and information. The following comments and the illustrative flowchart in the next section should be helpful.

1. In general, document symbols are necessary only when the document first appears in the system or reappears with a connector in the same flowchart. Document symbols for multiple copies would be repeated when the flow of one or more copies is different from the others.

2. When a new document is created from information included in another document, it should be shown alongside the document from which it is prepared and joined to it by an information flow line. The information used in creating the document should be written above the information flow line unless the nature of the information is obvious.

3. Use the appropriate annotations for numbered documents, multiple copies, and journals or ledgers. The number symbol (#) should appear on a document only after the document receives the number.

4. Because the flow of documents and information should be from top to bottom and left to right, arrowheads are usually not necessary. However, arrowheads may be used when the flow is bi-directional (information taken from and added to the same file), or when it is not possible to draw the flow from top to bottom or left to right.

5. Use processing symbols to identify procedures that are applied to documents.

6. Any time there is a comparison of information among documents, use the comparison symbol and information flow line. Write a brief description of the information being compared above the flow line.

7. It is not necessary to flowchart multiple copies of documents that do not affect accounting information (e.g., procedures applied to copies of sales orders by the marketing department).

The final step in drawing the flowchart is to indicate key attributes, system deficiencies, and supplemental narrative comments using the reference point symbol. Key attributes are those control procedures that support the evaluation of a specific control objective. On the other hand, system deficiencies might mean there is not reasonable assurance that a control objective is being achieved. The reference point symbol should be referenced to the specific control objective being evaluated.

Supplemental narrative comments are used to (1) clarify the importance of a key attribute that is not obvious on the face of the chart, (2) explain why a control procedure on the chart is not a key attribute when it appears to be one, or (3) describe system deficiencies (control weaknesses that may result in a specific control objective not being achieved). The notes column at the left of the flowchart is used for supplemental narrative comments. For each supplemental narrative comment, there must be a corresponding reference point.

Sometimes the preparer of a flowchart will observe significant procedures or other items that cannot be communicated or referenced in the flowchart. In these cases, separate memos should be written and included in the system documentation working papers.

Preparation of the flowchart is not complete until it has been checked for clarity and accuracy. Can someone unfamiliar with the accounting system read the flowchart and understand it? Have all significant information and document flows been presented? Have all key attributes and system deficiencies been referenced?

In addition to asking these questions, it may be desirable to trace one or two documents through the system. This is commonly known as a walk-through. A system walk-through helps to ensure that the document and information flows have been correctly mapped. Checking the flowchart is important and ordinarily is not time consuming.

Illustration

The flowchart in Figure 4B–1 was prepared from the following system description.

Upon receipt of a customer purchase order, the order department prepares a two-part order acknowledgement. After filing the customer's order alphabetically, the order department sends both copies of the order acknowledgement to the credit department, which indicates written credit approval or disapproval and returns both copies to the order department. If credit is disapproved, the order department destroys the first copy of the order acknowledgement and notifies the customer by mailing the second copy. If credit is approved, the second copy is mailed to the customer, and the first copy is forwarded to the sales department.

The sales department prepares a three-part shipping form ("shipper") using the information contained on the order acknowledgement. The information entered on the shipper includes the customer's number, name and address, and the stock number, description, and quantity. The sales department files its own sales department copy numerically and forwards the stock requisition copy to the warehouse and the packing slip copy to the shipping department.

The warehouse uses the stock requisition copy as authorization to release the goods and forwards both the goods and its copy of the shipper to the shipping department.

The shipping department receives the goods and stock requisition copy from the warehouse and the packing slip copy of the shipper from the sales department. After marking the quantity shipped on both the packing

FIGURE 4B–1   Illustration of Customer Order and Daily Sales System, The Nuflow Company

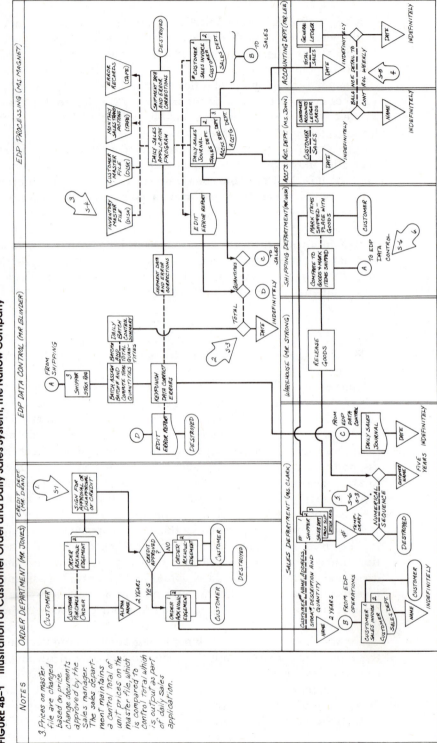

slip and stock requisition copies, the shipping department forwards the packing slip and goods to the customer and sends the stock requisition copy to EDP data control.

EDP data control batches the stock requisition copies and assigns batch numbers. Total quantities are accumulated per batch and entered into the batch control summary. Information from the stock requisition copies is keypunched and forwarded for processing by EDP processing.

EDP processing runs the daily sales application program to produce customer sales invoices and a daily sales journal. Three files are used in processing the application: (1) the inventory master file, which contains unit sales process; (2) the customer master file for the customers' names, addresses, special terms, and discounts; and (3) a cumulative month-to-date daily sales tape. Unit sales prices on the inventory master file are changed only upon submission of price change documents that are approved by the sales manager. The sales department maintains a control total of unit prices on the file, which is compared to the control total as part of the daily sales application. The shipping information (punched cards) and a magnetic tape of error records from previous runs serve as input to the application.

One copy of the daily sales journal and an edit error report are forwarded to EDP data control. The same person who prepared the original input compares total quantities shipped from the sales journal to the daily batch control summary and corrects any errors. Error corrections, which do not require independent approval, are processed the next day. The edit error report is destroyed and the daily sales journal and stock requisition copy of the shipper are forwarded to the sales department.

Customer invoices are sent to the sales department where one copy is promptly mailed to the customer and one copy is filed by customer name. The person who originally prepared the shipping documents accounts for the numerical sequence of the shippers by comparing the sales department copy to the stock requisition copy received from EDP data control. The sales department copy is destroyed, and the stock requisition copy is filed by customer name. The daily sales journal received from EDP data control is filed by date.

The accounts receivable department receives a copy of the daily sales journal which is used to update the customer account ledger cards. The accounting department also receives a copy of the daily sales journal from which it posts totals to the general ledger accounts. The detail customer ledger cards are balanced weekly to the general ledger control by the accounts receivable department.

QUESTIONS AND PROBLEMS

4–1. What is accounting control?

4–2. What is administrative control?

4–3. What is the independent auditor's responsibility for the client's system of internal control?

4–4. What is the concept of "reasonable assurance" as it relates to internal control?

4–5. Discuss the distinction that *SAS No. 16* makes between an error and an irregularity.

4–6. List some human limitations that can lessen the effectiveness of any system of internal control.

4–7. List five general control objectives that an accounting system should be expected to achieve to provide reasonable assurance that financial information is accurate and complete and assets are safeguarded.

4–8. How do general objectives relate to specific control objectives?

4–9. To effectively evaluate an accounting system, it is necessary to translate the general control objectives into specific control objectives for each aspect of the system. For the inventory audit area, consider the general control objective "Valuation":
   a. What specific control objectives are derived from valuation?
   b. What transactions and accounts are directly affected?

4–10. What are "key" system attributes?

4–11. Distinguish between "processing procedures" and "control procedures." How do they relate to "key attributes"?

4–12. What are the types of control procedures (key attributes) that often are key to achieving specific control objectives?

4–13. List some of the ways an auditor can identify key attributes.

4–14. What should an auditor do if convinced that there is *not* reasonable assurance that a specific control objective is being achieved?

4–15. What is the control environment and how does it affect the auditor's evaluation of whether a specific control objective is being achieved?

4–16. What should an independent auditor do if he or she suspects the existence of a material error or irregularity? Would your answer change if the auditor suspected the existence of an error or irregularity that was not material?

4–17. List and describe the various methods used by the auditor to document the review of accounting systems.

4–18. What is the effect of the systems evaluation on the preliminary audit approach?

4–19. An accounts payable clerk assembles a package that includes the vendor's invoice, receiving report, packing slip, and purchase order. The clerk compares the documents for agreement, checks the clerical accuracy of the vendor's invoice, assigns the account distribution, prepares a check, records the transaction in the cash disbursements register, and forwards the package to the controller. The controller reviews the package and signs the check. He then forwards the package to accounts payable for filing and gives the remittance copy of the vendor's invoice and check to his secretary for mailing.

Required:

List the processing procedures and the control procedures in this situation.

Processing   *Control*

4-20. The accounting department's secretary receives all customer remittances. Daily, the secretary lists the checks received, sends the checks to the accounts receivable department supervisor, and sends the listing to the accounts receivable clerks for application to customer accounts. The supervisor prepares the daily bank deposit from the checks. The company uses an online computer system to apply the receipts.

Required:

List the processing procedures and the control procedures in this situation.

Processing   *Control*

4-21. A payroll clerk receives the weekly timecards from all department managers. The clerk reviews the timecards for approval and prepares a batch ticket showing total hours worked. In addition, the clerk records the batch ticket data in the payroll department batch log. The timecards and batch ticket are then submitted to EDP for keypunching.

The EDP department maintains a master payroll disk file. This file includes each employee's name, number, wage rate, department number, and social security number. Only the personnel department may make changes to the file by means of file maintenance transactions, all of which must be approved by the director of personnel. The personnel department maintains a control total of wage rates and reconciles their total to the computer generated total produced with file maintenance update reports.

The master payroll file and the keypunched timecard data are processed, and payroll checks and a payroll register are generated. During the processing, payroll transactions are edited by the computer for (1) valid employee number, (2) valid department number, and (3) gross and net pay of more than $2,000 and $2,200, respectively. The payroll checks are sent directly to the department managers for distribution, and the payroll register is sent to the payroll clerk. The payroll clerk compares the total hours worked per the payroll register to total hours recorded in the payroll department batch log and reconciles any differences.

Required:

List the processing procedures and control procedures in this situation.

Processing   *Control*

4-22. An effective system of internal control (which consists of accounting and administrative controls) includes control procedures that have specific functions or purposes. For example, an accounting system may include key attributes that provide for all invoices to be checked for clerical accuracy, approved for propriety by reference to purchase authorizations and receiving records, and recorded in the accounting records before being paid. The system reduces the likelihood that (1) an invoice for an improper amount will be paid, (2) an invoice representing unauthorized purchases or materials not received will be paid, and (3) a properly approved invoice will not be paid.

Required:

Give the purposes or functions of each of the following procedures or techniques that may be included in an accounting system. Also, explain why each purpose or function may be considered a key attribute that provides reasonable assurance that a specific control objective is being achieved. (Use your background in this and other courses to answer.)

a. Fidelity bonding of employees.

b. Budgeting of capital expenditures. (AICPA, adapted)

4–23. Jordan Finance Company opened four personal loan offices in neighboring cities on January 2, 1985. Jordan makes small cash loans to borrowers who repay the principal with interest in monthly installments over a period not exceeding two years. Ralph Jordan, president of the company, uses one of the offices as a central office and visits the other offices periodically for supervision and internal auditing purposes.

Mr. Jordan is concerned about the honesty of his employees. He came to your office in December 1985 and stated, "I want to engage you to install a system to deter employees from embezzling cash." He also stated, "Until I went into business for myself I worked for a nationwide loan company with 500 offices and I'm familiar with that company's system of accounting and internal control. I want to describe that system so you can install it for me because it will absolutely prevent fraud."

Required:

a. How would you advise Mr. Jordan on his request that you install the large company's system of accounting and internal control for his firm? Discuss.

b. How would you respond to the suggestion that the new system would prevent embezzlement? Discuss. (AICPA, adapted)

4–24. The Kowal Manufacturing Company employs about 50 production workers and utilizes the following payroll procedures:

The factory foreman interviews applicants and on the basis of the interview either hires or rejects the applicants. When applicants are hired they prepare a W-4 form (Employee's Withholding Exemption Certificate) and give it to the foreman. The foreman writes the hourly rate of pay for the new employee in the corner of the W-4 form and then gives the form to a payroll clerk as notice that the worker has been employed. The foreman verbally advises the payroll department of rate adjustments.

A supply of blank timecards is kept in a box near the entrance to the factory. Workers take a timecard on Monday morning, fill in their name, and note in pencil on the timecard their daily arrival and departure times. At the end of the week the workers drop the timecards in a box near the door to the factory.

The completed timecards are taken from the box on Monday morning by a payroll clerk. Two payroll clerks divide the cards alphabetically between them, one taking the A to L section of the payroll and the other taking the M to Z section. The clerks are fully responsible for their section of the payroll. They compute the gross pay, deductions, and net pay, post the details to the employee's earnings records, prepare and number the payroll checks, and summarize weekly payroll information for submission to the chief accountant, who posts the information to the general ledger. Employees are automatically removed from the payroll when they fail to turn in a timecard.

The payroll checks are manually signed by the chief accountant and given to the foreman. The foreman distributes the checks to the workers in the factory and arranges for the delivery of the checks to the workers who are absent. The payroll bank account is reconciled by the chief accountant who also prepares the various quarterly and annual payroll tax reports.

Required:

List your suggestions for improving the Kowal Manufacturing Company's accounting systems for the factory hiring practices and payroll procedures.

(AICPA, adapted)

4–25. You have been asked by the board of trustees of a local church to review control procedures affecting accounting for collections and for members' pledges and contributions. As a part of this review you have prepared the following comments relating to the collections made at weekly services and recordkeeping for members' pledges and contributions.

The church's board of trustees has delegated responsibility for financial management and audit of the financial records to the finance committee. This group prepares the annual budget and approves major disbursements but is not involved in collections or recordkeeping. No audit has been considered necessary in recent years because the same trusted employee has kept church records and served as financial secretary for 15 years.

The collection at the weekly service is taken by a team of ushers. In order to facilitate the deposit, members who contribute by check are asked to draw their checks to "cash." The head usher counts the collection in the church office following each service. He then places the collection and a notation of the amount counted in the church safe. The next morning the financial secretary opens the safe and recounts the collection. He withholds about $100 to meet cash expenditures during the coming week and deposits the remainder of the collection intact. He then records the amount of the deposit in the church records.

At their request a few members are furnished prenumbered predated envelopes in which to insert their weekly contributions. The head usher removes the cash from the envelopes to be counted with the loose cash included in the collection and discards the envelopes. No record is maintained of issuance or return of the envelopes, and the use of the envelope system is not encouraged.

Each member is asked to prepare a contribution pledge card annually. The pledge is regarded as a moral commitment by the member to contribute a stated weekly amount. Based upon the amounts shown on the pledge cards, the financial secretary furnishes a letter to requesting members to support the tax deductibility of their contributions.

Required:

Describe control deficiencies and recommend improvements in control procedures for:

a. Collections made at weekly services.

b. Recordkeeping for members' pledges and contributions.   (AICPA, adapted)

4–26. Eastern Meat Processing Company buys and processes livestock for sale to supermarkets. In connection with your examination of the company's financial statements, you have prepared the following notes based on your review of procedures:

1. Livestock buyers submit a daily report of their purchases to the plant superintendent. This report shows the date of purchase and expected delivery date; the vendor; and the type, quantity, and weights of livestock purchased.

   As shipments are received, an available plant employee counts the number of each type received and places a check mark beside this quantity on the buyers report. When all shipments listed on the report have been received, the report is returned to the buyer.

   Vendors' invoices are received in the accounting department. After they are checked for clerical accuracy, they are sent to the buyer for approval and then returned to the accounting department. A disbursement voucher and a check for the approved amount are prepared in the accounting department.

   Checks are forwarded to the treasurer for a signature. The treasurer's office sends signed checks directly to the buyer for delivery to the vendor.

2. Livestock carcasses are processed by lots. Each lot is assigned a number. At the end of each day a tally sheet reporting the lots processed, the number and type of animals in each lot, and the carcass weight of the lot is sent to the accounting department where a perpetual inventory record of processed carcasses and their weights is maintained.

3. Processed carcasses are stored in a refrigerated cooler located in a small building adjacent to the employee parking lot. The cooler is locked when the plant is not open, and a company guard is on duty when the employees report for work and leave at the end of their shifts. Supermarket truck drivers wishing to pick up their orders have been instructed to contact someone in the plant if no one is in the cooler.

4. Substantial quantities of by-products are produced and stored, either in the cooler or elsewhere in the plant. By-products are initially accounted for when they are sold. At that time the sales manager prepares a two-part form; one copy serves as authorization to transfer the goods to the customer and the other becomes the basis for billing the customer. (Note: Assume billing procedures are satisfactory.)

Required:

For each of the numbered notes 1 to 4 above, state:

a. What the specific control objective(s) should be at the stage of the operating cycle described by the note.

b. The control deficiencies in the present procedures, if any.

c. Any suggestions for improvement.   (AICPA, adapted)

4–27. The customer sales and cash receipts functions of the Robinson Company, a small paint manufacturer, are attended to by a receptionist, an accounts receivable clerk, and a cashier who also serves as a secretary. The company sells its paint products to wholesale and retail stores.

The following describes the procedures performed by the employees of the Robinson Company pertaining to sales and cash receipts:

a. The receptionist opens the mail and forwards the customer puchase orders (between 15 and 20 each day) to the accounts receivable clerk. To expedite shipments, the accounts receivable clerk immediately prepares a five-copy sales invoice form, which is distributed as follows:

  (1) Copy 1, the customer billing copy, is held by the accounts receivable clerk until notice of shipment is received.

  (2) Copy 2, the accounts receivable copy, is held for posting the accounts receivable records.

  (3) Copies 3 and 4, the shipping copy and the packing slip, are sent to the shipping department.

  (4) Copy 5, the shipping authorization copy, is sent to the storeroom as authority for release of the goods to the shipping department.

b. After the storeroom forwards the goods to the shipping department, the shipping department packs the order, labels the cartons, prepares the bill of lading, and indicates quantities shipped on sales invoice copies 3 and 4. Sales invoice copy 4 is included in a carton as a packing slip. After the trucker has picked up the shipment, a customer copy of the bill of lading and sales invoice copy 3 are returned to the accounts receivable clerk. The Robinson Company copy of the bill of lading is filed in the shipping department. The company does not "back order" in the event of undershipments; customers are expected to reorder the merchandise.

c. Based on information included on sales invoice copy 3 and the customer copy of the bill of lading, the accounts receivable clerk completes sales invoice copies 1 and 2. Invoices are numbered; quantities shipped and unit prices inserted; and extensions, discounts, and totals calculated. The accounts receivable clerk then mails sales invoice copy 1 and the customer copy of the bill of lading to the customer. Sales invoice copies 2 and 3 are stapled together and filed in numeric order.

d. The accounts receivable clerk posts individual accounts receivable ledger cards from information contained on sales invoice copy 2. The posting is done on a bookkeeping machine, which simultaneously prepares the sales register. Monthly, the general ledger clerk summarizes the sales register for posting to the general ledger accounts.

e. The receptionist forwards all mail receipts and related correspondence to the accounts receivable clerk who examines the checks and determines that the accompanying vouchers or correspondence contains enough detail to permit posting of the accounts. The accounts receivable clerk then endorses the checks and gives them to the cashier who prepares the daily deposit. No currency is received in the mail, and no paint is sold over the counter at the factory.

f. The accounts receivable clerk uses the vouchers or correspondence that accompanied the checks to post the individual accounts receivable ledger cards. The bookkeeping machine simultaneously prepares a cash receipts register. Monthly, the general ledger clerk summarizes the cash receipts register for posting to the general ledger accounts.

g. The accounts receivable clerk corresponds with customers about unauthorized deductions for discounts, freight or advertising allowances, returns, etc., and prepares appropriate credit memos. Large disputed items are turned over to the sales manager for settlement. Each month the accounts receivable clerk prepares a trial balance of open accounts receivable and compares the total with the general ledger control account.

Required:

Identify deficiencies in control procedures related to sales and cash receipts and give examples of what could go wrong because of each deficiency.

(AICPA, adapted)

4–28. The following information describes the Inventory Accounts Payable System for the Black Crown Corporation.

    a. To initiate an inventory purchase, the various operating departments send an Inventory Materials Request (IMR) to the purchasing department (managed by Mr. Putt). The purchasing department reviews the IMR for approval by the department head, determines price(s), and prepares a four-part prenumbered purchase order (P.O.) from the IMR. Information obtained from the IMR includes the description and quantity of inventory items and the date they are needed. This information and prices are included on the P.O. The distribution of the P.O. is as follows:

        Original: vendor.

        Second copy: receiving department.

        Third copy: filed in the purchasing department by vendor name together with the IMR in the temporary open purchases file.

        Fourth copy: retained and filed numerically in the purchasing department for two years.

    b. The receiving department (supervised by Mr. Rough) temporarily files their copy of the P.O. by vendor name until inventory materials are delivered. When inventory materials are delivered, the receiving clerk pulls the receiving copy of the P.O. and writes the quantity of items and date received. The clerk makes one photocopy of the receiving copy of the P.O. if the full order has been received and two photocopies if only a partial shipment has been received. In the case of a partial shipment, the additional photocopy is refiled temporarily in the receiving department until the balance of the order is received, at which time the process is repeated. The original of the receiving copy of the P.O. is sent to the accounts payable department. The photocopy of the P.O. is sent to the purchasing department.

    c. The purchasing department compares the quantity and description of the items received per the photocopy of the P.O. with the related P.O. For partial shipments, the photocopy of the P.O., IMR, and P.O. are filed in the temporary open purchases file. When a photocopy of the P.O. is received for a complete shipment or for the completion of a prior partial shipment, it is filed by vendor name for two years along with the IMR, P.O., and any P.O. photocopies relating to prior partial shipments.

    d. The accounts payable department (supervised by Ms. Trap) maintains a temporary vendor name file for P.O.'s received from the receiving department. When a vendor invoice is received, an accounts payable clerk compares the invoice with the receiving copy of the P.O. as to description of material, quantities received, and price. The clerk then verifies the clerical accuracy of the invoice, assigns account distributions, and prepares a two-part sequentially numbered Voucher Ticket. The Voucher Ticket contains the vendor name and number, invoice amount, and account distribution. The first copy, along with the receiving copy of the P.O. and the vendor's invoice, is filed by vendor name for seven years. Another clerk batches the second copy of the Voucher Tickets daily, computes control totals, and prepares a Daily Batch Ticket. The Daily Batch Ticket reflects the number of Voucher Tickets, total dollar amount, and a hash total of account numbers. The clerk then forwards the Voucher Tickets and Daily Batch Ticket to the EDP department (supervised by Ms. Divot).

e. EDP processes the Daily Voucher Application using the information on the Voucher Tickets and two disk files, the General Ledger File and Accounts Payable Master File. In addition to updating these files, the Daily Voucher Application generates a one-part Daily Voucher Register. An independent control clerk in EDP compares control totals on the Daily Voucher Register to the Daily Batch Ticket and sends these two documents and the Voucher Tickets to Accounts Payable.

f. The accounts payable department files the Daily Voucher Register and Daily Batch Ticket together by date for 10 years and files the Voucher Tickets by voucher number for 3 years.

Required:

Prepare a flowchart of the Inventory Accounts Payable System.

4–29. The town of Commuter Park operates a private parking lot near the railroad station for the benefit of town residents. The guard on duty issues annual prenumbered parking stickers to residents who submit an application form and show evidence of residency. The sticker is affixed to the auto and allows the resident to park anywhere in the lot for 12 hours if four quarters are placed in the parking meter. Applications are maintained in the guard office at the lot. The guard checks to see that only residents are using the lot and that no resident has parked without paying the required meter fee.

Once a week the guard on duty, who has a master key for all meters, takes the coins from the meters and places them in a locked steel box. The guard delivers the box to the town storage building where it is opened, and the coins are manually counted by a storage department clerk who records the total cash counted on a "Weekly Cash Report." This report is sent to the town accounting department. The storage department clerk puts the cash in a safe, and on the following day the cash is picked up by the town's treasurer who manually recounts the cash, prepares the bank deposit slip, and delivers the deposit to the bank. The deposit slip, authenticated by the bank teller, is sent to the accounting department where it is filed with the "Weekly Cash Report."

Required:

Describe deficiencies in the existing system and recommend improvements to strengthen the control procedures over the parking lot cash receipts.

(AICPA, adapted)

4–30. Select the best answer for each of the following items.

a. When an independent auditor's examination of financial statements discloses special circumstances that make the auditor suspect that fraud may exist, the auditor's initial course of action should be to:

(1) Recommend that the client pursue the suspected fraud to a conclusion that is agreeable to the auditor.

(2) Extend normal audit procedures in an attempt to detect the full extent of the suspected fraud.

(3) Reach an understanding with the proper client representative as to whether the auditor or the client is to make the investigation necessary to determine if a fraud has in fact occurred.

(4) Decide whether the fraud, if in fact it should exist, might be of such magnitude as to affect the auditor's report on the financial statements.

b. In connection with the examination of financial statements, an independent auditor could be responsible for failure to detect a material fraud if:

(1) Statistical sampling techniques were not used on the audit engagement.

(2) The auditor planned the work in a hasty and inefficient manner.

(3) Accountants performing important parts of the work failed to discover a close relationship between the treasurer and the cashier.

(4) The fraud was perpetrated by one client employee, who circumvented the existing internal controls.

c. If an auditor were engaged to discover errors or irregularities and the auditor performed extensive detail work, which of the following could the auditor be expected to detect:

(1) Mispostings of recorded transactions.

(2) Unrecorded transactions.

(3) Counterfeit signatures on paid checks.

(4) Collusive fraud.

d. When preparing a record of a client's system of internal accounting control, the independent auditor sometimes uses a system flowchart, which can best be described as a—

(1) Pictorial presentation of the flow of instructions in a client's internal computer system.

(2) Diagram that clearly indicates an organization's internal reporting structure.

(3) Graphic illustration of the flow of operations that is used to replace the auditor's internal control questionnaire.

(4) Symbolic representation of a system or series of sequential processes.

e. Internal accounting control comprises the plan of organization and the procedures and records that are concerned with the safeguarding of assets and the—

(1) Decision processes of management.

(2) Reliability of financial records.

(3) Authorization of transactions.

(4) Achievement of administrative objectives.

f. Effective internal control in a small company that has an insufficient number of employees to permit proper division of responsibilities can *best* be enhanced by—

(1) Employment of temporary personnel to aid in the separation of duties.

(2) Direct participation by the owner of the business in the recordkeeping activities of the business.

(3) Engaging a CPA to perform monthly "write-up" work.

(4) Delegation of full, clear-cut responsibility to each employee for the functions assigned to each.   (AICPA, adapted)

EVALUATING COMPUTERIZED ACCOUNTING SYSTEMS

OVERVIEW

The significance of computerized accounting systems has been widely recognized by business people who are concerned about the impact on their operations of technological advances that allow easier access to computer files. Auditors too are concerned. *SAS No. 3,* "The Effects of EDP on the Auditor's Study and Evaluation of Internal Control" (AU 321.03), states that:

> When EDP is used in significant accounting applications . . . the auditor should consider the EDP activity in his study and evaluation of accounting control. This is true whether the use of EDP in accounting applications is limited or extensive and whether the EDP facilities are operated under the direction of the auditor's client or a third party.

From the auditor's perspective, the use of the computer in the accounting system has both advantages and disadvantages. In computerized accounting systems, many procedures previously performed manually are performed by computer programs. This virtually eliminates the possibility of processing errors resulting from lack of understanding of prescribed procedures or other human factors such as fatigue or carelessness. However, the centralized processing of accounting information in computerized systems also introduces concerns over segregation of duties not normally found in manual systems. Thus, centralized processing increases the opportunity for errors and irregularities unless effective computer controls are implemented.

As discussed in the preceding chapter, the auditor's objective in evaluating accounting systems is to identify key system attributes that reasonably assure the achievement of specific control objectives. In a computerized accounting system, these attributes are called "application controls" and might consist of (1) manual procedures in a user department, (2) manual procedures in the computer department, or (3) programmed procedures in a computer application. From the auditor's perspective, the data processing function is an integral part of the accounting system and should be evaluated along with all

5

other aspects of the accounting system. Evaluating the computerized portions of a company's accounting system is part of the program development phase of an audit and includes two distinct steps: (1) evaluating general controls and (2) evaluating application controls.

This chapter is divided into three sections. The first and second sections describe how auditors evaluate computerized accounting systems by reviewing general and application controls. The third section describes how certain data processing arrangements affect the auditor's evaluation process. The chapter focuses on the auditor's objective of evaluating whether a computerized accounting system provides reasonable assurance of preventing or detecting material errors or irregularities. In addition, Appendix 5A at the end of this chapter discusses companies' exposure to computer fraud and suggests some measures to prevent, detect, and limit it. In suggesting those measures, Appendix 5A expands on some of the general and application controls discussed in this chapter. Computer-assisted audit techniques are discussed in Chapter 7.

EVALUATING GENERAL CONTROLS

SAS No. 3 (AU 321.07) defines general controls as:

> . . . (a) the plan of organization and operation of the EDP activity, (b) the procedures for documenting, reviewing, testing, and approving systems or programs and changes thereto, (c) controls built into the equipment by the manufacturer (commonly referred to as "hardware controls"), (d) controls over access to equipment and data files, and (e) other data and procedural controls affecting overall EDP operations.

The auditor evaluates general controls whenever the computer is used to process transactions or maintain balances that are material to the financial statements. The objective of evaluating general controls is to determine whether the EDP environment promotes controlled computer applications. This determination is important to the auditor because it provides for an assessment of (1) the overall opportunity for errors and irregularities in the system and (2) whether any application controls that the auditor identifies are likely to operate effectively throughout the audit period.

For purposes of identifying and evaluating general controls, the general controls environment is divided into three basic categories:

1. *Segregation of duties.* The organization *within* the data processing function provides for segregating incompatible duties. Also, the segregation of responsibilities *between* the data processing function and user departments results in independence between data processing and users.
2. *Access and changes to programs.* The policies and procedures used in data processing provide reasonable assurance that only authorized programs are executed and that each program execution is authorized. Changes to programs are authorized, tested, and approved before being implemented.
3. *Access to data files.* Access to data files is restricted to authorized persons and programs to prevent accidental loss, intentional destruction, and unauthorized use or alteration.

In a batch processing environment, exercise of these controls is readily achievable by careful allocation of duties and basic safeguards. In online systems, any person with access to a terminal can function in several capacities (e.g., inputting the data, controlling the processing, and using the output). Such persons therefore have access to both programs and data and thus the potential to make unauthorized changes in either. In these situations, the even greater concentration of duties makes the designing of effective general controls particularly challenging.

Segregation of Duties

Segregation of Duties within EDP. Segregation of duties within an EDP department is important for the same reason it is important in a manual environment. The objective is to prevent employees from having incompatible duties. For example, in a manual system, an individual should not have access to both cash receipts and the accounts receivable subsidiary ledger. In computer environments, where much of the data recording and data processing activities become centralized, separation of duties is especially important. Similarly, an EDP department should be organized to segregate responsibility for transaction recording and handling of assets. For example, neither operators nor programmers should be involved in the data control function because this provides an opportunity to commit and conceal irregularities by initiating and processing transactions and then misappropriating the output (such as checks).

It is also important to segregate the operations and programming functions.

By mixing these duties, an individual who has enough knowledge about files and programs and access to computer equipment could make unauthorized changes to programs or data files without being detected. Programmers should not be allowed to run the computer, and operators should be prevented from programming. A good system of internal control will not allow programmers access to the computer room (or to terminals that effectively provide access) and also will not allow operators access to program documentation.

Segregation of Duties between the EDP Function and Users. Just as segregation is needed between data processing functions, it also is needed between the data processing department and user departments. Segregation is important because if data processing is under the direct control of a user, the user may have the opportunity to circumvent data processing controls.

Data processing employees should not have duties in user departments because an employee could initiate a transaction within the user department and also handle its processing within data processing. In addition, data processing employees should not be responsible for initiating information about assets or have access to the assets. For example, a data processing employee who is also a cashier or a stock clerk might thereby have control over both an asset and the related accounting records.

Access and Changes to Programs

One of the general objectives of accounting control—safeguarding—stresses that access to assets should be permitted only in accordance with management's authorization. In EDP environments, assets include accounting information on computer data files (which can be used to generate physical assets such as a check or an authorization to obtain inventory or other assets), the computer programs, and the computer equipment itself. Computer data files and programs cannot be altered without the use of computer equipment. Therefore, controlling access to computer equipment is an effective way to control access to computer programs and data files.

Although programs can be physically stored on a punched card, magnetic tape, or disk, they usually are stored on a disk. When stored on a disk, they often are grouped together into a file called a program library, which has a directory within it to identify each program. To execute a program, a person must have (1) the program name and location, (2) sufficient technical knowledge to run the program, and (3) access to the computer. Therefore, controls over program access focus on restricting one or more of these execution requirements. For example, restricting access to the computer room or terminals limits the number of people who can access programs. Prohibiting access by operators to program documentation prevents operators from learning program names and storage locations.

Other control techniques that may be used are passwords, special software librarian packages, and job accounting. It is becoming increasingly popular to establish security systems over files that require the user of the file to know not only its name but also a security code or password. In controlling access to program libraries, passwords are commonly used in conjunction with special software, which prevents unauthorized attempts to change programs. Job accounting provides an audit trail of machine activity through reports of jobs run on the computer, and it can be used to identify unauthorized execution of programs or unauthorized use of program libraries.

Access to Data Files

Controlling access to data files is important because it helps assure that the correct file is used in an application and that files are restricted to authorized users. In addition to maintaining a file library, external and internal file labels are commonly used. An external label affixed to magnetic tape and disk files helps the operator identify the correct file before processing transactions. The external label might include the file name, volume or serial number, date created, and version number. Some installations simply use a volume or serial number to prevent unauthorized individuals from readily identifying the contents of a file. Internal labels are entered on the file itself, such as a header label on a magnetic tape that identifies the file. Normally, these labels are automatically checked by the operating systems or application programs to help assure that the correct file is used.

General Control Deficiencies

There are two types of general control deficiencies—pervasive and specific. Pervasive general control deficiencies may affect all accounts and transactions for which computer processing is performed. For example, if program testing procedures are inadequate, a new or revised computer application could be subject to errors or irregularities. Figure 5–1 is an example of a working paper prepared by an auditor to describe the impact of a pervasive general control deficiency on certain specific control objectives. This working paper also identifies related manual controls, including an evaluation of their effectiveness in compensating for the deficiency in general controls.

Other general control deficiencies affect only certain specific accounts and transactions. For example, if data processing personnel have direct control over non-EDP assets, the potential errors or irregularities would be limited to accounts and transactions that directly affect those assets (e.g., payroll, inventory). Figure 5–2 illustrates an auditor's consideration of a specific general controls deficiency.

FIGURE 5-1 Summary of General Controls Evaluation—Pervasive Deficiency

Client ___XYZ Company___
Computer Installation ___Any location, USA___
Audit Date ___12/31/8x___

Prepared by/Date ___C.A. 4/30/8x___
Reviewed by/Date ___R.P.H. 6/15/8x___
Partner Review/Date ___J.G.B. 6/28/8x___

Item No.	Finding(s)	Specific Control Objectives Affected	Identify Compensating Manual Controls	Do Manual Controls Adequately Compensate for the Weakness (Yes/No)	Comments
1	The design of general controls indicates that there are no formal procedures that provide reasonable assurance that program changes are adequately tested to insure that they function as intended. As a result, inaccurate program changes made to the computerized billing or receivable systems could result in undetected errors or irregularities in any of the reports produced by these systems. However, access to all programs is appropriately restricted to application programmers. All program changes (whether authorized or unauthorized) must be made through a program library software package that records the current version number and the date of the last 99 changes for each program in the production library on a program history log.	S-2, S-3 S-4, S-5 S-6, S-7	While key attributes supporting the achievement of specific control objectives S-2, S-3, S-4, S-5, S-6, and S-7 were identified, they do not adequately compensate for the general controls deficiency.	NO	The preliminary audit approach for S-2, S-3, S-4, S-5, S-6 and S-7 includes procedures to: (1) Obtain a list of all changes made to the billing and receivable programs from the program history log and, through discussions with data processing, billing and receivable managers, evaluate whether all program changes were authorized; and (2) For each significant change, either: a. review available client test data (e.g., accounts receivable aging report before and after the program changes), if any, to evaluate whether the program change was accurate and that the program continues to function as intended, or b. use audit software (A32) to independently reconstruct essential computer reports (e.g., recompute sales by major product lines and recompute accounts receivable aging) and compare these results to client produced reports.

FIGURE 5-2 Summary of General Controls Evaluation—Specific Deficiency

Client ____ABC Manufacturing Co.____
Computer Installation ____Any Town, U.S.A.____
Audit Date ____12/31/8x____

Prepared by/Date ___C.A.___ 5/13/8x
Reviewed by/Date ___R.P.H.___ 6/3/8x
Partner Review/Date ___J.G.B.___ 6/5/8x

Item No.	Finding(s)	Specific Control Objectives Affected	Identify Compensating Manual Controls	Do Manual Controls Adequately Compensate for the Weakness (Yes/No)	Comments
1	It is common practice for the warehouse operators to leave the three warehouse CRT terminals, which have read/write access to the CURRENT QUANTITIES INVENTORY data file, logged on during normal working hours. As a result, it is possible for unauthorized changes to be made to inventory quantities maintained in this data file.	P-7	a) Monthly, the Quality Assurance Group prepares a report that summarizes (1) differences between actual and recorded quantities for a sample of inventory items, and (2) non-standard adjusting entries made to quantities [i.e., other than receipt or shipment of goods] that exceed $5,000. b) Monthly, the cost accounting manager prepares a condensed report that (1) analyzes all variance accounts, including "material usage" for any variances exceeding $5,000 and (2) contains any proposed adjustments to the standards. c) Monthly, the reports described above are reviewed with and approved by the plant manager and controller.	YES	Compensating manual controls identified for specific control objective P-7 and included as key attributes.

P-8		YES	Compensating manual controls identified for specific control objective P-8 and included as key attributes.
	a) The security guard checks goods leaving the premises for a valid shipping document and records the shipping number, destination, and date in the shipping log.		
	b) Quarterly, information in the shipping log is compared to the invoice register by the accounts receivable supervisor.		

Impact of General Control Deficiencies. Because of the pervasive nature of general controls, it is not always feasible to identify all the potential errors and irregularities that could occur when there is a deficiency. In addition to inadequate segregation of duties, the greatest potential for errors and irregularities occurs when access to programs or data files is not controlled.

Access to Programs. When access to programs is not controlled, unauthorized changes can be made to a program. The types of errors or irregularities that can occur depend on the type of program. Some examples follow:

1. Programs that read and edit input data

The edit criteria could be changed for all or selected records.

Editing could be suppressed for selected records.

For example, the edit criteria of a program that reads checks at a bank could be changed so that the program does not first determine the account balance before processing the check of a bank employee.

2. Programs that make calculations

The calculation could be changed for all or selected records.

3. Programs that update files

Unauthorized changes could be made to all or selected records on the file.

Records could be added to or deleted from the file.

For example, the credit limit of an employee account could be changed on the master file.

4. Programs that write output

Printing of selected information on reports could be suppressed.

Control totals on reports could be forced to agree with predetermined amounts.

A name on an output document (e.g., a check) could be changed without changing the same data on the master file.

Access to Data Files. Unauthorized access to data files could allow data files to be read, copied, and/or altered. Access to data files alone may not be considered critical, but when combined with the lack of controls over either program testing or program execution, such access may result in serious errors or irregularities.

EVALUATING APPLICATION CONTROLS

After evaluating the general controls, the auditor proceeds with the evaluation of the accounting system by identifying key attributes that reasonably assure the achievement of specific control objectives. While general controls relate to the overall operation of the computer department and usually have a pervasive impact, application controls relate to specific EDP tasks, such as the input of quantities shipped to the billing application. However, before beginning the review of an application, the auditor should first consider the effect of general control deficiencies on the application. If there are general control deficiencies, looking for application controls may be unproductive because there may be no basis for reliance on them throughout the audit period.

Computerized Key Attributes

The three types of general controls—related to (1) segregation of duties, (2) access and changes to programs, and (3) access to data files—can function as key attributes in a computerized system. When identified, they should be tested to provide a basis for reliance on the system.

In addition to general controls, *application controls* are attributes that directly contribute to the achievement of specific control objectives in computerized systems. Some application controls are *programmed procedures* within computer application programs and systems software (e.g., limit and reasonableness checks or the use of passwords). Others are *manual procedures* (discussed in Chapter 4) that are considered to be application controls because they are related to the use of the computer in the accounting system (e.g., review of output).

Types of Key Attributes	Manual	Computerized
Independent reviews	Check of one employee's work by another employee	Editing of input transactions for completeness and correctness
Approvals	Review of manually prepared documents	Comparisons of input to master file contents (e.g., valid part number or customer credit limit)
Comparisons	Comparison of manually prepared documents to source documents	Comparison of input or calculated items to a preprogrammed range or value
Recalculations	Recalculation of manually calculated items	Recalculation of batch totals or calculated items
Reconcilations	Reconcilation of manually prepared documents	Reconciliation of control totals, run-to-run totals, or record counts

An important characteristic of many key attributes is that they function as checks on other procedures. The auditor analyzes the flow of transactions through an accounting system and looks for independent reviews, approvals, comparisons, recalculations, and reconciliations. These are likely to be key attributes because they are intended to detect lack of adherence to previous processing procedures and serve to assure that data are authorized, complete, and accurate.

In identifying either user department or data processing procedures, the auditor is looking for the same types of key attributes, namely, independent reviews, approvals, comparisons, recalculations, and reconciliations. The table on page 149 shows examples of manual and computerized key attributes.

Application Functions

Application controls are divided into four functional categories: input, files, processing, and output. These functions are defined as follows.

Input function—transactions and data entering the application and the related edit, error, and balancing reports.

Processing function—new data generated or calculated by the application.

Output function—reports, documents, and data produced by the application.

Files function—master data files used in the application and the related file maintenance procedures.

These four functions—input, processing, output, and files—relate the application to the overall accounting system in terms of the accounting information it processes. This breakdown enables the auditor to assess how the particular application affects the accounting system and whether the achievement of a specific control objective may be reasonably assured by procedures that are part of that application.

Controls over Input. Input controls are designed to provide reasonable assurance that information accepted by the application from other parts of the accounting system is authorized, accurate, complete, and is processed only once. Many computer installations use batch processing, where transactions are accumulated in batches, arranged in sequence, and processed against one or more master files. In a batch processing environment, controls over input usually begin in user departments, where control is established through the use of batch controls. Batch controls usually involve a comparison of certain totals of data (e.g., total quantities shipped) before and after processing.

In addition to batch totals, input data may be checked for authorization, accuracy, and completeness by means of edit tests on the data. Examples of edit tests that may be performed in an application are:

1. Verifying that all required data are present.
2. Verifying proper data format.
3. Matching data to a set of allowable entries.
4. Matching data to a set of previously established values, such as a customer account number.
5. Checking the numerical sequence of the documents.
6. Recalculating check digits.
7. Performing reasonableness or limit tests.

Errors detected during the editing process may be handled in one of four different ways:

1. Edit errors in a batch result in the entire batch being rejected. Only batches containing no edit errors are processed beyond the edit routines.
2. Within a given batch, transactions with edit errors are rejected, but those without errors are accepted and processed.
3. Within a given batch, all transactions are accepted and processed. Those with edit errors are posted to a suspense account or file until a subsequent correction is posted. Unlocated differences also may be posted to the file until corrected.
4. Within a given batch, all transactions are accepted and processed. Those with edit errors are posted to the appropriate master or transaction file with some indication (such as a code) that the transaction contained an error. The code is removed when the error is subsequently corrected. Edit errors (except data conversion errors, such as keypunch errors) should be returned to user departments for correction and resubmission.

In an online system, where individual transactions are entered from remote terminals rather than batched, these same basic alternatives are possible. However, in online systems, each transaction is treated as a batch, so there is no distinction between the first two editing processes described above.

Controls over Processing. Processing controls are designed to provide reasonable assurance that accounting information calculated or generated by an application is accurate. The generation or calculation of new data is often done in a manner that is difficult for the user to verify. Manual processing controls generally consist of tests of items that have been calculated or generated, such as a review for reasonableness, manual recalculation of selected detail items, or manual recalculation of totals.

In some cases, programmed checks may be performed over calculated items, but, since they are usually subject to the same application development criteria as the original calculation, they do not provide the independence found in manual tests performed by the user. Furthermore, they can be difficult to identify and test for compliance. In general, programmed checks are similar to edits performed over input data. Typical checks include:

1. Verifying the proper format (e.g., numeric or alphabetical).
2. Verifying the range or sign of resulting values (positive, negative, zero balance).
3. Matching data to a set of allowable entries.
4. Reasonableness and limit tests.
5. Recalculation using different methods.

Controls over Output.   Output controls are designed to provide reasonable assurance that accounting information returned to other parts of the system is complete and accurate. Output can include printed reports, documents, special forms, and transaction (temporary) files. The completeness and accuracy of output depends on the quality of input information, the accuracy of data stored on master files used by the application, and the accuracy of processing performed by the application.

Control totals established by the user enable verification that all transactions have been completely recorded. Manual procedures, such as recalculation of amounts, comparison of certain data items to detailed manual records, or a visual scan or review, can be used to help determine that the output data are accurate.

Controls over Files.   There are two basic types of computer files: transactions files and master files. *Transaction files* contain information of a temporary nature such as daily sales transactions. *Master files* contain information that is of a more permanent nature, such as a customer number, name, address, credit limit, and terms.

The audit significance of master files is that many amounts calculated or generated by the application depend upon the accuracy of the data contained in the master file. The accuracy of invoice amounts, for example, depends upon the accuracy of the unit sales price for each part number stored in the sales price master file. Therefore, master file controls are designed to provide reasonable assurance that the data stored in master files remain authorized, accurate, and complete.

Changes to master files can occur in two ways. First, normal transactions processed by application programs can cause changes to master files, such as the updating of an accounts receivable master file from processing sales invoices, customer payments, and debit or credit memo transactions. Second, additions, deletions, and adjustments to master files may be caused by changes initiated outside the normal transaction flow. Examples include the addition of a new customer to an accounts receivable master file or the deletion of old inventory items from an inventory master file. Changes of this nature often are referred to as file maintenance transactions. Application controls over input, processing, and output apply to both types of master file changes.

To assure that the data on master files remain authorized, accurate, and complete, user departments generally obtain periodic reports of the contents

FIGURE 5-3 System Evaluation that Illustrates Application Controls

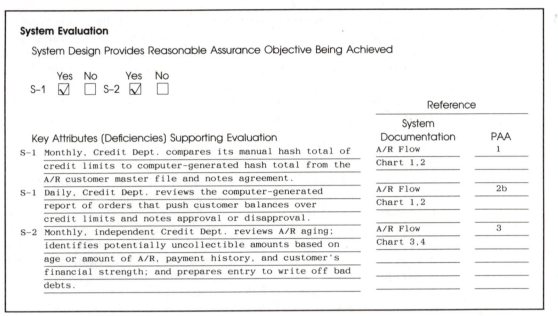

System Evaluation

System Design Provides Reasonable Assurance Objective Being Achieved

	Yes	No		Yes	No
S–1	☑	☐	S–2	☑	☐

Key Attributes (Deficiencies) Supporting Evaluation	Reference System Documentation	PAA
S–1 Monthly, Credit Dept. compares its manual hash total of credit limits to computer-generated hash total from the A/R customer master file and notes agreement.	A/R Flow Chart 1,2	1
S–1 Daily, Credit Dept. reviews the computer-generated report of orders that push customer balances over credit limits and notes approval or disapproval.	A/R Flow Chart 1,2	2b
S–2 Monthly, independent Credit Dept. reviews A/R aging; identifies potentially uncollectible amounts based on age or amount of A/R, payment history, and customer's financial strength; and prepares entry to write off bad debts.	A/R Flow Chart 3,4	3

of the master file. An aged trial balance of accounts receivable or a listing of current customers, for example, may be used to assure that customer information on the customer master file is authorized, accurate, and complete. Alternatively, user departments may obtain and review a listing of all changes to the master file.

Another important control is balancing the number of records and dollar amounts in the master file to other accounting records. Where more than one version of the file is maintained, there should be procedures to verify that the correct version is used for processing transactions. Computer department verification consists of adequate library procedures and internal and external file label checking. User verification of the correct file version might consist of such procedures as examination of application output and periodic review of master file contents.

Figure 5–3 shows an example of a system evaluation working paper prepared by an auditor that illustrates application controls.

SPECIAL EVALUATION CONSIDERATIONS

While the auditor's approach to evaluating computerized accounting systems, as described in the preceding pages, is useful in any computerized environment, there are some special considerations for certain types of computer installations. These are described on the pages that follow.

Online, Real-Time Systems

The advent of telecommunications and direct access files made possible real-time processing where the computer system can accept input at any time, execute the programs required to process the input, access and update the required master files, and respond to the user without any significant delay.

Real-time processing requires the use of online devices. An online system is one in which computer equipment and devices are in direct contact with the computer's central processing unit and usually under its direct control. The online devices usually are computer terminals that are remote from the central facility. A familiar example of online, real-time (OLRT) systems is one used by a commercial airline company for processing reservations.

OLRT systems have several audit implications. An important implication is the elimination of the time interval usually found in batch systems between the point where a transaction occurs and the point at which it is processed. In batch systems, this time period permits the examination of the transactions and the verification of balancing control totals. Another implication of OLRT systems is the potential loss of an audit trail from reduction (or elimination) of hard-copy source documentation. Another difference is that users of the terminals function as computer operators, bypassing the data control and operations functions that help control transactions processed in batch systems. Therefore, controls over authority to submit information must be a combination of user and system procedures, and it is the responsibility of the user to assure that input errors are corrected and all data are submitted for processing.

Not all online systems involve real-time processing. Some online systems permit users to enter data at any time, but the data are not processed until a fixed time period has elapsed or a predetermined number of transactions has been entered. This allows preprocessing reviews similar to those that can be made in a batch system. While this provides some control advantages, it also presents some disadvantages. For example, an online system for accounts receivable that does not include real-time processing of sales and cash receipts transactions permits a review of these transactions before processing but will not provide a completely current customer balance. Thus, transactions that cause a customer's balance to exceed established credit limits might nonetheless be approved.

Adequate online controls begin with procedures that limit access to the online terminals. User departments should have procedures that limit physical access to only authorized users. Also, the online systems software should require the use of a password or security code that identifies the user. Some online systems require thumbprints or plastic cards with magnetic strips to identify users. As a further control, the system may have several levels of passwords (terminal authority levels) in which the user's password permits only selected activities. For example, some users might be able to update a data file while others might only be permitted to obtain certain information from a file.

Unauthorized attempts to access computer information should be recorded and investigated. In some online systems, repeated unauthorized access attempts will cause the terminal to "lock" and prevent its further use until it is reactivated. To provide an audit trail, there should be a procedure to log input transactions. The methods commonly used include maintaining a manual log at the terminal site, attaching a printer to the terminal, or using a transactions log at the central facility where transactions entered into the system are recorded on magnetic tape or disk to provide an after-the-fact batch control.

Database Systems[1]

In conventional data processing systems, all data associated with a specific application are stored in separate files that relate only to that application. For example, the data stored in the inventory master file are used only by the specific programs of the inventory application. Since each application has its own files, there may be data redundancy. To illustrate, a bank might maintain information about a customer on several master files, such as the demand deposit master file, installment loan master file, and savings account master file. Redundancy in stored data has several disadvantages, such as extra storage costs and the requirement to update several master files whenever the data are changed.

Database systems reduce the amount of redundant data that are maintained on files. This reduction in data is achieved by storing the data in one central file (the database) and allowing appropriate applications to have access to that data. To illustrate, in the above example, all information about the bank customer might be stored on the database master file. Then each application program is allowed to use only the information on the file that is necessary to accomplish its processing function. A software package called the database management system (DBMS) controls the use of the database to prevent unauthorized access to the data. For example, a company might store all information about its employees on a database master file. However, the DBMS might be programmed to deny access to pay rates by an employee who is preparing a report on compliance with equal employment opportunity laws.

There are several control considerations for database systems. In conventional file systems, an error in master file data affects only transactions pro-

---

[1] This section is based in part on J. Hal Reneau, "Auditing in a Data Base Environment," *Journal of Accountancy*, December, 1977, pp. 59–65.

cessed by the specific application that uses that master file. Errors in data bases, however, can cause errors in several applications that use the data. Therefore, the validation of input data is critical. In addition to the general controls previously discussed, general controls in database systems involve the database administrator (DBA) and the DBMS. The DBA has custody of the data stored in the database and is responsible for controlling its use. The database administrator may be one person or a group of persons, but should be separate from the operations, data control, and the applications development and programming functions. If an application programmer wants to create a new data item or change a logical association, he or she should ask the DBA for permission. The DBA will then make the appropriate changes to the DBMS library. All changes should be approved and documented. The DBA should not be allowed to operate the computer or initiate transactions without user department approval. Application programmers should not have knowledge of data items that do not relate to their applications.

Minicomputers

Since their introduction in 1959, minicomputers have become increasingly popular. While there is no universally accepted definition of a minicomputer, they are typically less expensive and physically smaller than mainframe computers. Like larger mainframe computer systems, minicomputer systems consist of a central processing unit and input and output devices. Minicomputers are primarily designed for small and medium-sized businesses that use manual, mechanical, or punched-card data processing systems for bookkeeping and accounting functions. In large organizations, minicomputers are used to supplement mainframe computers, can be linked to each other, or both.

In reviewing computer controls in minicomputer environments, the auditor is likely to find apparent general control weaknesses. These weaknesses exist because it usually is impractical for small businesses (or small divisions of a large business) that use minicomputers to maintain many of the general computer controls that are practical in larger computer installations. Most minicomputer installations have few employees and little, if any, segregation of duties. In many cases, the person having responsibility for the computer also has responsibilities in user departments; thus, controls over access to the computer equipment, programs, and data files may be weak. On the other hand, there may be no employees who are capable of doing anything more than operate the programs supplied by a vendor. In these situations, the auditor will have less concern about unauthorized changes to programs than when the company either develops its own programs or has employees with the ability to alter purchased programs.

Microcomputers

Microcomputers usually are self-contained "desk top" or "personal" computers. Some are portable and are used by auditors at the client's office. They are relatively inexpensive and usually are used for different purposes than minicomputers or large mainframe computers. For example, most microcomputers have limited input (usually a keyboard and in some cases a telecommunication device called a "modem") and slower output devices. Thus, they cannot efficiently process large volumes of transactions, such as sales or cash disbursements.

Typically, microcomputers have been used for stand-alone applications that are not tied into a company's data processing network. However, in more and more cases, microcomputers are used as terminals that are linked to the company's main computer. Therefore, controls over access to a microcomputer and its programs may become an important audit consideration. When microcomputers are not used to process or maintain financial records, related controls are less important to the auditor.

While applications can be programmed for microcomputers, a high proportion of microcomputer applications are purchased software packages that assist management and employees in spreadsheet calculations, financial modeling, production control, word processing, and other administrative or technical functions. Microcomputers are used by auditors to perform certain computer audit assisted techniques such as recomputing a federal income tax provision or LIFO inventory calculations.

Distributed Data Processing

A data processing system may use centralized, decentralized, or distributed processing. Centralized processing means there is one central computer facility where data processing occurs. Although information may be transmitted from and to various geographic locations or management levels having online devices, no significant data processing occurs outside the central facility. Centralized processing is used when:

1. Users in all locations need access to the same data and need the most current version.
2. Data structures are designed to serve multiple applications.
3. Data are used by centralized applications.

Decentralized processing means that application processing occurs at several installations, usually in different geographic locations. In a decentralized system, the installations are not interconnected and do not operate in a cooperative manner. Each installation develops its application programs and data files independently of other locations. The decentralization philosophy was supported by the development of minicomputers, which made low-cost computer power available to more locations. Decentralized processing is used most often when:

1. Data are needed at one remote location and are rarely or never needed at other locations.
2. Data structures are designed to serve only one or two applications; therefore, the centralized system required by most database software is not needed.

Decentralized processing may lead to incompatible or duplicate programs, data files, and accounting systems within the organization. Further, there is often substantial duplication of accounting effort among user departments. These factors, plus the development of lower cost and more efficient telecommunication systems, led to the development of distributed processing.

Distributed processing involves the use of related computers to accomplish data processing needs. In a truly distributed system, data are captured, processed, and used at their source or point of origin and communicated to other computers only when the data must be further processed, stored, or made available in other areas of the organization. A typical distributed processing system consists of minicomputers, microcomputers, or intelligent terminals that can process data at the point of origination and communicate with other computers in the system. The system may be a "hierarchy" in which there is a larger computer at a central location, or a "network" in which there is no central location and any computer in the network can communicate with any other computer.

Distributed processing combines the advantages of centralization and decentralization. Remote users are allowed to have their own minicomputers, microcomputers, or intelligent terminals, but they are part of an interconnected system. They develop their own programs, but also can use the compilers, report generators, data, and software contained elsewhere in the system. Data can be kept and maintained locally, but it is structured according to the needs of the entire organization. Data are usually divided into those that are needed locally and those that are needed elsewhere. For example, the shipping address of a customer may be stored locally, but the customer's balance may be transmitted to a central location.

Computer controls are not dependent upon whether the data processing function is centralized, decentralized, or distributed. However, the scope of the auditor's evaluation is affected by the nature of processing. If centralized processing is used, there are no special audit considerations.

Where decentralized processing is used, the auditor decides which installations have significant application processing. Each of these installations are reviewed following the approach outlined earlier in this chapter. General controls are evaluated at each installation, and application controls are evaluated for the important applications at each location.

Essentially, the same considerations apply when the client has distributed processing. However, the use of telecommunications in a distributed system can result in the division of processing for a single application over two or more installations. Therefore, the auditor should consider not only the *significance* of the applications processed at each installation but also the *extent* of such processing. If the client has a truly distributed system, it usually will be necessary to first obtain information about the various applications and relate the application functions to the installations where processing occurs. The locations involved in a review of application controls will depend upon the extent of processing that occurs at the locations.

Computer Service Organizations

Many companies use computer service organizations to meet part or all of their data processing needs. The use of a service organization does not change the approach to evaluating accounting systems (the auditor still evaluates whether specific control objectives are achieved), but the auditor may obtain information and document controls differently. This is due to the practical considerations involved in evaluating controls at a remote location not under the control of the company and because other auditors may evaluate and report on the controls maintained by the service organization.

Auditors should obtain an understanding of the flow of transactions through the client's entire accounting system, including the portion that is maintained by service organizations. This helps the auditor determine whether the controls on which reliance is to be placed are maintained solely by either the client or a service organization, or are a combination of controls maintained by both the client and the service organization.

Sufficient Controls Maintained by the Client. Controls maintained by the client may be sufficient to achieve all the appropriate control objectives relating to particular accounting applications processed by a service organization. In such circumstances, it will not be necessary to further study the system of internal accounting control maintained by the service organization.

Controls Maintained Solely by a Service Organization. When substantially all controls are maintained solely by a service organization and the auditor plans to rely on them, the auditor should evaluate such controls. Generally, the most efficient way to evaluate these controls is by reference to a report on the internal accounting controls at the service organization[2] that is issued by the service organization's independent auditor (service audi-

---

[2] See *Statement on Auditing Standards, No. 44* (AU 324), "Special-Purpose Reports on Internal Accounting Control at Service Organizations" American Institute of Certified Public Accountants, 1982.

tor report), sometimes referred to as a "third-party" or "single-auditor" report. If such a report is not available, or is not acceptable, the auditor should attempt to review controls at the service organization. In many cases, service organizations will not permit an auditor of their customer to review controls at the service organization. If an on-site review is not possible, the auditor will be unable to rely on the portion of the accounting system that is maintained by the service organization. This means the auditor will have to obtain satisfaction as to the propriety of transactions processed by the service organization by using other audit procedures or qualify or disclaim an opinion because of the limitation on the scope of the examination.

Controls Maintained by Both the Client and a Service Organization. In many cases, a combination of controls is maintained by both the client and one or more service organizations to achieve specific control objectives. If the controls maintained by the client are not sufficient by themselves to achieve the specific control objectives, the service organization's controls should be evaluated. In such cases, the auditor should obtain a service auditor report. If a service auditor report is not available, the auditor should proceed in the manner described under "Controls Maintained Solely by a Service Organization" above.

Service Auditor Report. The scope of service auditor reports varies with the type of review. A service auditor may evaluate the design of the service organization's accounting controls but not perform any compliance tests. In these cases, the service auditor renders a "design only" type report. While this report may help the auditor understand the system, the auditor still must test compliance with the controls before relying on them. If the service auditor performs compliance tests, the report will be a "design and compliance" type report. This type of report can provide a basis for the auditor to rely on the service organization's controls.

A service auditor's review might cover all aspects of a ". . . segment of the service organization. . ."[3] such as a bank trust department or a division of a bank that performs the custodian and investment functions for pension plans. In these cases, the service auditor can issue a positive assurance report on the system of internal control taken as a whole. This type of report also provides a basis for an auditor to rely on the service organization's internal controls.

---

[3] Ibid., (AU 324.27).

APPENDIX 5A[4]

COMPUTER FRAUD

Computer fraud has rapidly become a multibillion dollar industry in the United States and throughout the world. It has grown to such proportions that almost any company with significant data processing applications has to regard the computer crime industry as one of its competitors. Why is computer fraud on the rise? Because from the perpetrator's standpoint, computer fraud offers some distinct advantages over other crimes: (1) it is relatively easy to commit, (2) it is difficult to detect and trace, and (3) the payoff can be much more lucrative.

The perpetrator of the "manual" fraud generally leaves such clues as handwriting, erasures, fingerprints, and the like, all of which point back to the culprit. The perpetrator of a computer fraud, however, can alter bits and bytes in magnetically coded data and not leave a single, identifiable trace. Recent statistics indicate that:

1. Computer fraud pays well—from $3 billion to $5 billion annually.[5]
2. The average return on a reported computer fraud is about 20 times the average return on old-fashioned manual frauds.[6]
3. The number of reported computer fraud cases resulting in criminal conviction is less than 10 percent.[7]

Further, the number of reported fraud cases may be deceiving, since not all computer frauds are reported. This appendix describes the characteristics of computer fraud and shows how companies can develop controls to prevent, detect, and limit it.

The FraudCube

There are many ways to commit computer fraud. The "FraudCube"—shown in Figures 5A–1 through 5A–4—is a three-dimensional block that represents the aggregate of all computer crime and fraud incidents. It has been developed as an aid to visualizing computer fraud and its characteristics. By dividing the FraudCube in different ways, we can demonstrate some of the important characteristics of computer fraud.

---

[4] This appendix is based on Ernst & Whinney copyrighted material. Another version, entitled "A Three-Dimensional Look at Computer Fraud," written by John G. Baab, Stephen M. Paroby, and William H. Marquard of Ernst & Whinney appeared in the October 1984 issue of the *Financial Executive,* pp. 21–23, 26–28.

[5] Laurence J. Ochs, "Is Your Computer Fraud Insurance Adequate?" *ABA Banking Journal,* November 1983, p. 112.

[6] Stanley Halper, "How to Thwart Computer Criminals," *Nation's Business,* August 1983, p. 61.

[7] Ibid.

162

FIGURE 5A-1 Relationship

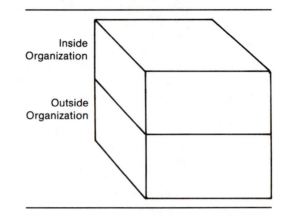

Inside
Organization

Outside
Organization

In one dimension, computer fraud is distinguished by the perpetrator's *relationship* to the victimized company. As Figure 5A–1 shows, computer fraud can be committed not only by people inside a company but also by people outside the organization.

In a second dimension, computer fraud is characterized by the level of computer *expertise* required to execute it. As Figure 5A–2 demonstrates, many computer crimes require a detailed knowledge of the workings of a computer system—its programs, access techniques, and data storage methods. But other computer frauds require nothing more than a knowledge of *how to use the existing system.*

FIGURE 5A-2 Expertise

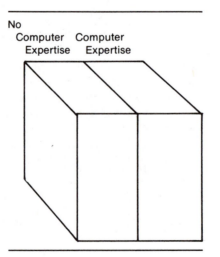

No
Computer   Computer
Expertise   Expertise

FIGURE 5A-3 Motivation

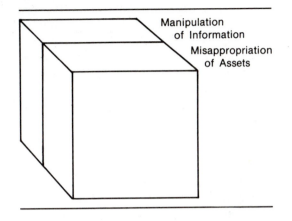

Figure 5A–3 illustrates that in a third dimension, computer fraud can be distinguished by the *motivation* or intent of the perpetrator. Some computer frauds have the misappropriation of assets as a direct goal. Other frauds are more concerned with delusion, misrepresentation, theft, or destruction of data—these frauds are concerned with the manipulation of information.

Thus, computer fraud can be classified in three dimensions: *relationship, expertise,* and *motivation.* Each of the eight blocks in the FraudCube in Figure 5A–4 represents a different combination of relationship, expertise, and motivation. The FraudCube offers some important insights into computer fraud. First, the perpetrator can be inside or outside the organization to commit

FIGURE 5A-4 The FraudCube

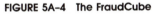

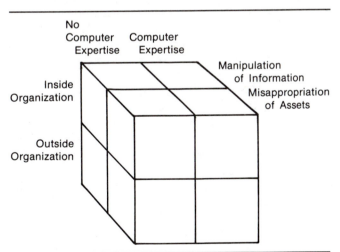

computer fraud. Second, he or she does not have to be a programmer or computer whiz kid to be successful. And third, the perpetrator can target the fraud at tangible company assets or intangible company information. An understanding of these computer fraud characteristics is important in designing a control environment to protect a computer system from fraudulent misuse.

The Fraud Control Matrix

The three advantages of computer fraud suggest three important objectives of the control environment to protect a computer system from fraudulent activity.

Since computer crime is relatively easy to commit, the first line of defense should be to try to *prevent* it. Prevention of computer fraud is primarily a function of access control and restriction, discussed in Chapter 5. A perpetrator's opportunities to compromise the computer system are effectively reduced, if not eliminated, by restricting access to the computer facility, computer terminals, data files, programs, and computer output.

Since computer fraud is difficult to discover or trace, the second line of defense should be a concerted effort to *detect* it. Even if a perpetrator has slipped past the established prevention mechanisms, the occurrence of fraud still should be detected and stopped—hopefully with minimal losses to the organization. Obviously, detection is an after-the-fact line of defense against fraud and certainly is not as desirable as prevention. Yet few, if any, control systems can completely prevent all fraud opportunities, so detection is an important objective of the fraud control system.

Finally, since computer fraud offers a lucrative payoff, the third line of defense should be *limitation* of fraud losses. The well-planned and well-executed fraud may avoid both preventive and detective measures. If this happens, the potential loss must at least be limited.

There are several approaches to implementing these control objectives. The approaches generally can be grouped under three classifications: physical controls, technical controls, and administrative controls. *Administrative controls* are internal control policies that establish a standard operating procedure for the computer installation. *Physical controls* involve the physical environment of the computer facility, including physical computer input media (e.g., terminals, cards) and output media (e.g., paper, checks). *Technical controls* employ the computer's processing facilities to restrict access to data files and programs.

Combining these administrative, physical, and technical control approaches with the computer control objectives of prevention, detection, and limitation results in a matrix of nine control objective/control approach combinations called the Fraud Control Matrix (see Figure 5A–5). Each square in the matrix represents a control objective/control approach combination,

FIGURE 5A–5 The Fraud Control Matrix

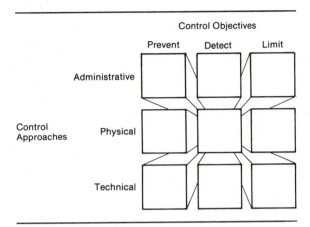

and any control measure established to protect the computer system from fraud can be classified into one or more of these nine squares.

Examining the Fraud Control Matrix

In this section we will examine each of the squares in the matrix and look at some specific instances of effective fraud control techniques. Many of these techniques also were described in Chapter 5 as general or application controls to prevent both errors *and* irregularities.

The first block, in the upper left-hand corner of Figure 5A–5, designates *administrative* controls designed to *prevent* computer fraud. Most of the control approaches in this category involve company policies designed to prevent unauthorized access to the computer system. Examples include:

1. *Security checks* on personnel prior to employment.
2. Proper *segregation of duties* among data processing employees and between data processing and user departments—i.e., no one individual may authorize, execute, and record a transaction.
3. An established *program change authorization* procedure—i.e., changes are made to programs only with the express authorization of the user department and after being thoroughly tested.

The second square in the matrix involves *physical* controls designed to *prevent* computer fraud. These controls primarily deal with physical access to the computer and its equipment. For example:

1. An *inconspicuous location* helps protect the computer facility from illegal intrusion. It is best to leave computer area entrances and locations unmarked and to avoid windows and public tours.
2. *Controlled access to a facility* through keys and magnetic cards physically restricts unauthorized users from computer terminals and from the computer facility.

A third square links *technical* controls with the *prevention* of computer fraud. These technical controls deal primarily with restricting access to hardware and data files. To illustrate:

1. *Encoding* is a technical means of storing or transmitting data in codified form. This control requires a perpetrator to "crack the code" before he or she can fraudulently manipulate the data.
2. *Access control software and passwords* are technical controls that allow a user access to a terminal, data file, program, or utility only after entering the correct password for that resource.

The first approach toward *detection* in the Fraud Control Matrix is through *administrative* measures. To illustrate:

1. A *review of access and execution logs* reveals—by both time and terminal—who has accessed the system and which programs have been executed.
2. A *program testing* procedure may be used to test a program after modifications are made, to ensure that fraudulent processes have not been introduced into the program.

Physical controls to *detect* fraud are probably the most difficult to implement and have the least chance of success, especially when one considers that the perpetrator does not have to be at the scene of the crime. Examples include:

1. A *computer room guard,* particularly during off-time hours.
2. A *manual building entry log,* which individuals must sign upon entering the computer facility.

Technical controls may be the most effective of the three approaches to *detecting* fraud because the perpetrator may not know they are in place or how to alter them. For example:

1. *Transaction logging* is the technical control that actually *produces* the reports, described above, that should be reviewed as an administrative approach to detecting fraud. Keep in mind that this control is of little use without that review on a regular basis. Program execution and program changes also may be logged.
2. Comparisons of *running totals* of dollar or amount fields in files and *hash totals* of nonamount fields, such as department numbers or part numbers, are effective in detecting fraudulent entries of data.

3. *Source code comparisons* involve using the computer to compare one source code version of a program to another to determine whether the programs match. By saving source code copies of important programs and comparing them regularly to the programs currently being run, one can determine if unauthorized modifications have been made to production programs.

Administrative controls are the first approach in the Fraud Control Matrix toward the *limitation* of fraud. To illustrate:

1. *Rotation of duties* within the data processing department should limit fraud losses, since an individual would be able to perpetrate a fraud only for a limited time.
2. *Established transaction limits* are administrative ceilings that limit potential fraud losses. For example, many banks place limits on the amounts that tellers or automatic teller machines may disburse.

Physical controls also may be instituted to *limit* potential fraud losses. Examples include:

1. *Preprinted limits on documents*—particularly asset-value documents such as checks. Even if a check is fraudulently prepared on the computer, a preprinted maximum value on the check will limit the potential loss.
2. Timely *data backup* does not necessarily limit an active fraud. However, it does limit the potential losses that may occur from fraudulently manipulated or destroyed data. Data backup facilitates the restoration of the destroyed data.

Technical controls also may be established to *limit* computer fraud. For example:

1. *Range checks* ensure that entered data fall within a range of permissible values and limit the losses that may occur from large unauthorized transactions.
2. *Reasonableness checks* determine whether an input or calculation is reasonable under the circumstances by comparing it to established standards.

Although each specific control technique has been described here under only *one* control objective/control approach combination, some techniques may fall into one or more additional combinations. Keep in mind that various approaches may be used to achieve the same control objective. No control system, however well designed, will protect a computer system completely. But careful attention to the control objectives of prevention, detection, and limitation as outlined in the Fraud Control Matrix should reduce the possibility of computer crime.

QUESTIONS AND PROBLEMS

5–1. Accounting controls in a computerized system can be classified into general controls and application controls. What are general controls? What do they include? What are application controls?

5–2. Regardless of the type of data processed or the kind of equipment used, all data processing involves four basic functions. Identify and describe these functions.

5–3. What are minicomputers? Where are they likely to be used? What are microcomputers and what are their typical uses?

5–4. "In reviewing computer controls in minicomputer environments, the auditor is likely to find general control weaknesses." Discuss the reasons why such weaknesses in general controls may exist.

5–5. What is distributed data processing?

5–6. Distinguish between transaction files and master files.

5–7. List and briefly discuss several audit implications of online, real-time systems.

5–8. For purposes of identifying and evaluating general controls, the general controls environment can be divided into three basic categories. List these categories.

5–9. In computer environments, why is it important to segregate the operations and programming functions?

5–10. Why is control over access to data files important?

5–11. Name and briefly explain the two types of general control deficiencies.

5–12. Select the best answer for each of the following items:
   a. Where computers are used, the effectiveness of internal accounting control depends, in part, upon whether the organizational structure includes any incompatible combinations of duties. Such a combination would exist when there is no separation of the duties between:
      (1) Documentation librarian and manager of programming.
      (2) Programmer and console operator.
      (3) Systems analyst and programmer.
      (4) Processing control clerk and key punch supervisor.
   b. Which of the following would lessen internal control in an electronic data processing system?
      (1) The computer librarian maintains custody of computer program instructions and detailed listings.
      (2) Computer operators have access to operator instructions and detailed program listings.
      (3) The control group is solely responsible for the distribution of all computer output.
      (4) Computer programmers write and debug programs that perform routines designed by the systems analyst.

    c. Accounting control procedures within the EDP activity may leave no visible evidence indicating that the procedures were performed. In such instances, the auditor should test these accounting controls by:

      (1) Making corroborative inquiries.

      (2) Observing the separation of duties of personnel.

      (3) Reviewing transactions submitted for processing and comparing them to related output.

      (4) Reviewing the run manual.

    d. The auditor's preliminary understanding of the client's EDP system is obtained primarily through:

      (1) Inspection.

      (2) Observation.

      (3) Inquiry.

      (4) Evaluation.   (AICPA, adapted)

5–13. Can general controls function as key attributes?

5–14. Does use of a computer service organization change an auditor's approach in evaluating accounting systems?

5–15. What is a "service auditor report"?

5–16. Payroll operations for Burns Corporation are processed on a computer. Some of the procedures are:

    a. The personnel department does the following:

      (1) Places new employees on the payroll.

      (2) Assigns each new employee a permanent employee number.

      (3) Initiates appropriate action for employee terminations or transfers.

    b. Timekeepers keep a daily record of the hours worked in each department.

    c. The payroll department keeps the deduction authorizations for all employees.

    d. Some employees have their paychecks mailed to their home.

    e. The EDP department prepares the entire payroll. It automatically pays each employee for a 40-hour week unless it is notified otherwise. The department also prepares the checks and the withholding stubs accompanying the checks.

Given these circumstances, discuss some of the controls that might be used to prevent *(a)* overpayment and *(b)* payment of nonexistent employees.

5–17. In converting an hourly payroll from a manual to a computer system, the rate file was established from rates received from the payroll department. Each rate combined the employee's base rate with a cost-of-living hourly bonus factor of $0.25. The program was written to pick up the combined rate from the file and add $0.25 before extending the rate times hours worked. As a result, each employee was paid $0.50 in cost-of-living instead of the approved $0.25. What procedures might have prevented this error?

5–18. Your company plans to have all payrolls processed by a local bank. At the end of each pay period, the company will give the bank a list of employees and the hours they worked during the period. Using the master rate file, the bank will calculate the net pay and deposit the net pay directly to each employee's bank account. The bank will prepare the payroll register, the quarterly and annual tax reports, and the annual W-2 statements. Identify several questions that might be asked regarding the company-bank procedures.

5–19. The Lake Utility District is installing an electronic data processing system. The CPA who conducts the annual examination of the Utility District's financial statements has been asked to recommend controls for the new system.

Required:

Discuss recommended controls over:
a. Program documentation.
b. EDP hardware.
c. Tape files and software. (AICPA, adapted)

5–20. George Beemster, CPA, is examining the financial statements of the Louisville Sales Corporation, which recently installed a computer. The following comments have been extracted from Mr. Beemster's notes on computer operations and the processing and control of shipping notices and customer invoices:

a. To minimize inconvenience, Louisville converted without change its existing data processing system, which utilized tabulating equipment. The computer company supervised the conversion and has provided training to all computer department employees (except keypunch operators) in systems design, operations, and programming.

b. Each computer run is assigned to a specific employee, who is responsible for making program changes, running the program, and answering questions. This procedure has the advantage of eliminating the need for records of computer operations because each employee is responsible for his or her own computer runs.

c. At least one computer department employee remains in the computer room during office hours, and only computer department employees have keys to the computer room.

d. System documentation consists of those materials furnished by the computer company—a set of record formats and program listings. These and the tape library are kept in a corner of the computer department.

e. The company considered the desirability of programmed controls, but decided to retain the manual controls from its existing system.

f. Company products are shipped directly from public warehouses, which forward shipping notices to general accounting. There a billing clerk enters the price of the item and accounts for the numerical sequence of shipping notices from each warehouse. The billing clerk also prepares daily adding machine tapes ("control tapes") of the units shipped and the unit prices.

g. Shipping notices and control tapes are forwarded to the computer department for keypunching and processing. Extensions are made on the computer. Output consists of invoices (in six copies) and a daily sales register. The daily sales register shows the aggregate totals of units shipped and unit prices, which the computer operator compares to the control tapes.

h. All copies of the invoice are returned to the billing clerk. The clerk mails three copies to the customer, forwards one copy to the warehouse, maintains one copy in a numerical file, and retains one copy in an open invoice file that serves as a detail accounts receivable record.

Required:

Describe weaknesses in internal control over information and data flows and the procedures for processing shipping notices and customer invoices. Recommend improvements in these controls and processing procedures.   (AICPA, adapted)

5–21. Discuss control weaknesses in the following four organizations:

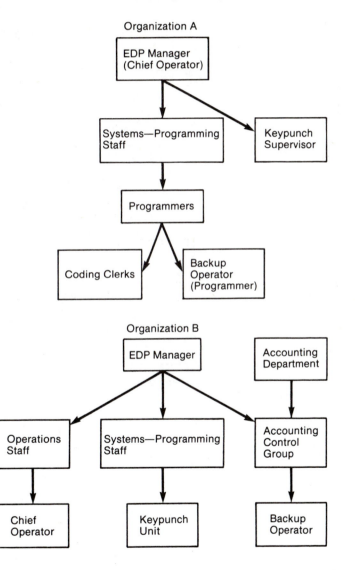

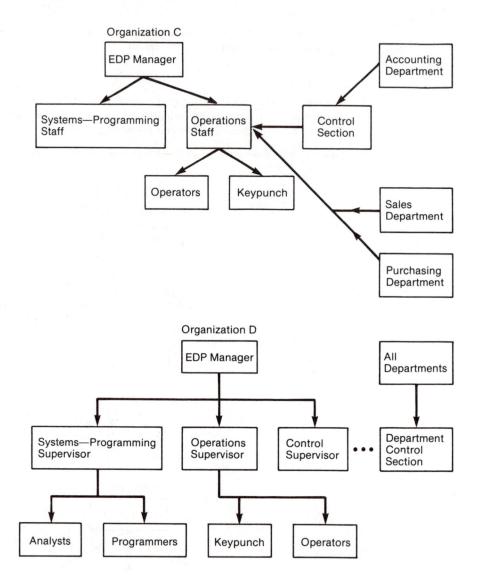

ANALYTICAL REVIEW

This chapter describes various types of analytical review procedures and how they are used in the three phases of the audit. Analytical review procedures include comparisons of key financial and operating data and relationships to prior periods, budgets, and industry statistics. These procedures can be used to summarize large amounts of data in a few simple calculations and therefore require less audit time. Figure 6–1 (page 176) summarizes the use of these procedures in each of the three phases of the audit.

SAS No. 23 (AU 318.02) states:

> Analytical review procedures are substantive tests of financial information made by a study and comparison of relationships among data. The auditor's reliance on substantive tests may be derived from tests of details of transactions and balances, from analytical review procedures, or from any combination of both. That decision is a matter of the auditor's judgment of the expected effectiveness and efficiency of the respective types of procedures. . . .

Although no specific analytical review procedures are required or suggested by *SAS No. 23* (AU 318), it indicates that such procedures can provide the kind of competent evidential matter required by generally accepted auditing standards. *To maximize effectiveness and efficiency, the auditor should be careful to select only those relationships that will produce meaningful results,* rather than compute every conceivable relationship.

The same analytical review procedure often can be used to achieve different audit objectives. A procedure used in one phase to identify potential problems (e.g., review of aging of interim accounts receivable to identify collectibility problems) also could be used at year-end to help determine the reasonableness of the balance (e.g., review of aging of year-end accounts receivable to support the adequacy of the year-end allowance for bad debts). The uses of analytical review procedures are limited only by the availability of information and creativity of the auditor.

6

TYPES OF ANALYTICAL REVIEW PROCEDURES

While some analytical review procedures should be applied in every audit, there is no formal body of defined procedures. Each audit will require the auditor to select or devise procedures that best fit the circumstances. Determining which financial relationships are important requires audit judgment and experience. Analytical review procedures should be sufficiently detailed to enable the auditor to identify significant fluctuations from the pattern expected as a result of the entity's experience. If planned properly, analytical review procedures will allow the auditor to (1) concentrate audit effort in the areas of greatest risk and (2) achieve audit efficiencies.

Client management frequently uses analytical review procedures to monitor and evaluate operations by focusing on unexpected fluctuations (or the absence of expected ones) in key ratios. Before performing analytical review procedures, the auditor should identify those used by management and determine if they are also useful for audit purposes. The auditor also should identify externally generated economic and industry statistics that management considers useful.

Some analytical review procedures that should be considered by an independent auditor are now discussed.

Financial and Operating Relationships

The analysis of financial and operating ratios is an effective method of enhancing the auditor's understanding of the client's business and assessing overall financial condition and profitability. This analysis provides quick insight into significant changes in a client's operations or financial characteristics. Ratio analysis also can be helpful in supporting the reasonableness of

FIGURE 6–1 Analytical Review Procedures Used during Audit Phases

Audit Phase	Type of Procedure	Timing	Use and Documentation
Initial planning	*Overall analytical review* of general financial condition and profitability trends to help identify changing circumstances. Analysis based primarily on inquiry of financial and operating management.	During the development of overall audit plan. Generally, during the second or third quarter of the client's fiscal year.	Helps in review of current developments and enhances understanding of client's industry and operations. Pertinent matters documented in permanent files and planning working papers.
Program development	*Detail analytical review* of period-to-period comparisons of financial statement amounts, operating and financial ratios, and other key data related to accounts affected by specific control objectives. Analysis based on expectations developed during initial planning and further inquiry of financial and operating management.	Concurrent with the system evaluation. Generally, during the third quarter of the client's fiscal year. For small clients, may be done concurrently with the overall analytical review.	Helps corroborate understanding of business and evaluation of system and identify areas requiring audit attention. Allows the auditor to measure effects of changes in conditions and circumstances. Documented in risk analysis and other planning working papers.
Program execution	*Direct tests* of account balances or transactions and final overall review of reasonableness of financial statement amounts. Analysis based on expectations developed during the risk analysis, investigation of responses to inquiries of management, and tests of underlying data.	During interim and year-end substantive testing.	Reduces or eliminates need for detail analysis of account balances or transactions. Documented in various working papers.

amounts that can be expected to vary with other financial statement amounts or operating data.

Financial ratios can be classified into four groups: (1) activity ratios, (2) profitability ratios, (3) liquidity ratios, and (4) solvency ratios. These ratios are discussed below.

Activity Ratios. These ratios are used to measure the client's operating efficiency, i.e., its success in using available resources. Activity ratios measure such things as the length of time required for conversion of certain current assets into cash and the average payment period of accounts payable. Because these ratios are calculated using specific accounts, they help to identify areas requiring further audit attention. Activity ratios include:

$$\text{Inventory turnover}[1] = \frac{\text{Cost of goods sold}}{\text{Average inventory}}$$

[1] For companies using LIFO, the auditor should consider restoring the LIFO reserves before computing this ratio and the next ratio (average age of inventory).

$$\text{Average age of inventory} = \frac{365 \text{ days}}{\text{Inventory turnover}}$$

$$\text{Accounts receivable turnover} = \frac{\text{Net sales}}{\text{Average accounts receivable}}$$

$$\begin{array}{l}\text{Average collection period} \\ \text{(also known as ``days'}} \\ \text{sales in receivables'')}\end{array} = \frac{365 \text{ days}}{\text{Accounts receivable turnover}}$$

$$\text{Average payment period} = \frac{365 \text{ days} \times \text{Average accounts payable}}{\text{Annual purchases of goods and services}}$$

A current inventory turnover rate that is significantly slower than either rates of prior years or rates of competitors could indicate obsolete, slow-moving, or overstock inventory. However, the auditor should be cautious when drawing conclusions from these ratios. Although a high inventory turnover (or low average age) may indicate efficient inventory management, it also may indicate problems (e.g., excessive markdowns). And a seasonal sales pattern also will influence the average age of inventory. For example, a lawn sprinkler manufacturer usually builds inventory in the winter in anticipation of the spring selling season.

The average collection period is one measure of the effectiveness of the client's credit and collection department—especially when compared to the client's general credit terms. For example, if the client extends 30-day credit terms to its customers, as a practical matter, an average collection period of 30 days is unlikely. But an average collection period of 35 to 45 days might indicate a well-managed credit and collection department. An increase in the collection period as compared to the prior year, or an average collection period that is significantly longer than industry averages, might indicate deficiencies in the client's credit and collection practices.

The average payment period provides an indication of the client's bill-paying patterns. Fluctuations in the average payment period also may indicate changes in liquidity or cash management philosophy.

Profitability Ratios. While the income statement is the primary tool in measuring profitability, the following ratios also may be useful in understanding changes in profitability:

$$\text{Gross margin} = \frac{\text{Net sales minus cost of goods sold}}{\text{Net sales}}$$

$$\text{Operating margin} = \frac{\text{Income before taxes and interest}[2]}{\text{Net sales}}$$

---

[2] To avoid being misled by seemingly significant changes, the auditor should consider the effect of unusual charges or credits when making comparisons of this ratio.

$$\text{Net profit margin} = \frac{\text{Net income}}{\text{Net sales}}$$

$$\text{Asset turnover} = \frac{\text{Net sales}}{\text{Total assets}}$$

$$\text{Return on assets} = \frac{\text{Net income}}{\text{Total assets}}$$

$$\text{Return on investment (ROI)} = \frac{\text{Net income}}{\text{Shareholders' equity}}$$

Comparisons of gross margins are particularly useful because they may indicate (1) a change in a company's ability to pass cost increases through to customers by raising prices, (2) shifts in sales mix, competition, or manufacturing efficiencies, or (3) financial statement errors. Generally, any significant change in the gross margin should be investigated because of the impact it has on operating income.

Return on assets measures how effectively the client's resources have been utilized in operations. Another way of expressing the return on asset ratio is the so-called "Dupont formula":

$$\text{Return on assets} = \text{Net profit margin} \times \text{Asset turnover}$$

This variation emphasizes the interaction of profitability and efficiency in the use of resources.

The return on investment ratio traditionally has been used as a measure of profitability. Although there are several variations, the most commonly used formula defines "investment" as shareholders' equity, which represents the resources of the shareholders used in generating net income.

Consideration should be given to using the inflation-adjusted current cost data maintained by many companies, as well as the historical data, for developing profitability ratios. For example, for companies using FIFO, current cost of sales eliminates the inventory profits. And the higher current cost depreciation charge may be indicative of the effect that replacing productive capacity will have on historical earnings.

Liquidity Ratios. These ratios are used to help measure the client's ability to satisfy current obligations as they become due. They may give the auditor some quick insight into changes in the company's management philosophy or operations. The primary ratios used to measure overall liquidity are:

$$\text{Current ratio} = \frac{\text{Current assets}}{\text{Current liabilities}}$$

$$\text{Quick ratio (also known as the "acid test" or liquidity ratio)} = \frac{\text{Cash, short-term marketable securities, and receivables (net)}}{\text{Current liabilities}}$$

The auditor should consider the effect that significant LIFO reserves or unrecorded commitments (e.g., significant payments required in the next year under noncancelable operating leases) might have on the current ratio.

The quick ratio measures the extent to which current liabilities are covered by highly liquid assets. Therefore, the quick ratio represents a more conservative evaluation of liquidity than the current ratio. It also provides a better indication of liquidity when inventory turnover is low. A quick ratio of less than 1 to 1 implies a dependency on inventory to liquidate current liabilities.

Working capital (current assets minus current liabilities) and working capital provided by operations (net income plus depreciation and other noncash charges) are other useful measures of liquidity. However, an increase in net income may only give rise to an increased investment in receivables and inventories (a common occurrence during times of high inflation), rather than greater cash flow. Changes in working capital or working capital provided by operations may not highlight this situation. To measure cash flow, working capital provided by operations should be adjusted for changes in receivables, inventories, payables, and accrued expenses.

The comparison of forecasted cash flow to cash requirements also can provide meaningful information about liquidity. In fact, the usefulness of working capital and the current and quick ratios for measuring liquidity depends on the predictability of future cash flow. The less predictable the cash flow, the greater the liquidity requirements.

Solvency Ratios. These ratios measure the long-term financial strength of the client. Prospective creditors often look at these ratios to determine the risk involved in lending funds. Potential investors look at these ratios to measure how effective management has been in using debt to leverage operating results, i.e., management's ability to generate earnings with borrowed funds. A company earning more on borrowed funds than it pays in interest may indicate efficient management. However, a highly leveraged company also may indicate higher risk and susceptibility to economic downswings. One or two loss periods could mean financial difficulty. A highly leveraged company also may have difficulty borrowing additional funds for expansion. The primary ratios used to measure solvency are:

$$\text{Debt-to-equity ratio} = \frac{\text{Long-term debt}}{\text{Shareholders' equity}}$$

$$\text{Ratio of earnings to fixed charges} = \frac{\text{Income before taxes, interest, and other fixed charges}}{\text{Annual interest expense and other fixed charges}}$$

$$\text{Debt service coverage} = \frac{\text{Net income, interest, depreciation, and other noncash charges}}{\text{Annual principal and interest payments}}$$

Liquidity and solvency ratios are widely used by creditors when establishing loan covenants. Often, the auditor will calculate these types of ratios when reviewing compliance with loan agreements. It may be appropriate to adjust these ratios to include significant other long-term liabilities, such as capital leases or commitments and contingencies that are not recorded under generally accepted accounting principles (GAAP) (e.g., noncancelable operating leases, unfunded pension obligations, loan guarantees), particularly if these ratios are used in evaluating a potential "going-concern" problem. *SAS No. 34* (AU 340) discusses other considerations when a question arises about an entity's continued existence.

Comparisons to Prior Periods

Generally, the best indicator of changes in circumstances and trends will be a comparison of a company's financial characteristics and operating results over a period of time. This comparison ordinarily should cover at least three years, but two years may be sufficient to identify changes requiring further investigation. For some accounts it may be necessary to review month-to-month data to identify fluctuations that are not obvious from a comparison of quarterly or annual data. In addition, because inflation or general growth or decline in business may distort dollar comparisons between current and prior periods, financial statement comparisons should include both dollar amounts and percentage relationships (e.g., balance sheet classifications as a percentage of total assets and income statement classifications as a percentage of net sales).

Many factors may affect comparisons. While the existence of a fluctuation or deviation from expected patterns does not necessarily indicate an error in the financial statements, it is important that the auditor understand why these fluctuations occurred. Factors that may affect interperiod comparability include:

1. Strikes.
2. Changes in production methods, customers, products, marketing strategy, or capitalization.
3. Disposal or acquisition of a line of business.
4. Accounting changes or account reclassifications.
5. Unusual charges or credits to operations.

Comparisons to Budgets

Analytical review of budgets should include: (1) comparison of the budget to prior years' operating results, (2) comparison of the budget to current year's operating results, and (3) analysis of major revisions to the budget. Before making budget comparisons and investigating variances, the auditor should evaluate the effectiveness of the client's approach to the budgetary process. For example, if the process includes a study of both present and past operating experience of the company and of general and industry economic conditions, and if past budgets have proven to be realistic, comparison to budgeted amounts can be a useful audit tool. But if budgets are inadequately prepared and historically subject to large variances, the auditor should limit or omit comparisons with budgets for analytical review purposes.

Comparisons to Industry Statistics

A comparison of financial statement amounts and relationships for the company or its segments to industry statistics can (1) improve the auditor's understanding of a client's business and industry, (2) indicate a client's financial strengths or problems, (3) highlight areas requiring audit attention, and (4) provide a basis for recommendations to management. Sources of industry statistics are discussed later in this chapter.

Comparisons to industry averages are especially useful in specialized industries because there is less variability in both the data reported and the structure of the companies. An industry average is not a "magic number" that means ideal performance. But significant variances from industry averages should be understood.

Making meaningful comparisons to industry data can be difficult for an auditor for a variety of reasons, including the following:

1. Each company has unique characteristics, such as product quality, customers, location, corporate structure, and capitalization.
2. The organization of industry statistics by Standard Industry Classification (SIC) code may result in diversified companies being compared with a company in one industry.

However, the variability of industry data does not diminish the usefulness of the comparisons. On the contrary, the principal value of comparisons may be the *questions* they raise. For example, such comparisons may reveal that the client uses an accounting method that is not predominantly used by the industry. As a further example, assume that the auditor compares the ratio of days' sales in accounts receivable for a tire manufacturer to prior periods and finds that the client's ratio has deteriorated. This indicates a potential problem with collectibility in general. But, when the client's performance is compared to that of the industry, the auditor finds that the industry ratio has steadily improved. This could suggest a specific problem for the client, such as a relaxation of customer credit policies, a weakening of credit and collection management, or perhaps a decline in tire quality control.

EVALUATING ANALYTICAL REVIEW RESULTS

An understanding of the client's business and industry should alert the auditor to likely fluctuations in the financial data. These fluctuations may be caused by (1) trends—general changes in business conditions, (2) seasonal patterns—changes in business activity caused by weather conditions or holidays, (3) cyclical patterns—changes in overall economic activity, or (4) dependent relationships—changes related to movements in other financial data. Underlying the use of analytical review procedures is the expectation that predictable relationships exist in the financial data. Therefore, the auditor should review results of analytical review procedures to determine whether the relationships make sense. In many cases, analytical review procedures will cover financial data for only part of the year, so the auditor should be particularly aware of seasonal factors that may distort comparability.

Fluctuations that cannot be explained from the auditor's knowledge of the client's business and industry (e.g., industry sales up 25 percent but client sales down 25 percent) or by known relationships with other financial data (e.g., sales down 25 percent but cost of sales up 5 percent) may result from nonrecurring transactions, erroneous accounting procedures or practices, or other factors. When unexpected fluctuations in amounts or relationships occur, or when expected ones do not, the auditor should find out why. The auditor's initial follow-up procedures should include discussions with operating executives as well as financial management. They already may have determined the cause of the variations, or if not, may save the auditor time by pursuing these matters. Of course, the auditor should consider the reasonableness of management explanations.

The auditor should be careful to avoid forming conclusions based upon significant variations or trends in one ratio—a single ratio rarely provides sufficient data to measure changes in conditions. However, changes in a group of related ratios may indicate matters of audit concern.

USE OF ANALYTICAL REVIEW IN AN AUDIT

Chapter 3 explained how overall analytical review is used during the initial planning phase to learn about changes in environmental factors. During initial planning, the auditor also plans the procedures which would be appropriate for the detail analytical review. It is important here to distinguish between the types of procedures performed during overall and detail analytical reviews.

Detail analytical review procedures, which are directed to specific accounts, are more comprehensive than overall analytical review procedures that are directed to overall financial condition and profitability. Although the same procedures are sometimes used in both the overall and detail analytical review, the data to which they are applied should be different. For example, in reviewing interim financial statements, the detail analytical review should focus on specific *components* of a financial statement amount. Also, to better understand the causes of fluctuations, a month-to-month comparison of levels of activity affecting the amount may be necessary. The following comments relating to specific control objectives further illustrate the difference:

> S–1, *"Customer orders require approval of credit and terms before acceptance,"* and S–2, *"Uncollectible amounts are promptly identified and provided for."* In the overall analytical review, the auditor might simply compare the total receivables balance to the prior year and relate the change to the general level of sales for the current year. This would help establish expectations about the condition of accounts and help confirm expectations based on knowledge of customer mix, economic conditions, and marketing strategy. In the detail analytical review, the auditor might review the aged trial balance for significant past due accounts and look at agings to design the preliminary audit approach.

> P–9, *"Obsolete, slow-moving, and overstock inventory is prevented or promptly detected and provided for."* In the overall analytical review, the auditor might review the interim financial statements for changes in inventory levels. Unexplained changes or unanticipated increases might lead the auditor to expect some problems in the area. In the detail analytical review, the auditor might separately calculate inventory turnover for raw materials and principal classes of finished goods inventories.

Overall analytical review and detail analytical review have different objectives. However, as a practical matter for many engagements, the overall and detail analytical review may be done at the same time. This is particularly true for small audits. But for large audits, where planning starts early in the year, the distinction is clearer.

The following sections discuss the use of (1) detail analytical review procedures as part of the risk analysis in the program development phase of the audit and (2) analytical review procedures as direct tests of balances in the program execution phase.

DETAIL ANALYTICAL REVIEW

The detail analytical review is one of the three inputs to the risk analysis. Its purpose is to:

1. Determine whether the numbers "make sense" in view of (a) the auditor's understanding of the client's business and industry, (b) expectations developed during initial planning, and (c) the evaluation of the accounting system. This will help identify areas where audit procedures may be limited because of the reasonableness of the amount.

2. Identify significant fluctuations or quantify transactions requiring further audit attention. This will lead the auditor to design a preliminary audit approach that includes specific audit procedures for these areas.

To help in deciding which detail analytical review procedures to use, Appendix III at the end of this textbook, provides examples of key data and ratios related to each specific control objective. The auditor should identify the purpose of each procedure before performing it. By answering the question "what will this procedure tell me?", the auditor should be able to avoid computing redundant or meaningless relationships. In some cases, certain aspects of interim financial statements may not be useful for detail analytical review procedures. For example, for many small businesses, interim costing procedures may not result in fairly stated inventory and cost of sales amounts. In these cases, analysis of interim gross margins would not be helpful.

Documenting Results of Detail Analytical Review

The analytical review procedures performed should be evidenced by appropriate working papers. Because many of the analytical review procedures utilize historical data, carry-forward schedules will be useful for performing these procedures, and they also provide a ready means of documenting the auditor's work. As in the case of environmental considerations, it may be convenient to document analytical review results by operating component.

To be useful, the information documented on the risk analysis working paper should be relevant to a specific control objective and should affect the preliminary audit approach for the related accounts. This makes the risk analysis more effective and easier to review.

Detail analytical review also should help the auditor establish the level of materiality and general audit approach for examining specific transactions and balances. For example, if the number or size of transactions in a particular area is small, the auditor may be able to conclude that evaluation of the accounting system is not an efficient or appropriate way of auditing the accounts or transactions affected. On the other hand, if an account contains items that the auditor wants to test, data that help define those key items and determine whether a representative sample is appropriate should be included in the Observations from Detail Analytical Review section of the risk analysis working paper.

To illustrate, in reviewing the aging of accounts receivable, the auditor might indicate the size and number of accounts in the over 90-day category to define key items for the collectibility review. In the inventory area, the auditor might indicate the number and dollar value of principal inventory items and their percentages of the total to define key items for a price test. The auditor also might include the approximate number of customers or inventory items and the average dollar amount of each to help justify and plan a representative sample. The sample risk analysis working paper in Chapter 2 illustrates how the detail analytical review helps determine the specific accounts to review for collectibility (see preliminary audit approach step 4).

When recording observations, the auditor should be as specific as possible and quantify the effects of changes. In many cases, the auditor will quantify factors already noted in the Environmental Considerations section. General comments such as "appears reasonable" or "nothing unusual noted" are not useful. Figure 6–2 illustrates appropriate comments in the risk analysis working paper.

Updating the Detail Analytical Review

In some cases, depending on the importance of the analytical review procedures to the risk analysis, it may be desirable for the preliminary audit approach to include procedures to update the detail analytical review information for the rest of the year to see if there are any significant changes. For example, if the results of the detail analytical review support only minimal procedures in an area, the auditor might want to review the same data through year-end to be sure that conditions still support the minimum effort planned.

FIGURE 6–2 Observations from Detail Analytical Review

Risk Analysis Prepared By/Date PWC 7–31
PAA Prepared By/Date RDH 8–15
Reviewed By/Date MG 8–20

Sales
S–1 Customer Orders Require Approval of Credit and Terms Before Acceptance
S–2 Uncollectible Amounts Are Promptly Identified and Provided for

Risk Analysis

Environmental Considerations Company sells construction materials to large commercial and residential contractors. Bad debts have been minor in the past. Commercial construction backlog is substantial. But high interest rates caused residential housing starts to decline dramatically in the last two quarters, adversely affecting residential contractors. Approximately 30% of outstanding receivables are from residential contractors.

Observations from Detail Analytical Review Accounts receivable have increased $570,000 (13%) over prior year. Days' sales in receivables at 6/30/X9 were 70 days (58 days at 12/31/X8). Over 60-day aging category increased $700,000, substantially all from residential contractors (including 20 accounts over $25,000). Only 2 commercial accounts were over 60 days old, both over $150,000. Allowance for doubtful accounts is $125,000 at 6/30/X9 ($100,000 at 12/31/X8). Write-offs through 6/30/X9 total $45,000 vs. $60,000 during all of 19X8.

Figure 6-2 *(concluded)*

Risk Analysis Prepared By/Date <u>PWC 7-31</u>
PAA Prepared By/Date <u>RDH 8-15</u>
Reviewed By/Date <u>MG 8-20</u>

Production or Service—Inventory Accountability and Physical Safeguards

P-8 Physical Loss of Inventory Is Prevented or Promptly Detected

Risk Analysis

Environmental Considerations In the first quarter, the client moved into a new wire manufacturing plant which had been under construction for 18 months. The transfer of inventory to the new facility was not well controlled--principally because the quantities removed from the Green St. plant were not counted before they were loaded or after the transfer. Copper rod, which has significant resale value, is the principal inventory item.

Observations from Detail Analytical Review April semi-annual inventory count resulted in a downward book-to-physical adjustment of $40,500 or 4% of the inventory balance (historically less than 1%). Using the current price (90¢/lb.) of copper, we estimate the adjustment represents a 40,000 pound loss (total copper inventory--1,050,000 pounds). The move to the new plant is blamed for most of the loss, but the client is still analyzing reasons for differences by product line.

Risk Analysis Prepared by/Date <u>PWC 7-31</u>
PAA Prepared by/Date <u>RDH 8-15</u>
Reviewed By/Date <u>MG 8-20</u>

Administration—Expenses and Related Liabilities

A-1 Expenses Are Incurred Only with Proper Authorization
A-2 Expenses and Related Liabilities Are Recorded Correctly as to Account, Amount, and Period

Risk Analysis

Environmental Considerations Client is not repeating last year's special magazine advertising and is curtailing new promotion programs due to anticipated general business downturn this year. Client has no plans to increase the research and development effort.

Observations from Detail Analytical Review Selling and G&A expenses for 6 months have declined to $18 million ($19 million last year); however, they increased slightly as a percentage of sales to 29.5% (29.0% last year). The largest SG&A expense, commissions, is 8.25% of sales (8.21% last year). Advertising and promotion expenses total $500,000 compared to $650,000 last year. Other components of G&A expenses have not changed significantly.

ANALYTICAL REVIEW AND TIMELY INTERIM REVIEWS

Although the discussion of analytical review in this chapter is directed to annual audits, the concepts also relate to timely interim reviews of financial information conducted in accordance with Statements on Auditing Standards. Many publicly held companies are required to have interim reviews (see Chapter 17), which may be performed on either a timely or a retrospective basis.

These review procedures are similar to the overall analytical review procedures used in the initial planning phase of the audit. Both procedures ordinarily include (1) analysis of financial relationships and operating results; and (2) comparisons to prior periods, budgets, and industry data. The purposes of the timely interim review and the initial planning phase of the audit also are similar: (1) to obtain a current understanding of the client's business, significant changes in circumstances, and other matters affecting the financial statements; and (2) to provide for timely attention to accounting and reporting issues.

To maximize efficiency, the auditor should try to coordinate timely interim reviews with the audit planning effort. Also, the auditor might schedule detail analytical review procedures at the same time as or immediately following a timely interim review to maximize the use of the updated analysis.

ANALYTICAL REVIEW PROCEDURES AS DIRECT TESTS

The use of analytical review procedures is appropriate in the audit process either as the primary direct test of a balance (substantive test) or as a corroborative test in combination with other procedures. Analytical review procedures provide an efficient alternative to detail analysis of account balances and they allow the auditor to consider whether the numbers make sense in view of his or her expectations.

In many cases, year-to-year comparisons of balances combined with tests of key attributes may comprise the entire audit effort for a particular area. For example, the risk analysis might indicate a low likelihood of material error related to authorization and recording of property additions. An analytical review of the level of additions for the year—comparison to prior year and capital budget—combined with the results of tests of key attributes for authorizing and recording additions through an interim date, could provide the auditor with sufficient evidence to conclude that the amount of property additions for the year is fairly stated. In other cases, analytical review procedures may supplement other direct tests of balances.

The extent to which analytical review procedures can be substituted for other audit procedures will depend on the persuasiveness of the analytical review evidence. There are various levels of persuasiveness. Year-to-year comparisons of account balances generally provide only corroborative evidence. For example, a year-to-year comparison of inventory turnover and levels provides some evidence as to the reasonableness of the inventory balance, but it does not provide sufficient evidence to allow a significant reduction of other audit procedures. Further, merely relating a change in one particular account to a change in another account may not be persuasive. For example, an auditor cannot conclude that an increase in inventory is reasonable merely because of increases in sales and accounts receivable. On the other hand, to establish a relationship between independent data and compare the relationship to prior periods may provide persuasive evidence. For example, a year-to-year comparison of the relationship of actual labor and overhead costs to materials put into production to the same relationship in the ending inventory might provide a reasonable basis for reducing the amount of price testing of standard costs otherwise necessary.

In testing the reasonableness of management's subjective estimates (e.g., allowance for doubtful accounts or accrual for warranty costs), analytical review procedures may provide the most effective test of the adequacy of the estimates. In some cases, analytical review procedures may provide the only method of testing. For example, where the client does not maintain an effective inventory costing system, overhead in the ending inventory might be approximated by relating actual overhead for the year to actual direct labor (assuming reliable direct labor reporting).

Because analytical review procedures may provide more comfort than tests of details of balances and often require much less time to perform, the auditor should maximize their use as direct tests of balances. Figure 6–3 includes examples of analytical review procedures that can be used as direct tests of balances.

TESTING UNDERLYING DATA USED IN ANALYTICAL REVIEW

Because the purposes of the overall and detail analytical reviews are only to increase the auditor's understanding of the client's business and identify areas that require further investigation, it is not necessary to test the data used in those reviews. However, if analytical review procedures are a significant element in the preliminary audit approach (i.e., they are the primary direct test of a balance), the auditor should test the reliability of the data to be used. If analytical review procedures are used to corroborate the results of other audit procedures, tests of the underlying data may not be necessary—especially when the data are generated independently of the accounting system. For example, production department yield statistics need not be tested when used to estimate the material content of finished goods and work in process.

FINAL OVERALL REVIEW

In the program execution phase, the auditor should perform a final overall review of the comparative financial statements near the conclusion of field work. The purpose of this analysis is to assure that (1) the auditor has

FIGURE 6–3   Examples of Analytical Review Procedures for Direct Tests of Balances

The following are examples of tests of reasonableness of account balances by reference to relationships with other financial data.

Provisions for bad debts by reference to aging of receivables, days' sales in receivables, or sales and historical charge-off percentage.

Inventory standard costs by comparing current standards to prior year standards adjusted by average inflation rate.

Material content of work in process and finished goods by relating raw materials put into production and quantities sold to standard yield factors.

Labor and overhead costs in ending inventory by relating actual labor and overhead for the year (reduced by idle plant, inefficiencies, and other noninventoriable costs) to material put into production (considering the effect of changes in product mix).

Overhead in ending inventory by relating actual overhead for the year to actual direct labor (assuming reliable direct labor reporting).

Finished goods inventory pricing by reference to selling prices less costs to dispose and "normal" gross margin.

Scrap income by relating standard cost scrap factor to pounds of material processed and applying the result to published scrap price per pound.

Provisions for depreciation by reference to asset balance, effect of additions and disposals, and average depreciation rate.

Payroll expense by reference to the average number of employees and the average pay per period.

Accrued payroll by reference to days accrued and average daily payroll or subsequent period gross payroll.

Commission expense by reference to rates and related sales.

Accruals for commissions or royalties by reference to terms of agreements and payment dates.

Defined benefit pension contribution payable by reference to applicable payroll and prior year contribution rate.

Interest expense and related accrual by reference to average debt outstanding, weighted-average interest rate, and payment dates.

Investment income by relating average amounts invested to an average interest or yield rate.

obtained explanations for fluctuations between years, (2) the numbers make sense in light of the auditor's understanding of the business and industry, and (3) the auditor is satisfied with the sufficiency of the audit procedures. This review often can be documented on a draft copy of the financial statements. It also will assist in preparing for closing conferences and audit committee meetings.

SOURCES OF INDUSTRY DATA

There are many sources of information that deal with national and local economic conditions and specific industries. Such information is available from government agencies, the National Association of Accountants, state CPA societies, and local libraries and chambers of commerce.

Copies of 10-Ks and 10-Qs (annual and quarterly reports of publicly held companies required to report to SEC), and proxy filings of competitors may be useful in reviewing financial statistics for other companies in the same industry. These filings can be obtained directly from the companies or from the SEC.

Examples of other sources that may be useful in locating financial statistics for industry comparisons are:

General Sources

Almanac of Business and Industrial Financial Ratios published by Prentice-Hall, Inc.

Annual Statement Studies published by Robert Morris Associates.

Cost of Doing Business in Corporations published by Dun & Bradstreet.

Specific Sources

American Trucking Trends published by American Trucking Association, Inc.

Basic Petroleum Data Book published by American Petroleum Institute.

Best Insurance Reports; Life-Health published by A. M. Best Company.

Electronic News Financial Fact Book & Directory published by Fairchild Publications.

Fairchild's Financial Manual of Retail Stores published by Fairchild Publications.

Polk's World Bank Directory published by R. L. Polk & Co.

QUESTIONS AND PROBLEMS

6–1. Generally accepted auditing standards require that an auditor obtain sufficient competent evidential matter. Can analytical review procedures provide such evidence?

6–2. Can the same analytical review procedure be used to achieve different audit objectives?

6–3. Are there set analytical procedures that must be used on every audit?

6–4. When is "detail analytical review" normally performed in an audit?

6–5. Which of the following would *not* be considered an activity ratio:
   a. Inventory turnover.
   b. Average payment period.
   c. Gross margin.
   d. Average age of inventory.
   e. Accounts receivable turnover.

6–6. Name some ratios that an auditor may use in understanding changes in profitability.

6–7. What is the "quick ratio" and what does it represent?

6–8. What are the primary ratios used to measure solvency?

6-9. Of what value is a comparison of a company's financial characteristics and operating results to prior periods?

6-10. Name some factors that may affect comparison of a company's financial characteristics and operating results to prior periods.

6-11. In general, what should be included in an analytical review of budgets?

6-12. "In performing an analytical review an auditor must always make budget comparisons." Comment on this statement.

6-13. What are the advantages of comparing financial statement amounts and relationships for a company or its segments to industry statistics?

6-14. Why are meaningful comparisons of client data with industry data difficult?

6-15. Name some sources of industry data and local economic conditions.

6-16. Compare and contrast analytical review for annual audits and for reviews of interim financial information.

6-17. Which of the following is *not* a key data, ratio, or relationship relating to the control objective "uncollectible amounts are promptly identified and provided for?"
a. Cost of sales to units shipped.
b. Average accounts receivable to net sales.
c. Bad debt write-offs to average accounts receivable.
d. Percentage composition of accounts receivable aging.

6-18. Select the *best* answer for each of the following questions:
a. Which of the following is *not* a typical analytical review procedure?
    (1) Study of relationships of the financial information with relevant nonfinancial information.
    (2) Comparison of the financial information with similar information regarding the industry in which the entity operates.
    (3) Comparison of recorded amounts of major disbursements with appropriate invoices.
    (4) Comparison of the financial information with budgeted amounts.
b. Analytical review procedures are
    (1) Statistical tests of financial information designed to identify areas requiring intensive investigation.
    (2) Analytical tests of financial information made by a computer.
    (3) Substantive tests of financial information made by a study and comparison of relationships among data.
    (4) Diagnostic tests of financial information which may *not* be classified as evidential matter.
c. One reason why the independent auditor makes an analytical review of the client's operations is to identify probable
    (1) Weaknesses of a material nature in the system of internal control.
    (2) Unusual transactions.
    (3) Noncompliance with prescribed control procedures.
    (4) Improper separation of accounting and other financial duties.

d. Significant unexpected fluctuations identified by analytical review procedures will usually necessitate
   (1) A consistency qualification.
   (2) A review of internal control.
   (3) Explanation in the representation letter.
   (4) Further investigation by the auditor.
e. Analytical review procedures may be classified as being primarily
   (1) Compliance tests.
   (2) Substantive tests.
   (3) Tests of ratios.
   (4) Detailed tests of balances.   (AICPA, adapted)

6–19. Below are some statistics that relate to the ABC Company.

ABC COMPANY

	Year Ended December 31			Industry Average
	1986	1985	1984	(1985)
Financial position relationships:				
Total liabilities to net worth	1.0	0.5	0.5	0.8
Current assets to current liabilities	2.5	2.2	2.3	2.0
Acid-test, quick assets to current liabilities	1.1	0.9	1.0	—
Inventory to working capital	0.9	1.1	1.0	0.6
Operating relationships:				
Net income to net worth	15.3%	10.4%	6.9%	5.6%
Net income per share of common stock	$13.10	$ 7.89	$ 4.87	—
Earnings retained (net income less dividends) to net income	77.2%	64.9%	46.9%	—
Number of days' sales in receivables (accounts receivable to average daily sales)	24.9	26.8	29.3	—
Merchandise turnover (cost of sales to average inventory)	8.9	8.3	7.2	8.2
Gross profit to sales	10.3%	9.5%	9.1%	—
Net income to sales	2.2%	1.7%	1.3%	1.3%
Sales per payroll dollar	$ 9.58	$ 8.69	$ 8.40	—

high variable costs

Required:

Comment on the general importance of the following financial relationships and make specific observations on those relationships for ABC.
a. Current assets to current liabilities. (ABC Company has a long-term debt covenant that requires a minimum ratio of 1.5:1.)
b. Inventory to working capital.
c. Net income to net worth.
d. Net income per share of common stock.
e. Number of days' sales in receivables (terms of sale is 30 days).
f. Gross profit and net income to sales (sales in 1986 increased by 30 percent).

6–20. The Core Corporation auditor's risk analysis working paper for specific control objectives P–11/P–12 ("Property, plant and equipment are purchased only with proper authorization;" and "Property, plant, and equipment purchases are recorded correctly as to account, amount, and period") contains the following detail analytical review data:

> Through June 30, 1985, purchases of PP&E totaled $250,000. Capital expenditures budget for the year is $380,000. Six purchases accounted for about half of the additions. The remainder consists of numerous smaller additions. Total costs of PP&E at December 31, 1984, and June 30, 1985, were $6,200,000 and $6,450,000, respectively.

How might these observations be more specific?

6–21. Use the data provided below to evaluate the reasonableness of 1985 total production wages.

a.

	1985	1984
Total production wages	$12,688,410	$10,159,800
Average number of production employees for the year	805	700

b. 100 new employees were hired early in 1985.

c. Nine percent and 9.5 percent wage increases went into effect on October 1, 1984, and 1985, respectively.

6–22. Assume the following about Tabbie Company:

	1985	1984	1983
Cash and short-term securities	$ 50,750	$ 20,325	$ 7,800
Accounts receivable	57,846	54,610	51,670
Inventories	135,194	101,583	88,200
Total current assets	261,390	194,299	165,780
Total current liabilities	243,988	205,015	154,329
Net sales	423,901	329,678	275,483
Cost of goods sold	281,208	198,199	176,254

Required:

a. Compute the following activity ratios for 1985 and 1984:
  (1) Inventory turnover.
  (2) Average age of inventory.
  (3) Accounts receivable turnover.
  (4) Average collection period.

b. Compute the following liquidity ratios for 1985 and 1984:
  (1) Current ratio.
  (2) Quick ratio.

c. What do the results of these ratios indicate?

6–23. Identify the primary specific control objective(s) to which the following analytical review observations relate:

a. Selling and administrative expenses, excluding administrative salaries, wages and commissions, bonuses, depreciation, and warranty expense, are $2,036,000 for the first half of 1985, versus $1,026,000 for the first half of 1984. This is almost $250,000 over budget and is attributed to unexpected high increases in general insurance expenses and promotional and additional insurance expenses associated with foreign marketing efforts.

b. At June 30, 1985, the company temporarily invested loan proceeds of $1.8 million in short-term certificates of deposit. These funds are expected to be used for new equipment purchases.

c. Net scrap expense was $150,000 during 1984. It is projected to be $165,000 for 1985.

d. During the first six months of 1985, inventory quantities decreased slightly while inventory costs increased by approximately 7 percent. Management plans to maintain the June 30, 1985, quantities through year-end. Gross margin through June 30, 1985, (33 percent) is comparable to 1984. Relationship of inventory components (materials—65 percent, labor—19 percent, overhead—16 percent) is also comparable to 1984.

The following is a summary of inventory by classification:

	6/30/85	12/31/84
Raw materials	$ 635,000	$ 612,000
Work in process	902,000	856,000
Finished goods	873,000	825,000
	$2,410,000	$2,293,000

e. Warranty reserves as of June 30, 1985, totaled $558,000, versus $315,000 at December 31, 1984. The increase is principally related to the substantial increase in revenues, though a defect in the uninterruptible power system caused a $150,000 addition to the reserve in the first quarter.

6–24. Assume the following facts:

a. The company uses straight-line depreciation for book purposes and records depreciation to the nearest month for additions and retirements. During 1985, assets were acquired and disposed of ratably throughout the year.

b. The ranges of useful lives are as follows:

Buildings	25–30 years
Machinery and equipment	8–15
Autos and trucks	3–6
Furniture and fixtures	5–10

c. Depreciation expense for 1984 was $711,000.

d. Depreciation on 1984 additions amounted to $100,000. Depreciation on these additions in 1985 totaled $200,000.

e. Except for autos and trucks, there are relatively few fully depreciated assets.

f. Most of the autos and trucks that were fully depreciated at December 31, 1984, were disposed of during 1985.

g. A property, plant, and equipment summary is shown below (in thousands).

	Balance 12/31/84	Additions	Deductions	Balance 12/31/85
Cost:				
Buildings	$ 2,963	$ 460		$ 3,423
Machinery and equipment	12,241	5,703	$ 907	17,037
Autos and trucks	1,652	611	401	1,862
Furniture and fixtures	122	22	6	138
	$16,978	$6,796	$1,314	$22,460
Accumulated depreciation:				
Buildings	$ 491	$ 124		$ 615
Machinery and equipment	4,372	856	$ 702	4,526
Autos and trucks	805	601	385	1,021
Furniture and fixtures	52	36	5	83
	$ 5,720	$1,617	$1,092	$ 6,245

Required:

Using the above facts, perform analytical review procedures to evaluate the reasonableness of 1985 depreciation expense.

6–25. Assume the following about Goode Company:

	1985	1984
Net sales	$423,901	$329,678
Cost of sales	281,208	198,199
Gross profit	$142,693	$131,479
Export rebates	3,821	5,587
	$146,514	$137,066
Other income	681	635
	$147,195	$137,701
Expenses:		
Selling	$ 25,876	$ 17,452
Personnel	44,071	62,253
Production	6,877	6,599
Interest	9,715	8,431
General	21,087	14,163
Exceptional expenses	12	34,572
	$107,638	$143,470
Income (loss) before taxes	$ 39,557	$ (5,769)
Tax expense (benefit)	21,600	(2,500)
Profit (loss) for year	$ 17,957	$ (3,269)
Total assets	$397,546	$315,645
Shareholders' equity	$ 42,082	$ 24,125

Required:

a. Compute the following profitability ratios for 1985 and 1984:
   (1) Gross margin.
   (2) Operating margin.
   (3) Net profit margin.

(4) Asset turnover.

(5) Return on assets.

(6) Return on investment.

b. What questions might the auditor ask based on these ratios?

c. What additional questions might the auditor ask based on the financial information presented?

6–26. Identify the primary specific control objective(s) to which the following analytical review observations relate:

a. Selling and administrative payroll approximated $936,000 through June 30, 1985, (approximately $7,510/employee) versus $849,000 through June 30, 1984, ($6,770/employee)—an almost 11 percent increase. Company is accruing $25,000/quarter for bonus payments.

b. The only change in equity accounts is due to net income.

c. Returns for 1983 and 1984 totaled $2,400 and $3,750, respectively. Returns for the first 6 months of 1985 are $95,000. Seven of the credits issued exceeded $12,000.

d. Taxes have been provided through June 30, 1985, at a rate of 40 percent, which is lower than the six months ended June 30, 1984, due to significant investment tax credits arising from the plant expansion program. Budgeted rate for year is 39 percent.

e. Depreciation was 6.7 percent of the average cost of depreciable assets for 1984. Depreciation for the six months ended June 30, 1985, annualized, projects to 7.0 percent. This is considered reasonable based on the level and timing of PP&E additions.

PREPARING THE AUDIT PROGRAM

This chapter describes how the auditor should consider the interaction of the three inputs to the risk analysis in assessing the likelihood of material error in the accounts affected by the specific control objectives and developing a preliminary audit approach and audit program. The chapter also offers guidance for determining the nature, timing, and extent of audit procedures. The concept of risk analysis is described in Chapter 2, and the inputs to the risk analysis are discussed in Chapters 3 through 6 ("Environmental Considerations" in Chapter 3, "System Evaluation" in Chapters 4 and 5, and "Detail Analytical Review" in Chapter 6). Each of these inputs contributes to the assessment of the likelihood of material error in the accounts affected by the specific control objectives.

Based on the risk analysis, and on the choices among alternative methods of accumulating sufficient competent evidential matter, the auditor outlines a preliminary audit approach for the accounts and transactions affected by the specific control objectives. A detailed audit program for each audit area (financial statement classification or transaction cycle) is then prepared from the preliminary audit approaches for related control objectives.

The preliminary audit approach should be an effective and efficient combination of audit procedures—both interim and year-end—for the accounts and transactions affected by the control objectives. It should be clear that audit emphasis is being directed to areas where the risk of material error is high, and audit effort is being minimized in areas where such risk is low.

ASSESSING THE LIKELIHOOD OF MATERIAL ERROR

The auditor's assessment of the likelihood of material error in the accounts affected by each specific control objective is a judgmental conclusion based on the risk analysis. For this purpose only, "error" also includes irregularities and judgmental differences.

For purposes of developing the preliminary audit approach and the audit program, it is important to understand the distinction between errors and irregularities (see Chapter 4). A properly developed and executed audit program should provide reasonable assurance of detecting material errors. However, irregularities may involve an effort to provide fictitious or altered evidence to cover up management override or collusion. Therefore, while the auditor should be alert to management's motivations and intentions, there can be no assurance that an examination conducted in accordance with generally accepted auditing standards will detect irregularities.

As previously indicated, in the assessment of the likelihood of material error the auditor should consider the effect of *all* three inputs to the risk analysis on the accounts affected by the specific control objective. When there are conflicts or mitigating effects among the inputs, the auditor should explain the conclusions in the risk analysis working paper. An explanation is essential so that it is clear how the auditor has assessed the relative importance of the three inputs and how the preliminary audit approach is responsive to the factors supporting the assessment of the likelihood of material error.

For example, the auditor may have reasonable assurance that the accounting system is designed to achieve a specific control objective, but a significant environmental factor, or an observation from detail analytical review which indicates that the numbers do not make sense, can make the likelihood of material error in the accounts affected moderate or high.[1]

In other circumstances, even though the accounting system is not designed to achieve the specific control objective, the likelihood of material error might be low. Consider a client with a small accounting department that lacks segregation of duties. The auditor may conclude that the accounting system does not provide reasonable assurance that a specific control objective is being achieved. Thus, control risk is high. Nevertheless, the auditor also may conclude that the likelihood of material error in the accounts affected

---

[1] Assessing the likelihood of material error as high does not indicate a potential violation of the Foreign Corrupt Practices Act unless the assessment is because the accounting system is not designed to achieve a specific control objective.

by the specific control objective is low because (1) the bookkeeper is competent and conscientious, (2) management provides supervision and reviews financial data, (3) no significant errors were noted during prior audits, and (4) the detail analytical review indicates that the financial information related to the accounts affected appears reasonable. In this case, there are environmental factors—supported by detail analytical review—that indicate a relatively low inherent risk, which mitigates the lack of segregation of duties. Thus, the amount of audit work should be less than if these factors did not exist.

In assessing the likelihood of material error, materiality should be considered relative to the financial statements taken as a whole. FASB *Statement of Financial Accounting Concepts No. 2,* "Qualitative Characteristics of Accounting Information," defines materiality as "the magnitude of an omission or misstatement of accounting information that, in the light of surrounding circumstances, makes it probable that the judgment of a reasonable person relying on the information would have been changed or influenced by the omission or misstatement."[2] This definition suggests that materiality should be viewed in terms of both qualitative and quantitative aspects.[3] As an example, many auditors set financial statement materiality at five percent of pre-tax income. However, when planning the audit and computing financial statement materiality, whether the auditor uses the prior year's actual income, an average of previous years' income, annualized current year-to-date income, or a forecast of current year income is a judgmental decision. In making that decision, the auditor should consider such things as current economic conditions, trend of earnings, and the company's historical ability to forecast income. Further, if the company is operating in a breakeven situation, a measure of materiality based on financial position may be more appropriate than one based on net income.

There may be potential errors (as defined above) in various areas which, in the aggregate, could be material to the financial statements taken as a whole. In these instances, it may be helpful to establish a specific audit materiality guideline in the form of an amount below which the auditor would not be concerned with potential errors. To illustrate, assume that financial statement materiality for a company is established at $250,000. In this case, the auditor might decide that any potential errors below $25,000 would not be of concern if the auditor can reasonably expect the aggregate effect of all such errors to be less than $250,000. The determination of a materiality guideline for this purpose should be based on current environ-

---

[2] Financial Accounting Standards Board, *Statement of Financial Accounting Concepts No. 2,* "Qualitative Characteristics of Accounting Information," 1980, p. xv. Copyright by Financial Accounting Standards Board, High Ridge Park, Stamford, Connecticut, 06905, U.S.A. Reprinted with permission. Copies of the complete document are available from the FASB.

[3] See Ibid., par. 125.

mental factors and the number and dollar amount of errors experienced in the past.

The auditor should distinguish the likelihood of material error from the concept of materiality itself. For example, property, plant, and equipment is frequently the largest balance sheet classification for a manufacturing client; however, ordinarily the auditor places considerably more audit emphasis on inventories because of the higher likelihood of material error.

PRELIMINARY AUDIT APPROACH

The preliminary audit approach is a list of the audit procedures to be performed for the aspects (e.g., validity, completeness, accuracy) of accounts or transactions affected by each specific control objective. The development of the preliminary audit approach on separate risk analysis working papers for each audit engagement provides the auditor an opportunity to focus attention on these aspects in developing the minimum audit effort necessary to become satisfied that the accounts or transactions are free of material error. Further, the preliminary audit approach allows the reviewer of the working paper and audit program to effectively challenge whether the planned approach is efficient and the combination of evidence to be provided will be sufficiently persuasive, thus holding detection risk to an acceptable level.

The preliminary audit approach should be responsive to the underlying reasons for the auditor's assessment of the likelihood of material error. For example, consider the situation where the likelihood of material error is low, principally because the auditor believes the system design achieves the specific control objective and *control risk* is low. In this case, the preliminary audit approach should include tests of the functioning of the key attributes that provide reasonable assurance of achieving the specific control objective. In other cases, the system evaluation may not be important to the assessment of the likelihood of material error. For example, the review of the environment may indicate that virtually all of a client's sales are made to several blue-chip customers and *inherent risk* is low. In this instance, evaluation and testing of the credit review function would not be necessary and the procedures might be limited to an analytical review of the year-end aging.

The preliminary audit approach should also be responsive to the risk analysis for each objective. For example, the inventory and production reporting systems may provide reliable information on usage and movement of physical quantities, but the pricing procedures may not be effective. The preliminary audit approach should provide for reliance on systems as to physical quantities and for performance of price tests designed to detect pricing errors.

The persuasiveness of audit evidence is derived from three variables: nature, timing, and extent of audit procedures. Each should be considered in designing a preliminary audit approach. The combinations are numerous, but the assessment of the likelihood of material error and the underlying risk analysis provide a basis for the auditor to choose the most efficient and effective mix of nature, timing, and extent.

Keep in mind that the auditor's overall goal is to obtain sufficient competent evidential matter to render an opinion on the financial statements taken as a whole. Making a judgment as to the likelihood of material error on each risk analysis working paper gives an indication of the degree of persuasiveness of evidence required to meet that overall goal. The auditor translates this into the audit tests necessary to become satisfied that the accounts affected by each specific control objective are free of material error. As a general rule, the higher the likelihood of material error, the more persuasive the evidence should be.

Different auditors will arrive at different conclusions as to the mix and timing of procedures. The risk analysis is not intended to result in a "canned" audit program. What is important is that (1) there be a rational and consistent approach for identifying the risks associated with each engagement and (2) an audit approach be developed that is responsive to these risks. The risk analysis should provide a reason for performing each procedure. As a result, the audit program should include all the necessary, but no unnecessary, procedures.

NATURE OF AUDIT PROCEDURES

The lists of audit procedures provided in Appendix II at the end of this textbook are good starting points for deciding on the nature of tests. However, to choose the most effective and efficient combination of procedures responsive to the likelihood of material error and the underlying risk analysis, the auditor should consider the evidence each procedure may provide.

As discussed in Chapter 2 (page 37) the auditing literature suggests that there are two types of audit procedures to choose from:

Compliance tests—to test the extent to which established controls and procedures are functioning as intended.

Substantive tests—to test or support the validity and the propriety of specific transactions or account balances.

Conceptually, this may be an important distinction; however, in practice the results of either type of test may contribute toward the purpose of the other. Errors having an impact on the financial statements may be discovered when conducting compliance tests, and compliance exceptions may be discovered when conducting substantive tests. Further, substantive tests can confirm or challenge the evaluation of the effectiveness of the accounting system, which is generally the purpose of compliance tests. Although a test may have a primary purpose (compliance or substantive), the same sample of transactions or balances often is used to obtain both types of evidence. These are sometimes referred to as "dual-purpose" tests.

The auditor achieves efficiency when performing tests that provide evidence about both the operation of key attributes and the validity and propriety of amounts. Many tests of transactions can be designed to enhance their capacity to yield both types of evidence. For example, tests of the key authorization and recording attributes related to cash disbursements can be designed to include large property additions through an interim date. As a result, year-end examination of invoices and other support for property additions might be significantly limited or omitted, and overall satisfaction might be obtained by an analytical review of the level of additions for the year.

Competence of Evidence

The selection among alternative audit procedures should consider the competence of the evidence they provide. This is illustrated by the choice between use of positive or negative accounts receivable confirmation requests and between requesting confirmation of balances or invoice amounts. For example, certain department stores and governmental agencies generally are not able to confirm account balances. Requests for confirmation of selected invoices would yield more competent evidence than requests for confirmation of balances mailed to those debtors. Similarly, negative confirmation requests would not yield competent evidence if there is reason to believe that request might fail to receive consideration or that the respondent would be unable to determine whether the information is correct. But negative requests are particularly useful for accumulating competent evidence when the likelihood of material error is low, a large number of small balances are involved, and there is reason to believe the request will receive consideration. For example, negative requests may be appropriate for magazine or cable TV subscriptions or retail store credit sales. Whether positive or negative requests are used, the auditor should be sure respondents have the information necessary to reply.

Testing Key Attributes

When the system evaluation indicates that there is reasonable assurance that specific control objectives are being achieved, the auditor should plan to obtain evidence that the key attributes identified are functioning. For example, the auditor may conclude that the system design provides reasonable assurance that the specific control objective, "Cash receipts are recorded correctly as to account, amount, and period and are deposited" is being achieved. The key attribute that supports the conclusion is an independent reconciliation of a prelisting of cash receipts to cash deposited and credits to accounts receivable. The auditor might test this key attribute by examining a representative sample of prelistings and reviewing evidence that they were reconciled to the bank deposit slips and the credits to accounts receivable. Or the auditor might use the sample of shipments selected for tests of credit review and billing procedures. In the latter case, the auditor would trace the subsequent cash receipt from the credit in Accounts Receivable to the applicable prelisting and the daily total to the reconciliation. The nature of audit procedures outlined in the preliminary audit approach will depend on the unique characteristics of the system. In any case, the preliminary audit approach should specify the key attributes to be tested and the nature and extent of the tests.

Frequently, key attributes do not leave documentary evidence. Therefore, the auditor cannot design tests to examine evidence that these procedures have been applied to transactions. The auditor can, however, obtain evidence of their functioning by observation of and discussion with employees involved in the process. For example, at the time the mail is opened, the office receptionist may prepare a daily listing of cash receipts which is sent to the president's secretary for comparison with the day's bank deposit. The prelisting is discarded after the amounts have been compared and reconciled, leaving no documentary evidence that the procedure ever took place. In this case, the auditor might inquire of the receptionist, accounts receivable bookkeeper, and employee responsible for preparing the bank deposit about the comparison process and the frequency with which questions arise. The auditor also should observe the prelisting and comparison processes.

When the auditor tests key attributes that relate to independent reviews, approvals, comparisons, recalculations, or reconciliations, inquiries should be made of the responsible individuals to determine that they understand their responsibilities and how exceptions are resolved. The auditor should do more than just examine documents and records, and the preliminary audit approach should reflect that.

In some cases, even though the system design provides reasonable assurance that control objectives are being achieved, the auditor may decide not to test key attributes. This is because the auditor may instead choose to perform direct tests of balances when this approach is a more efficient method of arriving at the same level of persuasive audit evidence. In other cases, the system evaluation may indicate that specific control objectives are not being achieved and tests of key attributes are not appropriate. In these cases, the auditor should plan to test transactions, but the purpose of the test would be to detect material errors rather than to test the functioning of key attributes.

Developing a Balance of Procedures

The preliminary audit approach should cover both interim and year-end procedures. Both tests of transactions and direct tests of balances may be performed at either time. The preliminary audit approach should lead to an audit program that provides sufficient evidence upon which to base an opinion at the least cost to the client. In many cases, this will involve (1) using tests of transactions to test both the functioning of key attributes (thus maximizing reliance on the client's system of internal control) and the correctness of balances and (2) limiting direct tests of balances (and using analytical review procedures as direct tests wherever possible). By integrating tests of transactions with direct tests of balances, the auditor maximizes the benefits provided by all audit procedures.

Understanding the interrelationship of specific transactions and accounts is critical to the development of an appropriate preliminary audit approach. Account balances result from a stream of transactions represented by the debits and credits to the accounts. Generally, transactions flow into and out of balance sheet accounts as they continue through the business cycle. On the other hand, income statement accounts generally contain an accumulation of transactions that have passed through one or more balance sheet accounts over a period of time. For example, the accounts receivable balance at any point in time is comprised of a series of sales, sales adjustments, and cash receipts transactions. Tests might be directed to the transactions, the balance, or both. Generally, a combination is appropriate, varying from extensive tests of transactions with only a review of reasonableness of the ending balance, to little or no tests of transactions and a detail analysis of the ending balance. The choice in each case will depend on the inputs to the risk analysis and the resulting assessment of the likelihood of error.

By recognizing how a transaction affects various accounts, the maximum benefit of tests of transactions can be achieved, and direct tests of balances needed to arrive at an audit conclusion can be limited. For example, in developing the preliminary audit approach for the accounts receivable of a client with effective sales and cash receipts systems the auditor might plan to:

1. Test sales, sales adjustments, and cash receipts transactions to establish the validity and the timely, accurate recording of the recurring debit and credit entries to accounts receivable.
2. Review credit approval and collection activity to determine the likelihood of uncollectible accounts occurring and not being provided for on a timely basis.
3. Limit direct tests of accounts receivable balance to analytical review, tests of cutoff, and a minimum of account circularization. In addition, when performing alternate procedures on nonreplies to confirmation requests, examination of remittance advices would not be required (because cash receipts were previously tested).

If the auditor's evaluation of the accounting system indicates that specific control objectives are not being achieved, the relative emphasis of planned tests of transactions and direct tests of balances would be different. The relative emphasis would depend on the nature of possible errors or irregularities and the effectiveness of audit procedures for detecting them. Specifically, when an objective is not achieved, the primary effects on the preliminary audit approach are:

Nature—direct tests of balances are substituted for certain tests of transactions.

Timing—direct tests of balances are performed closer to year-end.

Extent—certain tests are applied to more items.

TIMING OF AUDIT PROCEDURES

A timing decision is made for virtually every type of audit procedure. The decision is basically one of choosing to perform a procedure at an interim date or at year-end. The most difficult aspect of the timing decision is the determination of how early in the year audit procedures can be effectively and efficiently performed. Timing will depend primarily on the likelihood of material error—especially as it is affected by the system evaluation—and on the nature of the audit procedures. Timing also will depend on the auditor's schedule and client deadlines.

An effective control environment leads the auditor to expect that key attributes tested at an interim date will continue to function during the entire year. Thus, the effectiveness of the control environment helps the auditor judge how early in the year tests of key attiributes can be performed.

If the client requests that the auditor complete the audit shortly after year-end, performing a procedure as of an interim date and taking advantage of reliable accounting systems is often the only practical approach. And where there is a strong control environment and control objectives are being achieved, the auditor may decide to perform most direct tests of balances as of one, two, or even three months before year-end. Minimal testing of intervening transactions and year-end analytical review procedures can supply whatever other evidence the auditor considers necessary to be persuasive. However, this approach would not be appropriate where, for example, there is a history of substantial inventory adjustments, unless there is a reasonable basis for providing for the adjustment from the inventory date to year-end.

The timing of some procedures often will depend on the timing of other procedures. For example, the out-of-period search for amounts due to inventory suppliers should be performed as of the physical inventory date.

EXTENT OF TESTING CONSIDERATIONS

The number of items to be tested should be based upon the importance of the particular audit procedure in responding to the likelihood of material error in the accounts or transactions affected by each specific control objective [see *SAS No. 39,* "Audit Sampling" (AU 350.17)]. An audit procedure will be less important to the auditor's conclusion if it is part of a combination of procedures that will provide evidence for the same accounts and transactions. In this situation, the extent of each procedure may be limited. On the other hand, if the auditor plans a procedure that is to be the primary basis for the audit conclusion, more work is needed.

The importance of each audit procedure and the characteristics of the accounts or transactions being audited are the basis for determining the appropriate extent of testing. There are two extent of testing strategies: selecting and examining either (1) key items or (2) a representative sample. For compliance tests, a representative sample is appropriate. Either strategy may be used for substantive tests; frequently, a combination will be appropriate. *SAS No. 39* (AU 350.21) covers these strategies, which also are discussed below.

Key Items

The first step in selecting specific items for direct tests of balances (substantive tests) is to identify any transactions or accounts that are individually important either because of their size or because the auditor believes there is a high likelihood of error. These items are called key items and include:

1. Transactions having a high degree of management involvement (e.g., related party transactions).
2. Transactions requiring subjective judgments (e.g., allowance for loan losses in a bank, percentage of completion estimates for a contractor, claim reserves for an insurance company, or inventory valuation adjustments for a manufacturer).
3. Large or unusual transactions recorded as of or near year-end or an interim valuation date (e.g., large sales just before or after year-end or the physical inventory date).
4. Old items (e.g., past-due receivables or slow-moving inventory).
5. Other large or unusual transactions.

Sometimes examining key items will provide sufficient coverage so that there is little risk that the remaining items contain a material error. In these cases, no further testing is necessary.

Representative Samples

After performing direct tests of key items, there often remain items that are individually unimportant but are significant in total. These populations can consist of either transactions through a point in time (e.g., sales or cash disbursements through an interim date); items comprising an account balance at a point in time (e.g., individual parts in a year-end inventory or customer accounts receivable balances at an interim date); or key attributes applied to groups of transactions (e.g., reconciliations, edit reports, or batch controls).

For these populations, it will be necessary to audit a "representative" sample, unless other planned procedures, such as analytical review, provide sufficient evidence for concluding that the population is free of material error. A representative sample is one the auditor expects to reflect the characteristics of the population from which it is selected. Representative sampling allows the auditor to determine that (1) key attributes are functioning to provide reasonable assurance that specific control objectives are being achieved and/or (2) amounts comprising an account balance or class of transactions are free of material error.

The representativeness of a sample is a key assumption in drawing a conclusion about the population from which the sample was taken. There are two requirements for assuring that samples are representative:

1. The sample should be large enough.
2. Each item in the population should have a chance of selection.

Minimum Sample Size

The risk of drawing improper conclusions from the results of a representative sample varies inversely with the sample size; that is, the more items examined, the smaller the risk. Professional auditing literature [*SAS No. 39* (AU 350.33 and .36)] suggests a minimum representative sample size[4] to provide a basis for relying on the results. This minimum sample size will be appropriate *only* when:

1. No errors which would affect the audit conclusion about the population are expected; *and*
2. The test is only *one of the bases* for the audit conclusion (i.e., other audit procedures—tests of transactions and direct tests of balances, including analytical review—provide corroborative evidence that key attributes are functioning and/or account balances are free of material error).

Tests of less than the minimum are merely walk-throughs. They should be performed as part of the review of the systems documentation during program development. The auditor may learn something from these procedures but not enough to limit other procedures.

---

[4] In discussing tolerable error rates, *SAS No. 39* (AU 350.33) uses 10 percent as an example if less than substantial reliance is to be placed on a key attribute. Also, a footnote to AU 350.36 uses 10 percent as an example of risk level for a test of key attributes. Using attribute sampling theory (discussed in Chapter 8) and an expected error rate of zero with these parameters, results in a sample size of 22. We have adjusted this to 25 for setting a minimum sample size for either a compliance or a substantive test.

In testing key attributes, the auditor should plan a sample size of at least 25 or challenge the benefit to be gained from the test. If a sample of 25 seems like too much work, the auditor may be able to identify a better way of achieving the audit objective. In many cases, the auditor may find that the test is important and requires coverage of a representative sample of at least 25 items. The key questions the auditor should consider are "What am I trying to accomplish?" "Can the procedures on another sample be extended to cover the purpose of this limited test?" The use of one sample to accomplish several purposes can be particularly efficient. For example, the auditor should consider using a sample of shippers for testing credit approval, processing of sales, and recording of cash receipts. In this case, the auditor can use the same sample to test the transaction from its inception (order entry) to its consumation (receipt of cash).

As discussed in Chapter 8, the results from auditing most representative samples can be statistically evaluated. However, these results should be combined with the corroborative evidence obtained from other audit procedures—including analytical review. The auditor then can judgmentally conclude that (1) key attributes are functioning to provide reasonable assurance that specific control objectives are being achieved, and/or (2) amounts comprising an account balance or class of transactions are free of material error. If errors are detected, additional work will be necessary.

Representative Samples of More than the Minimum—Using Statistical Sampling

The "representative" portion of a test should include more than the minimum number of sample items under any of the following conditions:

1. *No errors are expected* and auditing the representative sample is the *primary basis* for a conclusion in an important audit area (i.e., the account balance or dollar value of transactions is clearly material, analytical review procedures are not particularly useful, and no other test of details is being performed).
2. *Errors are expected* and auditing the representative sample is *one of the bases* for a conclusion in an important audit area (i.e., the evidence from analytical review procedures and other tests of details is combined with the results of the representative sample to support the auditor's conclusion).
3. *Errors are expected* and auditing the representative sample is the *primary basis* for a conclusion in an important audit area.

The number of items to be included in any sample in excess of the minimum can be judgmentally determined. However, when the audit of a representative sample is to be the primary basis for the auditor's conclusion, there are statistical sampling techniques that are particularly useful for evaluating the results of the tests.

No Errors Expected and Audit Procedure Is Primary Basis for Conclusion. There are many situations where errors are not expected, but the audit of the representative sample is the primary basis for the auditor's conclusion in an audit area. This would be the case when the following conditions are present:

1. The account balance or class of transactions is clearly material.
2. Analytical review procedures are not particularly useful (either no relevant relationships exist or results would not be conclusive).
3. The evidence provided by auditing the representative sample can, by itself, be persuasive that no material error exists in the audit area.

Probability proportional to size (PPS) and discovery sampling (a form of attribute sampling) are statistical techniques that may be useful in these situations. These methods allow the auditor to specify a representative sample size that, if no errors are encountered, provides a desired level of assurance that there is no more than a certain dollar amount (PPS) or rate (discovery) of error in the population. Discovery and PPS sampling are described in Chapters 8 and 9, respectively.

Errors Expected. When errors are expected and the test is one of the bases for the auditor's conclusion, the auditor can select a representative sample of more than 25 items and project the results to estimate the total error in the population. Projection of errors is discussed further in "Quantifying Errors in Recorded Amounts" later in this chapter.

When errors are expected and the test is the primary basis for the auditor's conclusion, the auditor should use variables estimation sampling, a statistical technique used to estimate a dollar range within which the true audited value of the population lies. Variables estimation sampling is described in Chapter 9.

Figure 7–1 summarizes the strategies for extent of testing and may serve as a useful reference.

SELECTING REPRESENTATIVE SAMPLES

SAS No. 39 (AU 350.24) states that "sample items should be selected in such a way that the sample can be expected to be representative of the population. Therefore, all items in the population should have an opportunity to be selected. For example, random-based selection of items represents one method of obtaining such samples. . . ." *SAS No. 39* identifies the following four examples of random-based selection: "random sampling," "systematic sampling . . . with one or more random starts," "stratified random sampling," and "sampling with probability proportional to size." "Chapters 8 and 9 discuss each of these random selection techniques. To avoid biasing

FIGURE 7-1 Summary of Strategies for Extent of Testing

Conditions	Strategy	Number of Items
Individually important items because of size or likelihood of error	Key items	All
Remaining items individually unimportant but significant in total, and:		
No errors expected; test is one of the bases for conclusion	Minimum representative sample	At least 25*
No errors expected; test is primary basis for conclusion	Representative sample of more than minimum	More than 25
	Consider:	
	PPS sampling—to determine maximum dollar amount of error; concern is with higher value items	Based on desired reliability and tolerable error (e.g., 90 percent reliability and 3.3 percent of balance considered material— 70 items)
	or	
	Discovery sampling—to verify that percentage of items in error is within an acceptable range; no reason to emphasize higher value items	Based on desired reliability and tolerable error rate (e.g., 95 percent reliability and 5 percent acceptable error rate—60 items)
Errors expected; test is one of the bases for conclusion	Representative sample of more than minimum—to estimate dollar amount of error by projection	More than 25
Errors expected; test is primary basis for conclusion	Variables estimation sampling—to estimate dollar value of population or total dollar amount of error	Based on desired reliability, tolerable error, and population characteristics—at least 100 items
*Errors found	Expand sample to estimate either extent of noncompliance or amount of error	

Notes
(1) Tests of 1, 2, 5, or 10 items are walk-throughs made as part of the review of system documentation (*not* a basis for reaching a conclusion about the population or limiting other procedures).
(2) Many tests will cover key items and a representative sample of the remaining population.
(3) See Chapter 8 for an explanation of the concept of "tolerable error."

a sample, the use of block samples (groups of consecutive items) or judgmental samples should be avoided.

OTHER SAMPLING CONSIDERATIONS

Generally, the size of the population does not influence the size of a representative sample to be audited. However, for very small populations (e.g., 50 or 100 items), examining a representative sample to test key attributes is probably not an efficient way of supporting the related account balance or class of transactions. In these cases, analytical review procedures or direct tests of key items may provide greater comfort as to the reasonableness of the balance or the transaction total. For example, total payroll expense for a company with 50 or 100 employees can be estimated by extending average pay rates by the number of employees in each of the various classes and verifying pay for key employees by reference to approval by the board of directors.

Many key attributes are applied only once each day (e.g., reconciliations, edit reports, or batch controls). If it is an important procedure that will provide a basis for reducing the extent of other audit procedures, the auditor should examine evidence of at least 25 applications of the procedure. However, in these cases it is not necessary to verify all aspects of the procedure for 25 different days. Because the purpose of the test is to determine that the procedure is being performed, it ordinarily would be sufficient to support the details of only one and review the rest for unusual items.

For example, if the procedure is a daily reconciliation of shipping documents and customer invoices, the auditor should discuss the procedure with the personnel who are responsible for it and review one or two reconciliations thoroughly to determine that the personnel understand what they are doing. Then the auditor need only determine that the remaining reconciliations are being performed and that any unusual items are handled properly.

Similarly, with respect to monthly reconciliations, the auditor might verify one and merely examine the others for unusual reconciling items. For example, if independently prepared bank reconciliations are identified as a key attribute, the auditor might limit his or her work to (1) verification of the bank and book balances, deposits in transit, and outstanding checks for one interim month's reconciliation; (2) examination of remaining reconciliations (throughout the year or through an interim date) to ascertain that they were prepared independently of the cash receipts and disbursements functions and to identify any unusual items; (3) review of the year-end reconciliation and the items returned with the cutoff bank statement; and (4) confirmation of the year-end bank balance. In this case, there would be no need for more extensive procedures at interim (e.g., preparation of a proof of cash) or complete verification of the year-end reconciliation.

EVALUATING ERRORS IN AUDIT TESTS

It is important to remember that audit procedures are designed, in part, based on the auditor's expectations. Therefore, an important aspect of evaluating audit tests is to compare the results with the expectations upon which the tests were designed. Finding errors of any size when none were expected is more significant than finding errors when they were expected. This is true for both tests of key attributes and tests for correctness of recorded amounts.

Errors are known misstatements in recorded amounts based upon facts existing at the completion of the auditor's field work.[5] Errors also include lack of compliance with a key attribute. As stated earlier, the assessment of the likelihood of material error should consider errors and judgmental differences, i.e., potential misstatements based on differences in subjective estimates, the ultimate determination of which depends upon future events.

Qualitative Analysis

When the auditor finds an error (misstated recorded amount or lack of compliance with a key attribute), an attempt should be made to determine its cause before either dismissing it as inconsequential or expanding procedures. The auditor also should discuss the error with the client. Knowing the cause of an error will help determine the (1) potential for additional errors of a similar type and (2) need for changes in the audit program. The auditor might find that the error is either "systematic" or apparently random, and it may be either intentional or unintentional.

A "systematic" error—one that is expected to occur in every similar item in the population—would lead the auditor to review similar items. An apparently random occurrence is more difficult to evaluate. If it is believed to be an intentional circumvention of prescribed procedures, the auditor should attempt to find out how it occurred. The suspicion or detection of any defalcation or other irregularity should be carefully considered and investigated. Chapter 4 discusses the auditor's responsibilities in those situations.

If the auditor believes the error to be unintentional, attempts should be made to determine whether it resulted from a lack of understanding of prescribed procedures or from other human factors such as fatigue or carelessness. A misunderstanding could result in a systematic error (e.g., the use of an incorrect formula by a salesclerk for converting pounds to linear feet for billing purposes would result in errors in recording every sale that required such a conversion). Often, it will be necessary to have the client correct the effects of a systematic error.

When human error (due to fatigue, carelessness, etc.) is detected, the auditor should consider the probability that similar errors have occurred that might prevent reliance on the accounting system or cause a material error in the financial statements. If the auditor identifies what is believed to be an isolated instance of lack of compliance with a key attribute and plans to continue reliance on the accounting system, the auditor should

---

[5] *SAS No. 39* (AU 350.25) suggests that if an auditor is unable to apply planned audit procedures to a sample item (e.g., the supporting documentation is missing), it should be considered an error (rather than be replaced) when evaluating sample results. However, a selected item that is not part of the defined population (e.g., a void check or a customer account with a credit balance when the defined population is all positive customer balances) should be replaced and not considered an error.

increase the sample size to estimate the probable maximum error rate. Chapter 8 discusses this point further.

Quantifying Errors in Recorded Amounts

Errors may be quantified by specific identification, projection of sample results (statistical or nonstatistical), or approximation using analytical review where the likelihood of material error is either moderate or high.

If the auditor has tested key items and concludes that any errors found are systematic, the auditor should perform additional procedures or have the client perform procedures to quantify the total amount of these errors. If the auditor believes the error is clearly an isolated occurrence, the working papers should document the basis for that conclusion.

Any errors in key items for which the auditor is unable to determine the cause or that are otherwise apparently random may be indicative of similar errors in the remaining portion of the population. To quantify the potential amount of similar errors, the auditor should project the amount of the apparently random errors to the remaining portion of the population that was not tested. Alternatively, the auditor could examine a representative sample selected from the untested items. Errors in the representative sample should be projected to the portion of the population from which the sample was drawn, and the projected error should be added to the errors in the key items. If the auditor has tested a representative sample only, all errors should be projected to the population. These points are demonstrated in Figure 7–2. The techniques used in making these projections in statistical samples are discussed in detail in Chapters 8 and 9.

If the projected error exceeds the amount of error the auditor or the client is willing to tolerate, the auditor should consider whether a more precise approximation of the amount of error is needed. For example, if the initial sample was based on a low likelihood of material error, the auditor might test additional items or perform a different audit procedure.

If the auditor expands tests to include more items, the projection should be based upon the expanded sample. If the auditor obtains a more precise approximation of the error from a different audit procedure (e.g., analytical review), it may be used instead of the projection. Any difference between the auditor's estimate of the error based on all the available evidence and the amount of any correction recorded by the client should be aggregated with other possible misstatements in evaluating whether the financial statements may be materially misstated.

Approximations Using Analytical Review

Analytical review procedures that are used as the primary direct test of a balance ordinarily result in a difference from the recorded amount. If

FIGURE 7-2 Projecting Errors

Key Items Only

$$\frac{\text{Amount of error in key items}}{\text{Dollar amount of key items}} \times \frac{\text{Dollar amount of}}{\text{population}} = \frac{\text{Projected}}{\text{error}}$$

For example, if the auditor finds $15,000 of pricing errors in a test of large dollar inventory items with a recorded amount of $800,000 from a total inventory of $1,500,000, the projected error would be $28,125, calculated as follows:

$$\$15,000/\$800,000 \times \$1,500,000 = \$28,125$$

Representative Sample Only*

$$\frac{\text{Amount of error in representative sample}}{\text{Dollar amount of representative sample}} \times \frac{\text{Dollar amount of}}{\text{population}} = \frac{\text{Projected}}{\text{error}}$$

For example, if the auditor finds $300 of billing errors in a representative sample of $20,000 from total credit card receivables of $1,000,000, the projected error would be $15,000, calculated as follows:

$$\$300/\$20,000 \times \$1,000,000 = \$15,000$$

Key Items and a Representative Sample*

$$\frac{\text{Amount of error}}{\text{in key items}} + \left(\frac{\text{Amount of error in representative sample}}{\text{Dollar amount of representative sample}} \times \frac{\text{Dollar amount of}}{\text{population, excluding key items}} \right) = \frac{\text{Projected}}{\text{error}}$$

For example, if the auditor finds $8,000 of pricing errors in a test of large dollar inventory items with a recorded amount of $400,000 and $200 of errors in a representative sample of $40,000 from the remaining inventory of $2,000,000, the projected error would be $18,000, calculated as follows:

$$\$8,000 + (\$200/\$40,000 \times \$2,000,000) = \$18,000$$

* Chapter 9 discusses the techniques for making these projections when variables estimation and PPS sampling are used.

the auditor believes that the recorded amount is essentially correct because the likelihood of material error was assessed as low and the difference probably is due to the use of averages, the difference should not be considered an error. However, if the auditor believes the analytical review procedure provides a better approximation of the correct amount of the balance because the likelihood of material error was assessed as either moderate or high, any unadjusted difference should be considered an error. For example, the client may have an unreliable cost accounting and production reporting system—no key attributes relating to pricing of inventory and a history of large book-to-physical adjustments. The audit program might include an analytical review procedure to approximate the labor and overhead costs in ending inventory (e.g., by using the relationship of inventoriable labor and overhead costs for the year to materials put into production). In this case, any difference between the approximation and the recorded amount, after any client adjustments, is an audit difference that should be aggregated with other possible misstatements in evaluating whether the financial statements may be materially misstated.

Judgmental Differences.   Management is required to make estimates about the effect of future events on the valuation of certain amounts in its financial statements (e.g., allowances for bad debts and inventory obsolescence, accruals for warranty costs, losses from plant closing, and income taxes). The auditor's analysis of these estimates generally should lead to a range of acceptable amounts. For example, the auditor may believe the allowance for bad debts should be between $30,000 and $50,000. If management's recorded estimate falls within the auditor's acceptance range, the auditor ordinarily would conclude that the recorded amount is reasonable.

In other situations, management's recorded estimates will not fall within the acceptance range. Any amount outside the auditor's acceptance range that is due to different expectations about future events or what the auditor believes may be management's inappropriate consideration of relevant facts and circumstances is a judgmental difference. For example, from the analysis of specific problem accounts, aging of receivables, and recent trends of bad debt write-offs as a percent of sales, the auditor concludes that the allowance should be between $130,000 and $160,000. However, management believes that because of the addition of a new collection specialist, write-offs will decrease. Therefore, $100,000 is recorded as the allowance. The amount by which the recorded estimate falls outside of the auditor's acceptance range ($30,000) is an audit difference that should be aggregated with other possible misstatements in evaluating whether the financial statements may be materially misstated. Any amount outside the acceptance range that is due to mistakes in preparing the estimate (e.g., clerical errors) should be considered an error, not a judgmental difference.

The next section discusses one method of aggregating these differences.

Summary of Audit Differences

Differences encountered during the audit for which the client does not make adjustments should be summarized to evaluate the materiality of their aggregate effect on the financial statements. The auditor can document the process on a working paper, called a summary of audit differences. Audit differences include both errors and judgmental differences as defined in the sections above.

Format of the Summary. One format for a summary is to include separate columns for current year differences (both errors and judgmental differences), prior year errors, and prior year judgmental differences. It may show each type of item individually (e.g., inventory pricing errors, inventory quantity errors) or an appropriate combination of items (e.g., all items affecting inventory). Figure 7–3 is an example of such a summary.

Evaluation of Materiality. The auditor evaluates whether the individual or combined effect of items on the summary either cause the financial statements to be materially misstated or require consideration of additional disclosure. This evaluation involves both quantitative and qualitative considerations and requires the use of professional judgment. In addition to the effect of differences on net income, the auditor considers their effect on any other measurements that may be important, such as working capital, shareholders' equity, trend of earnings, or amounts related to debt covenant requirements. Other factors to consider (which are discussed below) include: (1) recurring differences and (2) the appropriateness of taking a more conservative position in certain circumstances.

Current Year Differences. As an initial point of reference in evaluating materiality of audit differences, the auditor considers the aggregate effect on current year net income (and any other important amounts) of errors and judgmental differences that remain unadjusted at the end of the year. For example, in Figure 7–3, the total effect on the income statement of correcting all audit differences is $30,600, or 2.9 percent. When evaluating the significance of recurring differences whose aggregate effects are currently immaterial but tend to increase each year (e.g., expense accruals), the auditor considers the likelihood of their having a material future effect (e.g., if the entity should decide to correct an entire difference by a charge to income in one year).

Prior Year Errors. Ordinarily, unadjusted errors (specifically identified, projected, or approximated) at the end of the prior year are considered in evaluating materiality because they may affect the fair presentation of current year net income. An immaterial unadjusted error from the prior year might cause current year net income to be materially misstated when it is considered along with current year differences. Or material current year differences might be immaterial when they are considered along with errors that are carried forward from the prior year. For example, if expenses are underaccrued by $10,000 at the end of 19X1, net income in 19X2 is understated because the expenses are erroneously charged in 19X2. If audit differences at the end of 19X2 cause net income to be overstated by $15,000, the combined effect is a $5,000 overstatement of 19X2 income.

FIGURE 7–3 Example of Summary of Audit Differences Working Paper

SUMMARY OF AUDIT DIFFERENCES
ABC MANUFACTURING CORP.
12/31/X5

	Increase (Decrease) Income		
		Prior Year	
	Current Year Differences	Errors	Judgmental Differences
Errors:			
Underaccrual of vacation pay	$(30,000)	$(24,000)	
Unrecorded payables	(21,000)	(28,000)	
Inventory cutoff	(10,000)	5,000	
	$(61,000)	$(47,000)	
Judgmental differences:			
Allowance for bad debts	$(30,000)		$(20,000)
Inventory obsolescence	(4,000)		
Plant closing overaccrual	35,000		35,000
	$ 1,000		$ 15,000
	$(60,000)	$(47,000)	$ 15,000
Tax effect	(29,400)	(23,000)	7,400
	$ 30,600	$(24,000)	$ 7,600
Judgmental difference in accrual for income taxes			15,000
Net effect	$(30,600)	$(24,000)	$ 22,600
	(2.9% of net income)		

CONCLUSION STATEMENT

The following factors have been considered in evaluating whether the financial statements are materially misstated:

1. The client intends to revise its policy for accruing vacation pay next year; so this error will not increase in future years.
2. Current year differences are immaterial to working capital and shareholders' equity and would not affect any debt covenant requirements.*
3. We also considered the following factors in evaluating whether current year net income is fairly stated:

Net effect of current year differences	$(30,600)
Eliminate $35,000 plant closing overaccrual from current year differences (facts and circumstances are essentially unchanged from the prior year), net of tax effect	(17,900)
Net effect of prior year errors on current net income	24,000
Reduction by the client of prior year overaccrual for income taxes during the current year with no change in circumstances	(15,000)
Possible overstatement of net income	$(39,500)
	(3.8% of net income)

Based on the above analysis, it is my opinion that the effects of audit differences, considering the other factors noted above, are not material to the financial statements of ABC Manufacturing Corp. for the year ended December 31, 19X5.

---

* If it is not obvious from the summary, the auditor should document the calculations to support this statement in the working papers.

In some cases, judgment regarding materiality may focus on financial position; so it may be inappropriate to offset prior year errors that reduce a current year overstatement of income. For example, auditors often take more conservative positions in evaluating the materiality of audit differences for companies that are in a troubled financial condition or are likely to be acquired.

Prior Year Judgmental Differences. Ordinarily, unadjusted judgmental differences at the end of the prior year are not considered in evaluating materiality in the current year. Differences between recorded estimates and the actual amounts ultimately required can be due to changes in conditions or different interpretations of facts and circumstances existing when the estimates were recorded. Changes in estimates are properly includible in the current year.

However, if the facts and circumstances regarding a recorded estimate from the prior year are essentially the same, it normally is appropriate to offset a prior year judgmental difference relating to the estimate against the current year differences when evaluating materiality. For example, an auditor may have concluded in the prior year that an accrual for a plant closing was overstated. If no changes occurred in the facts and circumstances during the current year and the overaccrual remains, it is appropriate to offset the prior overaccrual against the current overaccrual in evaluating materiality.

The auditor also should consider the effect on current year net income of any changes in prior year recorded estimates when they are made in the absence of any changes in circumstances since the prior year. For example, management may adjust prior year overaccruals (judgmental differences) to smooth earnings during a period of declining operations. In Figure 7–3, the reduction by the client of the prior year overaccrual for income taxes is an example. Further, there may be situations where unadjusted judgmental differences are immaterial in the year in which passed but have a material effect when adjusted in the following year without a change in circumstances. Although an auditor could conclude that the balance sheet is fairly stated in these circumstances (because no unadjusted current year differences remain), consideration is given to disclosing the income statement effect of the adjustments to keep the financial statements from being misleading.

Immaterial Changes in Accounting Principles. While auditors may conclude that these changes do not require separate disclosure, they consider their effect when combined with the net effect of items on the summary. For example, $100,000 of income from a change in accounting principle might be considered immaterial and not require disclosure. However, if the summary includes $100,000 of unadjusted differences that result in an overstatement of income, the combined effect might be material—especially to the trend of earnings. The auditor might therefore conclude that either separate disclosure of the change in accounting principle or an adjustment of the differences is necessary to keep the financial statements from being misleading.

Conclusion Statement

A conclusion statement explains the evaluation of the materiality of items in the summary, including consideration of other relevant factors, such as those discussed above.

COMPUTER-ASSISTED AUDIT TECHNIQUES[6]

When a company utilizes a computer in its accounting system, an auditor often is able to use it when performing audit procedures. The auditor may use the computer because it may in some instances be the most feasible means of performing tests or because the computer allows the efficient performance of otherwise time-consuming clerical audit procedures. Techniques employed by auditors to use the computer to perform audit procedures are called "computer-assisted audit techniques" (CAATs).

Generalized Audit Software

A generalized audit software package can be defined as a computer program or group of programs that can perform or assist the auditor in performing tests of key attributes, direct tests of balances, or analytical review procedures. For example, audit software applications can (1) perform calculations; (2) test records for correctness, consistency, and completeness; (3) compare data that are on separate files; (4) select and print key items or representative samples; and (5) summarize, stratify or reorganize data. Some advantages of using generalized audit software include:

1. Easily learned coding techniques can be utilized in writing applications.
2. The software is designed specifically to perform audit tasks.
3. The software produces audit documentation.
4. The software enables independent processing of live client data.
5. The software provides compatability with a variety of computer systems.

Use of audit software can help make audit tests (1) comprehensive, because each item in a file can be examined and subjected to a variety of tests, and (2) cost effective, because the computer is used to handle large volumes of data, thereby reducing time-consuming clerical tasks.

---

[6] A portion of this section was adapted from the Audit and Accounting Guide, "Computer-Assisted Audit Techniques" American Institute of Certified Public Accountants, 1979.

FIGURE 7-4   Examples of Computer Audit Software Applications for Accounts Receivable and Inventory

Specific Control Objective	Preliminary Audit Approach
S–1, S–2	Compare amounts due from individual customers with approved credit limits and print listing of customers with balances in excess of authorized amounts.
	Age accounts receivable master file and print amount in each aging category for comparison to company-prepared aging.
	Select and print representative sample of past due accounts and determine if follow-up procedures conform to company policy.
	Select and print all accounts overdue a specified number of days and that exceed a specified amount to help evaluate adequacy of allowance for doubtful accounts.
S–4, S–5, S–6	Foot accounts receivable master file and print total for comparison to general ledger.
	Select PPS* sample of customer invoices and print confirmation request for each invoice.
P–1, P–2	Select and print representative sample of cash disbursements during period and print all inventory purchases greater than a specified amount to test key system attributes (also can be used for transactions and accounts affected by F–3 and F–4).
P–6, P–7	Select and print representative sample of inventory items for price testing using estimation sampling and print all items which have extended value in excess of a specified amount.
	Merge prior year inventory with current year and print items with extended costs of more than a specified amount which also have increased by more than a specified percentage.
	Foot and extend inventory master file and print total for comparison to general ledger.
	Extend current year inventory quantities by current and prior year unit costs and print footed totals to support computation of LIFO index.
	Select and print representative sample of inventory items to be physically counted and reconciled to perpetual records.
	Account for sequence of inventory tag numbers and print missing numbers.
P–9	Print quantities on hand in excess of units sold during a specified period to detect potential overstock.
P–10	Print all items for which inventory cost exceeds selling price to detect valuation problems.

* A PPS sample is explained in Chapter 9.

Generalized audit software packages have been developed by both software vendors and some CPA firms. These software packages require minimum EDP knowledge so that an auditor can be quickly trained to utilize such packages. Figure 7–4 provides examples of how audit software could be used as part of the audit procedures for the specific control objectives that affect accounts receivable and inventory balances.

Test Decks

The test deck, which performs compliance tests of programmed procedures and controls, consists of test data either selected from previously processed transactions or created by the auditor. The test data are processed against the client's application programs and the actual results compared to the expected results. The expected results are independently determined on the assumption that the application contains effective programmed controls and will perform as specified in the program documentation. In using a test deck, the auditor is generally interested in determining that valid transactions are processed correctly and that invalid transactions are detected by the programmed controls. Although very effective for testing programmed controls, the use of a test deck has some shortcomings. For example, a test deck tests only preconceived situations and may not include all possible situations. Further, the tests lack objectivity because they are directed only toward documented controls.

Test deck transactions are not processed with regular input. However, a modification of the test deck, known as integrated test facility (ITF), creates a dummy entity (a fictitious customer, employee, or store) through which test transactions created by the auditor are processed with regular transactions through the client's records to the general ledger, at which point they are reversed by journal entry. The advantage of the ITF is that it tests the entire system, both the manual procedures and the programmed procedures. The principal disadvantage of ITF is that it involves considerable time to set up and execute.

Specialized Audit Software

Special audit programs may be written to perform specific audit tasks. They may be written by either the auditor or the client. If prepared by the client, the auditor should evaluate whether the program will perform what it is purported to perform.

Other Computer-Assisted Audit Techniques

Other computer-assisted audit techniques include the review and comparison of program logic, the use of time-sharing, and the application of utility programs. By reviewing and comparing program logic, the auditor can enhance his or her understanding of a particular program and identify any changes that have occurred during the audit period. Many major time-sharing vendors have libraries of programs that can be helpful to auditors, such as programs for statistical sampling and analytical review. Utility programs may be used by auditors to print all or part of a computer file or to support an audit software application by sorting records or creating a test file.

Internal auditors frequently use embedded audit modules, which are sections of program code that perform audit functions and are incorporated into regular application programs. This technique is most efficient when developed during the design of new applications.

Microcomputers

Microcomputers provide an auditor with powerful computer capability in a usable form at a reasonable cost. Microcomputers can (1) store, manipulate, summarize, and analyze large amounts of data; (2) perform mathematical calculations; (3) perform repetitive tasks; and (4) perform word processing. These types of activities are used in various aspects of audits. Consequently, microcomputers increase an auditor's ability to efficiently and accurately perform audit procedures. In contrast with large mainframe and minicomputers, software for microcomputers is not difficult to develop, and a number of software packages are available from outside vendors.

To illustrate, microcomputers may be used to:

1. Prepare separate trial balances from the general ledgers of each subsidiary or division and enter all audit and consolidation/elimination adjusting entries to arrive at a consolidated trial balance.
2. Perform analytical review computations (overall, detail, or as direct tests).
3. Calculate tax provisions (current and deferred).
4. Perform LIFO computations.
5. Compute earnings per share (both primary and fully diluted).
6. Prepare a summary of audit differences working paper.
7. Prepare financial statements from the trial balance.

CLIENT EXPECTATIONS

Occasionally, clients ask the auditor to perform procedures which go beyond the minimum requirements of the audit (e.g., confirm all receivables, examine expense reports for key personnel). Obviously, the auditor should not hesitate to perform these procedures; however, the preliminary audit approach should indicate clearly which tests are being performed to be responsive to client expectations.

DESCRIBING THE NATURE, TIMING, AND EXTENT OF AUDIT PROCEDURES

Steps in the preliminary audit approach should describe the nature, timing, and extent of the audit procedures. The auditor should be specific as to the procedures to be performed, when the procedure is to be performed, and the number of transactions to be tested or dollar amounts to be verified.

While the auditor performing the procedure should exercise judgment and challenge the program if it is believed to be inappropriate, efficient execution will be achieved only if the program steps are explicit as to nature, timing, and extent.

ASSEMBLING AND ORGANIZING THE AUDIT PROGRAM

The audit program should reflect the integration of preliminary audit approaches for various specific control objectives. For example, the audit program for sales and accounts receivable will be influenced by the following specific control objectives:

Reference No.	
S–1	Customer orders require approval of credit and terms before acceptance
S–2	Uncollectible amounts are promptly identified and provided for
S–3	Products shipped or services rendered are billed
S–4	Billings are for the correct amount
S–5	Revenues are recorded correctly as to account, amount, and period
S–6	Recorded billings are for valid transactions
S–7	Customer returns and other allowances are approved and recorded correctly as to account, amount, and period
F–1	Cash receipts are recorded correctly as to account, amount, and period and are deposited
F–2	Cash receipts are properly applied to customer balances

Because transactions affecting accounts receivable originate in two components of the business (Sales and Finance) and are subject to various system attributes and procedures, the preliminary audit approach is developed on several different pages of the risk analysis working paper. Development of the program in this manner (1) assures that all aspects of an account are given proper attention and (2) identifies specific audit procedures that serve several purposes.

In assembling the audit program, the auditor may find the same audit procedures outlined in several preliminary audit approaches. These procedures should be combined in the audit program to maximize the efficiency of performing tests. In those instances where different preliminary audit approaches call for different levels of persuasiveness from the same procedure, the audit program should reflect the most conservative approach (e.g., most extensive testing or performance closest to year-end).

Audit procedures applied to transactions often provide a basis for forming an opinion on related balance sheet classifications. Therefore, to the extent possible, the audit program should combine procedures applied to a class of transactions with direct tests of the related balances. For example combining audit procedures relating to sales, accounts receivable, and cash receipts often will be appropriate. And combining audit procedures for purchases, payables, and cash disbursements with the program for inventory; property, plant, and equipment; or operations (or cross-referencing certain steps in each section) may be helpful.

The following major program captions illustrate how an auditor might logically organize the audit program and the working papers:

1. Sales:
   Sales, receivables, and cash receipts

2. Production or service:
   Purchases (including selling and G&A expenses), cash disbursements
   Labor
   Inventory existence and valuation
   Property, plant, and equipment

3. Finance:
   Cash balances
   Investments
   Long- and short-term debt
   Shareholders' equity

4. Administration:
   Prepaid expenses, other assets, and accrued liabilities
   Income taxes
   Commitments and contingencies
   Other

5. General audit procedures

Major sections of this audit program organization cover transaction cycles and therefore cross component lines. As a result, this organization should lead to more efficient execution of the audit. The audit program for each section will be developed from the preliminary audit approaches for several specific control objectives that affect different aspects of a financial statement classification or transaction cycle. The organization described above also should be used for developing detailed time budgets and for filing working papers.

GENERAL AUDIT PROCEDURES

The audit program should include a section covering general audit procedures, most of which do not result from a risk analysis but are applicable to all audits. These include updating the system evaluation whenever tests of key attributes do not include the entire period under audit (covered in Chapter 4) and the final overall review (covered in Chapter 6). The other general audit procedures are discussed in Chapter 14.

CHANGES TO THE AUDIT APPROACH

The audit program should be prepared and approved prior to the program execution phase. As the auditor performs interim and year-end procedures, the audit program should be challenged. Changes in expectations due to new information or unanticipated results of tests and analyses (e.g., errors as discussed earlier) usually will cause the auditor to consider revising the nature, timing, or extent of the audit procedures.

New information may become available that represents a substantial change in the auditor's understanding of the business (e.g., the client unexpectedly disposes of a subsidiary or division or loses a major customer). In these instances, the auditor should revise the audit program relating to the aspects of accounts and transactions affected by the new information.

QUESTIONS AND PROBLEMS

7–1. The assessment of the likelihood of material error is based on what factors?

7–2. Student A made the following comment: "The likelihood of material error is greatest in the more material accounts." Comment on Student A's view of the relationship between the likelihood of material error and materiality.

7–3. What three variables affect audit procedures and, thus, the persuasiveness of audit evidence?

7–4. Give the purpose of compliance tests and the purpose of substantive tests.

7–5. What should an auditor do if a key attribute does not leave documentary evidence and the auditor cannot design tests to examine evidence that these procedures have been applied to transactions?

7–6. Give an example of an audit procedure that provides evidence about both the operation of key attributes and the validity and propriety of amounts.

7–7. What principal factors are relevant to the timing decision relating to audit procedures?

7–8. What are the two extent of testing strategies? Which strategy is used in compliance tests? Which is appropriate for substantive tests?

7–9. List the types of items that an auditor might consider key items.

7–10. What is a representative sample?

7–11. List two requirements for assuring that samples are representative.

7–12. The Wooden Corporation has a small accounting department that lacks segregation of duties. The corporation's auditor concludes that there is no reasonable assurance that certain specific control objectives are being achieved. Is it possible for the auditor to conclude that in these circumstances the likelihood of material error is low?

7–13. If an auditor's systems evaluation indicates that specific control objectives are not being achieved, what are the primary effects on the preliminary audit approach?

7–14. Distinguish between a systematic error and a random error in an audit.

7–15. List some examples of the capabilities of generalized audit software packages.

7–16. List some advantages of using generalized audit software.

7–17. Select the best answer for each of the following items:

a. The primary purpose of a generalized computer audit program is to allow the auditor to:

    (1) Use the client's employees to perform routine audit checks of the data processing records that otherwise would be done by the auditor's staff accountants.

    (2) Test the length of computer programs used in the client's electronic data processing systems.

    (3) Select larger samples from the client's electronic data processing records than would otherwise be selected without the generalized program.

    (4) Independently process client electronic data processing records.

b. An auditor can use a generalized computer audit program to verify the accuracy of:

    (1) Data processing controls.

    (2) Accounting estimates.

    (3) Totals and subtotals.

    (4) Account classifications.

c. In a daily computer run to update checking account balances and print out basic details on any customer's account that was overdrawn, the overdrawn account of the computer programmer was never printed. Which of the following control procedures would have been most effective in detecting this irregularity?

    (1) Use the test-deck approach by the auditor in testing the client's program and verification of the subsidiary file.

    (2) Use of a running control total for the master file of checking account balances and comparison with the printout.

    (3) A program check for valid customer code.

    (4) Periodic recompiling of programs from documented source decks and comparison with programs currently in use.

d. An auditor will use the EDP test data method to gain certain assurances with respect to the:

    (1) Input data.

    (2) Machine capacity.

    (3) Procedures contained within the program.

    (4) Degree of keypunching accuracy.

e. A primary advantage of using generalized audit packages in the audit of an advanced EDP system is that it enables the auditor to:

    (1) Substantiate the accuracy of data through self-checking digits and hash totals.

    (2) Utilize the speed and accuracy of the computer.

    (3) Verify the performance of machine operations which leave visible evidence of occurrence.

    (4) Gather and store large quantities of supportive evidential matter in machine readable form.   (AICPA, adapted)

7–18. What is an integrated test facility? What are its advantages and disadvantages?

7–19. CPA J is auditing the Fast Corporation. The controller asks J to perform certain procedures that go beyond the minimum requirements of the audit. Should J comply with controller's request?

7–20. Student A made the following comment: "Once the audit program is prepared and approved, it should not be changed." Is Student A correct?

7–21. May tests of transactions be integrated with direct tests of balances in the audit program?

7–22. Windy City, Inc., manufactures one product, which is sold only to three "blue-chip" customers. How important will the systems evaluation be to the auditor when considering specific control objective S–2, "Uncollectible amounts are promptly identified and provided for?"

7–23. The Jay Corporation is a small manufacturer with 25 employees. You are conducting the annual audit. In testing payroll, should you examine a representative sample? Explain.

7–24. CPA J has been engaged by Jennifer, Inc., to conduct the annual audit. CPA J is preparing the audit program. He determines that a key attribute is a reconciliation of shipping documents and customer invoices, performed once each working day. To properly test this key attribute, is it necessary for CPA J to completely examine at least 25 different reconciliations? Explain.

7–25. Below are eight audit procedures from risk analysis working papers. The procedures are part of the preliminary audit approach that has been developed. For each procedure (a) note any deficiencies in the extent of the test or the description of the extent and (b) prepare a revised procedure, if necessary, to conform to the extent of testing guidance in the chapter.

Procedures
1. Compare five daily lock-box reports to bank statement deposits.
2. Select two sales invoices from each location and determine if the following attributes are met. . . .
3. Select a block sample of 25 checks and examine each check to determine that the numerical sequence is accounted for. (Assume that the sequence checking of prenumbered checks was identified as a key attribute, and consider revising the audit procedure.)
4. Randomly select 10 employees from the payroll registers and perform the following. . . .
5. Test authorization for and recording of security purchases by reference to correspondence and bank advices for five investments made during the year.
6. Select a sample of the 25 largest dollar raw material items for a price test from the perpetual raw material inventory cards.
7. Request December 31 vendor statements from eight vendors with the largest outstanding balances on the November accounts payable trial balance.
8. Obtain and record 20 test counts for later tracing to the final inventory listing.

7–26. *a.* CPA T is testing a random sample of 25 purchases to test the functioning of various key attributes, including evidence that goods received are counted, inspected, and compared to the packing slip quantities. For the 15th item tested, CPA T notes that there is no packing slip or other receiving documentation. This is the second test item for which such evidence was not present and both are from Plant B, one of the company's three major plants. Should CPA T continue testing? Explain.

b. CPA B is testing a sample of 25 sales transactions to test the functioning of key attributes over credit approval. He notes that the documentary evidence for the key attribute he intends to rely on is missing for the third item tested. What should CPA B do?

7–27. *a.* CPA G has completed testing a random sample of payroll disbursements and has noted two errors in computation of gross pay. CPA G investigates the nature of the errors and learns that both were committed by a new payroll clerk hired in May, who did not understand that the company's office personnel were paid overtime at straight-time rates rather than at time-and-a-half like the factory workers. What additional information does CPA G need to decide if changes are needed in the audit program?

b. As part of the cash disbursements test, CPA H is comparing canceled checks to the cash disbursements register for agreement of check number, date, payee, and amount. The client cannot locate one check in CPA H's sample, but thinks that it will eventually turn up. CPA H will finish the interim work soon and is doubtful that the client will locate the check by then. The cash disbursements test is complete except for testing the missing item. What should CPA H do?

7–28. Elfand, Inc., is engaged in designing, manufacturing, and marketing solid state power conversion equipment. The Company cycle counts finished goods inventory throughout the year and takes an annual comprehensive physical inventory, which is observed by ABC and Associates, their outside auditors. You are assigned to the inventory portion of the December 31, 1985, annual audit and are asked to develop a preliminary audit approach relating to specific control objective P–9, "Obsolete, slow-moving, and overstock inventory is prevented or promptly detected and provided for." Assume that you find the following during your risk analysis:

1. *Environmental considerations:* The company's products are not susceptible to obsolescence because components can be substituted in related products. Parts considered defective by the materials manager are counted during the physical inventory and written off at year-end (and then scrapped).

2. *Observations from detail analytical review:* Net scrap expense was $40,000 during 1984, while $50,000 is projected for 1985.

3. *Systems evaluation:* Because of the insignificant amount of obsolete or otherwise unusable inventory, a systems evaluation is not considered necessary.

4. *Likelihood of material error in accounts affected:* Low.

Required:

Suggest a preliminary audit approach that is responsive to the risk analysis.

7-29. Refer to Elfand, Inc., in Question 7-28. Assume further that you are now assigned to develop a preliminary audit approach relating to specific control objective A–8, "Commitments and contingencies are identified, monitored, and, if appropriate, recorded or disclosed." Assume that you find the following during your risk analysis:

1. *Environmental considerations:* The company warrants its products for one year and provides a reserve for estimated future warranty expenses. No lawsuits are currently pending, per recent discussions with management. All legal matters are referred to outside counsel. The company is subject to OSHA and EPA regulations. Prior inspections by those agencies have not resulted in serious deficiencies.

2. *Observations from analytical review:* Warranty reserves as of June 30, 1985, totaled $558,000, versus $315,000 at December 31, 1984. The increase is principally related to the substantial increase in revenues, though a defect in one particular product caused a $150,000 addition to the reserve in the first quarter.

3. *System evaluation:* The system design provides reasonable assurance that commitments and contingencies are identified, monitored, and, if appropriate, recorded or disclosed. Legal matters are routed to outside counsel and the status of each item is regularly reviewed. Warranty reserves are reviewed quarterly for adequacy by the treasurer. Warranty claims are approved by the vice president–manufacturing and the treasurer.

4. *Likelihood of material error in accounts affected:* Although the system appears effective for warranties, uncertainty about the sufficiency of the reserve for the defective product and the potential for other product problems make the risk of material error moderate.

Required:

Suggest a preliminary audit approach that is responsive to the risk analysis.

AN INTRODUCTION TO STATISTICAL SAMPLING

Auditing procedures consist principally of tests of the accounting records. The theory of testing accounting records, as distinguished from complete and detailed checking, rests on the assumption that the demonstrated quality or amount of a properly selected sample is indicative of the probable quality or amount of the whole (population) from which the sample is selected.

The preceding chapter described the conditions when representative samples should include more than the minimum number of items. These conditions are:

1. No errors are expected and auditing the representative sample is the primary basis for a conclusion in an important audit area.
2. Errors are expected and auditing the representative sample is one of the bases for a conclusion in an important audit area.
3. Errors are expected and auditing the representative sample is the primary basis for a conclusion in an important audit area.

Statistical sampling techniques provide a useful approach to planning, selecting, and evaluating the results of these representative samples.

The use of statistical sampling techniques does not eliminate the use of judgments. In fact, statistical sampling requires that implicit judgments be explicitly quantified. Statistical sampling models use these judgments to set allowable levels of risk when making decisions based on sample evidence.

Chapters 8 and 9 discuss three different approaches to statistical sampling. They are: attribute sampling, probability proportional to size sampling, and variables estimation sampling. The appropriateness of a particular technique depends on the objective of the particular audit test.

ADVANTAGES OF USING STATISTICAL SAMPLING

SAS No. 39 (AU 350.45) states: "Statistical sampling helps the auditor *(a)* to design an efficient sample, . . . *(b)* to measure the sufficiency of the eviden-

8

tial matter obtained, and *(c)* to evaluate the sample results. By using statistical theory, the auditor can quantify sampling risk to assist himself in limiting it to a level he considers acceptable."

The advantages of using statistical sampling in an audit include:

1. It allows the auditor to quantify, and therefore control, the risk of making an incorrect decision based on sample evidence.
2. It provides a basis for determining the appropriate sample size, based on criteria established by the auditor.
3. It provides a mechanism for evaluating the sample information.

The remainder of this chapter reviews the fundamental concepts of statistical sampling. It assumes that the reader has taken a basic course in statistics. But even one who has not taken a recent course in statistics will be able to understand most of the concepts.

RISKS OF RELYING ON SAMPLE EVIDENCE

The audit risk[1] against which the auditor must guard is the risk that a material error will occur in an account balance and not be (1) prevented or detected by the system of internal control, or (2) detected by the audit procedures. The risk analysis process and the audit program are designed to minimize audit risk.

When a sample rather than all of the details of a particular account balance or class of transactions are tested, the risk that the decision as to its fairness will be incorrect is normally increased. This risk is due to the possibility that a sample does not closely represent the population from which it is drawn. We will now discuss the nature of this decision risk, referred to as *sampling risk,* and the audit judgments that are made to determine acceptable levels of it.

---

[1]*SAS No. 39* originally adopted the term *ultimate risk. SAS No. 45* amended it to *audit risk.* However, the term *ultimate risk* also may be found in the literature.

233

Audit Decisions and Risks

Every audit test is planned to result in one of two decisions. Direct tests of details of an account balance or class of transactions are designed *to accept* fairly stated recorded amounts or *to reject* materially misstated amounts. Tests of key attributes are designed to determine either that the attribute *is functioning* (and therefore can be relied on) or that it *is not functioning*. Whenever the auditor makes an audit decision from a specific audit test, a decision or sampling risk is incurred. *SAS No. 39* (AU 350.12) identifies the four types of sampling risk as the (1) "risk of incorrect rejection," (2) "risk of incorrect acceptance," (3) "risk of underreliance," and (4) "risk of overreliance."

Risks of Incorrect Rejection and Underreliance.   One type of risk is that of rejecting the account balance when it is fairly stated. The risk of making a decision error in this situation is called the *risk of incorrect rejection*. It is a concern whenever the auditor decides that a book value is not fairly stated. It is the risk that the amount is, in fact, fairly stated. Similarly, if as a result of a test of a key attribute, the auditor decides that the key attribute cannot be relied on or can be relied on to a lesser degree than planned, there is a risk that in fact it is functioning as originally perceived and could be relied on. The risk of incurring this decision error is called the *risk of underreliance*.

When an audit test indicates that the book value is materially misstated or that the key attribute is not functioning, the auditor's first reaction may be to modify the audit approach, which would usually result in a correction of an initially incorrect decision. Accordingly, the decision error resulting from the risks of incorrect rejection or underreliance generally will result only in more testing than would otherwise be required. As stated in *SAS No. 39* (AU 350.13), the risks of incorrect rejection or underreliance affect the *efficiency* of an audit and are often neither quantified nor controlled when performing tests. In these cases, the effectiveness of the audit is not impaired; however, the cost of the audit—to the auditor and/or the client—increases. Thus, there may be an economic impact.

When testing key attributes, or controls, if unexpected deviations are encountered, it is generally advisable to first reach the tentative decision that the key attribute is not functioning at the expected level and then decide if it would be more efficient to examine additional items for the key attribute or change the nature, timing, or extent of other planned audit procedures.

Risks of Incorrect Acceptance and Overreliance.   Another type of risk is the *risk of incorrect acceptance* of an account balance or class of transactions when in fact a material misstatement exists. The comparable risk relating to a test of key controls is the *risk of overreliance,* which is the risk of deciding to rely on a key attribute when in fact it is not functioning as perceived.

We previously stated that the auditor's natural reaction to a rejection or nonreliance decision is to perform additional audit work, which generally will compensate for and correct the decision error. However, if a sample, together with the results of other audit procedures, supports fair statement or reliance, an auditor normally will not do any additional audit work. This decision error may result in issuing an unqualified opinion on financial statements that include a material error. As stated in *SAS No. 39* (AU 350.14), this risk relates to the *effectiveness* of the audit. Because of the potential adverse consequences (e.g., lawsuits by users of the financial statements), the auditor is most concerned with controlling this risk.

Only one of these risks exists with respect to any particular audit decision. The audit decisions and related decision risks are summarized as follows:

Audit Decision	Decision (Sampling) Risk
Test of key attribute:	
Key attribute is not functioning	Risk of underreliance
Key attribute is functioning	Risk of overreliance
Direct test of balances:	
Recorded amount is materially misstated	Risk of incorrect rejection
Recorded amount is fairly stated	Risk of incorrect acceptance

The level of risk, which is generally expressed as a percentage, measures the probability or chance that a decision error will be made as a result of performing a specific audit procedure. However, a decision error will actually exist only when the auditor's decision is different from the true state of the account balance, a condition that is not known with certainty at the time of the test. When the audit decision agrees with the true state of the account balance, there is no decision error.

We have been using the terms *fairly stated* and *materially misstated* in defining these risk concepts. However, these risks relate to individual audit decisions about particular account balances, while *fair statement* and *material misstatement* are terms that generally refer to the status of financial statements taken as a whole. To discuss these factors in relation to a particular audit decision, we will introduce the concept of a tolerable error.

Tolerable Error

SAS No. 39 (AU 350.18) states: "When planning a sample for a substantive test of details, the auditor should consider how much monetary error in the related account balance or class of transactions may exist without causing the financial statements to be materially misstated. This maximum monetary error for the balance or class is called *tolerable error* for the sample. Tolerable error is a planning concept and is related to the auditor's preliminary estimates of materiality levels in such a way that tolerable error, combined for the entire audit plan, does not exceed those estimates." [Emphasis in original.]

Materiality should be considered relative to the financial statements taken as a whole. While one difference in an audit area may be immaterial, there may be several differences in various audit areas which, in the aggregate, could be material to the financial statements taken as a whole. Accordingly, it is helpful to establish a guideline in the form of an amount related to a particular aspect of an account below which the auditor would not be concerned with potential adjustments.

As an example, assume that financial statement materiality for a company is established at $500,000. When planning the test of inventory pricing, the auditor might decide that any potential adjustment below $50,000 would not be of concern. By setting tolerable error at $50,000, the auditor would reasonably expect that the effect of all such adjustments from all audit tests would be less than $500,000.

Tolerable error is associated with direct tests of balances. A comparable term for tests of key attributes is the *tolerable rate of occurrence*. The tolerable rate of occurrence is the maximum occurrence rate (a percentage) of exception to a key attribute that the auditor would be willing to accept without changing the planned reliance on that attribute.

We will now discuss the judgments that the auditor must make and how they can be correlated to determine acceptable levels of risk when planning or evaluating statistical samples. First, we will consider the risks in tests of key attributes. Then, the risks inherent in direct tests of balances will be discussed.

DETERMINING RISK LEVELS AND THE TOLERABLE RATE FOR TESTS OF KEY ATTRIBUTES

The objective of any test of a key attribute is to determine that it is functioning at a level that will permit the auditor to rely on it to prevent or detect material errors or irregularities. Both the tolerable rate of occurrence and the risk of overreliance are stated as percentages. The tolerable rate of occurrence and risk of overreliance percentages are then used in planning an audit procedure to apply to the appropriate number of items and in making an audit decision from the sample.

One reaction to finding more deviations or occurrences than the tolerable rate for a key attribute is to extend the test of the key attribute to additional sample items. More will be said about this later. An alternative to extending the test of a key attribute is to change the nature, timing, or extent of other tests in the audit program that relate to the same aspect of the account balance. When modifying the audit program in this way, it is important to recognize the result of the test of the key attribute that has been performed.

To illustrate, after testing the functioning of a key attribute, the auditor has some idea as to the level of its functioning. Rather than ignore that information, the auditor should use it to help in deciding the degree to which the nature, timing, and extent of other procedures should be changed. As the rate of occurrence in a sample increases, the reliance the auditor can place on the key attribute decreases. Thus, if the auditor finds very few errors, the degree to which the other procedures would change would be less than if many errors were found or the attribute was not tested at all.

Sometimes, a test of key attributes is the primary basis for a conclusion about an account balance. In this situation, the audit program may include only tests of key items or analytical review procedures, in addition to the test of key attributes. For example, in testing payroll expense and related accruals, a test of key attributes and an analytical review of total payroll expense based on the number of employees and average pay rates might be sufficient. In such a situation, the auditor should set the risk of overreliance and the tolerable error rate at low levels due to the heavy reliance placed on the test of key attributes.

DETERMINING RISK LEVELS FOR DIRECT TESTS OF BALANCES

As stated earlier, one of two risks exists in a direct test of balances, depending on the audit decision—risk of incorrect rejection or the risk of incorrect acceptance.

Risk of Incorrect Rejection

The risk of incorrect rejection relates to the efficiency of an audit. If an incorrect rejection error occurs, the auditor will generally extend the direct tests of balances to the degree necessary to correct the incorrect rejection error.

When the auditor is faced with a decision to reject based on the results of the original sample, the acceptable level for risk of incorrect rejection is determined by the difficulty in selecting and/or testing additional details of account balances. If it is relatively easy to select and test additional sample items (e.g., confirmation of accounts receivable balances), the auditor may accept a higher risk of incorrect rejection, perhaps as high as 20 percent. On the other hand, if additional sample items are difficult (but not impossible) to select or test, the auditor only may be willing to tolerate a much lower level of risk of incorrect rejection, such as 10 percent. In the situation where it is virtually impossible to select or test additional items after the initial test is completed, the auditor may wish to control the risk of incorrect rejection to a very small acceptable level, such as 2 percent. An example of this latter situation may be a test of quantities indicated in perpetual inventory records.

This risk is not always directly measured when using statistical sampling. However, it exists whenever a sample leads to the decision that the recorded amount is not fairly stated or key attributes should not be relied on.

Risk of Incorrect Acceptance

Determining the acceptable risk of incorrect acceptance requires that the auditor consider how the particular test being planned relates to other procedures that lead to an opinion about the aspect of the account balance being tested. The *risk of incorrect acceptance* for a particular sample for which the primary purpose is a direct test of a balance is one of the factors comprising the audit risk.

Accordingly, when determining what is an acceptable level of incorrect acceptance for a particular sample, the auditor should consider how the risk of incorrect acceptance relates to audit risk. Audit risk can be incurred only when errors larger than tolerable error actually occur *and* the following three events also occur:

1. The key attributes in the accounting system fail to detect and correct them.
2. The auditor's analytical review and audit procedures other than the sample fail to detect them.
3. The audit sample being planned also fails to detect them.

The following simple mathematical model, based on the Appendix to *SAS No. 39* (AU 350.47), expresses the relationship of the three factors that contribute to audit risk. For this model, the following notations should be used:

AuR—The allowable *Au*dit *R*isk. This is the risk (expressed as a percentage) that monetary errors greater than the tolerable error might remain undetected in the account after all audit procedures have been completed. The SAS implies a *maximum* acceptable audit risk of 5 percent.

IC—The auditor's assessment of the risk that the key attributes (*I*nternal Accounting *C*ontrol) would fail to detect errors larger than the tolerable error. The amount of this risk may be expressed as a percentage in the range of 10 percent (little risk) to 100 percent (no reliance can be placed on the system). The auditor may have to reevaluate this risk if any audit test subsequently indicates that key attributes are not functioning as expected.

AR—The auditor's assessment of the risk that *A*nalytical *R*eview and any planned substantive tests of balances other than the sample would fail to detect errors that are greater than the tolerable error amount, given that such errors have occurred and were not detected by the key attributes. The amount of this risk is expressed as a percentage in the range of 10 percent (very effective procedures) to 100 percent (the sample being planned is the only significant test to be performed).

TD—The allowable risk of incorrect acceptance for the *T*est of *D*etails being planned. The level of this risk can be computed from the three previously defined audit judgments.

To develop a formula for computing the allowable risk of incorrect acceptance, consider the definition of audit risk. Audit risk is incurred only when all three elements (*IC, AR,* and *TD*) fail to detect errors as large as the tolerable error. Therefore, the combined risk of failure is a joint probability and can be quantified as the product of the individual failure rates, or:

$$AuR = IC \times AR \times TD$$

This formula can then be rearranged to the following to compute the allowable risk of incorrect acceptance, given the other factors:

$$TD = \frac{AuR}{IC \times AR}$$

To illustrate these concepts, assume that the auditor is planning to select a sample of accounts receivable for confirmation. A test of key attributes is one of the bases for the auditor's conclusion. Thus, the auditor plans to place moderate, but not substantial, reliance on the accounting system. As a result, the auditor may conclude that there is a 30 percent risk that the key attributes will fail to detect errors as large as the tolerable amount. In addition, analytical review procedures will provide corroborative evidence, but will not be the primary basis for the auditor's conclusion (i.e., the procedures do not provide "highly persuasive" evidence). As a result, the auditor may conclude that there is a 70 percent risk that the analytical review procedures will fail to detect errors as large as the tolerable amount. Assuming the auditor wishes to limit audit risk to 5 percent, the allowable risk of incorrect acceptance can be computed from the formula:

$$TD = \frac{AuR}{IC \times AR}$$

by substituting values as follows:

$$TD = \frac{.05}{.30 \times .70} \cong .238 \text{ or } 23.8 \text{ percent}$$

To be conservative, the auditor may decide to round this risk level down to 20 percent and use that amount when planning the sample size for the confirmation test.

In many situations, the risks of these events occurring may not be explicitly stated as percentages. However, these factors always should be considered at least implicitly when designing the audit program.

The consideration of these factors is often performed from a positive standpoint by indicating the effectiveness of these factors in detecting errors rather than the risk that they would fail to detect errors. To convert a risk amount to an indicator of effectiveness, or vice versa, the known amount is simply subtracted from one. Thus, if the risk level is 20 percent, the effectiveness level is 80 percent.

Audit judgments are used to determine the appropriate risk levels for any audit test that is performed on only a sample of items. When statistical sampling techniques are used, the auditor is able to use the mathematical properties of the techniques to measure the risk inherent in an audit decision. The ability to measure the risk levels in a decision provides an opportunity for the auditor to limit the risk to acceptable levels.

RANDOM SAMPLING

Random samples are representative samples. Selection of a random sample is essential to be able to arrive at a statistical conclusion in an audit situation. However, as Chapter 7 described, random sampling is not the only way to select representative samples.

Random sampling is a sample selection procedure whereby each item making up the account balance or class of transactions has a *known chance* for selection. This chance is often an equal chance. However, some sample selection procedures require that individual items have a known but *unequal* chance for selection. An example is probability proportional to size selection (PPS— discussed in Chapter 9), also called dollar unit sampling (DUS). This selection technique requires each item to have a chance of selection that is proportional to its relative size (e.g., a $50 item has one tenth the chance of selection as a $500 item).

There are several ways to identify random samples. One of these is called random selection. Others are stratified random and probability proportional to size selection. Before discussing sampling techniques, some fundamental definitions should be clarified.

Definitions

A *population* is all items in a group about which a conclusion is desired. Cash disbursements, accounts receivable, and inventory are common examples of audit populations. A *frame* is the physical representation of the population. A *sampling unit* is the individual item within the frame. A *sample* is one or more items in the population selected from the frame.

An example will help put these concepts in perspective. Assume that the objective of an audit test is to determine whether cash disbursements are properly authorized. The population is all cash disbursements. The frame might be the cash disbursements register, since the cash disbursements register is a physical representation of the population of all recorded cash disbursements. The auditor could identify a sample from the population of cash disbursements by selecting sampling units from the frame, the cash disbursements register. A specific check (identified by a check number) would be the sampling unit.

The objective in testing a sample is to infer a conclusion about the population. From a technical standpoint, however, the conclusion applies only to the frame. Accordingly, it is very important that the frame includes all items in the population.

To determine the appropriateness of the frame, the auditor should consider whether it includes (1) all items from the population and (2) no items from other populations. In the cash disbursements example above, the auditor could not reach the conclusion that all disbursements are recorded. If items are selected from a frame of recorded disbursements (the cash disbursements register), unrecorded items are excluded from it. (However, the auditor could reach the conclusion that recorded disbursements were accounted for properly.) It also would be difficult for the auditor to conclude that property, plant, and equipment purchases are properly authorized based on a sample of cash disbursements, because the frame (cash disbursements register) includes many items that are not a part of the relevant population. Thus, it is important that the frame closely represent the population. Selecting a frame that differs from the population limits the potential for a valid sampling conclusion.

Random samples often are selected from only a portion of a population, most frequently when the extent of testing strategy includes tests of key items in a population. Key items are accounts or transactions in the population which are individually important because of their size or in which the auditor believes there is a high likelihood of error. Accordingly, key items always are included in the accounts or transactions to be tested and, if necessary, a representative sample is selected from the remaining portion of the population.

It may not be practicable to identify a frame for selecting a sample that excludes key items. This should not cause a significant problem for the selection of a random sample. However, when planning the sample selection, the auditor should be aware that those key items are included in the frame and take whatever action is necessary to ensure that a representative sample of the desired size—excluding key items—results from the sample selection procedure.

Selecting Random Samples

Simple random sampling generally means that each item in the population has an equal opportunity (probability) for selection. Random sampling can be further clarified by considering whether a sample item is returned to the frame before the next item is drawn. If the sample item is returned, the method is called *random sampling with replacement.* If the item is not returned, it is called *random sampling without replacement.* Since an audit test is applied to an individual item only once, it follows that audit samples generally are selected without replacement.

There are three techniques generally used by auditors to select random samples:

1. Random number tables.
2. Systematic selection procedures.
3. Computer software.

Each of these techniques assures random selection and has the advantages of being objective and easily documented.

Using Random Number Tables. *Random number tables* are published tables of numbers that typically are computer generated and subjected to statistical tests to ensure randomness. On an overall basis, these tables have an approximately equal distribution of the digits 0 through 9 in each continuous row or column.

To illustrate how to use a random number table, an excerpt is provided in Figure 8–1. Column and row references are indicated to facilitate discussion.

FIGURE 8-1 Random Number Table Excerpt

Row	Column						
	1	2	3	4	5	6	7
1	95889	38101	11618	57166	80481	80321	99538
2	62913	39641	91339	83620	04419	71429	52139
3	67667	84084	99396	16489	21436	36401	53783
4	24700	47418	57649	40333	97525	43648	71839
5	76479	43321	28977	82898	48102	83873	09351

There are four basic steps to follow when using a random number table to select a random sample.

1. *Find a method of proceeding* so that there is agreement between the numbers in the random number table and the population items in the frame.
2. *Select and record a starting point.* A random stab into the table can identify the starting point.
3. *Select and record a route through the table.* Random number tables can be read in any direction (e.g., up or down columns or across rows) and any portion or combination of the digits can be used, provided that the conventions are followed consistently. The route selected should be documented.
4. *Record the stopping point* so that a check can be made if the sample is to be reconstructed or to facilitate the selection of additional items should that become necessary.

To illustrate the use of the random number table in Figure 8–1, assume that you wish to take a random sample of six vouchers from the population of vouchers described in Figure 8–2.

FIGURE 8–2 A Population of 21 Vouchers

Voucher Number	Amount	Voucher Number	Amount	Voucher Number	Amount
14913	$ 109.76	14920	$ 52.50	14927	$ 15.46
14914	3,496.41	14921	70.31	14928	5,519.00
14915	891.36	14922	851.71	14929	4,000.00
14916	541.10	14923	1.29	14930	444.37
14917	21.76	14924	192.33	14931	387.11
14918	79.16	14925	5,642.39	14932	5.41
14919	916.41	14926	886.84	14933	91.88

The vouchers are in ascending numerical sequence, starting with number 14913. The list of all voucher numbers in the population (14913 through 14933) is the frame. We have chosen the last two digits of the voucher numbers to establish correspondence between the random number table (Figure 8–1) and the frame. For the first voucher this would be 13.

To find a starting place in the random number table, simply close your eyes and drop your pencil point on the table. This procedure is called a *random stab.*[2] For example, suppose the pencil pointed to column 2, row 3, of Figure 8–1. This is number 84084.

---

[2] When a large table of random numbers is used, a random number can be selected on one page by the random stab method, and that number used to identify a starting point—page, row, and column. However, this procedure is not required to ensure randomness.

Because the numbers that comprise the frame run from 13 to 33, any two digits of the digits in the table can be used. In this example, we will use the last two digits having values within the limits 13 to 33. The first number selected (84) is ignored since it is outside the limits of the frame (13 to 33). We also could have used the first two digits, the last digit in column 2 and the first digit in column 3, or any other convention we wished, as long as it was applied consistently.

The next number selected from the table should be based on the planned route through the random number table. We can specify selecting the number above or below, or to the left or right of the first number. In this example, assume the route was planned to read down the column. The next number down the column, 18, corresponds to voucher number 14918, which will be the first item in the sample. The next number is 21, corresponding to voucher number 14921.

Having reached the bottom of column 2, move to the top of column 3, row 1, and start down. The first number is 18, which would indicate that voucher number 14918 should be selected again for inclusion in the sample. If sampling with replacement, voucher number 14918 would be included again as if it were an entirely new item. If sampling without replacement, the number would be ignored. We continue through the table in this manner until the desired sample of 6 items has been selected.

Systematic Selection

Technically, systematic sampling is not a random sampling process. However, it is a practical approach to sample selection that closely approximates random sampling.

In *systematic sampling,* the first sample item is randomly chosen, a fixed number of items skipped, another item selected, the same fixed number of items skipped, the next sample item selected, and so on throughout the frame. The number of items counted before the next item is selected is called the *skip interval.* For instance, if the first random item selected is the second item, and the skip interval is seven, then the next item selected would be the ninth item.

To find the skip interval, divide the desired sample size into the number of items in the population and round down. If using more than one random starting point, the unrounded skip interval must be multiplied by the number of starts to give the skip interval for each. If necessary, the final skip interval is rounded down to the nearest integer. The more starting points used, the greater the assurance of obtaining a random sample. At least two starting points are recommended when a statistical conclusion is needed.

Selecting a sample with systematic selection is often easier than using random number tables, especially when the frame is on magnetic tape, a computer tab listing, a deck of keypunched cards, or a file of ledger cards or vouchers. Random numbers are required only to designate starting points. The items in the frame need not be numbered consecutively, as is necessary to correspond with a random number table.

However, to obtain the same results from systematic sampling as from random sampling, the auditor should be reasonably assured that the frame is arranged in random order with respect to the population characteristic being measured. For example, if accounts receivable amounts are being tested, systematic sampling might be used even though the accounts are filed alphabetically—provided the dollar amounts have no relation to the account names.

Suppose a random sample of six items is to be selected by systematic sampling from the population of 21 items in Figure 8–2. Using two random starts, the skip interval would be 7 [(21/6)(2)], i.e., every 7th item will be selected. To determine the starting points, random number tables should be used.

The starting points can be specified using a random stab technique as "the first two digits between 1 and 7 in the lefthand digit of column 5 in Figure 8–1." The first occurs at row 3 of column 5; the second occurs at row 5. The two numbers are 2 and 4, respectively. Therefore, the first voucher in the sample would be number 14914, because 14914 is the second voucher in the frame (corresponding to the random starting point of 2). From that random starting point, the next voucher selected would be number 14921 (the 7th item after number 14914). The following items would be selected for the sample:

Voucher	Number	Amount
1st start:		
2d voucher	14914	$3,496.41
9th voucher	14921	70.31
16th voucher	14928	5,519.00
2d start:		
4th voucher	14916	541.10
11th voucher	14923	1.29
18th voucher	14930	444.37

Computer Capabilities

An efficient way to select random samples is to use a computer. Most audit software packages can be used to assist in selecting random samples. Because audit software generally directly accesses the frame, or is provided with specifications describing the frame (e.g., checks numbered from 300 to 1,200), computer selected samples generally are easy to use and well documented.

To illustrate, one such software package used by auditors identifies sample items by applying systematic selection procedures with 10 random starting points. The auditor must provide the frame in machine-readable form, indicate the skip interval (assuming 10 starting points), and provide 10 different random numbers less than or equal to the skip interval. Since the system reads the frame, it directly identifies sample items. Other programs can then access the sample and perform arithmetic or other tests, create a magnetic tape of the records, prepare a printed report to facilitate the performance of audit procedures, or simply flag the sample items for future identification.

STRATIFIED RANDOM SAMPLING

Sometimes the sample selection procedure specified in the audit program requires stratifying the population. To stratify a population, stratification criteria must be defined and each item in the population categorized into its respective stratum. *A stratified random sample* is identified by selecting separate random samples from the population items in each stratum. The most common stratification criterion is the recorded amount of the individual items making up the population.

Stratified random samples can be difficult to select without using an audit software package that can stratify the population. Alternatively, a stratified random sample can be selected with a random number table or systematic selection procedure if the frame is arranged in an order that permits easy identification of the items that make up the various strata. Another method of random sampling, probability proportional to size (PPS), will be discussed in Chapter 9.

TYPES OF STATISTICAL SAMPLING TECHNIQUES

The three major statistical sampling techniques that are used by auditors are:

1. Attribute sampling.
2. Probability proportional to size sampling.
3. Variables estimation sampling.

Each of these techniques provides the auditor with the ability to measure, and therefore control, the risk of making an incorrect audit decision based on a sample. The remainder of this chapter describes attribute sampling. Chapter 9 discusses the other two sampling techniques.

ATTRIBUTE SAMPLING

Attribute sampling is a statistical sampling technique that provides an estimate of the maximum rate that a particular event (attribute) occurs or fails to occur, with measurable levels of risk of making a decision error.

Since this technique results in a measure of the rate of occurrence or nonoccurrence and does not provide information about the monetary effects of these occurrences, it is usually used for tests of key attributes. It also can be used for direct tests of balances in limited situations when the auditor is concerned about the frequency of occurrence of errors in an account in which the individual items are of comparable size. To illustrate, such a procedure can be used to detect understatement errors in the liability account for customer deposits.

The term *occurrence* rather than *error* is used here because an auditor might be interested in lack of compliance with a control procedure. Such lack of compliance is not an error, but the occurrence does have a possible effect on an account since an occurrence reflects on the effectiveness of key attributes related to the account. For example, the percentage of disbursements not having evidence of approval might lead an auditor to further investigate disbursements.

Definitions

Attribute sampling involves testing for the existence of a predefined quality or characteristic. When testing the functioning of key attributes, the characteristic usually is defined as the documented evidence of performance of the required control procedure (e.g., the appropriate person has initialed the invoice to indicate comparison of terms with those agreed to). The characteristic to be tested should be defined in the audit program.

Before beginning an audit test using attribute sampling, the auditor should understand the nature of the key attribute being tested *and* exactly what evidence will support the functioning of the control procedure with respect to the sample item. With a properly defined characteristic, the execution of the audit procedure is simply a matter of classifying each sample item as either possessing or not possessing the predefined quality.

Planning a test using attribute sampling requires defining a tolerable rate of occurrence (or exception) for key attributes. The *tolerable rate of occurrence,* expressed as a percentage, is the *maximum rate of exception* or deviation that the auditor would be willing to accept in the population without altering the planned reliance on the defined key attribute. If the rate of deviation for a key attribute is larger than the tolerable rate, the auditor should reevaluate the reliance placed on this key attribute in the audit program. This usually means increasing the extent of testing or changing the nature or timing of other audit procedures. The tolerable rate of occurrence is an audit judgment that is established during the program development phase of an audit. The tolerable rate of occurrence generally is placed at a relatively low level, such as 5 percent or 10 percent, since it makes little sense to test or rely on a control that does not function frequently.

The *expected rate of occurrence* (or expected rate of exception) is the rate (percent) of items in the population for which the auditor expects the key attribute not to be present (or not to function). If the expected rate exceeds the tolerable rate, the auditor should plan neither to test nor rely on the key attribute. The expected rate of occurrence is an audit judgment that is made when planning the attribute sampling test. It usually is based on judgment and prior experience in testing the same or a similar key attribute. Often, it is set at zero.

The *sample rate of occurrence* is the rate of exception to an attribute actually observed in the sample. It is the best estimate of the true, but unknown, *population rate of occurrence.*

The *risk of overreliance* is the risk (expressed as a percentage) that the attribute sampling test will indicate that the rate of exception in the functioning of a key attribute is less than the tolerable rate of occurrence when the true rate of occurrence exceeds the tolerable rate. It is the risk that the auditor will be misled by the attribute sampling test. If this occurs, the auditor will place more reliance on the key attribute than is warranted and, as a result, the nature, timing, or extent of the direct tests of balances may be inadequate.

Quantitatively, the risk of overreliance is directly related to *reliability (R)* in an attribute sampling test. Reliability indicates the percentage of the time that the auditor's conclusion that key attributes are functioning, based on an attribute sample of a specified size from the population, is correct. Therefore, its complement $(1 - R)$ is the risk of overreliance—the percentage of time that the conclusion is incorrect.

The risk of overreliance or reliability for a particular test is an audit judgment that is made during the program development phase of an audit. Generally, the risk of overreliance is set at a level of 10 percent or less, meaning reliability is 90 percent or greater. If either the risk of overreliance or reliability is given, the other can easily be computed by subtracting the given value from 100 percent.

The *achieved upper precision limit* is a statistical measure of the *maximum* rate of occurrence for an attribute, at a specified reliability level, based on the results of the test performed. It depends on the sample rate of occurrence, desired reliability (risk of overreliance), and the sample size. The achieved upper precision limit varies inversely with changes in reliability or sample size, given a specified number of observed occurrences. It always is larger than the sample occurrence rate and increases as additional occurrences are observed.

After determining the achieved upper precision limit (usually from a table), the auditor must compare it to the tolerable rate. If the achieved upper precision limit is less than or equal to the tolerable rate at the planned risk of overreliance, the auditor can conclude that the key attribute is functioning as expected and continue with the audit program as planned. On the other hand, if the achieved upper precision limit exceeds the tolerable rate, the auditor must reevaluate the planned reliance on the key attribute and modify the audit program accordingly.

A word of caution is in order before continuing. The use of statistical sampling (including attribute sampling) does not relieve the auditor of the responsibility to attempt to determine the cause of errors observed when performing an audit test. Chapter 7 discussed evaluating errors in audit tests.

APPROACHES TO APPLYING ATTRIBUTE SAMPLING

There are three possible approaches that an auditor may take to attribute sampling—use of formulas, use of computer programs, or use of tables. In this chapter we will illustrate the table approach.

The Table Approach for Attribute Sampling

Attribute sampling tables may be used to facilitate the use of attribute sampling in an audit environment. These tables are reproduced in Appendices 8A and 8B of this chapter. Appendix 8A contains tables that assist in determining the required sample size. The steps the auditor should follow for using Tables 8A–1 through 8A–5 are:

1. Select the applicable *table* based on the desired reliability level or risk of overreliance.
2. Identify the *column* for the tolerable rate of occurrence.
3. Identify the *row* corresponding to the expected rate of occurrence.
4. Read the sample size at the intersection of the column and row.

The following examples illustrate the use of these tables.

Example 1

Assume that when testing the account distribution of a sample of cash disbursements, an occurrence rate of 4 percent is expected, but the audit program indicates that a rate of 8 percent is tolerable. The auditor is willing to accept a risk of overreliance of no more than 5 percent. What sample size should be tested?

Answer: From Table 8A–4, the answer is 180 items.

Example 2

Assume the same situation as Example 1, except the auditor wants a risk of overreliance of no more than 1 percent. What is the required sample size?

Answer: From Table 8A–5, the answer is 280 items.

Evaluating Sample Results.   After executing the audit procedures for each sample item, the auditor can use the tables in Appendix 8B to find the achieved upper precision limit. The evaluation depends on reliability or risk of overreliance and sample size. To use those tables, the auditor should follow these steps:

1. Select the *table* corresponding to the desired reliability level or risk of overreliance.
2. Find the *row* corresponding to the sample size actually tested. Always be conservative. If the sample size tested falls between two rows, use the row with the *smaller* sample size.
3. In the row identified, find the *cell* corresponding to the *number* of occurrences in the sample. Always be conservative. If the number of occurrences in the sample falls between two cells, use the cell with the *higher* number of occurrences.
4. Read the upper precision limit percentage at the *top* of the *column* in which the cell appears.

The findings of an attribute sampling test generally should be stated in terms of: (1) the *estimated* population occurrence rate (which is the sample rate of occurrence), and (2) the achieved upper precision limit at a specified reliability level or risk of overreliance. The achieved upper precision limit will vary from the tolerable rate to the extent that the estimated rate of occurrence used in determining the sample size differs from the sample rate of occurrence.

For example, if in a given test the auditor specifies a reliability of 95 percent, a tolerable rate of 6 percent and an expected occurrence rate of 3 percent, the required sample size is determined to be 200 (Table 8A–4). However, if the auditor actually finds nine errors, Table 8B–4 indicates that the achieved upper precision limit would be 8 percent instead of the 6 percent which is the tolerable rate. In Table 8B–4, note that if the sample occurrence rate were less than or equal to the expected occurrence rate (3 percent), six or fewer occurrences would have been observed and the achieved upper precision limit would have been less than or equal to the tolerable rate of 6 percent.

The following examples further illustrate this concept.

Example 3

Under the conditions of Example 1 (5 percent risk of overreliance, 4 percent expected rate, 8 percent tolerable rate), the auditor selected 200 items (instead of 180) and found six occurrences for a sample occurrence rate of 3 percent. What is the achieved upper precision limit?

Answer: Because the sample occurrence rate (3 percent) was less than the expected rate (4 percent), the achieved upper precision limit would be expected to be less than the tolerable rate (8 percent). Table 8B–4 confirms this expectation by indicating an achieved upper precision limit of 6 percent.

Example 4

Assume the same conditions as Example 3 except that the auditor found 12 occurrences in the sample of 200 for a sample occurrence rate of 6 percent, what would be the achieved upper precision limit at 95 percent reliability?

Answer: From Table 8B–4, the answer is 10 percent, which as expected, is greater than the tolerable rate.

Example 4 illustrates that if the auditor initially estimates an expected rate of occurrence that is too low, the sample size will be too small to achieve an upper precision limit that is less than or equal to the tolerable rate of occurrence. This emphasizes the importance of being realistic when establishing the expected rate of occurrence. However, an estimate that is far too high requires a much larger sample than necessary and, therefore, wastes time.

If a test results in an achieved upper precision limit that exceeds the tolerable rate, it indicates that occurrences were observed in the sample at a rate exceeding the expected rate. After these occurrences have been qualitatively evaluated (i.e., they are determined to be neither systematic nor intentional), an auditor may conclude that the previously determined expected occurrence rate is closer to the true population rate of occurrence than is the sample rate of occurrence. In this case, it may be desirable to extend the test of the key attribute in an attempt to achieve an upper precision limit that is less than the tolerable rate.

In other situations, the auditor may have a very small expected rate and want to perform the minimum amount of testing to assure that the expectation is correct. In these circumstances, the auditor can prevent oversampling by determining the initial sample size based on an expected rate of occurrence of 0 percent. Then, if occurrences are observed, additional sample items can be selected to yield an upper precision limit less than or equal to the tolerable rate. This technique, which uses the tables in Appendix 8B, is a particular form of attribute sampling, often referred to as stop-or-go sampling.

Stop-or-Go Sampling.   Stop-or-go sampling is an attribute sampling plan that allows the auditor to determine the additional sample size that may achieve the desired results when the initial sample results are unacceptable. This approach is useful when (1) selecting and testing additional sample items is easy to perform, (2) a very small (or zero) rate of errors is expected, and (3) the auditor wishes to prevent oversampling. If additional sample items are difficult to select or supporting documents difficult to locate, it may not be practicable to use this approach.

The required additional sample size can be determined from the tables in Appendix 8B by following these steps:

1. Select the applicable *table* based on the desired reliability level or risk of overreliance.
2. Find the *column* for an upper precision limit less than or equal to a tolerable rate.
3. In the column identified find the *cell* that contains the number of errors already observed (or some greater number expected to be observed).
4. Read the required *total sample size* at the far left of the *row* in which the cell appears.
5. Subtract the sample size already tested from the required total sample size to obtain the additional required sample size.

Refer to Example 4 to illustrate the use of stop-or-go sampling. Remember that the risk of overreliance was 5 percent, the tolerable rate was 8 percent, and testing a sample of 200 items resulted in identifying 12 occurrences, thus establishing an upper precision limit of 10 percent (Table 8B–4).

An additional sample of 40 items is determined by entering Table 8B–4 at the column for an upper precision limit of 8 percent, locating the cell for 12 errors, and subtracting from the total required sample size (240) the 200 items already tested. However, before testing these 40 individual items, the auditor should challenge whether any additional occurrences might be observed. If additional occurrences are observed, the achieved upper precision limit still will be greater than the tolerable rate.

Figure 8–3 illustrates the steps that would be taken if stop-or-go sampling is to be used.

Assume the following:

Risk of overreliance	10%
Tolerable rate of occurrence	10%
Expected rate of occurrence	0%
Initial sample size (Table 8A–3)	25

FIGURE 8–3 Stop-or-Go Sampling

Cumulative Sample Size Table 8B–3	Stop-or-Go Sampling Strategy
25	If less than one occurrence, stop; if 1, expand to 40; if 2 or 3, expand to 70.
40	If less than 2 occurrences, stop; if 2 or 3, expand to 70.
70	If less than 4 occurrences, stop; if 4 or 5, expand to 100.

Before expanding any attribute sampling test indefinitely, consider whether it is realistic to expect to achieve the desired results in light of the sample rate of occurrence. It may be unlikely that an upper precision limit less than the tolerable rate will be achieved by extending the test.

When occurrences are found while executing a stop-or-go sampling plan, the auditor must decide among several alternatives. These include (1) increasing the sample size in hope of achieving an upper precision limit less than or equal to the tolerable rate or (2) otherwise changing the nature, timing, or extent of the planned audit procedures to adequately consider the internal control deficiency causing the occurrences. If the sample size is increased, the auditor should carefully consider the number of additional sample items and whether it is reasonable to expect to observe no additional occurrences.

Discovery Sampling

Discovery sampling is a term applied to an attribute sampling plan that is used when both the expected and tolerable error rates are very small. It is used by assuming an expected rate of zero and a small tolerable error rate (often 2 percent or less) at the desired reliability level.

Discovery sampling often is used during special purpose examinations. For example, after dismissing an employee, a company might wish to determine whether irregularities occurred in transactions over which the employee had control. If the former employee approved disbursements from a special bank account, the auditor might decide to test a sample of disbursements large enough to ensure that no more than 1 percent (tolerable rate) of the approved disbursements contained irregularities. In such a situation, a small risk of overreliance usually will be desired. If it were judgmentally determined to be 1 percent, Table 8A–5 indicates a required sample size of 460 disbursements. By testing a sample of this size, the auditor would be 99 percent confident (reliability) of finding an example of an irregularity if they actually occurred in 1 percent or more of the disbursements. In such a case, seeing one example of a fraudulent action normally would lead to expanding the investigation.

APPENDIX 8A

TABLES FOR DETERMINATION OF ATTRIBUTE SAMPLE SIZE

Tables 8A–1 to 8A–5 present the sample sizes required to achieve an upper precision limit less than or equal to the tolerable rate of occurrence assuming an expected occurrence rate at a specified risk of overreliance or reliability level. These tables are taken from the statistical sampling training material in the Ernst & Whinney Professional Development Program.

TABLE 8A–1

Reliability = 80% (Risk of Overreliance = 20%)
Required Sample Size

Expected Rate of Occurrence	Tolerable Rate of Occurrence															
	.5%	1%	2%	3%	4%	5%	6%	7%	8%	9%	10%	12%	14%	16%	18%	20%
0.00%	330	170	80	60	40	40	30	**	**	**	**	**	**	**	**	**
0.25	900	300	160	100	80	60	50	50	40	40	30	30	30	**	**	**
0.50	*	600	160	100	80	60	50	50	40	40	30	30	30	**	**	**
1.0		*	280	100	80	60	50	50	40	40	30	30	30	**	**	**
1.5			800	200	120	60	50	50	40	40	30	30	30	**	**	**
2.0			*	340	140	90	50	50	40	40	30	30	30	**	**	**
2.5				*	200	120	80	60	40	40	30	30	30	**	**	**
3.0					400	160	100	60	60	50	30	30	30	**	**	**
3.5					*	280	140	80	70	50	50	40	30	**	**	**
4.0						500	200	100	70	50	50	40	30	**	**	**
4.5						*	300	180	100	60	60	40	30	**	**	**
5.0							600	180	100	60	60	40	30	**	**	**
5.5							*	320	160	90	70	50	30	30	30	30
6.0								460	200	100	80	50	30	30	30	30
6.5								*	380	180	90	60	30	30	30	30
7.0									700	200	140	70	40	40	30	30
7.5									*	360	160	80	40	40	30	30
8.0										700	260	100	50	50	30	30
8.5										*	400	140	70	50	30	30
9.0											800	140	80	50	30	30
9.5											*	200	80	50	30	30
10.0												240	80	50	30	30
11.0												900	160	70	50	40
12.0												*	300	100	50	40
13.0													1000	160	90	50
14.0													*	300	100	50
15.0														*	160	80
16.0															360	100
17.0															*	200
18.0																360
19.0																*

Note: *more than 1,000 items.
**less than minimum representative sample of 25 items.

TABLE 8A-2

Reliability = 85% (Risk of Overreliance = 15%)
Required Sample Size

Expected Rate of Occurrence	Tolerable Rate of Occurrence															
	.5%	1%	2%	3%	4%	5%	6%	7%	8%	9%	10%	12%	14%	16%	18%	20%
0.00%	400	200	100	70	50	40	40	30	30	**	**	**	**	**	**	**
0.25	500	340	180	120	90	70	60	50	50	40	40	30	30	**	**	**
0.50	*	600	180	120	90	70	60	50	50	40	40	30	30	**	**	**
1.0		*	300	160	90	70	60	50	50	40	40	30	30	**	**	**
1.5			*	200	120	100	60	50	50	40	40	30	30	**	**	**
2.0				500	200	100	80	50	50	40	40	30	30	**	**	**
2.5				*	280	120	80	70	60	40	40	30	30	**	**	**
3.0					600	200	100	90	60	60	50	30	30	**	**	**
3.5					*	340	140	120	80	70	50	40	40	**	**	**
4.0						650	200	120	90	70	50	40	40	**	**	**
4.5						*	400	200	120	80	60	40	40	**	**	**
5.0							700	240	120	90	60	40	40	**	**	**
5.5							*	340	180	120	90	50	50	30	30	30
6.0								800	280	160	100	50	50	30	30	30
6.5								*	460	200	120	60	60	30	30	30
7.0									900	300	180	70	60	40	40	30
7.5									*	550	200	80	60	40	40	30
8.0										1000	300	100	60	50	40	30
8.5										*	550	140	70	60	40	30
9.0											*	200	100	60	40	30
9.5												240	120	60	40	30
10.0												340	120	60	40	30
11.0												*	200	90	60	50
12.0													400	140	80	50
13.0													*	200	100	60
14.0														500	140	70
15.0														*	220	100
16.0															500	160
17.0															*	240
18.0																500
19.0																*

Note: *more than 1,000 items.
  **less than minimum representative sample size of 25 items.

TABLE 8A-3

(Handwritten annotations around the table: "Specify lowest"; "Auditors Judgments PWP."; "Diff. between precision items"; "Threshold of Pain"; "Upper Precision Limit"; "% of error — alpha risk"; "wrong conclusion — 2nd highest"; "has to be Toto wide / too wide")

Reliability = 90% (Risk of Overreliance = 10%)
Required Sample Size

Expected Rate of Occurrence	Tolerable Rate of Occurrence															
	.5%	1%	2%	3%	4%	5%	6%	7%	8%	9%	10%	12%	14%	16%	18%	20%
0.00%	460	230	120	80	60	50	40	40	30	30	25	**	**	**	**	**
0.25	*	400	200	140	100	80	70	60	50	50	40	40	30	30	**	**
0.50		800	200	140	100	80	70	60	50	50	40	40	30	30	30	**
1.0		*	400	180	100	80	70	60	50	50	40	40	30	30	30	**
1.5			*	320	180	120	90	60	50	50	40	40	30	30	30	**
2.0				600	200	140	90	80	50	50	40	40	30	30	30	**
2.5			*	360	160	120	80	70	60	40	40	30	30	30		**
3.0				800	260	160	100	90	60	60	50	30	30	30		**
3.5				*	400	200	140	100	80	70	50	40	40	30		**
4.0					900	300	200	100	90	70	50	40	40	30		**
4.5					*	550	220	160	120	80	60	40	40	30		**
5.0						*	320	160	120	80	60	40	40	30		**
5.5							600	280	160	120	70	50	40	30		30
6.0							*	380	200	160	80	50	40	30		30
6.5								600	260	180	90	60	40	30		30
7.0								*	400	200	100	70	40	40		40
7.5									800	280	120	80	40	40		40
8.0									*	460	160	100	50	50		40
8.5										800	200	100	70	50		40
9.0										*	260	100	80	50		40
9.5											380	160	80	50		40
10.0											500	160	80	50		40
11.0											*	280	140	70		60
12.0												550	180	90		70
13.0												*	300	160		90
14.0													600	200		100
15.0													*	300		140
16.0														650		200
17.0														*		340
18.0																700
19.0																*

Note: *more than 1,000 items.
**less than minimum representative sample of 25 items.

TABLE 8A–4

Reliability = 95% (Risk of Overreliance = 5%)
Required Sample Size

Desired Upper Precision Limit (handwritten annotation)

Expected Rate of Occurrence	.5%	1%	2%	3%	4%	5%	6%	7%	8%	9%	10%	12%	14%	16%	18%	20%
							Tolerable Rate of Occurrence									
0.00%	600	300	150	100	80	60	50	50	40	40	30	30	**	**	**	**
0.25	*	650	240	160	120	100	80	70	60	60	50	40	40	30	30	30
0.50		*	320	160	120	100	80	70	60	60	50	40	40	30	30	30
1.0			600	260	160	100	80	70	60	60	50	40	40	30	30	30
1.5			*	400	200	160	120	90	60	60	50	40	40	30	30	30
2.0				900	300	200	140	90	80	70	50	40	40	30	30	30
2.5				*	550	240	160	120	80	70	70	40	40	30	30	30
3.0					*	400	200	160	100	90	80	60	50	30	30	30
3.5						650	280	200	140	100	80	70	50	40	40	30
4.0						*	500	240	180	100	90	70	60	40	40	30
4.5							800	360	200	160	120	80	60	40	40	30
5.0							*	500	240	160	120	80	60	40	40	30
5.5								900	360	200	160	90	70	50	50	30
6.0								*	550	280	180	100	80	50	50	30
6.5									1000	400	240	120	90	60	50	30
7.0									*	600	300	140	100	70	50	40
7.5										*	460	160	100	80	50	40
8.0											650	200	100	80	50	50
8.5											*	280	140	80	70	50
9.0												400	180	100	70	50
9.5												550	200	120	70	50
10.0												800	220	120	70	50
11.0												*	400	180	100	70
12.0													900	280	140	90
13.0													*	460	200	100
14.0														1000	300	160
15.0														*	500	200
16.0															*	300
17.0																550
18.0																*
19.0																

Note: *more than 1,000 items.
  **less than minimum representative sample of 25 items.

TABLE 8A-5

Reliability = 99% (Risk of Overreliance = 1%)
Required Sample Size

Expected Rate of Occurrence	.5%	1%	2%	3%	4%	5%	6%	7%	8%	9%	10%	12%	14%	16%	18%	20%
0.00%	920	460	230	160	120	90	80	70	60	50	50	40	40	30	30	30
0.25	*	*	340	240	180	140	120	100	90	80	70	60	50	40	40	40
0.50			500	280	180	140	120	100	90	80	70	60	50	40	40	40
1.0			*	400	260	180	140	100	90	80	70	60	50	40	40	40
1.5				800	360	200	180	120	120	100	90	60	50	40	40	40
2.0				*	500	300	200	140	140	100	90	70	50	40	40	40
2.5					1000	400	240	200	160	120	100	70	60	40	40	40
3.0					*	700	360	260	160	160	100	90	60	50	50	40
3.5						*	550	340	200	160	140	100	70	50	50	40
4.0							800	400	280	200	160	100	70	50	50	40
4.5							*	600	380	220	200	120	80	60	60	40
5.0								900	460	280	200	120	80	60	60	40
5.5								*	650	380	280	160	90	70	70	50
6.0									1000	500	300	180	100	80	70	50
6.5									*	800	400	200	120	90	70	60
7.0										*	600	240	140	100	70	70
7.5											800	280	160	120	80	70
8.0											*	400	200	140	100	70
8.5												500	240	140	100	70
9.0												700	300	180	100	90
9.5												1000	360	200	140	90
10.0												*	420	220	140	90
11.0													800	300	180	140
12.0													*	500	240	160
13.0														600	360	200
14.0														*	500	280
15.0															900	360
16.0															*	550
17.0																1000
18.0																*
19.0																

Note: *more than 1,000 items.

APPENDIX 8B

EVALUATION OF ATTRIBUTE
SAMPLE RESULTS

Tables 8B–1 through 8B–5 give the upper precision limit for any particular sample results at a specified risk of overreliance or reliability level. These tables are taken from the statistical sampling training material in the Ernst & Whinney Professional Development Program.

TABLE 8B–1

Reliability = 80% (Risk of Overreliance = 20%)
Number of Observed Occurrences

Sample Size	Upper Precision Limit																
	.5%	1%	2%	3%	4%	5%	6%	7%	8%	9%	10%	12%	14%	16%	18%	20%
25									0					1		
30							0				1		2		3	
40					0				1			2	3		4	5
50					0		1			2		3	4	5	6	7
60				0		1		2		3		4	5	6	7	8
70				0		1		2	3		4	5	6	8	9	10
80			0		1		2	3		4	5	6	8	9	10	12
90			0		1	2		3	4	5	6	7	9	10	12	14
100			0	1		2	3	4	5	6		8	10	12	14	16
120			0	1	2	3	4	5	6	7	8	10	13	15	17	19
140			0	1	3	4	5	6	7	9	10	13	15	18	20	23
160			1	2	3	5	6	7	9	10	12	15	18	21	24	27
180		0	1	2	4	6	7	9	10	12	14	17	20	24	27	30
200		0	1	3	5	6	8	10	12	14	15	19	23	27	30	34
220		0	2	3	5	7	9	11	13	15	17	21	25	30	34	38
240		0	2	4	6	8	10	12	15	17	19	24	28	33	37	42
260		0	2	4	7	9	11	14	16	18	21	26	31	36	41	46
280		0	3	5	7	10	12	15	18	20	23	28	33	39	44	49
300		1	3	5	8	11	14	16	19	22	25	30	36	42	47	53
320		1	3	6	9	12	15	18	20	23	26	32	39	45	51	57
340	0	1	4	7	10	13	16	20	22	25	28	35	41	48	54	61
360	0	1	4	7	10	13	17	20	23	27	30	37	44	51	58	65
380	0	1	4	8	11	14	18	21	25	28	32	39	46	54	61	68
400	0	1	5	8	12	15	19	23	26	30	34	41	49	57	65	72
420	0	1	5	9	12	16	20	24	28	32	36	44	52	60	68	76
460	0	2	6	10	14	18	22	28	31	35	40	48	57	66	75	84
500	0	2	6	11	15	20	24	29	34	39	43	53	62	72	82	91
550	0	2	7	12	17	22	27	32	38	43	48	59	69	80	90	101
600	1	3	8	13	19	24	30	36	41	47	53	64	76	87	99	111
650	1	3	9	15	21	27	33	39	45	51	58	70	83	95	108	120
700	1	4	10	16	23	29	36	42	49	56	62	76	89	103	116	130
800	1	5	12	19	26	34	41	49	57	64	72	87	103	118	134	149
900	1	5	13	22	30	38	47	56	64	73	81	99	116	134	151	169
1000	2	6	15	24	34	43	53	62	72	81	91	110	130	149	169	188

TABLE 8B-2

Reliability = 85% (Risk of Overreliance = 15%)
Number of Observed Occurrences

Sample Size	.5%	1%	2%	3%	4%	5%	6%	7%	8%	9%	10%	12%	14%	16%	18%	20%
25										0				1		
30								0				1		2		3
40						0				1		2		3	4	
50					0			1			2	3		4	5	6
60					0		1		2		3	4	5	6	7	8
70				0		1		2		3		5	6	7	8	10
80				0		1	2		3	4		6	7	8	10	11
90				0	1		2	3	4		5	7	8	10	11	13
100			0		1	2	3		4	5	6	8	9	11	13	15
120			0	1	2	3	4	5	6	7	8	10	12	14	16	18
140			0	1	2	3	5	6	7	8	9	12	14	17	20	22
160			0	2	3	4	6	7	8	10	11	14	17	20	23	26
180			1	2	3	5	7	8	10	11	13	16	19	23	26	29
200		0	1	3	4	6	8	9	11	13	15	18	22	26	29	33
220		0	1	3	5	7	9	10	12	14	16	20	24	29	33	37
240		0	2	3	5	8	10	12	14	16	18	23	27	32	36	41
260		0	2	4	6	8	11	13	15	18	20	25	30	34	39	44
280		0	2	4	7	9	12	14	17	19	22	27	32	37	43	48
300		0	3	5	8	10	13	15	18	21	24	29	35	40	46	52
320		0	3	5	8	11	14	17	20	23	25	31	37	43	49	56
340		1	3	6	9	12	15	19	21	24	27	34	40	46	53	59
360		1	3	6	10	13	16	19	22	26	29	36	43	49	56	63
380		1	4	7	10	14	17	20	24	27	31	38	45	52	60	67
400	0	1	4	7	11	15	18	22	25	29	33	40	48	55	63	71
420	0	1	4	8	12	15	19	23	27	31	35	43	50	58	66	75
460	0	1	5	9	13	17	21	27	30	34	38	47	56	64	73	82
500	0	2	6	10	14	19	24	28	33	37	42	51	61	71	80	90
550	0	2	7	11	16	21	26	31	36	42	47	57	68	78	88	99
600	0	3	7	13	18	23	29	35	40	46	51	63	74	86	97	109
650	0	3	8	14	20	26	32	38	44	50	56	68	81	93	106	118
700	0	3	9	15	22	28	35	41	48	54	61	74	87	101	114	128
800	1	4	11	18	25	33	40	48	55	63	70	85	101	116	131	147
900	1	5	13	21	29	37	46	54	63	71	80	97	114	132	149	167
1000	1	6	14	23	33	42	51	61	70	80	89	108	128	147	166	186

TABLE 8B–3

Reliability = 90% (Risk of Overreliance = 10%)
Number of Observed Occurrences

Sample Size	Upper Precision Limit															
	.5%	*1%*	*2%*	*3%*	*4%*	*5%*	*6%*	*7%*	*8%*	*9%*	*10%*	*12%*	*14%*	*16%*	*18%*	*20%*
25											0				1	
30									0				1		2	
40							0				1		2	3		4
50						0			1			2	3	4	5	
60					0			1		2		3	4	5	6	7
70					0		1		2		3	4	5	6	8	9
80				0		1		2		3	4	5	6	8	9	10
90				0		1	2		3	4		6	7	9	11	12
100				0	1		2	3	4		5	7	9	10	12	14
120			0		1	2	3	4	5	6	7	9	11	13	15	17
140			0	1	2	3	4	5	6	7	9	11	13	16	18	21
160			0	1	2	4	5	6	8	9	10	13	16	19	22	25
180			0	2	3	4	6	7	9	10	12	15	18	22	25	28
200			1	2	4	5	7	8	10	12	14	17	21	24	28	32
220			1	2	4	6	8	10	12	13	15	19	23	27	31	35
240		0	1	3	5	7	9	11	13	15	17	21	26	30	35	39
260		0	1	3	5	8	10	12	14	17	19	24	28	33	38	43
280		0	2	4	6	8	11	13	16	18	21	26	31	36	41	46
300		0	2	4	7	9	12	14	17	20	22	28	33	39	45	50
320		0	2	5	7	10	13	16	18	21	24	30	36	42	48	54
340		0	3	5	8	11	14	17	20	23	26	32	38	45	51	58
360		0	3	6	9	12	15	18	21	25	28	34	41	48	55	61
380		0	3	6	9	13	16	19	23	26	30	37	44	51	58	65
400		1	4	7	10	14	17	21	24	28	31	39	46	54	61	69
420		1	4	7	11	14	18	22	26	29	33	41	49	57	65	73
460	0	1	4	8	12	16	20	24	28	33	37	45	54	63	71	80
500	0	1	5	9	13	18	22	27	31	36	40	50	59	69	78	88
550	0	2	6	10	15	20	25	30	35	40	45	55	66	76	87	97
600	0	2	7	12	17	22	28	33	39	44	50	61	72	84	95	107
650	0	2	8	13	19	24	30	36	42	48	54	66	79	91	104	116
700	0	3	8	14	20	27	33	39	46	52	59	72	85	99	112	126
800	0	4	10	17	24	31	38	46	53	61	68	83	99	114	129	145
900	0	4	12	20	28	36	44	52	61	69	78	95	112	129	146	164
1000	1	5	13	22	31	40	49	59	68	77	87	106	125	144	164	183

TABLE 8B–4

Reliability = 95% (Risk of Overreliance = 5%)
Number of Observed Occurrences

Sample Size	.5%	1%	2%	3%	4%	5%	6%	7%	8%	9%	10%	12%	14%	16%	18%	20%
25												0				1
30											0			1		2
40									0			1		2		3
50							0				1		2	3	4	5
60						0			1			2	3	4	5	6
70						0		1		2		3	4	5	7	8
80					0		1		2		3	4	5	7	8	9
90					0		1	2		3	4	5	6	8	9	11
100				0		1		2	3	4		6	8	9	11	13
120				0	1		2	3	4	5	6	8	10	12	14	16
140				0	1	2	3	4	5	6	7	10	12	14	17	19
160			0	1	2	3	4	5	6	8	9	12	14	17	20	23
180			0	1	2	3	5	6	8	9	11	14	17	20	23	26
200			0	1	3	4	6	7	9	11	12	16	19	23	26	30
220			0	2	3	5	7	8	10	12	14	18	22	25	29	33
240			1	2	4	6	8	10	12	14	16	20	24	28	33	37
260			1	3	4	7	9	11	13	15	17	22	26	31	36	41
280			1	3	5	7	10	12	14	17	19	24	29	34	39	44
300		0	1	3	6	8	11	13	16	18	21	26	31	37	42	48
320		0	2	4	6	9	11	14	17	20	22	28	34	40	45	51
340		0	2	4	7	10	12	15	18	21	24	30	36	42	49	55
360		0	2	5	8	10	13	17	20	23	26	32	39	45	52	59
380		0	2	5	8	11	14	18	21	24	28	34	41	48	55	62
400		0	3	6	9	12	15	19	22	26	29	37	44	51	59	66
420		0	3	6	9	13	16	20	24	27	31	39	46	54	62	70
460		0	4	7	11	15	18	22	26	31	35	43	51	60	68	77
500		1	4	8	12	16	21	25	29	34	38	47	56	66	75	84
550		1	5	9	14	18	23	28	33	38	43	53	63	73	83	94
600	0	1	6	10	15	20	26	31	36	42	47	58	69	80	92	103
650	0	2	6	12	17	23	28	34	40	46	52	64	76	88	100	112
700	0	2	7	13	19	25	31	37	43	50	56	69	82	95	108	122
800	0	3	9	15	22	29	36	43	51	58	65	80	95	110	125	141
900	0	4	10	18	26	34	42	50	58	66	74	91	108	125	142	159
1000	1	4	12	20	29	38	47	56	65	74	84	102	121	140	159	178

TABLE 8B–5

Reliability = 99% (Risk of Overreliance = 1%)
Number of Observed Occurrences

Sample Size	.5%	1%	2%	3%	4%	5%	6%	7%	8%	9%	10%	12%	14%	16%	18%	20%
25																0
30														0		
40												0		1		2
50										0			1	2		3
60									0			1	2	3		4
70								0			1	2	3	4	5	6
80							0			1		2	4	5	6	7
90					0				1		2	3	5	6	7	9
100					0		1			2	3	4	6	7	9	10
120				0		1	2			3	4	6	8	9	11	13
140				0	1	2	3			4	5	7	10	12	14	16
160			0			1	2	3	5	6	7	9	12	14	17	20
180				0	1	2	3	4	6	7	8	11	14	17	20	23
200				0	1	3	4	5	7	8	10	13	16	19	23	26
220				0	2	3	5	6	8	10	11	15	18	22	26	30
240			0	1	2	4	6	7	9	11	13	17	21	25	29	33
260			0	1	3	5	6	8	10	12	14	19	23	27	32	36
280			0	2	3	5	7	9	12	14	16	21	25	30	35	40
300			0	2	4	6	8	10	13	15	18	23	28	33	38	43
320			0	2	4	7	9	11	14	17	19	24	30	35	41	47
340			1	3	5	7	10	13	15	18	21	26	32	38	44	50
360			1	3	6	8	11	14	16	19	22	28	35	41	47	54
380			1	3	6	9	12	15	18	21	24	30	37	44	50	57
400			1	4	7	10	13	16	19	22	26	32	39	46	54	61
420			2	4	7	10	14	17	20	24	27	35	42	49	57	64
460		0	2	5	8	12	15	19	23	27	31	39	47	55	63	72
500		0	3	6	10	13	17	21	26	30	34	43	52	60	70	79
550		0	3	7	11	15	20	24	29	34	38	48	58	68	78	88
600		0	4	8	13	17	22	27	32	37	43	53	64	78	86	97
650		0	4	9	14	19	25	30	36	41	47	58	70	82	94	106
700		1	5	10	16	21	27	33	39	45	51	64	76	89	102	115
800		1	7	13	19	25	32	39	46	53	60	74	89	103	118	133
900		2	8	15	22	29	37	45	53	61	69	85	101	118	135	152
1000	0	2	9	17	25	34	42	51	60	69	78	96	114	133	151	170

Upper Precision Limit

QUESTIONS AND PROBLEMS

8–1. Does the use of statistical sampling eliminate the use of judgment? Explain.

8–2. What are some advantages of using statistical sampling techniques in an audit?

8–3. Statistical sampling techniques are being used in auditing. A sample is taken and analyzed to draw an inference or reach a conclusion about a population, but there is always a risk that the inference or conclusion may be incorrect. What is the value, then, in using statistical sampling techniques?   (AICPA, adapted)

8–4. What are the four types of sampling risk?

8–5. What is meant by the terms *tolerable error* and *tolerable rate of occurrence?*

8–6. Describe what is meant by the term *audit risk.* How does the auditor control audit risk?

8–7. Assume that there is a 20 percent risk that the key attributes will fail to detect errors as large as the tolerable amount and a 60 percent risk that the analytical review and other audit procedures would fail to detect them. Assuming the auditor wishes to limit audit risk to a 5 percent level, calculate the allowable risk of incorrect acceptance.

8–8. Define the following terms:
  a. Population.
  b. Frame.
  c. Sampling unit.
  d. Sample.
  e. Simple random sampling.
  f. Systematic sampling.
  g. Stratified random sampling.

8–9. What three techniques may be used by auditors to select random samples?

8–10. One method used for drawing an unrestricted random sample is to use a random number table. List the steps to follow when using a random number table to select an unrestricted random sample.

8–11. What is the basic advantage systematic sampling has over simple random sampling?

8–12. A nonstratified sample of 80 accounts payable vouchers is to be selected from a population of 3,200. The vouchers are numbered consecutively from 1 to 3,200 and are listed, 40 to a page, in the voucher register. Describe some different techniques for selecting a random sample of vouchers for review.　　　(AICPA, adapted)

8–13. A CPA's client maintains perpetual inventory records. In the past, all inventory items have been counted on a cycle basis at least once during the year. Physical count and perpetual record differences have been minor. Now, the client wishes to minimize the cost of physically counting the inventory by changing to a sampling method in which many inventory items will not be counted during a given year. Under what circumstance will the auditor accept the sampling method?

(AICPA, adapted)

8–14. What is attribute sampling?

8–15. What is the nature of the characteristic being tested in attribute sampling?

8–16. If the risk of overreliance in an attribute sampling test is 30 percent, what is the reliability?

8–17. Assume that a CPA's sample shows an unacceptable error rate in a compliance test of internal control. Describe the various actions that the auditor may take based upon this finding.　　　(AICPA, adapted)

8–18. What is the nature of the achieved upper precision limit as used in attribute sampling?

When the achieved upper precision limit is compared to the tolerable rate at the planned risk of overreliance, what decision can the auditor make?

8–19. What three basic approaches may be used when applying a sampling technique?

8–20. For each of the following questions select the *best* answer:

a. What is the primary objective of using stratification as a sampling method in auditing?

(1) To increase the confidence level (reliability) at which a decision will be reached from the results of the sample selected.

(2) To determine the occurrence rate for a given characteristic in the population being studied.

(3) To decrease the effect of variance in the total population.

(4) To determine the precision range of the sample selected.

b. Which of the following is an advantage of systematic sampling over random number sampling?

(1) It provides a stronger basis for statistical conclusions.

(2) It enables the auditor to use the more efficient "sampling with replacement" tables.

(3) There may be correlation between the location of items in the population, the feature of sampling interest, and the sampling interval.

(4) It does not require establishment of correspondence between random numbers and items in the population.

c. For a large population of cash disbursement transactions, Smith, CPA, is testing compliance with internal control by using attribute sampling techniques. Anticipating an occurrence rate of 3 percent Smith found from a table that the required sample size is 400 with a desired precision limit of 5 percent and reliability of 95 percent. If Smith anticipated an occurrence rate of only 2 percent but wanted to maintain the same desired upper precision limit and reliability, the sample size would be closest to:

(1) 200.

(2) 400.

(3) 533.

(4) 800.

d. Which of the following best describes what the auditor means by the rate of occurrence in an attribute sampling plan?

(1) The number of errors that can reasonably be expected to be found in a population.

(2) The frequency with which a certain characteristic occurs within a population.

(3) The degree of confidence that the sample is representative of the population.

(4) The dollar range within which the true population total can be expected to fall.

e. The purpose of tests for compliance is to provide reasonable assurance that the accounting control procedures are being applied as prescribed. The sampling method that is most useful when testing for compliance is:

(1) Judgment sampling.

(2) Attribute sampling.

(3) Unrestricted random sampling with replacement.

(4) Stratified random sampling.

f. When using statistical sampling for tests of compliance, an auditor's evaluation of compliance would include a statistical conclusion concerning whether:
  (1) Procedural deviations in the population were within an acceptable range.
  (2) Monetary precision is in excess of a certain predetermined amount.
  (3) The population total is not in error by more than a fixed amount.
  (4) Population characteristics occur at least once in the population.

(AICPA, adapted)

8–21. An auditor believes that the error occurrence rate of expensing capital items is 2 percent, which will have an immaterial effect upon the financial statements. The maximum acceptable occurrence rate is 3 percent. What type of sampling plan should the auditor select in the circumstances? (AICPA, adapted)

8–22. Assume that an auditor is interested in appraising the effectiveness of the calculation of payroll taxes. Also, assume the auditor specifies a reliability of 95 percent and the tolerable rate of occurrence is 6 percent. The auditor, based on past experience with this client, feels that the expected error rate is 3 percent.

Required:

Using Appendix 8A, determine the size of the sample that the auditor should draw.

8–23. Referring to Question 8–22, the auditor finds 11 occurrences in the calculation. Using Appendix 8B, find the achieved upper precision limit given the specified reliability.

8–24. You are now conducting your third annual audit of the financial statements of Elite Corporation for the year ended December 31, 1984. You decide to employ unrestricted random number statistical sampling techniques in testing the effectiveness of the company's internal control procedures relating to sales invoices, which are all serially numbered. In prior years, after selecting one representative two-week period during the year, you tested all invoices issued during that period and resolved all of the errors which were found to your satisfaction.

Required:

a. Explain the statistical procedures you would use to determine the size of the sample of sales invoices to be examined.
b. Once the sample size has been determined, how would you select the individual invoices to be included in the sample?
c. Would the use of statistical sampling procedures improve the examination of sales invoices as compared with the selection procedure used in prior years?
d. Assume that the company issued 50,000 sales invoices during the year and the auditor specified a confidence level of 95 percent with a precision range of plus or minus 2 percent.
  (1) Does this mean that the auditor would be willing to accept the reliability of the sales invoice data if errors are found on no more than 4 sales invoices out of every 95 invoices examined? Discuss.
  (2) If the auditor specified a precision range of ±1 percent, would the confidence level be higher or lower than 95 percent assuming that the size of the sample remains constant? Why? (AICPA, adapted)

8–25. What are stop-or-go sampling and discovery sampling?

8-26. The use of statistical sampling techniques in an examination of financial statements does not eliminate judgmental decisions. Identify and explain at least four areas where judgment may be exercised by a CPA in planning a statistical sampling test.

(AICPA, adapted)

8-27. The Cowslip Milk Company's principal activity is buying milk from dairy farmers, processing the milk, and delivering it to retail customers. You are auditing the retail accounts receivable of the company and determine the following:

1. The company has 50 retail routes; each route consists of 100 to 200 accounts, the number that can be serviced by a driver in a day.
2. The driver enters cash collections from the day's deliveries to each customer directly on a statement form in record books maintained for each route. Mail remittances are posted in the route record books by office personnel. At the end of the month the statements are priced, extended, and footed. Photocopies of the statements are prepared and left in the customers' milk boxes with the next milk delivery.
3. The statements are reviewed by the office manager, who prepares a list for each route of accounts with 90-day balances or older. The list is used for intensive collection action.
4. The audit program used in prior audits for the selection of retail accounts receivable for confirmation stated: "Select two accounts from each route, one to be chosen by opening the route book at random and the other as the third item on each list of 90-day or older accounts." Your review of the accounts receivable leads you to conclude that statistical sampling techniques may be applied to their examination.

Required:

a. Since statistical sampling techniques do not relieve the auditor of responsibilities in the exercise of professional judgment, of what benefit are they to the auditor? Discuss.
b. Give the reasons why the audit procedure previously used for selection of accounts receivable for confirmation (as given in [4] above) would not produce a valid statistical sample.
c. What are the audit objectives or purposes in selecting 90-day accounts for confirmation? Can the application of statistical sampling techniques help in attaining these objectives or purposes? Discuss.
d. Assume that the company has 10,000 accounts receivable and that your statistical sampling disclosed 6 errors in a sample of 200 accounts. Is it reasonable to assume that 300 accounts in the entire population are in error? Explain.

(AICPA, adapted)

8-28. Answer the following questions using Appendices 8A and 8B.
a. Assume that you are testing a client's cash disbursements. Specifically, you are testing the propriety of account distributions. A sample occurrence rate of errors of 3 percent is expected, but the substantive tests of operations would have to be expanded only if the occurrence rate were above 8 percent. You want 95 percent reliability. What sample size should be used?
b. Under the conditions in *(a)* above, assume you selected the sample and found 4 occurrences of errors. What is the achieved upper precision limit?

PROBABILITY PROPORTIONAL TO SIZE AND VARIABLES ESTIMATION SAMPLING

This chapter describes two methods of statistical sampling that provide the auditor with a statistical conclusion regarding a recorded amount. The conclusion is based on substantive tests applied to a sample. The methods are probability proportional to size sampling and variables estimation sampling. Chapter 8 discussed attribute sampling, which enables the auditor to statistically evaluate a rate of occurrence in a population. On the other hand, variables estimation sampling enables the auditor to statistically evaluate the dollar value of a population. Probability proportional to size sampling is an extension of attribute sampling that enables the auditor to reach a conclusion in terms of dollars rather than in rate of occurrence. Probability proportional to size sampling has gained wide acceptance in recent years because it is relatively easy to use and results in an evaluation in terms that facilitate making audit decisions. However, each method has advantages and disadvantages, and each is appropriate in certain situations. In addition, computer programs are available that make even the complex calculations under variables estimation sampling manageable.

PROBABILITY PROPORTIONAL TO SIZE SAMPLING

Probability proportional to size (PPS) sampling or dollar unit sampling (DUS) is a statistical sampling technique that provides an estimate of the maximum amount of overstatement of a recorded amount with measurable levels of risk of making a decision error. This technique is most efficient when few, if any, differences are expected when performing the related audit procedure.

PPS sampling results in an estimate of the maximum probable overstatement of the recorded amount. Therefore, it is appropriate when the audit objective is to detect overstatements, such as during the tests of asset account balances. It is not appropriate if the objective is to test for understatements, since an understated item has less chance of being selected than if it was fairly stated. Also, if an item is not recorded, it cannot be selected. However, in some instances, PPS sampling can be effective in testing for understatements if applied to a reciprocal population. For example, in testing for unrecorded liabilities at year-end, the auditor might select a PPS sample of disbursements made subsequent to year-end to test for proper accrual of any liability. The sample would emphasize the larger disbursements in the population, and thus the more material potential liabilities. PPS sampling also can be used when testing key attributes when the auditor is concerned about the total dollar amount of transactions for which a key attribute did not function.

The PPS sampling technique allows the auditor to conclude that an account balance is fairly stated when the maximum probable overstatement ("net upper monetary bound of overstatement") is less than the tolerable error. As mentioned in Chapter 8, tolerable error is the maximum amount by which the account balance being tested can be overstated without the financial statements taken as a whole being materially misstated. The tolerable error for each audit area is an audit judgment that is determined during the program development phase of an engagement.

As discussed in Chapter 8, one of two sampling risks exist whenever the auditor makes a decision about an account balance based on sample evidence:

1. The risk of accepting a book value that is misstated by more than the tolerable error (risk of incorrect acceptance).
2. The risk of rejecting a book value that is fairly stated (risk of incorrect rejection).

When performing tests of key attributes, the same types of sampling risks exist and are referred to as the risk of overreliance (on the key attribute) and the risk of underreliance. Acceptable levels of sampling risks are based on audit judgments that are made during the program development phase of an engagement.

PPS sampling holds the risk of incorrect acceptance—the auditor's principal concern—to a specified level. The risk of incorrect rejection is not explicitly measured in PPS sampling. However, if the auditor expects to observe a few small differences in the sample, there is a technique to increase a PPS sample size to allow for differences in some sample items and still not make an incorrect rejection decision. Nonetheless, PPS sampling generally should be used only when errors are not expected.

SELECTING PPS SAMPLES

Probability proportional to size (PPS) samples are selected so that the probability of selecting an individual item is proportional to its relative size. In contrast, random samples are selected so that each item in the population has an equal probability of selection. With PPS sampling, an individual item with a recorded amount of $500 has 10 times the chance of being selected as an item with a recorded amount of $50.

PPS samples generally are selected by (1) defining a frame consisting of the individual one dollar units making up a population total; (2) computing a dollar value skip interval, based on tolerable error and desired risk of incorrect acceptance; (3) identifying a random sample of those dollars using the skip interval; and (4) systematically selecting the physical units containing the sample dollars for testing. It is unlikely that the frame of individual dollars would be in an order that introduces bias into the systematic selection process with PPS sampling. Therefore, the systematic PPS sample can be selected using only one random start.

To illustrate this process, consider an accounts receivable population containing 1,500 individual customer balances totaling $2,500,000, from which a PPS sample of customer accounts to be confirmed is desired. Correspondence is established by numbering the dollars making up the total balance from 1 to 2,500,000. Assume that the auditor computed a skip interval—based on formulas described later—of $38,461. The auditor then selects a random starting point between $1 and $38,461; assume it is $5,000. The selection process is then applied by identifying the customer accounts containing the 5,000th dollar and every 38,461st dollar after that. The presence of cumulative population totals for each individual item in the frame facilitates this process. The following illustrates the selection procedure:

Customer Account Number	Amount	Cumulative Balance	Amount of Selection Value	Sample Item
001	$ 1,200	$ 1,200		
002	8,043	9,243	$ 5,000	$ 8,043
003	728	9,971		
004	19,761	29,732		
005	4,222	33,954		
006	2,775	36,729		
007	3,896	40,625		
008	17,420	58,045	43,461	17,420
009	225	58,270		
010	8,799	67,069		
011	21,072	88,141	81,922	21,072
	.	.		
	.	.		
	.	.		
	.	.		
Total	$2,500,000	$2,500,000		

This example illustrates that a sample of individual dollars leads to the selection of individual population items for testing. Obviously, an individual dollar from a customer's balance cannot be confirmed. Therefore, once a dollar is selected, the entire item that includes the dollar is subjected to the audit test.

All items equal to or greater than the dollar value skip interval automatically will be selected (and therefore completely tested); thus the PPS sample will include larger value items. In fact, the skip interval serves as an upper boundary, and all items with balances equal to or greater than the upper boundary will be tested. Of course, the auditor can judgmentally choose to set an upper boundary lower than the calculated amount used to select a PPS sample from the remaining portion of the population.

The systematic selection technique can be used whether a sample is selected manually or with computer assistance. It requires accumulating the population values through the population and stopping each time a selection value is reached.

An audit population can be broken into any number of subpopulations for purposes of the systematic selection of a PPS sample. However, the same dollar value skip interval must be used for identification of sample items from each subpopulation. The sample size, skip interval, sample selection, and other necessary data can be determined using either tables (contained in Appendices 9A and 9B) or a computer. For large populations a computer is recommended.

CONTROLLING THE RISK OF INCORRECT ACCEPTANCE

An example of the conclusion that can be drawn from a PPS sample is:

As a result of the test, I am 90 percent confident that the accounts receivable balance of $3 million is not overstated by more than $60,000.

Accordingly, PPS sampling results in a reliability statement (90 percent confident) about the net upper monetary bound of overstatement (not more than $60,000). The *net upper monetary bound of overstatement* (NMB) is an estimate of the maximum overstatement that may exist in the account balance. NMB is similar to the achieved upper precision limit in attribute sampling, except that it is expressed as a dollar amount. An audit decision about the account balance is then made by comparing the computed NMB to the tolerable error. If NMB is less than or equal to the tolerable error, the sample evidence supports acceptance of the recorded amount.

As stated previously, reliability *(R)* expresses the probability (as a percent) that the actual errors in the population are less than or equal to the computed NMB. The only other condition that can exist is that the actual errors in the population exceed NMB, which, if greater than the tolerable error, would lead to incorrect acceptance of the misstated recorded amount. The complement of reliability $(1 - R)$ indicates the chance that actual errors exceed NMB.

When using PPS sampling, the risk of incorrect acceptance is controlled by the reliability level specified when planning and evaluating the test. To illustrate, assume the auditor is planning an accounts receivable confirmation test. The following facts and audit judgments have been given:

Total recorded amount	$4,500,000
Number of accounts	2,500
Tolerable error	$ 150,000
Risk of incorrect acceptance	20%

To control the risk of incorrect acceptance to the desired level of 20 percent, the auditor would specify a reliability level of 80 percent $(1 - .20 = .80$ or 80%) in computing the PPS sample size.

After performing the confirmation procedure and determining the audited value for each sample item, the PPS sampling technique provides a formula for determining the NMB at the specified reliability level. Comparing the computed NMB to the tolerable error permits a decision about the fair statement of the recorded amount within the desired level of risk.

The next section will discuss the first of these steps, planning to test enough sample items. Then we will discuss the evaluation of the sample results and the decision-making process.

DETERMINING THE PPS SAMPLE SIZE AND SKIP INTERVAL

The dollar value skip interval is the focal point of PPS sample selection. Although an approximate PPS sample size can be estimated from the dollar value skip interval, the use of the appropriate interval will result in enough sample items to achieve the desired objective, provided that the observed errors approximate those planned. Therefore, the auditor should not be concerned if the resulting PPS sample is smaller than the estimated sample size.

The first step in determining the dollar value skip interval for PPS sample selection is to convert the desired reliability level to an appropriate factor. The tables in Appendix 9A relate reliability and the expected numbers of errors to the appropriate factor. Different factors are used for overstatement and understatement errors. However, this should not be confused with testing for material understatement which, as previously stated, is not appropriate for PPS sampling. The understatement factors are used in evaluating the PPS sample results to estimate the impact of understatements found in particular sample items. When determining the PPS dollar value skip interval or estimated sample size, always use the overstatement reliability factors (Table 9A–1 in the Appendix).

If the auditor expects to find a few small errors when performing the audit test, two steps are necessary to determine the dollar value skip interval. First, the auditor should determine an interval without regard to the expected errors, i.e., use the overstatement reliability factor for zero errors. Second, that interval can be adjusted to reflect the auditor's expectation of errors.

In the previous example, the auditor wished to control the risk of incorrect acceptance to 20 percent. Therefore, the auditor should use the overstatement reliability factor for zero errors and 80 percent reliability. Table 9A–1 indicates that the factor is 1.61.

The dollar value skip interval can then be computed as follows:

$$\text{Dollar value skip interval} = \frac{\text{Tolerable error}}{\text{Reliability factor}}$$

Assume that the audit program for the confirmation tests indicates a tolerable error of $150,000. In that case, the dollar value skip interval would be $93,168 (rounded) ($150,000 ÷ 1.61).

The reliability factor for zero errors always should be used when initially computing the dollar value skip interval. If the auditor expects to observe a few differences in the sample, the tables in Appendix 9B should be used to adjust the dollar value skip interval to prevent an incorrect rejection decision if a few differences are discovered.

The tables in Appendix 9B depend on the reliability level and both the number and average relative size (stated as a percentage) of expected overstatement errors. These are estimated during the planning process. If the difference between the recorded and audited value of the sample items in error is expected to be 20 percent of the recorded value, then 20 percent is used as the relative error.

Once the auditor has computed the preliminary dollar value skip interval and determined the percentage sample size adjustment from Appendix 9B, the skip interval must be reduced by dividing it by the sum of 100 percent and the adjustment percentage. This adjusted skip interval should then be used to identify PPS sample items.

Determining Sample Size and Skip Interval— An Illustration

Continuing the confirmation example, assume that the auditor expects two or three differences with an average relative error of 10 percent to 20 percent. Using the sample size adjustment table in Appendix 9B for 80 percent reliability, and to be conservative, the higher number of errors (three) and relative error (20 percent), the percentage adjustment is 49 percent. Therefore, the skip interval of $93,168 will be divided by 149 percent (100% + 49%) to arrive at an adjusted skip interval of $62,529 (rounded). With this smaller skip interval, more sample items will be selected. Thus, the auditor will be able to accept the book value as fairly stated even if a few small errors are encountered in the sample. This adjusted skip interval should then be used to identify the PPS sample items.

Even though the dollar value skip interval will result in enough sample items, the auditor may wish to estimate the sample size before it is selected and tested. Since the dollar value skip interval will be used to identify the individual sample dollars in the population, the approximate number of individual sample items can be computed by dividing the population value by the skip interval. Accordingly:

$$\text{Estimated sample size} = \frac{\text{Population value}}{\text{Skip interval}}$$

In the example:

$$\$4,500,000 \div \$62,529 = 71.97 = 71 \text{ or } 72 \text{ customer accounts}$$

However, the estimated number of sample items must be reduced by the number of items in the population, if any, for which the recorded amount exceeds twice the skip interval. These items will be included in the estimated sample size as containing two or more sample dollars, although they obviously will be tested only once. Accordingly, the actual sample size will probably be different from the estimated sample size. This is not a problem as long as the appropriate skip interval was used to identify them.

In summary, the accounts receivable confirmation sample that results from the PPS selection procedure with a skip interval of $62,529 will be large enough to conclude that the recorded amount is not overstated by more than $150,000, with a risk of incorrect acceptance of 20 percent, even if three differences averaging 20 percent of the recorded amount are observed. Finding more than the equivalent of three 20 percent errors may prevent the auditor from concluding that the recorded amount is fairly stated.

Determining the appropriate PPS sample selection criteria is the first step in using this statistical technique. After sample items are selected and the audit test performed, an audit decision is made, within acceptable risk levels, based on the test results. The next section of this chapter discusses the PPS evaluation technique and decision making criteria.

EVALUATING PPS SAMPLE RESULTS

When evaluating the results of an audit procedure applied to only a sample of accounts or transactions, the auditor must project the results of testing the sample to the population. Obviously, there is a risk inherent in stating an audit decision about a population from testing only a sample. The statistical techniques of PPS sampling enable the auditor to make an audit decision and control the level or risk inherent in it.

When planning an audit test, the auditor judgmentally determines the tolerable error and an acceptable level of risk of incorrect acceptance. The PPS evaluation technique results in the net upper monetary bound of overstatement (NMB) at a specified reliability level. The auditor then compares NMB to the tolerable error *(TE)* to make an audit decision about the account balance. If NMB is less than or equal to *TE,* the auditor can conclude that the recorded amount is fairly stated with respect to the particular audit procedure. If not, this decision cannot be made and additional audit work may be required.

Simple formulas may be used to calculate NMB. They are illustrated in the following paragraphs.

The net upper monetary bound of overstatement is composed of three separate items:

Notation	Description
E_{UB}	The actual differences observed in the portion of the population that was completely tested (larger than the upper boundary).

Notation	Description
MB_U	The upper monetary bound of overstatement—an estimate of the maximum amount of overstatement indicated by overstatement errors observed in the sample.
MB_L	The lower monetary bound of understatement—an estimate of the minumum amount of understatement indicated by understatement errors observed in the sample.

The net monetary bound of overstatement is then computed by combining these factors as follows:

$$NMB = E_{UB} + MB_U - MB_L$$

Errors in the Portion of the Population Completely Tested (E_{UB})

The PPS sample selection technique uses a dollar value skip interval to identify sample items. The skip interval serves as a natural upper boundary; all items in the population that are greater than or equal to that amount will be selected for testing. Of course, the auditor could arbitrarily set some lower amount to be used as an upper boundary. In that case, the lower amount will be used to identify the portion of the population to be completely tested.

Since all of these population items are tested, they are key items. The auditor can determine with certainty the actual difference between audited and recorded amounts that exist in this portion of the population. This difference should be computed by netting understatement differences against overstatement differences to determine a net overstatement difference referred to as E_{UB}. If there is a net understatement difference in these items, E_{UB} will be negative.

Upper Monetary Bound of Overstatement (MB_U)

The objective in evaluating other overstatement differences is to estimate the maximum probable overstatement of the total recorded amount (MB_U) at the desired reliability level, indicated by the observed overstatement errors in the sample.

When evaluating these differences, the auditor gives greater weight to sample items for which the audited amount is zero, since these items are overstated by their entire book value. They are referred to as 100 percent errors, since their relative error is 100 percent. The portion of the upper monetary bound of overstatement attributable to 100 percent errors is computed by multiplying the skip interval times an overstatement reliability factor (from Table 9A–1) that is based on the (1) reliability level needed and (2) number of 100 percent errors noted.

In many audit situations, no 100 percent errors will be observed. This does not necessarily mean that none exists; it means only that the auditor did not observe any. In those situations, the reliability factor for zero errors would be used to compute that portion of MB_U.

The upper monetary bound of overstatement attributable to errors other than 100 percent errors is computed by considering the average relative error of these sample items. The relative error for each sample item is computed by dividing the recorded amount into the difference between the recorded and audited amounts. The average relative error is determined by totaling the individual relative errors and dividing the total by the number of errors. The average relative error is always less than 1.

The portion of MB_U attributable to errors other than 100 percent errors is then computed as follows:

1. From Table 9A–1, determine the overstatement reliability factor for the total number of overstatements noted in the sample (including 100 percent errors).
2. From the overstatement reliability factor obtained in (1) above, subtract the overstatement reliability factor for only 100 percent errors.
3. Multiply the difference in (2) above times both the average relative error and skip interval.[1]

These two portions of the formula (100 percent errors and other than 100 percent errors) are then combined to obtain the upper monetary bound of overstatement. If the skip interval is greater than the upper boundary actually used (i.e., arbitrarily set by the auditor), the ratio of the total recorded amount of the population less than the upper boundary to the actual number of sample items less than the upper boundary should be substituted for the skip interval in the above computation.

Lower Monetary Bound of Understatement (MB_L)

The upper monetary bound of overstatement was computed using reliability factors that estimated the maximum amount (or upper limit) of overstatement errors in the population. However, the overstatement orientation of PPS sampling dictates that MB_L be computed with reliability factors that estimate the *minimum* amount (or lower limit) of understatement errors in the population.

---

[1] If the auditor decides to set the upper boundary lower than the calculated skip interval (i.e., to test additional key items), then the ratio of the total population less than the upper boundary to the total number of sample items less than the upper boundary should be substituted for the skip interval.

The understatement reliability factors are much smaller than the overstatement factors. This minimizes the effect of understatement errors when they are "netted" against the effect of overstatement errors. Table 9A–2 in Appendix 9A contains the understatement reliability factors that are used when evaluating understatement errors. If no understatement errors are observed, there is no lower monetary bound to be netted against the upper monetary bound of overstatement.

The lower monetary bound of understatement is computed similarly to the upper monetary bound of overstatement except that there is no portion associated with 100 percent errors. All understatement errors are included in the average relative error computation. MB_U is then computed by multiplying understatement reliability factor from Table 9A–2 times the average relative error and the skip interval.

If the upper boundary is less than the skip interval, the ratio described above in computing MB_U is substituted again.

Evaluating Results—An Illustration

To illustrate the evaluation of a PPS sample using the computations described above, consider the previous example of the accounts receivable confirmations.

The auditor desired a reliability (R) of 80 percent and set tolerable error (TE) at $150,000. Because the auditor planned on seeing a few, small differences, the resulting skip interval was $62,529. Assume that using the skip interval of $62,529, the auditor obtained a sample of 69 items, plus two items that are equal to or greater than $62,529, and the total book value of these two items is $145,000. The total book value of the population excluding these 2 items is $4,305,000. Assume the following five differences were found.

Sample Items	Book Value	Audited Value	Difference
(1)	$ 1,892	$ 2,322	$ (430)
(2)	32,306	19,442	12,864
(3)	48,222	38,915	9,307
(4)	29,118	–0–	29,118
Items greater than or equal to $62,529:			
(5)	73,000	69,125	3,875

The first step is to compute the actual difference in items greater than or equal to the skip interval (E_{UB}). The auditor found one difference of $3,875 in these items. Therefore:

$$E_{UB} = \$3,875$$

Next, the auditor computes the upper monetary bound of overstatement (MB_U). The first thing to do is to segregate overstatement differences from understatement differences because of the different methods for evaluating these. In the example, the auditor noted one understatement difference [sample item (1)] and three overstatements. The next step is to determine the number of overstatement differences that are 100 percent differences. In this example, there is one sample item that is a 100 percent difference. The overstatement reliability factor for a reliability level of 80 percent and one error (from Table 9A–1) is 2.99. Multiplying this by the skip interval, $62,529, equals $186,962 (rounded). This is the portion of MB_U attributable to 100 percent errors.

Next, the auditor needs to compute the amount of MB_U attributable to other than 100 percent errors. There are two such errors in the example. The auditor computes the average relative error for these items as follows:

Sample Item	Difference/Book Value	Relative Error
(2)	$12,864/$32,306	.3982
(3)	$ 9,307/$48,222	.1930
	Total relative error	.5912

Dividing the total of the individual relative errors (.5912) by the number of these errors (2) results in an average relative error of .2956. The portion of MB_U attributable to errors other than 100 percent errors is computed as follows:

1. The overstatement reliability factor for a reliability level of 80 percent and three errors (from Table 9A–1) is 5.52.
2. The difference between the overstatement reliability factor for three errors and the factor for one 100 percent error (5.52 − 2.99) is 2.53.
3. The portion attributable to errors other than 100 percent errors (2.53 × .2956 × $62,529) is $46,763 (rounded).

Adding this $46,763 to the portion of the MB_U attributable to 100 percent errors ($186,962), results in MB_U of $233,725.

The next step is to determine the lower monetary bound of understatement (MB_L). There is one understatement error with a relative error of (430/1892) or .2273. Using Table 9A–2, the understatement reliability factor is .22. Thus, $MB_L = (.22)(.2273)(\$62,529)$ or $3,127 (rounded).

Finally, the auditor nets MB_L against MB_U and adds E_{UB} to determine the net upper monetary bound of overstatement at the 80 percent reliability level as follows:

$$\text{NMB} = E_{UB} + MB_U - MB_L$$
$$\text{NMB} = \$3,875 + \$233,725 - \$3,127$$
$$\text{NMB} = \$234,473$$

The auditor then compares NMB to the tolerable error *(TE)*. If NMB is less than or equal to *TE,* the auditor can conclude that the recorded amount is not misstated by more than tolerable error at the planned risk of incorrect acceptance (i.e., 20 percent in this example). In the example, NMB ($234,473) exceeds the amount of tolerable error ($150,000). Therefore, the sample evidence does not provide enough evidence to make that conclusion. In this case, the auditor has several choices:

1. Attempt to determine the nature and cause of the errors and consider whether additional audit evidence from supplemental audit procedures will allow the auditor to judgmentally determine the fairness of the book value based on the results of this sample and other relevant audit evidence.
2. Examine additional sample items, selected on a PPS basis, and combine the results of this sample with the original PPS sample.
3. Select and audit the largest previously unselected items. If no additional differences are discovered, the planned criteria will be met.
4. Suggest that the client adjust the book value of the population. NMB should be reduced by the amount of any such adjustment.

OTHER CONSIDERATIONS

PPS sampling is a statistical sampling technique that has many audit uses. Whenever the auditor is performing a test for which the principal objective is to detect overstatement and few, if any, errors are expected, the use of PPS sampling should be considered. The technique is relatively easy to use and results in an evaluation in terms that facilitate making audit decisions.

However, a word of caution is in order. This chapter began by noting that PPS sampling is appropriate when few or no errors are expected. The net upper monetary bound becomes large very quickly as differences are observed. Although this characteristic is very conservative, it leaves the auditor susceptible to making an incorrect rejection if unanticipated differences are observed.

If the auditor performs a PPS sampling application and encounters many unexpected differences (10 or more), there may be alternate methods of evaluating the sample results. Accordingly, if an auditor is in this situation and is unable to accept the recorded amount as being fairly stated, the auditor should consult with someone who is more knowledgeable about this statistical technique.

VARIABLES ESTIMATION SAMPLING

Variables estimation sampling is a statistical sampling technique that results in an estimate at a specified reliability of the dollar range within which the true audited value of the population lies. This technique is particularly well suited to audit situations where errors are expected and the auditor wishes to obtain evidence as to whether or not the errors are significant in total.

The Decision Interval

The decision-making process with variables estimation sampling is based on the comparison of an estimate of the true audited value (based on the sample) to a decision interval. If the estimate falls within the decision interval, the auditor concludes that the recorded amount is fairly stated, i.e., not misstated by more than tolerable error. If not, the statistical evidence indicates that a misstatement of more than the tolerable error may exist.

The *decision interval* is a range centered at the total recorded amount of the population and extends in both directions by an amount called *precision*. Using the notation B to represent the total recorded amount and A to signify the amount of precision, the decision interval can be illustrated on a number line as follows:

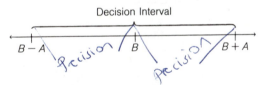

Decision Interval

$B - A$ Precision B Precision $B + A$

There are several ways to use the sample information to estimate the audited value of the population—referred to as the *population estimate*. The simplest method is to multiply the average audited amount in the sample by the number of items in the population. To illustrate, assume that the auditor has audited 100 sample items. If the total audited value for the 100 sample items, some of which differ from the recorded value, is $845,000, the average audited value is $8,450 ($845,000/100). If the number of items in the population is 10,000, the population estimate is $84,500,000 ($8,450 × 10,000).

To illustrate the use of the decision interval, assume further that the total recorded amount of this population is $85 million and that the precision is $1 million. In this case, the decision interval B plus or minus A and population estimate (X) appear as follows (in millions):

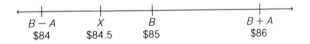

$B - A$	X	B	$B + A$
$84	$84.5	$85	$86

This sample indicates that the recorded amount is fairly stated since the population estimate is within the decision interval.

The precision amount is important because it is the principal basis for a decision about the fair statement of an account balance. The amount of precision depends on the sample results and is key to controlling the risks of relying on the sample evidence.

CONTROLLING RISKS WITH VARIABLES ESTIMATION SAMPLING

In the example above, the auditor computed the average audited value for all sample items and used it to compute the population estimate. Some of these sample items contained audit differences; others did not. Nonetheless, they all were used to compute the population estimate and to construct the decision interval.

We previously mentioned that precision is a key element in controlling the decision risks in variable estimation sampling. To consider how this is done, we use the following simple notation:

Population or sample characteristics:

N = The number of items in the population
S = A computed measure of the variability of the individual amounts in the sample—the standard deviation
n = Sample size

Audit judgments:

U = A factor to reflect the desired reliability level
A = Planned precision

Next, we examine the basic formula of the variable estimation technique. The formula can be arranged to compute either sample size or precision. The formula for each is:

Sample Size		Precision

$$n = \left(\frac{USN}{A}\right)^2 \quad \text{or} \quad A = \frac{U}{\sqrt{n}} SN$$

When using this formula, the auditor must use the conditions that exist in the population and sample *(N, S)* and provide the audit judgments *(U* and/or *A)*. The reliability factor *(U)* and either the desired precision *(A)* or the sample size *(n)* must be specified. Typically, the sample size is computed when planning the sample and then becomes a measure of the amount of work the auditor has done when evaluating its results. Therefore, when planning the sample, the amounts for *U* and *A* also are important audit judgments in determining the required sample size. These judgments provide the ability to control decision risks. In setting them, the auditor can control both the risk of incorrect acceptance and the risk of incorrect rejection.

To consider how these amounts are used to control risk, it is necessary to introduce an assumption. Assume that the auditor knows the true audited value of the population. The only way to actually know this value would be to test every item in the population—a task which would eliminate sampling risk. However, first assume that the true value *(T)* of the population equals the recorded amount *(B)*. After reviewing this assumption, we will consider the situation when the recorded amount *(B)* is overstated by more than the tolerable error amount *(TE)*.

When the first assumption is true *(B = T)*, an incorrect decision will be made whenever the sample results fail to support fair statement of the recorded amount (i.e., the population estimate is outside the decision interval). This would be an incorrect rejection decision. We will now consider how the risk of making that type of decision error is controlled.

Risk of Incorrect Rejection

The risk of incorrect rejection is the risk that the sample will indicate that the recorded amount is misstated by more than tolerable error when in fact it is fairly stated. We can use the first assumption (that the true value equals the recorded amount) to consider how to control this risk. It assumes the purest form of fair statement, i.e., exact equality *(B = T)*.

Statistical theory (specifically the central limit theorem) tells us that an estimate of the true value of a population will be within the precision distance from the actual population total. The percentage of the time this will be the case is stated as reliability. This means that R percent of the population estimates derived from *all* possible samples of a given size will be less than or equal to the precision distance away from the true value in either direction.

If the true value equals the recorded amount, this would mean that R percent of the time the auditor would reach the correct acceptance decision about the account balance. The following diagram illustrates this concept:

$$B - A = T - A \qquad\qquad B = T \qquad\qquad B + A = T + A$$

| R percent of the population estimates from all possible samples of a given size will be in this range.

The rest of the time $(1 - R)$ the auditor would conclude that the recorded amount is *not* fairly stated even though the true value is in fact equal to the recorded amount. This would result in an incorrect rejection of the recorded amount. Accordingly, in variables estimation sampling, the risk of incorrect rejection is controlled through the specification of reliability. The amount of incorrect rejection risk is the complement of reliability $(1 - R)$.

In addition to controlling the risk of incorrect rejection, variables estimation sampling also offers the opportunity to control the more dangerous risk of incorrect acceptance. We will now consider how that risk is controlled by examining the situation when the auditor is most vulnerable to making this type of decision error.

Risk of Incorrect Acceptance

The risk of incorrect acceptance is the risk that the sample will indicate that the recorded amount is fairly stated when in fact it is misstated by more than tolerable error. This would occur only when the population estimate falls within the decision interval and the true (but unknown) value differs from the recorded amount by more than the tolerable error amount.

The risk of incorrect acceptance is most easily understood by assuming that the true value of the population differs from the recorded amount by only slightly more, say one dollar, than the tolerable error amount. The larger the amount of actual error, the higher the likelihood that the sample will reveal the error. Accordingly, the auditor is most vulnerable to not detecting the misstatement when the true value differs from the recorded amount by slightly less than the tolerable error amount.

Remember, we previously noted that statistical theory tells us that a measurable percentage (R) of estimates of the population total will fall within the precision distance of the true value. It also tells us that the estimates from all possible samples of a given size will be distributed around the population's true value, i.e., a normal distribution. This means that approximately 50 percent of the population estimates resulting from samples of a given size will be greater than the true value and the other 50 percent will be less than the true value. More importantly, this same theory can be expanded to mathematically measure the percentage of population estimates that fall between any two points on a number line containing the true population value.

Since the decision interval is centered at the recorded amount, it is possible to determine a precision amount that will hold to an acceptable level the risk of obtaining a population estimate within the decision interval even though the recorded amount is misstated by slightly more than the tolerable error amount (risk of incorrect acceptance).

If the decision interval is represented by the recorded amount, plus or minus the tolerable error, then approximately 50 percent of all estimates from samples of a given size will support fair statement of the recorded amount even when the recorded amount is overstated by slightly more than the tolerable error. When this occurs, the auditor commits an incorrect acceptance. As the decision interval becomes smaller than tolerable error, there is less of a chance of obtaining a population estimate within the interval when the recorded value is overstated by more than the tolerable error. Remember that the length of the decision interval is determined by precision. Accordingly, *the risk of incorrect acceptance is controlled by the auditor's specification of precision in a variables estimation sampling plan.*

This conceptual understanding of the risk concepts and the basic principles of variables estimation sampling will be the foundation for the discussion of:

1. The computation of a sample size to control risks to the desired levels.
2. The evaluation of the sample results to make an audit decision within those risk levels.

When variables estimation sampling is used, the auditor has the ability to control both the risk of incorrect acceptance and the risk of incorrect rejection. The first step in controlling these risks is to plan to select a sample that is large enough. The next section will examine the steps in determining the appropriate sample size.

DETERMINING SAMPLE SIZE— USING A FORMULA

A variables estimation sample size should be large enough to permit making an audit decision within the desired risk levels. The variables and formula described earlier are summarized below:

	Notation	Description
Population characteristics	N	Number of items in the population.
	S	A measure of the variability of the recorded amounts of the population items. The statistical term for this amount is the standard deviation of the population.
Audit judgments	U	A statistical factor for the audit judgment for reliability or risk of incorrect rejection.
	A	The planned precision to reflect the judgments for the risk of incorrect acceptance and the tolerable error amount.
Computed amount	n	The number of sample items.

The above factors are related through the following formula to determine the required sample size:

$$n = \left(\frac{USN}{A}\right)^2$$

We will now consider each factor separately to illustrate how to determine the appropriate amounts to use in the formula.

Determining the Reliability Factor (U)— Using a Table

Previously, we indicated that reliability (stated as a percentage) is used to control the risk of incorrect rejection. The desired level of risk of incorrect rejection is an audit judgment, based in part, on the difficulty in identifying or testing additional sample items at a later date. This risk usually is stated in a range of 1 to 20 percent and is converted to a reliability level by subtracting it from 100 percent. For every reliability level, there is a corresponding factor (generally between one and three) called the reliability factor. Table 9–1 below contains factors for some of the more frequently used reliability levels and identifies the reliability factor (U) that corresponds to a desired reliability level or risk of incorrect rejection.

TABLE 9–1   Reliability Factors

Risk of Incorrect Rejection	Reliability (1 − Risk of Incorrect Rejection)	Reliability Factor (U)
1%	99%	2.58
5	95	1.96
10	90	1.65
20	80	1.28

Determining Planned Precision (A)—Using a Table

In Chapter 8, we used the notation TD to indicate the risk of incorrect acceptance for a sample used in a Test of Details of an account balance. As planned precision (A) gets smaller in relation to the tolerable error amount (TE), the risk of incorrect acceptance decreases. Accordingly, the risk of incorrect acceptance is controlled by specifying an amount for precision in the sample size formula relative to the tolerable error. How much smaller depends on the planned risk of incorrect acceptance.

The amount of precision to specify in the sample size formula can be determined once the auditor has made the necessary audit judgments for the risk of incorrect rejection, risk of incorrect acceptance, and the tolerable error amount. Table 9–2 assists in this determination. It indicates the relationship between planned precision *(A)* and the tolerable error amount *(TE)* to control the risk of incorrect acceptance and incorrect rejection to specified levels.

TABLE 9–2 Relationship of Precision to Tolerable Error *(A/TE)* at Given Risk Levels

	Risk of Incorrect Rejection			
	20%	10%	5%	1%
Risk of Incorrect Acceptance (TD)	Reliability factor:			
	1.28	1.65	1.96	2.58
1	.355	.413	.457	.525
2.5	.395	.456	.500	.568
5	.437	.500	.543	.609
7.5	.471	.532	.576	.641
10	.500	.561	.605	.668
15	.551	.612	.653	.712
20	.603	.661	.700	.753
25	.653	.708	.742	.791
30	.707	.756	.787	.829
35	.766	.808	.834	.868
40	.831	.863	.883	.908
45	.907	.926	.937	.952
50	1.000	1.000	1.000	1.000

To use Table 9–2, identify the appropriate row and column based on the audit judgments for desired risk levels and read the relationship of *A/TE* at their intersection. Then multiply the amount obtained by the tolerable error amount *(TE)* to obtain precision *(A)* to be specified when determining sample size.

The following example illustrates how to determine amounts for *U* and *A*. Assume that the audit program indicates the following for a test of inventory pricing for a retail grocery products warehouse:

Tolerable error amount *(TE)*	$100,000
Risk of incorrect acceptance *(TD)*	30%
Risk of incorrect rejection (1 − *R*)	10%

Table 9–1 indicates that the *U* factor for a 10 percent risk of incorrect rejection (90 percent reliability) is 1.65. Table 9–2 indicates that the ratio of precision to the tolerable error amount for a 30 percent risk of incorrect

acceptance and 10 percent risk of incorrect rejection is .756. Therefore, precision can be computed to be $75,600 (.756 × $100,000).

Once these amounts, which are based on audit judgment, are determined, the only remaining factors in the formula are characteristics of the population being tested.

Determining Population Characteristics— Using Formulas

The number of items in the population *(N)* is easily derived by counting or using another reliable source, such as a computer listing.

The standard deviation *(S)*, a measure of the variability of the population, is mathematically cumbersome, but not difficult to compute. It can be estimated by selecting a preliminary sample of at least 50 items from the population and:

1. Computing the average recorded amount.
2. Squaring the difference between each item's recorded amount and the average recorded amount and totaling these values.
3. Dividing this total by the preliminary sample size minus 1.
4. Computing the square root of the result.

The formula for calculating the standard deviation of a preliminary sample is:

$$S = \sqrt{\frac{\sum_{j=1}^{n} (x_j - \bar{x})^2}{n - 1}}$$

where

x_j = Recorded amount of the *j*th sample item
$\bar{x}$ = Average recorded amount of all sample items
n = Number of items in the preliminary sample

$\sum_{j=1}^{n} (x_j - \bar{x})^2$ Represents the process of totaling the individual values $(x_j - \bar{x})^2$ for each of the n sample items that are separately identified by the subscript *j*.

To illustrate the sample size formula, we continue our previous example. We were determining the sample size for an inventory price test of a grocery products distributor. The values for *U* and *A* were previously determined to be 1.65 and $75,600, respectively. Further, assume that by counting the pages and number of items on each page of the inventory listing the auditor has determined that there are 1,200 inventory line items. The auditor has randomly selected 50 line items and computed their average extended value to be $13,000, and their standard deviation *(S)* to be $410. Substituting these values in the sample size formula presented earlier would result in the following:

$$n = \left(\frac{USN}{A}\right)^2$$

$$= \left(\frac{1.65 \times \$410 \times 1{,}200}{\$75{,}600}\right)^2$$

$$\cong \underline{\underline{115}}$$

Therefore, a sample of at least 115 items would be tested to reach an audit decision about the fair statement of the inventory balance in regard to pricing, while planning to control the risk of incorrect rejection to 10 percent and the risk of incorrect acceptance to 30 percent.

The sample size formula reflects the two audit judgments in the manner you would expect. Smaller risks of either or both incorrect acceptance or incorrect rejection tend to increase the sample size.

Notice, however, that the sample size formula depends on neither the total nor average value in the population. The population characteristic which is most influential is S, a measure of variability of the population items around the average value. However, this measure is based on only a small presample of the *recorded* amounts in the population. Accordingly, as you will see, it is important to determine this amount when evaluating the sample results based on *audited* amounts.

One method of reducing the sample size is to adjust the sampling plan based on the variability of the population. This can sometimes be accomplished by dividing the population into several subpopulations (called strata) and determining a separate sample size for each. This process is called stratification, and the technique is called stratified variables estimation sampling.

Stratified Variables Estimation Sampling

The purpose of stratification is to divide a relatively heterogeneous population into relatively homogenous groups. As a result, where a population contains widely differing balances, stratification based upon recorded amounts is possible and may result in a smaller total sample size. This is the most common method of stratification.

Where another basis for stratification is used, there should be a belief that the stratification would achieve the desired objective. For example, inventory may consist of two very different types of products, and one type may be consistently more expensive or subject to error than the other. In this case, stratification of the two types of inventory may be appropriate.

When using stratified sampling, statistical theory is used to determine the required sample size for each strata. Strata with a large number of items and/or large standard deviations usually require testing proportionately more sample items than those with few items and/or small standard deviations.

The procedure of sample size allocation in stratified statistical sampling supports an intuitive judgment to place more emphasis on large items and less emphasis on small items. Formulas can be used to calculate how much more emphasis to give these items. They will not be covered here because stratification usually is accomplished with computer software.

EVALUATING SAMPLE RESULTS

When an audit procedure has been applied to a sample of the details of an account balance, the auditor uses the sample evidence to make a decision about the fair statement of the account total. With variables estimation sampling, this decision is made by comparing an estimate of the population's true audited value to a decision interval. A key element in constructing the decision interval is the amount used for precision, since this amount determines the endpoints of the decision interval within which the population estimate must fall to support fair statement of the recorded amount.

The size of the sample was determined by relating the audit judgments for risk of incorrect acceptance and risk of incorrect rejection, through precision (A) and the reliability factor (U), to the number of items in the population (N) and an estimate of the variability of the individual recorded amounts (S). Generally, the desired reliability and number of items in the population will not change. However, after testing the sample, the auditor must use the audited amounts of the sample items to make a decision. This requires computing a new value for S, based on the audited values of the sample items. Further, the sample size (n) is now given by the number of items actually tested. Accordingly, the auditor must compute a new value for precision that will reflect the variability of the audited amounts in the sample and the actual sample size. This precision is called *achieved precision* to indicate that it is achieved from the sample results. Its notation is A' (A prime).

Achieved precision reflects the results of auditing the sample. However, planned precision (A) was originally specified as a percentage of the tolerable error amount to control the risk of incorrect acceptance. Achieved precision (A') reflects only the sample results and does not consider the risk of incorrect acceptance.

If achieved precision (A') is larger than planned precision (A), the endpoint of the decision interval will be too close to the value of the recorded amount less the tolerable error amount. Accordingly, if the recorded amount is in fact overstated by more than the tolerable error amount, too high a percentage of all possible population estimates from samples from that misstated population will fall within the decision interval. This would lead to an incorrect acceptance decision too frequently. In such a situation, the risk of incorrect acceptance is larger than planned.

Alternatively, the achieved precision (A') might be smaller than the planned precision (A). In this case, a relatively low percentage of the population estimates that would be obtained if the true value was actually the recorded amount less the tolerable error amount would fall within the decision interval, resulting in a risk of incorrect acceptance that is lower than the auditor was originally willing to tolerate. Although this would be acceptable, it would place the endpoint of the decision interval too close to the recorded amount and, therefore, possibly result in the auditor rejecting a recorded amount that was not materially misstated (incorrect rejection).

Since neither of these situations is desirable, the achieved precision must be adjusted to reflect both the new information about the variability of the audited values and the planned risk of incorrect acceptance. This revised amount will be referred to as *adjusted precision or A''* (A double prime).

Adjusted precision *(A'')* can easily be computed from the following formula:

$$A'' = A' + TE(1 - A'/A)$$

where

A' = Achieved precision based on the sample results
A = Planned precision
TE = Tolerable error

If the population estimate falls within this decision interval, the auditor can conclude that the sample indicates that the recorded amount is fairly stated. This decision interval will control both incorrect acceptance risk and incorrect rejection risk to the planned levels.

If the population estimate falls outside the decision interval, the auditor cannot accept the recorded amount as being fairly stated. However, unlike the other statistical sampling methods that are used, the risk of making an incorrect rejection decision can be measured.

Calculating the Population Estimate

One of the keys to the decision making process is the population estimate. Previously, we illustrated using the average audited amount multiplied by the number of items in the population to estimate the total population audited value. Although this is the simplest method, there are several other more efficient ways of computing a population estimate.

Our previous discussion referred to the variability of the population as measured by the standard deviation *(S)*. This measure of variability must be made with respect to the population characteristic used to estimate the total audited value. There also are several methods of determining this amount.

Remember that when the standard deviation *(S)* changed from the estimate used in determining the required sample size, the achieved precision *(A')* differed from the planned precision *(A)*. Using a more efficient evaluation technique results in a better population estimate and a smaller achieved precision. These factors result in better decision making criteria.

An auditor can identify the evaluation technique that will lead to the most efficient decision interval by selecting the one with the smallest precision at a specified reliability level. Four methods can be used to determine the population estimate and related precision. The following paragraphs briefly describe the sample characteristics used by each. The sample characteristic is used to describe the method.

1. *Simple extension method.* This is the evaluation method previously illustrated. It uses the average audited value of the sample items to estimate the population total and the related achieved precision.
2. *Difference method.* This method uses the average difference between each sample item's recorded and audited amounts to estimate the population total and the related achieved precision.
3. *Ratio method.* This method uses the ratio of the sum of the audited amounts to the sum of the recorded amounts of the sample items to estimate the true value of the population and the related achieved precision.
4. *Regression method.* This method usually provides the most efficient population estimate, i.e., the greatest achieved precision and therefore the smallest range. It uses the mathematical properties of the simple extension, difference, and ratio estimation methods to develop a regression coefficient that correlates the average audited and recorded amounts of sample items with the total recorded amount of the population to obtain a population estimate and related achieved precision.

Variables estimation sampling can be used on either a stratified or unstratified basis. This decision is made when determining the total required sample size. The evaluation must be performed using the same strata boundaries.

Each evaluation technique can be used in either an unstratified or stratified approach. The words *separate* and *combined* are used to describe how the evaluation is performed. Therefore, the separate regression method indicates that the regression evaluation method was applied to the sample in each stratum whereas the combined regression method indicates the applicability of the regression method on a stratified basis.

The discussion of population estimates and the related precision intentionally has been from a very general perspective. To use variables estimation sampling in an audit situation requires that the auditor have only a general understanding of the technique but know how to use the concepts to make an audit decision. The computations required in variables estimation sampling can be quite complex. To facilitate the use of variables estimation sampling, computer programs have been developed to perform the complex arithmetic computations, summarize the results, and provide other information required to make an audit decision. Thus, an auditor usually should not attempt to perform manually the mathematical computations required with the use of this technique. However, the formula approach may be of interest in understanding the theory underlying the approach. Appendix 9C presents the formulas used in variables estimation sampling.

Evaluating Sample Results—An Illustration

To illustrate the evaluation of a variables estimation sample using the computations described above, consider the previous example of the inventory pricing test. The auditor desired a reliability of 90 percent (risk of incorrect rejection of 10 percent), a risk of incorrect acceptance of 30 percent, and set tolerable error at $100,000. Using the formula, planned precision was $75,600 and the required sample size was 115 items.
Assume the following additional information:

1. The recorded amount of inventory is $4 million.
2. A computer program analyzes the result of the auditor's tests of the pricing of the 115 sample items. Maintaining the planned reliability or confidence level, adjusted precision (A'') is computed as $69,750. The population estimate, based on the regression method, is $3,958,500.

Thus, the decision interval for the inventory account ranges from $3,930,250 to $4,069,750 (the recorded amount of $4 million plus or minus adjusted precision of $69,750). The population estimate of $3,958,500 falls within the decision interval. Accordingly, the auditor can conclude that the sample information supports fair statement of the inventory account balance at the planned risk of incorrect acceptance.

If the sample information does not support fair statement of the account balance, the auditor has three alternatives:

1. Increase the sample size based on the achieved precision.
2. Request that the account be revalued.
3. Attempt to determine the nature and cause of the errors and consider whether additional audit evidence from supplemental audit procedures will allow the auditor to judgmentally determine the fairness of the book value based on the results of this sample and other relevant audit evidence.

SAMPLING IN PRACTICE

The "art" of statistical sampling, discussed in Chapters 8 and 9, involves (1) precisely defining the particular objective of each audit test and (2) translating these objectives into statistically meaningful audit procedures.

As an example, consider inventories. The objectives in auditing inventories are to determine that they (1) physically exist, (2) are the property of the client, (3) are usable and salable, and (4) are priced in accordance with the client's established policies and with generally accepted accounting principles (GAAP). To accomplish these objectives, the audit program specifies a series of audit procedures. Suppose the auditor decides to use statistical sampling in the "price test." The purpose of the price test must be described so it can be translated into an appropriate sampling plan. The purpose might be one of the following:

1. To estimate the total dollar amount of pricing errors.
2. To estimate the percentage of items that have been priced incorrectly.
3. To discover some examples of pricing errors if they exist in a specified percentage of the items.

In many auditing situations, the auditor will wish to estimate the total dollar amount of pricing errors. Either probability proportional to size or variables estimation sampling may be used for this purpose.

To estimate the number of occurrences required by the second and third objectives noted above, attribute sampling or discovery sampling might be used.

Designing a Sampling Plan

Designing a sampling plan to accomplish audit objectives requires technical proficiency in statistics. It also requires a proficiency in the art of defining audit objectives and translating them into statistically meaningful audit procedures. If the auditor understands the principles in these chapters, appropriate sampling plans may be designed to cover many situations.

Time and Cost Considerations

In certain situations, the use of statistical sampling can save time, and therefore cost, but this should not be the sole consideration. One consideration should be the importance of a statistical conclusion to the overall audit evidence collected. Since there is nothing restrictive about an initial estimate of sample size, the auditor always should consider taking a few additional items whenever the sampling cost is small. An example would be accounts receivable confirmation requests where the cost of sending 25 additional requests (and performing alternative procedures on them, if necessary) might be nominal. Selecting enough sample items will be especially important if the auditor expects to find many differences; otherwise, there is a risk of not achieving the desired precision. It is almost always easier to select additional items initially rather than at a later date. For example, it would be difficult or impossible to go back to an open items account receivable file or work in process physical inventory weeks after the auditor initially selected a sample.

Of course, statistical sampling is not appropriate in every auditing situation. For instance, sampling usually will be relatively inefficient for small populations. Also, if the auditor suspects that certain items in the population are more likely to contain errors, these items should be segregated before sampling the remainder. Finally, statistical sampling generally should not be used to obtain information about rare events. If errors are rare, sampling may not provide much information about their occurrence rate or size.

SELECTING THE APPROPRIATE STATISTICAL TECHNIQUE

Statistical sampling techniques assist in determining a sample size and reaching an audit decision within allowable levels of decision risks. The selection of a particular statistical technique depends on:

1. The primary purpose of the test being planned.
2. Whether the primary concern is with understatement or overstatement.
3. Whether errors are expected to be encountered when performing the test.

The flowchart in Figure 9–1 describes the process leading to the use of a specific technique. Take a few minutes to look it over. It will help you

FIGURE 9–1 A Flowchart Describing the Process Used to Arrive at the Use of a Specific Sampling Technique

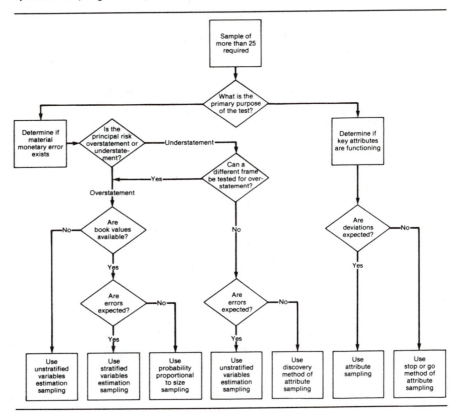

understand how the topics discussed in Chapters 8 and 9 relate to each other. Figure 9–1 mentions attribute sampling, probability proportional to size sampling, and variables estimation sampling as possible statistical techniques during an audit. Attribute sampling was covered in Chapter 8. Probability proportional to size sampling and variables estimation sampling were covered in this chapter.

APPENDIX 9A

TABLES FOR PROBABILITY PROPORTIONAL TO SIZE RELIABILITY FACTORS

Tables 9A–1 and 9A–2 give the probability proportional to size reliability factors for overstatement and understatement errors, respectively.

The steps in using these tables are:

1. Locate the appropriate tables based on whether overstatements or understatements are being evaluated. Always use the tables for overstatement errors when initially determining the required dollar value skip interval or sample size.
2. Locate the appropriate row based on the number of errors. Always assume zero errors when determining the dollar value skip interval or sample size.
3. Locate the appropriate column based on the desired reliability level or risk of incorrect acceptance.
4. Read the reliability factor at the intersection of the appropriate row and column.

TABLE 9A–1 Reliability Factors for Errors of Overstatement

Reliability:	99%	95%	93%	90%	85%	80%	75%	70%	60%	50%
Risk of Incorrect Acceptance:	1%	5%	7%	10%	15%	20%	25%	30%	40%	50%
Number of Over-statement Errors										
0	4.61	3.00	2.66	2.30	1.90	1.61	1.39	1.20	0.92	0.69
1	6.64	4.74	4.33	3.89	3.37	2.99	2.69	2.44	2.02	1.68
2	8.41	6.30	5.83	5.32	4.72	4.28	3.92	3.62	3.11	2.67
3	10.05	7.75	7.24	6.68	6.01	5.52	5.11	4.76	4.18	3.67
4	11.60	9.15	8.60	7.99	7.27	6.72	6.27	5.89	5.24	4.67
5	13.11	10.51	9.92	9.27	8.49	7.91	7.42	7.01	6.29	5.67
6	14.57	11.84	11.22	10.53	9.70	9.08	8.56	8.11	7.34	6.67
7	16.00	13.15	12.50	11.77	10.90	10.23	9.68	9.21	8.39	7.67
8	17.40	14.43	13.75	12.99	12.08	11.38	10.80	10.30	9.43	8.67
9	18.78	15.71	15.00	14.21	13.25	12.52	11.91	11.39	10.48	9.67
10	20.14	16.96	16.23	15.41	14.41	13.65	13.02	12.47	11.52	10.67
11	21.49	18.21	17.45	16.60	15.57	14.78	14.12	13.55	12.55	11.67
12	22.82	19.44	18.66	17.78	16.71	15.90	15.22	14.62	13.59	12.67
13	24.14	20.67	19.86	18.96	17.86	17.01	16.31	15.70	14.62	13.67
14	25.45	21.89	21.06	20.13	19.00	18.13	17.40	16.77	15.66	14.67
15	26.74	23.10	22.25	21.29	20.13	19.23	18.49	17.83	16.69	15.67
16	28.03	24.30	23.43	22.45	21.26	20.34	19.57	18.90	17.72	16.67
17	29.31	25.50	24.61	23.61	22.38	21.44	20.65	19.96	18.75	17.67
18	30.58	26.69	25.78	24.76	23.50	22.54	21.73	21.02	19.78	18.67
19	31.85	27.88	26.95	25.90	24.62	23.63	22.81	22.08	20.81	19.67
20	33.10	29.06	28.11	27.05	25.74	24.73	23.88	23.14	21.84	20.67

297

TABLE 9A–2 Reliability Factors for Errors of Understatement

Reliability: Risk of Incorrect Acceptance:	99% 1%	95% 5%	93% 7%	90% 10%	85% 15%	80% 20%	75% 25%	70% 30%	60% 40%	50% 50%
Number of Under-statement Errors										
1	0.01	0.05	0.07	0.11	0.16	0.22	0.29	0.36	0.51	0.69
2	0.15	0.36	0.43	0.53	0.68	0.82	0.96	1.10	1.38	1.68
3	0.44	0.82	0.94	1.10	1.33	1.54	1.73	1.91	2.29	2.67
4	0.82	1.37	1.53	1.74	2.04	2.30	2.54	2.76	3.21	3.67
5	1.28	1.97	2.18	2.43	2.79	3.09	3.37	3.63	4.15	4.67
6	1.79	2.61	2.85	3.15	3.56	3.90	4.22	4.52	5.09	5.67
7	2.33	3.29	3.56	3.89	4.35	4.73	5.08	5.41	6.04	6.67
8	2.91	3.98	4.29	4.66	5.15	5.58	5.96	6.31	6.99	7.67
9	3.51	4.70	5.03	5.43	5.97	6.43	6.84	7.22	7.95	8.67
10	4.13	5.43	5.79	6.22	6.80	7.29	7.73	8.13	8.90	9.67
11	4.77	6.17	6.56	7.02	7.64	8.16	8.62	9.05	9.86	10.67
12	5.43	6.92	7.34	7.83	8.48	9.03	9.52	9.97	10.83	11.67
13	6.10	7.69	8.12	8.65	9.34	9.91	10.42	10.90	11.79	12.67
14	6.78	8.46	8.92	9.47	10.19	10.79	11.33	11.82	12.75	13.67
15	7.48	9.25	9.73	10.30	11.06	11.68	12.24	12.75	13.72	14.67
16	8.18	10.04	10.54	11.14	11.92	12.57	13.15	13.69	14.69	15.67
17	8.89	10.83	11.35	11.98	12.79	13.47	14.07	14.62	15.66	16.67
18	9.62	11.63	12.18	12.82	13.67	14.37	14.99	15.56	16.63	17.67
19	10.35	12.44	13.00	13.67	14.55	15.27	15.91	16.50	17.60	18.67
20	11.08	13.25	13.84	14.53	15.43	16.17	16.83	17.44	18.57	19.67

APPENDIX 9B

TABLES FOR PROBABILITY PROPORTIONAL TO SIZE—PERCENTAGE SAMPLE SIZE ADJUSTMENT

Table 9B–1 gives the percentage increase in the required sample size to allow for examining up to 10 overstatement errors at a specified reliability level. Increasing the sample size by this factor will permit achieving a net upper monetary bound of overstatement that is less than or equal to the tolerable error, provided that the number and average relative size of observed differences is no greater than that planned for. Therefore, the auditor should be conservative in estimating the expected number and amount of errors. The steps in using these tables are:

1. Locate the appropriate tables based on the reliability level or risk of incorrect acceptance.
2. Specify the number of errors expected in the sample *(k)* and locate the appropriate row in the table.
3. Specify the expected average relative error of the errors and locate the appropriate column in the table.
4. Read the percentage adjustment at the intersection of the specified row and column.

The percentage adjustment amount indicates the percentage by which the estimated sample size must be increased to allow for the specified condition. The dollar value skip interval can be adjusted by dividing the preliminary amount by the sum of 100 percent and the indicated percentage adjustment.

TABLE 9B–1   Percent Sample Size Adjustment

99 Percent Reliability (1 Percent Risk of Incorrect Acceptance)

Expected Number of Errors	Expected Average Relative Error (percent)									
	10	20	30	40	50	60	70	80	90	100
1	4	9	13	18	22	26	31	35	40	44
2	8	17	25	33	41	50	58	66	74	83
3	12	24	35	47	59	71	83	95	106	118
4	15	30	46	61	76	91	106	122	137	152
5	18	37	55	74	92	111	129	148	166	185
6	22	43	65	87	108	130	151	173	195	216
7	25	49	74	99	124	148	173	198	223	247
8	28	56	83	111	139	167	195	222	250	278
9	31	62	92	123	154	185	216	246	277	308
10	34	67	101	135	169	202	236	270	304	337

95 Percent Reliability (5 Percent Risk of Incorrect Acceptance)

Expected Number of Errors	Expected Average Relative Error (percent)									
	10	20	30	40	50	60	70	80	90	100
1	6	12	18	23	29	35	41	47	53	58
2	11	22	33	44	55	66	77	88	99	110
3	16	32	48	64	79	95	111	127	143	159
4	21	41	62	82	103	123	144	164	185	206
5	25	50	75	100	125	151	176	201	226	251
6	30	59	89	118	148	177	207	236	266	295
7	34	68	102	136	169	203	237	271	305	339
8	38	76	115	153	191	229	267	305	344	382
9	42	85	127	170	212	255	297	339	382	424
10	47	93	140	186	233	280	326	373	420	466

93 Percent Reliability (7 Percent Risk of Incorrect Acceptance)

Expected Number of Errors	Expected Average Relative Error (percent)									
	10	20	30	40	50	60	70	80	90	100
1	6	13	19	25	31	38	44	50	57	63
2	12	24	36	48	60	72	83	95	107	119
3	17	34	52	69	86	103	121	138	155	172
4	22	45	67	89	112	134	156	179	201	223
5	27	55	82	109	137	164	191	219	246	273
6	32	64	97	129	161	193	225	258	290	322
7	37	74	111	148	185	222	259	296	333	370
8	42	83	125	167	209	250	292	334	375	417
9	46	93	139	186	232	278	325	371	418	464
10	51	102	153	204	255	306	357	408	459	510

90 Percent Reliability (10 Percent Risk of Incorrect Acceptance)

Expected Number of Errors	Expected Average Relative Error (percent)									
	10	20	30	40	50	60	70	80	90	100
1	7	14	21	28	34	41	48	55	62	69
2	13	26	39	52	66	79	92	105	118	131
3	19	38	57	76	95	114	133	152	171	190
4	25	49	74	99	124	148	173	198	222	247
5	30	61	91	121	151	182	212	242	273	303
6	36	71	107	143	179	214	250	286	322	357
7	41	82	123	164	206	247	288	329	370	411
8	46	93	139	186	232	279	325	371	418	464
9	52	103	155	207	258	310	362	414	465	517
10	57	114	171	228	285	341	398	455	512	569

TABLE 9B-1 (continued)

85 Percent Reliability
(15 Percent Risk of Incorrect Acceptance)

Expected Number of Errors	Expected Average Relative Error (percent)									
	10	20	30	40	50	60	70	80	90	100
1	8	16	23	31	39	47	54	62	70	78
2	15	30	45	60	74	89	104	119	134	149
3	22	43	65	87	108	130	152	174	195	217
4	28	57	85	113	142	170	198	226	255	283
5	35	70	104	139	174	209	243	278	313	348
6	41	82	123	165	206	247	288	329	370	411
7	47	95	142	190	237	285	332	379	427	474
8	54	107	161	215	268	322	376	429	483	537
9	60	120	180	239	299	359	419	479	539	598
10	66	132	198	264	330	396	462	528	594	660

80 Percent Reliability
(20 Percent Risk of Incorrect Acceptance)

Expected Number of Errors	Expected Average Relative Error (percent)									
	10	20	30	40	50	60	70	80	90	100
1	9	17	26	34	43	52	60	69	77	86
2	17	33	50	66	83	100	116	133	149	166
3	24	49	73	97	121	146	170	194	218	243
4	32	64	95	127	159	191	222	254	286	318
5	39	78	117	156	196	235	274	313	352	391
6	46	93	139	186	232	278	325	371	417	464
7	54	107	161	214	268	321	375	429	482	536
8	61	121	182	243	304	364	425	486	546	607
9	68	136	203	271	339	407	474	542	610	678
10	75	150	224	299	374	449	524	599	673	748

75 Percent Reliability
(25 Percent Risk of Incorrect Acceptance)

Expected Number of Errors	Expected Average Relative Error (percent)									
	10	20	30	40	50	60	70	80	90	100
1	9	19	28	38	47	57	66	75	85	94
2	18	37	55	73	91	110	128	146	165	183
3	27	54	81	107	134	161	188	215	242	269
4	35	71	106	141	176	212	247	282	317	353
5	44	87	131	174	218	261	305	348	392	435
6	52	103	155	207	259	310	362	414	466	517
7	60	120	180	239	299	359	419	479	539	599
8	68	136	204	272	340	408	475	543	611	679
9	76	152	228	304	380	456	532	608	683	759
10	84	168	252	336	420	504	587	671	755	839

70 Percent Reliability
(30 Percent Risk of Incorrect Acceptance)

Expected Number of Errors	Expected Average Relative Error (percent)									
	10	20	30	40	50	60	70	80	90	100
1	10	21	31	41	51	62	72	82	92	103
2	20	40	60	80	100	120	140	160	180	200
3	30	59	89	118	148	177	207	236	266	296
4	39	78	117	156	195	234	272	311	350	389
5	48	96	145	193	241	289	337	385	434	482
6	57	115	172	229	287	344	402	459	516	574
7	66	133	199	266	332	399	465	532	598	665
8	76	151	227	302	378	453	529	604	680	756
9	85	169	254	338	423	507	592	677	761	846
10	94	187	281	374	468	561	655	749	842	936

TABLE 9B–1 *(concluded)*

Expected Number of Errors	60 Percent Reliability (40 Percent Risk of Incorrect Acceptance) Expected Average Relative Error (percent)									
	10	20	30	40	50	60	70	80	90	100
1	12	24	36	48	60	72	84	97	109	121
2	24	48	72	96	119	143	167	191	215	239
3	36	71	107	142	178	213	249	285	320	356
4	47	94	141	189	236	283	330	377	424	472
5	59	117	176	235	293	352	411	469	528	587
6	70	140	210	281	351	421	491	561	631	701
7	82	163	245	326	408	489	571	652	734	816
8	93	186	279	372	465	558	651	744	837	930
9	104	209	313	417	522	626	730	835	939	1043
10	116	231	347	463	578	694	810	925	1041	1157

Expected Number of Errors	50 Percent Reliability (50 Percent Risk of Incorrect Acceptance) Expected Average Relative Error (percent)									
	10	20	30	40	50	60	70	80	90	100
1	14	28	43	57	71	85	99	114	128	142
2	29	57	86	114	143	171	200	229	257	286
3	43	86	129	172	215	258	301	344	387	430
4	57	115	172	230	287	344	402	459	516	574
5	72	144	215	287	359	431	503	574	646	718
6	86	172	259	345	431	517	604	690	776	862
7	101	201	302	403	503	604	705	805	906	1006
8	115	230	345	460	575	690	805	921	1036	1151
9	129	259	388	518	647	777	906	1036	1165	1295
10	144	288	432	576	720	863	1007	1151	1295	1439

APPENDIX 9C

AN EXAMPLE OF THE FORMULA
APPROACH TO VARIABLES ESTIMATION
SAMPLING

Formulas

1. Precision (using the population standard deviation):

$$\text{Precision} = U_R \cdot \frac{\sigma_{X_j}}{\sqrt{n}}$$

where

U_R = Reliability factor (number of standard deviations) corresponding to reliability of R percent
σ_{X_j} = Population standard deviation
n = Number of items in the sample

2. Precision interval (using the population standard deviation):

$$\text{Precision interval} = \bar{x} - \left(U_R \cdot \frac{\sigma_{X_j}}{\sqrt{n}} \right) \text{ to } \bar{x} + \left(U_R \cdot \frac{\sigma_{X_j}}{\sqrt{n}} \right)$$

where

$\bar{x}$ = Mean of the sample
U_R = Reliability factor
σ_{X_j} = Population standard deviation
n = Number of items in the sample

3. Precision (using the sample standard deviation):

$$\text{Precision} = U_R \cdot \frac{S_{X_j}}{\sqrt{n}}$$

where

U_R = Reliability factor corresponding to reliablity or R percent
S_{X_j} = Sample standard deviation
n = Number of items in the sample

4. Precision interval (using the sample standard deviation):

$$\text{Precision internal} = \bar{x} - \left(U_R \cdot \frac{S_{X_j}}{\sqrt{n}} \right) \text{ to } \bar{x} + \left(U_R \cdot \frac{S_{X_j}}{\sqrt{n}} \right)$$

where

$\bar{x}$ = Mean of the sample
U_R = Reliability factor
S_{x_j} = Population standard deviation
n = Number of items in the sample

5. Sample size for variables sampling:

$$n = \frac{(U_R \cdot S_{X_j} \cdot N)}{\text{Precision}^2}$$

where

n = Number of items in the sample
U_R = Reliability factor
S_{X_j} = Sample standard deviation
N = The number of items in the population

Precision is for the entire population, not for each item. If precision is expressed per item then the formula would be

$$n = \frac{(U_R \cdot S_{X_j})^2}{\text{Precision}^2}$$

6. Precision to be used in determining sample size:

$$A = \frac{TE}{1 + \dfrac{Z_{TD}}{Z_{\alpha/2}}}$$

where

α = Risk of incorrect rejection
A = Precision to be used in determining sample size (planned precision)
TE = Tolerable error
TD = Planned risk of incorrect acceptance as a percent
Z_{TD} = Normal table value of $.5 - TD$
$Z_{\alpha/2}$ = Normal table value of $.5 - \alpha/2$

Since this formula involves reading values from a table, an example may be helpful in explaining the concept.

Example—Calculation of Precision to Be Used in Determining Sample Size

Given:

Assume the auditor believes that a risk of incorrect rejection (α) of 5 percent and a risk of incorrect acceptance *(TD)* of 5 percent are acceptable and that tolerable error is $500,000.

Formula:

$$A = \frac{TE}{1 + \dfrac{Z_{TD}}{Z_{\alpha/2}}}$$

$$= \frac{\$500,000}{1 + \dfrac{Z.5 - .05}{Z.5 - .025}}$$

$$= \frac{\$500,000}{1 + \dfrac{Z.4500}{Z.4750}}$$

Next find the closest numbers in Table 9C–1 to the Z values .4500 for *TD* and .4750 for α. If the .4500 does not appear in the table (as it does not) use the next *higher* number. The number .4505 appears in the 1.6 row and .05 column which means that the Z value for *TD* is 1.65. The number .4750 does appear in the table in the 1.9 row and .06 column. Thus, the Z value for α is 1.96. If it had not appeared the next *lower* number should be used.

Now substitute the Z values in the formula as follows and solve:

$$A = \frac{\$500,000}{1 + \dfrac{1.65}{1.96}} \cong \$271,468$$

Thus, in this example $271,468 is the precision to be used in determining the sample size.

7. Achieved precision

$$A' = \frac{U_R S_{x_j}}{\sqrt{n}}$$

where

A' = Achieved precision

TABLE 9C-1 Normal Curve Area Table

σ	.00	.01	.02	.03	.04	.05	.06	.07	.08	.09
0.0	.0000	.0040	.0080	.0120	.0160	.0199	.0239	.0279	.0319	.0359
0.1	.0398	.0438	.0478	.0517	.0557	.0596	.0636	.0675	.0714	.0753
0.2	.0793	.0832	.0871	.0910	.0948	.0987	.1026	.1064	.1103	.1141
0.3	.1179	.1217	.1255	.1293	.1331	.1368	.1406	.1443	.1480	.1517
0.4	.1554	.1591	.1628	.1664	.1700	.1736	.1772	.1808	.1844	.1879
0.5	.1915	.1950	.1985	.2019	.2054	.2088	.2123	.2157	.2190	.2224
0.6	.2257	.2291	.2324	.2357	.2389	.2422	.2454	.2486	.2518	.2549
0.7	.2580	.2612	.2642	.2673	.2704	.2734	.2764	.2794	.2823	.2852
0.8	.2881	.2910	.2939	.2967	.2995	.3023	.3051	.3078	.3106	.3133
0.9	.3159	.3186	.3212	.3238	.3264	.3289	.3315	.3340	.3365	.3389
1.0	.3413	.3438	.3461	.3485	.3508	.3531	.3554	.3577	.3599	.3621
1.1	.3643	.3665	.3686	.3708	.3729	.3749	.3770	.3790	.3810	.3830
1.2	.3849	.3869	.3888	.3907	.3925	.3944	.3962	.3980	.3997	.4015
1.3	.4032	.4049	.4066	.4082	.4099	.4115	.4131	.4147	.4162	.4177
1.4	.4192	.4207	.4222	.4236	.4251	.4265	.4279	.4292	.4306	.4319
1.5	.4332	.4345	.4357	.4370	.4382	.4394	.4406	.4418	.4429	.4441
1.6	.4452	.4463	.4474	.4484	.4495	.4505	.4515	.4525	.4535	.4545
1.7	.4554	.4564	.4573	.4582	.4591	.4599	.4608	.4616	.4625	.4633
1.8	.4641	.4649	.4656	.4664	.4671	.4678	.4686	.4693	.4699	.4706
1.9	.4713	.4719	.4726	.4732	.4738	.4744	.4750	.4756	.4761	.4767
2.0	.4772	.4778	.4783	.4788	.4793	.4798	.4803	.4808	.4812	.4817
2.1	.4821	.4826	.4830	.4834	.4838	.4842	.4846	.4850	.4854	.4857
2.2	.4861	.4864	.4868	.4871	.4875	.4878	.4881	.4884	.4887	.4890
2.3	.4893	.4896	.4898	.4901	.4904	.4906	.4909	.4911	.4913	.4916
2.4	.4918	.4920	.4922	.4925	.4927	.4929	.4931	.4932	.4934	.4936
2.5	.4938	.4940	.4941	.4943	.4945	.4946	.4948	.4949	.4951	.4952
2.6	.4953	.4955	.4956	.4957	.4959	.4960	.4961	.4962	.4963	.4964
2.7	.4965	.4966	.4967	.4968	.4969	.4970	.4971	.4972	.4973	.4974
2.8	.4974	.4975	.4976	.4977	.4977	.4978	.4979	.4979	.4980	.4981
2.9	.4981	.4982	.4982	.4983	.4984	.4984	.4985	.4985	.4986	.4986
3.0	.49865	.4987	.4987	.4988	.4988	.4989	.4989	.4989	.4990	.4990
3.1	.49903	.4991	.4991	.4991	.4992	.4992	.4992	.4992	.4993	.4993

U_R = Reliability factor
S_{X_j} = Sample standard deviation
n = Number of items in the sample

8. Adjusted precision to be used whenever the achieved precision differs from the planned precision:

$$A'' = A' + TE(1 - A'/A)$$

where

A'' = Adjusted precision
A' = Achieved precision
TE = Tolerable error
A = Planned precision

An Example of Sampling for Variables

Assume that statistical sampling is used in conjunction with the confirmation of freight receivables for a motor carrier. At the balance sheet date, there are 5,000 bills outstanding totaling $1,500,000. Confirmations will be requested for a sample drawn from the freight bills based on a planned risk of incorrect acceptance of 28 percent and a reliability of 90 percent. The purpose of the confirmation requests is to test the validity of the $1,500,000 figure in freight bills receivable.

The 90 percent planned reliability is based on the auditor's willingness to accept a 10 percent risk of erroneously concluding that the book balance might be materially misstated when, in fact, it is reasonably stated.

The planned risk of incorrect acceptance is 28 percent based on the auditor's allowable ultimate risk level of 5 percent, the risk of internal controls failing to detect errors greater than tolerable error of 20 percent, and the risk that other audit procedures would fail to detect errors greater than tolerable error of 90 percent. The computation is as follows:

$$TD = \frac{UR}{(IC)(AR)} = \frac{.05}{(.2)(.9)} \cong 28\%$$

Planned precision is calculated as follows assuming $20,000 is the amount of tolerable error.

$$A = \frac{TE}{1 + \dfrac{Z_{TD}}{Z_{\alpha/2}}} = \frac{\$20,000}{1 + \dfrac{.59}{1.64}} = \$15,000 \text{ (rounded to the nearest thousand dollars)}$$

The $15,000 planned precision will be used when calculating a sample size that should prevent the auditor from incurring more than the allowable ultimate risk and risks of incorrect acceptance and incorrect rejection.

In dollar terms the average precision is $\pm\$3$ (that is, $15,000/5,000). The auditor draws a preliminary sample of 50 items in order to estimate the standard deviation of the population. The standard deviation is estimated to be $50.

Next we calculate sample size. If we label precision A, then:

$$n = \frac{(U_R \cdot S_{xj})^2}{A^2} = \frac{(1.65 \times 50)^2}{(3)^2} = 756.25$$

The above formula gives the sample size using sampling with replacement. Sample size for sampling without replacement can be found by using the following formula:

$$n = \frac{n'}{1 + \dfrac{n'}{N}}$$

where

> n' = Sample size with replacement
> N = Population size

When the fraction n/N is .05 or more a correction factor (explained later) should be made. When the fraction is less than .05, the use of a correction factor is optional since its effect is relatively immaterial.

In our example we will use sampling without replacement. Thus:

$$n = \frac{n'}{1 + \dfrac{n'}{N}} = \frac{756.25}{1 + \dfrac{756.25}{5,000}} \cong 657$$

Thus, the auditor must randomly sample at least another 607 accounts (657 less the 50 in the preliminary sample).

The auditor draws the sample, sends out the confirmation requests, and (after a second request to nonreplies to the first request) receives back all 657. Assume that the 657 confirmations received totaled $195,457. (In most circumstances not all confirmations sent out would be returned, and the auditor would use alternative procedures to test the balances of the nonreplies.) The average audited balance is $297 ($195,457 ÷ 657). If $297 is multiplied by the 5,000 bills, $1,485,000 is obtained. This represents the estimate of the audited value of the total freight bills.

At this point, the achieved precision (A') for the $1,485,000 estimated audited value may be established. The standard deviation of the audited sample values is calculated and found to be $40.

Achieved average precision can be determined from the following formula:

$$A' = \frac{U_R S_{x_j}}{\sqrt{n}} = \frac{1.65 \times \$40}{\sqrt{657}} \cong \$2.58$$

Since n/N is more than .05, and we are using sampling without replacement, a correction factor $\sqrt{1 - n/N}$ is multiplied by the achieved average precision. Thus, $2.58 is multiplied by $\sqrt{1 - n/N}$.

In our example, the correction factor is $\sqrt{1 - 657/5000} \cong .932$. Then,

$$.932 \times \$2.58 \cong \$2.40$$

The total achieved precision of the estimated audited value is found by multiplying $2.40 by N (in this example 5,000).

$$5,000 \times \$2.40 = \$12,000 = A'$$

Since the achieved precision is less than planned precision, we find adjusted precision A'' by the following formula:

$$A'' = A' + TE(1 - A'/A)$$

$$= \$12,000 + \$20,000 \left(1 - \frac{\$12,000}{\$15,000}\right)$$

$$= \$16,000$$

The decision interval becomes $\$1,500,000 \pm \$16,000$ or $\$1,484,000$ to $\$1,516,000$. Since the audited value of $\$1,485,000$ falls within the decision interval, the auditor can conclude that the sample information supports fair statement of the book value at the planned risk of incorrect acceptance of 28 percent. It is not necessary to measure the risk of incorrect rejection since the auditor has accepted the book value as fairly stated.

QUESTIONS AND PROBLEMS

9–1. Identify the statistical technique that should be used in each of the following situations (you may want to refer to Figure 9–1, page 295):

a. The auditor seeks to determine if key controls are functioning; many deviations are expected.

b. The same facts as in (a) exist except that few deviations are expected.

c. The auditor seeks to determine if material monetary errors exist, the principal risk is understatement, no different frame can be tested for overstatement, and errors are expected.

d. The same facts exist as in (c) except that no errors are expected.

e. The auditor seeks to determine if material monetary errors exist, the principal risk is overstatement, and few errors are expected.

f. The same facts exist as in (e) except that many errors are expected.

9–2. What information does the use of the probability proportional to size sampling technique provide the auditor concerning the recorded amount of the account balance? Give an example of an auditor's conclusion, using assumed data.

9–3. Is the probability proportional to size sampling method appropriate for detecting overstatements and understatements?

9–4. When does the PPS sampling technique indicate fair statement of an account balance?

9–5. What is tolerable error?

9–6. What are the two risks which exist whenever an auditor makes a decision about an account balance based on sample evidence? How and when are acceptable levels of these risks determined? Does PPS sampling control both of these risks?

9–7. Contrast a PPS sample with a random sample. What is another name for PPS sampling?

9–8. a. Describe how a PPS sample is selected assuming a sample of 40 items is to be selected from 500 individual accounts receivable balances totaling $140,000.

b. Given the facts in (a), determine the skip interval using the formula approach. If the random starting point is $1,000 how would the sample be selected?

c. Given the facts in (a) and (b), assume that the following balances comprise the accounts receivable total and show which of the identified items would be included in the PPS sample:

Item Number	Amount	Cumulative Balance
001	$ 600	$ 600
002	700	1,300
003	3,550	4,850
004	75	4,925
005	120	5,045
006	240	5,285
007	10	4,295
008	90	5,385
009	40	5,425
010	500	5,925
011	1,400	7,325
012	900	8,225
.	.	.
.	.	.
.	.	.
.	.	.
Total	$140,000	$140,000

9–9. Describe what is meant by the net upper monetary bound of overstatement and the reliability or confidence limit as used in PPS sampling.

9–10. If the risk of incorrect acceptance is 10 percent what reliability level should the auditor specify?

9–11.
a. Assume that an auditor wishes to control the risk of acceptance to 10 percent and expects zero errors. The tolerable error is $207,000. What would be the dollar value skip interval? (Use tables in Appendix 9A.)
b. Using the facts in (a), assume the auditor expects 3 or 4 differences with an average relative error of 20 percent to 30 percent. Using the tables in Appendix 9B, what would be the adjusted skip interval?
c. Given the facts in (a) and (b), what is the estimated sample size? Assume the population value is $2 million.
d. Given the above facts, what effect, if any, would it have on the auditor's decision if six errors averaging 30 percent of the recorded amount are observed while performing the confirmation procedure on the sample items?

9–12. Assume that PPS sampling will be used by the auditor. The population has 3,000 accounts with a total value of $8,500,000. A confidence level of 90 percent is desired and $500,000 is the tolerable error.
a. What skip interval should be used to identify items that should be tested?
b. What is the estimated sample size?
c. If the auditor wishes to allow for observing two errors averaging 20 percent, what is the required skip interval and estimated sample size?
d. When testing the sample items, the auditor noted the following two exceptions. (A skip interval of $218,000 was used to identify 38 sample items and one item larger than the interval.)

	Book Value	Audited Value
	$ 7,693	$ 6,741
	266,000	247,000

What conclusion can be drawn from this test? Have the objectives of the test been met? Explain your answer.

9–13. What is the final information result of using variables estimation sampling? Is the method useful when errors are expected?

9–14. What is the decision interval in variables estimation sampling? How is it used?

9–15. If the total recorded amount of a population is $50 million and precision is $2 million, what is the decision interval? If the population estimate is $49,100,000 is the recorded amount fairly stated?

9–16. Assume an auditor has audited 200 sample items. If the total audited value for the 200 items is $1 million and the number of items in the population is 15,000 what is the total estimated audit value of the population?

9–17. Potter Company asks its auditor for assistance in estimating the average gross value of the 5,000 invoices during June 1986. The CPA estimates the population standard deviation to be $8. If the goal is to achieve a precision of ±$10,000 with a 95 percent reliability level, what sample size should be drawn?   (AICPA, adapted)

9–18. How is the risk of incorrect rejection controlled in variables estimation sampling?

9–19. How is the risk of incorrect acceptance controlled in variables estimation sampling?

9–20. Assume that an audit program indicates the following for a test of inventory pricing for a clothing retailer:

Tolerable error amount *(TE)*	$200,000
Risk of incorrect acceptance	20%
Risk of incorrect rejection	5%

Calculate the precision amount.

9–21. Tom Murray, CPA, is conducting an audit of Jones Art Company. Mr. Murray plans to select sufficient inventory items for test counts and pricing tests so that he can make a rough estimate of total inventory cost.
  a. The standard deviation is a basic measure of variation. Define a standard deviation.
  b. Will wide variability (as measured by the population standard deviation) in the cost of the items being sampled affect the sample size? If so, in what manner?
                                                                        (AICPA, adapted)

9–22. What is the purpose of stratification of a variables estimation sample?

9–23. Differentiate the terms *planned precision (A)* and *achieved precision (A')*.

9–24. Describe the nature of *adjusted precision (A")*. How is it used?

9–25. Name four methods that may be used to determine a population estimate and related precision. Which method results in the most efficient estimate?

9–26. You want to evaluate the reasonableness of the book value of the inventory of your client, Jones, Inc. You satisfied yourself earlier as to inventory quantities. During the examination of the pricing and extension of the inventory, the following data were gathered using appropriate unrestricted random sampling with replacement procedures.

Total items in the inventory (N) = 12,700
Total items in the sample *(n)* = 400
Total audited value of items in the sample = $38,400

$$\sum_{j=1}^{400} (x_j - \bar{x})^2 = \$312,816$$

Formula for estimated population standard deviation:

$$S_{x_j} = \sqrt{\frac{\sum\limits_{j=1}^{j=n} (x_j - \bar{x})^2}{n-1}}$$

Formula for estimated standard error of the mean

$$SE = \frac{S_{x_j}}{\sqrt{n}}$$

Confidence level coefficient of the standard error of the mean at a 95 percent confidence (reliability) level = ±1.96.

Required:

a. Based on the sample results, what is the estimate of the total value of the inventory? Show computations in good form where appropriate.
b. What statistical conclusion can be reached regarding the estimated total inventory value calculated in *(a)* above at the confidence level of 95 percent?

(AICPA, adapted)

9–27. During the course of an audit engagement, a CPA attempts to obtain satisfaction that there are no material misstatements in the accounts receivable of a client. Statistical sampling is a tool that the auditor often uses to obtain representative evidence to achieve the desired satisfaction. On a particular engagement, an auditor determined that a material misstatement in a population of accounts would be $35,000. To obtain satisfaction, the auditor had to be 95 percent confident that the population of accounts was not in error by $35,000. The auditor decided to use unrestricted random sampling with replacement and took a preliminary random sample of 100 items *(n)* from a population of 1,000 items (N). The sample produced the following data:

Arithmetic mean of sample items *(x̄)* $4,000
Standard deviation of sample items *(SD)* $ 200

The auditor also has available the following information:

Standard error of the mean *(SE)* = $SD \div \sqrt{n}$
Population precision *(P)* = $N \times R \times SE$

Partial List of Reliability Coefficients

If Reliability Coefficient (R) Is	Then Reliability Is
1.70	91.086%
1.75	91.988
1.80	92.814
1.85	93.568
1.90	94.256
1.95	94.882
1.96	95.000
2.00	95.450
2.05	95.964
2.10	96.428
2.15	96.844

Required:

a. Define the statistical terms *reliability* and *precision* as applied to auditing.

b. If all necessary audit work is performed on the preliminary sample items and no errors are detected,

   (1) What can the auditor say about the total amount of accounts receivable at the 95 percent reliability level?

   (2) At what confidence level can the auditor say that the population is not in error by $35,000?   (AICPA, adapted)

9–28. Refer back to Question 9–27. Assume that the preliminary sample was sufficient. Compute the auditor's estimate of the population total.   (AICPA, adapted)

(Problems 29 and 30 are based on Appendix 9C)

9–29. Assume an auditor, in auditing an account, determines that 5 percent risk of incorrect rejection and a 25 percent risk of incorrect acceptance are acceptable. The auditor considers that for this account the tolerable error is $400,000.

Required:

   Determine the precision to be used in determining sample size so that the auditor can attain the acceptable risk of incorrect acceptance.

9–30. Assume the following data in the audit of accounts receivable of Smith Company:

Tolerable error	$ 100,000
Planned risk of incorrect rejection	5%
Population size	5,000
Allowable ultimate risk	5%
Internal control effectiveness	80%
Supplemental audit procedure effectiveness	20%
Estimated population standard deviation	$ 100
Book value	$5,080,000

Required:

a. Calculate the sample size for an unstratified variables estimation sample.

b. Assume 150 positive confirmations are sent out and returned. Also, assume the 150 returned confirmations total $150,000 with a standard deviation of $50. Is the account fairly stated?

AUDITING THE SALES COMPONENT

As discussed in earlier chapters, a typical commercial or industrial company can be divided into four basic operating components: sales, production or service, finance, and administration. In this chapter, we discuss the (1) specific control objectives relating to the sales component; (2) relationships of the specific control objectives to audit areas; and (3) audit procedures relating to the sales component.

The sales component relates to a company's marketing, distribution, billing, and collection efforts. The specific control objectives for the sales component are:

Reference No.	
S–1	Customer orders require approval of credit and terms before acceptance
S–2	Uncollectible amounts are promptly identified and provided for
S–3	Products shipped or services rendered are billed
S–4	Billings are for the correct amount
S–5	Revenues are recorded correctly as to account, amount, and period
S–6	Recorded billings are for valid transactions
S–7	Customer returns and other allowances are approved and recorded correctly as to account, amount, and period

Due to their relationship to sales transactions, two specific control objectives in the finance component are generally analyzed in conjunction with tests performed on sales transactions. These additional specific control objectives that relate to cash receipts are:

F–1	Cash receipts are recorded correctly as to account, amount, and period and are deposited
F–2	Cash receipts are properly applied to customer balances

10

The interrelationships among these specific control objectives are shown in Figure 10–1. For example, credits to accounts receivable can arise from bad debts (S–2), returns and allowances (S–7), and cash receipts (F–1, F–2).

The remainder of this chapter describes the audit of accounts and transactions in the sales component, including cash receipt transactions. It is important to note that not all of the procedures discussed in this chapter are performed on every audit. The nature, timing, and extent of the procedures performed on each audit are determined based on the auditor's risk analysis and assessment of the likelihood of material error, discussed earlier.

SALES, RECEIVABLES, AND CASH RECEIPTS

As stated in Chapter 7, whenever the system evaluation indicates that there is reasonable assurance that the specific control objective is being achieved and the auditor plans to rely on the system, the auditor should test the key attributes that provide that assurance.

The controls a company maintains over its sales and cash receipts transactions are very important. From a sales perspective, a company could find itself in a difficult operating situation if it did not bill its customers for all products shipped to them or it billed its customers at prices below established amounts. In addition, cash is the most liquid of all assets. If controls in this area are not adequate, funds easily can be misappropriated.

Testing Key Attributes over Sales, Receivables, and Cash Receipts

Dual purpose tests should be used to obtain evidence that a key attribute is both (1) functioning (compliance test) and (2) effective i.e., the transaction is recorded correctly (substantive test). It is not sufficient merely to verify

315

FIGURE 10–1   Relationship of Specific Control Objectives to Financial Statement Classifications—Sales Component

Balance Sheet

| | Control Objectives | | | | | | | |
	Debit				Credit			
Current assets:								
Cash	F–1,	F–2						
Accounts receivable	S–1,	S–3,	S–4,	S–5	S–2,	S–7,	F–1,	F–2
	S–6							
Allowance for doubtful accounts					S–1,	S–2		
Inventories	S–7				S–3,	S–5,	S–6	
Prepaid expenses and other assets								
Other assets:								
Notes receivable					F–1,	F–2		
Investments								
Goodwill and other intangibles								
Intercompany accounts								
Deposits and other assets								
Property, plant, and equipment:								
Land								
Buildings								
Machinery and equipment								
Allowances for depreciation								
Current liabilities:								
Notes payable								
Trade accounts payable and accrued liabilities								
Accrued payroll and related liabilities								
Taxes other than taxes on income								
Accrued interest								
Income taxes								
Long-term debt								
Deferred income taxes								
Shareholders' equity:								
Preferred stock								
Common stock								
Additional paid-in capital								
Retained earnings								
Commitments and contingencies								

Income Statement

| | Control Objectives | | | | | | |
	Debit				Credit		
Sales	S–1,	S–4,	S–7		S–1,	S–3,	S–4,
					S–5,	S–6,	F–1
Cost of sales	S–3,	S–5,	S–6,	S–7	S–7		
Selling, general, and administrative expenses	S–2						
Provision for income taxes							
Other							

316

that a transaction is correct and assume that the control functioned or vice versa.

Key attributes that are applied to individual transactions usually are tested by sampling from those transactions through an interim period. As each transaction is tested, the auditor should look for documentary evidence of the functioning of the key attribute. This can be in the form of signatures, initials, check marks, rubber stamps, and the like. For example, assume that the auditor concludes that the system design provides reasonable assurance that the specific control objective S–1, "Customer orders require approval of credit and terms before acceptance," is being achieved. One key attribute that the auditor concludes supports this assessment is that customer purchase orders are compared to approved schedules for credit limits, prices, discounts, payment terms, and delivery terms. The documentary evidence of this comparison is the initials of an order clerk on the customer purchase order. To test the *functioning* of this key attribute, the auditor might examine a sample of customer purchase orders noting the initials of the order clerk. The auditor also should make inquiries of the order clerks to determine that they understand their responsibilities and how exceptions are resolved. To test the *effectiveness* of the control, the auditor might compare the data on the purchase order to the appropriate schedules.

Certain control procedures are applied to groups of transactions (e.g., daily reconciliation of quantities shipped to quantities billed). In these cases, the auditor can either select (1) a sample of transactions and trace each to inclusion in the documentary evidence of the functioning of the key attribute (e.g., select a sample of invoices for tracing to the daily reconciliation schedules), or (2) a sample of the documentary evidence directly (e.g., select a sample of daily reconciliation schedules, support one reconciliation, and review the rest for reasonableness).

The auditor should make inquiries concerning control procedures applied to either individual transactions or groups of transactions. A few well-chosen questions directed to the right person can provide valuable insights about the effectiveness of the procedure. For example, the auditor might ask the credit manager for an explanation of his or her responsibilities and how exceptions are resolved. To accomplish this, the auditor might ask the following questions of the credit manager: "How do you perform the review? Do you review every order? How often are customer purchase orders turned down? Are customer purchase orders that do not meet approved credit criteria ever accepted? If so, who approves?" In some cases, it might be more effective to ask other personnel who are affected by the control procedure to provide information that would help evaluate the effectiveness of the credit manager's review. For example, the auditor might ask the sales manager "What do you do with customer purchase orders that are returned by the credit manager because customers do not meet the specific credit criteria?"

If the auditor learns that customer purchase orders are always accepted,

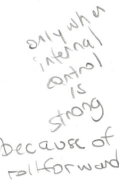
only when internal control is strong because of roll forward

control & subsidiary

even if they do not meet specified criteria, this may indicate that the control procedure is not what the auditor thought it was—even if there is documentary evidence in every case (i.e., the credit manager signs all of them). If this is the case, there is no point in continuing to gather evidence on the functioning of the attribute. The auditor should give effect to this new information by designing new procedures.

Use of prenumbered documents (e.g., shipping documents, invoices) by a client may assist in recording transactions in the proper period. However, prenumbering alone may not be a key attribute; the client must perform an independent sequence check. If such a control procedure exists, and the auditor decides that prenumbered documents represent a key attribute, the auditor should test the functioning of the attribute by reviewing how the client accounts for the numerical sequence (e.g., review numerical lists of shipping documents used during a day) and inquiring how the sequence check is performed.

As was noted in Chapter 7, in certain cases, key attributes do not leave documentary evidence (e.g., review and approval of account distribution without signing). The way the auditor obtains evidence of functioning of these key attributes is by observation and inquiry of the employee who performs the control procedure or other employees who are affected by it. To test the effectiveness of these key attributes, the auditor would examine a sample of transactions affected by the undocumented control.

Testing Sales, Receivables, and Cash Receipts Transactions

As mentioned above, in addition to accumulating evidence of the functioning of key attributes, the audit program may include certain procedures to test the effectiveness of the key attributes. In such cases, these procedures usually will be performed on a limited basis through an interim date.

On the other hand, if the system evaluation indicates there are no key attributes to be relied on, the same or similiar procedures might be performed to detect errors or irregularities in the recording of the transactions. In those cases, the auditor should test more transactions and select them from throughout most or all of the year.

The following procedures are designed to either (1) test the effectiveness of key attributes, or (2) detect errors or irregularities in the recording of transactions if no key attributes are functioning.

1. Testing adherence to established terms of sales. The auditor should compare the terms (prices, discounts, payment, delivery) of the sale included on the sales order or invoice to authorized terms. Sales and accounts receivable should be appropriately adjusted for any errors found. For example, underbillings (if collectible) should be recorded.

2. **Testing adherence to credit limits.** Companies frequently establish credit limits for their customers. Once a customer has reached the credit limit, further shipments normally are curtailed until payments on the existing balance are received. In testing the effectiveness of these policies, the auditor should evaluate the reasonableness of the criteria used and adequacy of the documentation required to establish customer credit limits. If the auditor concludes that the criteria are reasonable, customer balances should be compared to established credit limits to test adherence to the policies. The auditor should focus on what the client is doing about customers that have exceeded their established credit limit. If the client has taken appropriate action, then reliance on the credit limit policy is justified and the extent of the auditor's collectibility review can be limited.

3. **Comparing shipping records with sales records or invoices.** To evaluate whether the shipment of goods or rendering of services results in timely customer billings that are recorded in the correct period, the auditor should select a representative sample of shipping records and compare them with related sales invoices. The invoice should be dated on or very soon after the shipping date. Delay in recording shipments and preparing billings could slow down the company's collection cycle. Such delays also require the auditor to increase the length of the period covered by cutoff tests (discussed later in this chapter).

If the existence of client sequence checks of prenumbered documents is considered a key attribute and tested, as discussed earlier, the auditor can test the effectiveness of that control when performing other tests of documents. For example, the auditor should test whether the shipping records and sales invoices selected above are recorded in the proper sequence in the accounting records. If prenumbering is not considered a key attribute, the auditor can perform such a test to detect errors or irregularities in recording.

4. **Testing sales invoices for *(a)* quantities invoiced (by comparison with shipping records), *(b)* unit prices and discounts, and *(c)* clerical accuracy.** The purpose of this test is to determine the validity of the sale by ensuring that (1) the invoice reflects either the product actually shipped or the service rendered to the customer, (2) the correct price and discounts were used, and (3) no clerical errors were made in preparing the invoice. The auditor should compare the quantities and descriptions of goods on the invoice with the shipping documents. A bill of lading or copy of the shipping document signed by the customer, evidencing receipt of the inventory, are types of documentation that support the validity of a sale.

The auditor should compare prices on the invoice to authorized price lists, catalogs, contracts, or other price authorizations. In some cases, it may be necessary to convert prices from one unit of measure to another (e.g., pounds to feet, gallons to pounds). Where such conversions are common, the client probably maintains conversion tables that can be used to test the accuracy of the conversion.

Footings - add down
extension - multiply across

Billings that do not agree with sales contracts or price lists may be due to clerical errors, deliberate circumvention of company policy, or misappropriation of funds by withholding a portion of a customer's remittance and reducing the selling price. Alternatively, it is possible that management may have arranged special terms for that particular customer.

5. **Comparing sales invoices and credit memoranda with sales and accounts receivable records.**   To evaluate whether billings and related credits are properly recorded, the auditor should compare a sample of sales invoices and credit memoranda with the client's sales or credit journal and be sure that the transactions are included in the proper period for the correct amounts. Also, the auditor should trace each sale or credit to the accounts receivable records to test whether they are posted to the correct customer's account.

6. **Checking credit memoranda covering returned goods for (a) arithmetical accuracy, (b) quantities returned (by reference to receiving records), and (c) unit prices (by reference to the original invoice or record of the selling price).**   In commercial enterprises, credit is normally issued for goods returned or to correct errors in shipping (e.g., materials damaged during shipment) or billing. However, credit memos also can be used to conceal irregularities. For example, a credit memo could be issued to reduce a customer's account balance by the amount of the customer's payments that were misappropriated. By testing arithmetical accuracy, comparing to receiving records (customer name, date, description of merchandise, and quantities), and verifying prices, the auditor can evaluate whether the credit is proper.

In performing the test, the auditor also should note whether there is any significant time lag in issuing credits since this might result in an overstatement of sales and receivables. If a significant time lag exists, an allowance for unissued credits may need to be established at year-end.

7. **Examining cash receipts related to tested sales transactions.**   The auditor should test cash receipts to determine that they are deposited promptly and are recorded in the correct account and at the proper amount (including application to the correct customer account) in the proper period. Combining tests of cash receipts with tests of sales transactions provides an efficient method of sampling. It ordinarily is not practicable to select a representative sample of cash receipts, because they typically are not numbered and it is difficult to establish correspondence for selecting a representative sample. One way to overcome this problem is to use a representative sample of sales invoices for selecting a sample of cash receipts. To do this, the auditor could review a customer's account record to locate the cash receipt that paid the sales invoice selected in the test of sales transactions. This can only be done if the client applies cash received to specific invoices. The auditor then can test that cash receipt.

To test the cash receipt, the auditor should trace it from the customer account record to the cash receipts journal and bank deposit slip, ensuring that the dates on each are approximately the same. It also is important to note that the customer name and amount of the receipt is the same as on the deposit slip. This will test whether receipts are being deposited in the bank intact and also help detect lapping of individual receipts. *Lapping* is a type of fraud that involves embezzling receipts from one customer and covering the shortage with receipts from another customer. These, in turn, are covered with receipts which are received later from still other customers. Lapping may occur when there is poor segregation of duties between the cash receipts and accounts receivable accounting function (e.g., when the person responsible for processing cash receipts also has access to the accounts receivable records or vice versa).

Tests of cash receipts are appropriate whether the company uses a lockbox or receives customer payments directly. If the company uses a cash register, the auditor should compare cash register readings to recorded amounts.

It is important to remember that, in selecting the cash receipts sample in the above manner, the auditor's conclusion extends only to the population from which it was selected (cash receipts that are recorded in the customer accounts receivable records). If there are significant amounts of cash receipts from sources other than customers, those receipts will not be subjected to the tests described above. In this case, the auditor should test significant individual receipts (key items) from the various other sources. The tests described above also will not detect customer payments that are misappropriated. In this case, confirming balances directly with customers or reviewing customer correspondence files might detect a problem.

8. Testing of cash discounts and other allowances. The auditor's objective is to determine that discounts and other allowances given to customers are authorized, comply with the company's established terms, and are computed correctly. One common way to conceal a defalcation is by recording fictitious discounts and allowances to customer accounts. In testing allowances and discounts, the auditor should determine that the client is following established policies and procedures. For example, the propriety of allowances given to customers for the company's share of cooperative advertising should be verified through discussions with appropriate marketing executives.

In addition, the auditor should determine that discounts and other allowances are being recorded on a timely basis. If this is not the case, the auditor may have to increase the length of the period covered by cutoff tests.

9. Comparing recorded receipts with the bank statements. This procedure is performed by comparing the recorded receipts with the amounts shown on the bank statement, noting any unusual delays in making the deposits. While differences of one or two business days are common, unusual delays may be caused by an employee who is withholding cash receipts.

Reviewing Cash Receipts Records for Unusual Items

The auditor reviews the cash receipts records for a significant portion of the period under audit to detect significant cash receipts from unusual sources. For this test to be meaningful, the auditor must understand what constitutes an unusual item. What is considered unusual in one company may be considered commonplace in another. Examples of cash receipts that may be considered unusual are receipts from the client itself; receipts from banks or other lending institutions; large receipts in even-dollar amounts; and receipts from officers, directors, or employees.

Testing Clerical Accuracy

While executing the sales and cash receipts audit procedures, the auditor gains evidence that the amounts reflected in the sales and cash receipts registers are properly recorded. However, those records also should be tested for clerical accuracy and their postings should be traced to the general ledger. This is important because the general ledger is used to prepare the financial statements. If credit memoranda (for merchandise or billing corrections) are recorded separately, then the credit memo register also should be tested for clerical accuracy and the totals traced to the general ledger.

The extent of the clerical accuracy tests to be performed will vary. In general, the auditor will clerically test and trace one or two months' totals and rely on analytical review procedures for assurance that the remaining totals or related balances are reasonable.

ACCOUNTS RECEIVABLE—OTHER PROCEDURES

Trade accounts receivable result from credit sales to customers in the normal course of business. Accounts receivable usually represent a substantial asset on a commercial or industrial company's balance sheet. In the audit of accounts receivable, the auditor's objectives are to determine that the amount recorded as receivable accurately reflects the unpaid balance of sales made to or services performed for a customer and that such balance is collectible. In addition to testing key attributes and/or testing sales, receivable, and cash receipts transactions, the audit program for the sales component will include procedures for confirming and evaluating the collectibility of receivables.

Confirming Receivables

SAS No. 1 (AU 331.01) indicates that the confirmation of receivables is a "generally accepted auditing procedure." In practice, there are few instances where correspondence with debtors is not practicable. However, when it is not practicable to confirm the receivable balances or when no replies are received, the auditor must become satisfied as to the reasonableness of the receivables by the use of "alternative procedures." Examples of alternative procedures that may be employed by the auditor include the examination of purchase orders, shipping records, contracts, correspondence, and evidence of subsequent collection. Alternative procedures are discussed in more detail later in this chapter.

Statement on Auditing Standards No. 2, "Reports on Audited Financial Statements" (AU 509.12), notes that circumstances may make it impracticable or impossible for an auditor to confirm receivables. That *Statement on Auditing Standards* (AU 509.12) goes on to state that if the auditor is, ". . . able to satisfy himself as to . . . accounts receivable by applying alternative procedures, there is no significant limitation on the scope of his work, and his report need not include reference to the omission of the procedures or to the use of alternative procedures." If the auditor is not satisfied with the results of the alternative procedures, *Statement on Auditing Standards No. 2* (AU 509.10–.12) suggests that this limitation on the work should be referred to in the scope paragraph, described in an explanatory paragraph, and be referred to in either a qualified opinion or disclaimer of opinion. The same is true if confirmation of receivables is practicable and is not done because of the client's wishes.

SAS No. 1 (AU 331.03) points out that the method and timing of requesting confirmations and the number of confirmations to be requested are to be determined by the auditor. Further, *SAS No. 1* (AU 331.03) notes that "such matters as the effectiveness of internal control, the apparent possibility of disputes, inaccuracies, or irregularities in the accounts, the probability that requests will receive consideration or that the debtor will be able to confirm the information requested and the materiality of the amounts involved are factors to be considered by the auditor in selecting the information to be requested and the form of confirmation, as well as the extent and timing of his confirmation procedures."

Methods of Confirmation.   Accounts receivable may be confirmed by either the positive request method, the negative request method, or by a combination of the two methods. With the positive request method, the debtor is asked to reply directly to the auditor and state whether the balance as indicated on the request is correct or incorrect; and, if it is incorrect, to indicate the correct balance and any possible explanation of the difference. A positive request typically is used (1) for individual account balances that are material in amount, (2) when the auditor suspects there is a strong possibility that the accounts contain errors and/or irregularities, (3) when the auditor suspects that there is disagreement between the client and customers as to the accounts, (4) when variables estimation sampling techniques are em-

FIGURE 10-2 Positive Confirmation Request Form Prepared for Mailing

---

RECEIVABLE CONFIRMATION REQUEST

Our auditors, Ernst & Whinney, are making an examination of our financial statements and wish to obtain direct confirmation of the amount owed us as of the date indicated below. Please compare the balance shown below with your records as of the date indicated and note the details of exceptions (if any) in the space provided below or on an attachment. Then please sign this request in the space provided and return it in the enclosed reply envelope direct to Ernst & Whinney, _153 East 53rd Street, New York, New York 10022_

<table>
<tr><td></td><td>Powertronics Inc.</td></tr>
<tr><td></td><td>Company Aldo Count</td></tr>
<tr><td>To: Alster Corp.</td><td>Signature</td></tr>
<tr><td>13507 Lake Dr.</td><td>Treasurer-Controller 11/16/X5</td></tr>
<tr><td>Dayton, OH 45423</td><td>Title   Date</td></tr>
</table>

This is not a request for payment and remittances should not be sent to Ernst & Whinney.

Confirmation Date __10/31/X5__

Account Balance __$190,000__

Ernst & Whinney:
The account balance shown above is correct as of the date indicated. (If not correct, note exceptions below or on an attachment.)

_____

_____

_____

Signature _____

Title   Date

---

ployed, or (5) where there is reason to believe that a negative request will not receive adequate consideration.[1] Positive confirmations are requested on either a standard or specially printed form or on the client's letterhead. Figure 10–2 is an example of a standard positive request form.

When the negative request method is used, the debtor is asked to reply only if the balance stated on the request is not in agreement with the debtor's records. Circularization on a negative basis is appropriate only when (1) the likelihood of material error is low, (2) where there are many small balances, and (3) there is reason to believe the request will receive consideration.[2] For example, negative requests may be appropriate for magazine or cable TV subscriptions or retail store credit sales.

Where the negative request method is used, the request may be either rubber-stamped or attached in the form of a sticker on the company's regular statement to the customer, or it may be a special form or business reply

---

[1] See *SAS No. 1* (AU 331.05).

[2] Ibid.

FIGURE 10-3   Negative Confirmation Request Form

Please Examine This Statement Carefully

If it does not agree with your records, report any differences in writing to our auditors

Ernst & Whinney
Suite 2000
Wachovia Building
Winston-Salem, North Carolina 27111

who are making an examination of our financial statements. If no differences are reported to them, this statement will be considered correct. Payments should *not* be sent to Ernst & Whinney but should be made to us in the usual manner.

card enclosed with the statement. Figure 10-3 is an example of a negative request. Often both positive and negative requests are used by the auditor during the course of the same examination (see *SAS No. 1*, AU 331.06).

The usual form of confirmation requests will not be acknowledged by some organizations (e.g., the U.S. government and certain retail stores), because it is not convenient for them to verify the balance shown. In those instances, a confirmation request may be tailored to assist the debtor in replying. For example, the auditor may find that a particular debtor will respond to a request that lists purchase orders for all unpaid items, unpaid invoices, or cash remittances where the account has been paid after the confirmation date. If the auditor suspects that a confirmation request will not be acknowledged, the client should be asked to communicate with the debtor prior to preparing the confirmation request to find out what information should be included on the request.

Steps in the Confirmation Process

There are six basic steps in the application of accounts receivable confirmation or circularization procedures: (1) preliminary planning, (2) selecting accounts for circularization, (3) recording accounts circularized, (4) preparing and controlling confirmation requests, (5) investigating differences reported in confirmation replies, and (6) performing alternative procedures.

Preliminary Planning.   Planning the accounts receivable circularization is important for several reasons. Many businesses do not send out statements of all open items; rather, they send invoices as the goods are shipped or services are performed. On certain engagements, the auditor may confirm individual invoice amounts. On other engagements, the auditor may confirm the total amounts owed, so it will be necessary to send statements. In those situations, the auditor and the client should agree on when the statements are to be prepared and what the statements will contain.

The auditor also must plan for the format of the confirmation request before the confirmation date. The auditor should decide such things as: Should the negative confirmation request be stamped on the statement or included in the envelope as a separate form? Should the positive confirmation request be on the client's letterhead or should a standard form be used?

Additional planning is required if a statistical sampling technique will be used to infer sample results to the total receivable balance. The auditor must make sure that a valid statistical sample can be selected. Also, the auditor may plan to use computer-assisted audit techniques to select the items in the sample.

Selecting Amounts for Circularization. During the program development phase, the auditor must decide, based on the inputs to the risk analysis working papers, whether to use positive, negative, or a combination of the two confirmation methods. In addition, the auditor must determine the number of accounts or invoices to be selected and the method of selection. The auditor also should define key items to be confirmed.

Key items include accounts that are individually important due to their size and accounts that the auditor believes have a higher likelihood of error. Older accounts may have a higher likelihood of error. Using the aged trial balance, the auditor can identify old unpaid balances or invoices. These may signal that a dispute exists with the customer or that the customer is experiencing financial difficulties and the account may be uncollectible.

In many instances, after key accounts have been segregated and confirmed, there remains a large population of accounts that are individually unimportant but significant in total. For these accounts, the auditor often confirms a representative sample if analytical review procedures or tests of key attributes are not sufficiently persuasive to enable the auditor to conclude that there is no material error in the population. In many instances, computer software can be utilized to select a statistical sample for circularization.

When working with a statistical sample of accounts to be circularized in the positive form, it is important to remember that all sample items must be substantiated for the results to be statistically valid. Substantiation can be either by direct response from the customer or, in the absence of such a response, by some form of alternative procedures performed by the auditor.

Either positive or negative confirmations may be used when confirming a representative sample of account balances. It is important to note that use of negative confirmations does not provide a basis for quantifying how many requests receive consideration; yet, it is the requests that receive consideration that provide the basis for the audit conclusion. Therefore, when using negative confirmation requests, the auditor should estimate a *consideration rate*, i.e., the number of customers in the sample (stated as a percentage) who will actually read and consider the negative confirmations received.

The number of negative requests to mail is the desired sample size[3] divided by this rate. The following approach should be used to estimate the consideration rate:

1. In the first year negative confirmations are to be sent, the auditor should use the response rate to first requests for positive confirmations sent in the previous year.[4] For example, assume the minimum sample size of 25 is desired in 1984, and 1983's first response rate on positive requests was 50 percent. The number of negative confirmations the auditor should mail in 1984 would be 50 (25 divided by the estimated consideration rate of .50).
2. Some or all of the current year negative requests should be worded as positives so that the response rate on these can be used to determine the number of requests to mail in the subsequent year.

Under this approach, all requests, including those worded as positives, should be evaluated as negative confirmations, so no alternative procedures are required on nonresponses. However, the conclusion should be based on the desired sample size expected to be considered (total number mailed times the planned—or actual—consideration rate)—*not the number of requests mailed.* The audit program should clearly state that any confirmation requests worded as positives were done so only to determine the number of negative requests to mail in the subsequent year.

The above approach to sending negative confirmations can be used with (1) representative samples for which no statistical conclusion is planned, or (2) attribute, discovery, or PPS sampling. *However, the approach is only appropriate when the criteria for using negative confirmations are met.* For example, negative confirmations should not be used for key items or variables estimation sampling because the criteria (e.g., errors expected, large balances) for these strategies differ from those for using negatives.

Recording Accounts Circularized. The auditor should include a record of the accounts selected for circularization in the working papers. If negative requests are used, notations on the copy of the detailed accounts receivable listing or an adding machine tape of these accounts will serve this purpose. For positive requests, notations on the copy of the detailed listing, copies of the requests, or a worksheet listing the customer names, addresses, and account balances are appropriate. A working paper used to record the positive confirmations mailed also may be used to document the results of the confirmation procedures. Figure 10–4 is an example.

---

[3] The minimum of 25 (with no statistical conclusion) or the number necessary to achieve the desired parameters in a statistical sampling application should be used.

[4] If positive confirmations were not previously sent (e.g., in a new engagement), the auditor should word all the current year requests as positives and assume a low response rate (e.g., 30 percent).

FIGURE 10–4 Accounts Receivable Confirmation Working Paper

			Name	Date			
		Prepared	*Jack*	12/15/xx			
		Approved					

Accounts Receivable Confirmations
Hexitron Manufacturing Corporation   Page 5 of 5
December 31, 19xx (Confirmation date – 10/31/19xx)

Account Name	Acct No.	Confirmation Number	Confirmation Mailing Date First/Second	Account Balance per Books	Account Balance per Customer	Unconfirmed Balance
Shields Equipment Co.	23851	46	N/A N/A	2341'26'52 △	2341'26'52 ∅	
Stahr Industrial Sales Corp.	24799	47	11/21	91'260'08 △		91'260'08
Summit Associates	24869	48	11/21	35251'1'29 △	35606'66'33 ∅	
Teakline Sales, Inc.	25601	49	N/A	128282'68'84 △	149430'1'42 ∅	
Trombold Equipment Co.	25978	50	N/A	64684'29 △	54684'29 ∅	
				1580172'5'45	1335143'1'25	34754'42'30

△ Traced to 10/31/19xx A/R Listing.

∅ Per confirmation returned.

✓ See SA-3.

T Based on our risk analysis, these differences were expected. Client handles the differences correctly at year-end and our audit program provided procedures for reviewing these year-end procedures.

✓x On page cross-reference.

	Percentage of Accts Receivable		
	Accts	Amount	Response Rate
	32%	75%	88%

Alternative Procedures Cash Receipts	Alternative Procedures Shipping Advices	Balance Supported by Alternative Procedures	Audited Book Balance	Balance Over (Under) Book Balance	Detail of Difference	Explanation of Difference
			−0−			
72,102.76 ✓	19,157.32 ✓	91,260.08	−0−			
				3,555.04	3,555.04 ✓X	This amount represents one invoice. The merchandise was shipped 10/31 but was recorded as a November sale. Shipping documentation was examined. This shipment was made from the Seattle Division which closes sales early on an interim basis.
				211,474.58	163,650.37	The customer confirmation covered this balance of EMC International, a Sackline Sales subsidiary. Agrees in amount with EMC balance on page 2 of Accounts Receivable Confirmations.
					47,824.21 ✓X	Same as for confirmation No. 48 above.
					211,474.58	
				(10,000.00)	(10,000.00) ✓X	Customer deposit. This balance was traced to the detail listing of Accounts Payable.
2,933,738.20	541,704.10	3,415,442.30	(1,025,148.10)	(1,025,148.10)		

Percentage to Total

84%	16%	100%

Total Difference ✓X = T
180,984.42

Percentage to Balance Confirmed

1.15%

SA-2

Preparing and Controlling Confirmation Requests. The client usually prepares the confirmation requests (e.g., types positive requests or stamps statements with negative requests). However, the auditor mails the requests. Before the auditor mails the customer statements and confirmation requests, they should be compared with the trial balance of the accounts (prepared by either the auditor or the client) or with the company's detailed accounts receivable records (e.g., customer ledger cards) to determine that the balances, customers' name, and addresses are in agreement and that no statements have been withheld or altered by the client. The company's employees also may assist in stuffing envelopes for the auditor. In such cases, the auditor needs to directly supervise them to maintain control over the confirmations.

When using positive requests, the auditor should mail second requests to customers who do not reply after a reasonable time (e.g., two weeks). If a reply to the second request is not received, the auditor should consider mailing a third request. For those customers who fail to reply to positive requests, the auditor should perform alternative procedures.

Occasionally, during the preparation of the confirmation requests, a company employee may ask to see a statement before it is mailed—for example, to attach a "past-due" notice. Such requests are generally valid; however, the auditor should make a record of the statement withdrawn (name, address, and amount) and be sure that it is returned, unaltered, for mailing.

In some cases, a client may request that the auditor not confirm a customer's balance—even though it would be practicable to do so. For example, the client may not want to send the customer a confirmation reflecting a credit balance, or an account may be in dispute. In these cases, if not confirming the balance significantly limits the scope of the examination, it also may be necessary to change the standard auditors' report.

To assure that all statements selected for circularization will either reach the addressee or be returned to the auditor by the post office, the auditor must maintain physical control over them from the time they are prepared until they are mailed. If the auditor does not maintain physical control, the client or an employee of the client could circumvent the circularization procedures in an attempt to cover irregularities by removing statements with the incorrect balances, altering balances to cover the manipulation of accounts, or changing addresses so that the statements are not received by the customer.

If the client's envelopes are used, their return address should be blocked out on all envelopes and replaced with the auditor's. This ensures that no statements are returned to the company and identifies undeliverable confirmations.

The auditor documents performance of the circularization procedures in the working papers. This documentation should include:

1. The coverage obtained through circularization of key items.
2. A description of how any representative samples were selected.

3. A description of any accounts not circularized at the client's request, including the reasons.
4. A description of how customer statements were controlled until mailed.

An example of a memorandum covering circularization procedures is shown in Figure 10–5.

Investigating Differences Reported in Confirmation Replies. In reply to confirmation requests, some customers will report differences. Most differences result from normal business reasons, such as shipments or customer payments that are in-transit. But differences also might indicate audit problems, such as unrecorded credits or allowances, disputes between the client and the customer, or clerical errors.

All reported differences should be investigated. Usually, the auditor will ask the client to investigate the differences. The auditor should keep a list or copies of replies given to the client for investigation. The auditor should review the client's reconciliation of the reported difference(s) and examine support for the reconciling items as necessary.

The auditor must consider the impact of these differences on total accounts receivable. In other words, besides obtaining satisfactory explanations for the differences in the accounts circularized, the auditor should challenge whether the same type of differences may exist in the remaining accounts that were not circularized. While many of these differences (such as payments or shipments that are in-transit) will not affect the financial statements, other differences may indicate a deficiency in the client's accounting system and accordingly may have a significant impact on the financial statements and the audit procedures. Such differences could result from not granting credit for payments made (other than in-transit payments) or for merchandise returned before the cutoff date, warranty problems, or customer disputes.

Refer again to Figure 10–4. Confirmation numbers 48 and 49 reveal that Hexitron's Seattle division was cutting off sales early on an interim basis. Many companies have early cutoffs for various reasons. One reason might be to enable management to have monthly financial reports prepared on a timely basis. However, this procedure is at variance with proper accounting and should be corrected at year-end, so that the audited income statement includes all the current year sales.

The "Explanation of Difference" column for Confirmation Number 50 refers to a $10,000 deposit being carried in accounts payable. Deposits generally are recorded in a deposit account or are applied to the customer's account receivable balance at appropriate times. This is a confirmation exception that should be followed up to identify additional audit considerations.

Performing Alternative Procedures. Alternative procedures must be performed by the auditor to substantiate the balances of any customers who fail to respond to positive confirmation requests. As with all audit procedures,

FIGURE 10–5 Memorandum Regarding Circularization Procedures

Prepared _Smith_ 9/30/X1
Approved _____ _____

Circularization of Accounts Receivable   1 of 2
Moore Machine Company
9/30/X1

Customer accounts receivable of Moore Machine Company were circularized as of the balance sheet date 9/30/X1.

All accounts with balances in excess of $50,000 were circularized using the positive method. This amounted to nine accounts, comprising 46.1% of the total accounts receivable balance — see working paper SA 4.5. All remaining accounts, except as noted in the following paragraph, were circularized using the negative method.

It is the client's policy not to mail statements to any customer with credit balances. Accordingly, at the client's request we did not circularize any credit balance accounts. A listing of the accounts, totaling ($3,750.19) is included on working paper SA 4.15. Copies of these customer statements are also enclosed.

Customer statements remained under my control from the time received from the client until mailing. Two client employees under my supervision assisted in preparing confirmation requests, stuffing envelopes, and blocking out the company's return address using the Ernst & Whinney block out stamp. At the time of mailing, the total number of confirmation requests prepared was reconciled to the total number of accounts on the aged trial balance without exception. A schedule showing this reconciliation is included on working paper SA 4.16.

FIGURE 10–5 *(concluded)*

	Name Date Prepared *Smith* 9/30/X1 Approved ___ ___

Circularization of Accounts Receivable   2 of 2

Moore Machine Company

9/30/X1

    Based on the results of the procedures performed, it is my opinion that all accounts were circularized in accordance with the audit program.

the extent of the procedures performed is based on the risk analysis. If the auditor has established reliance on the cash receipts system, the procedures may be limited to reviewing the activity in the customer's account balance for evidence of subsequent payments. If reliance on the cash receipts system has not been established, the auditor should perform the following alternative procedures:

1. Support collections subsequent to the confirmation date by inspecting incoming checks or remittance advices (verify that subsequent receipts relate to sales made prior to the confirmation date).
2. Trace collected amounts to the record of cash receipts.
3. If payment has not been received from the customer, the auditor should:
   a. Examine shipping records to determine that the materials invoiced to the customer were shipped.
   b. Examine evidence as to the existence of the recorded debtor (if there is any doubt).

Client assistance should be obtained in performing alternative procedures. This assistance could include scheduling cash received subsequent to the confirmation date and obtaining, for the auditor's review, the various supporting documents such as remittance advices, duplicate deposit slips, shipping advices, and customer purchase orders.

Reconciliation of the Accounts Receivable Trial Balance to the General Ledger

If the accounts receivable trial balance (prepared by either the auditor or the client) used to circularize receivables does not agree with the general ledger as of the circularization date, a reconciliation should be prepared. This reconciliation normally will be prepared by the client. Examples of reconciling items include adjustments to accounts receivable made after the date that the detailed trial balance was prepared and cash received on or prior to the confirmation date that was not posted to customer balances until after the detailed trial balance was prepared (commonly referred to as "unapplied cash").

The auditor should examine underlying support for any significant reconciling items. Examples of supporting documentation include invoices, shipping documents, customer correspondence, credit memos, and books of original entry (e.g., sales journal, cash receipts journal).

Accounts Receivable Rollforward

If confirmation procedures are performed prior to the balance sheet date, it is necessary to review and/or test activity that occurs between the date of circularization and year-end (the rollforward period). In addition, it may be necessary to circularize significant account balances that result from subsequent sales transactions.

In reviewing transactions between the circularization date and the balance sheet date, the auditor should perform some or all of the following:

1. Obtain analyses of the entries in the general ledger control account for the intervening months.
2. Compare the level of activity during the rollforward period to prior periods.
3. Trace the entries from the analyses to the books of original entry that were tested as part of the tests of key attributes.
4. Test significant transactions from unusual sources by examining supporting documentation.

Figure 10–6 is an example of a typical rollforward audit schedule. Note the audit procedures described in the tick mark explanations at the bottom of the schedule.

Sales Cutoff

While auditing accounts receivable, the auditor tests whether sales are recorded in the proper accounting period. Sales cutoff may be tested by examining key invoices and shipping documents (e.g., all sales over $10,000) or a representative sample from the sales transactions for several days prior to and subsequent to the period under review. These documents are then traced to the sales and accounts receivable records for the appropriate period.

It should be evident how the results of the audit procedures in one area have a direct bearing on other audit steps. For example, two accounts in Figure 10–4 (Nos. 48 and 49) were incorrect because of an early sales cutoff. This finding could have a significant effect on both the nature and extent of the sales cutoff test. If the auditor's follow-up to the confirmation procedures indicate that client personnel at a shipping location do not accurately cutoff sales at month-end, the auditor may perform an extensive sales cutoff review for that location. Many of these additional procedures can be performed only if the auditor is aware of the situation during the early stages of field work.

The sales cutoff test performed in connection with the examination of accounts receivable should be related to the cutoff tests performed in connection with the examination of inventories. These tests are discussed in Chapter 12.

Evaluating the Collectibility of Receivables

To conform with generally accepted accounting principles (GAAP), accounts receivable should be reported in the financial statements at their

FIGURE 10–6 Typical Rollforward Audit Schedule

	Name	Date
Prepared	Arnold	1/19/XX
Approved		

Accounts Receivable Rollforward
Hepitron Manufacturing Corporation
December 31, 19XX

				Prior Year
Accounts receivable balance @ 10/31/19XX			2106896593	1902957600
(confirm date)			G/L	
November Activity				
Increases			Δ	
Sales		R	27,1848283.39	2446363200
JE 11/13 (to record NSF checks)		I	5275.12	754300
JE 11/25 (to record pricing error on det. inv. #390733)		I	2070000	
Decreases			Δ	
Cash receipts		R	26486285.25	2378240000
Credit memos		I	58769.11	6054300
Accounts receivable balance @ 11/30/19XX			2173471307	1966285800
			G/L	
December Activity				
Increases			Δ	
Sales		R	2930662443	2757681000
JE 12/13 (to record NSF check)		I	11749.72	847200
Decreases			Δ	
Cash receipts		R	3000586713	2768011000
Credit memos		I	65713.82	51125.00
JE 12/20 (to apply deposits to A/R)		⌁	5000000	
Balance @ 12/31/19XX			2093310627	1951690500
			TB	

G/L Agrees with the general ledger

Δ Agrees with the sales or cash receipts journal.

* Per last year's working papers

I Amount immaterial or appears reasonable compared with the prior year.

R Amount appears reasonable based on comparison to prior months of
current year and same month of prior year taking into account the
current trends in operation.

⌁ Examined sales contract and traced deposit amount to details of
liability accounts. appears proper.

TB agrees with trial balance

Conclusion: I have examined the rollforward of trade accounts
receivable balances from the confirmation date to the balance
sheet date in accordance with the audit program. In my
opinion, these balances are fairly stated.

336

estimated realizable amount. The auditor determines that the gross amount of the receivables is fairly stated by obtaining satisfaction that (1) uncollectible accounts have been properly written off and (2) adequate provision has been made for potentially uncollectible amounts, discounts, allowances, and other possible credits. In reviewing the collectibility of accounts receivable and evaluating the adequacy of the allowance for doubtful accounts, the auditor will refer to various client records and other information. This discussion of evaluating collectibility is divided into the following topics: aging of accounts, review of individual account balances, review of subsequent credits, prior experience of the company and changes in nature of customers, comparison of current year's statistics with prior experience, and changes in the external environment.

Aging of Accounts. Customer accounts are aged to determine the length of time that amounts have been outstanding. Generally, the longer an account is past due, the more likely it is to be uncollectible. Therefore, the aging of receivables is of interest to the auditor in evaluating the adequacy of the allowance for uncollectible accounts. The auditor often finds it useful to compare the current percentage of past-due accounts with that of prior years.

The aging often is prepared by the client and may be done as of the confirmation date, the balance sheet date, or both. If the receivables include a large number of small accounts, a list of only those amounts that are past due may be acceptable. If the aging is prepared by the client, the auditor should test the clerical accuracy of the aging amounts by reference to the individual accounts and should reconcile the total to the general ledger. The aged trial balance should be included as a part of the auditor's working papers, and information obtained concerning the collectibility of accounts should be noted on it (e.g., payments of past-due amounts, discussions with the credit manager). Figure 10–7 is an example of an aged trial balance of accounts receivable.

Review of Individual Account Balances. After an initial review of the aged trial balance, the auditor may select certain accounts for further investigation. The auditor should discuss collectibility of the amounts with the credit manager or other responsible company official(s) and summarize the results of the discussions in the working papers. The auditor also should check collections of past-due amounts since the balance sheet date and should examine correspondence with customer, collection agency reports, and other relevant data included in the client's credit files. It also may be advisable to obtain Dun & Bradstreet reports or independent information from other sources relating to customers whose accounts are material.

Review of Subsequent Credits. The auditor should examine credit memos issued and recorded subsequent to year-end to ascertain whether these credit

FIGURE 10-7 Aged Trial Balance of Accounts Receivable

Accounts Receivable—October 31, 19X5

| | | | | Prepared | P.C. 11-25-x5 |
| | | | | Approved | M.G. 11-25-x5 |

Customer Balance	Balance	0–30 Days	31–60 Days	61–90 Days	Over 90 Days
ASP Inc.	$ 16,000				$ 16,000✓
Advant Corp.	30,000	$ 25,000	$ 5,000		
Almay Homes Inc.	18,500	16,000	2,500		
Americana Corp.	13,000	1,500		$11,500✓	
Arsada Corp.	21,000	16,700	1,000		3,300
Avenly Company	19,000	15,000	4,000		
Bashko Company	22,900	22,000			900
Batens Company	11,500	10,000	700		800
Biotex Corp.	36,700	31,000	5,000		700
Bostar Manufacturing Co.	12,000	11,000	1,000		
Brunch Industries Inc.	1,000			1,000	
Bruel Industries Inc.	3,500	1,750		1,750	
Budd International	27,000				27,000
Cabanz Enterprises Inc.	22,000	16,000	6,000		
Calarco Inc.	12,700	8,400	2,300		2,000
Wagner Manufacturing Co.	17,300	10,000	7,300		
Warwick Industries	20,800				20,800
Wilcox Watch Co.	26,500	26,500			
	$2,145,870 ¢	$1,793,300	$147,400	$54,400	$153,770
	''	''	''	''	''

'' Foots.
¢ Crossfoots.
✓ This account has been paid, per review of cash receipts journals, through November 21.

memos affect the period under audit and therefore require adjustment. The auditor also should be alert for any indication of additional credits that may be required for the period under audit and propose an adjustment to record any noted. The review for pending unissued credits should include inquiry of client personnel outside the accounting department (e.g., customer service, sales, engineering).

Prior Experience of the Company and Changes in Nature of Customers.   The prior collection experience of the client may indicate future collection experience. However, the auditor should be alert for any changes in the nature of the client's business or type of customer. For example, if a company that was selling its product solely to jobbers in the past decides to sell directly to retail outlets, its previous collection experience would probably be of little or no use in predicting its future experience.

Comparison of Current Year's Statistics with Prior Experience.   Comparison of current statistics with those of the prior year can highlight potential weaknesses in the company's collection efforts that may have an impact on the overall collectibility of accounts receivable. For example, the auditor should consider performing the following analytical review procedures:

1. Compare the allowance for doubtful accounts to the total accounts receivable for current and prior periods.
2. Compare the bad debt provision to credit sales for current and prior periods.
3. Compare bad debt write-offs to the average accounts receivable for current and prior periods.
4. Compare the percentage composition of accounts receivable aging to prior periods.
5. Compare the number of days' sales in receivables with the prior period.

Change in External Environment.   The auditor should be alert to changes in business conditions occurring after the audit is planned. For example, the increased likelihood of business failures during a period of economic recession and rising interest rates may affect the adequacy of the allowance for doubtful accounts.

Other Analytical Review Procedures

There are various other analytical review procedures that may be performed in the audit of sales and accounts receivable. Comparing gross margins to prior periods may provide the auditor with evidence that billings are for the correct amount and are recorded in the proper account and period. If sales returns and allowances are not significant, a comparison of sales returns and allowances to sales for the current and prior periods may provide all the evidence needed to conclude that total returns and allowances are reasonably stated.

QUESTIONS AND PROBLEMS

10–1. Why are the controls a company maintains over its sales and cash receipts transactions important?

10–2. Why would an auditor test sales invoices for *(a)* quantities invoiced, *(b)* unit prices and discounts, and *(c)* clerical accuracy?

10–3. Why should an auditor test cash discounts and other allowances?

10–4. Describe positive and negative confirmation procedures. When should each be used?

10–5. May positive and negative confirmation procedures be used on the same audit?

10–6. In some instances the usual form of confirmation requests will not be acknowledged. In these instances, may a confirmation request be tailored so as to bring a reply?

10–7. List six basic steps involved in the application of accounts receivable confirmation procedures.

10–8. May the client assist the auditor in preparing confirmation requests?

10–9. CPA K is working on the accounts receivable portion of the audit of the Reach Corporation. During the preparation of the confirmation requests, a client employee asks to see one statement before it is mailed to attach a "past-due" notice. What should K do?

10–10. CPA J is working on the accounts receivable portion of the audit of the Arbor Company. J is sending positive requests to a portion of the accounts. What should J do if some of the customers do not respond to the initial request?

10–11. When the auditor documents the accounts receivable circularization procedures in the working papers, what should the documentation include?

10–12. In general, what kinds of differences will be reported by customers in reply to confirmation requests?

10–13. What alternative procedures need to be performed by the auditor in the cases where positive confirmations are unanswered?

10–14. Can client assistance be used in performing alternative procedures?

10–15. If confirmation procedures are performed prior to the balance sheet date, what review procedures should be performed of activity that occurs between the date of circularization and the balance sheet date (the rollforward period)?

10–16. Select the best answer for each of the following:
  a. Which of the following would be the *best* protection for a company that wished to prevent the "lapping" of trade accounts receivable?
    (1) Segregate duties so that the bookkeeper in charge of the general ledger has no access to incoming mail.
    (2) Segregate duties so that *no* employee has access to both checks from customers and currency from daily cash receipts.
    (3) Have customers send payments directly to the company's depository bank.
    (4) Request that customer's payment checks be made payable to the company and addressed to the treasurer.
  b. The use of the positive (as opposed to the negative) form of receivables confirmation is indicated when:
    (1) Internal control surrounding accounts receivable is considered to be effective.
    (2) There is reason to believe that a substantial number of accounts may be in dispute.
    (3) A large number of small balances are involved.
    (4) There is reason to believe the requests will be answered.
  c. It is sometimes impracticable or impossible for an auditor to use normal accounts receivable confirmation procedures. In such situations the *best* alternative procedure the auditor might resort to would be:

      (1)   Examining subsequent receipts of year-end accounts receivable.

      (2)   Reviewing accounts receivable aging schedules prepared at the balance sheet date and at a subsequent date.

      (3)   Requesting that management increase the allowance for uncollectible accounts by an amount equal to some percentage of the balance in those accounts that cannot be confirmed.

      (4)   Performing an overall analytical review of accounts receivable and sales on a year-to-year basis.   (AICPA, adapted)

10–17.   What is a sales cutoff test? How is it performed?

10–18.   What analytical review procedure may provide evidence needed in auditing sales returns and allowances?

10–19.   You are considering using the services of a reputable outside mailing service for the confirmation of accounts receivable balances. The service would prepare and mail the confirmation requests and remove the returned confirmations from the envelopes and give them directly to you.

Required:

    What reliance, if any, could you place on the services of the outside mailing service? Discuss and state the reasons in support of your answer.

(AICPA, adapted)

10–20.   Dodge, CPA, is examining the financial statements of a manufacturing company with a significant amount of trade accounts receivable. Dodge is satisfied that the accounts are properly summarized and classified and that allocations, reclassifications, and valuations are made in accordance with generally accepted accounting principles. Dodge is planning to use accounts receivable confirmation requests to satisfy the third standard of field work as to trade accounts receivable.

Required:

    a.   Identify and describe the two forms of accounts receivable confirmation requests and indicate what factors Dodge will consider in determining when to use each.

    b.   Assume Dodge has received a satisfactory response to the confirmation requests. Describe how Dodge could evaluate collectibility of the trade accounts receivable.   (AICPA)

10–21.   The Meyers Pharmaceutical Company, a drug manufacturer, has the following system for billing and recording accounts receivable:

    1.   An incoming customer's purchase order is received in the order department by a clerk who prepares a prenumbered company sales order form in which is inserted the pertinent information, such as the customer's name and address, customer's account number, quantity, and items ordered. After the sales order form has been prepared, the customer's purchase order is stapled to it.

    2.   The sales order form is then passed to the credit department for credit approval. Rough approximations of the billing values of the orders are made in the credit department for those accounts on which credit limitations are imposed. After investigation, approval of credit is noted on the form.

3. Next, the sales order form is passed to the billing department, where a clerk types the customer's invoice on a billing machine that cross-multiplies the number of items and the unit price and then adds the automatically extended amounts for the total amount of the invoice. The billing clerk determines the unit prices for the items from a list of billing prices.

   The billing machine has registers that automatically accumulate daily totals of customer account numbers and invoice amounts to provide "hash" totals and control amounts. These totals, which are inserted in a daily record book, serve as predetermined batch totals for vertification of computer inputs.

   The billing is done on prenumbered, continuous, carbon-interleaved forms having the following designations:

   a. "Customer's copy."

   b. "Sales department copy," for information purposes.

   c. "File copy."

   d. "Shipping department copy," which serves as a shipping order. Bills of lading are also prepared as carbon copy by-products of the invoicing procedure.

4. The shipping department copy of the invoice and the bills of lading are then sent to the shipping department. After the order has been shipped, copies of the bill of lading are returned to the billing department. The shipping department copy of the invoice is filed in the shipping department.

5. In the billing department, one copy of the bill of lading is attached to the customer's copy of the invoice and both are mailed to the customer. The other copy of the bill of lading, together with the sales order form, is then stapled to the invoice file copy and filed in invoice numerical order.

6. A keypunch machine is connected to the billing machine so that punched cards are created during the preparation of the invoices. The punched cards then become the means by which the sales data are transmitted to a computer.

   The punched cards are fed to the computer in batches. One day's accumulation of cards comprises a batch. After the punched cards have been processed by the computer, they are placed in files and held for about two years.

Required:

List the procedures that a CPA would employ in the examination of the selected audit samples of the company's:

a. Typed invoices, including the source documents.

b. Punched cards.

(The listed procedures should be limited to the verification of the sales data being fed into the computer. Do not carry the procedures beyond the point at which the cards are ready to be fed to the computer.)   (AICPA, adapted)

10–22. You have examined the financial statements of the Heft Company for several years. The system of internal control for accounts receivable is very satisfactory. The Heft Company is on a calendar year basis. An interim audit, which included confirmation of the accounts receivable, was performed at August 31 and indicated that the accounting for receivables was very reliable.

The company's sales are principally to manufacturing concerns. There are about 1,500 active trade accounts receivable, of which about 35 percent in number represent

65 percent of the total dollar amount. The accounts receivable are maintained alphabetically in five subledgers which are controlled by one general ledger account.

Sales are machine-posted in the subledgers by an operation that simultaneously produces the customer's ledger card, his monthly statement, and the sales journal. All cash receipts are in the form of customer's checks and are machine-posted simultaneously on the customer's ledger card, his monthly statement, and cash receipts journal. Information for posting cash receipts is obtained from the remittance advice portions of the customer's checks. The bookkeeping machine operator compares the remittance advices with the list of checks that was prepared by another person when the mail was received.

Summary totals are produced monthly by the bookkeeping machine operations for posting to the appropriate general ledger accounts such as cash, sales, accounts receivable, etc. Aged trial balances by subledger are prepared monthly.

Sales returns and allowances and bad debt write-offs are summarized periodically and recorded by standard journal entries. Supporting documents for these journal entries are available. The usual documents arising from billing, shipping, and receiving are also available.

Required:

Prepare in detail the audit program for the Heft Company for the year-end examination of the trade accounts receivable. Do not give the program for the interim audit.   (AICPA)

10–23. You are making an examination of the accounts of the Hardy Corporation. Accounts receivable represent a significant proportion of the total assets of the company. At the beginning of the audit you mailed out positive confirmations on a test basis. Included in your tests were confirmations requested from several U.S. government departments; the confirmation requests for these accounts were returned along with the following notations:

"Your confirmation letter is returned herewith without action inasmuch as the type of information requested therein cannot be compiled by this office with sufficient accuracy to be of any value."

Your test also included customers whose accounts payable systems were either decentralized or who used a voucher system which made it impossible or impractical to give the requested information. These customers either informed you of their inability to comply with the request or did not reply.

Required:

Assuming the number and amount of responses to confirmation requests are unsatisfactory, what additional auditing procedures would you apply?

(AICPA, adapted)

10–24. You have been assigned to the audit of Sever, Inc., a medium-sized manufacturer of machine parts, whose fiscal year ended October 31. You and the senior accountant arrive on Monday, November 13, to start the field work for the completion of the audit. The senior accountant gives you a copy of the accounts receivable aging schedule prepared by the company, the audit program, and a folder containing all working papers in connection with circularization of receivables performed on November 2. The folder contains the following information:

Adding machine tape of accounts receivable at October 31.

A list showing the name, address, and balance of 12 customers to whom positive requests for confirmation were mailed.

Five positive requests which have been returned by customers confirming the balances as being correct.

Eight negative confirmations which have been returned with notations made thereon by customers.

Two positive and one negative requests returned by the post office marked "unknown" or similar designation.

The senior accountant introduces you to the controller, the credit manager, the accounts receivable bookkeeper, and the billing clerk. You are then instructed to proceed with the tests of the aging schedule and completion of the audit work on the accounts receivable, as outlined in the audit program. The senior accountant will return tomorrow to answer any questions you have with respect to the accounts receivable and to review any items you think should be discussed.

The senior accountant informs you that the adding machine tape was prepared by the accounts receivable bookkeeper for your use in sending out the confirmation requests. Another member of your firm checked the customers' statements to the tape but did not check the total by re-adding the tape. However, you note that the total at the bottom of the tape does agree with the total shown on the aging schedule prepared by the company. The senior accountant also tells you that either positive or negative requests were sent to all of the 50 accounts.

The aging schedule appears on the page 345. You are to assume that the internal accounting control is good. You should study the aging schedule and answer the questions which follow. The normal credit terms are net 30.

Required:

Using the information presented in this problem, perform the following:
a. List the items on the aging schedule that you would select for further examination and describe why.
b. Describe what you would do with the adding machine tape prepared at the time the confirmations were mailed.
c. List the items you would select for discussion with the senior accountant.
d. Describe what you would do with the five positive requests which were returned indicating no exceptions.
e. Describe what you would do with the requests returned by the post office marked "unknown" or similar designation.
f. Describe what you would do with the negative requests returned with notations made thereon by customers.

10–25. You performed interim audit procedures at Novak Piston Company as of October 31. You have returned to Novak Piston Company in January. The senior on the engagement has assigned you to perform the year-end accounts receivable audit procedures. The procedures include reviewing the interim transactions between October 31 to December 31. In addition to the October 31 aged accounts receivable listing that you obtained at the time of the accounts receivable circularization, with

SEVER, INC.
Aged Trial Balance—Accounts Receivable
October 31

	Balance Dr.	Balance Cr.	Oct.	Sept.	Aug.	May June–July	Prior
ABC Investment Brokerage	$ 14,750.00		$ 14,750.00				
Allied Products Co.	12,618.32				$12,618.32		
American Manufacturing Co.		$ 612.00					
B & D Machinery, Inc.	57,538.79		35,123.76	$10,078.12	6,312.45	$ 6,024.46	
Beat Equipment, Inc.	1,098.45		198.45				$ 900.00
Cooper, Frank M. (Employee)	5,000.00					5,000.00	
Chalmera Motors, Inc.	7,445.83			1,263.17	2,376.28	3,806.38	
Davidson Engineering Company	3,573.35					3,573.35	
Drake Press Division	78,396.21		78,396.21				
Erie Machine Works, Inc.	6,215.63						6,215.63
Evans and Co. (Deposit)	10,000.00		10,000.00				
Franklin Motors, Inc.	17,624.91		11,784.16	5,840.75			
Franklin Motors, Inc. (Note)	25,000.00				25,000.00		
Globe Machinery, Inc.	30,248.65		25,932.40				4,316.25
Globe Machinery, Inc. (Consignment)	103,487.98		50,116.73	28,745.27	12,678.93	8,319.00	3,628.05
	$495,444.00	$5,612.00	$328,577.92	$53,932.36	$66,768.92	$31,104.88	$15,059.93

	Balance Dr.	Balance Cr.	Oct.	Sept.	Aug.	May June–July	Prior
Watkins Company	4,728.16		4,728.16				
Whitman, Inc.	16,512.54		16,512.54				
Young Machinery Co.	8,378.05		6,873.00	1,505.05			

345

a balance of $506,918.04, client personnel have provided you with the following information.

Sales:	
November	$286,492.10
December	299,032.88
Cash disbursements:	
November	$181,000.01
December	287,787.29
Cash receipts:	
October	$173,360.09
November	251,121.63
December	304,004.40
Credit memos:	
October	$2,220.23
November	3,553.20
December	2,785.15
Consigned inventory (company has not recorded as a receivable nor sale):	
November	$11,018.35
December	21,814.60
Journal entries:	
November:	
#13—Goode Corporation—credit not recorded by Novak	$ 5,800.00
#14—error in recording invoice W-49623; posted as $44,882, correct amount $48,428	3,546.00
#21—NSF checks (November)	868.26
December:	
#7—Pure Plastics Company—discount taken and recorded; however, subsequently disallowed by Novak	$ 101.12
#12—NSF checks (December)	217.64
#14—Consigned inventory incorrectly priced in favor of consignee	2,953.00
#17—Write off of uncollectible accounts	8,666.40

Required:

Using the information given, perform the following.

a. Prepare an accounts receivable rollforward analysis.
b. Describe the audit procedures you might perform in support of the interim transactions, depending upon the audit program.

10–26. In the past, records to be evaluated in an audit have consisted of printed reports, listings, documents, and written papers, all of which are visible output. However, in fully computerized systems which employ daily updating of transaction files, output and files are frequently in machine-readable forms such as cards, tapes, or disks. Thus, they often present the auditor with an opportunity to use the computer in performing an audit.

Required:

Discuss how the computer can be used to aid the auditor in examining accounts receivable in such a fully computerized system. (AICPA)

AUDITING THE PRODUCTION OR SERVICE COMPONENT— MATERIALS, OVERHEAD, AND LABOR

The specific control objectives relating to the production or service component (as shown in Figure 11–1) can be divided into the following categories— materials and overhead; labor; inventory accountability and physical safeguards; and property, plant, and equipment.

In Chapter 4, we noted that most transactions originate in one of the four basic operating components (sales, production or service, finance, and administration) and are completed in another component. For example, purchases of office supplies usually originate in the administration component while inventory purchases originate in the production or service component and are subject to different controls. However, when the related invoices are received for payment, these transactions generally are entered into the accounts payable/cash disbursements system under the same controls. In this example, it is more efficient to combine the testing of the accounts payable/cash disbursements system for office supplies and inventory purchases into one test. Figure 11–2 categorizes the production or service component specific control objectives—plus the relevant additional specific control objectives not included in the production or service component—into areas of overall audit emphasis. Figure 11–3 demonstrates the relationship of these specific control objectives to the financial statement classifications.

Chapters 11 and 12 will deal with how the production or service component is audited. Chapter 11 covers materials and overhead and labor, while Chapter 12 covers inventory accountability; physical safeguards; and property, plant, and equipment. It is important to note that not all of the procedures discussed in this chapter are performed on every audit. The procedures performed on each audit are determined based upon the risk analysis.

PURCHASES, CASH DISBURSEMENTS, AND ACCOUNTS PAYABLE

Figure 11–2 lists the specific control objectives commonly covered by tests of purchases, cash disbursements, and accounts payable. As Chapter 7 indicated, whenever the system evaluation indicates that there is reasonable assurance that the specific control objective is being achieved, the auditor should test each key attribute that was identified. The testing of key attributes related to purchases and cash disbursements generally are performed concurrently and therefore will be discussed together. Purchases and cash disbursements audit procedures generally are performed as of an interim date; whereas a portion of the accounts payable procedures are generally performed as of year-end, with the remainder performed at either interim or year-end. As with all audit procedures, the exact timing and extent of work to be performed is indicated in the audit program.

Testing Key Attributes Related to Purchases, Expenses, and Cash Disbursements

Tests of purchases, expenses, and cash disbursements are among the most significant tests performed. Using one sample, it may be possible to obtain satisfaction that controls over authorization and recording of transactions affecting inventories, property, plant and equipment, cash, expenses, and accounts payable are operating effectively, and that the related transactions are properly authorized and recorded. Before performing the audit procedures in this area, it is important for the auditor to obtain an understanding of the key attributes in the purchasing and cash disbursements system by reviewing the accounting system documentation and risk analysis working papers.

Dual purpose tests should be used to obtain evidence that a key attribute is both (1) functioning (compliance test) and (2) effective (substantive test— i.e., the transaction is recorded correctly). It is not sufficient merely to verify that a transaction is correct and assume that the control functioned properly.

Key attributes that are applied to individual transactions usually are tested by sampling from those transactions through an interim period. As each transaction is tested, the auditor should look for documentary evidence of

FIGURE 11-1 Production or Service Operating Component Specific Control Objectives

*Reference
No.*

Materials and Overhead

P-1   Goods or services are purchased only with proper authorization

P-2   Goods or services received are recorded correctly as to account, amount, and period

Labor

P-3   Salary, wage, and benefit expenses are incurred only for work authorized and performed

P-4   Salaries, wages, and benefits are calculated at the proper rate

P-5   Salaries, wages, benefits, and related liabilities are recorded correctly as to account (department, activity, cost center, etc.), amount, and period

Inventory Accountability and Physical Safeguards

P-6   Costs are assigned to inventory in accordance with the stated valuation method

P-7   Usage and movement of inventory is recorded correctly as to account, amount (quantities and dollars), and period

P-8   Physical loss of inventory is prevented or promptly detected

P-9   Obsolete, slow-moving, and overstock inventory is prevented or promptly detected and provided for

P-10 Inventory is carried at the lower of cost or market

Property, Plant, and Equipment

P-11 Property, plant, and equipment are purchased only with proper authorization

P-12 Property, plant, and equipment purchases are recorded correctly as to account, amount, and period

P-13 Disposals, retirements, trade-ins, idle plant and equipment, and other losses are identified and recorded correctly as to account, amount, and period

P-14 Physical loss of property, plant, and equipment is prevented

P-15 Depreciation is calculated using proper lives and methods

the functioning of the key attribute. This can be in the form of signatures, initials, check marks, rubber stamps, and the like. For example, assume that the auditor concludes that the system design provides reasonable assurance that the specific control objective P-2, "goods or services received are recorded correctly as to account, amount, and period," is being achieved. One key attribute is the controller's approval of the account distribution assigned by an accounts payable clerk. The documentary evidence of this comparison is the initials of the controller on the voucher. To test the functioning of this key attribute, the auditor might examine a sample of vouchers noting the initials of the controller. To test the effectiveness of the control, the auditor might compare the description of the item purchased on the invoice to the chart of accounts noting that the account distribution is reasonable.

Certain control procedures are applied to groups of transactions (e.g., daily

FIGURE 11-2   Specific Control Objectives by Audit Area—Production or Service

---

Purchases (including material, overhead, administrative expenses, property acquisitions, and prepaid expenses), accounts payable, and cash disbursements:

P–1* A–1   Goods or services are purchased only with proper authorization

P–2* A–2   Goods or services received are recorded correctly as to account, amount, and period

P–11   Property, plant, and equipment are purchased only with proper authorization

P–12   Property, plant, and equipment purchases are recorded correctly as to account, amount, and period

F–3   Cash disbursements are for goods or services authorized and received

F–4   Cash disbursements are recorded correctly as to account, amount, and period

Labor, employee benefit expenses, accrued payroll, pension, and related liabilities, and cash disbursements:

P–3* A–3   Salary, wage, and benefit expenses are incurred only for work authorized and performed

P–4* A–4   Salaries, wages, and benefits are calculated at the proper rate

P–5* A–5   Salaries, wages, benefits, and related liabilities are recorded correctly as to account (department, activity, cost center, etc.), amount, and period

F–3   Cash disbursements are for goods or services authorized and received

F–4   Cash disbursements are recorded correctly as to account, amount, and period

Inventory existence and valuation:

P–6   Costs are assigned to inventory in accordance with the stated valuation method

P–7   Usage and movement of inventory is recorded correctly as to account, amount (quantities and dollars), and period

P–8   Physical loss of inventory is prevented or promptly detected

P–9   Obsolete, slow-moving, and overstock inventory is prevented or promptly detected and provided for

P–10   Inventory is carried at the lower of cost or market

Property, plant, and equipment:

P–11   Property, plant, and equipment are purchased only with proper authorization

P–12   Property, plant, and equipment purchases are recorded correctly as to account, amount, and period

P–13   Disposals, retirements, trade-ins, idle plant and equipment, and other losses are identified and recorded correctly as to account, amount, and period

P–14   Physical loss of property, plant, and equipment is prevented

P–15   Depreciation is calculated using proper lives and methods

---

* These control objectives also may relate to "inventory existence and valuation."

reconciliation of dollar value of purchases submitted to EDP for processing to the daily voucher report). In these cases, the auditor can select either (1) a sample of transactions and trace each to inclusion in the documentary evidence of the functioning of the key attribute (e.g., select a sample of vendor invoices for tracing to daily reconciliation schedules), or (2) a sample of the documentary evidence directly (e.g., select a sample of daily reconcilia-

Balance Sheet

	Control Objectives	
	Debit	Credit
Current assets:		
Cash		F–3, F–4
Accounts receivable		
Allowance for doubtful accounts		
Inventories	P–1, P–2, P–3, P–4, P–5, P–6, P–7	P–7, P–8, P–9, P–10
Prepaid expenses and other assets		
Other assets:		
Notes receivable		
Investments		
Goodwill and other intangibles		
Intercompany accounts		
Deposits and other assets		
Property, plant, and equipment:		
Land	P–11, P–12	P–13
Buildings	P–11, P–12	P–13, P–14
Machinery and equipment	P–11, P–12	P–13, P–14
Allowances for depreciation	P–13, P–14	P–15
Current liabilities:		
Notes payable		
Trade accounts payable and accrued liabilities	F–3, F–4	A–1, A–2, P–1, P–2, P–11, P–12
Accrued payroll and related liabilities	F–4	P–4, P–5
Taxes other than taxes on income	F–4	
Accrued interest		
Income taxes		
Long-term debt		
Deferred income taxes		
Shareholders' equity:		
Preferred stock		
Common stock		
Additional paid-in capital		
Retained earnings		
Commitments and contingencies		

Income Statement

	Control Objectives	
	Debit	Credit
Sales		
Cost of sales	P–1, P–2, P–3, P–4, P–5, P–6, P–7, P–8, P–9, P–10, P–15	
Selling, general, and administrative expenses	A–1, A–2, P–15	
Provision for income taxes		
Other	P–13, P–14	P–8, P–13

tion schedules and support one reconciliation and review the rest for reasonableness).

The audit program should include inquiry procedures concerning control procedures applied to either individual transactions or groups of transactions. A few well-chosen questions directed to the right person can provide valuable insights about the effectiveness of the procedure. For example, the auditor might ask the controller for an explanation of his or her responsibilities and how exceptions are resolved. To accomplish this, the auditor might ask the following questions of the controller: "How do you perform the review? Do you look at every item or only large items? How often do you find discrepancies? How are they resolved?" In some cases, it might be more effective to ask other personnel who are affected by the control procedure to provide information that might help evaluate the effectiveness of the controller's review. For example, the auditor might ask the accounts payable clerk, "What do you do with vouchers that are returned by the controller because of errors in account distribution?"

If the auditor learns that vouchers always are accepted even if there are errors in the account distribution, this indicates the control procedure is not what the auditor thought it was—even if there is documentary evidence in every case (i.e., the controller signs all of them). If this is the case, there is no point in continuing to gather evidence of the functioning of the attribute. The auditor should give effect to this new information by designing additional audit procedures.

Use of prenumbered documents (e.g., purchase orders, checks) by a client may assist in recording transactions in the proper period. However, prenumbering alone may not be a key attribute; the client must perform an independent sequence check. If such a control procedure exists, and the auditor decides that prenumbered documents represent a key attribute, the auditor should test the functioning of the attribute by reviewing how the client accounts for the numerical sequence (e.g., review numerical sequence of checks issued during a day) and inquiring how the sequence check is performed. As was noted in Chapter 7, in certain cases, key attributes do not leave documentary evidence (e.g., review of account distribution without indicating approval). The way the auditor obtains evidence of the functioning of these key attributes is by observation and inquiry of the employee who performs the control procedure or other employees who are affected by it. To test the effectiveness of these key attributes, the auditor would examine a sample of transactions affected by the undocumented control.

Testing Purchases, Expenses, and Cash Disbursements Transactions

As mentioned above, in addition to accumulating evidence of the functioning of key attributes, the audit program will include certain procedures to test the *effectiveness of the key attributes.* In these cases, the audit procedures usually will be performed on a limited basis through an interim date.

On the other hand, if the system evaluation indicates that there are no key attributes to be relied on, the same or similar procedures might be performed to detect errors or irregularities in recording the transactions. In these cases, the auditor should test more transactions and select them from throughout most or all of the year.

The following procedures are designed to either (1) test the effectiveness of key attributes or (2) detect errors or irregularities in the recording of transactions if no key attributes are functioning.

1. Examining checks. To test whether the disbursements journal accurately reflects the disbursement, the auditor should examine the canceled check and compare it to the cash disbursements record noting that the check date, check number, payee, and amount are in agreement. The auditor also should note whether: (1) the check is signed by an authorized check signer (a list of the company's authorized check signers should be included in the permanent file working papers), (2) the check was endorsed by the payee to assure that the payment was received by the proper person, and (3) the check was canceled within a reasonable period after issuance. Finally, to reduce the amount of work related to outstanding checks on the year-end bank reconciliations, the auditor might test whether they are correctly included in or excluded from month-end bank reconciliations.

When examining voided checks, the auditor should note whether the check has been defaced sufficiently to prevent its unauthorized reissuance. Checks may be defaced in a number of ways. One effective way is to tear off the signature block.

2. Examining supporting documentation. The auditor should examine documentation in support of each cash disbursement tested to determine that each disbursement is for a valid business purpose. Ordinarily, this includes examining the invoice, noting that the (1) check amount agrees with the amount of the invoice, (2) account distribution reflected in the cash disbursements journal or voucher register makes sense in light of the description of items on the vendor's invoice, (3) invoice is clerically accurate, and (4) invoice has been canceled in some manner to prevent duplicate payment (many companies perforate or mark invoices "paid").

The auditor also should test whether the disbursement is authorized. If the item selected for testing is for inventory or other purchases of supplies or materials, the auditor should examine the related purchase order (P.O.) noting that the item description, quantity, and unit price entered on the order are in agreement with the invoice. For other purchases, the auditor may find the purchase authorized or approved on a purchase requisition or on the invoice itself.

3. Determining that goods or services were received. For purchases of inventory or other goods, the auditor should examine receiving reports or other evidence of goods received (e.g., vendor packing slips), noting that quantities received are in agreement with quantities ordered (per the purchase order) and quantities invoiced. In many cases, there is no evidence of receipt of services (e.g., heat, power, light, outside services). Approval of suppliers' invoices often will be the only documentary evidence. The auditor also should determine whether invoices are recorded in the proper accounting period by comparing the date of recording to the date of receipt of the related merchandise or service.

If the existence of client sequence checks of prenumbered documents is considered a key attribute and tested, as discussed earlier, the auditor can test the effectiveness of that control when performing other tests of documents. For example, the auditor could test whether checks selected in the test of cash disbursements are recorded in the proper sequence in the accounting records. If prenumbering is not considered a key attribute, the auditor can perform such a test to detect errors or irregularities in recording.

4. Determining that the charge was recorded in the proper general ledger account. The auditor should test whether the account distribution reflected in the cash disbursements journal makes sense in light of the description on the vendor's invoice. This will require reference to the client's chart of accounts. A copy of the current chart of accounts should be included in the permanent file working papers. Testing account distribution is very important, since recording expenses in the incorrect account classification may lead to significant misstatements. For example, the manufacturing overhead absorption rate will be affected if manufacturing costs are improperly recorded as administrative expenses or vice versa. Improper account distribution also could affect the results of other audit procedures. For example, a review of legal fees to determine the possible existence of any unrecorded or contingent liabilities is not meaningful unless the auditor can be reasonably assured that all legal expenses incurred have been correctly classified.

5. Testing other records. If the purchasing system is tied into the inventory accounting system, tests of transactions may include: (1) tracing quantities received to entries in the perpetual inventory records, (2) tracing material costs for work-in-process to job order cost records, and (3) testing the calculation and recording of price variances between standard cost and actual cost.

Reviewing Cash Disbursements Records for Unusual Items

To perform this procedure effectively, the auditor first should develop an understanding of what constitutes an unusual item. Examples are payments to officers, directors, and employees (other than for compensation);

checks made payable to "cash" or "bearer"; payments to banks or other lending institutions; and unusually large payments.

Testing Clerical Accuracy

The voucher register (invoice register) or cash disbursements journal should be tested for clerical accuracy, and the totals should be traced to the general ledger. The extent of the clerical accuracy tests to be performed usually will be established in the audit program. However, it ordinarily would not be necessary to clerically test the books of original entry for every month and trace each month's totals to postings in the general ledger. Rather, the auditor might clerically test and trace one or two months' totals and rely on analytical review procedures to be satisfied that the remaining totals are reasonable.

Accounts Payable

Most effort in the audit of accounts payable is spent determining that all significant liabilities have been recorded. Generally, liabilities are more likely to be understated than overstated. Invoices are usually received after related goods or services are received. Thus, a company must "hold the books open" for a specified time subsequent to the end of the period to assure that all invoices related to goods received or services rendered prior to the end of the period have been received and recorded. If the company's procedures for establishing an accurate cutoff are not adequate, then liabilities often will be recorded in the wrong period.

As discussed later in this chapter, an inaccurate cutoff may have a significant impact on both the balance sheet and income statement. The auditor also should be aware that understating liabilities may be a deliberate attempt to present a misleading picture, known as "window dressing." By understating both assets and the related liabilities, without affecting income, management can create an artificially strong current ratio and an appearance of high liquidity.

The first step in auditing payables is to obtain a detailed listing, or trial balance, of trade accounts payable from the client. The form of listing will vary from company to company. It may be either a computer printout or a manual listing of all unpaid items in the voucher register or unpaid invoices file. In some instances, the trial balance will simply be an adding machine tape of the unpaid items. The auditor generally should begin by testing the clerical accuracy of the detailed listing. If there is a difference between the total per the detailed listing and the general ledger, this difference should be investigated. Depending upon the amount of the difference, the client may be requested to reconcile the two amounts.

The auditor also should review the detail of the accounts payable trial balance for possible items that might require specific disclosure or reclassification (e.g., accounts with affiliates; amounts payable to officers, directors, or stockholders; taxes payable). Appropriate reclassification entries should be prepared and recommended to the client. Debit balances in vendors' accounts, if significant either individually or in the aggregate, should be examined and tested in the same manner as customer accounts receivable. For example, it may be necessary to request written confirmations from the vendors or examine subsequent cash realizations. Debit balances of a substantial amount should be reclassified in an appropriate asset category (e.g., accounts receivable).

The next step in auditing payables is to perform a search for unrecorded liabilities (out-of-period search).

Search for Unrecorded Liabilities.   The search for unrecorded liabilities is designed to detect any material amounts of unrecorded liabilities. The search for unrecorded liabilities normally will include:

1. Review of transactions recorded after the balance sheet date to determine whether any significant transactions apply to the period under audit.
2. Review of unprocessed invoices for items that should be included in the period under audit.
3. Review of vendors' statements (described below).
4. Examination of unmatched receiving reports for items received on or prior to the balance sheet date.
5. Inquiry of accounting and purchasing personnel about any significant unrecorded liabilities.
6. Review of consignment sales records to ascertain whether the liability and related expense have been recorded in the proper period.

In executing these procedures, the auditor should compare the documents or information examined to the client's payables listing to identify any additional items that should be on the list.

Review of Vendors' Statements.   The search for unrecorded liabilities usually includes review and reconciliation of vendors' statements to the year-end accounts payable trial balance. The auditor may ask the company to save any vendors' statements it receives at year-end. In addition, the company may request key vendors, selected by the auditor, to send statements directly to the auditor.

Because the main objective of obtaining vendors' statements directly from vendors and reconciling them to the accounts payable detailed listing is to identify any unrecorded amounts, the auditor should not necessarily request statements from only those vendors with large account balances at year-end. Statements should be requested from principal suppliers (regardless of the size of the *recorded* account balance at the balance sheet date), from those with past-due balances, and from those with amounts in dispute.

A current list of vendors usually can be obtained from the purchasing department. Information as to the identity of major vendors also may be obtained from tests of key attributes working papers, inventory price tests, reviews of voucher registers during the year, prior years' working papers, and discussions with employees in the accounts payable and purchasing departments.

Each request for vendors' statements (see Figure 11–4) should include the (1) exact name of the client (including division and location, if applicable), (2) date as of which the statement is requested, (3) address of the auditor's office to which the statement is to be mailed, and (4) signature of the client employee authorized to make the request. A business reply envelope with the auditor's address usually is included with the request. The request should be mailed by the auditor. The return address on the client's envelope should be blocked out with a clear imprint of the auditor's address.

Vendors' statements should be requested at an early date so they will be received before the field work is completed. It usually is desirable to mail requests on or prior to the balance sheet date. If a vendor does not reply, the auditor should consider mailing a second request.

Differences between amounts shown on the accounts payable trial balance and amounts shown on the vendors' statements received should be investigated. In most instances, company personnel should prepare the vendor reconciliations. Normally, these are tested by tracing payments in-transit to the cash disbursements records, examining correspondence and other supporting documents for debit memos that have not been processed by the

FIGURE 11–4 Request for Statement of Account

REQUEST FOR STATEMENT OF ACCOUNT

Our auditors, Ernst & Whinney, are making an examination of our financial statements and wish to obtain a complete statement of our account with you as of December 31, 1985. Please furnish Ernst & Whinney with details of our indebtedness to you on open account, notes, acceptances, loans, or contracts. If you hold any collateral, liens, or security agreements in connection with our indebtedness to you, please specify the nature and amount of assets pledged. Please send this information in the enclosed reply envelope direct to Ernst & Whinney, 2700 Arco Tower, 515 South Flower Street, Los Angeles, CA 90071.

Acme Manufacturing Co.
Company

Joe Sparkman
Signature

To: Wolston Hardware Co.
105 Main Street
Los Angeles, California

Accounts Payable
Supervisor   Dec. 20, 1985
Title   Date

vendor, and by obtaining explanations and examining supporting documentation for any other reconciling differences. In some cases, the differences are the result of unrecorded liabilities.

A Final Comment on Unrecorded Liabilities.   A schedule of all unrecorded liabilities noted during the search should be prepared and totaled. This schedule ordinarily should show the name of the vendor, date of the invoice, date the goods or services were received, amount, and the general ledger account that should have been charged. To properly evaluate the materiality of the unrecorded amounts, the total impact on the balance sheet and income statement should be shown on the schedule and reviewed separately.

If the company counts its inventory at an interim date, the auditor should perform the search for unrecorded liabilities related to above procedures related to inventory payables (including requesting vendor statements) as of that date.

It may be helpful at this point to contrast the audit of receivables (discussed in Chapter 10) and the audit of accounts payable. When auditing accounts receivable, the auditor does not often utilize documentation created by third parties. Therefore, confirmation of receivables is the usual procedure; the auditor reviews documentation only as an alternative procedure. In contrast, when auditing accounts payable, the auditor has greater access to documentation created by third parties. Thus, the auditor's procedures utilize that documentation and rely less on confirmations from third parties.

LABOR, EMPLOYEE BENEFIT EXPENSES, ACCRUED PAYROLL AND RELATED LIABILITIES, AND CASH DISBURSEMENTS

Payroll and employee benefit expenses are major costs for most companies and have a significant effect on a company's operations. Payroll and payroll-related costs affect several accounts including payroll expense, inventories, payroll tax expense, withholding taxes payable, and cash. The company's payroll system should be sufficient to assure that salary, wage, and benefit expenses are: (1) incurred only for work authorized and performed; (2) calculated at the proper rate; and (3) recorded correctly as to account, amount, and period.

Testing Key Attributes Related to Payroll Transactions

As discussed in "Testing Key Attributes Over Purchases, Expenses, and Cash Disbursements," dual purpose tests should be used to obtain evidence that a key attribute is both functioning and effective.

Key attributes that are applied to individual payroll transactions usually are tested by sampling from those transactions through an interim period. For example, assume that the auditor concludes that the system design provides reasonable assurance that the specific control objective P–3, "Salary, wage, and benefit expenses are incurred only for work authorized and performed," is achieved. One key attribute that the auditor concludes supports this assessment is that timecards are approved by the employee's supervisor. The documentary evidence of this comparison is the initials of the supervisor on the timecard. To test the functioning of this key attribute, the auditor might examine a sample of payroll checks, obtain the timecard relating to the hours covered by the check, and note the initials of the supervisor on the timecard. The auditor also should make inquiries of the supervisors to determine (1) that they understand their responsibilities and (2) how exceptions are resolved. To test the effectiveness of the control, the auditor might compare the number of hours worked per the timecard to the number of hours paid per the payroll register and the check. Certain control procedures are applied to groups of transactions (e.g., weekly reconciliation of hours per the timecards to hours paid in the payroll register). In these cases, the auditor can select either (1) a sample of payroll transactions and trace each to inclusion in the documentary evidence of the functioning of the key attribute (e.g., select a sample of timecards for tracing to the weekly reconciliation schedules), or (2) a sample of the documentary evidence directly (e.g., select a sample of weekly reconciliation schedules and test the details of one reconciliation and review the rest for reasonableness).

Of course, the audit program also should include inquiry of client personnel to gain insight about the effectiveness of control procedures applied to either individual or groups of transactions.

Testing Payroll Transactions

The following procedures are designed to either (1) test the effectiveness of key attributes or (2) detect errors or irregularities in the recording of payroll transactions if no key attributes are functioning.

1. Checking the recorded pay against the original record of hours worked or units produced. To test whether employees are paid for actual work performed, the auditor should compare the employee's name, clock number, department number, and recorded time or units produced as shown on the original record (e.g., clock card, time sheet, production report) with the payroll journal.

2. Comparing the rates paid with authorization forms, union contracts, or other pertinent data. To determine whether employees are being paid at the proper rate, the auditor should compare the rate paid with the company's authorized rates of pay. One type of source documentation is a union contract. Not all organizations have unions and, in those that do, not all employees are covered. When applicable, a contract should be used as the source for testing wage rates. Other types of source documents include wage authorization forms, internal memos, and letters of employment agreement. The auditor should include in the working papers a precise description of the documentation examined in support of the wage rates.

3. Checking the computation of payroll. The pay of plant employees usually is determined by either of two basic methods: (1) an hourly or daily rate plan or (2) a piece-rate plan. An understanding of these methods is essential to effectively test payroll calculations. Before testing the computation of gross pay, the auditor should be familiar with the company's policies governing the normal work week and compensation for overtime. A description of these policies normally is included in the permanent file working papers.

4. Checking the personnel records. The purpose of this procedure is to ascertain whether the persons paid were actually employed during the pay period tested. An obvious method for an employee to obtain funds fraudulently would be to falsify the time records for a terminated employee and misappropriate the paycheck. One way the auditor may check for this is by tracing a representative sample of names from the payroll records to employment records maintained independently of the payroll department. The auditor should note the employee name, clock number, hiring date, and, if applicable, termination date. Also, the auditor should obtain information on new and terminated employees from the personnel department and determine whether prompt action has been taken to add their names to or remove them from the payroll records.

5. Checking expense distribution. To determine that the expense distribution is proper, the auditor should compare the expense account charged (e.g., department, activity, or cost center) to the employee's position description in the personnel file.

6. Examining the canceled payroll checks. The purpose of this procedure is to determine whether the proper employees received their paychecks and whether amounts are in agreement with the payroll journal. The auditor should compare the check number, payee, and amount with the payroll journal. Further, the auditor should check the names of the check signers (which must be the authorized signers), the payee's endorsement, and the date the check cleared the bank (which should be within a reasonable period after issuance). The auditor also should determine that the check has been properly included in or excluded from the month-end bank reconciliations.

The auditor is not expected to be able to recognize a forged endorsement. However, checks that bear more than one endorsement or lack an endorsement deserve special consideration. In many instances, the second endorsement will be that of a local businessman, which is not unusual. If the second endorser is an individual associated with the company and, in particular, an employee associated with the preparation or distribution of the payroll, the auditor should note the item for further investigation. If a paycheck requires further investigation, the auditor may want to ascertain whether properly approved time records support the check and whether records show the payee was employed during the period.

Attending Payroll Payoffs

In addition to the procedures performed for payroll transactions, another procedure that may be performed to determine that only legitimate employees receive pay is to observe the actual paying of employees. This procedure, sometimes called a "payroll payoff," normally is used when internal accounting control is considered deficient. This procedure was more common in the past than it is today. With the increasing awareness of the importance of strong internal accounting controls by the business community, the necessity of performing payroll payoffs has significantly decreased. In certain engagements, however, such as large governmental units, this procedure may be very appropriate.

When performing a payoff, the auditor should check the identification of the employees being paid (e.g., a badge that includes the employee's picture). The auditor should compare the amount paid with the payroll journal and observe the employee signing a receipt for the check. A responsible official from the company should be with the auditor during the payoff.

If any checks remain unclaimed at the end of the payoff, the auditor should list the payee's name and the amount and number of the check. The auditor should inquire of the company representative and/or others present at the payoff as to the whereabouts of these individuals.

Testing Clerical Accuracy

The auditor should test the clerical accuracy of the payroll journal to determine that the details of the payroll have been summarized properly and the totals have been recorded correctly in both the subsidiary and general ledgers. In a manufacturing company, the subsidiary ledgers may include manufacturing expense ledgers or job cost ledgers. Financial information from these ledgers affects inventory valuations, profit determination, and managerial control. Thus, proper distribution of direct and indirect labor expenses and department allocations of indirect labor is important, since it affects reported net income. The auditor should test the reasonableness of the distribution of payroll expense by reference to the client's chart of accounts.

The extent of the clerical accuracy tests to be performed should be established in the audit program. However, it ordinarily would not be necessary to clerically test the books of original entry for every month and trace each month's totals to postings in the general ledger. Rather, the auditor might clerically test and trace one or two months' totals and rely on analytical review procedures to be satisfied that the remaining totals are reasonable.

Payroll Expense and Employee Benefit Expenses

The tests of key attributes relating to payroll provide the auditor with evidence concerning the functioning of the client's payroll system. In addition to or in lieu of these procedures, the auditor sometimes performs analytical review procedures on total payroll and other employee benefit expenses. These assist the auditor in evaluating the reasonableness of certain financial data in a minimal amount of time.

The following are types of analytical review procedures that may be used:

1. Compare payroll expense with the prior period and budgeted amounts.
2. Compare payroll expense to sales for the current and prior periods.
3. Compare employee benefits to gross pay for the current and prior periods.
4. Compare pension expense for the current and prior periods.
5. Compare employee benefit expenses to direct labor cost, hours worked, or the number of employees for the current and prior periods.
6. Compare average compensation per employee with prior periods.

Accrued Payroll and Related Liabilities

The tests performed on accrued payrolls and related liabilities generally involve either obtaining detailed analyses of the account balances or performing analytical review procedures. As with all audit procedures, the exact nature, timing, and extent of procedures to be performed on an individual engagement are indicated in the audit program.

In testing the related payroll liability accounts (e.g., federal withholdings, state withholdings, and FICA), an analysis similar to the one shown in Figure 11–5 may be helpful. If the client prepares the analysis, the auditor should first determine that the schedule accomplishes the intended objective and is clerically accurate and then determine that the balance agrees with the trial balance. The types of supporting documentation examined in auditing these analyses include: (1) payroll journals from which the total amounts withheld for individual payrolls can be verified, (2) payroll tax returns that identify the periods for which withholdings have been reported and paid to the government, and (3) canceled checks, which evidence payment. On many engagements, these analyses are not obtained. Instead, the auditor reviews the balances in the related accounts for overall reasonableness. This review generally is performed by comparing the current year balance with the prior year balance and discussing differences with client personnel when such comparisons do not appear to make sense. Auditing these accounts

FIGURE 11-5   Working Paper for Accrued Payroll Account

	Client		
		Name	Date
	Prepared	Hudson	1/12/XY
	Approved		

Accrued Payroll
CCH Corporation
December 31, 19XX

Accrued Payroll - acct #2157				
Payroll #26 - paid on 1/2/XY				
covers the period 12/15/XX-12/28/XX			√	224,976.52
Payroll #27				
covers the period 12/29/XX-1/11/XY:				
estimated total payroll	$230,000.00			
To accrued as of year end	N 30%			69,000.00
Total Accrued Payroll @ 12/31/XX			T/B	293,976.52
				F

T/B   Traced to and agrees with the trial balance

F   Footed

√   Traced to the gross payroll amount for payroll #26 per the
payroll journal. Amounts agreed.

√   Agreed the net pay amount per the payroll journal with
the net funds transferred to the payroll bank account
on 1/2/XY.

N   The company's operations are mainly limited to the
weekdays. Therefore, the client accrued the estimated
payroll for 12/29, 12/30 and 12/31 using 10 days as the
total number of workdays in the pay period. This
resulted in a 30% accrual of the total estimated
payroll for the pay period which appears reasonable.

4   The actual payroll per the payroll register for the period
ended 1/11/XX was $234,598. The year end accrual is,
therefore, understated by $1,378. See the Summary
of Audit Differences.

through comparisons is much more efficient than auditing details of the balance.

QUESTIONS AND PROBLEMS

11–1. List the four categories into which the specific control objectives for the production or service component can be divided.

11–2. Discuss the basic steps taken by an auditor when examining trade accounts payable.

11–3. What audit procedures should be applied to debit balances in vendors' accounts?

11–4. How is a search for unrecorded trade accounts payable conducted by the auditor?

11–5. What is the main objective of an auditor obtaining vendors' statements directly from vendors and reconciling them to the client's detailed accounts payable listing?

11–6. What should an independent auditor do to identify a client's major vendors?

11–7. List some types of analytical review procedures that may be used in the audit of a client's payroll expenses.

11–8. What kinds of audit tests are usually performed on accrued payrolls and related liabilities?

11–9. Select the *best* answer for each of the following items:

    a. It would be appropriate for the payroll accounting department to be responsible for which of the following functions?
        (1) Approval of employee time records.
        (2) Maintenance of records of employment, discharges, and pay increases.
        (3) Preparation of periodic governmental reports as to employee's earnings and withholding taxes.
        (4) Distribution of paychecks to employees.

    b. A surprise observation by an auditor of a client's regular distribution of paychecks is primarily designed to satisfy the auditor that:
        (1) All unclaimed payroll checks are properly returned to the cashier.
        (2) The paymaster is not involved in the distribution of payroll checks.
        (3) All employees have in their possession proper employee identification.
        (4) Names on the company payroll are those of bona fide employees presently on the job.

    c. Under which of the following circumstances would it be advisable for the auditor to confirm accounts payable with creditors?
        (1) Internal accounting control over accounts payable is adequate and there is sufficient evidence on hand to minimize the risk of a material misstatement.
        (2) Confirmation response is expected to be favorable and accounts payable balances are of immaterial amounts.
        (3) Creditor statements are not available and internal accounting control over accounts payable is unsatisfactory.
        (4) The majority of accounts payable balances are with associated companies.

d. Which of the following is the most efficient audit procedure for the detection of unrecorded liabilities?

    (1) Compare cash disbursements in the subsequent period with the accounts payable trial balance at year end.

    (2) Confirm large accounts payable balances at the balance sheet date.

    (3) Examine purchase orders issued for several days prior to the close of the year.

    (4) Obtain a "liability certificate" from the client.   (AICPA, adapted)

11–10. You were in the final stages of your examination of the financial statements of Ozine Corporation for the year ended December 31, 1983, when you were consulted by the corporation's president who believes there is no point to your examining the 1984 voucher register and testing data in support of 1984 entries. He stated that (1) bills pertaining to 1983 which were received too late to be included in the December voucher register were recorded as of the year-end by the corporation by journal entry, (2) the internal auditor made tests after the year-end, and (3) he would furnish you with a letter certifying that there were no unrecorded liabilities.

Required:

a. Should a CPA's test for unrecorded liabilities be affected by the fact that the client made a journal entry to record 1983 bills which were received late? Explain.

b. Should a CPA's test for unrecorded liabilities be affected by the fact that a letter is obtained in which a responsible management official certifies that to the best of his knowledge all liabilities have been recorded? Explain.

c. Should a CPA's test for unrecorded liabilities be eliminated or reduced because of the internal audit test? Explain.

d. Assume that the corporation, which handled some government contracts, had no internal auditor but that an auditor for a federal agency spent three weeks auditing the records and was just completing his work at this time. How would the CPA's unrecorded liability test be affected by the work of the auditor for a federal agency?

e. What sources in addition to the 1984 voucher register should the CPA consider to locate possible unrecorded liabilities?   (AICPA, adapted)

11–11. Mincin, CPA, is the auditor of the Raleigh Corporation. Mincin is considering the audit work to be performed in the accounts payable area for the current year's engagement.

The prior year's working papers show that confirmation requests were mailed to 100 of Raleigh's 1,000 suppliers. The selected suppliers were based on Mincin's sample that was designed to select accounts with large dollar balances. A substantial number of hours were spent by Raleigh and Mincin resolving relatively minor differences between the confirmation replies and Raleigh's accounting records. Alternate audit procedures were used for those suppliers who did not respond to the confirmation requests.

Required:

a. Identify the accounts payable audit objectives that Mincin must consider in determining the audit procedures to be followed.

b. Identify situations when Mincin should use accounts payable confirmations and discuss whether Mincin is required to use them.

c. Discuss why the use of large dollar balances as the basis for selecting accounts payable for confirmation might not be the most efficient approach and indicate what more efficient procedures could be followed when selecting accounts payable for confirmation.   (AICPA, adapted)

11–12. Arthur, CPA, is auditing the RCT Manufacturing Company as of February 28, 1985. As with all engagements, one of Arthur's initial procedures is to make overall checks of the client's financial data by reviewing significant ratios and trends so that he has a better understanding of the business and can determine where to concentrate his audit efforts.

The financial statements prepared by the client with audited 1984 figures and preliminary 1985 figures are presented below in condensed form.

RCT MANUFACTURING COMPANY
Condensed Balance Sheets
February 28, 1985, and 1984

	1985	1984
Assets		
Cash	$ 12,000	$ 15,000
Accounts receivable, net	93,000	50,000
Inventory	72,000	67,000
Other current assets	5,000	6,000
Plant and equipment, net of depreciation	60,000	80,000
	$ 242,000	$ 218,000
Liabilities and Equity		
Accounts payable	$ 38,000	$ 41,000
Federal income tax payable	30,000	14,400
Long-term liabilities	20,000	40,000
Common stock	70,000	70,000
Retained earnings	84,000	52,600
	$ 242,000	$ 218,000

RCT MANUFACTURING COMPANY
Condensed Income Statement
Years Ended February 28, 1985, and 1984

	1985	1984
Net sales	$1,684,000	$1,250,000
Cost of goods sold	927,000	710,000
Gross margin on sales	$ 757,000	$ 540,000
Selling and administrative expenses	682,000	504,000
Income before federal income taxes	$ 75,000	$ 36,000
Income tax expense	30,000	14,400
Net income	$ 45,000	$ 21,600

Additional information:

a. The company has an insignificant amount of cash sales.

b. The end of year figures are comparable to the average for each respective year.

Required:

For each year, compute the current ratio. Based on the ratio, identify and discuss audit procedures that should be included in Arthur's audit of accounts payable.

(AICPA, adapted)

11–13. One of the auditor's primary means of verifying payroll transactions is by a detailed payroll test. You are making an annual examination of the Joplin Company, a medium-sized manufacturing company. You have selected a number of hourly employees for a detailed payroll test. The following worksheet outline has been prepared.

Column Number	Column Heading
1	Employee number
2	Employee name
3	Job classification
	Hours worked
4	Straight time
5	Premium time
6	Hourly rate
7	Gross earnings
8	Deductions (list)
9	Amount of check
10	Check and check number
11	Account number charged
12	Description of account

Required:

a. Using the column numbers above as a reference, state the principal way(s) that the information in each column would be verified.

b. In addition to the payroll test, the auditor uses a number of other audit procedures in the verification of payroll transactions. List five additional procedures which may be employed. (AICPA, adapted)

11–14. The Generous Loan Company has 100 branch loan offices. Each office has a manager and four or five subordinates who are employed by the manager. Branch managers prepare the weekly payroll, including their own salaries, and pay employees from cash on hand. The employee signs the payroll sheet signifying receipt of his salary. Hours worked by hourly personnel are inserted in the payroll sheet from timecards prepared by the employees and approved by the manager.

The weekly payroll sheets are sent to the home office along with other accounting statements and reports. The home office compiles employee earnings records and prepares all federal and state salary reports from the weekly payroll sheets.

Salaries are established by home office job-evaluation schedules. Salary adjustments, promotions, and transfers on full-time employees are approved by a home office salary committee based upon the recommendations of branch managers and area supervisors. Branch managers advise the salary committee of new full-time employees and terminations. Part-time and temporary employees are hired without referral to the salary committee.

Required:

a. Based upon your review of the payroll system, how might funds for payroll be diverted?

b. Prepare a payroll audit program to be used in the home office to audit the branch office payrolls of the Generous Loan Company. (AICPA)

AUDITING THE PRODUCTION OR SERVICE COMPONENT— INVENTORY ACCOUNTABILITY AND PHYSICAL SAFEGUARDS; PROPERTY, PLANT, AND EQUIPMENT

INVENTORIES

Inventories may be defined as those items of tangible personal property held by a company that are: (1) held for a sale in the ordinary course of business; (2) in the process of production for sale in a business; or (3) to be consumed in the production of goods for sale in a business.[1] Figure 11–2 on page 351 lists the specific control objectives relating to inventories. The audit of inventory can be complex depending on the sophistication of the client's inventory system.

The objective of the examination of inventories is for the auditor to determine whether inventories are presented fairly in the financial statements in conformity with generally accepted accounting principles (GAAP) applied on a consistent basis. Thus, the auditor must determine that the inventories (1) physically exist, (2) are the property of the company, (3) are usable and salable, and (4) are priced correctly. This involves investigating the care and accuracy with which the company has counted the inventories, the method and basis that have been followed in pricing them, and the arithmetical accuracy of the computations made. The auditor must also determine whether adequate provision has been made for obsolete and slow-moving inventory. There are numerous types of inventories and many methods of costing and evaluating them. Thus, inventories are one of the most difficult assets of the business to audit.

---

[1] Committee on Accounting Procedure, *Accounting Research Bulletin No. 43,* "Restatement and Revision of Accounting Research Bulletins" American Institute of Certified Public Accountants, 1953, p. 27.

CHAPTER 12

Methods of Determining Cost

The primary basis of accounting for inventories is cost. The cost of inventories is the sum of all the expenditures and charges incurred, directly or indirectly, in bringing inventory items to their present condition and location. *Accounting Research Bulletin No. 43* states "cost for inventory purposes may be determined under any one of several assumptions as to the flow of cost factors (such as first-in first-out, average, and last-in first-out); the major objective in selecting a method should be to choose the one which, under the circumstances, most clearly reflects periodic income."[2] ". . . Standard costs are acceptable if adjusted at reasonable intervals to reflect current conditions so that at the balance-sheet date standard costs reasonably approximate costs computed under one of the recognized bases."[3] "In some situations a reversed mark-up procedure of inventory pricing, such as the retail inventory method, may be both practical and appropriate."[4]

A departure from the cost basis of pricing inventory is required when the utility of the goods is no longer as great as their original cost. *Accounting Research Bulletin No. 43* states:

> . . . Where there is evidence that the utility of goods, in their disposal in the ordinary course of business, will be less than cost, whether due to physical deterioration, obsolescence, changes in price levels, or other causes, the differences should be recognized as a loss in the current period. This is generally

---

[2] Ibid, p. 29.

[3] Ibid., p. 30.

[4] Ibid.

accomplished by stating such goods at a lower level commonly designated as *market*.[5] [Emphasis in original.]

Determining that Inventories Physically Exist

SAS No. 1 (AU 331.01) indicates that the observation of inventories is a "generally accepted auditing procedure." In practice, the client's physical count of the inventories is almost always observed and tested by the auditor. However, if it is impracticable or impossible to observe the physical inventory, the auditor must become satisfied as to the fairness of the inventory balances by the use of alternative procedures. *SAS No. 1* (AU 331.09) further states:

> When inventory quantities are determined solely by means of a physical count, and all counts are made as of the balance-sheet date or as of a single date within a reasonable time before or after the balance-sheet date, it is ordinarily necessary for the independent auditor to be present at the time of the count, and, by suitable observation, tests and inquiries, satisfy himself respecting the effectiveness of the methods of inventory-taking and the measure of reliance which may be placed upon the client's representations about the quantities and physical condition of the inventories.

SAS No. 1 (AU 331.10 and .11) notes that when the client has reliable perpetual records that are compared periodically with physical counts, the auditor's observation procedures usually can be performed at any time, not necessarily at year-end. If a client uses statistical sampling to determine inventory quantity, the auditor must be satisfied with the sampling plan, counting procedures, and the counts (by observation).

SAS No. 2 (AU 509.12) notes that circumstances may make it impracticable or impossible to observe physical inventory. If the auditor is, however, ". . . able to satisfy himself as to inventories . . . by applying alternative procedures, there is no significant limitation on the scope of his work, and his report need not include reference to the omission of the procedures or to the use of alternative procedures."

In using alternative procedures, *SAS No. 1* (AU 331.12) notes that the auditor's procedures should include making or observing physical counts of inventory, testing intervening inventory transactions, and reviewing the client's counts and procedures relating to the physical inventory of the balance sheet inventory figure. *SAS No. 2* (AU 509.10–.12) suggests that if the auditor is not satisfied with the results of the alternative procedures, this limitation on his or her work should be referred to in the scope paragraph, described in an explanatory paragraph, and referred to in either a qualified

---

[5] Ibid. (The AICPA lower-of-cost-or-market method defines "market" as replacement cost but sets an upper limit of selling price less costs to complete and sell and a lower limit of selling price less both costs to complete and sell and earn a normal profit.)

opinion or disclaimer of opinion. The same is true if observation of inventory is practicable and it is not done because of the client's wishes.

Physical inventories are observed to determine that the stated quantities (as shown in the inventory listings) fairly represent the actual quantities on hand at the date the physical inventory was taken. The audit program contains the procedures to be performed during the observation process. Those procedures are discussed in greater detail below.

Review of the Client's Inventory Plan.   It is important that the auditor become familiar with the client's plan for taking the physical inventory. In a typical manufacturing company, the inventory may consist of hundreds or thousands of individual items. These items may be in various stages of completion and may be located in several areas. The count and identification of these items must be completed accurately. As a part of the procedures used to examine inventories, the auditor should review a copy of the company's inventory instructions. Complete instructions normally include:

1.   Names of the persons drafting and approving the instructions.   Usually the controller or some other responsible client executive will approve the instructions.

2.   Dates and times of the inventory taking.   Many companies take a complete physical inventory at the end of their fiscal year. If a company's inventory controls are reliable, it is acceptable to take the physical inventory prior to year-end. This practice is usually desirable because it allows the company to complete a major part of its work in closing its books before the end of its fiscal year.

3.   Names of the employees responsible for supervising the taking of the inventory.

4.   Plans for rearranging and segregating stock, including the precaution of clearing work in process to natural cutoff points.   Stock should be arranged in an orderly manner to make the counts easier for the inventory teams. When different items are intermingled or are at difficult-to-reach locations, the company's risk of counting the same item twice or overlooking items increases.

5.   Provisions for control of receiving and shipping during the inventory count period and, if the plant is not shut down, provisions for handling stock movement.   Although not always practical, it is helpful if the receiving and shipping departments are cleared of all stock. If items must be transferred between departments, there should be procedures to assure that each item is counted only once.

6.   Instructions as to the use of inventory tags or sheets and their distribution, collection, and control.   Generally, prenumbered tags are used, and they should be accounted for after the inventory count is completed.

7. Detailed instructions for accurate description of items and for determination of quantities by count, weight, or other measurement. Normally, all information recorded on the inventory tag should be checked or reviewed by an employee who did not participate in the original count. To obtain assurance that all information is recorded properly, some companies require a "blind" second count. After the first employee records a count and the count portion of the tag has been removed, a second employee, without knowing what the first employee has recorded, counts the item and separately records the count. Then, a third employee compares the two counts and investigates any differences.

8. Instructions for identifying and segregating obsolete and slow-moving items of inventory.

9. Plans for determining quantities at outside locations and for segregating any consigned stock.

10. Methods of transcribing original counts to final inventory sheets or summaries.

11. Methods followed in pricing inventory quantities, including the extent of rechecking prices.

12. Instructions for making extensions and footings and the extent of recheck.

13. Instructions for review and approval of inventory by department heads or other supervisory personnel.

Observation of Taking the Physical Inventory. An auditor must plan for an inventory observation carefully. In planning the nature, timing, and extent of the observation and testing procedures, the auditor should be familiar with the client's inventory, the approximate volume, the proper units of measure, and where the valuable items are located. The auditor should pay particular attention to the company's instructions regarding count procedures and control of inventory tags. In addition, the auditor should know when to arrive at the inventory location, who to ask for upon arrival, and the areas of the plant for which he or she is responsible (plant layout sketches are helpful). It is helpful to arrange a tour of the storage area with the client in advance and discuss suitable clothing to wear.

When arriving at the client's plant, the auditor should meet with a supervisory employee of the client and discuss last-minute instructions at that time. Also, it is good practice for the auditor to meet all the company's inventory supervisors and know where they can be contacted if needed. It is important to note that the auditor does not "take," "determine," or "supervise" a physical inventory, but rather "observes" and "tests" the inventory-taking procedures. The nature of the auditor's responsibility to "observe" and "test" must be clearly understood. It is important to note that the auditor does not give instructions to client personnel but reports any problems noted to the appropriate supervisor.

The auditor's responsibility to observe the taking of the inventory involves a number of important considerations:

1. Has the company made adequate preparations for taking the inventory? Stock should be arranged in an orderly manner. Shipping and receiving cutoffs (discussed later in this chapter) should be established. Movement of stock should be kept to a minimum.
2. Do employees taking inventory appear to be conscientious and familiar with the stock and their duties? Are they adequately supervised?
3. Are the inventory-counting teams following the company's inventory instructions? Any deviations should be noted in the working papers and reported to the proper supervisor. Company procedures may require two independent counts of each inventory item; the results of these independent counts should be reviewed immediately.

The auditor should be alert for any possible double counts of inventory items. Inventories are sometimes counted twice when inventory teams skip around instead of counting items in location sequence. The use of inventory tags assists in avoiding double counts. However, items still may be counted twice when the contents of several bins or boxes are recorded on a single inventory tag or listing.

The auditor also should be alert for any items not counted. Sometimes entire sections of a department may be missed inadvertently. To prevent this, inventory crews should place inventory tags on each item or inventory sheets in each location.

The auditor must be alert for "hollow squares" (empty spaces between stacks of boxes) and empty containers. The auditor may request that containers be opened or piles of inventory be moved (although such requests normally are made on a limited basis).

Also, the auditor should watch for apparently unsalable, damaged, slow-moving, and obsolete items and discuss those with the client personnel who are responsible for the inventory. In some circumstances, it may be difficult to recognize such items, but any that appear to be questionable should be noted in the working papers for further investigation.

While observing the inventory, the auditor also should test the effectiveness of the procedures used by the client in taking the inventory by performing test counts of selected items. Special attention should be given to items of high extended value, but a sample from the counts made by each inventory team and of all types of inventory from all departments normally should be included. There are no specific rules for the number of items to be counted. The nature of the inventory, the general arrangement of the stock, the type and extent of errors made by the inventory crews, and similar factors will all determine the extent of the tests made by the auditor. Chapter 7 describes the considerations relating to the extent of audit tests.

To count items that cannot be accumulated as individual units, special

FIGURE 12–1 Inventory Test Count Worksheet

							NAME	DATE
						APPROVED BY *Williams*		2-23-86

INVENTORY TEST COUNTS

E & WR REPRESENTATIVE *J. Sanders*		NAME OF CLIENT *Moore Machine Company*						PAGE 4 OF 4
PLANT OR WAREHOUSE *Denver*		BUILDING *Main St.*	FLOOR 1	SECTION		DEPARTMENT *Machine Assembly*		
DATE *12-30-85*		TIME FROM *2:30 P.M.* TO *4:00 P.M.*		STAGE OF COMPLETION. DESCRIPTION. CONDITION. ETC.				

TAG NUMBER	PART NUMBER	UNIT	QUANTITY *(all counted)*				
1100	6072-51	ea.	⋎ 1	4"-6" Modified press - w/o mounts			
1112	301-10	pcs.	⋎ 310	1/4" x 18" x120" Stainless			
1157	304-13	pcs.	⋎ 36	1/2" round - 6 ft. lengths - Stainless			
1210	410-21	boxes	Ⓐ 121	6" Mounting bolts - Heat treated			
1260	4896-00	boxes	⋎ 7	Pulley shaft - 1½" - 4 to a box			
1262	7882-95	ea.	⋎ 13	5" Rollers for Model 7820-10 mill			

1862	3620-10	doz.	⋎ 5	2 Ton fastening mounts			
1921	1420-08	ea.	⋎ 10	8" Mill housing - Last operation #972			

⋎ – Traced to final inventory listing – Allen.

Ⓐ – Represents a portion of this item. Footed tags 1201, 1210, 1460, and 1692, and traced the total to the final inventory listing. – Allen

A-9 PRINTED IN U.S.A.

techniques or equipment may be used (e.g., scales, comparison with like items already counted, estimating tonnage of bulk storage items, aerial surveys of timber tracts and log storage ponds, and photographs of construction projects). Of course, the auditor must understand and become satisfied with the procedures used.

When test counts disclose isolated or minor errors made by an inventory crew, the auditor should bring them to the attention of an employee who is able to correct the error on the spot. It usually is not necessary to report minor errors to company supervisory personnel. However, if the auditor encounters a situation that might have a significant effect on the accuracy of the inventory, company supervisory personnel should be notified immediately so that corrective action can be taken. Examples of such situations include disregard of inventory instructions, general carelessness, or existence of excessive errors.

The auditor should record some of the test counts on working papers (see Figure 12–1). The working papers also should include information relating to the numerical sequence of tags used, details of unused or voided tags in that sequence, and details of any obsolete or slow-moving items and large quantity items. The auditor should indicate clearly those items that were counted. At a later date, the auditor will trace the information to the final inventory listing prepared by the client to test the reliability of the procedures used by the company in compiling the final inventory. To make the subsequent audit tests easier, the information listed should be both complete and accurate. Generally, the following information should be included: (1) name of the auditor performing the tests, (2) name of the client, (3) page number, (4) location of items (plant, building, floor, etc.), (5) date of the count, (6) time of inventory observation, (7) tag number (if applicable), (8) quantity and unit of count, and (9) description of item. Regarding the description of inventory items, the auditor should use the same description that the company uses. Where applicable, part numbers, last completed operation, and other pertinent information also should be listed.

Obtaining Receiving and Shipping Cutoff Information. During the physical inventory count, the auditor should list receiving and shipping cutoff information. At a later date, the auditor should trace the information into the company's accounting records. The objective is to ascertain whether (1) all items received up to the cutoff date and included in the physical inventory are charged to the purchases or inventory accounts (receiving cutoff), and (2) all items shipped up to the cutoff date and excluded from the physical inventory have been recorded as sales in the period.

Depending on the company's procedures, the following audit procedures may be used to test the cutoff:

1. Visit the receiving and shipping areas to observe whether a clear separation has been achieved between items included in the physical inventory and those excluded.

2. When the client maintains shipping and receiving logs, the auditor may request copies of such logs or select a representative sample of shipments and receipts for later testing. Usually the following receiving information is gathered: (1) vendor name, (2) receiving report number, (3) date received, (4) quantity and description of items received, and (5) name of the shipper.

   For shipments, the following information usually is gathered: (1) customer name, (2) shipping report or invoice number, (3) date shipped, (4) quantity and description of items shipped, (5) name of the shipper, and (6) if available, the invoice amount. For both receipts and shipments, the auditor should indicate whether the items were included in the physical inventory.

3. When prenumbered receiving or shipping tickets are used, note the last number used preceding the cutoff. Also note any prior unused numbers. If the company receives or ships materials in freight cars, truck trailers, or sea vessels, include a listing of full and empty cars, trailers, or vessels at the client's location and indicate their inventory status. (In most cases, this requires special attention because of the substantial amounts involved.)

4. When the client does not use receiving or shipping tickets or maintain related logs, the auditor should request that such information be maintained for a period prior and subsequent to the physical inventory date.

5. The auditor also should obtain information concerning shipment and receipts occurring subsequent to the physical inventory. Generally, at the time of the physical inventory, the auditor should request that the client send to the auditor receiving and shipping cutoff information for a specified period subsequent to the physical inventory date so that tests of inventory cutoff may be completed.

Preparing Vendor Statement Requests. As discussed earlier, reconciliation of vendor statements is an important part of the examination of accounts payable. Reconciliation of vendor statements also is an important part of the inventory receiving cutoff work. The auditor should plan the timing and extent of vendor statement requests so that the objectives of both audit areas are met.

Summarizing the Inventory Observation Procedures. At the conclusion of the observation and tests, a memorandum may be prepared that describes the work done and the conclusions reached. Alternatively, a checklist that serves the same purpose can be completed. As an example, Figure 12–2

FIGURE 12–2 Excerpts from an Inventory Observation Checklist

<table>
<tr><td></td><td>Name</td><td>Date</td></tr>
<tr><td>Prepared by _____</td><td>_____</td></tr>
<tr><td>Approved by _____</td><td>_____</td></tr>
</table>

INVENTORY OBSERVATION CHECKLIST

NAME OF COMPANY _____
SUBSIDIARY/DIVISION _____
LOCATION/DEPARTMENT _____
DATE(S) OF INVENTORY TAKING _____ DATE(S) OF OBSERVATION _____
CPA FIRM REPRESENTATIVE(S) _____
COMPANY REPRESENTATIVE IN CHARGE OF INVENTORY (OR DEPARTMENT)
_____

The purposes of the inventory observation are to determine that the (1) inventory physically exists, (2) stated quantities fairly represent the actual quantities on hand at the date of the observation, and (3) inventory is in a usable and saleable condition (e.g., not damaged or obsolete).

Inventory Instructions

	Yes	No	Explanation

(1) Were adequate written instructions prepared covering each phase of the physical inventory procedures? (Describe deficiencies noted, if any.)

Obtain a copy of the instructions for the work papers and consider the following in evaluating their adequacy:

(a) Names of persons drafting and approving instructions.
(b) Dates and times of inventory taking.
(c) Names of persons responsible for supervising inventory taking.
(d) Plans for arranging and segregating inventory, including precautions taken to clear work-in-process to cutoff points.
(e) Provisions for control of receiving and shipping during inventory taking period and, if plant is not shut down, provisions for handling inventory movements.
(f) Instructions for recording description of items and how quantities are to be determined (e.g., count, weight, or other measurement).
(g) Instructions for identifying obsolete, damaged, and slow-moving items.
(h) Instructions for identifying, segregating, and counting goods held on consignment from others and reconciling counts to consignment records.

Company Counting Procedures

	Yes	No	Explanation

(6) Were inventory crews assigned to count material for which they normally are responsible?
If not, were the crews familiar with the inventory?

(7) Were inventory crews denied reference to perpetual records during the counting? Will someone subsequently compare counts to the perpetual records and investigate differences?

FIGURE 12–2 *(concluded)*

	Yes	No	Explanation
Cutoff Procedures			
(13) Was production suspended during inventory taking? (If not, describe the procedure used to control the movement of materials.)			
(14) Were shipping and receiving operations suspended during the inventory taking? (If not, describe procedure employed to assure an accurate cutoff.)			

	Yes	No	Explanation
Obsolescence and Safeguarding			
(17) Briefly describe the Company's procedure for identifying obsolete and slow-moving items.	N/A	N/A	
(18) Briefly describe deficiencies noted (if any) in the Company's physical safeguards over inventory items.	N/A	N/A	
Test Count Procedures			
(19) Were counting and recording procedures actually observed?			
(20) Were independent test counts made and listed in the work papers?			

	Yes	No	Explanation
Compilation Information			
(33) If quantities counted will be converted to a different unit of measure on the final inventory listing, have we obtained sufficient information to test the conversion?			
(34) Will details of Company count combinations be available when our test counts are traced to the final inventory listing? (If not, describe how we can reconcile our counts to the final listing.)			

CONCLUSION STATEMENT (based on the results of your tests and observations). Indicate your opinion as to whether the Company's inventory documentation (e.g., tags, count sheets, or perpetual records) fairly represents the actual quantities on hand at the date of the observation. Also conclude as to the inventory's usability and saleability.

includes excerpts from such a checklist. If a memorandum is prepared it should normally include the following:

1. Location, time of visit, and departments covered.
2. Whether the company's employees followed the inventory instructions.
3. Comments about the company's "housekeeping" (e.g., whether the inventory items were neatly arranged).
4. Description of the procedures followed in selecting a representative sample of inventory items for test counts.
5. Procedures followed in observing and making test counts. Degree of accuracy indicated by test counts. Any unusual items or conditions observed, such as obsolete or slow-moving stock, damaged merchandise, consigned stock, and production or stock movement during the taking of physical inventory.
6. Description of procedures used by the company to obtain accurate shipping and receiving cutoff and information obtained for future cutoff testing.
7. An opinion, based on the results of tests and observations, whether the recorded quantities reasonably represent the quantities actually on hand.

Figure 12–3 is an example of a memo covering an inventory observation.

Testing Perpetual Inventory Records.   Companies often maintain detailed perpetual inventory records of quantities on hand at all times. The perpetual records may be in the form of ledger cards maintained in the stockroom or computer printouts updated periodically (e.g., daily or weekly) from receiving and usage reports. Some forms of perpetual inventory systems include only quantities, while others also include inventory prices. Rather than take a complete physical inventory, many companies that use perpetual records make counts of individual items from time to time throughout the year (cycle counts). Then the quantities shown on the perpetual records are used as quantities for compiling an inventory listing, which is priced and compared to the book inventory.

Procedures normally employed during the tests of perpetual records include the following:

1. Review and evaluate the perpetual recordkeeping system. This normally is performed when the accounting system is evaluated.
2. Obtain a listing of the physical quantities on hand as shown by the perpetual records at the book-to-perpetual comparison date. Test the listing by comparing it to the final compiled inventory listing for agreement.
3. Test quantities in the perpetual records through physical examination. Test count procedures should include (a) selecting items from the records

FIGURE 12–3   Inventory Observation Memorandum

Name   Date

Prepared David 12/31/X1

Approved _____ ____

Inventory Observation
Mor-Sam Machine Parts Company
12/31/X1   1 of 2

    I was present at the Mor-Sam Machine Parts Company on December 31, 19X1, to observe their physical inventory, which consists of raw steel, work-in-process, and finished machine parts.

    I had previously read the Mor-Sam Inventory Instructions and inventory section of the audit program, and met with L. Smith, E & W senior, to discuss the physical inventory observation procedures. Upon arrival at Mor-Sam I met Mr. Jack Green, the production control engineer, who was in charge of the physical inventory. We toured all plant areas and I observed that the inventory, which was still being counted by the inventory crews, was neatly arranged which facilitated the inventory taking.

    I observed the procedures used by the four inventory teams. The teams appeared familiar with the inventory items and appeared to be conscientious in counting and recording the quantities and descriptions of inventory items. Based on these observations, I made twenty test counts of items recorded by each team. I listed all test counts which had a value in excess of $3,500 (35 in total) for subsequent tracing to the final inventory listing. During the observation I noted that count team C failed to list the last operation as part of the description. I brought this matter to the attention of Mr. Green, who had the tags corrected.

    My comments about material that may be obsolete and data for testing Mor-Sam's inventory tag control and cutoff procedures are attached.

FIGURE 12–3 *(concluded)*

	Name	Date
Prepared	David	12/31/X1
Approved		

Inventory Observation

Nor—Sam Machine Parts Company

12/31/X1   2 of 2

    Based on my observations, it is my opinion that the attached "Inventory Instructions" were followed and that the quantities and descriptions of items recorded on the inventory tags reasonably represent the actual quantities on hand as of December 31, 19X1.

and supporting quantities by physical examination and count and (b) selecting items from the floor and tracing the quantity back to the records. Both of these tests are necessary to test whether all items listed on the perpetual records physically exist, and all items physically in inventory are recorded on the perpetual records. List test counts made on a test count worksheet.

4. Perform other procedures normally undertaken during the physical inventory observation, such as obtaining cutoff information, touring the inventory areas, and making note of potentially obsolete items.

5. Review the client's perpetual inventory records and investigate any significant quantity adjustments.

Tracing Test Counts, Checking Cutoffs, and Testing Clerical Accuracy

When taking of the physical inventory has been completed, the client will price the inventory, multiply (extend) quantities by unit prices, and accumulate the extensions to arrive at a total inventory amount. The auditor tests the final inventory to determine that it has been compiled and summarized accurately. The auditor's procedures include (1) tracing test counts, (2) checking cutoffs, and (3) testing clerical accuracy.

Tracing Test Counts into Final Inventory Listing. The auditor should trace the test counts that were made and listed in the working papers during the observation of physical inventory to the company's final inventory listing. This test is made to determine that the quantities listed on the final inventory summary accurately represent the physical quantities on hand at the inventory date. Often the final inventory is simply a listing of quantities noted on each inventory tag. However, some companies may use intermediate worksheets, adding machine tapes, or the computer may be used to aggregate items by part number (or some other logical arrangement).

In some instances, only totals by part number appear on the final inventory listing, and this may complicate the auditor's task. In this situation, the auditor may trace the test counts to the applicable inventory tags (accounting for all tags), total the quantities on all the tags for a particular item, and compare this total to the quantity shown on the inventory listing.

Checking Receiving and Shipping Cutoff Procedures. The inventory account included in the general ledger must, of course, include all transactions that affect the status of the physical inventory at the time of the count; otherwise, the financial statements will be distorted. Therefore, it is important to ascertain that proper cutoffs were made. The test of the company's receiving and shipping cutoff procedures determines whether: (1) all materials received have been included in inventories, (2) liabilities have been recorded for all materials purchased on account and included in the inventories, (3) liabilities have not been recorded for any items excluded from the inventory, (4) receivables have been recorded for all products sold on account, (5) all products sold have been excluded from inventory, and (6) receivables have not been recorded for products included in the inventory.

Particular attention should be given to inventory in transit, either from vendors or from branches, divisions, or subdivisions of the client. The auditor must determine whether these items have been recorded properly in the accounts. As part of this test, the auditor will use receiving and shipping cutoff data obtained during the taking of the physical inventory. The purchasing and receiving records and the sales and shipping records of the company also will be tested.

Testing Clerical Accuracy. Extensions and footings of inventories always should be tested by the auditor. Even though the calculations may have been performed on a computer, rechecked by client personnel, or made by an outside service organization under the control of the company, the auditor must test clerical accuracy. The extent of the auditor's tests will depend upon such factors as the procedures used by the client in compiling the final inventory listing, the care used by the client in making and checking the calculations, and the number and dollar amounts of the inventory items.

Some of the more common clerical errors that are made by a client in summarizing inventories include: transposition errors, misplaced decimal points, incorrect conversions and/or units of measure, errors in extensions, failure to carry page totals onto summary sheets, errors in footings, and errors in pricing.

When the auditor must perform a significant amount of clerical accuracy testing, an outside service organization may be engaged or the computer may be used. If a service organization is employed, the auditor should direct and supervise their work. When using the computer, the auditor may obtain the assistance of EDP specialists, who use computer programs specifically developed for this purpose (see "Computer-Assisted Audit Techniques" in Chapter 7).

When the auditor performs tests of clerical accuracy, the work should be done carefully, but as efficiently as possible. Since the auditor is primarily concerned with material errors, the tests are normally done on an approximate basis—that is, it is seldom necessary to prove extensions or footings to the exact dollar. For transpositions, misplaced decimals, and footings, the time-saving technique of sight testing (i.e., visually noting the reasonableness of the total) often is used. Large dollar or quantity items usually are checked for clerical accuracy. Where there are conversions (e.g., from feet to pounds), the auditor should test the source of information used for the conversion as well as the conversion itself. Although not all pages of the inventory detail are usually footed, all page totals are ordinarily traced to the summary, and the summary is footed. The working papers should include a description of the tests of clerical accuracy made by the auditor and a summary of the findings and conclusions.

Review of Final Inventory Listing

After tracing the test counts to, and testing the clerical accuracy of, the final inventory listing, the auditor should review the listing for unusual items. Examples of unusual items include: (1) an inventory item that appears to have a significantly larger quantity on hand than other inventory items, (2) an inventory item that appears to have an unusual per unit cost, (3) an extended value that is very large or very small in light of the quantities on hand and its unit cost, and (4) page totals that appear unusually large in relation to the other page totals in the listing.

Inventory Valuation

The auditor must determine whether the basis of pricing used by the client conforms to GAAP and whether it has been applied consistently. The price test of inventory cost usually is performed separately for each segment of the inventory, i.e., raw materials and purchased parts, work in process, and finished goods.

Raw Materials and Purchased Parts. The price test of raw materials and purchased parts is the most objective inventory valuation test. The test itself involves supporting the unit cost of selected items in inventory by reference to vendors' invoices. The two approaches taken to test pricing for raw materials and purchased parts are (1) select key items and/or a representative sample of items from the detailed inventory listing and support the costs of each item, or (2) select a representative sample of raw materials and parts purchased from throughout the year (or an interim period) for testing key attributes.

Testing the Detailed Inventory Listing. When performing the price test of raw materials and purchased parts, the auditor should begin by preparing a working paper listing the items selected for testing from the detailed inventory listing. The working paper should show the description of the item, stock (part) number, quantity in inventory, unit price, and extended amount. Space should be left between the description of the items to be tested in case the auditor needs to list several vendors' invoices to account for the total quantity in inventory. An example of a price test working paper is illustrated in Figure 12–4. When examining the vendor invoices, the auditor should note the following:

1. *Date received.* Assuming the client uses the first-in, first-out (FIFO) method to price inventories, the invoice immediately preceding the inventory date should be listed first. Then list progressively older invoices until the quantity in the ending inventory has been accounted for. If there are no current invoices, there is a possibility that the item is obsolete, slow-moving, or unsalable. This should be noted for further analysis during tests for obsolete inventory.

2. *Quantity.* Invoices examined should cover the total quantity in inventory.

3. *Unit price.* The unit price should include the vendor's invoice price plus any indirect charges for freight, insurance, etc. Rebates and trade discounts should be deducted from the unit price. When units of measurement on the vendor's invoice differ from the units in the inventory (for example, steel purchased by the pound but priced in linear feet in the inventory), standard conversion tables should be used to test the conversion and to determine the unit price.

When performing these procedures, the auditor also should be alert for possible obsolete or slow-moving inventory. For example, assume that no purchases were made at any time during the year for one of the inventory items selected for price testing and that there was very limited usage of this item during the year (the auditor could determine the usage by comparing this year's quantity on hand with last year's). Thus, it appears that this item may be obsolete or slow-moving.

Price Tests Combined with Tests of Key Attributes. On many engagements, raw materials and purchased parts will be tested in conjunction with the tests of key attributes related to purchases and cash disbursements. In these cases, the auditor is not concerned with examining a sufficient number of invoices to support the quantity of the item in inventory. Instead, the auditor is concerned with tracing the inventory cost for each purchase into the client's inventory system and testing the key attributes for the purchase. The nature of these procedures will vary significantly from client to client due to differences in inventory accounting systems. Therefore, an understanding of the client's inventory system is essential before attempting to undertake any of these procedures.

The auditor also tests whether the company priced its inventory at "cost or market, whichever is lower." A satisfactory way to check the market value of purchased items is to review the price paid for recent purchases. However, if a commodity is subject to declining prices or rapid market fluctuations, supplementary tests and inquiries should be made. One source

FIGURE 12-4 Purchased Items Price Test

Purchased Items Price Test
Moore Machine Co.
12/31/X1

	Name	Date
Prepared	Clelland	2/9/X2
Approved		

page 4/4*

Inst By #/Item #	Description	Per Inventory Quantity	Unit Price	Extension	Date	Per Vendor's Invoice Quantity	Unit Price	Extension	Inventory Over/Under	Vendor/Comments
40/5	#462 – 2¼" x 36" x 320'	36716 lbs	5385/lb	$19768	12/2/X1 ✓	Ⓐ 32600 lbs	5385/lb	$17555	$ (32)	Big Steel
					12/3/X1 ✓	Ⓐ 4110 lbs	5463/lb	2245		Martin Co.
						36710		$ 19800		
62/16	#628 – 2½" x 36" x 120'	28880 lbs	5591/lb	16147	12/29/X1 ✓	21000 lbs	5591/lb	$ 11741	168	Lantel Steel
					11/30/X1 ✓	Ⓐ 7880 lbs	5378/lb	4238		Lantel Steel
						28880		$ 15979		
184/40	#667 – 92-3" Stainless Bolts	914 boxes	590/box	539	11/2/X1 ✓	Ⓐ 914 boxes	590/box	$ 539	–0–	Substantial Corp
188/29	#722 – 2 Wing Supports	987 pcs	5.787/ea	5712	12/22/X1 ✓	Ⓐ 987 pcs	5.787/ea	$ 5712	–0–	Smith, Inc
260/1	#1086 – 28 Windows	620 pcs	1.20/ea	744	12/29/X1 ✓	620 pcs	1.20/ea	$ 744	–0–	Large Glass Works
720/32	#3626 – 10 Hydraulic Pumps	20 pcs	365.50/ea	7310	12/29/X1 ✓	20 pcs	365.50/ea	$ 7310	–0–	Curtiss Company
840/36	#721 Door Bolts & Nuts	500 pcs	.65/ea	325	12/3/X1 ✓	350 pcs	.50/ea	$ 175		
					11/28/X1 ✓	100 pcs	.65/ea	65		
					10/2/X1 ✓	Ⓐ 50 pcs	.70/ea	35		
						500		275		
920/16	#480 Rivets	2000 lbs	.50/lb	1000	12/20/X1 ✓	1400 lbs	.50/lb	$ 700	1	Jones & Company
					11/15/X1 ✓	Ⓐ 600 lbs	.485/lb	291		Jones & Company
						2000		991		
1200/4	#820 Seats	10 pcs	600.00/ea	6000	12/3/X1 ✓	1 pc	600.00/ea	$ 600	675	Barton Corp
					10/15/X1 ✓	Ⓐ 9 pcs	525.00/ea	4725		Barton Corp
						10		$ 5325		
1261/31	#910-4 4" Bolts (heat treated)	10 doz	6.00/doz	60	12/11/X1 ✓	120 pcs	6.00/ea	720	(660)Ⓒ	Barton Corp
1300/19	#1200 – 1A Compartment Lights	100 pcs	3.00/ea	300	12/2/X1 ✓	100 pcs	3.00/ea	300	–0– Ⓓ	Philip Electric
				$ 115810 *					$ 419 Ⓑ	

Percent of Purchased Items Inventory Tested   37.5%

Ⓐ The quantity represents that portion of the quantity per the invoice needed to equal inventory quantity on hand.

Ⓑ Posted projected error for the entire purchased items inventory of $1133 to the Master Accepts Schedule, estimated as follows:
[419 ÷ 115,810] × 313,150 (total purchased items inventory per trial balance)

Ⓒ Item counted in dozens, priced at ea.

Ⓓ Per random number listing on PA-26.

✓ Examined vendor's invoice.

PA-25

*Author's note: Figures shown on this page do not sum to totals since this is page 4 of four pages. The other three pages are not shown.

of information is published quotations in financial and trade publications; another is the suppliers' price lists. The purchasing agent of the company also may be able to give helpful information.

Work in Process and Finished Goods.   The cost of work in process and finished goods will include a material component, a labor component, and a manufacturing overhead component. Before performing the price test for work in process and finished goods, the auditor must understand the client's cost accounting system. An analysis of the client's cost system usually is included in the permanent file working papers and is updated annually as part of the auditor's evaluation of the accounting systems. There are two basic types of cost systems that an auditor will commonly encounter: job order cost and process cost. Either actual costs or standard costs can be used with these systems. The general characteristics of each are discussed in the following paragraphs.

Under a job order cost system, the cost is determined for each separate order or unit of production. Material costs are compiled from material requisitions and from invoices for specific purchases. Direct labor charges are accumulated from employee payroll data. Overhead is usually applied as a percentage of the direct labor cost or at a fixed rate for each direct labor-hour.

The process cost system differs from the job order cost system in that costs are not accumulated by specific order or by unit of production but rather by state of production. Process cost systems usually are used by companies whose product is manufactured in a continuous operation. Examples include oil refineries and pulp and paper manufacturers. Under a process cost system, cost and units of production are accumulated over a period of time (e.g., daily, weekly, monthly) by department or manufacturing operation. Unit costs to be used for inventory valuation purposes can then be computed using these accumulated costs.

Standard costs are used by many companies to obtain current operating information and to simplify accounting procedures. Standard costs are used in combination with either a job order or a process cost system. Under a standard cost system, cost rates of labor, material, and overhead for each operation on each item manufactured are predetermined and represent normal or ideal rates under assumed conditions. Differences between standard and actual costs normally are charged or credited to variance expense accounts. In such a system, the auditor must determine whether the standard costs will properly value the inventory. The standard cost system must approximate actual cost to be a proper basis for valuing inventory.

One effective way to determine the difference between standard and actual costs is to review the variance accounts. If the variance account balance is relatively insignificant, then it would appear that standard cost, in the aggregate, approximates actual cost. However, if the variance account balance is large, a potential misstatement of inventory cost may exist. An adjustment may then be required to restate the standard cost in inventory to more closely approximate actual cost. Before these determinations can be made, certain tests of the cost system must be performed to assure that the variance accounts do reflect the accumulated differences between standard and actual cost.

An important factor in performing a price test of work in process and finished goods, as previously stated, is understanding the company's cost accounting system. Once understood, appropriate tests can be designed to test the system. These tests typically involve examination of supporting documentation such as vendors' invoices and payroll records for material and labor content and the review and test of overhead calculations. The specific audit procedures employed will vary from client to client and depend primarily on the company's cost accounting system.

Reviewing for Slow-Moving or Obsolete Items

Companies should have adequate procedures to control, remove from inventory, and determine the estimated realizable value of obsolete or slow-moving items. Such items should be reduced to their net realizable value. If a company does not employ such procedures, the auditor frequently will be required to perform extensive tests. The auditor's tests of inventory for slow-moving and obsolete stock normally include the following procedures:

1. Discuss with responsible company personnel the procedures used to determine the quantities of such inventory and the related adjustments to inventory cost and test the reasonableness of the company's determination.
2. Search for such items during the physical inventory observation and check at a later date to see whether such items were considered by the company in its determination.
3. Review raw materials and purchased parts price-test working papers for evidence of such items.
4. Check to determine that the current year inventory does not include items excluded from the prior year inventory.
5. Review inventory records on a test basis for items that appear to be inactive.
6. Evaluate inventory quantities in light of expected usage to determine that quantities on hand are not excessive. Turnover ratios, sales forecasts, current sales, and unfilled orders sometimes are used as bases for estimating usage.

Testing for Lower of Cost or Market

The auditor should test the market price for items in work in process and finished goods in order to determine that adequate provision has been made for losses in disposing of inventories, whether they are on hand or are committed to be acquired. The price may be the (1) cost of replacement, (2) selling price less the cost to complete and sell the item, or (3) selling price less (a) the cost to complete and sell the item and (b) a normal profit.[6] The selling prices may be obtained from the company's price lists, contracts, catalogs, or recent sales invoices. The auditor must be alert for trade discounts that reduce the listed selling price. Also, as previously discussed, the auditor should inquire about the existence of damaged, slow-moving, overstocked, and obsolete inventories.

Physical Inventory Adjustments

When the amount of adjustment from book to physical inventory is considered abnormal, the company should find the reasons for the adjustment and prepare a summary of the reconciling items. The auditor should review the reconciliation and be satisfied as to the reasonableness of the items. A review of monthly gross profit margins, standard cost variances, methods of costing sales, provisions for inventory shrinkage, and methods of accounting for freight and discounts may help explain the adjustment.

Inventory Rollforward

If physical inventories are taken, priced, and compiled before the balance sheet date, the auditor should determine that the proper adjustments have been recorded as of the inventory date. Also, tests should be made of the inventory transactions that occurred during the period from the physical inventory through the balance sheet date (rollforward period). The test of rollforward transactions normally includes:

1. Tests of entries included in the inventory control accounts by reference to purchase journals, labor distributions, overhead allocations, and other related records.
2. Review of the reasonableness of activity levels (i.e., materials receipts, production, cost of goods sold, scrap) to earlier period and/or budgeted amounts.
3. Comparison of the gross profit margins of the current period with those of prior periods. Unusual variations should be investigated and explained in the working papers.

---

[6] Ibid., p. 31.

Consignments; Purchase and Sales Commitments

The auditor should determine whether the company has established adequate control over merchandise that has been either received or shipped on consignment. Confirmation of quantities on hand may be requested by corresponding with outside consignors or consignees. In certain instances, the auditor also may personally observe this inventory. The auditor should ascertain that the consigned stock has been properly included in the inventory if it is a consignment out to another firm or excluded if it is a consignment in from another firm.

The auditor should discuss with appropriate company officials the existence of any possible purchase commitments for quantities in excess of normal requirements or at prices in excess of current market. Purchase contracts may be examined on a test basis. The auditor should determine whether a provision for losses from unfavorable commitments is required in the circumstances.

The auditor also should review with company officials the possible existence of any commitments to sell products at prices below the cost of production and disposal. Sales contracts may be examined on a test basis, and the auditor should determine whether a provision for losses from these unfavorable commitments is required.

Analytical Review Procedures

There are many analytical review procedures that may be used by the auditor in the analysis of inventory and cost of goods sold. Analytical review procedures may provide audit evidence to assist the auditor in concluding, among other things, whether costs assigned to inventory are determined in accordance with the stated valuation method and whether usage and movement of inventory is recorded correctly as to account, amount, and period. Examples of analytical review procedures frequently performed in this area include:

1. Comparing overhead costs to direct labor for current and prior periods.
2. Comparing units purchased to units sold.
3. Comparing the current period's percentage composition of inventory components with the percentage composition in prior periods.
4. Comparing gross margin percentages by product line for the current period with prior periods.
5. Comparing direct labor and overhead to materials put into production for the current and prior periods.

PROPERTY, PLANT, AND EQUIPMENT

Property, plant, and equipment are tangible assets used in the operations of a company's trade or business that have a useful life of more than one year. Property, plant, and equipment should be recorded at cost. Cost includes acquisition or production cost plus all other expenditures (e.g., freight, handling charges, installation costs) necessary to place the asset in use. The cost of the asset should be charged to operations ratably over its estimated useful life.

The specific control objectives addressed in auditing property, plant, and equipment are listed in Figure 11–2. What may not be evident from a review of these specific control objectives is that the auditor's examination of property, plant, and equipment also may include gathering additional information needed for (1) reporting to the SEC, (2) auditing the income tax provision, and (3) preparing the company's income tax returns, if part of the engagement. Although gathering tax information is part of all phases of an audit, it is an especially significant part of the examination of property, plant, and equipment because of the greater number of tax-related matters applicable to property transactions. Property, plant, and equipment is an area where there can be a great difference between the accounting used for financial statement purposes and the accounting used for income tax purposes.

The Economic Recovery Tax Act of 1981 introduced the Accelerated Cost Recovery System (ACRS) for income tax purposes. As a result, most companies have different accounting methods for financial reporting and income tax purposes for almost all of their assets placed in service after 1980 because of different asset lives. Many companies maintain two separate sets of property, plant, and equipment records—one for books and the other for tax. Audit working papers may contain two sets of audit schedules that reflect each of the methods.

The audit procedures employed during the examination of property, plant, and equipment generally include: (1) testing additions and disposals, (2) testing reasonableness of depreciation expense, (3) testing for items improperly charged to expense (e.g., repairs and maintenance), (4) summarizing property transactions for the period under audit, and (5) gathering information needed to audit the income tax provision and prepare the income tax returns.

The auditor always should be alert for indications of properties not on the books, unrecorded property disposals or retirements, or evidence that title to any property does not rest with the client. Evidence of these situations may be noted in other parts of the audit such as in the inspection of tax bills, rent receipts, or insurance policies.

Testing Additions and Disposals

Ordinarily, the examination of property, plant, and equipment accounts involves reviewing and testing changes in the account balances during the period under audit. Changes in property, plant, and equipment accounts may result from (1) additions of new property, plant, and equipment, (2) renovation or modification of existing assets that extends their useful lives, or (3) disposals. In testing additions, the auditor examines documentation in support of cost. In testing disposals, the auditor determines whether asset retirements by sale or abandonment are properly recorded; whether fully depreciated assets are eliminated from the accounts (if it is the company's policy to do so); and whether assets that have become obsolete because of changes in the nature of the company's operations have been properly eliminated from the accounts.

Before beginning the audit procedures, the auditor should review the risk analysis working papers relating to property, plant, and equipment and related system documentation, including details of the client's accounting practices and policies. Attention should be given to the company's policies for authorizing acquisitions and retirements. These policies often will be formally documented and included in an accounting procedures manual. Authorization policies typically will vary depending on the size of the addition. For example, the purchase of a new adding machine probably would have to be approved by a department head, whereas the construction of an addition to the manufacturing facility normally would be approved by the board of directors.

Additions. In testing asset additions, the auditor may (1) test key attributes by examining a representative sample of property acquisitions (concurrently with test of cash disbursements) through an interim date and review any unusually large property acquisitions from the interim date to year end, (2) select and test specific property, plant, and equipment acquisitions (e.g., key items), or (3) perform a combination of (1) and (2).

In testing key attributes, the auditor examines evidence of the controls that assure that the (1) addition was authorized and approved, (2) recorded amount agrees with the invoice and contract order, (3) addition was recorded in the correct account, and (4) addition was recorded in the correct period. These controls are very similar to those tested during the purchases and cash disbursements procedures previously discussed, which makes it efficient to combine the tests.

In testing a specific fixed asset acquisition, the auditor will examine documentation in support of the asset cost. For example, if a company acquired a machine for $10,000 and expended an additional $1,000 in labor and overhead costs installing and testing it, the cost of the asset would be $11,000.

The auditor generally performs the following procedures when testing specific acquisitions to property, plant, and equipment:

1. Obtain from the client a listing of asset additions by account (land, buildings, building improvements, furniture and fixtures, office equipment, manufacturing equipment, vehicles). This listing should contain the vendor, date and amount of the invoice, and a description of the item capitalized.

2. Examine vendor's invoice for date of purchase, cost, description of the asset, and name of the client.
3. Support other costs by reference to direct labor reports, timecards, or payroll reports.
4. Determine whether the purchase was authorized in accordance with company policies.
5. Examine data evidencing receipt of the asset.
6. For major purchases of land or buildings, examine the deed, title policy, closing statement, and similar documents to establish ownership.
7. Determine whether the asset life and salvage value set by the company are reasonable.
8. Determine if the addition is eligible for the investment tax credit.
9. Where additions represent replacements, inquire as to corresponding retirements.

The working paper in Figure 12–5 is a typical analysis of property, plant, and equipment additions (in this case for building additions purchased from outside vendors). Note the miscellaneous items that have been grouped together. The auditor generally does not examine support for all additions. To limit the extent of the audit work to specific acquisitions, the auditor supports only items exceeding a certain limit—in the case of Figure 12–5, $500. The limit is established during the program development phase of the audit.

Companies often construct their own additions to property, plant, and equipment. The construction cost usually will be accounted for in a manner similar to the accounting for work in process inventory under a job order cost system. Construction cost includes material, purchased services, labor, overhead, and interest. The method of allocating overhead to self-constructed plant and equipment varies among companies. Some companies allocate only variable (direct) overhead, while others follow the full absorption method of allocating both fixed (indirect) and variable amounts.

In testing assets constructed by the company, the auditor should perform the following tests in addition to those procedures outlined above:

1. Review the company's procedures for accumulating production costs.
2. Support labor costs by reference to payrolls, direct labor reports, and timecards.
3. Support the computation of the application of overhead. Ascertain that the method of applying overhead is consistent with that used in prior years and is reasonable.
4. Support the interest capitalized.

Disposals. The cost and related accumulated depreciation amounts of all assets sold, traded, scrapped, or disposed of in any other manner should be removed from the asset and accumulated depreciation accounts. The audi-

FIGURE 12–5 Working Paper for Building Additions

	Client	Name	Date
		Prepared Simon	7/2/XX
		Approved _____	_____

Building Additions — Outside Vendors
MNO Corporation
June 30, 19XX

Book and Tax Bases

Date	Vendor	Description	
8/15	Fred Loyd Bright	Architect for new spray room	15 000 00 ✓
Various	Carter-Coffee, Inc.	Construction of spray room	167 151 00 ✓
2/17	Gowen Electric Supply	Mercury vapor fixtures	11 389 00 ✓
5/19	Fire Protection Company	Installation of sprinkle system	7 935 00 ✓
	Miscellaneous items—each less than $500		6 945 00 ⌀
			208 420 00 S
			F

F Footed

S Traced to summary of property, plant, and equipment

✓ Examined vendor's invoice—item properly capitalized

⌀ Examined final billing indicating total contract price—item properly capitalized. Building addition was placed in service 6/29/XX.

⌀ Depreciation lapse schedule scanned. No items other than those listed above were over $500.

tor should be familiar with the company's policies and procedures regarding disposals. In testing disposals of fixed assets, the auditor may perform the following:

1. Obtain from the client a schedule of all disposals by account classification.
2. Examine evidence that the disposal was properly approved in accordance with company policy.
3. Support sales price by reference to contract, sales invoice, remittance advice, correspondence, or cash receipts records.
4. Support cost and accumulated depreciation amounts by reference to the company's detail property records.
5. Support the computation of gain or loss. If the company used different methods of depreciation for tax and book purposes, the computation of both tax and book gain or loss should be tested.
6. Determine whether the cost of assets acquired through trade-ins has been recorded correctly.
7. Gather all information needed to compute investment credit and depreciation recapture and to prepare Form 4797 and Schedule D of the corporate income tax return.

Figure 12–6 is a typical analysis of equipment disposals, in this case of automotive equipment. If the company's controls over the disposal of assets are inadequate, there is a possibility that an asset may be disposed of without the cost being removed from the accounts. The auditor should review miscellaneous income accounts to determine if the proceeds from any sales of equipment have been credited directly to income without removing the cost of the asset and related accumulated depreciation amounts from the accounts. In addition, the auditor should scan miscellaneous cash receipts records and investigate large or unusual amounts.

Testing Reasonableness of Depreciation Expense

For financial reporting purposes, there are several acceptable methods of computing the current provisions for depreciation. The depreciation method utilized by a company primarily will be a function of the accounting and tax policies of its management. Regardless of the method used, the auditor is concerned primarily with determining that the estimated useful lives are reasonable, that the same method of computation used in prior years is being used in the current period, and that the calculations are accurate.

The annual provision for depreciation is an estimate based on some important assumptions (e.g., estimated useful lives, depreciation methods) and there is no single correct answer. The auditor's primary purpose is to test

FIGURE 12-6   Automotive Equipment Disposal Schedule

				Client Name	Date
				Prepared *Simon*	7/8/XX
				Approved _____	____

Disposal of Automotive Equipment
MNO Corporation
June 30, 19XX

Book Basis

Date acq/disp	Description	Proceeds	Cost	Accumulated Depreciation	Gain (Loss)
2/28/XX-5/1/XX⁴	Ford Sed. No. 3372468C802⁴	1050000⁴	1325892✓	1293303✓	1017411
6/1/XX-4/1/XX⁴	Mercury Sed. No. 224889V5177⁴	200000⁴	487262✓	248904✓	(38358)
		1250000 F	1813154⁵ F	1542207⁵ F	979053 F ⁱ/F
					T/B

F Footed

ⁱF Crossfooted

5 Traced to summary of property, plant, and equipment

4 Verified by examination of sales contract

✓ Traced to depreciation lapse schedule

T/B Traced to trial balance acct. No. 8076 - agreed

398

the overall reasonableness of the client's estimate. The reasonableness of a company's provision for depreciation depends on:

1. The reasonableness of the estimated economic useful lives established by the company for depreciable assets or leasehold improvements. Leasehold improvements should be written off over the life of the lease or the useful life of the improvement, whichever is shorter.
2. The reasonableness and consistency of the depreciation methods used by the company.
3. The reasonableness of the depreciation calculations.

To test the reasonableness of the useful lives assigned to assets, the auditor might review the lives assigned to major property additions during the year. Those lives should be considered in relation to the lives used for other similar assets, considering the average length of service of such assets. Also, when reviewing sales or trade-ins of plant and equipment, a consistent pattern of large gains might indicate that assets are being depreciated over lives that may be too short. Consistent losses might indicate that net book values are too high because useful lives are too long.

The method of depreciation selected by the company also has a significant impact on depreciation expense. The auditor should keep in mind that the accelerated methods (e.g., double declining balance, sum-of-the-year's digits, ACRS) that may be permitted for tax purposes might not be appropriate for financial reporting purposes. This is a highly judgmental issue and the auditor should be alert for depreciation methods that do not fairly reflect economic reality. A consistent pattern of gains when assets are sold might be caused not only by assigning useful lives that are too short but also by using an accelerated method when the straight-line method better reflects economic reality.

A word of caution is in order here. A gain or loss on sale of an asset does not necessarily mean that the useful life or depreciation method used was wrong. But if all or most of the assets sold are resulting in large gains or losses—that is, there is a *consistent pattern*—then that should cause the auditor to challenge the reasonableness of the useful lives or depreciation methods.

The reasonableness of the depreciation calculations usually can be tested on an overall basis using analytical review. Analytical review usually is preferable to testing the individual calculations because it is difficult to test more than a very small percentage of the annual provision by testing depreciation expense for individual assets, and analytical review procedures can provide the auditor with persuasive evidence as to the reasonableness of the current year's depreciation. Figure 12–7 is an example of a reasonableness test using analytical review.

To evaluate the consistency of the client's depreciation methods, the auditor needs to know the depreciation methods and asset lives used in prior

FIGURE 12–7 Working Paper for Reasonableness Tests—Depreciation Expense

	Asset Balances			Useful	
	Beginning A	Ending A	Average B	Life C	Depr. D
Land Improvements	16560	16560	16560	(5)	3312
Buildings	413660	1253503	833581	(40)	20840
Machinery and Factory Equipment	371587	438119	404853	(10)	40485 (High)
				(15)	26990 (Low)
Office Equipment	59088	58416	58752	(5)	11750 (High)
				(10)	5875 (Low)
Automotive	25272 E	21594	23433	(3)	7811
				High	84198 F
	Actual	71874 A			
				Low	64828 F

A Obtained from the property, plant, and equipment summary working paper.

B Computed by averaging beginning and ending balances.

C Agreed to useful life guidelines established by corporate policy statements included in permanent file.

D Computed by dividing B by C.

E Reduced by $6,027 to reflect fully depreciated automobile.

F Represents summation of the high and low depreciation ranges.

Conclusion
Since actual balance falls within potential depreciation range, the amount appears reasonable.

Prepared MKa 8/3/XX

Depreciation Expense—Reasonableness Test
MNO Corporation
June 30, 19XX

years and how the client computes depreciation for assets in the year they are purchased and sold. Many companies provide one half of a year's depreciation on all assets acquired or disposed of during the year, while other companies provide a full year's depreciation in the year of acquisition and none in the year the asset is sold. These accounting procedures are only time-saving short cuts. If depreciation is materially different using the actual time the asset was in service, depreciation calculated using one of the shortcut methods would not be acceptable.

Testing for Items Improperly Charged to Expense

GAAP require that plant and equipment having useful lives of more than one year be capitalized and that their cost be charged to expense ratably over their estimated useful lives. In addition, companies often establish a lower dollar limit for capitalization. Acquisitions costing less than the established dollar amount are charged directly to expense. The dollar amount varies from company to company.

The practice of establishing a dollar limit for capitalizing additions is acceptable if the overall effect on the financial statements is not significant. For example, if a company has established a lower limit of $100 and has charged the cost of a new office chair costing $75 directly to expense, the auditor need not be concerned that this is a departure from GAAP even though the estimated useful life of the chair may be 10 years. However, these limits should not be followed routinely without applying common sense. For example, if the company above had acquired 100 new chairs, costing $75 each and charged the acquisition directly to expense, the auditor should propose that an adjustment be made to capitalize and depreciate the cost of the chairs.

To test whether plant and equipment acquisitions have been improperly charged to expense, the auditor reviews charges to repairs and maintenance and supplies accounts. Generally, only amounts in excess of the company's capitalization limit would be tested. In certain situations, the testing of repairs and maintenance will be limited to comparing the amount expensed to the prior year's repair and maintenance expenditures and the current year's budget.

Summarizing Property Transactions

The auditor normally obtains a summary of the beginning and ending balances in the asset and related allowance accounts and the intervening transactions from the client. This summary should be prepared showing beginning balances, additions to asset accounts, current provision for depreciation, disposals, and ending balances. An example of the format of a fixed asset summary is shown in Figure 12–8.

FIGURE 12–8 Property, Plant, and Equipment Summary Schedule

Client Name _____ Date _____
Prepared _Mar. 19XX_
Approved _____

Property, Plant and Equipment Summary
MNO Corporation
June 30, 19XX

Acct. No.	Account Name	COST					Acct. No.	ACCUMULATED DEPRECIATION				
		Opening Balance	Additions	Retirements	Other	Ending Balance		Opening Balance	Charges	Disposals	Other	Ending Balance
250	Land	5500 — T				5500 — TB						
251	Land Improvements	1651042 T				(651042) TB	451	91/1951 T	331212	✓		1250603 TB
252	Buildings	4/365476 T	209420 — ✓	631142522 2	120350817 TB	452	104116714 T	2073764 ✓			1249055 TB
253	Machinery	24/59946 T	734/549 ✓	2/4799a ɸ	3/362503 TB	453	13227405 T	2259700	2/4799a		5209313 TB
254	Factory Equipment	10997753 T	923744	6091621	24594445 TB	454	5155350 T	957897	6091621		55045426 TB
255	Office Equipment	5902930 T	923744	9196/22 ɸ	5094/6a4 TB	455	1101637 T	5181197	9961122		1225754 TB
256	Autos — T====	3/3791a T	892647	1513/54	2/53405 TB	456	1058046 T	1044650 ✓	1542207		542418 TB
257	Building Construction	55500/195 T	76421357	(63/42322) 2	—0— TB						
		1452647/3 F	33963742 F	—0— F	17936/3/6 c/f		32942646 F	7187350 F	53/4442 F	—0— F	34430/054 c/f

	Depreciation Liab. W.E. No.	
	4491	331212 TB
	4492	2073764 TB
	4493	2259700 TB
	4494	957897 TB
	5055	754456 TB
	5056	14/1997 TB
	5070	14/1936 TB
		5181197 TB
		7187350 F

F Footed.
‡ Crossfooted.
TB Agrees with trial balance.
T Traced to prior year's audit report.
✓ Traced to detailed analysis of this item in this file.
ɸ Traced to detailed analysis of this account in this file.
✓ Traced to reasonableness test performed on P.B-15.
2 Transferring cost of building of plant in service on January 1, 19X2.

If the company uses different depreciation methods for book and tax purposes, a summary of each should be obtained. A schedule showing the reconciliation between book and tax bases of the asset accounts, provision for depreciation, accumulated depreciation, and gains or losses on disposal also should be obtained or prepared and included in the working papers.

QUESTIONS AND PROBLEMS

12–1. Define inventories.

12–2. What is the objective of the audit of inventories?

12–3. What is the "cost" of inventories?

12–4. In determining inventory cost, what should be the objective in selecting among assumptions as to the flow of cost factors?

12–5. When is a departure from the cost basis of pricing inventory acceptable?

12–6. What should be observed by the auditor during the taking of an inventory?

12–7. What should be done with the auditor's test counts that were made and listed in the working papers during the physical inventory?

12–8. What is the purpose of testing the company's receiving and shipping cutoff procedures?

12–9. List the audit procedures an auditor can employ to determine whether slow-moving or obsolete items are included in the inventory.   (AICPA, adapted)

12–10. When a CPA has accepted an engagement from a new client who is a manufacturer, it is customary for the CPA to tour the client's plant facilities. Discuss the ways in which the CPA's observations made during the course of the plant tour would be of help in planning and conducting the audit.   (AICPA, adapted)

12–11. Describe the steps normally taken by the auditor to:
 a. Support additions to property, plant, and equipment.
 b. Test assets constructed by the company.
 c. Test a recorded disposal.
 d. Test provisions for depreciation.

12–12. List and briefly discuss the purpose of the audit procedures that might reasonably be taken by an auditor to determine that all property, plant, and equipment retirements have been recorded on the books.   (AICPA, adapted)

12–13. Select the *best* answer for each of the following items:
 a. In violation of company policy, the Jefferson City Company erroneously capitalized the cost of painting its warehouse. The CPA examining Jefferson City's financial statements most likely would learn of this by:
  (1) Reviewing the listing of construction work orders for the year.
  (2) Discussing capitalization policies with the company controller.

(3) Observing, during his physical inventory observation, that the warehouse had been painted.

(4) Examining in detail a sample of construction work orders.

b. Which of the following is a customary audit procedure for the verification of the legal ownership of real property?

(1) Examination of correspondence with the corporate counsel covering acquisition matters.

(2) Examination of ownership documents registered and on file at a public hall of records.

(3) Examination of corporate minutes and resolutions concerning approval to acquire property, plant, and equipment.

(4) Examination of deeds and title guaranty policies on hand.

c. Which of the following is the best audit procedure for the discovery of damaged merchandise in a client's ending inventory?

(1) Compare the physical quantities of slow-moving items with corresponding quantities of the prior year.

(2) Observe merchandise and raw materials during the client's physical inventory taking.

(3) Review the management's inventory representation letter for accuracy.

(4) Test overall fairness of inventory values by comparing the company's turnover ratio with the industry average.

d. When verifying debits to the perpetual inventory records of a nonmanufacturing company, an auditor would be most interested in examining a sample of purchase:

(1) Approvals.

(2) Requisitions.

(3) Invoices.

(4) Orders.

e. To best ascertain that a company has properly included merchandise that it owns in its ending inventory, the auditor should review and test the:

(1) Terms of the open purchase orders.

(2) Purchase cutoff procedures.

(3) Contractual commitments made by the purchasing department.

(4) Purchase invoices received on or around year end.

f. The primary objective of a CPA's observation of a client's physical inventory count is to:

(1) Discover whether a client has counted a particular inventory item or group of items.

(2) Obtain direct knowledge that the inventory exists and has been properly counted.

(3) Provide an appraisal of the quality of the merchandise on hand on the day of the physical count.

(4) Allow the auditor to supervise the conduct of the count so as to obtain assurance that inventory quantities are reasonably accurate.

g. An auditor usually will trace the details of the test counts made during the observation of the physical inventory taking to a final inventory schedule. This audit procedure is undertaken to provide evidence that items physically present and observed by the auditor at the time of the physical inventory count are:

(1) Owned by the client.

(2) Not obsolete.

(3) Physically present at the time of the preparation of the final inventory schedule.

(4) Included in the final inventory schedule. (AICPA, adapted)

12-14. To check a company's handling of the sales cutoff at the close of the fiscal year ended December 31, 19X1, you have compiled the data listed on the schedule on the next page. This includes all sales of significant amounts from December 27, 19X1, to January 4, 19X2, inclusive.

The company realized a gross profit of 40 percent on each sale, and all sales were recorded as of the invoice dates. The company's preliminary net sales and net profit for the year were $10,000,000 and $500,000, respectively. The company took its physical inventory on October 31, 19x1.

The item marked A represents the sale of a replacement test device which is included in one of the client's machines. The client asked its supplier to ship the device direct to the customer. The invoice totaling $3,900 from the supplier was accrued at December 31, 19x1.

The items marked B represent sales that were ready for shipment on the 31st, but the truck hired to deliver the equipment to the customers did not appear until January 3, 19x2. This was confirmed by our representative who was at the client's plant on December 31, 19x1. A review of last year's working papers revealed that the client excluded from sales items ready for shipment but not shipped by year-end.

The item marked C represents a delivery by a salesperson who neglected to turn in the paperwork until the following week.

Required:

Complete the schedule on the next page by showing the suggested adjustment, if any, for items A, B, and C.

12-15. While testing the clerical accuracy of Belcher Foundry's March 31 inventory, you noted the following matters which you plan to discuss with the accountant in charge.

1. You were unable to locate in the compiled inventory these items test-counted by our representative:

Tag No.	Quantity	Description	Dept.
0183	387 pcs.	Gear plates	39
0764	2,185 lbs.	Steel grit	52
0287	62 lbs.	Western bentonite	39
1347	500 pcs.	Fire brick	51
0891	8 lbs.	Plastic wood	52
0777	1,350 ft.	Leather fillet	52
0253	41 ea.	Disc sanders	39

2. Your footing of the compiled inventory is $27,000 more than the client's figure. (You have carefully checked your work.)

3. You found the following extension errors:

Description	Count Unit	Price	Extension as Recorded
Molybdenum	854 lbs.	$ 2.04/lb	174.22
Grinding wheel	21 ea.	59.60 ea.	1,215.60
Sandpaper	310 ea.	8.35/C.	2,588.50
Ferro chrome	4,500 lbs.	.1967/lb.	1,062.18

Sales Cutoff Test
ACS Company
12/31/X1

Name ____
Date ____
Prepared ____
Approved ____

Description	Billing Amount	Invoice Date	Shipping Date	Recorded in Proper Period Yes (A)	Adjustment Debit A/R (A)	Inventory Dr. (A)	Credit Sales A/R (A)
a	8,000	12/29/X1	12/29/X1				
b	9,000	12/30/X1	12/30/X1				
c (A)	5,000	12/29/X1	1/3/X2				
d	6,000	12/31/X1	12/31/X1				
e	7,000	12/31/X1	12/31/X1				
f	9,000	12/31/X1	1/3/X2				
g (B)	4,000	12/31/X1	1/3/X2				
h	5,000	12/31/X1	1/3/X2				
i	6,000	1/3/X2	1/4/X2				
j	5,000	1/4/X2	1/5/X2				
k	3,000	1/4/X2	1/5/X2				
l	6,000	1/5/X2	1/6/X2				
m (C)	2,000	1/6/X2	12/31/X1				

4. On a test basis, you compared the current year's unit prices with the previous year's and noted the following items:

Description	Quantity	Current Year's Cost	Previous Year's Cost
Steel scrap	3,300 lbs.	$ 65.50 N.T.	$67.80 G.T.
Pig iron	300 lbs.	8.00 N.T.	78.00 N.T.
73XTRB4	3 ea.	1,715.00 ea.	Unable to find in previous year's inventory
Kitchen sink	1 ea.	57.00 ea.	Unable to find in previous year's inventory

N.T.—Net ton.
G.T.—Gross ton.

Required:

Using the information presented:

a. Describe the probable causes of the errors in the above items.

b. Describe which clerical accuracy tests you think should be expanded (or employed) because of your findings.

c. List specific recommendations you would make for changes in the accounting system and procedures for this client to follow in observing and compiling next year's physical inventory if you believe any changes are desirable.

d. Based solely on the information in this problem, outline the points you would include in a "clerical accuracy tests" memorandum for the working papers.

12–16. Your audit client, Household Appliances, Inc. operates a retail store in the center of town. Because of lack of storage space Household keeps inventory that is not on display in a public warehouse outside of town. The warehouseman receives inventory from suppliers and, on request from your client by a shipping advice or telephone call, delivers merchandise to customers or to the retail outlet.

The accounts are maintained at the retail store by a bookkeeper. Each month the warehouseman sends to the bookkeeper a quantity report indicating opening balance, receipts, deliveries, and ending balance. The bookkeeper compares book quantities on hand at month end with the warehouseman's report and adjusts his books to agree with the report. No physical counts of the merchandise at the warehouse were made by your client during the year.

You are now preparing for your examination of the current year's financial statements in this recurring engagement. Last year you rendered an unqualified opinion.

Required:

a. Prepare an audit program for the observation of the physical inventory of Household Appliances, Inc. (1) at the retail outlet and (2) at the warehouse.

b. As part of your examination would you verify inventory quantities at the warehouse by means of:

(1) A warehouse confirmation? Why?

(2) Test counts of inventory at the warehouse? Why?

   c. Since the bookkeeper adjusts books to quantities shown on the warehouseman's report each month, what significance would you attach to the year-end adjustments if they were substantial? Discuss.

   d. Assume you are unable to satisfy yourself as to the inventory at the audit date of Household Appliances, Inc. Could you render an unqualified opinion? Why?

                           (AICPA)

12–17. On January 10, 1984, you were engaged to make an examination of the financial statements of Kahl Equipment Corporation for the year ended December 31, 1983. Kahl has sold trucks and truck parts and accessories for many years, but has never had an audit. Kahl maintains good perpetual records for all inventories and takes a complete physical inventory each December 31.

   The Parts Inventory account includes the $2,500 cost of obsolete parts. Kahl's executives acknowledge these parts have been worthless for several years but they have continued to carry the cost as an asset. The amount of $2,500 is material in relation to 1983 net income and year-end inventories but not material in relation to total assets or capital at December 31, 1983.

Required:

   a. List the procedures you would add to your inventory audit program for new trucks because you did not observe the physical inventory taken by the corporation as of December 31, 1983.

   b. Should the $2,500 of obsolete parts be carried in inventory as an asset? Discuss.

                         (AICPA, adapted)

12–18. Ace Corporation does not conduct a complete annual physical count of purchased parts and supplies in its principal warehouse but uses statistical sampling instead to estimate the year-end inventory. Ace maintains a perpetual inventory record of parts and supplies and believes that statistical sampling is highly effective in determining inventory values and is sufficiently reliable to make a physical count of each item of inventory unnecessary.

Required:

   a. Identify the audit procedures that should be used by the independent auditor that change or are in addition to normal required audit procedures when a client utilizes statistical sampling to determine inventory value and does not conduct a 100 percent annual physical count of inventory items.

   b. List at least 10 normal audit procedures that should be performed to verify physical quantities whenever a client conducts a periodic physical count of all or part of its inventory.   (AICPA)

12–19. One of your clients, Bonded Warehousing Company, recently incorporated a subsidiary company to field warehouse petroleum products at a nearby industrial area. The parent company has engaged in terminal warehousing of lubricating oils and greases for a nearby petroleum refinery for some time. The refinery attempted to borrow against its light oil inventory but could do so only through a field warehousing arrangement. Bonded Warehousing was asked to field warehouse gasoline and diesel fuel for the refinery. The subsidiary leased the refinery's tank farm and undertook the field warehousing activity. The tank farm, which has adequate capacity for the refinery's output, has fifty tanks containing meters, alternate gauging openings, and protection devices such as valve locks. There are also burglar and fire alarms, and fire fighting equipment. Only nonnegotiable warehouse receipts are issued.

The subsidiary employs only a stock record clerk, who keeps perpetual inventory records and issues warehouse receipts, and four yardmen, who do all loading and unloading of the tanks and take inventories. The parent company's home office receives all cash, writes all checks, and maintains all the records for the subsidiary company for a small monthly fee, and the home office internal control for these is excellent.

Required:

List the features which you believe would be desirable in a system of internal control over inventories for the subsidiary.

Classify these controls in the following categories:

a. Controls at the field warehouse over receipts and releases of goods.
b. Other inventory controls at the field warehouse.
c. Specific controls which should be exercised by the home office after subsidiary operations are commenced.
d. Other related organizational or administrative matters which should be considered by the home office on or before the date subsidiary operations are begun.
(AICPA)

12–20. Late in December 1985 your CPA firm accepted an audit engagement at Rich Jewelers, Inc., a corporation that deals largely in diamonds. The corporation has retail jewelry stores in several Eastern cities and a diamond wholesale store in New York City. The wholesale store also sets the diamonds in rings and in other quality jewelry.

The retail stores place orders for diamond jewelry with the wholesale store in New York City. A buyer employed by the wholesale store purchases diamonds in the New York diamond market, and the wholesale store then fills orders from the retail stores and from independent customers and maintains a substantial inventory of diamonds. The corporation values its inventory by the specific identification cost method.

Required:

Assume that at the inventory date you are satisfied that Rich Jewelers, Inc., has no items left by customers for repair or sale on consignment and that no inventory owned by the corporation is in the possession of outsiders.

a. Discuss the problems the auditor should anticipate in planning for the observation of the physical inventory on this engagement because of the:
  (1) Difficult locations of inventories.
  (2) Nature of the inventory.
b. (1) Explain how your audit program for this inventory would be different from that used for most other inventories.
  (2) Prepare an audit program for the verification of the corporation's diamond and diamond jewelry inventories, identifying any steps which you would apply only to the retail stores or to the wholesale store.
c. Assume that a shipment of diamond rings was in transit by corporate messenger from the wholesale store to a retail store on the inventory date. What additional audit steps would you take to satisfy yourself as to the gems that were in transit from the wholesale store on the inventory date? (AICPA, adapted)

12–21. Often an important aspect of a CPA's examination of financial statements is the observation of the taking of the physical inventory.

Required:

a. What are the general objectives or purposes of the CPA's observation of the taking of the physical inventory? (Do not discuss the procedures or techniques involved in making the observation.)

b. For what purposes does the CPA make and record test counts of inventory quantities during the observation of the taking of the physical inventory? Discuss.

c. A number of companies employ outside service companies that specialize in counting, pricing, extending, and footing inventories. These service companies usually furnish a certificate attesting to the value of the inventory. Assuming that the service company took the inventory on the balance sheet date:

(1) How much reliance, if any, can the CPA place on the inventory certificate of outside specialists? Discuss.

(2) What effect, if any, would the inventory certificate of outside specialists have upon the type of report the CPA would render? Discuss.

(3) What reference, if any, would the CPA make to the certificate of outside specialists in the audit report? (AICPA, adapted)

12–22. The processing operations of Smith Company, your client, require a basic raw material, colgum, which is imported and refined by several domestic suppliers. Colgum is combined with other raw materials of the same general category to produce the finished product. Smith Company has been disturbed by the unreliability of the supply because of the international situation and labor troubles of the suppliers and has stockpiled a large supply of colgum to assure continued operations. This supply of colgum is a substantial portion of Smith's inventory and you determine that it is a three-year supply. Colgum is a staple commodity widely used in manufacturing operations. Smith has consistently applied the lower-of-cost-or-market rule to the valuation of its total inventory. The year-end market price of colgum is less than Smith's cost.

Required:

a. What effect, if any, would this excess supply have upon the financial statements and your report? Discuss briefly.

b. What effect, if any, would this excess supply have upon the application of the rule of "cost or market, whichever is lower" to the valuation of individual items as against category totals in the total inventory? Discuss briefly.

(AICPA, adapted)

12–23. Coil steel comprises one half of the inventory of the Metal Fabricating Company. At the beginning of the year the company installed a system to control coil steel inventory.

The coil steel is stored within the plant in a special storage area. When coils are received, a two-part tag is prepared. The tag is prenumbered and each part provides for entry of supplier's name, receiving report number, date received, coil weight, and description. Both parts of the tag are prepared at the time the material is received and weighed and the receiving report prepared. The "A" part of the tag is attached to the coil and the "B" part of the tag is sent to the stock records department with the receiving report. The stock records department files the tags numerically by coil width and gauge. The stock records department also maintains perpetual stock cards on each width and gauge by total weight; in a sense, the cards are a control record for the tags. No material requisitions are used by the plant, but as coils are placed into production, the "A" part of the tag is removed from the coil and sent to stock records as support of the production report which is the basis of entries on the perpetual inventory cards.

When the "A" part of the tag is received by the stock records department, it is matched with the "B" part of the tag and the "A" part is destroyed. The "B" part is stamped with the date of use, processed, and retained in a consumed file by width and gauge. The coils are neatly stacked and arranged and all tags are visible.

The balance of the inventory is examined by standard procedures and you are satisfied that it is fairly stated. Physical inventories are taken on a cycle basis throughout the year. About one twelfth of the coil steel inventories are taken each month. The coil steel control account and the perpetual stock cards are adjusted as counts are made. Internal control of inventories is good in all respects.

In previous years, the client had taken a complete physical inventory of coil steel at the end of the year (the client's fiscal year ends December 31) but none is to be taken this year. You are engaged for the current audit in September. You audited the financial statements last year.

Required:

Assuming that you decide to undertake some preliminary audit work before December 31, prepare audit programs for:

a. The verification of coil steel quantities previously inventoried during the current year.

b. Observation of physical inventories to be taken in subsequent months.

(AICPA, adapted)

12–24. In connection with his examination of the financial statements of Knutson Products Company, an assembler of home appliances for the year ended May 31, 1985, Ray Abel, CPA, is reviewing with Knutson's controller the plans for a physical inventory at the company warehouse on May 31, 1985.

Note: In answering the two parts of this question do not discuss procedures for the physical inventory of work in process, inventory pricing, or other audit steps not directly related to the physical inventory taking.

1. Finished appliances, unassembled parts and supplies are stored in the warehouse, which is attached to Knutson's assembly plant. The plant will operate during the count. On May 30, the warehouse will deliver to the plant the estimated quantities of unassembled parts and supplies required for May 31 production, but there may be emergency requisitions on May 31. During the count, the warehouse will continue to receive parts and supplies and to ship finished appliances. However, the appliances completed on May 31 will be held in the plant until after the physical inventory.

2. Warehouse employees will join with accounting department employees in counting the inventory. The inventory takers will use a tag system.

Required:

   a. What procedures should the company establish to ensure that the inventory count includes all items that should be included and that nothing is counted twice?

   b. What instructions should the company give to the inventory takers?

(AICPA, adapted)

12–25. Line-Rite Manufacturing Company, Inc., is a moderate-sized company manufacturing equipment for use in laying pipelines. The company has prospered in the past, gradually expanding to its present size. Recognizing a need to develop new products if its growth is to continue, the company created an engineering research and development section. During 1986, at a cost of $70,000, this section designed, patented, and successfully tested a new machine which greatly accelerates the laying of small-sized lines.

In order to adequately finance the manufacture, promotion, and sale of this new product, it has become necessary to expand the company's plant and to enlarge inventories. Required financing to accomplish this has resulted in the company engaging you in April 1986 to examine its financial statements as of September 30, 1986, the end of the current fiscal year. This is the company's initial audit.

In the course of your preliminary audit work, you obtain the following information:

1. The nature of the inventory and related manufacturing processes do not lend themselves well to taking a complete physical inventory at year-end or at any other given date. The company has an inventory team that counts all inventory items on a cycle basis throughout the year. Perpetual inventory records, maintained by the accounting department, are adjusted to reflect the quantities on hand as determined by these counts. At year-end, an inventory summary is prepared from the perpetual inventory records. The quantities in this summary are subsequently valued in developing the final inventory balances.

2. The company carries a substantial parts inventory that is used to service equipment sold to customers. Certain parts are also used in current production. The company considers any part to be obsolete only if it shows no usage or sales activity for two consecutive years. A reserve of $10,000 exists at present for parts in this category. Your tests indicate that obsolescence in inventories might approximate $50,000.

As part of your audit you must deal with each of the foregoing matters.

Required:

   a. With respect to inventories, define the overall problem involved in this first audit.

   b. Outline a program for testing inventory quantities.

   c. Enumerate and discuss the principal problems involved in inventory obsolescence for the company assuming the amount involved was significant with respect to the company's financial position. (AICPA, adapted)

12–26. A processor of frozen foods carries an inventory of finished products consisting of 50 different types of items valued at approximately $2,000,000. About $750,000 of this value represents stock produced by the company and billed to customers prior to the audit date. This stock is being held for the customers at a monthly rental charge until they request shipment and is not separated from the company's inventory.

The company maintains separate perpetual ledgers at the plant office for both stock owned and stock being held for customers. The cost department also maintains a perpetual record of stock owned. The above perpetual records reflect quantities only.

The company does not take a complete physical inventory at any time during the year since the temperature in the cold storage facilities is too low to allow one to spend more than 15 minutes inside at a time. It is not considered practical to move items outside or to defreeze the cold storage facilities for the purpose of taking a physical inventory. Due to these circumstances, it is impractical to test count quantities to the extent of completely verifying specific items. The company considers as its inventory valuation at year-end the aggregate of the quantities reflected by the perpetual record of stock owned, maintained at the plant office, and priced at the lower of cost or market.

Required:

a. What are the two principal problems facing the auditor in the audit of the inventory? Discuss briefly.

b. Outline the audit steps that you would take to enable you to render an unqualified opinion with respect to the inventory. (You may omit consideration of a verification of unit prices and clerical accuracy.) (AICPA)

12–27. The accounting and internal control procedures relating to purchases of materials by the Branden Company, a medium-sized concern manufacturing special machinery to order, have been described by your junior accountant in the following terms:

After approval by manufacturing department foremen, material purchase requisitions are forwarded to the purchasing department supervisor who distributes such requisitions to the several employees under his control. The latter employees prepare prenumbered purchase orders in triplicate, account for all numbers, and send the original purchase order to the vendor. One copy of the purchase order is sent to the receiving department where it is used as a receiving report. The other copy is filed in the purchasing department.

When the materials are received, they are moved directly to the storeroom and issued to the foremen on informal requests. The receiving department sends a receiving report (with its copy of the purchase order attached) to the purchasing department and sends copies of the receiving report to the storeroom and to the accounting department.

Vendors' invoices for material purchases, received in duplicate in the mail room, are sent to the purchasing department and directed to the employee who placed the related order. The employee then compares the invoice with the copy of the purchase order on file in the purchasing department for price and terms and compares the invoice quantity with the quantity received as reported by the shipping and receiving department on its copy of the purchase order. The purchasing department employee also checks discounts, footings, and extensions, and initials the invoice to indicate approval for payment. The invoice is then sent to the voucher section of the accounting department where it is coded for account distribution, assigned a voucher number, entered in the voucher register, and filed according to payment due date.

On payment dates, prenumbered checks are requisitioned by the voucher section from the cashier and prepared except for signature. After the checks are prepared they are returned to the cashier, who puts them through a check signing machine, accounts for the sequence of numbers, and passes them to the cash disbursement bookkeeper for entry in the cash disbursements books. The cash disbursements book-keeper then returns the checks to the voucher section which then notes payment dates in the voucher register, places the checks in envelopes, and sends them to the mail room. The vouchers are then filed in numerical sequence. At the end of each month, one of the voucher clerks prepares an adding machine tape of unpaid items in the voucher register and compares the total thereof with the general ledger balance and investigates any difference disclosed by such comparison.

Required:

Discuss the weaknesses, if any, in the internal control of Branden's purchasing and subsequent procedures, and suggest supplementary or revised procedures for remedying each weakness with regard to:

a. Requisition of materials.
b. Receipt and storage of materials.
c. Functions of the purchasing department.
d. Functions of the accounting department.   (AICPA)

12-28. You are working on an audit in which the audit program calls for supporting all property additions over $100,000 through August 31. In executing this audit step, you examined the following section of the property ledgers for project 830–10. This project is part of the expansion of the productive capacity of the company's Custom Power division.

Project 830–10

LAND

Date	Explanation	Ref.	Debit	Credit	Balance
2/1	Purchase for cash	CD	$200,000		$200,000
3/1	Purchase for cash	CD	55,000		255,000

BUILDINGS

Date	Explanation	Ref.	Debit	Credit	Balance
2/1	Purchase for cash	CD	$800,000		$ 800,000
3/1	Purchase for cash	CD	45,000		845,000
4/1	Building razed	GJ		$45,000	800,000
8/31	Transfer from construction in progress	GJ	500,000		1,300,000

Further examination of the records and inquiries of the executives of the corporation result in the following factual determinations:

As of February 1, land and a building located near the Custom Power division's current plant were purchased for cash of $1 million. The building was about 10 years old and was deemed to have a remaining useful life of 25 years. The aggregate purchase price was allocated $200,000 to land and $800,000 to building by the management.

On March 1, property adjoining this plant site was acquired for a purchase price of $100,000. There was a building in good condition on the property. Based on the relationship of assessed valuations for local property tax purposes, the purchase price was allocated $55,000 to land and $45,000 to building. Since the company could not use the building economically, it was demolished on April 1 at a cost of $5,000, which was charged to operating expenses. The $45,000 allocated cost of the building was charged to operations.

During the period from April 1 to August 28, the company's maintenance department constructed a building on the newly acquired property at a cost of $500,000. The monthly cost of $25,000 for direct labor and $75,000 for materials was paid on the first day following each of the five months of construction (first payment was made on May 1). The maintenance department has an overhead rate of 40 percent of direct labor dollars. The building was placed in service on August 30.

On February 1, the company borrowed $400,000 at 12 percent annual interest to finance this construction. Interest earned on these funds until they were used totaled $10,000.

The building was appraised at $650,000 for insurance purposes. Assume that the company has no other debt.

Required:

a. Describe the types of audit evidence that could be examined to determine that:
   (1) The company holds unencumbered title to the properties.
   (2) The properties are stated on the basis of cost.
   (3) The properties are properly classified.
b. Prepare any adjusting journal entries which you would propose as of December 31. Explain the basis for each of the entries and show your computations.
c. The supervisor of property accounting mentioned to you that he believes that the company has been too conservative in capitalizing only the direct costs of the building constructed by company employees and believes that the building cost should be recorded at $650,000, the amount of the lowest bid received from outside contractors. How would you respond?

12–29. A manufacturing company whose records you are auditing has $1 million of Buildings and $3 million of Machinery on its books. During the year you are covering in your audit, additions amounted to $100,000 for Buildings and $500,000 for Machinery. All additions were made through construction orders controlled by a Construction Work in Progress account, which had a balance of $20,000 at the close of last year and $55,000 at the close of this year. Some of the additions were purchased and a number were constructed by the company. You are to state in detail the audit procedures you would follow in verification of the fixed asset additions during the year. Assume that your firm also performed the audit for the prior year.

(AICPA, adapted)

12–30. Terra Land Development Corporation is a closely held family corporation engaged in the business of purchasing large tracts of land, subdividing the tracts, and installing paved streets and utilities. The corporation does not construct buildings for the buyers of the land and does not have any affiliated construction companies. Undeveloped land is usually leased for farming until the corporation is ready to begin developing it.

The corporation finances its land acquisitions by mortgages; the mortgagees require audited financial statements. This is your first audit of the company and you have now begun the examination of the financial statements for the year ended December 31, 1984.

Your preliminary review of the accounts has indicated that the corporation would have had a highly profitable year except that the president and vice president, his son, were reimbursed for exceptionally large travel and entertainment expenses.

Required:

The corporation has three tracts of land in various stages of development. List the audit procedures to be employed in the verification of the physical existence and title to the corporation's three landholdings. (AICPA, adapted)

12–31. In connection with a recurring examination of the financial statements of the Louis Manufacturing Company for the year ended December 31, 1984, you have been assigned the audit of the Manufacturing Equipment, Manufacturing Equipment—Accumulated Depreciation, and Repairs to Manufacturing Equipment accounts. Your review of Louis's policies and procedures has disclosed the following pertinent information:

1. The Manufacturing Equipment account includes the net invoice price plus related freight and installation costs for all of the equipment in Louis's manufacturing plant.

2. The Manufacturing Equipment and Manufacturing Equipment—Accumulated Depreciation accounts are supported by a subsidiary ledger which shows the cost and accumulated depreciation for each piece of equipment.

3. An annual budget for capital expenditures of $1,000 or more is prepared by the budget committee and approved by the board of directors. Capital expenditures over $1,000 which are not included in this budget must be approved by the board of directors and variations of 20 percent or more must be explained to the board. Approval by the supervisor of production is required for capital expenditures under $1,000.

4. Company employees handle installation, removal, repair, and rebuilding of the machinery. Work orders are prepared for these activities and are subject to the same budgetary control as other expenditures. Work orders are not required for external expenditures.

Required:

a. Cite the major objectives of your audit of the Manufacturing Equipment, Manufacturing Equipment—Accumulated Depreciation, and Repairs to Manufacturing Equipment accounts. Do not include in this listing the auditing procedures designed to accomplish these objectives.

b. Prepare the portion of your audit program applicable to the review of 1984 additions to the Manufacturing Equipment account. (AICPA, adapted)

12–32. While auditing an urban bus company in a city with a population of 50,000, you encounter the following situation:

a. You have checked an authorization for the purchase of five engines to replace the engines in five buses.

b. The cost of the old engines was removed from property and that of the new engines properly capitalized. The work was done in the company garage.

c. You find no credits for salvage or for the sale of any scrap metal at any time during the year. You have been in the garage and did not see the old engines.

d. The accountant is also treasurer and office manager. He is an authorized check signer and has access to all cash receipts. Upon inquiry, he says he does not recall the sale of the old engines nor of any scrap metal.

Required:

Assuming that the engines were sold as scrap, outline all steps that this fact would cause you to take in connection with your audit. Also mention steps beyond those related directly to this one item. (AICPA, adapted)

12–33. The Irving Manufacturing Company uses a system of shop orders in its plant. This system includes a series of orders for construction and installation of fixed assets, another series for retirement of assets, and a third series for maintenance work. There are "standing order" numbers for minor repetitive maintenance items and special orders for unusual or major maintenance items.

In connection with a regular annual audit of the Irving Manufacturing Company, prepare a program for work to be done on the maintenance orders. Assume that there appears to be reasonable internal control in the company. Prepare the program to avoid doing any more work than is necessary to meet acceptable auditing standards and explain the purpose or objective of each of your proposed steps.

(AICPA, adapted)

12–34. In the audit of fixed assets an auditor has several problems. For example, the auditor must be satisfied that all of the owned assets are recorded. Also, the auditor must be satisfied that the amounts at which the assets are recorded are in accordance with generally accepted accounting principles.

In connection with the annual audit of the fixed assets of a medium-sized manufacturing company, state the general procedures by which the auditor can be satisfied (a) that all of the owned assets are recorded, and (b) that the recorded amounts are proper. Briefly explain how each procedure will help to satisfy the auditor and to which of the two problems it is applicable. Do not include depreciation provisions as a part of these problems. (AICPA, adapted)

AUDITING THE FINANCE COMPONENT

The specific control objectives for the finance component are listed in Figure 13–1 (page 420). The finance component deals with the management of a company's financial resources. As you can see in Figure 13–2 (page 421), the audit areas associated with this component are cash balances, investments and related income, debt and related accrued interest and interest expense, and shareholders' equity. The audit procedures relating to specific control objectives F–2 and F–3 are integrated with the procedures performed in the sales and production or service components, respectively. They have been excluded from Figure 13–2 and are not addressed in this chapter.

The interrelationship of the finance-related specific control objectives to financial statement classifications is illustrated in Figure 13–3 (page 422). The finance component impacts most accounts in the financial statements. However, not all of the procedures discussed in this chapter are performed on each audit. The procedures to be performed on each audit are determined based upon the three inputs to the risk analysis and the assessment of the likelihood of material error documented on the risk analysis working papers.

CASH BALANCES

The tests of cash balances (both cash on hand and cash on deposit) are designed to assure that the amount reported as cash in the financial statements fairly represents the amount of cash that is available to the company for disbursement, investment, and other purposes. Since cash is very susceptible to misappropriation, the auditor should be alert for indications that the cash balance is not under the client's control. Although the detection of fraud is not the auditor's primary objective, care should be exercised in all phases of the examination.

13

Cash on Deposit

Cash on deposit includes demand deposits and time deposits. Time deposits normally represent investments of cash not needed to meet daily operating needs and usually will be stated separately in the balance sheet, either as current or noncurrent assets depending on the nature and intended holding period of the investments. The audit procedures designed to test time deposits normally will include confirmation of the balances through direct correspondence with banks and, if the activity during the year is significant, a review and test of related transactions (including interest earned).

Demand deposits (checking accounts) usually comprise the major portion of a company's cash balance. Most of the audit procedures employed during the examination of cash are designed to test demand deposit account balances. These procedures include (1) preparation and mailing of bank confirmation requests and requests for cutoff bank statements, (2) use of bank confirmations and cutoff statements received, (3) testing client bank reconciliations, and (4) testing transfers between different bank accounts.

Preparation and Mailing of Requests for Bank Confirmations and Cutoff Bank Statements.   The bank confirmation inquiry (Figure 13–4, page 423), generally is mailed to all banks with which the company had deposits or loans during the current year. The information regarding which banks should be requested to confirm deposits or loans can be obtained through a review of prior years' working papers, inquiry of company personnel, and a review of the company's general ledger trial balance. Requests sometimes are mailed even if the deposit account was closed or if the loan was paid off during the year in order to confirm that the company has no undisclosed remaining obligations with the bank. If practicable, the confirmation requests should be mailed to the banks a few days before the balance sheet date.

The information supplied by the client on the request (items circled in Figure 13–4) include the:

1. Bank name and address.
2. Date as of which the information is requested.
3. Account name and number (according to the bank records).
4. Authorized signature (usually an authorized check signer).

To assure that the requests are not altered by the client prior to mailing, bank confirmation requests should be mailed by the auditor. The requests, along with the auditor's self-addressed reply envelope, should be mailed in an envelope bearing the auditor's return address. A record of confirmation inquires mailed should be maintained. If the auditor has not received a response within a reasonable period of time, the client should be asked to call the bank or the auditor should send a second request, whichever is the most expedient and appropriate method for getting a response.

A cutoff bank statement is a bank statement showing transactions for a specified number of days following the normal bank statement date. The period to be covered by the cutoff statement should be stated in the audit program. The information that the client includes in a request for a cutoff bank statement should include:

1. A brief description of the reason for the cutoff statement.
2. The specific period for which the statement is to be prepared.
3. Instructions for the bank to mail the statement directly to the auditor.
4. A description and identifying number of the bank account.

FIGURE 13-1 Finance Operating Component Specific Control Objectives

Reference No.	
F-1	Cash receipts are recorded correctly as to account, amount, and period and are deposited
F-2	Cash receipts are properly applied to customer balances
F-3	Cash disbursements are for goods or services authorized and received
F-4	Cash disbursements are recorded correctly as to account, amount, and period
F-5	Debt and lease obligations and related expenses are authorized and recorded correctly as to account, amount, and period
F-6	Equity transactions are authorized and recorded correctly as to account, amount, and period
F-7	Investments in and advances to/from subsidiaries and other affiliates are authorized and recorded correctly as to account, amount, and period
F-8	Investment transactions are authorized and recorded correctly as to account, amount, and period
F-9	Income earned on investments is recorded correctly as to account, amount, and period
F-10	Loss in value of investments is promptly detected and provided for
F-11	Physical loss of investments is prevented or promptly detected

FIGURE 13-2 Specific Control Objectives by Audit Area—Finance Component

---

Cash balances:

F–1   Cash receipts are recorded correctly as to account, amount, and period and are deposited

F–4   Cash disbursements are recorded correctly as to account, amount, and period

Investments, including intercompany accounts, and related income:

F–7   Investments in and advances to/from subsidiaries and other affiliates are authorized and recorded correctly as to account, amount, and period

F–8   Investment transactions are authorized and recorded correctly as to account, amount, and period

F–9   Income earned on investments is recorded correctly as to account, amount, and period

F–10 Loss in value of investments is promptly detected and provided for

F–11 Physical loss of investments is prevented or promptly detected

Long- and short-term debt and related accrued interest and expense:

F–5   Debt and lease obligations and related expenses are authorized and recorded correctly as to account, amount, and period

Shareholders' equity:

F–6   Equity transactions are authorized and recorded correctly as to account, amount, and period

---

5. The signature of an official of the company authorized to make such a request.

Figure 13–5 (page 424) is an example of such a request.

Use of Bank Confirmations and Cutoff Statements. Bank confirmations and cutoff statements are used in testing the accuracy and completeness of the client's bank reconciliations. The information on the bank confirmation also is used to test notes payable and long-term debt balances and to confirm related information about collateral, payment terms, and interest rates that is needed for financial statement disclosure. In addition, the confirmation includes information about contingent liabilities of the client as endorser of notes discounted or as a guarantor of other loans, letters of credit, etc. The auditor should note the disposition of all information listed on the confirmation; for example, confirmed balances should be traced to bank reconciliations and loan balances should be cross-referenced to long-term debt working papers. Indications of contingent liabilities should be considered for financial statement disclosure.

Immediately upon receipt of the bank confirmation, the auditor should review it for completeness. If the confirmation is not complete, the auditor should ask the client to call the bank and request an amended copy of the confirmation. Occasionally, the amount reported by the bank on the confirmation does not agree with the amount shown on the bank statement.

FIGURE 13–3   Relationship of Specific Control Objectives to Financial Statement Classifications—Finance Component

Balance Sheet

	Control Objectives	
	Debit	*Credit*
Current assets:		
Cash	F–1, F–5, F–6, F–8, F–9	F–3, F–4, F–8
Accounts receivable		F–1, F–2
Allowance for doubtful accounts		
Inventories		
Prepaid expenses and other assets		
Other assets:		
Notes receivable	F–4	F–1, F–2
Investments	F–8	F–8, F–10, F–11
Goodwill and other intangibles	F–7	
Intercompany accounts	F–7	F–7
Deposits and other assets		
Property, plant, and equipment:		
Land		
Buildings		
Machinery and equipment		
Allowances for depreciation		
Current liabilities:		
Notes payable	F–4	F–5
Trade accounts payable and accrued liabilities	F–3, F–4	
Accrued payroll and related liabilities	F–4	
Taxes other than taxes on income	F–4	
Accrued interest	F–4	F–5
Income taxes	F–4	
Long-term debt	F–4	F–5
Deferred income taxes		
Shareholders' equity:		
Preferred stock		F–6
Common stock		F–6
Additional paid-in capital		F–6
Retained earnings	F–6	F–6
Commitments and contingencies		

Income Statement

	Control Objectives	
	Debit	*Credit*
Sales		
Cost of sales		
Selling, general, and administrative expenses	F–5	
Provision for income taxes		
Other	F–8, F–10, F–11	F–1, F–8, F–9

FIGURE 13–4 Standard Bank Confirmation Inquiry

BANK CONFIRMATION INQUIRY

DUPLICATE
To be mailed to accountant

Your completion of the following information report will be appreciated. If the space provided is inadequate, please enter totals hereon and attach a statement giving full details as called for by the columnar headings identified below. **If the answer to any item is "none," please so indicate.** Please sign this request in the space provided below and return the duplicate copy in the enclosed reply envelope direct to Ernst & Whinney, 153 East 53rd Street, New York, New York 10022 .

To: Sixth National Bank
5763 Perry Place
Matawan NY 14003

Powertronics, Inc.
Account Name Per Bank Records
Aldo Count
Authorized Signature

1. At the close of business of December 31 19 85 our records showed the following balance(s) to the *credit* of the above named customer. In the event that we could readily ascertain whether there were any balances to the credit of the customer not designated in this request, the appropriate information is given below.

Amount	Account Name	Account Number	Subject to With-drawal by Check?	Interest Bearing? Give Rate
$ 244,962.19	General	1068-423	Yes	No
1,425.92	Salary	5741-076	Yes	No
2,541.64	Hourly	5741-075	Yes	No

2. Notes, securities, or accounts receivables, etc., held by us for collection as of the close of business on that date were_____
   None   .

3. The customer was directly liable to us in respect of loans, acceptances, etc., at the close of business on that date in the total amount of $589,256.23 as follows:

Amount	Date of Loan or Discount	Due Date	Interest Rate	Interest Paid To	Description of Liability, Collateral, Security Interests, Liens, Endorsers, Etc.
$ 161,813.22	1/1/81	1/1/89	7.6%	6/30/85	Office Building
425,443.01	9/1/80	9/1/90	8.0%	8/31/85	Main Plant

4. The customer was contingently liable as endorser of notes discounted and/or as guarantor at the close of business on that date in the total amount of $_____, as below:

Amount	Name of Maker	Date of Note	Due Date	Remarks
$	None			

5. Other direct or contingent liabilities, open letters of credit, and related collateral, were_____
   None

6. Security agreements under the Uniform Commercial Code, financing statements, or any other agreements providing for restrictions, not noted above, were as follows (if officially recorded, indicate date and office in which filed):_____
   None

Sixth National Bank of Matawan   Henry Farsdail   1/15/86
Bank   Authorized Signature   Date
A-4   VP - Corporate Accounts

If the bank is in error, the auditor should obtain a corrected written confirmation from the bank.

If the cutoff statement received covers a period shorter than that requested, consideration should be given to obtaining an additional cutoff statement from the bank. Also, if the bank cutoff statement has been received by the client rather than the auditor, the following additional audit procedures are required: (1) compare the beginning balance on the cutoff bank statement to the amount shown on the bank confirmation, (2) examine the cancellation

FIGURE 13-5   Request for Cutoff Bank Statements

REQUEST FOR CUTOFF BANK STATEMENT

Our auditors, Ernst & Whinney, are making an examination of our financial statements and wish to obtain a detailed statement of our account(s) shown below with your bank, including cancelled checks and advices, for the period from <u>January 1, 1985</u> to the close of business on <u>January 12, 1985</u>. Please forward this data direct to Ernst & Whinney, <u>153 East 53rd Street, New York, New York 10022</u>

Account Name(s) <u>General   Salary   Hourly</u>
Account Number(s) <u>1068-423 57141-076 5741-075</u>

Powertronics, Inc.
Company Aldo Corent

To: <u>Sixth National Bank</u>
<u>5763 Perry Place</u>
<u>Matawan, NY 14003</u>

Authorized Signature
Treasurer   Jan. 3, 1985
Title   Date

---

dates on all checks to determine if the checks have been canceled in the period covered by the cutoff statement and that the dates on the checks agree with the dates of the disbursements in the cash disbursements records, and (3) foot the checks and reconcile the total with the total charges on the bank statement. (The auditor also may decide to compare individual checks with the entries on the bank statement and the cash book.)

Testing Bank Reconciliations. Testing a company's bank reconciliation involves several audit procedures. Generally, the auditor will perform some or all of the following:

1. Test the clerical accuracy of the client-prepared reconciliation and outstanding check list. (Copies of the reconciliations should be included in the working papers.)
2. Trace the bank balance on the reconciliation to the bank confirmation.
3. Trace book balances to the general ledger or trial balance.
4. Support deposits in transit by performing two separate procedures: (1) trace the deposit amount to entries in the cash receipts records prior to the date of the cash reconciliation, and (2) trace the deposit amount to the cutoff bank statement. Any unusual delay between the time the deposit was recorded on the books and the date it cleared the bank should be investigated. If the deposit in transit represents a bank transfer (discussed later), cross-reference the amount to the bank transfer schedule and to the outstanding check list of the transferring bank account.
5. Support outstanding checks by reference to checks returned with the cutoff bank statement. The auditor should examine the cancellation date

and issuance date on the check to determine that it was properly classified as outstanding. Also, the checks returned in the cutoff bank statement should be reviewed to determine whether the checks issued prior to the account reconciliation date were properly included on the outstanding check list.

6. Prepare a list of any large or unusual outstanding checks. Examples include checks drawn payable to cash, officers, employees (other than regular payroll checks), and affiliates. The auditor should review the list to determine whether any additional audit procedures should be performed, such as examining supporting documentation for the disbursements.

7. Examine invoices, vouchers, or other supporting documentation for large checks not returned with the cutoff bank statement. If a large number of outstanding checks are not returned with the cutoff statement, the auditor may wish to request an additional cutoff statement directly from the bank.

8. Prepare a list of checks that have been outstanding for an unusual length of time (e.g., three months or more). The auditor should review the list to determine whether any additional audit procedures should be performed—such as contacting the payee to ascertain why the check was not cashed or examining the documentation supporting the disbursement.

9. Examine supporting documentation for any other significant reconciling items, such as unrecorded credit or debit advices.

The primary objective of the procedures outlined above is to determine that the stated cash balance is correct. However, several of the procedures also may detect irregularities if they exist. Defalcations often are concealed through manipulation of the outstanding check list. This can be accomplished by omitting checks from the list, changing amounts on the list, or simply understating the total through incorrect footing. The auditor should keep these possible manipulations in mind when testing outstanding checks. Also, any transactions noted in inactive accounts should be investigated, since balances in inactive accounts may be convenient sources of theft or unauthorized borrowing by personnel having access to those accounts.

Proof of Cash.   On many engagements, a proof of cash may be prepared for a period to determine that cash receipts and disbursements are recorded correctly. An example of a proof of cash is shown in Figures 13–6A and 13–6B. The proof of cash includes bank reconciliations as of the beginning and end of the applicable period. The activity occurring during that period also is scheduled. This activity consists of credits to the cash account per the bank, charges to the account per the bank, cash receipts per the company's books, and cash disbursements per the company's books. Any differences

FIGURE 13–6A Proof of Cash

	Client	Name	Date
	Prepared	*Goode* 12/11/X1	
	Approved	_____	___ ___

October Proof of Cash – First Nat'l Bank
Regular Acct
RST, Inc.
12/31/X1

1 of 2

	Beginning Bank Reconciliation 9/30/X1	Receipts	Disbursements	Ending Bank Reconciliation 10/31/X1
Per bank statement	65,117.60 A	1,421,117.68 A	1,565,570.54 A	506,723.14 A
Deposits in transit:				
Beginning deposited 10/1/X1 T booked 9/30/X1 B	23,714.04 T/B	(23,714.04) T/B		
Ending		X -0-		X -0-
Outstanding checks:				
Beginning	(211,584.83) ✓		(211,584.83) ✓	
Ending			210,207.78 ✓	(210,207.78) ✓
Other reconciling items:				
NSF check charged 10/15/X1, redeposited 11/2/X1			(2,073.61) ∅	2,073.61 ∅
Per books	463,305.21	1,397,403.64	1,563,119.88	297,588.97
	F GL	F C	F D	F&CF GL

F&CF Footed and crossfooted.
A Per bank statement.
T Examined bank statement noting date and amount.
B Examined cash receipts journal noting date and amount.
✓ Traced to outstanding check list (Figure 13-6B)
∅ Examined NSF advice and duplicate deposit ticket dated 11/2/X1.
C Traced to October cash receipts journal.
D Traced to October cash disbursements journal.
GL Traced to general ledger.

FIGURE 13–6B Proof of Cash

Client	Name	Date	
Prepared	Goode	12/11/X1	
Approved			

October Proof of Cash – First Nat'l Bank
Regular account
PST, Inc.
12/31/X1

2 of 2

Outstanding Check Lists

September 30, 19X1

Payee	Check Number	Description of Purchase	Amount
HWA Corporation	14578 ✓	Office Furniture	1856901 ✓
	14585 T		74233 T
ABC Incorporated	14609 ✓	Aluminum Casting	4462189 ✓
Department of Water	14610 ✓	Utilities	188989 ✓
	14611 ✓		27925 ✓
	14612 ✓		6274 ✓
Custom Incorporated	14613 ✓	High Speed Press	14485505 ✓
			Ⓐ
			21158483
			F

October 31, 19X1

Payee	Check Number	Description of Purchase	Amount
	14585 ⁊		74253 ⁊
AXZ Realty	15233 ⁊	Land Purchase 50 acres	15500000 ⁊
	15234 ⁊		28900 ⁊
ABC Incorporated	15235 ⁊	Aluminum Casting	4982010 ⁊
	15236 ⁊		25000 ⁊
	15237 ⁊		72500 ⁊
CTX Leasing	15238 ⁊	Company Cars	256040 ⁊
	15240 ⁊		34615 ⁊
	15241 ⁊		47480 ⁊
			Ⓐ
			21020978
			F

F Footed.
✓ Examined cancelled check noting number, payee,
   amount, and that dated prior to 10/1/X1 and paid
   subsequent to 9/30/X1.
T Traced to 10/31/X1 outstanding checklist.
⁊ Examined cancelled check noting number, payee,
   amount, and that dated prior to 11/1/X1 and paid
   subsequent to 10/30/X1.
Ⓐ Traced to proof of cash [Figure 13-6A]

between the credits and charges per the bank and per the company's books are reconciled.

The reconciliation of the cash receipts and disbursements per the bank's records and the company's records for the period covered by the proof of cash sets the proof of cash apart from a regular bank reconciliation. Bank credits and charges are supported with bank statements. The company's cash receipts and disbursements should be traced to the books of original entry (e.g., cash receipts and cash disbursements journals). Any reconciling items between book and bank receipts and disbursements also usually appear as reconciling items in the beginning or ending bank reconciliations and are therefore audited when the bank reconciliations are audited.

Bank Transfers.   When the company maintains more than a single bank account, a schedule of bank transfers (Figure 13–7) generally is prepared. This schedule is used to detect "kiting" (recording the transfer as a deposit in the receiving bank prior to recording the disbursement in the paying bank) and to help ascertain whether cash balances are properly stated. The transfer schedule should include all transfers of funds between bank accounts for several business days before and after the balance sheet date. When testing the bank transfer schedule, there are two factors the auditor should be alert for. First, the book disbursement and bank deposit should be recorded in the same period. If the recorded dates are not in the same period, an understatement or overstatement of cash has occurred. For example:

Situation	Amount	Disbursed per Books	Deposited per Books
A	$1,000	12/30	1/2
B	$1,000	1/3	12/30

In situation A, the client's books would be understated by $1,000 because a disbursement was recorded without recording the corresponding deposit. In situation B, cash would be overstated. The second item to be alert for is that if the dates of the bank charge for the disbursement and the credit for the deposit occur in different periods, the check or deposit should be a reconciling item on the appropriate bank reconciliation. For example:

Situation	Disbursement Book Date	Disbursement Bank Date	Deposit Book Date	Deposit Bank Date
A	12/31	1/5	12/31	1/2
B	12/29	1/3	12/29	12/30

FIGURE 13-7 Schedule of Bank Transfers

Client Name Date
Prepared Allen 1/21/X2
Approved

Year-End Bank Transfers
RST, Inc.
12/31/X1

Payor	Check #	Amount	Date Paid per Books	Date Paid per Bank	Payee	Date Deposited per Books	Date Deposited per Bank
First Nat'l Bank—reg. acct.	51085	46096.54	4 12/21	12/22 z	1st National Payroll	4 12/21	12/21 z
" " " " "	51086	90000.00	4 12/21	12/22 z	2nd " "	4 12/21	12/21 z
" " " " "	51210	47243.24	4 12/28	12/29 z	1st " "	4 12/28	12/28 z
" " " " "	51211	35000.00	4 12/28	✓ 1/2/1 z	2nd " "	4 12/28	12/29 z
" " " " "	52690	49204.11	4 1/4	1/5 z	1st " "	4 1/4	1/4 z
" " " " "	52783	75000.00	4 1/5	1/8 z	2nd " "	4 1/5	1/5 z
" " " " "	52910	47303.10	4 1/11	1/12 z	1st " "	4 1/11	1/11 z

4 Agrees with date paid or deposited, as appropriate, per the books
z Agrees with date per the appropriate bank statement
✓ Traced to 12/31/X1 outstanding check list—agrees

Note:
I reviewed the company's cash disbursement records and bank statements covering the period 12/20–1/13. All bank transfers noted during this review appear properly scheduled by the client.

Conclusion:
Based upon the procedures performed, it is my opinion that the client has properly recorded its bank transfers during the period of 12/20–1/13.

In situation A, both the disbursement and deposit are reconciling items. Given these facts, the auditor should find the amount as an outstanding check in the disbursing bank account reconciliation and a deposit in transit in the depository bank account reconciliation. Situation B reflects the fact that a check cleared the depository bank before the disbursing bank. In this case, only the disbursement should appear as a reconciling item.

The evidence examined in auditing a bank transfer schedule consists mainly of tracing the dates the transfers were reflected in the company's and bank's records to the company's cash receipts and cash disbursements journals and to the appropriate bank statement. In situations where a transfer is recorded in different periods, the auditor should determine that the transfer has been properly included on the outstanding check list or as a deposit in transit on the respective bank reconciliations.

General Considerations. The auditor should review cash transactions for a few days prior to the balance sheet date and from that date to the completion of the field work, noting any significant unusual items. Payments to or from officers or affiliates, a temporary reduction in notes payable, evidence of new financing, delays in deposits of cash in transit, large receipts from sources other than trade receivables, or payments to vendors other than recognized suppliers are all items that ordinarily should be investigated. These items could indicate subsequent events that should be disclosed in the financial statements, unrecorded liabilities, or possible manipulation of cash.

Cash on Hand

Cash on hand includes petty cash funds, change funds, and undeposited receipts. The audit procedures relating to cash on hand may be performed at year-end or during an interim examination, depending on the circumstances of the engagement.

Cash Count Procedures. Most imprest and change funds are small and will take only a few minutes to count. On many engagements, these funds will not be counted; the auditor should do so only if called for by the audit program. In certain businesses, such as department stores or banks, these funds often amount to many thousands of dollars. In such cases, it is sometimes sufficient to account for all the bundles of currency and wrapped coin and count the contents of only a representative number of bundles.

Figure 13–8 is an example of a form that may be used by the auditor in making a cash count. The details of other cash items should be listed on the form and tested at a later date. Other common cash items are checks for deposit, advances, undistributed disbursements, and bad checks.

After completing the cash count, the auditor should obtain a receipt *signed in ink* from the employee to whom the fund is returned. The actual amount

FIGURE 13–8 Cash Count

	Name	Date
Approved *Williams*		10-29-X1

CASH COUNT **PETTY CASH**
(Name of Fund)

CLIENT **RST, INC.** AUDIT DATE **12-31-X1**

COUNTED BY **Greg Allen** DATE **10-15-X1** TIME **8:30 A.M.**

	QUANTITY	AMOUNT	TOTAL
CURRENCY			
Fifties			
Twenties	20	400 00	
Tens	20	200 00	
Fives	27	135 00	
Twos			
Ones	115	115 00	850 00
COIN			
Dollars			
Halves	12	6 00	
Quarters	44	11 00	
Dimes	22	2 20	
Nickels	51	2 55	
Pennies	75	75	22 50
WRAPPED COIN	$10.00		

Checks for Deposit	list attached	*K.C. Carr 10-13-X1 payable to RST Inc.*	125 00
Cash Items	" "		
Advances	" "		
Undistributed Disbursements	" "		
Bad Checks	" "		
Other	" "	*Stamps*	1 40
		TOTAL	998 90

Above listed cash and cash items in the amount of *Nine hundred ninety-eight and* $^{90}/_{100}$ —— Dollars

($ **998.90**) were returned to me after count by a representative of Ernst & Whinney. All cash and cash items for which

I am accountable to **RST INC.**

have been presented for inspection and count.

10-15-X1	*G. F. Drew*
Date	Signature of Custodian

(THIS RECEIPT MUST BE PREPARED IN INK)

BAL. PER FUND	$ 1,000.00
✓ PER COUNT	998.90
	1.10 NOT ADJUSTED

A-5 PRINTED IN U.S.A.

of the fund should be indicated on the receipt. This receipt serves as acknowledgment of the return of the fund.

When differences between the actual count and the recorded amount are noted, the auditor should include a full explanation of the differences in the working papers. The auditor should discuss these differences with appropriate client personnel. Any unusual items in the fund, such as the custodian's checks, old personal checks, or officers' checks, also should be discussed with the appropriate company personnel. A memorandum of the discussion should be included in the working papers.

Undeposited Receipts. Undeposited cash receipts consist of checks and currency. Cash on hand usually is significant in businesses that deal routinely with cash, such as banks and department stores. When undeposited receipts are significant, they should be counted at an interim date or on the balance sheet date and traced to the bank statement for the following period to determine that the checks cleared the bank and are appropriately classified as cash.

General. Cash counts always should be made in the presence of the fund custodian. The custodian should observe the count. If the employee is called away before the count is completed, the auditor should return the cash to the employee immediately.

NOTES RECEIVABLE

A note receivable is a written contractual arrangement that should include an unconditional promise to pay a certain sum of money under terms clearly specified in the contract. Most notes are negotiable, which makes them transferable (i.e., they can be sold, assigned, discounted, or pledged as collateral), and notes usually are interest bearing. Notes are distinguishable from regular trade accounts in that the latter typically are covered by informal contracts (which are supported by invoices and shipping documents), are not interest bearing, and have shorter terms (e.g., 30 days).

Notes often are used as a credit instrument when:

1. The goods sold have a high unit value and the buyer wants an extended payment term.
2. Loans are made by banks or finance companies.
3. Trade customers in troubled financial condition request extended terms.
4. Property, plant, and equipment or a segment of the business is sold.

Audit Procedures

The auditor normally obtains or prepares a schedule of notes, acceptances and other instruments evidencing indebtedness to the client. The schedule should include the name of the debtor, interest rate, date of note, date due, payment terms, beginning note balance, additions, payments, and ending note balance. Also, the schedule should show the related interest income and receivable for each note including the beginning interest receivable, additions, interest income for the period, and ending interest receivable. In addition, the schedule should describe any collateral and notes discounted, assigned with recourse, or otherwise pledged.

As with any audit procedures, the nature, timing, and extent of audit procedures performed on notes receivable should be established in the audit program. The audit procedures that the auditor might perform include:

1. *Confirmation.*   Notes may be confirmed as of an interim date or year-end. If the confirmation date is other than year-end, the auditor should review the transactions in the intervening period. The confirmation request should include the note principal balance, interest rate, and collateral, if any. Alternative procedures should be performed on those notes for which no reply is received.
2. *Inspection.*   Notes may be inspected to determine whether the client has sold (assigned) any to another party. For example, assume the client sold a note to a third party without notifying the debtor. The sale would not necessarily be detected by confirmation procedures, because the debtor may not be aware of the sale.
3. *Collectibility.*   The auditor should review the notes receivable schedule to determine whether the debtors are meeting the payment terms. If a debtor has not met the payment terms, the auditor should inquire about the collectibility of the balance outstanding.
4. *Clerical accuracy and analytical review.*   These procedures might include recalculating the accrued interest receivable or unearned interest receivable. Analytical review procedures can be used instead of detail tests to test interest income and accrued or unearned interest receivable.

MARKETABLE SECURITIES AND RELATED INCOME

Marketable securities include both short-term and long-term investments. *Short-term investments* include all securities that have a ready market and that management intends to convert to cash within a short period of time. They are held as a temporary investment of excess funds and generally are classified as a current asset. *Long-term investments* are held for either long-term capital appreciation or to influence or control another company and are classified as a noncurrent asset.

The auditor's objective in examining securities owned by the company is to be satisfied that they are fairly presented on the balance sheet and that any related income also is fairly stated. Specifically, the auditor should determine whether the securities are in the company's possession or held by others for the account of the company, that they are owned by the company, and that the basis at which they are carried and income is recognized conforms with generally accepted accounting principles applied on a consistent basis.

Audit Procedures

If investments are held by a third party, they generally are confirmed directly with the third party. If held by the client, they are physically examined and counted by the auditor. As with any audit procedure, the nature, timing, and extent of the procedure is established in the audit program. However, investments may be confirmed as of an interim date or year-end, but any counting of investments usually is performed at or near year-end. If the date of the count is other than the balance sheet date, the auditor should account for transactions in the intervening period. However, if the securities are in a safe deposit box, a letter from the safe deposit company attesting to nonentry to the box during the interim period may eliminate the need to account for intervening transactions.

Many of the cash count procedures discussed earlier apply to securities counts. The physical examination and count of securities always should be made in the presence of an authorized client representative. After the count is completed, the auditor should obtain a signed receipt, *in ink,* from the client representative. The receipt should indicate that all securities were returned to the client intact. If securities are held in more than one location, arrangements generally are made to count securities at all locations at the same time. This avoids the possibility of securities being transferred from one location to another in an attempt to cover up theft or unauthorized use or to overstate securities held.

When making a physical examination of securities, the auditor should note that:

1. Stock certificates and registered bonds are made out in the name of the client.
2. The number of shares, face amount of bonds, certificate numbers, description, interest rates, and maturity dates agree with the information on the listing of securities obtained from the client.
3. All coupons for coupon bonds have been clipped to the date of the securities count, and coupons have not been clipped in advance of maturity dates.

When investments are held by others for the account of the client, the holder of the securities should be requested to supply the auditor with the following information:

1. Name of issuer.
2. Description of security.

3. Certificate number or bond number.
4. Number of shares or face amount of bonds.
5. Date through which interest (e.g., on bonds) has been paid.

As with other confirmation requests, the request for confirmation of securities should include instructions to mail the reply directly to the auditor. The auditor should mail the request.

The auditor should compare the information obtained from the confirmation of securities to the information on a listing of securities obtained from the client. Differences noted should be investigated. In making this comparison, the auditor should take special care to ascertain that the certificate numbers on the listing agree with those noted during the physical examination or listed on the confirmation. Differences in the certificate numbers may mean that there have been unauthorized or unrecorded securities transactions during that year in which common stock or bonds were sold and later replaced with certificates of the same issuer.

Once the auditor has ascertained that the securities listed on the schedule are under the control of the client, the auditor should test the cost of the investments and the realized gain or loss on sales made during the year. In doing this, the auditor generally will:

1. Obtain a listing from the client of all securities transactions made during the year. The listing should show a detailed description of the securities purchased or sold, cost, sales price, and realized gain or loss on sale.
2. For securities owned at the balance sheet date, support the carrying amount by (a) reference to prior year working papers for those securities acquired in prior years and (b) examination of brokers' advices for securities acquired during the current period under audit. When examining brokers' advices, the auditor should note the description of the security, name of the issuer, certificate number, number of shares or face amount, and cost.
3. Support other transactions made during the year as shown on the client's listing by reference to brokers' advices.
4. Test the computation of realized gain or loss and trace the total to the trial balance. Note whether cost used in computing the gain or loss is determined using the first-in first-out method, specific certificate method, or average cost method. Also note whether the method used is consistent with that used in prior years. Remittance advices may be examined to support the proceeds from the sale of investments. However, if the auditor has previously established reliance on the cash receipts system, the auditor can trace the proceeds to the cash receipts records.
5. By reference to the prior year's working papers, ascertain that all securities owned at the beginning of the year have been accounted for either as sales during the year (included on the schedule of transactions entered into during the year) or as owned at the balance sheet date.

The examination of marketable securities also should include tests of dividend and interest income and accrued interest receivable. In performing the tests of investment income received and receivable, the auditor may:

1. Review the reasonableness of interest income through the use of an estimated average interest rate applied to the average balance of investments. This procedure may provide sufficient evidence to make detail tests of interest income (e.g., steps 3, 4, and 5 below) unnecessary.
2. Test dividends received by reference to dividend reports included in Standard and Poor's, Moody's, or other financial publications and by reference to the client's cash receipts records. The auditor should ascertain whether all dividends declared on stocks owned have been received. Differences should be investigated.
3. Test interest received by tracing the amounts to the cash receipts records.
4. Test the computation of accrued interest receivable.
5. Compare the level of investment income and rate of return with prior periods.
6. Compare the total accrued interest receivable with prior periods.

Reporting Requirements

When performing the audit of securities, the auditor should be sure that all information needed for financial statement disclosure is included in the working papers. This information includes a summary of marketable equity securities (cost and market) by current and noncurrent asset classification and a summary of realized and unrealized gains and losses by current and noncurrent classification.

Market value at the balance sheet date and as of the date of the auditor's report should be tested by reference to market quotations included in periodicals such as *The Wall Street Journal,* or the National Association of Securities Dealers Automatic Quotations System (NASDAQ quotations), or by requesting from a broker confirmation of market prices on securities not regularly quoted.

DEBT AND LEASE OBLIGATIONS AND RELATED EXPENSE

The objective in this audit area is to determine that (1) the amount of indebtedness at the balance sheet date is fairly stated, (2) the accrual of interest thereon is fairly stated, (3) all of the provisions of the indenture or other agreement have been met, and (4) adequate disclosure is made in the financial statements. As in many other audit areas, confirmation procedures are performed to substantiate the balances. Long- and short-term debt may be confirmed using either a bank confirmation inquiry or developing a confirmation tailored to the auditor's specific situation. In many cases, the auditor only needs to update the prior year's confirmation request and give it to the client to be typed on their stationery and signed by an appropriate company official. Information commonly requested from a lender includes the unpaid principal balance as of the confirmation date, interest rate, terms for repayment, date through which interest has been paid, any collateral, and the nature of any defaults.

Once the confirmation requests have been typed and signed by the client, the auditor should maintain control over them until mailing. The procedures to control these requests are the same as those discussed previously. Attempts should be made to mail this correspondence several days prior to the confirmation date. If responses are not received within a reasonable period of time (e.g., two weeks), second requests should be mailed.

A separate request need not be sent to a bank that is already receiving a bank confirmation inquiry through the cash balances audit procedures, since the bank should confirm the existence of the debt on that confirmation. A reference to the appropriate cash balance audit working papers should be made in these situations.

The client should provide the auditor with a schedule of long-term and short-term debt. This schedule might include the following information: (1) name of the debt, (2) interest rate, (3) unpaid balance, (4) current and long-term portions, (5) date through which interest was paid, (6) interest expense, and (7) related accrued interest payable.

The schedule should be tested for clerical accuracy and the total debt outstanding should be traced to the general ledger or trial balance. The appropriate information on the schedule should agree with the information included on the responses to confirmation requests. Any differences noted should be investigated. Other audit procedures related to debt and lease obligations include:

1. Test changes in long-term debt during the period by examining supporting documents.
2. Read the bond indentures or other agreements noting the principal provisions affecting the financial statements (particularly such features as sinking fund or redemption requirements), requirements as to current or other asset amounts and/or related ratios, dividend or surplus restrictions, pledge of assets and deposits of proceeds from disposition thereof, and insurance requirements. The auditor must determine if such requirements or restrictions have been met. Copies of all agreements normally are included in the permanent file working papers.
3. Inspect bonds redeemed, retired, or surrendered during the period, including those held by the company in the treasury. Obtain confirmation of bonds retired or held by the trustee in sinking funds or other funds.
4. Determine the amount of long-term debt maturing within one year.

Determine the amount, if any, that is required to be paid into sinking funds or other funds within one year.

5. Test the computation of interest expense for the period including the amortization of any premium or discount and test the accrued interest at the end of the period.
6. Classify indebtedness as to secured and unsecured obligations and as to type or classification—such as to banks, affiliates, officers, and stockholders.
7. Review the classification of leases as either capital or operating.

There are several nonroutine transactions and events that can affect a company's debt structure. Several of these transactions have been addressed by the Accounting Principles Board and the Financial Accounting Standards Board and have resulted in the following pronouncements:

1. *APB Opinion No. 26*, "Early Extinguishment of Debt."
2. *FASB Statement No. 4*, "Reporting Gains and Losses from Extinguishment of Debt."
3. *FASB Statement No. 6*, "Classification of Short-Term Obligations Expected to be Refinanced."
4. *FASB Statement No. 15*, "Accounting by Debtors and Creditors for Troubled Debt Restructurings."
5. *FASB Statement No. 47*, "Disclosure of Long-Term Obligations."
6. *FASB Statement No. 64*, "Extinguishments of Debt Made to Satisfy Sinking Fund Requirements."
7. *FASB Interpretation No. 8*, "Classification of a Short-Term Obligation Repaid Prior to Being Replaced by a Long-term Security."
8. *FASB Statement No. 76*, "Extinguishment of Debt."
9. *FASB Statement No. 78*, "Classification of Obligations that are Callable by the Creditor."

An in-depth discussion of these areas is beyond the scope of this book. However, the auditor should recognize circumstances when these pronouncements are applicable and be able to research the accounting and auditing requirements for a specific situation.

SHAREHOLDERS' EQUITY

A company's equity includes its capital stock (common and preferred), paid-in capital, and retained earnings. The most common transactions impacting equity are issuance of stock, exercise of stock options, a company's acquisition of its own stock, donated capital, cash dividends, stock dividends, and income or loss for the period. In auditing shareholders' equity, the auditor should determine the (1) propriety of the charges and credits to the accounts, (2) propriety of the presentation of the accounts on the balance sheet, and (3) company's compliance with legal requirements.

Trace to Board meetings (handwritten margin note)

Analyses of the various equity accounts for the year generally are obtained from the client, including the changes in the number of shares outstanding and the number of shares held in treasury. The analyses are tested for clerical accuracy, the beginning balances are agreed with the prior year's working papers, and the ending balances are agreed with the trial balance.

If the company uses an independent registrar or transfer agent, a confirmation usually is sent to them. The type of information confirmed includes the number of shares of the various classes of stock authorized, issued and outstanding; the number of shares held in treasury; the amount of cash dividends paid; and the stock dividends issued.

The transactions included on the analyses of the equity accounts generally are supported as follows:

1. Any stock issuances, repurchases, retirements, dividends, or options are traced to authorization by the board of directors or other committee.
2. Information confirmed by the transfer agent or registrar is agreed with the working papers.
3. The recorded amount of dividends paid is tested by multiplying the number of shares outstanding times the amount of the cash dividend paid or the percentage stock dividend issued.
4. When a stock dividend is issued, the amount of equity capitalized from retained earnings is tested by multiplying the number of shares distributed times the market value of the stock.
5. If the company does not have a registrar or transfer agent, the number of shares outstanding is reconciled with stock certificate stubs and certificates representing unissued, retired, or treasury shares. If the auditor examines any certificates, including treasury stock, the auditor should obtain a signed receipt, *in ink,* from the custodian of the certificates, for the return of any certificates examined and counted. A listing of all certificates examined, which contains the number of shares and their certificate numbers, should be prepared. The total number of certificates issued, purchased and retired during the year should be added to the balance of shares outstanding at the beginning of the year, and the result should agree with the year-end balance.
6. Review canceled stock certificates to determine that they have been defaced in a manner that prevents reuse.
7. If a company pays its own dividends directly to its shareholders, cancelled dividend checks may be examined for agreement with the company's records.

QUESTIONS AND PROBLEMS

13–1. What is included in cash on deposit?

13–2. To which banks should an auditor mail bank confirmation inquiries?

13–3. What information should be included on a bank confirmation inquiry?

13–4. What information should be included on a request for a cutoff bank statement?

13–5. For what purposes is a bank confirmation used on an audit?

13–6. What is included in cash on hand?

13–7. What are short-term marketable securities?

13–8. When making a physical examination of securities what should be noted?

13–9. If investments are held by others for the account of a client, what information should the auditor request of the holder?

13–10. What procedures may an auditor use to test investment income received and receivable?

13–11. What is the auditor's objective in auditing long-term and short-term debt and the related accrued interest and expense?

13–12. Select the best answer for each of the following items:
  a. On the last day of the fiscal year, the cash disbursements clerk drew a company check on bank A and deposited the check in the company account in bank B to cover a previous theft of cash. The disbursement has not been recorded. The auditor will best detect this form of kiting by:
    (1) Comparing the detail of cash receipts as shown by the cash receipts records with the detail on the confirmed duplicate deposit tickets for three days prior to and subsequent to year-end.
    (2) Preparing from the cash disbursements book a summary of bank transfers for one week prior to and subsequent to year-end.
    (3) Examining the composition of deposits in both banks A and B subsequent to year-end.
    (4) Examining paid checks returned with the bank statement of the next accounting period after year-end.
  b. The cashier of Safir Company covered a shortage in the cash working fund with cash obtained on December 31 from a local bank by cashing, but not recording, a check drawn on the company's out-of-town bank. How would the auditor discover this manipulation?
    (1) Confirming all December 31 bank balances.
    (2) Counting the cash working fund at the close of business of December 31.
    (3) Preparing independent bank reconciliations as of December 31.
    (4) Investigating items returned with the bank cutoff statements.
  c. During the course of an audit, a CPA observes that the recorded interest expense seems to be excessive in relation to the balance in the long-term debt account. This observation could lead the auditor to suspect that:
    (1) Long-term debt is understated.
    (2) Discount on bonds payable is overstated.
    (3) Long-term debt is overstated.
    (4) Premium on bonds payable is understated.
  d. The auditor's program for the examination of long-term debt should include steps that require the:

(1) Verification of the existence of the bondholders.

(2) Examination of any bond trust indenture.

(3) Inspection of the accounts payable subsidiary ledger.

(4) Investigation of credits to the bond interest income account.

e. If a company employs a capital stock registrar and/or transfer agent, the registrar or agent, or both, should be requested to confirm directly to the auditor the number of shares of each class of stock:

(1) Surrendered and canceled during the year.

(2) Authorized at the balance sheet date.

(3) Issued and outstanding at the balance sheet date. *diff T. stock*

(4) Authorized, issued, and outstanding during the year.

f. An audit program for the examination of the retained earnings account should include a step that requires verification of the:

(1) Gain or loss resulting from disposition of treasury shares.

(2) Market value used to charge retained earnings to account for a two-for-one stock split.

(3) Authorization for both cash and stock dividends.

(4) Approval of the adjustment to the beginning balance as a result of a write-down of an account receivable. (AICPA, adapted)

13–13. XYZ operates sales divisions in several cities throughout the country. In addition to other activities, the sales divisions are responsible for the collection of local receivables; each division maintains a bank account in which all collections are deposited intact. Twice a week these collections are transferred to the home office by check; no other checks are drawn on this bank account. Except for cash receipts and cash disbursements journals, no accounting records are kept at the sales offices, but all cash records are retained by them in their files.

As part of your year-end audit you wish to include an audit of cash transfers between the sales divisions and the main office. It is intended that your representative will visit all locations.

Required:

a. What are the purposes of the audit of cash transfers?

b. Assuming that your representative has a full knowledge of audit procedures for regular cash collection that he will perform at each location, design only such additional specific audit steps as he will be required to perform to audit the cash transfers from each sales division to home office. (AICPA)

13–14. When you arrive at your client's office on January 11, 1986, to begin the December 31, 1985, audit, you discover the client had been drawing checks as creditors invoices became due but not necessarily mailing them. Because of a working capital shortage, some checks may have been held for two or three weeks.

The client informs you that unmailed checks totaling $27,600 were on hand at December 31, 1985. He states these December-dated checks had been entered in the cash disbursements book and charged to the respective creditors' accounts in December because the checks were prenumbered. Heavy collections permitted him to mail the checks before your arrival.

The client wants to adjust the cash balance and accounts payable at December 31 by $27,600 because the cash account had a credit balance. He objects to submitting to his bank your audit report showing an overdraft of cash.

Required:

a. Submit a detailed audit program indicating the procedures you would use to satisfy yourself of the accuracy of the cash balance on the client's statements.

b. Discuss the propriety of reversing the indicated amount of outstanding checks.

(AICPA, adapted)

13–15. The Patrick Company had poor internal control over its cash transactions. Facts concerning its cash position at November 30, 1985, were as follows:

The cash books showed a balance of $18,901.62, which included undeposited receipts. A credit of $100 on the bank's records did not appear on the books of the company. The balance per bank statement was $15,550. Outstanding checks were: No. 62 for $116.25, No. 183 for $150.00, No. 284 for $253.25, No. 8621 for $190.71, No. 8623 for $206.80, and No. 8632 for $145.28.

The cashier misappropriated all undeposited receipts in excess of $3,794.41 and prepared the following reconciliation:

Balance per books, November 30, 1985		$18,901.62
Add: Outstanding checks:		
8621	$190.71	
8623	206.80	
8632	145.28	442.79
		$19,344.41
Less: Undeposited receipts		3,794.41
Balance per bank, November 30, 1985		$15,550.00
Deduct: Unrecorded credit		100.00
True cash, November 30, 1985		$15,450.00

Required:

a. Prepare a supporting schedule showing how much the cashier misappropriated.

b. How did he attempt to conceal his theft?

c. Taking only the information given, name two specific features of internal control that apparently were missing.

d. If the cashier's October 31 reconciliation is known to be in order and you start your audit on December 5, 1984, what specific auditing procedures would uncover the theft? (AICPA, adapted)

13–16. In connection with your audit of the ABC Company at December 31, 1985, you were given a bank reconciliation by a company employee which shows:

Balance per bank	$15,267
Deposits in transit	18,928
	$34,195
Checks outstanding	21,378
Balance per books	$12,817

As part of your verification you obtain the bank statement and canceled checks from the bank on January 15, 1986. Checks issued from January 1 to January 15, 1986, per the books were $11,241. Checks returned by the bank on January 15th amounted to $29,219. Of the checks outstanding December 31st, $4,800 were not returned by the bank with the January 15th statement, and of those issued per the books in January 1986, $3,600 were not returned.

a. Prepare a schedule showing the above data in proper form.

b. Suggest four possible explanations for the condition existing here and state what your action would be in each case, including any necessary journal entry.

(AICPA, adapted)

13–17. Mr. William Green recently acquired the controlling financial interest of Importers and Wholesalers, Inc., importers and distributors of cutlery. In his review of the duties of employees, Mr. Green became aware of loose practices in the signing of checks and the operation of the petty cash fund.

You have been engaged as the company's CPA and Mr. Green's first request is that you suggest a system of sound practices for the signing of checks and the operation of the petty cash fund. Mr. Green prefers not to acquire a check-signing machine.

In addition to Mr. Green, who is the company president, the company has 20 employees including four corporate officers. About 200 checks are drawn each month. The petty cash fund has a working balance of about $200 and about $500 is expended from the fund each month.

Required:

Prepare a letter to Mr. Green containing your recommendations for good internal control procedures for:

a. Signing checks. (Mr. Green is unwilling to be drawn into routine check signing duties. Assume that you decided to recommend two signatures on each check.)

b. Operation of the petty cash fund. (Where the effect of the control procedure is not evident, give the reason for the procedure.) (AICPA, adapted)

13–18. A surprise count of the Y Company's imprest petty cash fund, carried on the books at $5,000, was made on November 10, 1985.

The company acts as agent for an express company in the issuance and sale of money orders. Blank money orders are held by the cashier for issuance upon payment of the designated amounts by employees. Settlement with the express company is made weekly with its representative who calls at the Y Company office. At that time he collects for orders issued, accounts for unissued orders, and leaves additional blank money orders serially numbered.

The count of the items presented by the cashier as composing the fund was as follows:

Currency (bills and coin)		$2,200
Cashed checks		500
Vouchers (made out in pencil and signed by recipient)		740
NSF checks (dated June 10 and 15, 1985)		260
Copy of petty cash receipt vouchers:		
Return of expense advance	$200	
Sale of money orders (#C1015–1021)	100	300
Blank money orders—claimed to have been purchased for $100 each from		
the Express Company (#C1022–1027)		600

At the time of the count there was also on hand the following:

Unissued money orders #C1028–1037.

Unclaimed wage envelopes (sealed and amounts not shown).

The following day the custodian of the fund produced vouchers aggregating $400 and explained that these vouchers had been temporarily misplaced the previous day. They were for wage advances to employees.

a. Show the proper composition of the fund at November 10, 1985.
b. State the audit procedures necessary for the verification of the items in the fund. (AICPA, adapted)

13–19. In connection with an audit you are given the following work sheet:

Bank Reconciliation
December 31, 1985

Balance per ledger, December 31, 1985		$17,174.86
Add:		
Collection received on the last day of December and charged to "cash in bank" on books but not deposited		2,662.25
Debit memo for customer's check returned unpaid (check is on hand but no entry has been made on the books)		200.00
Debit memo for bank service charge for December		5.50
		$20,142.61
Deduct:		
Checks drawn but not paid by bank (see detailed list below)	$2,267.75	
Credit memo for proceeds of a note receivable that had been left at the bank for collection but has not been recorded as collected	400.00	
Check for an account payable entered on books as $240.90 but drawn and paid by bank as $419	178.10	2,945.85
Computed balance		$17,196.76
Unlocated difference		200.00
Balance per bank (checked to confirmation)		$16,996.76

Checks Drawn but Not Paid
by Bank

No.	Amount
573	$ 67.27
724	9.90
903	456.67
907	305.50
911	482.75
913	550.00
914	366.76
916	10.00
917	218.90
	$2,267.75

Required:

a. Prepare a corrected reconciliation.
b. Prepare journal entries for items that should be adjusted prior to closing the books. (AICPA, adapted)

13–20. One audit procedure that can be used to detect "kiting" at year-end is the reconciliation of all bank activity with the books (for all bank accounts) for the period just before and just after the year-end. Certain detailed comparisons can be avoided if this reconciliation is accomplished in summary form.

 a. Using the following data, devise a good working paper form to achieve the above-stated objective and reconcile thereon the bank balances at the three dates shown and the bank activity for the period December 1, 1984, to January 12, 1985. (Your working papers must include a "proof of cash transactions" but need not show the corrected balances or totals.)

 b. For each item on the working papers, you are to show by appropriate symbols all audit procedures you would take in completing your audit.

 c. Prepare journal entries needed as a result of your work.

ABC Corporation	11/30/84	12/31/84	1/12/85
Balance per bank statement	$27,324.08	$20,383.89	$29,514.84
Balance per cash book and general ledger	21,214.95	16,689.86	
Outstanding checks	7,324.13	8,231.12	3,172.50
Deposits in transit	2,200.00	3,750.00	1,625.00

	Period 12/1/84–12/31/84	Period 1/2/85–1/12/85
Receipts per cash book	$88,546.50	$21,473.26
Credits per bank statement	86,324.00	24,372.10
Disbursements per cash book	93,071.59	9,980.03
Charges per bank statement	93,264.19	15,241.15

The client obtained bank statements for November 30 and December 31, 1984, and reconciled the balances. You obtained the statements of January 12, 1985, directly and obtained the necessary confirmations. You have found that there are no errors in addition or subtraction in the books.

The following information was obtained:

1. Bank service charges of $11.50 were charged on the November 30, 1984, statement and recorded in the cash disbursements on December 5, 1984. Charges of $13.25 were charged on the December 31, 1984, statement and recorded in the cash disbursements on January 6, 1985.

2. A check (#28890) for $22.48 cleared the bank in December at $122.48. This was found in proving the bank statement. The bank made the correction on January 8.

3. A $1,000 note sent to the bank for collection on November 15, 1984, was collected and credited to the account on November 28, 1984, net of a collection fee, $3.50. The note was recorded in the cash receipts on December 10, 1984. The collection fee was then entered as a disbursement.

4. The client records returned checks in red in the cash receipts book. The following checks were returned by the bank.

Customer	Amount	Date Returned	Date Recorded	Date Redeposited
A. Black	$327.50	12/6/84	(Note)	12/8/84
C. Denny	673.84	12/27/84	1/3/85	1/15/85

Note: No entries made in either receipts or disbursement books for this item.

5. Two payroll checks for employees' vacations totaling $215.75 were drawn on January 3 and cleared the bank on January 8. These checks were not entered on the books since semimonthly payroll summaries (from payroll disbursement records) are entered in the disbursements on the 15th and 31st only. (AICPA, adapted)

13–21. Glattelet Rural Electric Power Cooperative issues books of sight drafts to the foremen of its 10 field crews. The foremen use the drafts to pay the expenses of the field crews when they are on line duty requiring overnight stays.

The drafts are prenumbered and, as is clearly printed on the drafts, are limited to expenditures of $300 or less. The foremen prepare the drafts in duplicate and send the duplicates, accompanied by expense reports substantiating the drafts, to the general office.

The draft duplicates are accumulated at the general office and a voucher is prepared when there are two or three draft duplicates on hand. The voucher is the authority for issuing a company check for deposit in an imprest fund of $5,000 maintained at a local bank to meet the drafts as they are presented for payment. The cooperative maintains a separate general ledger account for the imprest fund.

The audit of the voucher register and cash disbursements disclosed the following information pertaining to sight drafts and the reimbursement of the imprest fund:

1. Voucher No. 10524 dated December 31, 1984, paid by Check No. 10524 dated December 31, 1984, for the following drafts:

Draft No.	Date	Crew No.	Explanation	Amount
6001	12/24/84	3	Expenses, 12/22–24	$160
2372	12/28/84	6	Expenses, 12/26–28	310
5304	12/30/84	7	Cash advance to foreman	260
			Voucher total	$730

2. Voucher No. 10531 dated December 31, 1984, paid by Check No. 10531 dated January 3, 1985, for the following drafts:

Draft No.	Date	Crew No.	Explanation	Amount
4060	12/29/84	1	Expenses, 12/27–29	$150
1816	1/3/85	4	Expenses, 1/1–3	560
			Voucher total	$710

3. Voucher No. 23 dated January 8, 1985, paid by Check No. 23 dated January 8, 1985, for the following drafts:

Draft No.	Date	Crew No.	Explanation	Amount
1000	12/31/84	9	Expenses, 12/28–31	$270
2918	2/3/85	10	Expenses, 12/28–31	190
4061	1/7/85	1	Expenses, 1/4–6	210
			Voucher total	$670

4. All of the above vouchers were charged to Travel Expense.

5. Examination of the imprest fund's bank statement for December, the January cutoff bank statement, and accompanying drafts presented for payment disclosed the following information:

a. Reimbursement Check No. 10524 was not credited on the December bank statement.

b. The bank honored Draft No. 2372 at the established maximum authorized amount.

c. Original 1984 drafts drawn by foremen but not presented to the client's bank for payment by December 31, 1984, totaled $1,600. This total included all 1984 drafts itemized above except No. 4060 and No. 2372, which were deducted by the bank in December.

d. December bank service charges listed on the December bank statement but not recorded by the client amounted to $80.

e. The balance per the bank statement at December 31, 1984, was $5,650.

Required:

a. Prepare the auditor's adjusting journal entry to correct the books at December 31, 1984. (The books have not been closed.) A supporting working paper analyzing the required adjustments should be prepared in good form.

b. Prepare a reconciliation of the balance per bank statement and the financial statement figure for the imprest cash account. The first figure in your reconciliation should be the balance per bank statement.   (AICPA, adapted)

13–22. Toyco, a retail toy chain, honors two bank credit cards and makes daily deposits of credit card sales in two credit card bank accounts (Bank A and Bank B). Each day Toyco batches its credit card sales slips, bank deposit slips, and authorized sales return documents, and keypunches cards for processing by its electronic data processing department. Each week detailed computer printouts of the general ledger credit card cash accounts are prepared. Credit card banks have been instructed to make an automatic weekly transfer of cash to Toyco's general bank account. The credit card banks charge back deposits that include sales to holders of stolen or expired cards.

The auditor conducting the examination of the 1984 Toyco financial statements has obtained the following copies of the detailed general ledger cash account printouts, a summary of the bank statements and the manually prepared bank reconciliations all for the the week ended December 31, 1984.

TOYCO
Detailed General Ledger Credit Card
Cash Account Printouts
For the Week Ended December 31, 1984

	Bank A	Bank B
	Dr. or (Cr.)	Dr. or (Cr.)
Beginning balance:		
December 24, 1984	$12,100	$ 4,200
Deposits:		
December 27, 1984	2,500	5,000
December 28, 1984	3,000	7,000
December 29, 1984	0	5,400
December 30, 1984	1,900	4,000
December 31, 1984	2,200	6,000
Cash transfer:		
December 27, 1984	(10,700)	0
Charge-backs:		
Expired cards	(300)	(1,600)
Invalid deposits (physically deposited in wrong account)	(1,400)	(1,000)
Redeposit of invalid deposits	1,000	1,400
Sales returns for week ending December 31, 1984	(600)	(1,200)
Ending balance:		
December 31, 1984	$ 9,700	$29,200

TOYCO
Summary of the Bank Statements
For the Week Ended December 31, 1984

	Bank A	Bank B
	(Charges) or Credits	
Beginning balance:		
December 24, 1984	$10,000	$ 0
Deposits dated:		
December 24, 1984	2,100	4,200
December 27, 1984	2,500	5,000
December 28, 1984	3,000	7,000
December 29, 1984	2,000	5,500
December 30, 1984	1,900	4,000
Cash transfers to general bank account:		
December 27, 1984	(10,700)	0
December 31, 1984	0	(22,600)
Charge-backs:		
Stolen cards	(100)	0
Expired cards	(300)	(1,600)
Invalid deposits	(1,400)	(1,000)
Bank service charges	0	(500)
Bank charge (unexplained)	(400)	0
Ending balance:		
December 31, 1984	$ 8,600	$ 0

TOYCO
Bank Reconciliations
For the Week Ended December 31, 1984

Code No.		Bank A	Bank B
		Add or (Deduct)	
1.	Balance per bank statement—December 31, 1984	$8,600	$ 0
2.	Deposits in transit—December 31, 1984	2,200	6,000
3.	Redeposit of invalid deposits (physically deposited in wrong account)	1,000	1,400
4.	Difference in deposits of December 29, 1984	(2,000)	(100)
5.	Unexplained bank charge	400	0
6.	Bank cash transfer not yet recorded	0	22,600
7.	Bank service charges	0	500
8.	Charge-backs not recorded—Stolen cards	100	0
9.	Sales returns recorded but not reported to the bank	(600)	(1,200)
10.	Balance per general ledger—December 31, 1984	$9,700	$29,200

Required:

Based on a review of the December 31, 1984, bank reconciliations and the related information available in the printouts and the summary of bank statements, describe what action(s) the auditor should take to obtain audit satisfaction for each item on the bank reconciliations.

Assume that all amounts are material and all computations are accurate.

Organize your answer sheet as follows using the appropriate code number for each item on the bank reconciliations:

Code No.	Action(s) to Be Taken by the Auditor to Obtain Audit Satisfaction
1.	

(AICPA, adapted)

13–23. The following information was obtained during your audit of cash at the Chatman Corporation for the month of October:

1. Information per bank statement:
   Balance September 30 $525,750
   Balance October 31   498,475
   Disbursements for October   228,745
   Receipts for October   201,470
2. Deposit in transit at September 30   43,870
3. Deposit in transit at October 31   12,890
4. Outstanding checks September 30   47,115
5. Outstanding checks October 31   23,607
6. Information per general ledger:
   Balance September 30   530,005
   Balance October 31   485,280
7. Receipts recorded in cash receipts journal on September 28, recorded as a deposit by the bank in the payroll account rather than this regular account on September 30, corrected by bank on October 5   10,000
8. Service charge made by the bank in October recorded by journal entry on November 5   22
9. Deposit of Chatman Corporation recorded on books October 2 but not credited by bank until October 31   29,370

10.	Deposit of the Smith Corporation credited by the bank on September 30, corrected by bank on November 3 by debit memo	2,500
11.	Information per cash journals:	
	Cash receipts for October	160,490
	Cash disbursements for October	205,215
12.	Check issued by another company charged to client by bank in error on October 9; corrected by bank on October 27	50
13.	Check No. 646 issued by client September 20 was returned by the payee October 20. The check was voided and an entry was made in the journal to reverse the entry of September 20	50

Required:

a. Prepare a four-column proof of cash.

b. Assume the reconciliation was given to you by the client. List the audit procedures you would perform, except those relating to tests of recorded receipts and disbursements, using tick marks to key them to the reconciliation.

13–24. You are in charge of your second yearly examination of the financial statements of Hillsboro Equipment Corporation, a distributor of construction equipment. Hillsboro's equipment sales are either outright cash sales or a combination of a substantial cash payment and one or two 60- or 90-day nonrenewable interest-bearing notes for the balance. Title to the equipment passes to the customer when the initial cash payment is made. The notes, some of which are secured by the customer, are dated when the cash payment is made (the day the equipment is delivered). If the customer prefers to purchase the equipment under an installment payment plan, Hillsboro arranges for the customer to obtain such financing from a local bank.

You begin your field work to examine the December 31 financial statements on January 5 knowing that you must leave temporarily for another engagement on January 7 after outlining the audit program for your assistant. Before leaving, you inquire about the assistant's progress in his examination of notes receivable. Among other things, he shows you a working paper listing the makers' names, the due dates, the interest rates, and amounts of 17 outstanding notes receivable totaling $100,000. The working paper contains the following notations:

1. Reviewed system of internal control and found it to be satisfactory.
2. Total of $100,000 agrees with general ledger control account.
3. Traced listing of notes to sales journal.

The assistant also informs you that he is preparing to request positive confirmation of the amounts of all outstanding notes receivable and that no other audit work has been performed in the examination of notes receivable and interest arising from equipment sales. There were no outstanding accounts receivable for equipment sales at the end of the year.

Required:

a. List the additional audit procedures that the assistant should apply in his audit of the account for notes receivable arising from equipment sales (Hillsboro has no other notes). No subsidiary ledger is maintained.

b. You ask your assistant to examine all notes receivable on hand before you leave. He returns in 30 minutes from the office safe where the notes are kept and reports that 1986 notes on hand total only $75,000. List the possible explanations that you would expect from the client for the $25,000 difference. (Eliminate fraud or misappropriation from your consideration.) Indicate beside each explanation the audit procedures you would apply to determine if each explanation is correct.   (AICPA, adapted)

13–25. In your audit of the Longmont Company you prepared a schedule of notes receivable. This company, a manufacturer, does not have many notes receivable and therefore does not keep a note register. All notes have resulted from sales to customers. The following schedule was prepared:

Column No.	Column Heading
1	Name of maker
2	Names of endorsers
3	Date of note
4	Due date
5	Principal
6	Interest rate
	Discounted (to the bank)
7	Date
8	Rate
9	Amount of discount
	Interest
10	Collected
11	Accrued
12	Prepaid
13	Payment on principal
14	Balance due
15	Collateral held

Required:

Draw a line down the middle of a lined sheet(s) of paper.

a On the left of the line, state the specific source(s) of information to be entered in each column and, where required, how data of previous columns are combined.

b. On the right of the line state the principal way(s) that such information would be verified.   (AICPA)

13–26. As a result of highly profitable operations over a number of years, Eastern Manufacturing Corporation accumulated a substantial short-term investment portfolio. In his examination of the financial statements for the year ended December 31, 1984, the following information came to the attention of the corporation's CPA:

1. The manufacturing operations of the corporation resulted in an operating loss for the year.
2. In 1984, the corporation placed the securities making up the short-term investment portfolio with a financial institution which will serve as custodian of the securities. Formerly the securities were kept in the corporation's safe-deposit box in the local bank.
3. On December 22, 1984, the corporation sold and then repurchased on the same day a number of securities that had appreciated greatly in value. Management stated that the purpose of the sale and repurchases was to establish a higher cost and book value for the securities and to avoid the reporting of a loss for the year.

Required:

a. List the objectives of the CPA's examination of the Short-term Investment account.

b. Under what conditions would the CPA accept a confirmation of securities on hand from the custodian in lieu of inspecting and counting the securities himself?

c. What disclosure, if any, of the sale and repurchase of the securities would the CPA recommend for the financial statements? If the client accepts the CPA's recommendations for disclosure, what effect, if any, would the sale and repurchase have upon the CPA's opinion on the financial statements? Discuss.

(AICPA, adapted)

13–27. You are in charge of the audit of the financial statements of the Demot Corporation for the year ended December 31, 1986. The corporation has had the policy of investing its surplus funds in short-term investments. Its stock and bond certificates are kept in a safe-deposit box in a local bank. Only the president or the treasurer of the corporation has access to the box.

You were unable to obtain access to the safe-deposit box on December 31 because neither the president nor the treasurer was available. Arrangements were made for your assistant to accompany the treasurer to the bank on January 11 to examine the securities. Your assistant has never examined securities that were being kept in a safe-deposit box and requires instructions. He should be able to inspect all securities on hand in an hour.

Required:

a. List the instructions that you would give your assistant regarding the examination of the stock and bond certificates kept in the safe-deposit box. Include in your instructions the details of the securities to be examined and the reasons for examining these details.

b. When he returned from the bank your assistant reported that the treasurer had entered the box on January 4. The treasurer stated that he had removed an old photograph of the corporation's original building. The photograph was loaned to the local Chamber of Commerce for display purposes. List the additional audit procedures that are required because of the treasurer's action.

(AICPA, adapted)

13–28. You are engaged in the audit of the financial statements of the Sandy Core Company for the year ended December 31, 1986. Sandy Core Company sells lumber and building supplies at wholesale and retail; it has total assets of $1 million and a stockholders' equity of $500,000.

The company's records show an investment of $100,000 for 100 shares of common stock of one of its customers, the Home Building Corporation. You learn that Home Building Corporation is closely held and that its capital stock, consisting of 1,000 shares of issued and outstanding common stock, has no published or quoted market value.

Examination of your client's cash disbursements records reveals an entry of a check for $100,000 drawn on January 23, 1986, to Mr. Felix Wolfe, who is said to be the former holder of the 100 shares of stock. Mr. Wolfe is president of the Sandy Core Company. Sandy Core Company has no other investments.

Required:

List the auditing procedures you would employ in connection with the $100,000 investment of your client in the capital stock of the Home Building Corporation.

(AICPA, adapted)

13–29. In connection with his examination of the financial statements of Belasco Chemicals, Inc., Kenneth Mack, CPA, is considering the necessity of inspecting securities on the balance sheet date, May 31, 1985, or at some other date. The securities held by Belasco include negotiable bearer bonds, which are kept in a safe in the treasurer's office, and miscellaneous stocks and bonds kept in a safe-deposit box at The Merchants Bank. Both the negotiable bearer bonds and the miscellaneous stocks and bonds are material to proper presentation of Belasco's financial position.

Required:

a. What are the factors that Mr. Mack should consider in determining the necessity for inspecting these securities on May 31, 1985, as opposed to other dates?
b. Assume that Mr. Mack plans to send a member of his staff to Belasco's offices and The Merchants Bank on May 31, 1985, to make the security inspection. What instructions should he give to this staff member as to the conduct of the inspection and the evidence to be included in the audit working papers? (Note: Do not discuss the valuation of securities; the income from securities; or the examination of information contained in the books and records of the company.)
c. Assume that Mr. Mack finds it impracticable to send a member of his staff to Belasco's offices and The Merchants Bank on May 31, 1985. What alternative procedures may he employ to assure himself that the company had physical possession of its securities on May 31, 1985, if the securities are inspected on (1) May 28, 1985? (2) June 5, 1985? (AICPA, adapted)

13–30. The cashier of a bank is also treasurer of a local charity. He is authorized to purchase $10,000 in U.S. bonds for the bank and a similar amount for the charity. He makes both purchases but misappropriates the bonds belonging to the charity. When an audit is made of the charity, the treasurer borrows the bonds from the bank and places them in the charity's safe-deposit box.

Required:

Discuss the internal controls you would recommend for the charity to prevent the occurrence of this manipulation. (AICPA, adapted)

13–31. You are making a regular annual audit of a small, but growing, manufacturing corporation. As a result of inadequate working capital, the corporation has borrowed from its bank on short-term notes and has occasionally given notes to suppliers for overdue accounts payable. Prepare an audit program for notes payable.

(AICPA, adapted)

13–32. In connection with various steps, other than those concerned directly with notes and mortgages payable in the usual annual audit, the auditor's verification work assists in determining all the notes and mortgages payable are properly recorded on the books of the client. List five of these procedures, stating the manner in which each procedure aids in determining that notes and mortgages payable are correctly recorded. (AICPA, adapted)

13–33. You were engaged on May 1, 1986, by a committee of shareholders to perform a special audit as of December 31, 1985, of the shareholders' equity of the Major Corporation, whose stock is actively traded on a stock exchange. The group of shareholders who engaged you believe that the information contained in the shareholders' equity section of the published annual report for the year ended December 31, 1985, is not correct. If your examination confirms their suspicions, they intend to use the report in a proxy fight.

Management agrees to permit your audit but refuses to permit any direct confirmation with shareholders. To secure cooperation in the audit, the committee of shareholders has agreed to this limitation and you have been instructed to limit your audit in this respect. You have been instructed also to exclude the audit of revenue and expense accounts for the year.

Required:

a. Prepare a general audit program for the usual examination of the shareholders' equity section of a corporations's balance sheet, assuming no limitation on the scope of your examination of revenue and expense accounts.

b. Describe any special auditing procedures you would undertake in view of the limitations and other special circumstances of your examination of the Major Corporations's shareholders' equity accounts. (AICPA, adapted)

13–34. You are a CPA engaged in an examination of the financial statements of Pate Corporation for the year ended December 31, 1985. The financial statements and records of Pate Corporation have not been audited by a CPA in prior years.

The shareholders' equity section of Pate Corporation's balance sheet as of December 31, 1985, follows:

Shareholders' equity:

Capital stock—10,000 shares of $10 par value authorized; 5,000 shares issued and outstanding	$ 50,000
Capital contributed in excess of par value of capital stock	32,580
Retained earnings	47,320
Total shareholders' equity	$129,900

Pate Corporation was founded in 1979. The corporation has 10 stockholders and serves as its own registrar and transfer agent. There are no capital stock subscription contracts in effect.

Required:

a. Prepare the detailed audit program for the examination of the three accounts comprising the shareholders' equity section of Pate Corporation's balance sheet. (Do not include in the audit program the verification of the results of the current year's operations.)

b. After every other figure on the balance sheet has been audited by the CPA it might appear that the retained earnings figure is a balancing figure and requires no further verification. Why does the CPA verify retained earnings as he does other figures on the balance sheet? Discuss. (AICPA, adapted)

AUDITING THE ADMINISTRATION COMPONENT AND GENERAL PROCEDURES

AUDITING THE ADMINISTRATION COMPONENT

The specific control objectives for the administration component are listed in Figure 14–1 (page 458). The administration component deals with the control and support of the company's operating activities and related costs. This component also covers (1) income taxes and (2) commitments and contingencies that relate to the various operating components (see Figure 14–2, page 458). The audit areas associated with the administration component include general and administrative expenses, which cover prepaid and deferred items as well as other assets and accrued liabilities. Specific control objectives F–3 and F–4, which were discussed in Chapters 11 and 13, also are related to this component. The relationship of the administration component specific control objectives to financial statement classifications are shown in Figure 14–3 (page 459).

This section of the chapter will emphasize audit procedures that might be performed on accounts and transactions relating to the administration component. Not all of the procedures discussed would be performed on each audit. The actual procedures to be performed will depend on the assessment of the likelihood of material error in the accounts affected by each specific control objective, considering the three inputs to the risk analysis.

General and Administrative Expenses, Prepaid and Deferred Items, Other Assets, and Accrued Liabilities

Figure 14–2 lists the specific control objectives that relate to general and administrative expenses, prepaid and deferred items, other assets, and accrued liabilities. The tests in these audit areas may be performed at either an interim date (e.g., in conjunction with tests of key attributes of a purchas-

14

ing or cash disbursement system) or at year-end (e.g., direct test of balances). As previously mentioned, the nature, timing, and extent of the work to be performed should be described in the audit program.

Testing Key Attributes

As is the case when auditing any of the operating components, it is important for the auditor to understand the accounting systems. Whenever the system evaluation indicates that the system provides reasonable assurance that a specific control objective is being achieved, the auditor should test each key attribute associated with that control objective.

Dual purpose tests should be used to provide evidence that a key attribute is both (1) functioning (compliance test) and (2) effective (substantive test— i.e., the transaction is recorded correctly). It is not sufficient merely to verify that a transaction is correct and assume that the control functioned.

Key attributes that are applied to individual transactions usually are tested by sampling from those transactions through an interim period. As each transaction is tested, the auditor should look for documentary evidence of the functioning of the key attribute. Such evidence can be in the form of signatures, initials, check marks, and so on. For example, assume that the auditor concludes that the system design provides reasonable assurance that the specific control objective A–1, "Expenses are incurred only with proper authorization," is being achieved. One key attribute that the auditor might conclude supports this assessment is that sales commission expense requests are reviewed for compliance with company policy. The documentary evidence for this review is the marketing manager's initials. To test the functioning of this key attribute, the auditor might examine a sample of sales commission expense requests, noting the marketing manager's initials. To test the effectiveness of this control, the auditor might recompute the amount of sales commission expense based on the company policy.

FIGURE 14-1 Administration Operating Component Specific Control Objectives

Reference No.

A-1 Expenses are incurred only with proper authorization

A-2 Expenses and related liabilities are recorded correctly as to account, amount, and period

A-3 Salary, wage, and benefit expenses are incurred only for work authorized and performed

A-4 Salaries, wages, and benefits are calculated at the proper rate

A-5 Salaries, wages, benefits, and related liabilities are recorded correctly as to account (department, activity, etc.), amount, and period

A-6 Amortization or loss in value of intangibles is recorded correctly as to account, amount, and period

A-7 Provisions for income taxes and related liabilities and deferrals are recorded correctly as to account, amount, and period

A-8 Commitments and contingencies are identified, monitored, and, if appropriate, recorded or disclosed

Certain control procedures are applied to groups of transactions (e.g., weekly reconciliations of sales quantities on commission reports to quantities billed). In these cases, the auditor can select either (1) a sample of transactions and trace to inclusion in the documentary evidence that supports functioning of the key attribute (e.g., select a sample of sales commission expense requests

FIGURE 14-2 Relationship of Specific Control Objectives to Audit Areas—Administration Component

General and administrative expenses, prepaid and deferred items, other assets, and accrued liabilities:

A-1 Expenses are incurred only with proper authorization

A-2 Expenses and related liabilities are recorded correctly as to account, amount, and period

A-3 Salary, wage, and benefit expenses are incurred only for work authorized and performed

A-4 Salaries, wages, and benefits are calculated at the proper rate

A-5 Salaries, wages, benefits, and related liabilities are recorded correctly as to account (department, activity, etc.), amount, and period

A-6 Amortization or loss in value of intangibles is recorded correctly as to account, amount, and period

F-3 Cash disbursements are for goods or services authorized and received

F-4 Cash disbursements are recorded correctly as to account, amount, and period

Income taxes:

A-7 Provisions for income taxes and related liabilities and deferrals are recorded correctly as to account, amount, and period

Commitments and contingencies:

A-8 Commitments and contingencies are identified, monitored, and, if appropriate, recorded or disclosed

FIGURE 14-3 Relationship of Specific Control Objectives to Financial Statement Classifications—Administration Component

Balance Sheet

| | Control Objectives | |
	Debit	Credit
Current Assets:		
Cash		
Accounts receivable		
Allowance for doubtful accounts		
Inventories		
Prepaid expenses and other assets	A–1, A–2	A–2
Other Assets:		
Notes receivable		
Investments		
Goodwill and other intangibles	A–1, A–2	A–6
Intercompany accounts		
Deposits and other assets	A–1, A–2	A–2
Property, Plant, and Equipment:		
Land		
Buildings		
Machinery and equipment		
Allowances for depreciation		
Current Liabilities:		
Notes payable		
Trade accounts payable and accrued liabilities	F–3, F–4	A–1, A–2
Accrued payroll and related liabilities		A–3, A–4, A–5
Taxes other than taxes on income		A–1, A–2
Accrued interest		
Income taxes	A–7	A–7
Long-Term Debt		
Deferred Income Taxes	A–7	A–7
Shareholders' Equity:		
Preferred stock		
Common stock		
Additional paid-in capital		
Retained earnings		
Commitments and Contingencies	A–8	A–8

Income Statement

| | Control Objectives | |
	Debit	Credit
Sales		
Cost of sales	A–8	
Selling, general, and administrative expenses	A–1, A–2, A–3, A–4, A–5, A–6, A–8	
Provision for income taxes	A–7	A–7
Other		

for tracing to the weekly reconciliations) or, (2) a sample of the related documentary evidence itself to test (e.g., select a sample of weekly reconciliations, test one reconciliation to support functioning of the key attribute, and review the rest for reasonableness).

The audit program should include inquiries concerning control procedures applied to either individual or groups of transactions. A few well-chosen questions directed to the right person can provide valuable insights about both the functioning and the effectiveness of a procedure. For example, the auditor might ask the marketing manager for an explanation of his or her responsibilities and how exceptions are resolved. To accomplish this, the auditor might ask the following questions of the marketing manager: "How do you perform the review? Do you review every sales commission expense request? Are sales commission expense requests that do not meet approved commission rates ever accepted?" In some instances, it might be useful to ask other personnel who are affected by the control procedure to provide information that might assist in evaluating the reasonableness of the marketing manager's review. For example, an auditor might ask the sales clerk, "What do you do with sales commission expense requests that are returned by the marketing manager due to incorrect commission rates?"

If the auditor learns that sales commission expense requests are always accepted even if they have incorrect commission rates, the control procedure obviously is not functioning—even if there is documentary evidence to the contrary in every case (i.e., the marketing manager signs all of them). If this is the case, there is no point in continuing to gather evidence of the functioning of the attribute. The auditor should give effect to this new information by designing other audit procedures.

In certain cases, the functioning of key attributes does not result in documentary evidence of performance (e.g., review and approval of sales commission without indicating approval). The auditor obtains evidence of the functioning of these key attributes by observation and inquiry of the employee who performs the control procedures or other employees who are affected by it. To test the effectiveness of these key attributes, the auditor would examine a sample of transactions affected by the undocumented control.

Testing Transactions

As mentioned above, in addition to gathering evidence of the functioning of key attributes, the audit program should include procedures to test the effectiveness of the key attributes. In these cases, the audit procedures usually will be performed on a limited basis through an interim date.

On the other hand, if the system evaluation indicates that there are no key attributes to be relied on, the same or similar procedures might be performed to detect errors or irregularities in recording the transactions. In those cases, the auditor should test more transactions and select them from throughout most or all of the year.

The audit procedures performed in those audit areas are similar to those described in the "Purchases, Cash Disbursements, and Accounts Payable" section of Chapter 11. The similarities include examining canceled checks and supporting documentation; determining that items were recorded in the proper general ledger account and period; reviewing cash disbursement records for unusual items; and performing clerical accuracy tests. The procedures are commonly performed on accounts and transactions in the administration component; however, because of their similarities, administration and production component expenses often are combined and tested as part of the same sample.

Documents that may be examined in support of prepaid expenses, deferred items, other assets, and other liabilities include rental or lease agreements, insurance policies, tax receipts and returns, contracts (e.g., royalty), and employment agreements (e.g. advance, deferred compensation, bonus, and commission). The period in which the charge was incurred can be identified while examining the invoice, receiving report, or other documentation. The period reflected on these documents should be compared with the company's books and records for agreement.

Confirmation Procedures

Confirmations may be requested for items such as deposits and miscellaneous receivables, including amounts due from employees. These confirmation procedures are no different from the positive confirmation procedures performed on trade accounts receivable, discussed in Chapter 10. However, a confirmation tailored to the specific situation may have to be developed. Confirmation also may be requested of insurance companies for life insurance policies on behalf of a client officer or other employee. The confirmation will aid in supporting the cash surrender value and any policy loans. As with other confirmations, the auditor must supervise any client assistance and maintain control of the confirmations until physically mailed.

Testing Clerical Accuracy

In addition to the clerical accuracy tests previously discussed, other related audit procedures might include testing the computation of: unexpired portions of insurance premiums; prepayments of interest, rent, advertising, taxes and royalties; and amortization of patents, goodwill, and bond discount and expense. When testing the computation of amortization, the auditor also should review the method used for consistency.

Analytical Review Procedures

The following are some analytical review procedures that may be used as direct tests of balances for accounts in the administration component:

1. Compare specific or total administrative and/or selling expenses for the current period with prior periods and with budgeted amounts.
2. Compare total administrative or selling expenses to sales.
3. Compare specific expense items to sales.
4. Compare prepaid expenses, other assets, and accrued liabilities account balances for the current period with prior periods.

Search for Unrecorded Liabilities

The procedures performed in the search for unrecorded ("out-of-period") liabilities relating to administrative expenses (e.g., professional fees, rents, advertising) are the same as those performed in an inventory purchases out-of-period search. These procedures, discussed in detail in Chapter 11, include:

1. Reviewing transactions recorded after the balance sheet date to determine whether any significant transactions apply to the period under audit.
2. Reviewing unprocessed invoices for items that should be included in the period under audit.
3. Inquiring of accounting and purchasing personnel whether they know of any significant out-of-period liabilities.

In executing these procedures, the auditor compares the documents or information examined to the client's records to determine whether the items that apply to the period under audit are properly accrued.

As previously noted, requests for vendors' statements usually are made in conjunction with the inventory purchases out-of-period search. These requests usually are not sent to vendors associated with the administration function because those related accruals typically are not as significant as inventory-related payables. However, if vendor statements are requested to audit administrative expense accruals, the procedures performed are similar to those described in Chapter 11 for inventory-related payables.

Salaries, Wages, Benefits, and Related Liabilities

In the administration component, the tests of payroll transactions relate to a client's office, sales, and executive personnel. The audit procedures performed are similar to, and in many cases combined with, those discussed for production or service described in Chapter 11. The following audit procedures also may be appropriate.

Office and Executive Payroll. Officers' salaries normally will be tested by reference to the minutes of the board of directors meetings or employment agreements. In most organizations, information about office and executive payroll is confidential. While the auditor is expected to maintain the confidential nature of *all* information pertaining to a company, payroll information is particularly sensitive.

Analytical Review. Analytical review procedures that may be performed include:

1. Compare administrative payroll dollars to number of administrative employees.
2. Compare the administrative payroll to sales.
3. Compare the administrative payroll to direct labor.
4. Compare administrative employee benefits to administrative payroll.
5. Compare administrative pension contribution to covered administrative employees.
6. Compare administrative payroll taxes to administrative gross payroll.
7. Compare the salary, wage, and benefit accruals for the current period with prior periods.

Intangible Assets

The auditor's objective in examining intangible assets is to determine whether such assets have value to the company and whether the accounting for them, including their amortization, is in conformity with generally accepted accounting principles consistently applied. Intangibles include such items as patents, licenses, and goodwill arising from the acquisition of a business. The auditor should examine any documents supporting the existence and amount of these types of intangible assets and test the calculation of the amortization for the period. The key point in auditing any intangible asset is to challenge, through inquiry and other evidence, the future benefit to be derived from the asset.

Income Taxes

Federal, state, and foreign income taxes have an important effect on both the income statement and the balance sheet. In auditing income taxes, the auditor should:

1. Obtain an analysis of changes in the income tax liability accounts during the period under review and
   a. Reconcile additions to the accrual with the appropriate expense account.

    b. Examine paid checks or other evidence of payment to support the nature of payments and the year to which they apply.

2. Obtain and test data necessary for allocation of income to various states, possessions, or foreign countries. The auditor should investigate the possibility of liability for income or similar taxes for which returns have not been filed by the client.

3. Review the computation of the provision for income taxes, including any deferred taxes, for the period under review.

4. Determine the status of returns filed for prior years. The extent to which returns have been examined by taxing authorities should be noted. Information should be obtained on changes made by taxing authorities and the effect of any unsettled matters. The auditor should give consideration to the effect of questionable items that may be present in returns filed but not examined on current and future years.

COMMITMENTS AND CONTINGENCIES

Loss Contingencies

FASB Statement No. 5, "Accounting for Contingencies," defines a contingency as:

> . . . an existing condition, situation, or set of circumstances involving uncertainty as to possible gain [gain contingency] . . . or loss [loss contingency] . . . to an enterprise that will ultimately be resolved when one or more future events occur or fail to occur. [par. 1][1]

FASB Statement No. 5 was issued to limit the variability of accounting practices that had developed with respect to contingencies, particularly contingent liabilities—loss contingencies that arise as the result of incurring a liability. A loss contingency includes possible impairment of assets as well as contingent liabilities.[2] Loss contingencies arise, for example, from endorsements of others' notes, guarantees of indebtedness of others, repurchase commitments, pending litigation, probable tax assessments, decisions to self-insure, threat of expropriation, or establishment of a warranty policy.

The auditor should be alert to the existence of loss contingencies during all phases of an audit. Bank confirmations may disclose the existence of guarantees and endorsements of loans and open letters of credit. The review of contracts, lease agreements, sales and purchase commitments, and minutes

---

[1] *Statement of Financial Accounting Standards No. 5,* "Accounting for Contingencies," Financial Accounting Standards Board, 1975. Copyright by the Financial Accounting Standards Board, High Ridge Park, Stamford, Connecticut, 06905, U.S.A. Reprinted with permission. Copies of the complete document are available from the FASB.

[2] See Donald E. Kieso and Jerry J. Weyganndt, *Intermediate Accounting,* 4th ed. (New York: John Wiley & Sons, 1983), p. 454.

of meetings also may disclose loss contingencies. Letters from a client's attorneys (discussed in the next section) may also be a useful source of information relating to loss contingencies.

FASB Statement No. 5, "Accounting for Contingencies," indicates that loss contingencies should be accrued only if both of the following exist:

 a. Information available prior to issuance of the financial statements indicates that it is probable that an asset has been impaired or a liability has been incurred at the date of the financial statements . . . It is implicit in this condition that it must be probable that one or more future events will occur to confirm the fact of the loss.

 b. The amount of the loss can be reasonably estimated. [par. 8][3]

If the above conditions are not met, *FASB Statement No. 5* indicates that ". . . disclosure of the contingency shall be made when there is at least a reasonable possibility that a loss or an additional loss may have been incurred. . . ." [par. 10][4]

Litigation, Claims, and Assessments

SAS No. 12, "Inquiry of a Client's Lawyer Concerning Litigation, Claims, and Assessments" (AU 337.04), states that the auditor should obtain the following evidential matter regarding litigation, claims, and assessments:

 a. The existence of a condition, situation, or set of circumstances indicating an uncertainty as to the possible loss to an entity arising from litigation, claims, and assessments.

 b. The period in which the underlying cause for legal action occurred.

 c. The degree of probability of an unfavorable outcome.

 d. The amount or range of potential loss.

Management is the primary source of information about litigation, claims, and assessments. *SAS No. 12* (AU 337.05 –.06) notes that the auditor should:

 1. Question and discuss with management the policies and procedures ". . . for identifying, evaluating, and accounting for litigation, claims, and assessments."

 2. Obtain from management a description and evaluation of such items ". . . that existed at the date of the balance sheet being reported on, and during the period from the balance-sheet date to the date the information is furnished, including an identification of those matters referred to legal counsel, and obtain assurances from management, ordinarily

---

[3] Copyright by the Financial Accounting Standards Board, High Ridge Park, Stamford, Connecticut, 06905, U.S.A. Reprinted with permission. Copies of the complete document are available from the FASB.

[4] Ibid.

in writing, that they have disclosed all such matters required to be disclosed by *Statement of Financial Accounting Standards No. 5."*

3. Examine all documents in the client's possession concerning such items, including correspondence and invoices sent by any attorney.

4. Obtain assurance from management (ordinarily in writing), that all unasserted claims have been disclosed ". . . that the lawyer has advised them are probable of assertion and must be disclosed in accordance with *Statement of Financial Accounting Standards No. 5."* With the client's permission, the auditor ". . . should inform the lawyer that the client has given the auditor this assurance."

5. Request management to send a letter of inquiry to any lawyer with whom management consulted regarding such items.

In addition, *SAS No. 12* (AU 337.07) suggests that audit procedures performed for other purposes may disclose litigation, claims, and assessments. Some of the examples of such procedures suggested by *SAS No. 12* include: (1) reading the minutes of meetings (e.g., board of directors, shareholders); (2) reading various client legal documents (e.g., contracts, lease agreements) and correspondence with government agencies; and (3) looking at bank confirmations for information concerning guarantees.

SAS No. 12 (AU 337.08) suggests that letters of inquiry to the client's lawyer ask for corroboration of the information furnished by management concerning litigation, claims, and assessments. Figure 14–4 describes items that should appear in such a letter. *SAS No. 12* (AU 337.14) states that "a lawyer may be unable to respond concerning the likelihood of an unfavorable outcome of litigation, claims, and assessments or the amount or range of potential loss, because of inherent uncertainties." In such a case, *SAS No. 12* (AU 337.14) notes that the auditor normally ". . . will conclude that the financial statements are affected by an uncertainty concerning the outcome of a future event which is not susceptible of reasonable estimation." If material, the auditor normally will conclude that an unqualified opinion cannot be given. Chapter 16 discusses this further.

OTHER GENERAL PROCEDURES

In addition to audit procedures related to one of the four operating components, the audit program also includes what are known as "general procedures." These are procedures that (1) do not result from the risk analysis, (2) are administrative in nature, and/or (3) only are required for certain engagements. The remaining sections of this Chapter discuss these procedures, which are divided into procedures performed on all audits and procedures performed on certain audits.

FIGURE 14–4 Items that Should Appear in an Inquiry of a Client's Lawyer

The matters that should be covered in a letter of audit inquiry include, but are not limited to, the following:

a. Identification of the company, including subsidiaries, and the date of the examination.

b. A list prepared by management (or a request by management that the lawyer prepare a list) that describes and evaluates pending or threatened litigation, claims, and assessments with respect to which the lawyer has been engaged and to which he has devoted substantive attention on behalf of the company in the form of legal consultation or representation.

c. A list prepared by management that describes and evaluates unasserted claims and assessments that management considers to be probable of assertion, and that, if asserted, would have at least a reasonable possibility of an unfavorable outcome, with respect to which the lawyer has been engaged and to which he has devoted substantive attention on behalf of the company in the forms of legal consultation or representation.

d. As to each matter listed in item b, a request that the lawyer either furnish the following information or comment on those matters as to which his views may differ from those stated by management, as appropriate:
   (1) A description of the nature of the matter, the progress of the case to date, and the action the company intends to take (for example, to contest the matter vigorously or to seek an out-of-court settlement).
   (2) An evaluation of the likelihood of an unfavorable outcome and an estimate, if one can be made, of the amount or range of potential loss.
   (3) With respect to a list prepared by management, an identification of the omission of any pending or threatened litigation, claims, and assessments or a statement that the list of such matters is complete.

e. As to each matter listed in item c, a request that the lawyer comment on those matters as to which his views concerning the description or evaluation of the matter may differ from those stated by management.

f. A statement by the client that the client understands that whenever, in the course of performing legal services for the client with respect to a matter recognized to involve an unasserted possible claim or assessment that may call for financial statement disclosure, the lawyer has formed a professional conclusion that the client should disclose or consider disclosure concerning such possible claim or assessment, the lawyer, as a matter of professional responsibility to the client, will so advise the client and will consult with the client concerning the question of such disclosure and the applicable requirements of *Statement of Financial Accounting Standards No. 5*.

g. A request that the lawyer confirm whether the understanding described in item f is correct.

h. A request that the lawyer specifically identify the nature of and reasons for any limitation on his response.

Inquiry need not be made concerning matters that are not considered material, provided the client and the auditor have reached an understanding on the limits of materiality for this purpose.

Source: Quoted from *Statement on Auditing Standards No. 12*, "Inquiry of a Client's Lawyer Concerning Litigation, Claims, and Assessments," American Institute of Certified Public Accountants, 1976, (AU 337.09).

PROCEDURES PERFORMED ON ALL AUDITS

Related Party Transactions[5]

During the course of the audit examination, the auditor should be alert to the possibility of the existence of related party transactions that could have a material effect on the financial statements. *FASB Statement No. 57,* "Related Party Disclosures," defines related parties as including:

> . . . Affiliates of the enterprise; entities for which investments are accounted for by the equity method by the enterprise; trusts for the benefit of employees, such as pension and profit-sharing trusts that are managed by or under the trusteeship of management; principal owners of the enterprise; its management; members of the immediate families of principal owners of the enterprise and its management; and other parties with which the enterprise may deal if one party controls or can significantly influence the management or operating policies of the other to an extent that one of the transacting parties might be prevented from fully pursuing its own separate interests. Another party also is a related party if it can significantly influence the management or operating policies of the transacting parties or if it has an ownership interest in one of the transacting parties and can significantly influence the other to an extent that one or more of the transacting parties might be prevented from fully pursuing its own separate interests. [par. 24]

SAS No. 45 indicates that the auditor should realize ". . . that the substance of a particular transaction could be significantly different from its form and that financial statements should recognize the substance of particular transactions rather than merely their legal form." Further, "the auditor should view related party transactions within the framework of existing accounting pronouncements, and place primary emphasis on the adequacy of disclosure."

Audit Procedures. *SAS No. 45* recommends the following specific audit procedures to determine the existence of related parties:

a. Evaluate the company's procedures for identifying and accounting for related party transactions.
b. Request from appropriate management personnel the names of all related parties and inquire whether there were any transactions with those parties during the period.
c. Review filings by the client with the Securities and Exchange Commission and other regulatory agencies for the names of related parties and for

---

[5] This section is based in part on *Statement of Financial Accounting Standards No. 57,* "Related Party Disclosures," Financial Accounting Standards Board, 1982. Copyright by Financial Accounting Standards Board, High Ridge Park, Stamford, Connecticut, 06905, U.S.A. Reprinted with permission. Copies of the complete document are available from the FASB. Also, it is based in part on *Statement on Auditing Standards No. 45,* "Omnibus Statement on Auditing Standards—1983," American Institute of Certified Public Accountants, 1983.

other businesses in which officers and directors occupy directorship or management positions.

d. Determine the names of all pension and other trusts established for the benefit of employees and the names of their officers and trustees. . . .

e. Review shareholder listings of closely held companies to identify principal shareholders.

f. Review prior years' working papers for the names of known related parties.

g. Inquire of predecessor, principal, or other auditors of related entities as to their knowledge of existing relationships and the extent of management involvement in material transactions.

h. Review material investment transactions during the period under examination to determine whether the nature and extent of investments during the period create related parties.

To identify transactions with related parties, *SAS No. 45* suggests that the auditor:

1. Give audit personnel the names of all related parties.
2. "Review the minutes of meetings. . . ."
3. "Review proxy and other material filed with the [SEC]. . . ."
4. "Review conflict-of-interests statements obtained by the company from its management. . . ."
5. "Review the extent and nature of business transacted with major customers, suppliers, borrowers, and lenders for indications of previously undisclosed relationships."
6. "Consider whether any transactions are not being given accounting recognition . . ." (e.g., the client receiving services at no cost).
7. "Review the accounting records for large, unusual, or nonrecurring transactions or balances . . ." (especially transactions occurring near the end of a reporting period).
8. "Review confirmations of compensating balance arrangements for indications that balances are or were maintained for or by related parties."
9. "Review invoices from law firms that have performed . . ." services for the client.
10. "Review confirmations of loans receivable and payable for indications of guarantees. . . ."

SAS No. 45 indicates that if related party transactions have been identified, additional audit procedures may be needed to determine ". . . the purpose, nature, and extent of these transactions and their effect on the financial statements." Further, *SAS No. 45* states that the auditor should consider the following:

a. Obtain an understanding of the business purpose of the transaction. . . .

b. Examine invoices, executed copies of agreements, contracts, and other pertinent documents, such as receiving reports and shipping documents.

c. Determine whether the transaction has been approved by the board of directors or other appropriate officials.

d. Test for reasonableness the compilation of amounts to be disclosed, or considered for disclosure, in the financial statements.

e. Arrange for the audits of intercompany account balances to be performed as of concurrent dates, even if the fiscal years differ, and for the examination of specified, important, and representative related party transactions by the auditors for each of the parties with an appropriate exchange of relevant information.

f. Inspect, confirm, or otherwise obtain satisfaction as to the transferability and value of collateral.

Disclosure. *SAS No. 45* indicates that the auditor should be satisfied that material related party transactions are adequately disclosed in the financial statements. *FASB Statement No. 57* states that disclosure should include:

a. The nature of the relationships involved.

b. A description of the transactions, including those to which no amounts or nominal amounts were ascribed for each of the periods for which income statements are presented, and such other information deemed necessary to an understanding of the effects of the transactions on the financial statements.

c. The dollar amounts of transactions for each of the periods for which income statements are presented and the effects of any change in the method of establishing the terms from that used in the preceding period.

d. Amounts due from or to related parties as of the date of each balance sheet presented and, if not otherwise apparent, the terms and manner of settlement. [par. 2]

SAS No. 45 indicates that sometimes the client includes a representation in the financial statements that a related party transaction was consummated on approximately the same terms as if the transaction had been with an unrelated party. If the auditor cannot reach a conclusion as to the propriety of this representation, depending upon the materiality in the situation either a qualified or adverse opinion should be given.

Illegal Acts by Clients[6]

During the course of an audit, the independent auditor may find evidence of possible illegal acts (e.g., bribes, illegal political contributions). *SAS No. 17*, "Illegal Acts by Clients" (AU 328), discusses the independent auditor's responsibilities in such circumstances as well as how much attention an auditor should give to the possibility that illegal acts actually may have occurred.

SAS No. 17 (AU 328.03) indicates that an audit conducted in accordance with generally accepted auditing standards does not guarantee that all illegal

---

[6] This section is based in part on *Statement on Auditing Standards No. 17*, "Illegal Acts by Clients," American Institute of Certified Public Accountants, 1977.

acts will be uncovered. The independent auditor is not an expert in determining what is or is not illegal. However, an auditor may be able to identify an illegal act in the course of an examination.

Transactions that appear to be unusual or questionable should raise an auditor's concern about the possibility of an illegal act. *SAS No. 17* (AU 328.07–.08) suggests procedures and inquiries that may identify illegal acts:

1. Consideration by an auditor of laws and regulations that may directly affect the financial statements (e.g., tax laws).
2. Inquiry of client's management and legal counsel concerning loss contingencies.
3. Inquiries about the client's compliance with laws and regulations and policies for preventing illegal acts.
4. Examination of the client's internal communications regarding compliance with laws and regulations.

Materiality. The auditor should consider the materiality of an illegal act. Such a consideration would include an evaluation of possible effects on the financial statements. Illegal acts can result in fines, penalties, damages, or other sanctions by regulatory bodies, and may result in a risk in relation to revenue that is material in amount (e.g., possible loss of an important business relationship or loss of assets). Material effects should be adequately disclosed in the financial statements.

Once the auditor has determined that an illegal act has occurred, *SAS No. 17* (AU 328.13) suggests that:

> . . . the auditor should report the circumstances to personnel within the client's organization at a high enough level of authority so that appropriate action can be taken by the client with respect to—
> a. consideration of remedial actions;
> b. adjustments or disclosures that may be necessary in the financial statements;
> c. disclosures that may be required in other documents (such as a proxy statement).

The Auditor's Report. The discovery of the occurrence of an illegal act may require the independent auditor to modify the audit report. *SAS No. 17* (AU 328.14) notes that the auditor may be unable to:

> . . . determine the amounts associated with certain events, taken alone or with similar events, of which he becomes aware, or whether an act is, in fact, illegal, because of an inability to obtain sufficient competent evidential matter. . . . For example, the act may have been accomplished by circumventing the internal control system and may not be properly recorded. . . . In those circumstances, the auditor should consider the need to qualify his opinion or disclaim an opinion because of the scope limitations. . . .

Alternatively, if the effect of an event is material and is not properly accounted for or disclosed, it may be necessary to give a qualified opinion or adverse opinion. Finally, if the effect of an illegal act on the financial statements cannot be estimated, then the auditor should modify the report in the manner used for disclosing uncertainties (see Chapter 16). If in the situations mentioned above the client is unwilling to accept the appropriate modified report, the auditor should consider withdrawing from the engagement and reporting the situation to the client's board of directors.

Other Considerations.   If an auditor finds an illegal act, regardless of its materiality, the auditor must carefully consider management's response once the matter is brought to their attention. Unless appropriate consideration is given to the reported illegal act, the auditor should consider withdrawing from the engagement.

It is up to the client's management to notify parties other than personnel within the client's organization of the existence of an illegal act. *SAS No. 17* (AU 328.19) states that "generally, the auditor is under no obligation to notify those parties. However, if the auditor considers the illegal act to be sufficiently serious to warrant withdrawing from the engagement, he should consult with his legal counsel as to what other action, if any, he should take."

Foreign Corrupt Practices Act.   The Foreign Corrupt Practices Act of 1977 (FCPA) prohibits all U.S. companies (as well as their officers, directors, agents, employees, and shareholders who are acting on behalf of the company) from bribing foreign governmental or political officials. Additionally, publicly held corporations are required to meet certain requirements concerning internal control and recordkeeping.

The FCPA prohibits any U.S. company from using interstate commerce to offer, pay, promise to pay, or authorize giving anything of value to any of the following to induce the recipient to misuse official position in order to wrongfully assist in obtaining, retaining, or directing business to any company or person:

1. Foreign official, including any person acting in an official capacity for a foreign government, department, agency, or instrumentality.
2. Foreign political party, or official or candidate for foreign political office.
3. Other person, while knowing or having reason to know, that the offer or payment will ultimately go to either of the above two categories.

Penalties for conviction of such acts include fines and/or imprisonment.

Internal Control and Recordkeeping.   The law also amends the Securities Exchange Act of 1934 by requiring public companies to

> . . . devise and maintain a system of internal accounting control sufficient to provide reasonable assurance that—

(i)   transactions are executed in accordance with management's general or specific authorization;

(ii) transactions are recorded as necessary (I) to permit preparation of financial statements in conformity with generally accepted accounting principles or any other criteria applicable to such statements, and (II) to maintain accountability for assets;

(iii) access to assets is permitted only in accordance with management's general or specific authorization; and

(iv) the recorded accountability for assets is compared with the existing assets at reasonable intervals and appropriate action is taken with respect to any differences.

These objectives were taken from *SAS No. 1* (AU 320.28) and were incorporated in Section 13(b) of the 1934 Act. Consequently, the management and employees of a public company may be subject to civil and criminal liability under the federal securities laws for failure to maintain a sufficient system of internal control.

The FCPA also requires public companies to ". . . make and keep books, records, and accounts, which, in reasonable detail, accurately and fairly reflect the transactions and dispositions of the assets of the issuer. . . ." Congress intended the internal control section of the law to strengthen the antibribery provisions. However, the internal control provision of the law is not limited to the detection or prevention of foreign bribery—and it affects all public companies whether or not they are involved in foreign trade.

Management's Responsibility under the FCPA.   Corporate management is responsible for seeing that corrupt practices do not occur in the conduct of their business. Businesses may want to establish codes of conduct for the guidance of officers and employees in their business activities. Companies (especially those involved in international activities) may want to monitor compliance with such codes of conduct. Internal or external auditors may be asked to review compliance with certain policies.

Management also is responsible for the establishment and maintenance of the system of internal control (discussed in Chapters 4 and 5).

Auditor's Responsibility under the FCPA.   An independent audit does not guarantee detection of an illegal act. However, *SAS No. 16* (AU 327.06) notes that the ". . . auditor's plan for an examination . . . is influenced by the possibility of material errors or irregularities." And *SAS No. 17* (AU 328.08) states "the auditor should . . . inquire about the client's compliance with laws. . . ." Thus, the auditor may become aware of possible violation of the FCPA.

An AICPA auditing interpretation, "Scope of Study and Evaluation of Accounting Control and the Foreign Corrupt Practices Act" (AU 9328.02) states that ". . . there is nothing in the Act or the related legislative history that purports to alter the auditor's duty to his client or the purpose of his study and evaluation of internal accounting control. The Act creates express new duties only for companies subject to the Securities Exchange Act of 1934, not for auditors."

As discussed in Chapter 18, *SAS No. 20* (AU 323), as amended by *SAS No. 30* (AU 642), requires the auditor to inform the client of material weaknesses in internal accounting control disclosed during the audit. In addition, two AICPA auditing interpretations, "Material Weaknesses in Accounting Control and the Foreign Corrupt Practices Act" (AU 9328.04–.05) and "Compliance with the Foreign Corrupt Practices Act of 1977" (AU 9642.12–.13) discuss the auditor's responsibilities in communicating with management concerning material weaknesses, as follows:

1. ". . . the standards for determining a violation of the Act may differ from those applied by an auditor in determining material weaknesses. . . ." Thus, ". . . the auditor may wish to include a statement to that effect in any communication concerning internal accounting control." Furthermore, "the auditor should not issue a report that provides assurance on compliance with the internal accounting control provision of the Act." [AU 9642.12–.13]

2. If an auditor finds a material weakness in internal accounting control, the matter should be discussed with the client's management and legal counsel to determine if the weakness violates the Act. Consideration should be given to corrective action. However, "if management has concluded that corrective action for a material weakness is not practicable, consideration should be given to the reasons underlying that conclusion, including management's evaluation of the costs of correction in relation to the expected benefit to be derived. . . . If it is determined that there has been a violation of the Act and appropriate consideration is not given to the violation, the auditor should consider withdrawing from the current engagement or dissociating himself from any future relationship with the client. . . ." [AU 9328.04–.05]

Minutes of Shareholders, Board of Directors, and Committee Meetings

Corporate minutes are a record of meetings and actions of the shareholders, board of directors, or any other group entrusted with the responsibility of administering corporate affairs. While the day-to-day, ordinary business activities of a company are seldom the subject of corporate resolutions, the minutes may contain authorizations to borrow money, references to contracts that obligate the company, mention of claims or lawsuits, authorization of dividends, approval of executive compensation, or approval of major capital acquisitions. Authorization for bank signatories and the opening or closing of bank accounts also will appear in the minutes. Matters considered and actions taken by the shareholders or board of directors may impact the financial statements, so the auditor should have knowledge of them. Such knowledge provides evidence of the validity of the accounts affected by the actions of the board of directors or shareholders.

Whenever possible, the auditor should obtain from the client complete copies of minutes of meetings of shareholders, directors, and executive and other important committees. If the copies given to the auditor are not signed, the copies should be compared with the originals to make sure they are both accurate and complete. The minutes should be made a permanent part of the working papers.

If it is not possible to obtain copies of the minutes, the minute books should be read and summarized by the auditor. The excerpts recorded for the working papers should be those that may affect the financial statements.

If the client is unwilling to make the minutes available at all, the auditor should explain to the client the importance of the minutes to the audit examination. The client should be told that, without such access, a disclaimer of opinion may be necessary.

General Ledger and Journal Entries

The auditor should review all large, nonstandard postings to the general ledger and also any client working paper entries made solely to prepare the financial statements. The purpose is to identify any large or unusual postings from unfamiliar sources and other unusual entries that might not have been identified through other audit procedures (e.g., the purchase and sale of a significant item of equipment in the same year).

This review should be performed by an auditor who is familiar with the recurring journal entries and other posting sources so that unusual items will be detected. It usually is beneficial to set a dollar limit below which entries need not be investigated. For publicly held companies that issue interim reports to shareholders and neither issue a separate fourth quarter report nor disclose fourth quarter results in the annual report, the auditor should be alert to significant fourth quarter transactions or adjustments that may require disclosure. These disclosures are required by *APB Opinion No. 28*, "Interim Financial Information."

Subsequent Events

The auditor's report based on the examination of financial statements relates to the financial position as of a given date and the results of operations and changes in financial position for a period ended on that date. Certain events and transactions occurring after the balance sheet date may have a significant impact on the financial statements; therefore, audit procedures should extend into the subsequent period. In certain instances, subsequent events may require changes in the statements or in the related footnotes.

Generally, the period covered by the post balance sheet date procedures extends from the date of the balance sheet to the date used in the auditor's report, which in most cases is the date of completion of the field work. When preparing registration statements for the SEC, this period is extended to the date of the registration statement.

Types of Subsequent Events.   There are two types of subsequent events that should be considered:

1. *Events that affect the financial statements at the balance sheet date and should be reflected therein.*   If subsequent information is acquired in time to permit its use, if the information provides a basis for more accurate estimates or provisions, and if the information would have been utilized had it been available at the balance sheet date, appropriate adjustments should be made in the financial statements. Examples are collection or settlement of receivables or determination or settlement of liabilities on a substantially different basis than previously anticipated, or events that make large portions of the inventory or investments in stock or plant assets worthless.

2. *Events that relate to occurrences that arose subsequent to the balance sheet date.*   These are events that do not require adjustment of the financial statements but whose effect in the future may be such that disclosure is advisable. Examples are changes in short- and long-term debt and capital stock, restrictive covenants relating to dividends or other matters, mergers or acquisitions, disposal of a substantial portion of the productive assets, or serious losses from flood, fire, or other casualty. *SAS No. 1* (AU 560.05) notes that "occasionally . . . an event may be so significant that disclosure can best be made by supplementing the historical financial statements with pro forma financial data giving effect to the event, as if it had occurred on the date of the balance sheet." Further, *SAS No. 1* (AU 560.09) states that when such events are very material ". . . the auditor may want to include in his report an explanatory paragraph directing the reader's attention to the event and its effects. . . ."

Certain events do not require adjustment of the financial statements and usually do not require disclosure. Examples are war, strikes, unionization, management changes, marketing agreements, or loss of important customers. Even if these events had occurred before the balance sheet date, they typically would not be commented on in the financial statements. Further, the reasons for disclosure of such events may not be clear, and financial statement users could draw incorrect inferences from such disclosures.

Auditing Procedures in the Subsequent Period. The auditor's search for the occurrence of subsequent events should include the following steps [see *SAS No. 1* (AU 560.12)]:

1. Scan cash receipts journal for evidence of proceeds of loans or significant sales of productive assets.
2. Scan cash disbursements journal for unusual payments and payment of liabilities not recorded as of the balance sheet date.
3. Review general journal entries.
4. Review collections of accounts receivable.
5. Review credit memoranda issued for sales returns and allowances. Ascertain that there is no important time lag in issuing the credits.
6. Review the various corporate minutes. Inquire about matters covered at meetings for which minutes are not yet available.
7. Review the client's most recent interim financial statements.
8. "Inquire of client's legal counsel concerning litigation, claims, and assessments. . . ." (*SAS No. 1*—560.12, as amended by *SAS No. 12*)
9. Question management about the occurrence of subsequent events. Ask management to comment in the letter of representations (this letter is discussed below) concerning events that may have occurred.

Subsequent Discovery of Facts. The auditor's responsibility generally ends as of the date of the audit report. However, at a later date, the auditor may discover facts not previously known, that existed at the date of the audit report. *SAS No. 1* (AU 561.05) states that the auditor's actions in such situations depend on whether ". . . (a) his report would have been affected if the information had been known to him at the date of his report and had not been reflected in the financial statements and (b) he believes there are persons currently relying or likely to rely on the financial statements who would attach importance to the information." The procedures the auditor should follow in such a situation are described in detail in *SAS No. 1* (AU 561).

Financial Statement Review Procedures

In addition to the various tests of the accounting records, the auditor should review the financial statements for clerical accuracy and completeness. Each financial statement amount should be traced to the trial balance or other working papers (e.g., worksheet for the statement of changes in financial position; computation of earnings per share, if applicable). Financial data included in the footnotes to the financial statements should be traced to appropriate detail working papers.

Certain companies are required to present supplemental information (e.g., segment data, interim financial data, oil and gas reserves) in footnotes to the financial statements or elsewhere in their annual reports to shareholders. The procedures required for auditing or reviewing this information are discussed later in this chapter.

Clients often publish other information along with financial statements. While not the subject of the auditor's report, this information may relate to the audit examination or to the propriety of the auditor's report. Consequently, the auditor should read such other information and consider whether it is consistent with the information presented in the financial statements. *SAS No. 8* covers the auditor's responsibility for other financial information. Chapter 16 discusses how *SAS No. 8* and the other information affects the auditor's report.

Letter of Representations[7]

A required procedure in an audit is to obtain written representations from company management to (1) confirm information given to the auditor orally and (2) supplement information the auditor has obtained from the books and records of the company. The letter of representations is addressed to the auditor and signed by the client (although the letter often is drafted by the auditor).

Figure 14–5 lists the areas commonly covered in the letter of representations. The written representations are an important part of the working papers. They give the company's management an opportunity to consider whether all important matters have been disclosed to the auditor and also remind management of its primary responsibility for the fair presentation of the financial statements. However, the representations do not relieve the auditor of the responsibility to follow generally accepted auditing standards in the examination.

Generally, written representations may be limited to items that are considered material to the financial statements either individually or in total. However, materiality criteria do not apply to certain items (e.g., items 1, 2, 3, and item 7, as it relates to individuals significantly involved in the system of internal accounting control) in Figure 14–5.

The letter of representations should be addressed to the auditor and dated as of the date of the audit report. The letter should be signed by members of management responsible for the matters discussed—generally the chief financial officer and chief executive officer. However, depending on the circumstances, the auditor may want to obtain representations from others. For example, an auditor might want to obtain representations about the

---

[7] This section is based on *Statement on Auditing Standards No. 19*, "Client Representations," American Institute of Certified Public Accountants, 1977.

FIGURE 14-5 Areas Commonly Covered in a Client's Letter of Representations

1. Management acknowledgment of its responsibility for the fair presentation of the financial statements.
2. The availability of all financial records and any related data.
3. The completeness and availability of all minutes of meetings of shareholders, directors, and committees of directors.
4. The nonexistence of errors or unrecorded transactions in the financial statements.
5. Information concerning related party transactions.
6. Information concerning noncompliance with contracts that may affect the financial statements.
7. Irregularities involving the client's management or employees.
8. Communications that the client received from regulatory agencies relating to noncompliance with, or deficiencies in, financial reporting practices.
9. The client's plans or intentions that may affect the carrying value or classification of assets or liabilities.
10. The disclosure of compensating balances or other arrangements involving restrictions on cash balances and disclosure of line-of-credit or similar arrangements.
11. Reducing inventory that is obsolete to net realizable value.
12. Losses as a result of sales commitments.
13. Status of title to assets.
14. Obligations to repurchase assets that were previously sold.
15. Losses from purchase commitments for inventory quantities in excess of requirements or at prices in excess of market.
16. Violations or possible violations of laws or regulations whose effects should be considered for disclosure in the financial statements or as a basis for recording a loss contingency.
17. Information relating to subsequent events.
18. Other liabilities and gain or loss contingencies that are required to be accrued or disclosed by *FASB Statement No. 5.*
19. Unasserted claims or assessments that the client's lawyer has advised are probable of assertion and must be disclosed in accordance with *FASB Statement No. 5.*
20. Capital stock repurchase options or agreements or capital stock reserved for options, warrants, conversions, or other requirements.
21. Unaudited interim financial information included in audited financial statements.
22. Other matters that the auditor may determine, based on the circumstances of the engagement, should be included in written representations from management.

Source: Adapted from *Statement on Auditing Standards No. 19,* "Client Representations," American Institute of Certified Public Accountants, 1977, (AU 333).

completeness of the minutes of board of directors meetings from the person responsible for keeping such records.

Management's failure to comply with an independent auditor's request for written representations on material matters may be a scope limitation that would impact the auditor's report.

PROCEDURES PERFORMED ON CERTAIN AUDITS

Effect of Internal Audit

In Chapter 4, we pointed out that an internal audit staff is part of an effective control environment. *SAS No. 9*, "The Effect of an Internal Audit Function on the Scope of the Independent Auditor's Examination" (AU 322), describes how the auditor should consider the work of internal auditors in determining the overall audit plan. If the normal duties of the internal auditors affect the audit plan or if they perform work at the independent auditor's request, their competence and objectivity should be reviewed and evaluated and their work should be tested. However, *SAS No. 9* (AU 322.01) precludes the substitution of internal auditors' work for the work of the independent auditor.

During initial planning, the independent auditor should plan to use the work of internal auditors to reduce the amount of work the independent auditor performs in the examination. Ordinarily, this requires meeting with the internal auditors before they complete their work schedule for the year. Discussions with the internal auditors should cover the scope and findings of their work to date and their plans for the remainder of the year. These discussions should provide the basis for a tentative determination of the effect of the internal audit function on the overall audit plan. Early consideration of the adequacy of the internal auditors' documentation standards and the compatability of their working papers with the independent auditor's working papers should provide for further audit efficiency.

The internal audit function can affect the independent auditor's overall audit plan in the following ways:

1. Internal audit activities may include the testing of important accounting systems. These activities should be considered as part of the control environment.
2. Internal auditors may function as an integral part of the accounting system in a specific area (e.g., preparation of monthly bank reconciliations). The auditor may conclude that these procedures are key to achievement of specific control objectives. The preliminary audit approach should include tests to determine whether these key attributes are functioning.
3. Internal auditors may provide direct assistance to the independent auditor by performing tests under the independent auditor's supervision. Following audit programs prepared or approved by the independent auditor, the internal auditors might examine part of an entity's operations (e.g., a plant, division, branch, or subsidiary) or specific financial statement classifications (e.g., property accounts at various locations), or per-

form specified procedures (e.g., test key attributes, reconcile vendors' statements, or summarize credit information for loans made by a bank).

Competence and Objectivity.   On engagements where there is an internal audit function that can affect the overall audit plan, the independent auditor should evaluate the competence and objectivity of the internal audit staff. Section IV of the questionnaire in Appendix 4A is an example of a document that can be used to help in such an evaluation.

Competence is affected by formal education (including continuing professional education), professional certifications, and prior and current work experience. Information concerning these factors may be obtained by inquiry of appropriate client personnel. Working with the internal auditors, reviewing their working papers for adequacy of documentation, discussing audit methods and problems, and assessing the quality of internal auditors' recommendations also provide information for evaluating their competence.

Competence also can be affected by the level of supervision, particularly when an internal audit department has staff members with varying levels of experience. The adequacy of supervision may be evaluated by reviewing the (1) guidance provided in the audit programs, (2) nature and extent of reviews of working papers and reports, (3) extent to which more experienced auditors work with less experienced auditors, and (4) ratio of supervisors to staff members.

Objectivity relates to internal auditors' abilities to perform their functions without being influenced or restricted by those to whom they report or those they audit. For example, internal auditors who report directly to the president or an executive vice president are likely to be more independent than those reporting to the controller. Often there is more than one line of reporting. The independent auditor should consider the effects on objectivity of an organizational structure that provides for the internal auditors to report the results of their work to one level and administratively to another level. For example, objectivity would be enhanced by internal auditors reporting the results of their work to the audit committee of the board of directors.

However, the objectivity of the internal audit function should not be judged solely on the organizational structure. Other procedures for evaluating objectivity might include:

1. Reviewing internal audit program scope restrictions and determining who established those restrictions.
2. Discussing with internal audit management their perception of the influence to those to whom they report and those they audit on the determination of audit assignments, scope, procedures, and reports.
3. Determining whether all relevant facts and recommendations in working papers are included in reports.

4. Reviewing responses to report recommendations by those being audited and evaluating reasons for any recommendations not implemented.

Objectivity also may be affected by personal relationships among the internal auditors and those they audit. Inquiries should be made concerning family relationships (e.g., are any of the internal auditors or members of their families related to other employees?). The independent auditor also should be alert to situations that may indicate other relationships that may affect objectivity.

Evaluations of Internal Auditors' Work. When internal auditors function as part of the control environment, the independent auditor should reach conclusions regarding the effectiveness of the accounting systems by reviewing and testing their work. Internal audit programs, working papers, and reports should be reviewed carefully. In coming to conclusions, the independent auditor should consider the (1) appropriateness of the audit scope, (2) adequacy of the audit programs and working papers, and (3) consistency of the reports with the results of the work.

Testing the work of the internal auditors should be accomplished by (1) discussing the work performed and working papers prepared with the individuals responsible and (2) examining several of the same or similar transactions or account balances. Similar transactions are ones that are processed by substantially the same procedures within a system (or in substantially the same type of system) of internal accounting control. Similar account balances are those that result from such processing. Examples of similar transactions are:

1. Installment loan transactions of each branch of a bank or finance company having centralized accounting systems.
2. Property additions recorded at a company's various plants, each of which maintains its own records under uniform prescribed accounting and control procedures.

To evaluate the internal auditors' conclusions regarding the effectiveness of the accounting systems, it ordinarily should not be necessary to test the work of each internal auditor in an internal audit department or to test transactions or account balances at each location when the internal auditors have performed the same procedures at a number of locations.

SAS No. 9 (AU 322.08) notes that testing the work of internal auditors should be done by examination of "documentary evidence." However, in certain instances, testing of procedures by observation may be appropriate (e.g., observation of internal auditors' checking of physical inventories in a manufacturing plant or counting of cash and securities in a bank).

When Providing Direct Assistance. When internal auditors provide direct assistance to the auditor, their work should be evaluated carefully. In addition, the independent auditor should reexamine several of the same transactions or account balances that the internal auditors examined. The extent of reexamination will be affected by the degree of audit judgment that the internal auditors are required to exercise and the degree of supervision that the independent auditor provides.

The independent auditor has sole responsibility for the audit report and, therefore, should judge the effectiveness of internal accounting control, the sufficiency of tests performed, the materiality of transactions, and other matters affecting the audit report. When the internal auditors' work affects the examination, the independent auditor's testing and evaluation of their work, together with other procedures performed, should be extensive enough to enable the independent auditor to make judgments and reach conclusions as to these matters. The extent to which the internal audit function can affect the independent auditor's overall audit plan ultimately depends on the independent auditor's evaluation of the risk that significant audit adjustments or financial statement disclosures may be required in a particular audit area.

Specifically, the independent auditor should not rely on internal auditors to perform a substantial part of the examination of (1) key account balances or transactions (e.g., evaluation of the allowance for loan losses for a bank, percentage-of-completion estimates for a construction contractor, significant property sale by a land developer), (2) material unusual transactions, or (3) any subsidiary's financial statements on which the auditor plans to express a separate opinion.

The independent auditor's working papers should include a memorandum that describes the normal duties of the internal auditors and documents the independent auditor's evaluation of their competence and objectivity and the effect of their work on the overall audit plan. When internal auditors function as part of the control environment, the independent auditor should obtain copies of their reports that relate to important audit areas or that include comments on significant deficiencies in controls. When internal auditors directly assist the independent auditor, the working papers should be retained by the independent auditor.

Using an Outside Specialist[8]

It may be necessary for the independent auditor to employ a person or firm with a particular skill or knowledge (outside of accounting and auditing) to aid in the conduct of an audit. Examples of such outside specialists include geologists, engineers, appraisers, actuaries, and attorneys. The employment of such individuals or firms raises a number of questions including: (1)

---

[8] This section is based on *Statement on Auditing Standards No. 11,* "Using the Work of a Specialist," American Institute of Certified Public Accounts, 1976.

when an outside specialist is needed; (2) how to select an outside specialist; (3) how to use the findings of an outside specialist; and (4) how the use of an outside specialist can affect the auditor's report.

When a Specialist Is Needed. Examples of audit situations where the assistance of a specialist is appropriate include:

1. Valuation of assets (e.g., jewelry)—an appraiser.
2. Evaluation of amounts derived by actuarial determinations (e.g. pension costs, insurance reserves)—an actuary.
3. Interpretation of contractual agreements or regulations—an attorney.
4. Percentage-of-completion estimates (e.g., government contract)—an engineer.

Selection of a Specialist. The independent auditor should evaluate the professional reputation and qualifications of the outside specialist. Consideration should be given to factors such as the (1) specialist's license or certification, (2) reputation of the specialist in his or her profession, and (3) relationship of the specialist to the auditor's client. The specialist should be independent of the client.

Using the Specialist's Findings. The independent auditor may use the work and findings of the outside specialist as evidential matter supporting some aspect of the financial statements. Consequently, the auditor should understand the methods and assumptions that the specialist uses. The auditor should be satisfied that these methods and assumptions are valid for purposes of providing evidence regarding the items being tested. The auditor should consider testing any accounting data furnished to the specialist by the client (e.g., payroll data furnished to an actuary for purposes of making pension plan calculations). Further, the auditor should evaluate whether the conclusions of the specialist support the client's representations. If the auditor is satisfied that the specialist's work is reasonable, then it is appropriate to rely on that work. *SAS No. 11* (AU 336.08) states that in cases in which the specialist is related to a client ". . . the auditor should consider performing additional procedures with respect to some or all of the related specialists' assumptions, methods, or findings to determine that the findings are not unreasonable or engage an outside specialist for that purpose."

Effect on the Auditor's Report. If the outside specialist's findings support the client's representations, the auditor may conclude (assuming no other information to the contrary) that sufficient competent evidence has been obtained. In such a situation, an unqualified opinion should be given in the auditor's report, without any reference to an outside specialist.

If there is a material difference between the client's representations and the specialist's findings (or if the auditor believes the specialist's findings are not reasonable), the auditor should apply additional procedures. If additional procedures do not resolve the differences, the auditor should consider engaging another specialist. If it appears that sufficient competent evidence cannot be obtained, *SAS No. 11,* (AU 336.09) states that the auditor should ". . . qualify his opinion or disclaim an opinion because the inability to obtain sufficient competent evidential matter as to an assertion of material significance in the financial statements constitutes a scope limitation. . . ." Alternatively, if the auditor concludes after additional procedures or obtaining results from a second specialist that the client's representations are not in accordance with generally accepted accounting principles (GAAP), then a qualified or adverse opinion should be given. Chapter 16 discusses these various modifications of the auditor's report. If a modified auditor's report is given because of the report or findings of a specialist, the auditor may make reference to and identify the specialist in the audit report.

Audit Aspects of Segment Information[9]

FASB Statement No. 14, "Financial Reporting for Segments of a Business Enterprise," requires that certain information concerning the client's operations in various industries, foreign operations, export sales, and major customers be included in the annual financial statements.[10] Independent auditors then must apply certain audit procedures and report on segment information. Auditing segment information is discussed here; reporting on segment information is discussed in Chapter 16.

SAS No. 21 (AU 435.03) states that "the objective of auditing procedures applied to segment information is to provide the auditor with a reasonable basis for concluding whether the information is presented in conformity with *FASB Statement No. 14* in relation to the financial statements taken as a whole." *SAS No. 21* further states that the auditor ". . . is not required to apply auditing procedures that would be necessary to express a separate opinion on the segment information."

Materiality. *SAS No. 21* (AU 435.05) states that materiality in considering segment information should be evaluated in terms of dollar magnitude of the information in relation ". . . to the financial statements taken as a whole." However, qualitative factors as well as quantitative factors should be considered in judging materiality. *SAS No. 21* (AU 435.08) lists the following qualitative factors that an auditor may want to consider:

---

[9] This section is based on *Statement on Auditing Standards No. 21,* "Segment Information," American Institute of Certified Public Accountants, 1977.

[10] *FASB Statement Nos. 18, 21, 24, and 30* amend *FASB Statement No. 14.* As a result of *Statement No. 21,* the financial statements of nonpublic enterprises are no longer subject to the requirements of *Statement No. 14.*

[1] The significance of a matter to a particular entity (for example, a misstatement of the revenue and operating profit of a relatively small segment that is represented by management to be important to the future profitability of the entity),

[2] [T]he pervasiveness of a matter (for example, whether it affects the amounts and presentation of numerous items in the segment information), and

[3] [T]he impact of a matter (for example, whether it distorts the trends reflected in segment information). . . .

Modification of Regular Audit Procedures. *SAS No. 21* (AU 435.06) states that "in planning his examination, it may be necessary for the auditor to modify or redirect selected audit tests to be applied to the financial statements taken as a whole. For example, the auditor may decide to select inventories for physical observation on the basis of industry segments or geographic areas." *SAS No. 21* gives examples of factors that should be considered in determining whether procedures should be modified or redirected:

a. Internal accounting control and the degree of integration, centralization, and uniformity of the accounting records.

b. The nature, number, and relative size of industry segments and geographic areas.

c. The nature and number of subsidiaries or divisions in each industry segment and geographic area.

d. The accounting principles used for the industry segments and geographic areas.

SAS No. 21 (AU 435.06) states that ". . . the tests of underlying accounting records normally applied in an examination of financial statements should include a consideration of whether the entity's revenue, operating expenses, and identifiable assets are appropriately classified among industry segments and geographic areas."

Procedures Applied to Segment Information. *SAS No. 21* (AU 435.07) suggests that the following procedures be applied to segment information:

1. Discuss with management its method of determining segment information. Consider the reasonableness of the method relative to *FASB Statement No. 14.*

2. "Inquire as to the bases of accounting for sales or transfers between industry segments and between geographic areas, and test, to the extent considered necessary, those sales or transfers for conformity with the bases of accounting disclosed."

3. "Test the disaggregation of the entity's financial statements into segment information."

4. "Inquire as to the methods of allocating expenses incurred and identifiable assets used jointly by two or more segments, evaluate whether those

methods are reasonable, and test the allocations to the extent considered necessary."

5. "Determine whether the segment information has been presented consistently from period to period and, if not, whether the nature and effect of the inconsistency are disclosed and, if applicable, whether the information has been retroactively restated in conformity with paragraph 40 of *FASB Statement No. 14*."

Supplementary Information Required by the FASB[11]

*SFC = yes
AICPA = no*

The FASB requires certain information to be provided by management outside the basic financial statements. *SAS No. 27* (AU 553.06) states that the FASB regards such information ". . . an essential part of the financial reporting of certain entities. . . . Accordingly, the auditor should apply certain limited procedures to supplementary information required by the FASB and should report deficiencies in, or the omission of, such information."

SAS No. 27 (AU 553.07) suggests that the auditor apply the following procedures to such information:

add a middle paragraph will not qualify opinion

a. Inquire of management regarding the methods of preparing information, including (1) whether it is measured and presented within guidelines prescribed by the FASB, (2) whether methods of measurement or presentation have been changed from those used in the prior period and the reasons for any such changes, and (3) any significant assumptions or interpretations underlying the measurement or presentation.

b. Compare the information for consistency with (1) management's responses to the foregoing inquiries, (2) audited financial statements, and (3) other knowledge obtained during the examination of the financial statements.

c. Consider whether representations on supplementary information required by the FASB should be included in specific written representations obtained from management. . . .

d. Apply additional procedures, if any, that other Statements prescribe for specific types of supplementary information required by the FASB.

e. Make additional inquiries if application of the foregoing procedures causes the auditor to believe that the information may not be measured or presented within applicable guidelines.

Chapter 16 discusses how the results of the review of the supplementary information affects the auditor's report.

In addition, the Auditing Standards Board has issued three SAS's that supplement *SAS No. 27*. They are *SAS No. 28*, "Supplementary Information on the Effects of Changing Prices" (AU 554), *SAS No. 33*, "Supplementary

---

[11] This section is based on *Statement on Auditing Standards No. 27*, "Supplementing Information Required by the Financial Accounting Standards Board," American Institute of Certified Public Accountants, 1979.

Oil and Gas Reserve Information" (AU 555), and *SAS No. 40*, "Supplementary Mineral Reserve Information" (AU 556).

Interim Financial Information[12]

This section discusses the auditor's objectives and procedures that should be applied when engaged by a client to review interim financial information. *SAS No. 36* (AU 722.02) notes that the review may be of interim financial information ". . . presented alone, including interim financial statements and summarized interim financial data that purport to conform with the provisions of *Accounting Principles Board Opinion No. 28*, as amended, and that is issued by a public entity to stockholders, boards of directors, or others, or contained in reports filed with regulatory agencies. . . ." Alternatively, the *SAS* indicates the review may be of interim financial information which ". . . accompanies, or is included in a note to, audited financial statements of a public or nonpublic entity."

Objective of a Review. *SAS No. 36* (AU 722.03) states:

> The objective of a review of interim financial information is to provide the accountant, based on objectively applying his knowledge of financial reporting practices to significant accounting matters of which he becomes aware through inquiries and analytical review procedures, with a basis for reporting whether material modification should be made for such information to conform with generally accepted accounting principles.

The *SAS* indicates a review is not an audit in accordance with generally accepted auditing standards. Further while significant matters may come to the auditor's attention during a review, there is no assurance that all of such matters that would be disclosed by an audit will be disclosed by a review.

Nature of Procedures for a Review. *SAS No. 36* (AU 722.06) notes that the procedures used in ". . . a review of interim financial information consist primarily of inquiries and analytical review procedures concerning significant accounting matters. . . ." *SAS No. 36* indicates that usually these procedures include:

1. "Inquiry concerning (1) the accounting system, to obtain an understanding of the manner in which transactions are recorded, classified, and summarized in the preparation of interim financial information and (2) any significant changes in the system of internal accounting control, to ascertain their potential effect on the preparation of interim financial information."

[12] This section is based on *Statement on Auditing Standards No. 36*, "Review of Interim Financial Information," American Institute of Certified Public Accountants, 1981.

2. "Application of analytical review procedures to interim financial information to identify and provide a basis for inquiry about relationships and individual items that appear to be unusual. Analytical review procedures for purposes of this section, consist of (1) comparison of the financial information with comparable information for the immediately preceding interim period and for corresponding previous periods, (2) comparison of the financial information with anticipated results, and (3) study of the relationships of elements of financial information that would be expected to conform to a predictable pattern based on the entity's experience. In applying these procedures, the independent accountant should consider the types of matters that in the preceding year or quarters have required accounting adjustment."

3. "Reading the minutes of meetings of shareholders, board of directors, and committees of the board of directors to identify actions that may affect the interim financial information."

4. "Reading the interim financial information to consider, on the basis of information coming to the independent accountant's attention, whether the information to be reported conforms with generally accepted accounting principles."

5. "Obtaining reports from other independent accountants, if any, who have been engaged to make a review of the interim financial information of significant components of the reporting entity, its subsidiaries, or other investees. . . ."

6. Inquiring of management personnel responsible ". . . for financial and accounting matters concerning (1) whether the interim financial information has been prepared in conformity with generally accepted accounting principles consistently applied, (2) changes in the entity's business activities or accounting practices, (3) matters as to which questions have arisen in the course of applying the foregoing procedures, and (4) events subsequent to the date of the interim financial information that would have a material effect on the presentation of such information."

7. Obtaining written representations from management on matters the accountant feels are appropriate (e.g., subsequent events).

Timing and Extent of Procedures. *SAS No. 36* suggests that the accountant carefully plan the review of interim information. Consideration should be given to accomplishing some of the work before the end of the interim period.

SAS No. 36 (AU 722.08–.15) indicates that the extent of the application of the procedures for a review is a function of a variety of factors, including:

1. The accountant's familarity with the client's accounting and financial reporting practices.

2. The accountant's awareness of the client's internal control system and any weaknesses in that system.

3. The accountant's awareness of ". . . changes in the nature or volume of the client's business activities or accounting changes."

4. Questions raised during a review that may require the accountant to make additional inquiries or perform additional procedures.

5. The results of the procedures used in the regular audit of financial statements. Such procedures may result in the modification of the procedures used in the review of interim financial statements.

SAS No. 36 also discusses reporting on interim financial information, which is covered in Chapter 17.

QUESTIONS AND PROBLEMS

14–1. List some documents that the auditor may examine in support of transactions when auditing the administration component.

14–2. When auditing the administration component, for what items might the auditor request confirmation?

14–3. List some examples of analytical review procedures that may be used as direct tests of balances for accounts in the administration component.

14–4. What are the auditor's objectives in examining intangible assets? Give some examples of intangible assets.

14–5. Describe the audit procedures that would generally be followed in establishing the propriety of the recorded liability for federal income taxes of an established corporation that you are auditing for the first time. Consideration should be given to the status of (a) the liability for prior years and (b) the liability arising from the current year's income. (AICPA, adapted)

14–6. What evidence should the auditor obtain regarding litigation, claims, and assessments?

14–7. What should the auditor be alert for regarding related party transactions?

14–8. What specific audit procedures may an auditor use to identify the existence of related party transactions?

14–9. Once related party transactions have been identified, what additional audit procedures may be needed to determine (a) the purpose, nature, and extent of the transactions, and (b) the effect of the transactions on financial statements? (AICPA, adapted)

14–10. The auditor should be satisfied that material related party transactions are adequately disclosed in the financial statements. Discuss items that should appear in such a disclosure.

14–11. List some specific audit procedures that may identify illegal acts.

14–12. The auditor's discovery of the occurrence of an illegal act may result in a modification of the audit report. Discuss these possible modifications.

14–13. Jane Smith, CPA, is a partner of the CPA firm of XYZ CPA's. During the course of her annual audit of the Small Company, Smith uncovers an illegal act committed by the head of purchasing. Smith reports the act to Small's president and board of directors. Since the effect of the act is not material, the president and board decide to do nothing. What should Smith do?

14–14. List the procedures that an independent auditor might use in searching for the occurrence of subsequent events.

14–15. Discuss some ways in which the internal audit function can affect the independent auditor's overall audit plan.

14–16. In evaluating the competence of a client's internal audit staff, the independent auditor will look at several factors. List some of these factors.

14–17. The objectivity of the internal audit function should not be judged solely on the organizational structure. List other procedures for evaluating objectivity.

14–18. What is the auditor's objective in examining segment information?

14–19. Is an auditor required to audit supplemental information that the FASB requires management to provide outside the basic financial statements?

14–20. What is the auditor's objective in making a review of interim financial information for a client?

14–21. List the procedures that an auditor may use in reviewing interim financial information.

14–22. Comment on the timing of an accountant's review of interim information.

14–23. Discuss the extent of the application of the procedures of a review of interim information.

14–24. Select the *best* answer for each of the following questions:
   a. Which of the following audit procedures would be *least* effective for detecting contingent liabilities?
      (1) Summarizing the minutes of the meetings of the board of directors.
      (2) Reviewing the bank confirmation letters.
      (3) Examining confirmation letters from customers.
      (4) Confirming pending legal matters with the corporate attorney.
   b. A CPA has received an attorney's letter in which *no* significant disagreements with the client's assessments of contingent liabilities were noted. The resignation of the client's lawyer shortly after receipt of the letter should alert the auditor that:
      (1) Undisclosed unasserted claims may have arisen.
      (2) The attorney was unable to form a conclusion with respect to the significance of litigation, claims, and assessments.
      (3) The auditor must begin a completely new examination of contingent liabilities.
      (4) An adverse opinion will be necessary.

    c. Auditors often request that the client send a letter of inquiry to those attorneys who have been consulted with respect to litigation, claims, or assessments. The primary reason for this request is to provide the auditor with:

        (1) An estimate of the dollar amount of the probable loss.

        (2) An expert opinion as to whether a loss is possible, probable, or remote.

        (3) Information concerning the progress of cases to date.

        (4) Corroborative evidential matter.

    d. For a reporting entity that has participated in related party transactions that are material, disclosure in the financial statements should include:

        (1) The nature of the relationship and the terms and manner of settlement.

        (2) Details of the transactions within major classifications.

        (3) A statement to the effect that a transaction was consummated on terms no less favorable than those that would have been obtained if the transaction had been with an unrelated party.

        (4) A reference to deficiencies in the entity's system of internal accounting control.

    e. The objective of a review of the interim financial information of a publicly held company is to:

        (1) Provide the accountant with a basis for the expression of an opinion.

        (2) Estimate the accuracy of financial statements based upon limited tests of accounting records.

        (3) Provide the accountant with a basis for reporting whether material modifications should be made.

        (4) Obtain corroborating evidential matter through inspection, observation, and confirmation.

    f. Which of the audit procedures listed below would be *least* likely to disclose the existence of related party transactions of a client during the period under audit?

        (1) Reading "conflict-of-interest" statements obtained by the client from its management.

        (2) Scanning accounting records for large transactions at or just prior to the end of the period under audit.

        (3) Inspecting invoices from law firms.

        (4) Confirming large purchase and sales transactions with the vendors and/or customers involved.

    g. An example of a transaction that may be indicative of the existence of related parties is:

        (1) Borrowing or lending at a rate of interest that equals the current market rate.

        (2) Selling real estate at a price that is comparable to its appraised value.

        (3) Making large loans with specified terms as to when or how the funds will be repaid.

        (4) Exchanging property for similar property in a nonmonetary transaction.

                                 (AICPA, adapted)

14–25. During the course of your examination of the financial statements of Hawthorn Inc., for the year ended December 31, 19X1, your post–balance sheet examination disclosed the following items:

1. January 3, 19X2: The state government approved plans for the construction of an expressway. The plan will result in the appropriation of a portion of the land owned by Hawthorn, Inc.'s Welco Division. Construction will begin in late 19X2. No estimate of the condemnation award is available.

2. January 7, 19X2: The mineral content of a shipment of ore to Hawthorn en route on December 31, 19X1, was determined to be 72 percent. The shipment was recorded at year-end at an estimated content of 50 percent by a debit to Raw Material Inventory and a credit to Accounts Payable in the amount of $20,600. The final liability to the vendor is based on the actual mineral content of the shipment.

3. January 15, 19X2: Culminating a series of personal disagreements between Johnson, the president, and his brother-in-law, the treasurer, the latter resigned, effective immediately, under an agreement whereby the corporation would purchase his 10 percent stock ownership at book value as of December 31, 19X1. Payment is to be made in two equal amounts in cash on January 31 and July 31, 19X2.

4. January 31, 19X2: As a result of reduced sales, production was curtailed in January and some workers were laid off at both of the company's divisions. On February 5, 19X2, all remaining workers went on strike. To date the strike is unsettled.

5. February 10, 19X2: A contract was signed whereby Carlton, Inc., purchased from Hawthorn, Inc., all of the Welco Division's fixed assets (including rights to receive the proceeds of any property condemnation) and inventories. The effective date of the transfer will be March 1, 19X2. The sale price was $500,000, subject to adjustment following the taking of a physical inventory. Important factors contributing to the decision to enter into the contract were the policy of the board of directors of Carlton, Inc., to diversify the company's activities and the report of a survey conducted by an independent market appraisal firm which revealed a declining market for Welco's products. The Welco Division accounted for approximately 45 percent of Hawthorn's revenues.

Assume that the preceding items came to your attention prior to completion of your audit on February 15, 19X2, and that you will render a standard audit report.

Required for each of the above items:

a. State the audit procedures, if any, that would have brought the item to your attention. Indicate other sources of information that may have revealed the item.

b. Discuss the disclosure you would recommend for the item, listing details that you would suggest be disclosed. Indicate those items or details, if any, that should not be disclosed. Present your reasons for recommending or not recommending disclosure of the items or details.

14–26. Windek, a CPA, is nearing the completion of an examination of the financial statements of Jubilee, Inc., for the year ended December 31, 1986. Windek is currently concerned with determining the occurrence of subsequent events that may require adjustment or disclosure essential to a fair presentation in conformity with GAAP.

Required:

a. Briefly explain what is meant by the phrase "subsequent event."

494

   b. How do those subsequent events that require financial statement adjustment
      differ from those that require financial statement disclosure?
   c. What are the procedures that should be performed in order to determine the
      occurrence of subsequent events?   (AICPA, adapted)

14–27. Loman, CPA, who has examined the financial statements of the Broadwall Corpora-
       tion, a publicly held company, for the year ended December 31, 1986, was asked
       to perform a limited review of the financial statements of Broadwall Corporation
       for the period ending March 31, 1987. The engagement letter stated that a limited
       review does not provide a basis for the expression of an opinion.

Required:

   a. Explain why Loman's limited review will *not* provide a basis for the expression
      of an opinion.
   b. What are the review procedures that Loman should perform, and what is the
      purpose of each procedure?   (AICPA, adapted)

SMALL BUSINESSES

The concepts discussed in the previous chapters are applicable to all audits. However, these concepts require modification when applied to small businesses. Typically, these small businesses are privately owned, although the approach to auditing small subsidiaries, divisions, or branches of publicly held companies also may warrant modification. This chapter discusses how to audit small businesses. It also describes financial statement reviews and compilations, which may be alternatives to independent audits for privately owned businesses.

AUDITS OF SMALL BUSINESSES

Larger businesses typically develop systems of internal control that provide segregation of duties and reasonable assurance that errors or irregularities will be prevented or detected. In a typical small business, the methods of recording transactions are relatively uncomplicated, and any control-oriented procedures that do exist may not by themselves provide reasonable assurance that errors or irregularities will be prevented or detected. This is because there often is an overall lack of segregation of duties in a small business. This is typically the case where (1) there are only a few individuals (e.g., two or three) who principally do the accounting work, and (2) various personnel have access to both assets and the related accounting records. However, close involvement in the accounting process by one key individual in a small business—usually the owner/manager—often minimizes the likelihood of material error.

In audits of small businesses, the above conditions mean it generally will not be appropriate to evaluate whether there are key attributes that provide reasonable assurance that control objectives are being achieved. Instead, the auditor should determine the effect of owner/manager involvement and other control-oriented procedures on the likelihood of material error. As a

15

result, the risk analysis discussed in previous chapters requires modification—principally in the approach to the system evaluation.

Risk Analysis

The risk analysis for small businesses is based on the interaction of three inputs. Two of the inputs—Environmental Considerations and Observations from Detail Analytical Review—are the same as in the risk analysis used in audits of larger businesses. The third input is labeled control considerations. It covers the effect of owner/manager involvement and other control-oriented procedures on the assessment of risk. If these procedures reduce the risk of material error, the audit effort can be reduced accordingly.

Specific Control Objectives. Chapter 2 described how control objectives provide convenient points of reference for considering the inputs to the risk analysis and assessing the combined effect on the accounts and transactions affected. The chapter also introduced the 41 specific control objectives that have been defined for a typical commercial or industrial business. The typical small business is involved in fewer and less complex activities, so some of these objectives have been combined and others have been eliminated. The following specific control objectives have been defined for a typical small commercial or industrial business:

Risk Analysis Working Paper		
1	S–1	Customer orders require approval of credit and terms before acceptance
	S–2	Uncollectible amounts are promptly identified and provided for
2	S–3	Products shipped or services rendered are billed

Risk Analysis
Working Paper

	S–4	Billings are for the correct amount
	S–5	Revenues are recorded correctly as to account, amount, and period
	S–6	Recorded billings are for valid transactions
3	S–7	Customer returns and other allowances are approved and recorded correctly as to account, amount, and period
4	P–1 P–11 A–1	Expenditures for goods and services are made only with proper authorization
	P–2 P–12 A–2	Expenditures for goods and services are recorded correctly as to account, amount, and period
5	P–3 A–3	Salary, wage, and benefit expenses are incurred only for work authorized and performed
	P–4 A–4	Salaries, wages, and benefits are calculated at proper rate
	P–5 A–5	Salaries, wages, benefits, and related liabilities are recorded correctly as to account (department, activity, cost center, etc.), amount, and period
6	P–6	Costs are assigned to inventory in accordance with the stated valuation method
	P–7	Inventory quantities are accurately recorded and extended
	P–8	Physical loss of inventory is prevented or promptly detected
7	P–9	Obsolete, slow-moving, and overstock inventory is prevented or promptly detected and provided for
	P–10	Inventory is carried at the lower of cost or market
8	P–13	Disposals, retirements, trade-ins, idle plant and equipment, and other losses are identified and recorded correctly as to account, amount, and period
	P–14	Physical loss of property, plant, and equipment is prevented
	P–15	Depreciation is calculated using proper lives and methods
9	F–1	Cash receipts are recorded correctly as to account, amount, and period and are deposited
	F–2	Cash receipts are properly applied to customer balances
10	F–3	Cash disbursements are for goods or services authorized and received
	F–4	Cash disbursements are recorded correctly as to account, amount, and period
11	F–5	Debt and lease obligations and related expenses are authorized and recorded correctly as to account, amount, and period
	F–6	Equity transactions are authorized and recorded correctly as to account, amount, and period
12	A–7	Provisions for income taxes and related liabilities and deferrals are recorded correctly as to account, amount, and period
13	A–8	Commitments and contingencies are identified, monitored, and, if appropriate, recorded or disclosed

Specific control objectives for investments (F–7, F–8, F–9, F–10, F–11) and amortization of intangibles (A–6) have not been included for small businesses. However, if the client is involved in these activities, the auditor should take into consideration the related control objectives and complete a risk analysis working paper.

The small business approach also can be used for a not-for-profit entity. This usually requires adding the control objectives for investments and eliminating the control objectives relating to inventories (P–6 through P–10) and sales (S–1 through S–7), except for one objective relating to revenue recognition (S–5) and, in some cases, uncollectible amounts (S–2).

Risk Analysis Working Paper.   The risk analysis working paper for small businesses differs from the working paper for commercial and industrial companies introduced in Chapter 2 as follows:

1. *Combined specific control objectives.*   As indicated above, the specific control objectives for certain activities have been combined. For example, as noted on page 498, risk analysis working paper No. 4 covers the initiation and recording of various types of expenditures (i.e., production materials and overhead, selling and administrative expenses, and equipment purchases). Further combinations also might be appropriate. For example, in some small businesses, expenditures for goods and services are recorded only when the related cash disbursements are recorded. In these cases, it may be most efficient to combine risk analysis working papers No. 4 and No. 10.
2. *Control considerations.*   The System Evaluation section of the standard risk analysis working paper has been replaced with a section labeled "Control Considerations." This section covers the effect of owner/manager involvement and other control-oriented procedures in the accounting process on the assessment of risk.

Figure 15–1 describes how to complete a small business risk analysis working paper.

Planning and Environmental Considerations

The discussion of audit planning in Chapter 3, including acquiring an understanding of the client's business and industry, also is applicable to audits of small businesses. Although it usually will require less time to obtain an understanding of these businesses, environmental considerations are no less important. For example, the influence of a major customer or the reliance on one or a few suppliers can have a significant impact on the operations of a small business.

Ownership Influences and Management Characteristics.   One of the most significant environmental considerations in many small business audits is

FIGURE 15–1 How to Complete the Risk Analysis Working Paper for Small Businesses

Production or Service—Materials and Overhead,
    Property, Plant, and
    Equipment

Administration—Expenses and Related Liabilities

Prepared By/Date _____
Reviewed By/Date _____

P–1, P–11, A–1 Expenditures for Goods and Services are Made Only with Proper
    Authorization

P–2, P–12, A–2 Expenditures for Goods and Services are Recorded Correctly as
    to Account, Amount, and Period

Risk Analysis

Environmental Considerations _____
_____
_____
_____
_____
_____

Observations from Detail Analytical Review _____
_____
_____
_____
_____
_____
_____

1. Summarize the external and internal environmental factors and their potential impact on accounts or transactions affected by the control objectives. These factors may increase or decrease the likelihood of material error and lead the auditor to emphasize specific audit areas or help justify reduced audit effort.

2. Summarize pertinent information obtained from analytical review of interim financial and operating data. Quantify changes in conditions and circumstances and cover important trends and relationships that confirm or challenge our understanding of the environment. Indicate specific amounts and percentages relating to accounts and transactions that the auditor wants to test (e.g., indicate number of items and amounts or range of amounts for key items).

3. Summarize the effect of owner/manager involvement and other control-oriented procedures on the likelihood of material error in the accounts and transactions affected by the specific control objectives. The important procedures are obtained from the Control Information Form.

4. Assess the likelihood of material error occurring in the accounts affected by the control objectives, based on the interaction of the inputs to the risk analysis. When there is a conflict among the inputs, or the conclusion is otherwise unclear, include an explanation.

5. Develop a preliminary audit approach for the transactions and accounts affected by each control objective. The preliminary audit approach should be responsive to the risks identified and include both tests of transactions and direct tests of balances. Cross-reference the preliminary audit approach to steps in the audit program.

Control Considerations _____

_____

_____

_____

_____

_____

Likelihood of Material Error in Accounts Affected (Conclusion based on Risk Analysis. Explain if not obvious.) _____

☐ High
☐ Moderate
☐ Low

_____

_____

Audit Program Reference

Preliminary Audit Approach Responsive to Risk Analysis

_____

_____

_____

_____

_____

_____

_____

_____

(P–1, P–11, A–1, P–2, P–12, A–2)

501

the pervasive influence of one key individual—the owner/manager. This influence can affect the entire business, from the determination of which customers will be granted credit to the decision as to the amount, form, and source of additional financing for the business.

Larger companies usually develop systems of internal control to assure that financial information is complete and accurate. However, the owner/manager of a small business typically is able to execute and might be able to conceal improper transactions. Therefore, the auditor's consideration of the motivations and integrity of the owner/manager is particularly important in the audit of a small business.

The auditor should accept and retain only clients whom he or she believes are honest. However, even an honest owner might have certain philosophies or motivations that require a higher level of professional skepticism on the auditor's part. The following are examples of factors and motivations that might affect the audit of a small business:

Desire to minimize income to reduce taxes.

External financing dependent upon presenting favorable results.

Significant leveraging of owner's personal finances to provide sufficient capital to operate the business.

Charging personal expenses to the business to obtain tax deductions.

If the one key individual who dominates the operations of the small business is the owner of the company, the auditor should consider the factors and motivations as described above. However, in some instances, the owner may not be the manager. For example, an owner who is merely an investor and is not involved in the operation of the business might delegate responsibility for day-to-day operations to a manager. If the manager is control conscious, the auditor generally would expect fewer problems. If the manager is not control conscious, the auditor's expectations of material error may be increased. In either case, the auditor should determine how the absentee owner monitors operations. In addition, the auditor should consider the factors discussed under "Management Characteristics" in Chapter 3.

If events or circumstances raise doubts about management that might affect particular audit areas, the circumstances should be summarized or referred to in the Environmental Considerations section of the applicable risk analysis working paper. The documentation should avoid generalizations about management's competence or integrity. Rather, it should describe specific circumstances that raise concerns.

In the case of a small subsidiary, division, or branch of a larger entity, consideration should be given to the effect of parent company control over these operations. In many cases, standardized financial reporting requirements, monitoring of reported results, and internal audit visits can reduce the likelihood of material error.

Control Considerations

Control Environment in a Small Business. In audits of larger companies, the auditor reviews the control environment to evaluate whether it is appropriate to plan for reliance on key attributes—that is, whether their continued functioning is enhanced by the environment in which they operate. An effective control environment leads the auditor to expect that key attributes tested at an interim date will continue to function during the entire year. Thus, the effectiveness of the control environment helps judge how early in the year audit procedures can be performed.

In audits of small businesses, key attributes ordinarily are not expected to be found because of an overall lack of segregation of duties. In these cases, the auditor should evaluate the nature and effect of factors that are present in the accounting process that might allow justification of minimum audit procedures. Many of these factors (e.g., monitoring of operating results) are similar to those that are identified as the control environment in a large business. For a large business, their influence is more general in effect because of the complexity of operations and the large volume of transactions.

In contrast, for a small business these factors—particularly the degree of owner/manager supervision and review—will have a direct effect on the accuracy of the accounting records. Therefore, the focus should be on the involvement of the owner/manager as well as other control-oriented procedures in the accounting process to determine whether any of these factors reduce the likelihood that material errors could occur without detection. If the assessment is favorable, the auditor can reduce the extent of audit procedures. For example, the auditor might use a minimum representative sample to test certain types of transactions.

While owner/manager involvement in the accounting process ordinarily is considered a positive influence, the auditor should be alert to the effect that the factors and motivations described earlier might have on the owner/manager's performance of control-oriented procedures. In addition, the auditor should recognize that it is easier for management to override the accounting process in a small business. For example, assume the owner/manager reviews account distribution, but the auditor's experience from prior audits is that personal expenses may be charged to the business or that job costs may be misclassified between construction contracts to improve profitability. In this case, experience negates the effect of the owner/manager's review of account distribution. Both factors should be documented on the risk analysis working paper—the auditor's knowledge, from prior experience, in the Environmental Considerations section and the owner/manager's review in the Control Considerations section.

Control Information Form. *SAS No. 1* (as amended by *SAS No. 43*) (AU 320.54) indicates that after a preliminary review of the accounting system, the auditor may conclude that the system cannot be relied on to reduce the extent of substantive tests. In those instances, that *SAS* suggests that the auditor document the reasons for such a conclusion. The Control Information Form (see Appendix 15A) is used to document the auditor's understanding of the control environment and the flow of transactions in small businesses; it also evidences the auditor's judgment not to rely on key attributes.

The Control Information Form is divided into four sections. The first section provides for identifying the key accounting employees and their primary responsibilities. The second section covers key accounting records and requires an indication of whether they are prepared manually or by a computer. The third section covers overall control environment considerations (e.g., monitoring of operating results) that typically relate to more than one specific control objective. The fourth is used to document who, if anyone, performs certain procedures in the flow of each significant type of transaction affected by the specific control objectives or groups of objectives identified in this chapter. All four sections of the Control Information Form are utilized by the auditor to perform the risk analysis. Although the auditor's expectations would be favorable if the owner/manager is performing these procedures, he or she also should be interested if others (e.g., the accountant/bookkeeper or someone else) are performing procedures that reduce the likelihood of material error. For example, if the bookkeeper reconciles quantities shipped to quantities billed, the likelihood of unbilled shipments is reduced. The risk analysis should reflect this favorable expectation.

If a computer assists in the performance of a procedure, this should be indicated in the Control Information Form. Information about the involvement of the computer in the flow of transactions should help the auditor design appropriate audit procedures.

Information necessary to complete the Control Information Form should be obtained by observation and inquiry of client personnel. Narratives and flow charts are not necessary, unless they would be helpful to supplement information in the Form (e.g., to describe a complex inventory valuation).

Many of the procedures listed in the Control Information Form are similar to items in the reference lists for "System Attributes to Consider" in Appendix II at the end of this textbook. However, in a small business, these procedures usually cannot be key attributes because of the overall lack of segregation of duties. Rarely is it practical to separate access to assets from the recordkeeping functions in a small business. Therefore, even if the procedures have elements of control (e.g., owner's secretary reconciles bank accounts), the lack of segregation of duties (e.g., owner's secretary also makes the daily bank deposits) usually means these are not key attributes on which the auditor may rely. Nonetheless, if key attributes exist and it would be efficient to rely on them, the auditor should do so.

Summarizing Control Considerations on the Risk Analysis Working Paper. The important procedures documented in the Control Information Form that significantly impact the assessment of risk are summarized in the risk analysis working paper section labeled "Control Considerations." In a small business, these considerations can be a significant input to the assessment of the likelihood of material error in specific accounts and transactions, especially in those areas involving a large volume of recurring transactions (e.g., sales, cash receipts, cash disbursements). Figure 15–2 shows an example of a completed Control Considerations section of the risk analysis working paper and the related page of the Control Information Form from which the information was derived. As indicated in the example, all procedures being performed are not summarized in the risk analysis working paper—only those that the auditor believes will significantly reduce the likelihood of material error. In certain areas, there may not be any procedures that the auditor believes will reduce the likelihood of material error. In those cases, "None" should be indicated in the Control Considerations section.

Computerized Accounting Records. The approach to examining computerized accounting records in a small business is to understand what is being done by the computer and how it can be used to perform audit procedures. For small businesses, information about the computer installation and functions performed by the computer is documented in the Control Information Form. In the example in Figure 15–2, note that where the computer assists in the performance of a procedure, a "C" is indicated next to the "X" in the "Performed By" column. The availability of computerized records offers the opportunity to use the computer to perform audit procedures such as footing files, selecting samples, and performing analytical tests.

Analytical Review

For many small businesses, the overall and detail analytical review will be completed during the same visit to the client. Chapter 6 states that the purpose of detail analytical review is to:

1. Determine whether the numbers "make sense" in view of (a) the auditor's understanding of the client's business and industry, (b) expectations developed during initial planning, and (c) the evaluation of the accounting system. This will help identify areas where audit procedures may be limited because of the reasonableness of the amount.
2. Identify significant fluctuations or quantify transactions requiring further audit attention. This will lead the auditor to design a preliminary audit approach that includes specific audit procedures for these areas.

FIGURE 15–2   Excerpt from Control Information Form and Related Risk Analysis Working Paper

---

P–3   **Salary, Wage, And Benefit Expenses Are Incurred Only For Work Authorized**
A–3   **And Performed**

P–4   **Salaries, Wages, And Benefits Are Calculated At The Proper Rate**
A–4

P–5   **Salaries, Wages, Benefits, And Related Liabilities Are Recorded Correctly**
A–5   **As To Account (Department, Activity, Cost Center, Etc.), Amount, And Period**

	Owner/ Manager	Bookkeeper/ Accountant	Plant Mgr.	Secretary	Not Done
1. Personnel records maintained				X	
2. Approval of payroll:					
(a) New hires	X				
(b) Changes in pay rate	X				
(c) Overtime pay	X				
(d) Termination	X				
(e) Bonuses	X				
3. Time cards, time reports, or piece-work records approved			X		
4. Time paid reconciled to time worked weekly		X C*			
5. Work paid reconciled to work produced (if pay is tied to production)					N/A
6. Distribution of hours (direct and indirect) to activity or department reviewed or approved					X
7. Compensation for sick leave, vacation, and holidays approved	X				
8. Clerical accuracy of payroll register checked		X C*			
9. Payroll register reviewed for unusual amounts	X				
10. Payroll checks:					
(a) Signed by	X				
(b) Distributed by				X	

The columns "Owner/Manager", "Bookkeeper/Accountant", "Plant Mgr.", and "Secretary" are grouped under **Performed By**, with "Plant Mgr." and "Secretary" under **Other**.

* "C" indicates that a computer is involved in the performance of this procedure.

Excerpt from Risk Analysis Working Paper for P–3, A–3/P–4, A–4/P–5, A–5

Control Considerations The owner hires all employees and approves all wage rates. Time cards are approved by the plant manager. In addition, the owner reviews the payroll register for unusual amounts and knows every employee, so the possibility of fictitious employees or "padded" payroll is considered remote.

Often the nature and extent of interim financial and operating data might limit the auditor's ability to accomplish these purposes. For example, interim financial statements might not include properly computed cost of sales (e.g., standard gross profit percentages are used) or appropriate accruals. However, in many cases, adjustments are necessary only in a few audit areas, such as income taxes or warranties. The key question is: What interim financial and operating information does the owner/manager use to monitor operations? This information might help the auditor plan the nature and extent of work in specific audit areas. If there are no interim financial statements, the auditor can scan the general ledger to obtain information for planning the audit effort. Other records (e.g., trade accounts receivable ledger or an aged trial balance) also can be scanned to identify balances or transactions that might require audit attention.

As Chapter 6 indicates, the detail analytical review also should help establish materiality for examining specific transactions and balances. If an account contains items that the auditor wants to test, that information should be quantified in the Observations from Detail Analytical Review section of the risk analysis working paper (e.g., indicate number of items and amounts or range of amounts). As pointed out in Chapter 6, Appendix III at the end of this textbook provides examples of detail analytical review information related to various specific control objectives.

Preparing the Audit Program

Assessing the Likelihood of Material Error.   As in other audits, the assessment of the likelihood of material error in the accounts affected by each specific control objective should consider the effect of all three inputs to the risk analysis. Even though the auditor usually does not find key attributes in small businesses, the likelihood of material error may be low. For example, consider the situation where (1) the bookkeeper is competent and no significant errors were noted during past audits, (2) the auditor's detail analytical review indicates that the operating and financial data appear to be reasonable, and (3) the owner/manager reviews all transactions in the area. In this case, all three inputs indicate a low expectation of error in the accounts affected, so the amount of audit work should be less than if these factors did not exist.

On the other hand, the example of the owner/manager who reviews account distribution in the "Control Environment in a Small Business" section above, illustrates that unfavorable environmental considerations can negate the effect of owner/manager involvement in the accounting process. Obviously, the divergent effects of owner/manager involvement make the assessment of their combined impact a highly judgmental process.

Nature of Audit Procedures.   As described earlier in this chapter, due to the lack of segregation of duties in small businesses, the auditor ordinarily would not perform a system evaluation for these engagements. Accordingly, when deciding on the nature of procedures to perform, the auditor should select procedures that provide evidence as to the validity and propriety of accounting for transactions and balances (substantive tests)—rather than those that provide evidence of the functioning of key attributes (compliance tests).

The lists of audit procedures provided in Appendix II at the end of this textbook are good starting points for deciding on the nature of tests. Because the accounting system is not being relied on, the auditor should use the procedures listed under "If Objective Not Achieved." These procedures typically require more extensive testing to discover errors that may have occurred. However, the auditor should keep in mind that the risk analysis may justify less work. In many cases, favorable control considerations will enable the use of certain of the less extensive procedures listed under "If Objective Achieved."

Control Considerations. Owner/manager review and other control-oriented procedures in a small business are not key attributes because of an overall lack of segregation of duties. Therefore, it is not necessary to include steps in the preliminary audit approach to obtain direct evidence of the functioning of each of the procedures listed in the Control Considerations section of the risk analysis working paper. However, when performing audit procedures, the auditor should be alert for any indications that the control considerations listed on the risk analysis working paper are not effective. Specifically, the auditor should make inquiries of the owner/manager and accounting personnel regarding the control-oriented procedures they perform and how exceptions are resolved. And the auditor should observe them performing these procedures during the course of the audit.

Further, the auditor should determine whether any errors identified in the audit tests resulted from lack of performance of the control-oriented procedures considered in the risk analysis. If so, the auditor should reconsider the nature and extent of the audit procedures. For example, if the Control Considerations section of the risk analysis working paper indicates that the owner/manager approves customer credit limits, but the auditor finds instances where such limits are exceeded without approval, the auditor should challenge the sufficiency of the preliminary audit approach to reviewing the collectibility of receivables.

Tests of Transactions. While key attributes will rarely be identified and tested in the audits of small businesses, the auditor will frequently test transactions to obtain evidence as to the accuracy, validity, and completeness of the accounting records. For example, the auditor might examine a sample of shipping documents from throughout the period under audit to test whether all shipments have been billed. In other cases, the auditor might be able to use an analytical review procedure to obtain persuasive evidence that an account balance or class of transactions is fairly stated, so that a test of transactions is not necessary.

Timing of Audit Procedures.   The lack of reliable accounting systems usually dictates that most or all of the audit procedures for small businesses will be performed after year-end. However, if certain procedures (e.g., confirmation of receivables, observations of inventory) are performed prior to the balance sheet date, analytical review procedures or detail tests of intervening transactions should be performed to assure that no material errors occurred in the intervening period. Because the auditor ordinarily does not test key attributes, the tests of transactions usually should cover all or substantially all of the period under audit.

Extent of Testing Considerations.   The extent of testing considerations in Chapter 7 are equally applicable to the audits of small businesses. The discussion of small populations in the "Other Sampling Considerations" section of Chapter 7 is particularly relevant for a small business. The principal point to remember is that auditing a representative sample may not be an efficient strategy for achieving the audit objective for many small populations. As a more efficient alternative, consider using analytical review or a combination of tests of key items and analytical review instead of a sample. For example, for companies that have a small number of employees, the auditor could estimate total payroll for the year by extending the average authorized pay rate/salary by the hours (or months) in the year. This could be done in much less time than it would take to audit a sample of payroll transactions. This analytical review strategy is not only more efficient than sampling, but it also provides 100 percent coverage of payroll for the year.

In the areas where representative sampling is considered necessary, the considerations in Chapter 7 for sample size and methods of selection are applicable to small business audits. For example, if the auditor expects no errors in the sample because of effective owner/manager involvement and other inputs to the risk analysis and the sample is not the primary basis for the audit conclusion, the minimum representative sample can be used.

If there is a lack of effective involvement by the owner/manager in an area with a high volume of transactions (e.g., sales, cash receipts, cash disbursements), the auditor needs to test more than the minimum. In these cases, favorable environmental considerations and observations from detail analytical review are not enough to justify a low expectation of material error. As a result, at least 60 transactions should be tested or, if errors are expected, the auditor should use statistical sampling. This approach may allow the auditor to limit year-end direct tests of related balances.

Final Overall Review.   A final overall analytical review is especially useful in the audit of a small business whose operations tend to be relatively uncomplicated. As a result, the reasons for variations from period to period can be more readily understood. In many cases, discussion with the owner/ manager can be helpful in establishing the overall reasonableness of operating results and financial position.

REVIEWS AND COMPILATIONS

Historically, clients engaging CPAs for financial statement services had to choose between two alternative services—"audited" or "unaudited." As explained in Chapter 1, in an audit the CPA firm expresses an opinion on the fairness of the financial statements. Or a company could have received unaudited financial statements, which contained no assurance whatsoever from the CPA firm. In most cases, this lack of any assurance limited the usefulness of unaudited financial statements—particularly to outsiders, such as creditors, who had an interest in how well the company was doing.

However in 1979, a new AICPA committee, the Accounting and Review Services Committee (ARSC), began issuing *Statements on Standards for Accounting and Review Services (SSARS)*. These standards cover unaudited financial statements and other accounting services for nonpublic entities. *SSARS No. 1,* "Compilation and Review of Financial Statements" (AR 100.04), *as amended by SSARS No. 2,* defines a nonpublic entity as:

> . . . any entity other than *(a)* one whose securities trade in a public market either on a stock exchange (domestic or foreign) or in the over-the-counter market, including securities quoted only locally or regionally, *(b)* one that makes a filing with a regulatory agency in preparation for the sale of any class of its securities in a public market, or *(c)* a subsidiary, corporate joint venture, or other entity controlled by an entity covered by *(a)* or *(b)*.

As a result of *SSARS No. 1,* nonpublic entities may engage independent accountants to perform either of two services related to unaudited financial statements. Those services are reviews of financial statements or compilations of financial statements. The level of service selected depends on the entity's needs. Audited financial statements offer the highest level of credibility. However, reviews and compilations are alternatives to an audit.

Reviews of Financial Statements

SSARS No. 1 (AR 100.04) states that a review of financial statements consists of:

> Performing inquiry and analytical procedures that provide the accountant with a reasonable basis for expressing limited assurance that there are no material modifications that should be made to the statements in order for them to be in conformity with generally accepted accounting principles or, if applicable, with another comprehensive basis of accounting.

To issue a review report *SSARS No. 1* (AR 100.38) indicates that an accountant must be independent. In addition, *SSARS No. 1* states that:

1. "The accountant should possess a level of knowledge of the accounting principles and practices of the industry in which the entity operates and an understanding of the entity's business . . . that will provide him, through the performance of inquiry and analytical procedures, with a reasonable basis for expressing limited assurance that there are no material modifications that should be made to the financial statements. . . ." (AR 100.24)

2. "The accountant's understanding of the entity's business should include a general understanding of the entity's organization, its operating characteristics, and the nature of its assets, liabilities, revenues, and expenses. This would ordinarily involve a general knowledge of the entity's production, distribution, and compensation methods, types of products and services, operating locations, and material transactions with related parties." (AR 100.26)

The objective of a review differs from the objective of an audit. *SSARS No. 1* (AR 100.04) distinguishes between the two as follows:

> . . . The objective of an audit is to provide a reasonable basis for expressing an opinion regarding the financial statements taken as a whole. A review does not provide a basis for the expression of such an opinion because a review does not contemplate a study and evaluation of internal accounting control, tests of accounting records and of responses to inquiries by obtaining corroborating evidential matter through inspection, observation or confirmation, and certain other procedures ordinarily performed during an audit. A review may bring to the accountant's attention significant matters affecting the financial statements, but it does not provide assurance that the accountant will become aware of all significant matters that would be disclosed in an audit.

SSARS No. 1 (AR 100.27) suggests that the independent accountant's inquiry and analytical review procedures in a review consist of:

> *a.* Inquiries concerning the entity's accounting principles and practices and the method followed in applying them. . . .
>
> *b.* Inquiries concerning the entity's procedures for recording, classifying, and summarizing transactions, and accumulating information for disclosure in the financial statements. . . .
>
> *c.* Analytical procedures designed to identify relationships and individual items that appear to be unusual. For the purposes of this statement, analytical procedures consist of (1) comparison of the financial statements with statements for comparable prior period(s), (2) comparison of the financial statements with anticipated results, if available (for example, budgets and forecasts), and (3) study of the relationships of the elements of the financial statements that would be expected to conform to a predictable pattern

based on the entity's experience. In applying these procedures, the accountant should consider the types of matters that required accounting adjustments in preceding periods. Examples of relationships of elements in financial statements that would be expected to conform to a predictable pattern may be the relationships between changes in sales and changes in accounts receivable and expense accounts that ordinarily fluctuate with sales, and between changes in property, plant, and equipment and changes in depreciation expense and other accounts that may be affected, such as maintenance and repairs.

d. Inquiries concerning actions taken at meetings of shareholders, board of directors, committees of the board of directors, or comparable meetings that may affect the financial statements.

e. Reading the financial statements to consider, on the basis of information coming to the independent accountant's attention, whether the financial statements appear to conform with generally accepted accounting principles.

f. Obtaining reports from other independent accountants, if any, who have been engaged to audit or review the financial statements of significant components of the reporting entity, its subsidiaries, and other investees. . . .

g. Inquiries of persons having responsibility for financial and accounting matters concerning (1) whether the financial statements have been prepared in conformity with generally accepted accounting principles consistently applied, (2) changes in the entity's business activities or accounting principles and practices, (3) matters as to which questions have arisen in the course of applying the foregoing procedures, and (4) events subsequent to the date of the financial statements that would have a material effect on the financial statements.

Some of the procedures that independent accountants follow when auditing inventories and when reviewing them are contrasted below.

	Audit	Review
Physical existence	Observe taking of inventory, review for obsolete or damaged items, record selected counts, and ultimately trace these to the final inventory listings.	Inquire how inventory quantities were determined—by physical count or some other procedure.
	Obtain direct confirmation from third parties holding consigned inventory or storing company inventory.	Inquire if inventory on consignment or stored elsewhere was included in final inventory total.
	Test receiving and shipping records to verify proper purchase and sales cutoffs.	Inquire whether proper receiving and shipping cutoff was obtained.

	Audit	Review
Clerical tests	Test the clerical accuracy of final inventory listings.	Inquire if final inventory listings were double-checked for clerical accuracy.
	Trace totals from the inventory listings to the general ledger and statements.	Inquire if the general ledger was adjusted to the physical inventory.
Pricing	Test the inventory valuation method by reference to appropriate invoices and other records. Test reasonableness of labor content and rates. Also test the overhead accumulation and allocation bases.	Inquire as to the inventory valuation method used. Also inquire whether the inventory includes applicable labor and overhead costs.
	Review subsequent sales and sales contracts to test whether the inventory is salable at prices in excess of cost.	Inquire as to the salability of the inventory at prices above cost.
		Perform selected analytical procedures (e.g., compare total inventory, gross margin, and inventory turnover to prior periods and anticipated results).

While a review does not provide the same assurance as an audit, some financial statement users find the review to be an acceptable alternative. The form of the independent accountant's review report is discussed in Chapter 17.

Compilation of Financial Statements

SSARS No. 1 (AR 100.04) states that a compilation consists of "Presenting in the form of financial statements . . . information that is the representation of management (owners) without undertaking to express any assurance on the statements." Ordinarily, accountants provide this service in conjunction with other professional assistance, such as tax services. The accountant does not have to be independent to perform a compilation.

In a compilation engagement, an accountant is not required to perform any specific tests or to make inquiries or analyses. However, *SSARS No. 1* states that:

1. "The accountant should possess a level of knowledge of the accounting principles and practices of the industry in which the entity operates

that will enable him to compile financial statements that are appropriate in form. . . ." (AR 100.10)

2. "To compile financial statements, the accountant should possess a general understanding of the nature of the entity's business transactions, the form of its accounting records, the stated qualifications of its accounting personnel, the accounting basis on which the financial statements are to be presented, and the form and content of the financial statements. . . ." (AR 100.11)

3. "Before issuing his report, the accountant should read the compiled financial statements and consider whether such financial statements appear to be appropriate in form and free from obvious material errors [mistakes in compilation]. . . ." (AR 100.13)

The form of the accountant's compilation report is discussed in Chapter 17.

APPENDIX 15A

CONTROL INFORMATION FORM—SMALL BUSINESSES*

Control Information Form

Small Businesses

Client Name _____

Subsidiary or Division _____

Year-End _____

Prepared by	Date	Reviewed by	Date
Updated by	Date	Reviewed by	Date

Instructions

1. This form should be used to document an understanding of the control environment and the flow of transactions in small businesses. It focuses on the nature and extent of owner/manager involvement and other control-oriented procedures in the accounting process. If present, these procedures may reduce the likelihood of material error in the accounts affected by the specific control objectives.

2. Place an "X" in the appropriate "Performed By" column to indicate who performs the indicated procedure. Other important accounting procedures used by the client should be described in the space provided. If a computer assists in the performance of a procedure, place a "C" next to the "X."

3. If a particular procedure is not applicable due to the nature of the client's business, place an "N/A" in the column marked "Not Done."

4. Where an asterisk (*) appears, indicate in the blank space how often (e.g., daily, monthly, quarterly) the procedure is performed.

5. This Form can provide most or all of the system documentation necessary for the audit of a small business. In certain cases (e.g., complex inventory valuations), narratives may be necessary to supplement information in the Form.

6. This Form is a carryforward document which should be updated each year. If there are significant changes, a new Form should be prepared.

Note: The purpose of this form is to identify control-oriented procedures that reduce the likelihood of material error in the accounts affected by the respective specific control objectives; these should be summarized in the Control Considerations section of the risk analysis working paper. The fact that a listed procedure is not present does not necessarily indicate a deficiency.

Many of the procedures indicated in this form are similar to items in the Reference Lists of System Attributes to Consider in Appendix II at the end of this textbook. However, segregation of duties is implicit in the examples in the Reference Lists. In a small business, the limited number of personnel involved in the accounting process and access to both assets and the related accounting records make it impractical to have an effective segregation of duties. As a result, the procedures listed in this form usually are not key attributes on which the auditor may rely.

Individuals Performing Key Accounting Functions

List the names of key accounting personnel in the spaces provided. In the column below each name, indicate with an "X" the functions performed by that individual. In a separate memorandum, summarize the qualifications of these individuals (include background and number of years in present position).

Names

_____ _____ _____ _____ _____ _____

_____ _____ _____ _____ _____ _____

Function

General ledger

Accounts receivable

Accounts payable

Cashier

Credit

Shipping

Billing

Purchasing

Receiving

Payroll

Cost Accounting

Personnel

Income Taxes

Computer

Other

Key Accounting Records

Record	Manual	Computerized

1. If any accounting records are computerized, describe the data processing equipment:
   Manufacturer _____ Series/Model _____

   Input/Output Devices: Disks ____ Diskettes ____ Tapes ____
   Terminals ____ Cassettes ____
   Other ____ (Describe) _____

2. Are application programs:
   Obtained from outside vendors? ____
   Developed in-house? ____
3. Who is authorized and/or trained to:
   Operate the equipment? _____
   Write or change programs? _____
   Purchase software from vendors? _____

Overall Control Considerations

	Yes	No
1. Personal funds, income, and expenses of the owner/manager and key accounting personnel completely segregated from business	_____	_____
2. Owner/manager uses operating budgets and cash projections and compares these with actual results _____*	_____	_____
3. Comparative financial reports prepared _____* which are sufficiently informative to highlight abnormalities	_____	_____
4. Non-standard journal entries approved by owner/manager	_____	_____
5. Background checks made for new employees	_____	_____
6. Employees who handle cash, securities, and other valuable assets covered by fidelity bonds	_____	_____
7. Owner/manager requires bookkeeper to take annual vacations and assigns someone else to perform bookkeeping duties during that time	_____	_____
8. Physical security sufficient to protect inventory and equipment	_____	_____
9. If a subsidiary, division, or branch:		
a. Standardized financial report packages used	_____	_____
b. Abnormalities in reported financial results followed up on a timely basis by group management	_____	_____
c. Periodic examinations made by group internal auditors. If yes, describe results of recent audits._____	_____	_____

_____
_____
_____
_____

Other

Accounting Procedures

S–1 Customer Orders Require Approval of Credit and Terms before Acceptance
S–2 Uncollectible Amounts Are Promptly Identified and Provided for

	Performed By				Not Done
	Owner/ Manager	Bookkeeper/ Accountant	Other		
1. Credit approved prior to shipment	_____	_____	_____	_____	_____
2. Customer orders approved as to price, discount, payment, and delivery terms	_____	_____	_____	_____	_____
3. Quotes or price estimates approved	_____	_____	_____	_____	_____
4. Aged listings of customer accounts:					
(a) prepared _____ *	_____	_____	_____	_____	_____
(b) reviewed _____ *	_____	_____	_____	_____	_____
(c) compared to credit limits _____ *	_____	_____	_____	_____	_____
5. Delinquent accounts and unusual items investigated _____ *	_____	_____	_____	_____	_____
6. Bad debt write-offs and other adjustments approved _____ *	_____	_____	_____	_____	_____

Other

Accounting Procedures

S–3 Products Shipped or Services Rendered Are Billed
S–4 Billings Are for the Correct Amount
S–5 Revenues Are Recorded Correctly as to Account, Amount, and Period
S–6 Recorded Billings Are for Valid Transactions

	Performed By			Not Done
	Owner/ Manager	Bookkeeper/ Accountant	Other	

1. Shipping documents issued in pre-numbered order and sequence checked _____ *

2. Order log reviewed for orders not shipped _____ *

3. Materials leaving premises checked for appropriate shipping documents

4. Direct shipments reviewed to assure that customers are billed _____ *

5. Quantities shipped reconciled to quantities billed _____ *

6. Price lists approved _____ *

7. Invoices issued in prenumbered order and sequence checked _____ *

8. Invoices checked for accuracy and agreement with approved price lists, discounts, written quotes, etc.

9. Invoices compared to shipping documents _____ *

10. Invoices compared to approved sales orders _____ *

11. Unused and voided billing forms controlled

12. Accounts receivable trial balance reconciled to control account _____ *

13. Statements mailed to all customers _____ *

14. Customer complaints and responses
    to statements followed up   _____ _____ _____ _____ _____

<u>Other</u>

Accounting Procedures

S-7 Customer Returns and Other Allowances Are Approved and Recorded Correctly as to Account, Amount, and Period

	Performed By			Not Done
	Owner/ Manager	Bookkeeper/ Accountant	Other	

1. Credits for returns, allowances, price changes, and discounts approved before issuance   _____ _____ _____ _____ _____

2. Credit memos issued in prenumbered order and sequence checked _____*   _____ _____ _____ _____ _____

3. Credit memos compared to receiving/ inspection report for returned goods or to other approval document before issuance   _____ _____ _____ _____ _____

4. Non-cash credits to receivables reviewed _____*   _____ _____ _____ _____ _____

<u>Other</u>

Accounting Procedures

P–1   **Expenditures for Goods and Services Are**
P–11   **Made Only with Proper Authorization**
A–1

P–2   **Expenditures for Goods and Services Are**
P–12   **Recorded Correctly as to Account, Amount,**
A–2   **and Period**

	Owner/ Manager	Bookkeeper/ Accountant	Other		Not Done
1. Expenses incurred or purchases made above specified dollar limit approved (Describe _____)					
2. Goods counted, inspected, and compared to packing slip or invoice before acceptance					
3. Receiving documentation, purchase order, and invoice matched before recording purchase					
4. Record of returned goods matched to vendor credit memos					
5. Invoice additions, extensions, and pricing checked					
6. Unmatched receiving reports and invoices investigated for inclusion in estimated liability at close of period					
7. (a) Account distribution assigned (b) Account distribution reviewed					
8. Vendor statements reconciled to accounts payable detail _____ *					
9. Accounts payable detail reconciled to control account _____ *					
10. Expense reports reviewed					
11. Commissions approved					
12. Commissions reconciled to recorded sales _____ *					

Performed By

Other

Accounting Procedures

P–3   Salary, Wage, and Benefit Expenses Are
A–3   Incurred Only for Work Authorized
and Performed

P–4   Salaries, Wages, and Benefits Are
A–4   Calculated at the Proper Rate

P–5   Salaries, Wages, Benefits, and Related
A–5   Liabilities Are Recorded Correctly
as to Account (department, activity, cost
center, etc.), Amount, and Period

	Owner/ Manager	Bookkeeper/ Accountant	Other		Not Done
1. Personnel records maintained					
2. Approval of payroll:					
(a) New hires					
(b) Changes in pay rate					
(c) Overtime pay					
(d) Termination					
(e) Bonuses					
3. Time cards, time reports, or piece-work records approved					
4. Time paid reconciled to time worked _____ *					
5. Work paid reconciled to work produced (if pay is tied to production)					

(Performed By spans Owner/Manager, Bookkeeper/Accountant, Other columns)

6. Distribution of hours (direct and indirect) to activity or department re-
   viewed or approved   _____ _____ _____ _____ ____

7. Compensation for sick leave, vaca-
   tion, and holidays approved   _____ _____ _____ _____ ____

8. Clerical accuracy of payroll register
   checked   _____ _____ _____ _____ ____

9. Payroll register reviewed for unusual
   amounts   _____ _____ _____ _____ ____

10. Payroll checks:
    (a) Signed by   _____ _____ _____ _____ ____
    (b) Distributed by   _____ _____ _____ _____ ____

Other

Accounting Procedures

**P–6   Costs Are Assigned to Inventory in Accordance
        with the Stated Valuation Method**
**P–7   Inventory Quantities Are Accurately Recorded
        and Extended**
**P–8   Physical Loss of Inventory Is Prevented or
        Promptly Detected**

	Performed By			Not Done
	Owner/ Manager	Bookkeeper/ Accountant	Other _____	

1. (a) Costs assigned to physical inven-
       tory quantities   _____ _____ _____ _____ ____
   (b) Costs reviewed   _____ _____ _____ _____ ____

2. Actual costs compared with produc-
   tion cost budgets _____ *   _____ _____ _____ _____ ____

3. Written instructions for inventory counts prepared   _____ _____ _____ _____ _____

4. Responsible for physical inventory taking   _____ _____ _____ _____ _____

5. Actual quantities compared to perpetual inventory records _____ *   _____ _____ _____ _____ _____

6. Differences between physical counts and perpetual records investigated   _____ _____ _____ _____ _____

7. Inventory accounts adjusted for results of periodic _____ * physical counts   _____ _____ _____ _____ _____

8. Inventory adjustments approved   _____ _____ _____ _____ _____

9. Written stores requisition or shipping orders used for all inventory issues   _____ _____ _____ _____ _____

10. Materials leaving premises checked for appropriate shipping documents   _____ _____ _____ _____ _____

11. Results of scrap gathering, measuring, recording, storing, and disposal/recycling reviewed _____ *   _____ _____ _____ _____ _____

Other

Accounting Procedures

**P–9   Obsolete, Slow-Moving, and Overstock
Inventory Is Prevented or Promptly Detected
and Provided for**

**P–10   Inventory Is Carried at the Lower of
Cost or Market**

	Performed By				Not Done
	Owner/ Manager	Bookkeeper/ Accounting	Other		
1. Stock levels and usability reviewed _____ *					
2. Production and existing stock levels related to forecasts of market and technological changes					
3. Inventory on hand reviewed for "old" items _____ *					
4. Carrying value compared to net realizable value; adjustments recorded, if necessary _____ *					

<u>Other</u>

Accounting Procedures

P–13 Disposals, Retirements, Trade-ins, Idle Plant and Equipment, and Other Losses Are Identified and Recorded Correctly as to Account, Amount, and Period

P–14 Physical Loss of Property, Plant, and Equipment Is Prevented

P–15 Depreciation Is Calculated Using Proper Lives and Methods

	Performed By				Not Done
	Owner/ Manager	Bookkeeper/ Accountant	Other		
1. Disposals authorized					
2. Gain or loss on sale amounts recorded with related disposals					
3. Replaced assets and trade-ins removed from accounts as part of recording related acquisition					
4. Property ledgers maintained and reconciled to control accounts _____ *					
5. Adequacy of property insurance coverage reviewed _____ *					
6. Asset lives and depreciation methods for property additions assigned					
7. Depreciation lapse schedules maintained					
8. Depreciation calculations checked for accuracy and overall reasonableness _____ *					

Other

Accounting Procedures

F–1 Cash Receipts Are Recorded Correctly as to Account, Amount, and Period and Are Deposited

F–2 Cash Receipts Are Properly Applied to Customer Balances

	Performed By				Not Done
	Owner/ Manager	Bookkeeper/ Accountant	Other		
1. Mail opened by	______	______	______	______	______
2. (a) Record of checks and cash received prepared ______ *	______	______	______	______	______
(b) If so, list subsequently compared to daily deposits	______	______	______	______	______
3. Cash register tape totals compared with amount of cash in drawer	______	______	______	______	______
4. Cash refunds approved	______	______	______	______	______
5. Each day's receipts deposited intact and without delay (If not daily, indicate frequency ______ ______)	______	______	______	______	______
6. Checks restrictively endorsed upon receipt	______	______	______	______	______
7. Cash receipts posted to customer ledger from:					
(a) Checks and cash received	______	______	______	______	______
(b) Remittance advices	______	______	______	______	______
(c) Receipts listing	______	______	______	______	______
(d) Lockbox report	______	______	______	______	______
8. Cash receipts applied to specific invoices rather than to current balance	______	______	______	______	______
9. Total cash receipts on account reconciled to credit to accounts receivable ______ *	______	______	______	______	______
10. Miscellaneous receipts (scrap sales, rents, dividends) monitored	______	______	______	______	______
11. Bank accounts reconciled monthly	______	______	______	______	______

Other

Accounting Procedures

F–3 Cash Disbursements Are for Goods or Services Authorized and Received
F–4 Cash Disbursements Are Recorded Correctly as to Account, Amount, and Period

	Owner/ Manager	Bookkeeper/ Accountant	Other		Not Done
1. Checks prepared only when receipt of goods or services and approval documented	___	___	___	___	___
2. Extensions, additions, discounts, and pricing checked	___	___	___	___	___
3. Supporting documents reviewed before signing check	___	___	___	___	___
4. Propriety of account distribution reviewed before signing check	___	___	___	___	___
5. Supporting documents cancelled to prevent duplicate payments	___	___	___	___	___
6. Access to unissued checks limited to	___	___	___	___	___
7. Authorized check signers (Describe dual signature requirements _____ _____ _____)	___	___	___	___	___
8. Access to check signing machine and signature plates restricted to	___	___	___	___	___
9. Signed checks mailed by	___	___	___	___	___

The "Performed By" heading spans the Owner/Manager, Bookkeeper/Accountant, and Other columns.

10. Checks issued and recorded in numerical sequence

11. Check sequence accounted for when reconciling bank accounts

12. Bank accounts reconciled monthly

Other

Accounting Procedures

F–5 Debt and Lease Obligations and Related Expenses Are Authorized and Recorded Correctly as to Account, Amount, and Period

F–6 Equity Transactions Are Authorized and Recorded Correctly as to Account, Amount, and Period

	Performed By				Not Done
	Owner/ Manager	Bookkeeper/ Accountant	Other		

1. Debt and leases authorized according to specified dollar limits (Describe _____)

2. Notes payable register maintained

3. Compliance with loan covenants and lease agreements monitored _____ *

4. Leases reviewed for classification as capital or operating _____ *

5. Interest expense posted _____ *

6. Books of stock certificate stubs and unissued certificates in custody of specified official

7. Surrendered certificates cancelled and
retained _____ _____ _____ _____ _____

Other

Accounting Procedures

A–7 Provisions for Income Taxes and Related Liabilities and Deferrals Are Recorded Correctly as to Account, Amount, and Period

	Performed By			Not Done
	Owner/ Manager	Bookkeeper/ Accountant	Other	
1. Applicable taxing authorities identified	_____	_____	_____ _____	_____
2. Calendar maintained or other method used to assure all returns prepared, filed timely, and payments made	_____	_____	_____ _____	_____
3. Tax provisions prepared	_____	_____	_____ _____	_____
4. Tax returns prepared	_____	_____	_____ _____	_____

Other

Accounting Procedures

A–8 Commitments and Contingencies Are Identified, Monitored, and, If Appropriate, Recorded or Disclosed

	Performed by			Not Done
	Owner/ Manager	Bookkeeper/ Accountant	Other	
1. Files of contracts, correspondence, legal judgments, etc., maintained and reviewed _____ *				
2. Records of costs incurred under product warranties maintained				
3. Adequacy of insurance coverage reviewed _____ *				

Other

QUESTIONS AND PROBLEMS

15–1. Describe the most common differences between systems of internal control in large and small businesses.

15–2. What characteristic in a small business' system of internal control often minimizes the likelihood of material error?

15–3. Define Control Considerations.

15–4. Describe the similarities and differences between the inputs to the risk analysis for small businesses and larger businesses.

15–5. What is the use of the Control Information Form?

15–6. Describe the purpose of a detail analytical review as it relates to small businesses.

15-7. What procedures should the auditor perform to be alert for indications that the control considerations listed on the risk analysis working paper are not effective?

15-8. Select the best answer for each of the following items.

a. The risk analysis is based on the interaction of three inputs. In addition to environmental considerations and observations from detail analytical review, the third input for small businesses is:

(1) A summary of the overall analytical review and current developments.
(2) Control considerations.
(3) System evaluation.
(4) Planning considerations.

b. Events or circumstances that raise doubts about management and might affect particular audit areas should be summarized in which section of the risk analysis working paper?

(1) Control considerations.
(2) Observations from detail analytical review.
(3) Environmental considerations.
(4) Likelihood of material error in accounts affected.

c. The Control Information Form is divided into four sections, one of which:

(1) Provides for identifying the key accounting employees and their primary responsibilities.
(2) Covers overall system considerations that relate to one or more specific control objectives.
(3) Documents the results of the overall analytical review as well as detail analytical review.
(4) Provides for identifying all accounting employees and their responsibilities.

d. Ordinarily the auditor would not perform a system evaluation for a small business because of:

(1) The low likelihood of material error.
(2) The favorable control environment.
(3) The lack of segregation of duties.
(4) The significant owner influence.

e. In the audit of a small business the auditor will frequently test transactions to obtain evidence as to:

(1) Accuracy.
(2) Validity.
(3) Completeness.
(4) All of the above.

f. In the audit of a small business, if certain audit procedures are performed prior to the balance sheet date, the auditor should:

(1) Review intervening transactions to assure that no material errors occurred in the intervening period.
(2) Perform analytical review procedures of intervening transactions to assure that no material errors occurred in the intervening period.
(3) Perform confirmation procedures as of the balance sheet date to assure that no material errors occurred in the intervening period.
(4) Perform detail tests or analytical review procedures of intervening transactions to assure that no material errors occurred in the intervening period.

15–9. Distinguish between a review and a compilation.

15–10. Discuss the nature of audit procedures for small businesses.

15–11. Describe the extent of testing considerations when there is a lack of effective involvement by the owner/manager in an area with a high volume of transactions and the environmental considerations and observations from detail analytical review are positive.

15–12. Mor-Sam is a manufacturer of electronic components. The Company's primary customers are large manufacturing concerns that produce stereo units, radios, and televisions for the home. Mor-Sam has approximately 150 customers of whom 50 percent account for 75 percent of the company's $5 million in revenue. Following is an excerpt from the working papers describing Mor-Sam's sales, accounts receivable, and cash receipts accounting system.

"All orders received are forwarded to the billing clerk for approval. Once the order is approved, the billing clerk prepares a shipping document (shipper) and forwards it to the vice president for approval. Once approved, one copy of the shipper is sent to the shipping department and the other to the billing clerk for preparation of the customer invoice. A copy of each customer invoice is sent to the general ledger bookkeeper for posting to the accounts receivable ledger and sales journal. Weekly, the billing clerk accounts for the numerical sequence of shippers and summarizes and reconciles products shipped to those invoiced. All receipts are given to the general ledger bookkeeper for posting and deposit. The general ledger bookkeeper also prepares the monthly bank account reconciliation. Components that are returned by customers are reviewed by the vice president and, if approved, a credit memo for returned goods is prepared by the general ledger bookkeeper."

Required:

To aid Mor-Sam in their reevaluation of internal controls over sales, accounts receivable, and cash receipts, prepare a schedule that illustrates how the responsibilities are currently allocated. Use the format shown below. Also describe the impact Mor-Sam's current system would have on the auditor's audit procedures.

Duties	*General Ledger Bookkeeper*	*Billing Clerk*	*Vice President*

15–13. National Control's invoices are numbered as used. Customers are billed monthly, except for the five largest customers who account for 75 percent of National's revenues and are billed twice a month. The invoices are comprehensive and include all deliveries during the billing period. For the most part, revenues represent numerous small charges and have increased 23 percent from the same period of the previous year with a gross margin of approximately 9.5 percent. Price lists do not exist, as most agreements are negotiated individually with the customers by the president. The services provided by National are recurring, with the majority of new business coming from existing customers. However, there are isolated instances of "one-time" customers.

Customer complaints and inquiries are resolved by one of the accounting clerks if routine in nature and by the president if more serious. The same accounting clerk reconciles the accounts receivable subsidiary ledger to the general ledger monthly. On average, accounts receivable represent more than 50 percent of total assets.

Required:

For specific control objectives S–3, "Products shipped or services rendered are billed;" S–4, "Billings are for the correct amount;" S–5, "Revenues are recorded correctly as to account, amount, and period;" and S–6, "Recorded billings are for valid transactions;" identify the environmental considerations and control considerations. Also, determine the likelihood of material error in the accounts affected.

15–14. DHM National services approximately 200 customers with 5 customers accounting for approximately 75 percent of its annual revenue ($3,500,000). One customer alone accounts for approximately 25 percent of the revenue. Customer rates are negotiated individually by the president. Accounts receivable turn over approximately once a month. The aged trial balance is prepared annually. However, because of the small number of customers, delinquencies are readily identifiable and customers are contacted on a timely basis. Customer invoices outstanding for more than 60 days are considered to be unusual. DHM National reviews its accounts receivable for collectibility annually, prior to year-end. The president must approve any adjustment. As of year-end, DHM wrote off $7,500 in an effort to clean up its accounts receivable.

Required:

For specific control objectives S–1, "Customer orders require approval of credit and terms before acceptance;" and S–2, "Uncollectible amounts are promptly identified and provided for;" identify the environmental and control considerations. Also, describe the impact the environmental and control considerations have on the audit procedures.

15–15. Craig Enterprises is generally uncharacteristic of a small business in that its control environment contains sound segregation of duties. As a result, key attributes are present in the accounting system. Craig employs approximately 125 people and has an average weekly payroll of approximately $30,000. The majority of the employees are salaried. The vice president/treasurer maintains all personnel records and approves all new hirings, terminations, pay rates, and overtime, holiday, vacation, and sick leave pay. Payroll checks are signed by the vice president/treasurer and distributed by the controller, who knows the employees. The controller also checks the clerical accuracy of the payroll register and reviews it for unusual amounts. Bonuses, approved by the president, are paid annually. Employees generally work 40 hours per week. However, salaried employees may earn additional wages by providing administrative assistance (e.g., processing orders) at night and on weekends.

Required:

For specific control objectives P–3, A–3, "Salary, wage, and benefit expenses are incurred only for work authorized and performed;" P–4, A–4, "Salaries, wages, and benefits are calculated at proper rate;" and P–5, A–5, "Salaries, wages, benefits, and related liabilities are recorded correctly as to account (department, activity, cost center, etc.), amount, and period;" identify the environmental and control considerations. Also, describe the impact the environmental and control considerations have on the audit procedures.

15–16. Celmor Manufacturing began using a lockbox for its cash receipts at the beginning of the year. The president's secretary prepares a list of cash (checks) received directly by the company, which for the most part are insignificant. Cash receipts received directly by Celmor approximate $55,000 annually, or 2 percent of their total receipts. Receipts received by the company are deposited by the president weekly, or more often if the amount is significant. The controller prepares the deposit ticket. Also, the controller compares the lists of deposits prepared by the bank and the president's secretary to the bank deposits. Receipts are posted to the accounts receivable customer ledger by a clerk from remittance advices or lockbox report. The commercial bank account is reconciled monthly by the controller.

Required:

For specific control objectives F–1, "Cash receipts are recorded correctly as to account, amount, and period and are deposited;" and F–2, "Cash receipts are properly applied to customer balances;" identify the environmental and control considerations. Also, describe the impact environmental and control considerations have on the audit procedures.

15–17. Domor Manufacturing anticipates no major disposals of property, plant, and equipment for the year. Additions to date have been $385,496 or 8 percent of total assets. Disposals and additions require the approval of the operations supervisor. Domor intends to close its Greenville manufacturing facility and move the equipment to its main manufacturing facility. The company intends to lease the building. The EPA has recently completed an investigation at Domor; no fines have been assessed, and no equipment changes are necessary. The controller maintains the depreciation lapse schedules and reconciles them quarterly.

Required:

For specific control objectives P–13, "Disposals, retirements, trade-ins, idle plant and equipment, and other losses are identified and recorded correctly as to account, amount, and period;" P–14, "Physical loss of property, plant, and equipment is prevented;" and P–15, "Depreciation is calculated using proper lives and methods;" identify the environmental and control considerations. Also, describe the impact the environmental and control considerations have on the audit procedures.

15–18. Dan Industries is a job order shop in which all jobs are estimated and bid. The vice president of operations is responsible for correct billing of the sales contract and for movement of materials from production through shipment. Also, he has the ultimate authority to accept or reject all orders up to $1 million. Orders in excess of $1 million are approved or rejected by the president. Each job is priced on an individual basis based on accepted estimates. Sales have decreased 28 percent over the prior year with gross margins decreasing 3 percent. Shipping documents are issued in prenumbered order as are invoices. The sequences are verified daily by an accounting clerk. Accounts receivable are closely monitored; statements are mailed to customers monthly.

Required:

For specific control objectives S–3, "Products shipped or services rendered are billed;" S–4, "Billings are for the correct amount;" S–5, "Revenues are recorded correctly as to account, amount, and period;" and S–6, "Recorded billings are for valid transactions;" identify the environmental and control considerations. Also, determine the likelihood of material error in accounts affected.

15–19. P&M, Inc., manufactures its products to customer specifications. If the specifications are not met, the products are rejected by the customer. Each P&M location issues their own credit memos, which are reviewed by the vice president of finance after issuance. P&M issues credit memos totaling 8 to 10 percent of total sales ($3,900,000) per year. Management expects that rejections will increase during the slow economic times that P&M is experiencing. Some of the goods returned are reworked, but for the most part they are scrapped. Scrap sales for the last two years have been relatively constant at $29,525 and $31,005, respectively. The controller applies credits along with other noncash items to customer open receivables and accordingly adjusts salesmen's commissions for credit memos issued.

Required:

For specific control objective S–7, "Customer returns and other allowances are approved and recorded correctly as to account, amount, and period," describe the impact that the environmental considerations, observations from detail analytical review, and the control considerations have on the audit procedures.

15–20. The auditor should accept and retain only clients whom he or she believes are honest. However, an honest owner might have certain philosophies or motivations that require a higher level of professional skepticism on the auditor's part. List four examples of factors and motivations that might affect the audit of a small business.

THE AUDITOR'S REPORT

The auditor's report is the means by which the auditor communicates to financial statement users an opinion as to the fairness of the financial statements based on the results of the examination. It is important that the report describe clearly and concisely the nature of the auditor's examination and the degree of responsibility being taken. The specific form the report will take depends on the circumstances.

Chapter 1 identified the various types of audit reports and presented an example of the standard audit report. The standard audit report consists of a scope paragraph and an opinion paragraph. The scope paragraph provides a general statement of the work performed by the auditor, and it identifies the financial statements and the period covered. The opinion paragraph states the auditor's opinion on the financial statements.

When circumstances require a variation from the standard report, the auditor will usually include a middle paragraph—between the scope and opinion paragraphs—in which an explanation of the departure from the standard report is given. The auditor's opinion, or a statement (and reason) that the auditor is disclaiming one, is included in the third paragraph.

Figure 16–1 summarizes the criteria for the standard audit report and the various departures from the standard report. This chapter discusses the criteria in detail and presents examples of these various types of reports.

THE STANDARD REPORT

The auditor's report generally includes the balance sheet, income statement, and statements of retained earnings and changes in financial position. When the auditor has formed the opinion (on the basis of an examination made

16

in accordance with generally accepted auditing standards) that the reporting entity's financial statements present fairly the financial position, results of operations, and changes in financial position in conformity with generally accepted accounting principles (GAAP) applied on a basis consistent with that of the preceding period, an unqualified opinion should be issued. Following is the standard wording for an unqualified opinion from *SAS No. 2*, "Reports on Audited Financial Statements" (AU 509.07):

(Scope Paragraph)

We have examined the balance sheet of X Company as of [at] December 31, 19XX, and the related statements of income, retained earnings[1] and changes in financial position for the year then ended. Our examination was made in accordance with generally accepted auditing standards and, accordingly, included such tests of the accounting records and such other auditing procedures as we considered necessary in the circumstances.

(Opinion Paragraph)

In our opinion, the financial statements referred to above present fairly the financial position of X Company as of December 31, 19XX, and the results of its operations and the changes in its financial position for the year then ended, in conformity with generally accepted accounting principles applied on a basis consistent with that of the preceding year.

---

[1] Authors' note: If the financial statements include a statement of shareholders' equity instead, it may be identified in the scope paragraph.

FIGURE 16-1   Criteria for the Standard Audit Report and the Various Departures from the Standard Report

STANDARD REPORT
Unqualified Opinion

1. The examination was conducted in accordance with generally accepted auditing standards.
2. The financial statements are fairly presented.

DEPARTURES FROM THE STANDARD REPORT
Unqualified Opinion

1. The auditor refers to reliance on another independent auditor for performance of part of the audit.
2. The auditor believes that departure from a promulgated accounting principle is justified to prevent a misleading statement.
3. Consistency (change in accounting principle for which prior year financial statements are retroactively restated).
4. The auditor emphasizes a matter.

Qualified Opinion

1. Limitation on scope.*
2. Departure from generally accepted accounting principles.*
3. Consistency (change in accounting principle for which prior year financial statements are not restated).
4. Uncertainty* ("subject to" opinion).

Adverse Opinion

1. Departure from generally accepted accounting principles.*

Disclaimer of Opinion

1. Limitation on scope.*
2. Uncertainty.*
3. Auditor not independent.

*When one criterion is applicable to more than one type of report (e.g., limitation on scope—qualified or disclaimer, departure from GAAP—qualified or adverse), the materiality of the item should determine the type of opinion.

Comparative Financial Statements[2]

If the audited financial statements include financial statements of one or more preceding years for comparative purposes, the auditor's report should refer to the prior year(s) statements. *SAS No. 15* (AU 505.02) notes that a continuing auditor (a current auditor who has examined one or more immedi-

---

[2] This section is based on *Statement on Auditing Standards No. 15*, "Reports on Comparative Financial Statements," American Institute of Certified Public Accountants, 1976; and *Statement on Auditing Standards No. 26*, "Association with Financial Statements," American Institute of Certified Public Accountants, 1979.

ately preceding periods) should update his or her report on the financial statements for prior period(s) (i.e., reexpress the previous opinion or express a different opinion) when those financial statements are presented on a comparative basis with the current financial statements. Such an update is not necessary ". . . if only summarized comparative information of the prior period(s) is presented."

SAS No. 15 (AU 505.03) suggests the following example of an auditor's report on comparative statements for two periods:

> We have examined the balance sheets of the ABC Company as of December 31, 19X2 and 19X1, and the related statements of income, retained earnings, and changes in financial position for the years then ended. Our examinations were made in accordance with generally accepted auditing standards and, accordingly, included such tests of the accounting records and such other auditing procedures as we considered necessary in the circumstances.
>
> In our opinion, the financial statements referred to above present fairly the financial position of ABC Company as of December 31, 19X2 and 19X1, and the results of its operations and the changes in its financial position for the years then ended, in conformity with generally accepted accounting principles applied on a consistent basis.

SAS No. 15 (AU 505.04) also suggests that during the audit of the current period, the auditor should be alert for anything that might relate to prior period statements that are presented with the current statements.

Different Opinions. *SAS No. 15* (AU 505.05) permits different opinions for the various years included in comparative financial statements. However, the auditor should explain all substantive reasons for departures from an unqualified opinion in an explanatory paragraph. The explanatory paragraph is not needed, however, when the exception is due to a change in accounting principle.

Differing Update Report. In the process of updating a report from a prior period, the auditor should consider anything that may affect the financial statements of that period. *SAS No. 15* (footnote 4) states that:

> . . . An updated report on prior-period financial statements should be distinguished from a reissuance of a previous report . . . since in issuing an updated report the continuing auditor considers information that he has become aware of during his examination of the current-period financial statements . . . and because an updated report is issued in conjunction with the auditor's report on the current-period financial statements.

SAS No. 15 (AU 505.06) suggests that the following likely will cause a different opinion on financial statements of a prior year from that expressed in an earlier report:

1. An uncertainty of a prior period for which the auditor modified or disclaimed an opinion is resolved in a subsequent period.
2. During the current examination the auditor finds an uncertainty that affects the financial statements of a prior period.
3. The auditor initially issued a modified opinion due to a departure from generally accepted accounting principles and then in a subsequent period the client restates the financial statements to conform to generally accepted accounting principles.

SAS No. 15 (AU 505.07) indicates that the auditor should explain the substantive reasons for the change in the report in a separate paragraph.

Predecessor Auditor. *SAS No. 15* (AU 505.08) notes that a predecessor auditor may reissue a report on statements of a prior period at the request of a former client. Before doing so, the predecessor auditor should determine if the report is still appropriate. According to *SAS No. 15* (AU 505.09), this may be accomplished by:

1. Reading the current financial statements. The auditor should ". . . compare the prior-period financial statements that he reported on with the financial statements to be presented for comparative purposes. . . ."
2. Obtaining a letter from the current auditor that comments on whether the current audit revealed anything that might have a material effect on the financial statements reported on by the predecessor auditor. The predecessor auditor's report, however, should not mention the current auditor's work. The predecessor might want to consider the independence and professional standing of the current auditor. This may be done by employing techniques similar to those a principal auditor would use when part of an audit is conducted by another auditor (discussed later in this chapter).

If the predecessor auditor becomes aware of something occurring subsequent to his or her report that affects that report, *SAS No. 15* (AU 505.10) suggests that the predecessor auditor should make such inquiries and perform such procedures as are needed. The predecessor auditor should then decide if the report needs to be changed.

One Period Unaudited. *SAS No. 26* (AU 504.15) indicates that if unaudited financial statements are presented comparatively with audited statements, the unaudited statements should be clearly labeled "unaudited," and either the (1) prior period report should be reissued or (2) current period report should contain a separate paragraph describing the responsibility assumed for the prior period financial statements. *SAS No. 26* (AU 504.16) presents the following example of a separate paragraph to be used in the current period report when the prior period statements are audited and the current period is unaudited:

> The financial statements for the year ended December 31, 19X1, were examined by us (other accountants) and we (they) expressed an unqualified opinion on them in our (their) report dated March 1, 19X2, but we (they) have not performed any auditing procedures since that date.

Note that the paragraph indicated that (1) the statements for the year ended December 31, 19X1, had been previously examined, (2) an unqualified opinion was expressed, (3) the report was dated March 1, 19X2, and (4) no audit procedures had been performed after the date of the previous report. If the prior report was other than unqualified, the reasons for the lack of an unqualified opinion also should be noted in the paragraph.

SAS No. 26 (AU 504.17) notes that when the prior period financial statements are unaudited and the current audit report contains a separate paragraph concerning the prior year, the paragraph should include:

1. A statement concerning the service performed in the prior period and the date of the report of that service.
2. A notation of any material modifications indicated in the prior period report.
3. An indication that the service was not an audit, and consequently, there is no basis for giving an audit opinion.
4. A disclaimer of opinion or a description of the review, if the client is a public entity.
5. A description of the service performed (review or compilation) if the client is a nonpublic entity.

SAS No. 26 (AU 504.17) provides the following example of a separate paragraph describing a review:

> The 19X1 financial statements were reviewed by us (other accountants) and our (their) report thereon, dated March 1, 19X2, stated we (they) were not aware of any material modifications that should be made to those statements for them to be in confirmity with generally accepted accounting principles. However, a review is substantially less in scope than an audit and does not provide a basis for the expression of an opinion on the financial statements taken as a whole.

Separate Financial Statements

If the auditor is not asked to examine all of the basic financial statements, only those that were examined should be referred to in the auditor's report. For example, when the examination includes only the balance sheet, the following wording is suggested:

> We have examined the balance sheets of The National Company as of December 31, 19X2 and 19X1. Our examinations were made in accordance with generally accepted auditing standards and, accordingly, included such tests of the

accounting records and such other auditing procedures as we considered necessary in the circumstances.

In our opinion, the accompanying balance sheets present fairly the financial position of The National Company at December 31, 19X2 and 19X1, in conformity with generally accepted accounting principles applied on a consistent basis.

Consolidated Financial Statements

The following wording is suggested in auditors' reports that accompany consolidated financial statements:

> We have examined the consolidated balance sheets of The United Corporation and subsidiaries at December 31, 19X2 and 19X1, and the consolidated results of their operations and changes in their financial position for the years then ended. Our examinations were made in accordance with generally accepted auditing standards and, accordingly, included such tests of the accounting records and such other auditing procedures as we considered necessary in the circumstances.
>
> In our opinion, the financial statements referred to above present fairly the consolidated financial position of The United Corporation and subsidiaries at December 31, 19X2 and 19X1, and the consolidated results of their operations and changes in their financial position for the years then ended, in conformity with generally accepted accounting principles applied on a consistent basis.

It usually is not necessary to identify the subsidiaries by name. However, if it is necessary, the form could be *The United Corporation and consolidated subsidiaries, X Company and Y Company.*

If the consolidated subsidiaries can be concisely described to distinguish them from the unconsolidated subsidiaries, it is preferable to use such a description, both in the auditor's report and in the heading of the financial statements (e.g., wholly owned subsidiaries, wholly owned domestic subsidiaries). The auditor should be careful to select a description that is mutually exclusive and not equally applicable to one or more of the unconsolidated subsidiaries.

Parent Company Financial Statements

Ordinarily, only the consolidated financial statements will be issued to present financial position, results of operations, and changes in financial position of a corporation and its subsidiaries, and the auditor's opinion will extend only to these statements. However, there may be instances where separate financial statements of the parent company also will be issued (e.g., certain reports to creditors, filings with the SEC).

DEPARTURES FROM THE STANDARD REPORT

SAS No. 2 (AU 509.09) suggests seven principal reasons why an independent auditor may depart from the wording of the standard report. These are:

1. Limitations on the scope of the auditor's examination.
2. Reliance on the report of another auditor.
3. Lack of conformity with GAAP.
4. A departure from an accounting principle set by the body designated to establish such principles.
5. Lack of consistency.
6. Uncertainties.
7. Emphasis of a matter.

As illustrated in Figure 16–1, an auditor can deviate from the standard report and still issue an unqualified opinion. Items 2, 4, 5, and 7 are examples.

Limitations on Scope

SAS No. 2 (AU 509.10) notes that in order to express an unqualified opinion on the financial statements being examined, the auditor must use all audit procedures that are necessary in the circumstances. Further, this *SAS* indicates that limitations on the scope of the auditor's examination may result in a qualified opinion or a disclaimer of opinion. Such limitations may be due to (1) restrictions imposed by the client, (2) circumstances (e.g., timing of the audit), (3) lack of competent evidence, or (4) poor accounting records.

SAS No. 2 (AU 509.11) notes that the decision as to whether a qualification or disclaimer of opinion is necessary depends on the importance of the procedures omitted to the auditor's ". . . ability to form an opinion on the financial statements examined. This assessment will be affected by the nature and magnitude of the potential effects of the matters in question and by their significance to the financial statements. If the potential effects relate to many financial statement items, this significance is likely to be greater than if only a limited number of items is involved."

In a related area, *SAS No. 19*, "Client Representations," (AU 333) requires that an auditor obtain certain written representations from management (see Chapters 2 and 14). Refusal by management to provide a letter of representations is a scope limitation that would result in a qualification or disclaimer of opinion.

Other Auditors

Sometimes a part of an audit will be conducted by another independent auditing firm. For example, the principal auditor may not have an office in the city where a large subsidiary of a client is located. Under these circumstances, the subsidiary may be audited by another CPA firm.

The principal auditor has a choice as to whether and how to refer to the other auditor in the (principal auditor's) report. First, the principal auditor may choose to make no reference to the other auditor. Under these circumstances, the principal auditor becomes responsible for the other auditor's work. *SAS No. 1* (AU 543.05) states that the principal auditor usually will make no reference to the other auditor when:

1. The other auditor is: (a) associated with the principal auditor, or (b) a correspondent of the principal auditor.
2. The principal auditor hired, supervised, or guided the other auditor.
3. The principal auditor becomes satisfied as to the other auditor's work.
4. The work of the other auditor is not material in relation to the financial statements.

Alternatively, the principal auditor may wish to refer to the other auditor in the report. In those cases, both the scope and opinion paragraphs of the audit report should refer to the other auditor and indicate the extent of the responsibility of the other auditor for the report. The principal auditor may name the other auditor only if (1) the other auditor has given permission, and (2) the other auditor's report also is presented. Although the authoritative literature permits an auditor to specifically name the other auditor, mentioning the name generally is not done in practice. Reference to the other auditor is a departure from the standard report, but is not a qualification of the auditor's opinion.

Whether reference is made to the other auditor or not, *SAS No. 1* (AU 543.10) suggests that the principal auditor should consider:

1. Inquiring of professional organizations, practitioners, bankers, and others as to the professionalism of the other auditor.
2. Obtaining a representation from the other auditor that he or she is independent.
3. Making sure that the other auditor is familiar with generally accepted auditing standards and the reporting requirements of regulatory agencies. Also making sure that the other auditor realizes that the work will be relied on by the principal auditor.
4. Coordinating the activities of the two auditors to facilitate the review of items that may affect the consolidation of the accounts.

In addition, if no reference is made to the other auditor's work, *SAS No. 1* (AU 543.12) suggests that the auditor should think of possibly performing one, two, or all of the following:

    a. Visit the other auditor and discuss the audit procedures followed and results thereof.

b. Review the audit programs of the other auditor. In some cases, it may be appropriate to issue instructions to the other auditor as to the scope of his audit work.

c. Review the working papers of the other auditor, including his evaluation of internal control and his conclusions as to other significant aspects of the engagement.

If the principal auditor believes that the work of the other auditor cannot be relied upon, *SAS No. 1* (AU 543.11) suggests that the principal auditor qualify the opinion or disclaim an opinion and state the reasons for the exception. This situation is in effect similar to a scope limitation.

Lack of Conformity with GAAP

SAS No. 2 (AU 509.15) notes that if the auditor believes that the financial statements materially depart from GAAP, the auditor should issue a qualified opinion or an adverse opinion. *SAS No. 2* (AU 509.16) also notes that deciding whether the departure is ". . . sufficiently material to require either a qualified or an adverse opinion . . ." will depend on the dollar size of the departure and qualitative factors such as the significance of the item to the client's business, whether the misstatement is pervasive, and how the misstatement affects the financial statements taken as a whole.

SAS No. 32, "Adequacy of Disclosure in Financial Statements," (AU 431.03) states that "if management omits from the financial statements, including the accompanying notes, information that is required by generally accepted accounting principles, the auditor should express a qualified or an adverse opinion and should provide the information in his report, if practicable, unless its omission from the auditor's report is recognized as appropriate by a specific Statement on Auditing Standards. . . ."

Departure from an Accepted Authoritative Principle

In Chapter 19, it is noted that Rule 203 of the Code of Ethics states:

> A member shall not express an opinion that financial statements are presented in conformity with generally accepted accounting principles if such statements contain any departure from an accounting principle promulgated by the body designated by Council to establish such principles which has a material effect on the statements taken as a whole, unless the member can demonstrate that due to unusual circumstances the financial statements would otherwise have been misleading. In such cases his report must describe the departure, the approximate effects thereof, if practicable, and the reasons why compliance with the principle would result in a misleading statement.

SAS No. 2 (AU 509.19) suggests that if the auditor believes that such unusual circumstances are present, an unqualified opinion can be given unless there is some other reason to modify the audit report. However, the departure and its effects must be described in a separate paragraph.

Consistency

SAS No. 1 (AU 546.01) notes that a change in accounting principle makes it necessary for an auditor to describe the inconsistency in the audit report. *SAS No. 1* further notes that the auditor generally should indicate agreement with the change or lack thereof. If the auditor makes no comment, this will mean the auditor concurs with the change.

SAS No. 1 (AU 546.01) also states that "the form of modification of the opinion depends on the method of accounting for the effect of the change. . . ." *SAS No. 1* (AU 546.02) states that if the change in accounting principle ". . . should be reported by restating the financial statements of prior years,[3] the appropriate reference to consistency is that the statements are consistent after giving retroactive effect to the change." It also presents the following example of such an opinion covering one year:

> . . . applied on a basis consistent with that of the preceding year after giving retroactive effect to the change, with which we concur, in the method of accounting for long-term construction contracts as described in Note X to the financial statements.

In addition, *SAS No. 1* (AU 546.03) presents the following example of an opinion covering one year, when a change in accounting principle in that year should be reported by a means other than restating prior year statements:

> . . . in conformity with generally accepted accounting principles which, except for the change, with which we concur, in the method of computing depreciation as described in Note X to the financial statements, have been applied on a basis consistent with that of the preceding year.

SAS No. 1 (AU 546.05 and .06) also states that if the new accounting principle or the method of accounting for the effect of the change are not in conformity with GAAP, a qualification or adverse opinion due to departure from GAAP may be in order. In addition, if the auditor is not satisfied with management's reason for the change in accounting principles, a qualification may be needed.

Uncertainties

In discussing uncertainties, *SAS No. 2* (AU 509.22) states:

> In certain instances, the outcome of matters that may affect the financial statements or the disclosures required therein is not susceptible of reasonable estima-

---

[3] *APB Opinion No. 20,* "Accounting Changes," indicates which accounting changes should be reported by restating prior years and which should not.

tion. . . . When such uncertainties exist, it cannot be determined whether the financial statements should be adjusted, or in what amounts.

Examples of uncertainties include the results of lawsuits or the effects of income tax adjustments. When material uncertainties exist, the auditor should consider qualifying the opinion or even disclaiming an opinion.

The following opinion paragraph is suggested by *SAS No. 2* (AU 509.39), as amended by *SAS No. 43*, "Omnibus Statement on Auditing Standards," when a qualified opinion is necessary because of an uncertainty:

> In our opinion, subject to the effects on the financial statements of such adjustments, if any, as might have been required had the outcome of the uncertainty referred to in the preceding paragraph been known, the financial statements referred to above present fairly. . .

Note that the words *subject to* are used. Uncertainties are the only instances in which such a phrase may be used. In other types of qualifications, the phrase *except for* is usually proper. *SAS No. 2* (AU 509.24) notes that the auditor need not modify the opinion because of the existence of an uncertainty when it is concluded ". . . that there is only a minimal likelihood that resolution of the uncertainty will have a material effect on the financial statements."

Uncertainties concerning an entity's ability to continue in existence are addressed in *SAS No. 34*, "The Auditor's Considerations When a Question Arises About an Entity's Continued Existence (AU 340)." That *SAS* (AU 340.03) points out that the auditor does not look for evidence concerning an entity's future existence. The auditor is entitled to assume the entity can continue in existence unless there is information to the contrary. Contrary information suggested by *SAS No. 34* (AU 340.04) includes information that may:

1. Suggest solvency problems.
2. ". . . raise a question about continued existence without necessarily indicating potential solvency problems . . ." (e.g., departure of key personnel, litigation, or legislation that may affect an entity's capacity to continue in operation).

SAS No. 34 (AU 340.05) also suggests factors that may mitigate the importance of contrary information noted above (e.g., ability to dispose of assets, availability of debt financing, availability of more equity capital). *SAS No. 34* (AU 340.07–.08) indicates that the auditor should consider such mitigating factors along with any contrary information that arises. Additional considerations by the auditor often are warranted too. Those considerations mainly involve management plans that address the conditions observed.

SAS No. 34 (AU 340.11) suggests that after evaluating contrary information, the mitigating factors, and management's plans, the auditor must determine whether a substantial doubt remains about the entity's ability to continue in existence. If it does, the auditor ". . . should consider the recoverability and classification of recorded asset amounts, and the amounts and classification of liabilities. . . ." *SAS No. 34* (AU 340.11) further states that "identifying the point at which uncertainties about recoverability, classifications, and amounts require the auditor to modify his report is a complex professional judgment. No single factor or combination of factors is controlling."

Emphasis of a Matter

SAS No. 2 (AU 509.27) points out that, in certain situations, an auditor may wish to emphasize a certain matter but still issue an unqualified opinion. For example, the auditor may wish to:

1. ". . . point out that the entity is a component of a larger business enterprise . . ."
2. ". . . call attention to an unusually important subsequent event or to an accounting matter affecting the comparability of the financial statements with those of the preceding period."

Such information may be included in a separate paragraph in the report but should not be referred to in the opinion paragraph.

Lack of Independence

Another reason for a departure from the standard report is where the auditor is not independent. *SAS No. 26* (AU 504.09) states:

> When an accountant is not independent, any procedures he might perform would not be in accordance with generally accepted auditing standards, and he would be precluded from expressing an opinion on such statements. Accordingly, he should disclaim an opinion with respect to the financial statements and should state specifically that he is not independent.

The auditor is not required to indicate the reason for his or her lack of independence.

QUALIFIED OPINIONS, ADVERSE OPINIONS, AND DISCLAIMERS

This section discusses the various types of departures from the unqualified opinion and presents illustrations of the auditor's report in those circumstances.

Qualified Opinion

SAS No. 2 (AU 509.29) suggests a qualified opinion in the following circumstances:

1. The auditor expresses certain reservations concerning the scope of the audit.
2. There is a material departure from generally accepted accounting principles.
3. There is a material change in accounting principles or their application between periods (i.e., consistency).
4. Significant uncertainties exist.

SAS No. 2 (AU 509.32-.33) suggests that in issuing a qualified opinion, the auditor should clearly explain the reasons for the qualification and (except for qualifications due to consistency) the effect, if any, on the financial statements in one or more middle paragraphs. If the effect cannot be determined, that should be noted. *SAS No. 2* (AU 509.33) states that "if such disclosures are made in a note to the financial statements, the explanatory paragraph(s) may be shortened by referring to it." This *SAS* also suggests that the auditor state in the middle paragraph whether the exception is due to an uncertainty that depends on future events or a disagreement between the auditor and the client about whether an adjustment to the financial statements is necessary.

SAS No. 2 (AU 509.34) suggests that qualifications based on scope should be described only in the auditor's report (not in a footnote to the financial statements) because they relate to the auditor's examination, not the financial statements. Further, a scope qualification should be mentioned in an explanatory paragraph and noted in the scope and opinion paragraphs.

SAS No. 2 (AU 509.35) states that ". . . a qualified opinion should include the word 'except' or 'exception' in a phrase such as 'except for' or 'with the exception of,' unless the qualification arises because of an uncertainty affecting the financial statements; then the expression 'subject to' should be used."

Qualification because of Scope Limitation.   An example regarding receivables if the auditor has decided that the significance of the effect[4] of the limitation does not necessitate a disclaimer of opinion follows:

(Separate Paragraph)

In accordance with your instructions, we did not request confirmation of certain past-due accounts receivable aggregating $_____. We were unable to satisfy ourselves as to these receivables by alternative methods.

(Opinion Paragraph)

In our opinion, except for the effect of such adjustments, if any, as might have been determined to be necessary had we been able to request confirmations of the accounts receivable, the financial statements referred to above. . . .

---

[4] See *SAS No. 2.*

The wording "except for the effect of such adjustments, if any . . ." is necessary because the auditor does not know whether the accounts receivable are (1) fairly stated, (2) misstated, but by an immaterial amount, or (3) not fairly stated. *SAS No. 2* (AU 509.40) notes that other "wording such as 'In our opinion, except for the above-mentioned limitation on the scope of our examination . . .' bases the exception on the restriction itself, rather than on the possible effects on the financial statements, and therefore is unacceptable."

Qualification because of Departure from a Generally Accepted Accounting Principle. An example of such a report from *SAS No. 2* (AU 509.36) follows (assuming the auditor has decided an adverse opinion is not necessary):

(Separate Paragraph)

The Company has excluded from property and debt in the accompanying balance sheet certain lease obligations, which, in our opinion, should be capitalized in order to conform with generally accepted accounting principles. If these lease obligations were capitalized, property would be increased by $_____, long-term debt by $_____, and retained earnings by $_____ as of December 31, 19XX, and net income and earnings per share would be increased (decreased) by $_____ and $_____, respectively, for the year then ended.

(Opinion Paragraph)

In our opinion, except for the effects of not capitalizing lease obligations, as discussed in the preceding paragraph, the financial statements present fairly. . . .

AU 509.37 indicates that the separate paragraph can be shortened if the pertinent information is included in a note to the financial statements.

Qualification because of a Change in Accounting Principles or Their Application between Periods. As discussed in the "Consistency" section earlier in this chapter, when a change in accounting principle is reported by a means other than restating prior year statements, the auditor should modify the opinion as to consistency and describe the nature of the change. An example of such a report is included in that section.

Qualification because of Uncertainty. The following is an example from *SAS No. 2* (AU 509.39) (as amended by *SAS No. 43*) of a report qualified because of an uncertainty (assuming the auditor has decided a disclaimer of opinion is not necessary):

(Separate Paragraph)

As discussed in Note X to the financial statements, the Company is defendant in a lawsuit alleging infringement of certain patent rights and claiming royalties and punitive damages. The Company has filed a counter action, and preliminary hearings and discovery proceedings on both actions are in progress. Company officers and counsel believe the Company has a good chance of prevailing, but the ultimate outcome of the lawsuits cannot presently be determined, and no provision for any liability that may result has been made in the financial statements.

(Opinion Paragraph)

In our opinion, subject to the effects on the financial statements of such adjustments, if any, as might have been required had the outcome of the uncertainty referred to in the preceding paragraph been known, the financial statements referred to above present fairly. . . .

Adverse Opinion

According to *SAS No. 2* (AU 509.41), in an adverse opinion, the auditor states that the financial statements as a whole are not presented fairly in conformity with GAAP. Further, the auditor has concluded that the exceptions are so material that a qualified opinion cannot be issued. The auditor should have definite evidence of lack of fair presentation.

SAS No. 2 (AU 509.42, .44) indicates that the auditor should explain the reasons for the adverse opinion and discuss the effects of the exception on the financial statements in one or more middle paragraphs. When such effects are not determinable, this should be noted. Finally, since a reference to consistency in the opinion paragraph implies that GAAP have been used, an auditor should not refer to consistency in the opinion paragraph if an adverse opinion is given. If an auditor does have consistency exceptions, these exceptions also should be discussed in the report.

Using our previous example of a departure from GAAP that required a qualified opinion, if the effects are so significant that the financial statements as a whole are not presented in conformity with GAAP, the following adverse opinion is appropriate:

(Separate Paragraph)

The Company has excluded from property and debt in the accompanying balance sheet certain lease obligations, which, in our opinion, should be capitalized in order to conform with generally accepted accounting principles. If these lease obligations were capitalized, property would be increased by \$_____, long-term debt by \$_____, and retained earnings by \$_____ as of December 31, 19XX, and net income and earnings per share would be increased (decreased) by \$_____ and \$_____, respectively, for the year then ended.

(Opinion Paragraph)

In our opinion, because of the effects of the matters discussed in the preceding paragraph, the financial statements referred to above do not present fairly, in conformity with generally accepted accounting principles, the financial position of X Company at December 31, 19XX, or the results of its operations and changes in its financial position for the year then ended.[5]

---

[5] This opinion paragraph is quoted from *SAS No. 2* (AU 509.43).

Disclaimer of Opinion

Sometimes an auditor is unable to form an opinion as to the fairness of the financial statements and thus disclaims an opinion. *SAS No. 2* (AU 509.45) indicates that when disclaiming an opinion, the auditor should explain the reasons for the disclaimer in a separate paragraph. A disclaimer may be necessary due to a limitation on the scope of the auditor's examination, a material uncertainty, or if the auditor is not independent.

Disclaimer because of a Scope Limitation. The following example of a disclaimer from *SAS No. 2* (AU 509.47) is appropriate when sufficient competent evidence is not obtained:

(Scope Paragraph)

. . . Except as set forth in the following paragraph, our examination was made in accordance with generally accepted auditing standards and accordingly included such tests of the accounting records and such other auditing procedures as we considered necessary in the circumstances.

(Separate Paragraph)

The Company did not take a physical inventory of merchandise, stated at $_____ in the accompanying financial statements as of December 31, 19XX, and at $_____ as of December 31, 19X1. Further, evidence supporting the cost of property and equipment acquired prior to December 31, 19XX, is no longer available. The Company's records do not permit the application of adequate alternative procedures regarding the inventories or the cost of property and equipment.

(Disclaimer Paragraph)

Since the Company did not take physical inventories and we were unable to apply adequate alternative procedures regarding inventories and the cost of property and equipment, as noted in the preceding paragraph, the scope of our work was not sufficient to enable us to express, and we do not express, an opinion on the financial statements referred to above.

Disclaimer because of an Uncertainty. When expressing a disclaimer because of an uncertainty, the auditor should explain all of the substantive reasons for the disclaimer in a separate paragraph. An example of such a report follows:

(Separate Paragraph)

As more fully described in Note X to the financial statements, the Company is the defendant in a civil action alleging patent infringement relating to its principal product. The action seeks to recover $50,000,000 in damages, costs and attorney's fees together with injunctive relief. The civil suit was filed in November 19X2, and the ultimate liability, if any, cannot now be determined.

(Disclaimer Paragraph)

Because of the possible material effect on the financial statements of the lawsuit discussed in the preceding paragraph, we cannot and do not express an opinion on the financial statements referred to above.

OTHER REPORTING MATTERS

Other Information[6]

Companies often publish other information along with financial statements. In Chapter 14, we stated that the auditor should read the other information and consider whether it is consistent with the information presented in the financial statements. *SAS No. 8* (AU 550.04) states:

> If the auditor concludes that there is a material inconsistency, he should determine whether the financial statements, his report, or both require revision. If he concludes that they do not require revision, he should request the client to revise the other information. If the other information is not revised to eliminate the material inconsistency, he should consider other actions such as revising his report to include an explanatory paragraph describing the material inconsistency, withholding the use of his report in the document, and withdrawing from the engagement.

If the auditor believes there is a material misstatement of fact, rather than an inconsistency, this should be discussed with the client. *SAS No. 8* (AU 550.06) states that if after discussing the matter with the client, ". . . the auditor concludes that a material misstatement of fact remains, the action he takes will depend on his judgment in the particular circumstances. He should consider steps such as notifying his client in writing of his views concerning the information, and consulting his legal counsel as to further appropriate action in the circumstances."

Segment Information[7]

The auditor's standard report also covers segment information included in the financial statements covered by the report. *SAS No. 21* (AU 435.08) states that the auditor should refer to segment information only if the audit disclosed one of the following:

1. ". . . [A] misstatement or omission, or a change in an accounting principle, relating to the segment information that is material in relation to the financial statements as a whole. . . ."
2. A restriction on the scope of the examination.

---

[6] This section is based on *Statement on Auditing Standards No. 8,* "Other Information in Documents Containing Audited Financial Statements," American Institute of Certified Public Accountants, 1976.

[7] This section is based on *Statement on Auditing Standards No. 21,* "Segment Information," American Institute of Certified Public Accountants, 1977.

Misstatement or Omission. *SAS No. 21* (AU 435.09–.10) states that if a misstatement in segment information is material in relation to the financial statements as a whole, the auditor should modify the opinion due to a departure from GAAP. On the other hand, if the client does not include all or part of the needed segment information, the auditor should modify his or her opinion due to inadequate disclosure. The auditor need not present the omitted information in the audit report, but should describe the kind of information omitted.

Scope. Sometimes an auditor is unable to reach a conclusion as to whether the client needs to disclose segments as required by *FASB Statement No. 14,* "Financial Reporting for Segments of a Business Enterprise," and the client fails to develop information that would be needed to reach such a conclusion. *SAS No. 21* (AU 435.15) notes that the auditor should describe this situation in the scope paragraph and then qualify the report on the financial statements. A qualification also is necessary if the auditor is unable to apply the necessary auditing procedures to reported segment information (AU 435.16).

See Chapter 14 for discussion of the audit aspects of segment information.

REPORTING ON INFORMATION ACCOMPANYING THE BASIC FINANCIAL STATEMENTS IN AUDITOR-SUBMITTED DOCUMENTS[8]

An independent auditor occasionally issues a document that contains information in addition to the client's basic financial statements. *SAS No. 29* (AU 551.03) notes that this accompanying information may include, for example, ". . . additional details or explanations of items in or related to the basic financial statements, consolidating information, historical summaries of items extracted from the basic financial statements, statistical data, and other material, some of which may be from sources outside the accounting system or outside the entity." *SAS No. 29* (AU 551.05) indicates that the other information consists of representations of the client's management. The auditor's report should indicate the type of examination the auditor has performed as well as the degree of responsibility that the auditor is assuming for this information.

SAS No. 29 (AU 551.06) suggests the following guidelines for the auditor's report on such information:

1. "The report should state that the examination has been made for the purpose of forming an opinion on the basic financial statements taken as a whole."

---

[8] This section is based on *Statement on Auditing Standards No. 29,* "Reporting on Information Accompanying the Basic Financial Statements in Auditor-Submitted Documents," American Institute of Certified Public Accountants, 1980.

2. "The report should identify the accompanying information. . . ."
3. "The report should state that the accompanying information is presented for purposes of additional analysis and is not a required part of the basic financial statements. . . ."
4. "The report should include either an opinion on whether the accompanying information is fairly stated in all material respects in relation to the basic financial statements taken as a whole or a disclaimer of opinion, depending on whether the information has been subjected to the auditing procedures applied in the examination of the basic financial statements. The auditor may express an opinion on a portion of the accompanying information and disclaim an opinion on the remainder."
5. "The report on the accompanying information may be added to the auditor's standard report on the basic financial statements or may appear separately in the auditor-submitted document."

If the auditor expressed a qualified opinion on the basic financial statements, the report should clearly describe the effects of that qualification on the accompanying information. Further, if the auditor expresses an adverse opinion or disclaims an opinion on the basic financial statements, the auditor generally should not express any opinion on the accompanying information. [*SAS No. 29* (AU 551.10)]

Reporting Examples

SAS No. 29 (AU 551.12) gives the following example of an unqualified opinion on accompanying information:

> Our examination was made for the purpose of forming an opinion on the basic financial statements taken as a whole. The (identify accompanying information) is presented for purposes of additional analysis and is not a required part of the basic financial statements. Such information has been subjected to the auditing procedures applied in the examination of the basic financial statements and, in our opinion, is fairly stated in all material respects in relation to the basic financial statements taken as a whole.

SAS No. 29 (AU 551.14) presents the following example of a report on accompanying information when the auditor's report on basic financial statements is a qualified opinion:

> Our examination was made for the purpose of forming an opinion on the basic financial statements taken as a whole. The schedules of investments (page 7), property (page 8), and other assets (page 9) as of December 31, 19XX, are presented for purposes of additional analysis and are not a required part of the basic financial statements. The information in such schedules has been subjected to the auditing procedures applied in the examination of the basic financial statements; and, in our opinion, except for the effects on the schedule of investments of not accounting for the investments in certain companies by the equity method as explained in the second preceding paragraph

[second paragraph of our report on page 1], such information is fairly stated in all material respects in relation to the basic financial statements taken as a whole.

SUPPLEMENTARY INFORMATION REQUIRED BY FASB

SAS No. 27 "Supplementary Information Required by the Financial Accounting Standards Board" (AU 553), suggests procedures to be performed by the auditor in reviewing supplementary information required by the FASB. Those procedures are discussed in Chapter 14. *SAS No. 27* (AU 553.08) notes that an expansion of the auditor's report is needed if the (1) required supplementary information has been omitted, (2) measurement or presentation of the information provided materially departs from the FASB's guidelines, or (3) auditor has not been able to complete the audit procedures.

In addition, *SAS No. 29* (AU 551.15) notes that if ". . . supplementary information required by the FASB is presented outside the basic financial statements in an *auditor-submitted document,* the auditor should disclaim an opinion on the information unless he has been engaged to examine and express an opinion on it. . . ." (Emphasis added.) In such a situation, *SAS No. 29* suggests the following disclaimer:

> The (identify the supplementary information) on page XX is not a required part of the basic financial statements but is supplementary information required by the Financial Accounting Standards Board. We have applied certain limited procedures, which consisted principally of inquiries of management regarding the methods of measurement and presentation of the supplementary information. However, we did not audit the information and express no opinion on it.

QUESTIONS AND PROBLEMS

16–1. What is included in the scope and opinion paragraphs of the auditor's standard report?

16–2. If the audited financial statements of a client include last year's financial statements, what reference should be made to the latter in the accountant's report?

16–3. For what reasons would a middle paragraph be added to the auditor's standard report?

16–4. For what reasons should an independent auditor depart from the wording of the auditor's standard report?

16–5. Under what circumstances should the following opinions be expressed by the auditor:
a. Qualified.
b. Adverse.
c. Disclaimer.

16–6. Under what circumstances may the principal auditor be willing to assume responsibility for the work of another auditor?

16–7. Can an independent CPA rely on another independent CPA to audit a subsidiary of a client? Explain.

16–8. If a client publishes other information along with its financial statements, must the auditor audit this other information?

16–9. Does the auditor's standard report also cover segment information included in the financial statements?

16–10. CPA X, who practices in Philadelphia, has a client located in Philadelphia. The client has a large division in Georgia. Since CPA X does not have an office in Georgia he has another firm, ABC, do the audit of the division in Georgia. ABC, in fact, does a lot of correspondent work for CPA X in the southeast area. Due to the long and close relationship between CPA X and ABC, X decides not to make reference to ABC in the audit report. Since X will make no reference to ABC, should X perform any additional procedures?

16–11. Balsam Corporation is engaged in a hazardous trade and cannot obtain insurance coverage from any source. A material portion of the corporation's assets could be destroyed by a serious accident. The corporation has an excellent safety record and has never suffered a catastrophe. Assume that the audit examination was made in accordance with generally accepted auditing standards, that GAAP were applied on a consistent basis, and the disclosure was adequate.

Required:

What type of opinion should be rendered? (AICPA, adapted)

16–12. Select the best answer for each of the following items:

a. In which of the following circumstances would an auditor be required to issue a qualified report with a separate explanatory paragraph?

   (1) The auditor satisfactorily performed alternative accounts receivable procedures because scope limitations prevented performance of normal procedures.

   (2) The financial statements reflect the effects of a change in accounting principles from one period to the next.

   (3) A particular note to the financial statements discloses a company accounting method which deviates from GAAP.

   (4) The financial statements of a significant subsidiary were examined by another auditor, and reference to the other auditor's report is to be made in the principal auditor's report.

b. The annual report of a publicly held company presents the prior year's financial statements which are clearly marked "unaudited" in comparative form with current year audited financial statements. The auditor's report should:

   (1) Express an opinion on the audited financial statements and contain a separate paragraph describing the responsibility assumed for the financial statements of the prior period.

   (2) Disclaim an opinion on the unaudited financial statements, modify the consistency phrase, and express an opinion on the current year's financial statements.

  (3) State that the unaudited financial statements are presented solely for comparative purposes and express an opinion only on the current year's financial statements.

  (4) Express an opinion on the audited financial statements and state whether the unaudited financial statements were compiled or reviewed.

c. When an adverse opinion is expressed, the opinion paragraph should include a direct reference to:

  (1) A footnote to the financial statements which discusses the basis for the opinion.

  (2) The scope paragraph which discusses the basis for the opinion rendered.

  (3) A separate paragraph which discusses the basis for the opinion rendered.

  (4) The consistency or lack of consistency in the application of GAAP.

d. An auditor need not mention consistency in the audit report if:

  (1) The client has acquired another company through a "pooling of interests."

  (2) An adverse opinion is issued.

  (3) This is the first year the client has had an audit.

  (4) Comparative financial statements are issued.

e. Jones, CPA, is the principal auditor who is auditing the consolidated financial statements of his client. Jones plans to refer to another CPA's examination of the financial statements of a subsidiary company but does *not* wish to present the other CPA's audit report. Both Jones' and the other CPA's audit reports have noted no exceptions to GAAP. Under these circumstances the opinion paragraph of Jones' consolidated audit report should express:

  (1) An unqualified opinion.

  (2) A "subject to" opinion.

  (3) An "except for" opinion.

  (4) A principal opinion.

f. The principal auditor is satisfied with the independence and professional reputation of the other auditor who has audited a subsidiary but wants to indicate the division of responsibility. The principal auditor should:

  (1) Modify the scope paragraph of the report.

  (2) Modify the scope and opinion paragraphs of the report.

  (3) Not modify the report except for inclusion of an explanatory middle paragraph.

  (4) Modify the opinion paragraph of the report.

g. A limitation on the scope of the auditor's examination sufficient to preclude an unqualified opinion will *always* result when management:

  (1) Engages an auditor after the year-end physical inventory count.

  (2) Refuses to furnish a letter of representations.

  (3) Knows that direct confirmation of accounts receivable with debtors is not feasible.

  (4) Engages an auditor to examine only the balance sheet.

h. An auditor is confronted with an exception considered sufficiently material as to warrant some deviation from the standard unqualified auditor's report. If the exception relates to a departure from GAAP, the auditor must decide between expressing a (an):

  (1) Adverse opinion and a "subject to" opinion.

  (2) Adverse opinion and an "except for" opinion.

(3) Adverse opinion and a disclaimer of opinion.

(4) Disclaimer of opinion and a "subject to" opinion.   (AICPA, adapted)

16–13. The auditor's report must contain an expression of opinion or a statement to the effect that an opinion cannot be expressed. Four types of opinions which meet these requirements are generally known as:

1. An unqualified opinion.
2. A qualified opinion.
3. An adverse opinion.
4. A disclaimer of opinion.

Required:

For each of the following situations, indicate the type of opinion which you would render. Unless there is an implication to the contrary in the situation as stated, you may assume that the examination was made in accordance with generally accepted auditing standards, that the financial statements present fairly the financial position, results of operations, and changes in financial position in conformity with GAAP applied on a consistent basis, and that the statements include information disclosure necessary so as not to be misleading.

a. During the course of the examination, the CPA suspects that a material amount of the assets of the client, Ash Corporation, have been misappropriated through fraud. The corporation refuses to allow the auditor to expand the scope of the examination sufficiently to confirm these suspicions.

b. Dogwood Corporation owns properties which have substantially appreciated in value since the date of purchase. The properties were appraised and are reported in the balance sheet at the appraised values with full disclosure. The CPA believes that the values reported in the balance sheet are reasonable.

c. Subsequent to the close of Holly Corporation's fiscal year, a major debtor was declared bankrupt due to a rapid series of events. The debtor had confirmed the full amount due to Holly Corporation at the balance sheet date. Since the account was good at the balance sheet date, Holly Corporation refuses to disclose any information in relation to this subsequent event. The CPA believes that all accounts were stated fairly at the balance sheet date.   (AICPA, adapted)

16–14. The auditor's standard report usually contains a sentence like this: "Our examination was made in accordance with generally accepted auditing standards and, accordingly, included such tests of the accounting records and such other auditing procedures which we considered necessary in the circumstances."

a. Distinguish between auditing procedures and auditing standards.

b. Quote or state in your own words four generally accepted auditing standards.

(AICPA, adapted)

16–15. At the beginning of your examination of the financial statements of the Efel Insurance Company, the president of the company requested that in the interest of efficiency you coordinate your audit procedures with the audit being conducted by the state insurance examiners for the same fiscal year. The state examiners audited the asset accounts of the company while you audited the accounts for liabilities, stockholders' equity, income, and expenses. In addition, you obtained confirmations of the accounts receivable and were satisfied with the results of your audit tests. Although you had no supervisory control over the state examiners, they allowed you to review and prepare extracts from their working papers and report. After reviewing the state examiners' working papers and report to your complete satisfaction, you are now preparing your report.

Required:

What effect, if any, would the above circumstances have on your auditor's report? Discuss. (AICPA, adapted)

16–16. Following are the financial statements of the Young Manufacturing Corporation and the auditor's report of their examination for the year ended January 31, 1985. The examination was conducted by John Smith, an individual practitioner, who has examined the corporation's financial statements and reported on them for many years.

YOUNG MANUFACTURING CORPORATION
Statements of Condition
January 31, 1985, and 1984

Assets	1985	1984
Current assets:		
Cash	$ 43,822	$ 51,862
Accounts receivable—pledged—less allowances for doubtful accounts of $3,800 in 1985 and $3,000 in 1984 (see Note)	65,298	46,922
Inventories—pledged—at average cost, not in excess of replacement cost	148,910	118,264
Other current assets	6,280	5,192
Total current assets	$264,310	$222,240
Fixed assets:		
Land—at cost	$ 38,900	$ 62,300
Buildings—at cost, less accumulated depreciation of $50,800 in 1985 and $53,400 in 1984	177,400	150,200
Machinery and equipment—at cost less accumulated depreciation of $30,500 in 1985 and $25,640 in 1984	95,540	78,560
Total fixed assets	$311,840	$291,060
Total assets	$576,150	$513,300

Liabilities and Shareholders' Equity		
Current liabilities:		
Accounts payable	$ 27,926	$ 48,161
Other liabilities	68,743	64,513
Current portion of long-term mortgage payable	3,600	3,600
Income taxes payable	46,840	30,866
Total current liabilties	$147,109	$147,140
Long-term liabilities:		
Mortgage payable	90,400	94,000
Total liabilities	$237,509	$241,140
Shareholders' equity:		
Capital stock par value $100, 1,000 shares authorized, issued and outstanding	$100,000	$100,000
Retained earnings	238,641	172,160
Total shareholders' equity	$338,641	$272,160
Total liabilities and shareholders' equity	$576,150	$513,300

Note: I did not confirm the balances of the accounts receivable but satisfied myself by other auditing procedures that the balances were correct.

YOUNG MANUFACTURING CORPORATION
Income Statements
For the Years Ended January 31, 1985, and 1984

	1985	1984
Income:		
Sales	$884,932	$682,131
Other income	3,872	2,851
Total	$888,804	$684,982
Costs and expenses:		
Cost of goods sold	$463,570	$353,842
Selling expenses	241,698	201,986
Administrative expenses	72,154	66,582
Provision for income taxes	45,876	19,940
Other expenses	12,582	13,649
Total	$835,880	$655,999
Net income	$ 52,924	$ 28,983

Mr. Paul Young, President   March 31, 1985
Young Manufacturing Corporation

I have examined the balance sheet of the Young Manufacturing Corporation and the related statement of income and retained earnings.

These statements present fairly the financial position and results of operations in conformity with consistent generally accepted principles of accounting. My examination was made in accordance with generally accepted auditing standards, and accordingly included such tests of the accounting records and such other auditing procedures as I considered necessary in the circumstances.

(Signed) John Smith

Required:

List and discuss the deficiencies of the auditor's report prepared by John Smith. Your discussion should include justifications that the matters you cited are deficiencies. (Do not check the addition of the statements. Assume that the addition is correct.)   (AICPA, adapted)

16–17. The complete opinion included in the annual report of The Modern Department Store for 1986 is reproduced below:

Auditor's Certificate
DOE & DOE
New City, New State

To whom it may concern:

In our opinion, the accompanying balance sheet and related statements of income, retained earnings, and changes in financial position present fairly the financial position of The Modern Department Store and the results of its operations and the changes in its financial position. Our examination of these financial statements was made in accordance with generally accepted auditing standards and accordingly included such tests of the accounting records and such other auditing procedures as we considered necessary, except that we did not confirm accounts receivable, but instead accounted for subsequent collections in the accounts, and we did not observe the taking of the physical inventory because it was taken prior to our appointment as auditors.

Required:

List and discuss the deficiencies of the "Auditor's Certificate" prepared by Doe & Doe.

16–18. You are the independent auditor for the Claren Corporation. The president's salary has been increased substantially over the prior year by action of the board of directors. His present salary is much greater than salaries paid to presidents of companies of comparable size and is clearly excessive. You determine that the method of computing the president's salary was changed for the year under audit. In prior years, the president's salary was based on net income before income taxes. The Claren Corporation is in a cyclical industry and would have had an extremely profitable year except that the increase in the president's salary siphoned off much of the income that would have accrued to the stockholders. The president is a substantial stockholder.

Required:

a. Discuss your responsibility for disclosing this situation.
b. Discuss the effect, if any, that the situation has upon your auditor's opinion as to:
   (1) The fairness of the presentation of the financial statements.
   (2) The consistency of the application of accounting principles.

(AICPA, adapted)

16–19. About two years ago you were engaged to conduct an annual audit of Pierson Company. This was shortly after the majority stockholders assumed control of the company and discharged the president and several other corporate officers. A new president canceled a wholesaler's contract to distribute Pierson Company products. The wholesaler is a Pierson Company minority stockholder and was one of the discharged officers. Shortly after you commenced your initial audit, several law suits were filed against Pierson Company by the wholesaler. Pierson Company filed countersuits.

None of the suits have been decided. The principal litigation is over the canceled contract and the other suits are claims against the company for salary, bonus, and pension fund contributions. Pierson Company is the plaintiff in suits totaling approximately $300,000 and defendant in suits totaling approximately $2 million. Both amounts are material in relation to net income and total assets. Pierson's legal counsel believes the outcome of the suits is uncertain and that all of the suits are likely to be "tied up in court" for an extended time.

You were instructed by the board of directors each year to issue an audit report only if it contained an unqualified opinion. Pierson Company refuses to provide for an unfavorable settlement in the financial statements because legal counsel advised the board of directors that such a provision in the financial statements could be used against Pierson by the opposition in court. The pending litigation was fully disclosed in a footnote to the financial statements, however.

You did not issue a report on the completion of your audit one year ago and you have now completed your second annual audit. The scope of your audits was not restricted in any way, and you would render unqualified opinions if there were no pending litigation. You have attended all meetings of the stockholders and the directors and answered all questions directed to you at these meetings. You were promptly paid for all work completed to the current date. The board of directors of Pierson Company invited you to deliver to them an audit report containing an unqualified opinion or to attend the annual meeting of the stockholders one week hence to answer questions concerning the results of your audit if you are unwilling to render an unqualified opinion.

Required:

a. Discuss the issues raised by the fact that the auditor attended the stockholders' and directors' meetings and answered various questions. Do not consider the propriety of the failure to issue a written audit report.

b. Should a CPA issue the audit report promptly after completing the examination? Why?

c. (1) What kind of auditor's opinion would you render on Pierson Company's financial statements for the year just ended? Why? (You need not write an auditor's opinion.)

   (2) Write the middle paragraph that you would include in your auditor's standard report for Pierson Company's financial statements for the year just ended.   (AICPA, adapted)

16–20. The following draft of an auditor's report has been submitted for review.

To: Eric Jones, Chief Accountant
     Sunshine Manufacturing Company

We have examined the balance sheet of the Sunshine Manufacturing Company for the year ended August 31, 1986, and the related statements of income, retained earnings, and changes in financial position. Our examination included such tests of the accounting records and such other auditing procedures as we considered necessary in the circumstances except that, in accordance with your instructions, we did not count the buyers' cash working fund.

In our opinion, subject to the limitation on our examination discussed above, the accompanying balance sheet and statements of income, earned surplus, and changes in financial position present fairly the financial position of the Sunshine Manufacturing Company at August 31, 1986, and the results of its operations and changes in its financial position for the year then ended.

                                                                    Frank George & Company
                                                                    August 31, 1986

It has been determined that:

1. Except for the omission of the count of the buyers' cash working fund, there were no scope restrictions placed in the auditor's examination.

2. The Sunshine Manufacturing Company has been in continuous operation for 30 years, but its financial statements have not previously been audited.

Required:

a. Assuming that Frank George & Company was able to perform alternative auditing procedures to satisfactorily substantiate the buyers' cash working fund and purchases through the fund, identify and discuss the deficiencies in the auditor's report.

b. Assuming that Frank George & Company was unable to satisfactorily substantiate the buyers' cash working fund and purchases through the fund by alternative auditing procedures, discuss the appropriateness of the opinion qualification proposed by Frank George & Company's report.

c. Discuss the potential consequences to the CPA of issuing a substandard report or failing to adhere in the examination to generally accepted auditing standards.

(AICPA, adapted)

16–21. Charles Burke, CPA, has completed field work for his examination of the Williams Corporation for the year ended December 31, 1986, and now is in the process of determining whether to modify his report. Presented below are two independent, unrelated situations which have arisen.

Situation I

In September 1986, a lawsuit was filed against Williams to have the court order it to install pollution-control equipment in one of its older plants. Williams's legal counsel has informed Burke that it is not possible to forecast the outcome of this litigation; however, Williams's management has informed Burke that the cost of the pollution-control equipment is not economically feasible and that the plant will be closed if the case is lost. In addition, Burke has been told by management that the plant and its production equipment would have only minimal resale values and that the production that would be lost could not be recovered at other plants.

Situation II

During 1986, Williams purchased a franchise amounting to 20 percent of its assets for the exclusive right to produce and sell a newly patented product in the northeastern United States. There has been no production in marketable quantities of the product anywhere to date. Neither the franchisor nor any franchisee has conducted any market research with respect to the product.

Required:

In deciding the type of report modification, if any, Burke should take into account such considerations as follows:

Relative magnitude.

Uncertainty of outcome.

Likelihood of error.

Expertise of the auditor.

Pervasive impact on the financial statements.

Inherent importance of the item.

Discuss Burke's type-of-report decision for each situation in terms of the above and other appropriate considerations. Assume each situation is adequately disclosed in the notes to the financial statements. Each situation should be considered independently. In discussing each situation, ignore the other. It is not necessary for you to decide the type of report which should be issued. (AICPA, adapted)

16–22. Presented below is an independent auditor's report. The corporation being reported on is profit oriented and publishes general-purpose financial statements for distribution to owners, creditors, potential investors, and the general public. The report contains deficiencies.

Auditor's Report

We have examined the consolidated balance sheet of Belasco Corporation and subsidiaries as of December 31, 1985, and the related consolidated statements of income and retained earnings and changes in financial position for the year then ended. Our examination was made in accordance with generally accepted auditing standards and accordingly included such tests of the accounting records and such other auditing procedures as we considered necessary in the circumstances. We did not examine the financial statements of Seidel Company, a major consolidated subsidiary. These statements were examined by other auditors whose report thereon has been furnished to us and our opinion expressed herein, insofar as it relates to Seidel Company, is based solely upon the report of the other auditors.

In our opinion, except for the report of the other auditors, the accompanying consolidated balance sheet and consolidated statement of income and retained earnings and changes in financial position present fairly the financial position of Belasco Corporation and subsidiaries at December 31, 1985, and the results of its operations and the changes in its financial position for the year then ended, in conformity with generally accepted accounting principles applied on a basis consistent with that of the preceding year.

Required:

Describe the reporting deficiencies of the auditor's report, explain the reasons therefore, and briefly discuss how the report should be corrected. Do not discuss the addressee, signatures, and date. Also, do not rewrite the auditor's report.

(AICPA, adapted)

16–23. Nancy Miller, CPA, has completed field work for her examination of the financial statements of Nickles Manufacturers, Inc., for the year ended March 31, 1985, and now is preparing her auditor's report. Presented below are two independent, unrelated assumptions concerning this examination.

Assumption 1

The CPA was engaged on April 15, 1985, to examine the financial statements for the year ended March 31, 1985, and was not present to observe the taking of the physical inventory on March 31, 1985. Her alternative procedures included examination of shipping and receiving documents with regard to transactions during the year under review as well as transactions since the year-end, extensive review of the inventory-count sheets, and discussion of the physical inventory procedures with responsible company personnel. She has also satisfied herself as to inventory valuation and consistency in valuation method. Inventory quantities are determined solely by means of physical count. (Note: Assume that the CPA is properly relying upon the examination of another auditor with respect to the beginning inventory.)

Assumption 2

As of April 1, 1985, Nickles has an unused balance of $1,278,000 of federal income tax net operating loss carryforward that will expire at the end of the company's fiscal years as follows: $432,000 in 1986, $870,000 in 1987, and $76,000 in 1988. Nickles's management expects that the company will have enough taxable income to use the loss carryforward before it expires.

Required:

For each assumption described above discuss:

a. In detail, the appropriate disclosures in the financial statements and accompanying footnotes.

b. The effect, if any, on the auditor's standard report. For this requirement assume that Nickles makes the appropriate disclosures, if any, recommended in *(a)*.

Note: Complete your discussion (both [*a*] and [*b*]) of each assumption before beginning discussion of the next assumption. In considering each independent assumption, assume that the other situation did not occur. (AICPA, adapted)

16–24. Roscoe, CPA, has completed the examination of the financial statements of Excelsior Corporation as of and for the year ended December 31, 1985. Roscoe also examined and reported on the Excelsior financial statements for the prior year. Roscoe drafted the following report for 1985:

March 15, 1986

We have examined the balance sheet and statements of income and retained earnings of Excelsior Corporation as of December 31, 1985. Our examination was made in accordance with generally accepted accounting standards and accordingly included such tests of the accounting records as we considered necessary in the circumstances.

Roscoe, CPA
(signed)

Other information:

a. Excelsior is presenting comparative financial statements.

b. Excelsior does not wish to present a statement of changes in financial position for either year.

c. During 1985, Excelsior changed its method of accounting for long-term construction contracts and properly reflected the effect of the change in the current year's financial statements and restated the prior year's statements. Roscoe is satisfied with Excelsior's justification for making the change. (The change was discussed in a footnote to the financial statements.)

d. Roscoe was unable to perform normal accounts receivable confirmation procedures but alternate procedures were used to satisfy Roscoe as to the validity of the receivables.

e. Excelsior Corporation is the defendant in litigation, the outcome of which is highly uncertain. If the case is settled in favor of the plaintiff, Excelsior will be required to pay a substantial amount of cash which might require the sale of certain fixed assets. The litigation and the possible effects have been properly disclosed in a footnote to the financial statements.

f. Excelsior issued debentures on January 31, 1984, in the amount of $10 million. The funds obtained from the issuance were used to finance the expansion of plant facilities. The debenture agreement restricts the payment of future cash dividends to earnings after December 31, 1990. (Excelsior declined to disclose this essential data in the footnotes to the financial statements.)

Required:

Consider all facts given and rewrite the auditor's report in acceptable and complete format incorporating any necessary departures from the standard audit report.

Do not discuss the draft of Roscoe's report but identify and explain any items included in "Other Information" that need not be part of the auditor's report.

(AICPA, adapted)

16–25. The following tentative auditor's report was drafted by a staff accountant and submitted to a partner in the accounting firm of Better & Best, CPAs:

To the Audit Committee of American Widgets, Inc.

We have examined the consolidated balance sheets of American Widgets, Inc., and subsidiaries as of December 31, 1984, and 1983, and the related consolidated statements of income, retained earnings, and changes in financial position, for the years then ended. Our examinations were made in accordance with generally accepted auditing standards as we considered necessary in the circumstances. Other auditors examined the financial statements of certain subsidiaries and have furnished us with reports thereon containing no exceptions. Our opinion expressed herein, insofar as it relates to the amounts included for those subsidiaries, is based solely upon the reports of the other auditors.

As discussed in Note 4 to the financial statements, on January 8, 1985, the company halted the production of certain medical equipment as a result of inquiries by the Food and Drug Administration, which raised questions as to the adequacy of some of the company's sterilization equipment and related procedures. Management is not in a position to evaluate the effect of this production halt and the ensuing litigation, which may have an adverse effect on the financial position of American Widgets, Inc.

As fully discussed in Note 7 to the financial statements, in 1984 the company extended the use of the last-in, first-out (LIFO) method of accounting to include all inventories. In examining inventories, we engaged Dr. Irwin Same (Nobel Prize winner 1982) to test check the technical requirements and specifications of certain items of equipment manufactured by the company.

In our opinion, except for the effects, if any, on the financial statements of the ultimate resolution of the matter discussed in the second preceding paragraph, the financial statements referred to above present fairly the financial position of American Widgets, Inc., as of December 31, 1984, and the result of operations for the years then ended in conformity with generally accepted accounting principles applied on a basis consistent with that of the preceding year.

To be signed by Better & Best, CPAs March 1, 1985, except for Note 4 as to which the date is January 8, 1985.

Required:

Identify deficiencies in the staff accountant's tentative report that constitute departures from the generally accepted standards of reporting. (AICPA, adapted)

SPECIAL REPORTS AND UNAUDITED FINANCIAL STATEMENTS

Chapter 16 considered the various issues relating to the auditor's standard report. This chapter discusses special reports and reports that accompany unaudited financial statements.

SPECIAL REPORTS[1]

This section discusses those situations where the standard report is not suitable.

SAS No. 14 (AU 621.01) states that special reports are appropriate for:

    a. Financial statements that are prepared in accordance with a comprehensive basis of accounting other than generally accepted accounting principles. . . .

    b. Specified elements, accounts, or items of a financial statement. . . .

    c. Compliance with aspects of contractual agreements or regulatory requirements related to audited financial statements. . . .

    d. Financial information presented in prescribed forms or schedules that require a prescribed form of auditor's report. . . .

Special reports should serve a useful purpose and be prepared in a manner that is appropriate to the nature of the reporting entity. For example, a statement of cash receipts and disbursements might serve a useful purpose and be appropriate in reporting the operations of a charitable organization, but it would not be suitable for reporting the operations of a manufacturing company.

Basis Other than GAAP

SAS No. 14 (AU 621.04) states that the following are the cases in which a comprehensive basis other than GAAP may be used.

---

[1] This section is based on *Statement on Auditing Standards No. 14,* "Special Reports," American Institute of Certified Public Accountants, 1976.

17

a. A basis of accounting that the reporting entity uses to comply with the reporting requirements or financial reporting provisions of a government regulatory agency to whose jurisdiction the entity is subject. . . .

b. A basis of accounting that the reporting entity uses or expects to use to file its income tax return for the period covered by the financial statements.

c. The cash receipts and cash disbursements basis of accounting, and modifications of the cash basis having substantial support, such as recording depreciation on property and equipment or accruing income taxes.

d. A definite set of criteria having substantial support that is applied to all material items appearing in financial statements. . . .

SAS No. 14 (AU 621.05) requires that an auditor's report in any of the above instances include *all* of the following:

1. A scope paragraph.
2. An explanatory paragraph that (a) describes (or refers to a note to the statements that describes) the basis on which the statements are presented, (b) refers to the note that indicates how the basis differs from GAAP, and (c) states that the statements are not intended to conform with GAAP.
3. An opinion paragraph that states (a) whether the current ". . . statements are fairly presented in conformity with the basis of accounting described . . ." and (b) whether that basis of accounting was applied consistently with the prior period. Any departure from an unqualified opinion should be explained in an additional paragraph or paragraphs.

SAS No. 14 further states that "when reporting on financial statements prepared in accordance with the requirements or financial reporting provisions of a government regulatory agency . . . , the auditor may use the form of reporting . . . [described above] only if the financial statements are intended solely for filing with a regulatory agency or if additional distribution is recognized as appropriate by an AICPA accounting or audit guide or auditing interpretation. . . ."

Terms such as *balance sheet* or *income statement* are generally understood to be associated with statements that are based on GAAP. Consequently, the auditor should consider whether the financial statement titles accurately display the meaning of the financial statements. *SAS No. 14* (AU 621.08) provides examples of titles that may be used when the basis of accounting is other than GAAP. For example, a cash basis entity might use the title "statement of revenue collected and expenses paid" instead of income statement.

Reports on Specific Elements, Accounts, or Items

Expressing an Opinion. *SAS No. 14* (AU 621.10–.12) indicates that an auditor may express an opinion on specific elements, accounts, or items in financial statements as either a separate engagement or as part of an examination of financial statements. However, in the latter case, if an adverse opinion or disclaimer of opinion is given for the financial statements as a whole, the auditor's report on the specific elements, accounts, or items should not encompass a major portion of the financial statements. Also, the report should not accompany the entire financial statements.

SAS No. 14 (AU 621.13) requires that a report on specific elements, accounts, or items:

a. Identify the specified elements, accounts, or items examined.
b. State whether the examination was made in accordance with generally accepted auditing standards and, if applicable, that it was made in conjunction with an examination of financial statements. (Also, if applicable, any modification of the auditor's standard report on those statements should be indicated.)
c. Identify the basis on which the specified elements, accounts, or items are presented and, when applicable, any agreements specifying such basis.
d. Describe and indicate the source of significant interpretations made by the client in the course of the engagement relating to the provisions of a relevant agreement.
e. Indicate whether the specified elements, accounts, or items are presented fairly on the basis indicated.
f. If applicable, indicate whether the disclosed basis has been applied in a manner consistent with that of the preceding period.

Applying Agreed-Upon Procedures. *SAS No. 35*, "Special Reports—Applying Agreed-Upon Procedures to Specified Elements, Accounts, or Items of a Financial Statement" (AU 622.01), states that a CPA also can report on ". . . applying to one or more specified elements, accounts, or items of a financial statement agreed-upon procedures . . . that are not sufficient to enable him to express an opinion on the specified elements, accounts, or items, provided *(a)* the parties involved have a clear understanding of the procedures to be performed and *(b)* distribution of the report is to be restricted to named parties involved. . . ." Examples of such procedures suggested by *SAS No. 35* include reconciling cash on deposit and reviewing the aged trial balance of accounts receivable (and possibly mailing confirmation requests) in connection with a proposed acquisition. *SAS No. 35* provides examples of a CPA's report in those situations.

Reports on Compliance

Entities may be required by contracts (e.g., bond indentures) or regulatory agencies to provide compliance reports by independent auditors. According to *SAS No. 14* (AU 621.18), the auditor can give negative assurance relative to the items in question either ". . . in a separate report or in one or more paragraphs of the auditor's report accompanying the financial statements. Such assurance, however, should not be given unless the auditor has examined the financial statements to which the contractual agreements or regulatory requirements relate."

SAS No. 14 (AU 621.19) also states that the

> . . . negative assurance should specify that it is being given in connection with an examination of the financial statements. The auditor may also wish to state that the examination was not directed primarily toward obtaining knowledge regarding compliance. A separate report giving negative assurance should contain a paragraph stating that the financial statements have been examined, the date of the report thereon, and whether the examination was made in accordance with generally accepted auditing standards.

SAS No. 14 (AU 621.19) includes examples of compliance reports.

Prescribed Forms

Some authorities may require that financial statements be prepared on preprinted forms that also specify the wording of the auditor's report. In some instances, the auditor may believe that the wording of the prescribed form is not in conformity with the reporting standards of the profession. *SAS No. 14* (AU 621.21) points out that whenever printed forms would force the auditor to make an assertion that is believed to be unjustified in the circumstances, the auditor has no alternative but to reword that portion of the form or to submit a separate report.

OTHER TYPES OF REPORTS

Reports on Interim Financial Information Not Presented with Audited Financial Statements[2]

An independent accountant who conducts a review of interim financial data may issue a report to be included in a written communication that

---

[2] This section and the next section are based on *Statement on Auditing Standards No. 36,* "Review of Interim Financial Information," American Institute of Certified Public Accountants, 1981.

sets forth interim financial information. *SAS No. 36,* "Review of Interim Financial Information" (AU 722.17), notes that the independent accountant's report should:

1. State that the review was performed in accordance with applicable standards.
2. Identify the interim financial information that was reviewed.
3. Describe the procedures for such a review.
4. State ". . . that a review of interim financial information is substantially less in scope than an examination in accordance with generally accepted auditing standards, . . . and accordingly, no opinion is expressed. . . ."
5. State whether the accountant ". . . is aware of any material modifications that should be made to the accompanying financial information so that it conforms with generally accepted accounting principles."

The report should usually be dated as of the completion of the review and each page of the interim financial data should be marked "unaudited." *SAS No. 36* (AU 722.18) presents the following example of such a report.

> We have made a review of (describe the information or statements reviewed) of ABC Company and consolidated subsidiaries as of September 30, 19X1, and for the three-month and nine-month periods then ended, in accordance with standards established by the American Institute of Certified Public Accountants.
>
> A review of interim financial information consists principally of obtaining an understanding of the system for the preparation of interim financial information, applying analytical review procedures to financial data, and making inquiries of persons responsible for financial and accounting matters. It is substantially less in scope than an examination in accordance with generally accepted auditing standards, the objective of which is the expression of an opinion regarding the financial statements taken as a whole. Accordingly, we do not express such an opinion.
>
> Based on our review, we are not aware of any material modifications that should be made to the accompanying financial (information or statements) for them to be in conformity with generally accepted accounting principles.

A modification of the accountant's report is necessary if there is a departure from GAAP and related disclosure requirements or a change in accounting principle that is not in conformity with GAAP. However, an uncertainty or lack of consistency in applying accounting principles affecting interim financial information will not require a modified report if appropriately disclosed in the financial statements.

In the case of a departure from GAAP, the accountant's report should describe the departure and, if possible, its effect on interim financial information. If a departure is due to inadequate disclosure, the report should, if possible, include the needed information.

SAS No. 36 (AU 722.21) presents the following example of an accountant's report modified due to a departure from GAAP:

(Explanatory third paragraph)

Based on information furnished us by management, we believe that the Company has excluded from property and debt in the accompanying balance sheet certain lease obligations that should be capitalized in order to conform with generally accepted accounting principles. This information indicates that if these lease obligations were capitalized at September 30, 19X1, property would be increased by $＿＿＿, and long-term debt by $＿＿＿, and net income and earnings per share would be increased (decreased) by $＿＿＿, $＿＿＿, $＿＿＿, and $＿＿＿, respectively, for the three-month and nine-month periods then ended.

(Concluding paragraph)

Based on our review, with the exception of the matter(s) described in the preceding paragraph(s), we are not aware of any material modifications that should be made to the accompanying financial (information or statements) for them to be in conformity with generally accepted accounting principles.

SAS No. 36 (AU 722.22) also presents the following modification due to inadequate disclosure:

(Explanatory third paragraph)

Management has informed us that the Company is presently contesting deficiencies in federal income taxes proposed by the Internal Revenue Service for the years 19XX through 19XY in the aggregate amount of approximately $＿＿＿, and that the extent of the company's liability, if any, and the effect on the accompanying (information or statements) are not determinable at this time. The (information or statements) fail to disclose these matters, which we believe are required to be disclosed in conformity with generally accepted accounting principles.

(Concluding Paragraph)

Based on our review, with the exception of the matter(s) described in the preceding paragraph(s), we are not aware of any material modifications that should be made to the accompanying financial (information or statements) for them to be in conformity with generally accepted accounting principles.

Interim Financial Information Accompanying Audited Financial Statements

SAS No. 36 (AU 722.24) notes that some companies are required by the SEC ". . . to include selected quarterly financial data in annual reports or other documents filed with the SEC that contain audited financial statements . . . ." Other companies may voluntarily include such quarterly data. In either case, the review procedures noted in Chapter 14 should be applied.

Placement of Interim Information. *SAS No. 36* (AU 722.26) states that generally, interim information ". . . would be presented as supplementary information outside the audited financial statements. If management chooses to present the interim financial information in a note to the audited financial statements, the information should be clearly marked as unaudited."

Timing of Review. The auditor may review interim information either before the issuance of quarterly data ("timely review") or at the time of the annual audit ("retrospective review").

Audit Report. Generally, the audit report need not refer to the interim data. However, the auditor's report should be expanded when the interim data required by the SEC are either (1) omitted or (2) not reviewed. *SAS No. 36* (AU 722.29) provides suggested additions to the auditor's report in such situations.

SAS No. 36 (AU 722.30) indicates the auditor's report also should be expanded if interim information is voluntarily provided or required by the SEC and the:

1. Interim information is presented in a note that is not marked as unaudited;
2. Information required by the SEC that is voluntarily presented has not been reviewed and is not so marked;
3. Interim information is not presented in conformity with generally accepted accounting principles;[3] or
4. "Interim financial information includes an indication that a review was made but fails to state that the review is substantially less in scope than an examination in accordance with generally accepted auditing standards, the objective of which is an expression of opinion regarding the financial statements taken as a whole, and accordingly, no such opinion is expressed."

In 3 and 4 above, the audit report need not be expanded if a separate report based on the auditor's review discusses the circumstances and is presented with the interim information.

Condensed Financial Statements[4]

SAS No. 42 (AU 552), permits an auditor to report on condensed financial statements that are taken from a public entity's audited financial statements.

---

[3] See *APB Opinion No. 28*, "Interim Financial Reporting," for description of generally accepted accounting principles as they relate to interim information.

[4] The next two sections are based on *Statements on Auditing Standards No. 42*, "Condensed Financial Statements and Selected Financial Data," American Institute of Certified Public Accountants, 1982.

For purposes of this *SAS,* a public entity is one that is required to file audited financial statements with a regulatory agency at least annually (e.g., an SEC registrant). However, condensed financial statements may not fairly present financial position, results of operations, and changes in financial position. Therefore, an auditor's report on condensed financial statements is not the same as the report on the financial statements that they were taken from.

SAS No. 42 (AU 552.05) notes that the auditor's report should indicate:

1. ". . . that the auditor has examined and expressed an opinion on the complete financial statements. . . ."
2. ". . . the date of the auditor's report on . . ." that examination.
3. ". . . the type of opinion expressed. . . ."
4. The auditor's opinion as to whether the information in the condensed financial statements ". . . is fairly stated in all material respects in relation to the complete financial statements from which it has been derived. . . ."

SAS No. 42 (AU 552.06) provides the following example of an auditor's report on condensed financial statements:

> We have examined, in accordance with generally accepted auditing standards, the consolidated balance sheet of X Company and subsidiaries as of December 31, 19X0, and the related consolidated statements of income, retained earnings, and changes in financial position for the year then ended (not presented herein); and in our report dated February 15, 19X1, we expressed an unqualified opinion on those consolidated financial statements. In our opinion, the information set forth in the accompanying condensed consolidated financial statements is fairly stated in all material respects in relation to the consolidated financial statements from which it has been derived.

SAS No. 42 (AU 552.08) also permits issuance of a report on condensed financial information presented on a comparative basis with interim financial information of a subsequent period accompanied by an auditor's review report (e.g., quarterly report to the SEC). The *SAS* provides an example of such a report, which essentially combines an accountant's review report with the above example.

Selected Financial Data

SAS No. 42 (AU 552.09) permits an auditor to report on selected financial data in a client-prepared document that contains audited financial statements (e.g., selected financial data required in the annual shareholders report of an SEC registrant). *SAS No. 42* applies to both public and nonpublic entities.

The auditor's report should be limited to data obtained from audited statements. If the data also include other information, the auditor should indicate that it is not covered by the audit report.

SAS No. 42 (AU 552.09) notes that the auditor's report should indicate:

1. "... that the auditor has examined and expressed an opinion on the complete financial statements...."
2. "... the type of opinion expressed...."
3. The auditor's opinion as to whether the information "... in the selected financial data is fairly stated in all material respects in relation to the complete financial statements from which it has been derived...."

SAS No. 42 (AU 552.10) provides the following example of a paragraph that may be added to the auditor's standard report to express an opinion on selected financial data (see the *SAS* for full text of this report):

> We have also previously examined, in accordance with generally accepted auditing standards, the consolidated balance sheets as of December 31, 19X3, 19X2, and 19X1, and the related consolidated statements of income, retained earnings, and changes in financial position for the years ended December 31, 19X2 and 19X1 (none of which are presented herein); and we expressed unqualified opinions on those consolidated financial statements. In our opinion, the information set forth in the selected financial data for each of the five years in the period ended December 31, 19X5, appearing on page xx, is fairly stated in all material respects in relation to the consolidated financial statements from which it has been derived.

Forecasts

In 1975, the AICPA's Accounting Standards Executive Committee issued *Statement of Position 75–4 (SOP 75–4),* "Presentation and Disclosure of Financial Forecasts." *SOP 75–4* makes the following distinction between financial forecasts, financial projections, and feasibility studies:

1. *Financial forecast:* "... an estimate of the most probable financial position, results of operations and changes in financial position for one or more future periods."
2. *Financial projection:* "... an estimate of financial results based on assumptions which are not necessarily the most likely."
3. *Feasibility study:* "... an analysis of a proposed investment or course of action. A feasibility study may involve the preparation of financial projections and/or a financial forecast."

SOP 75–4 provides presentation and disclosure guidance for entities issuing financial forecasts. However, it notes that financial forecasts are not part of the basic financial statements. The reader should refer to *SOP 75–4* for the details of the recommendations on presentation and disclosure. Briefly, some of the major suggestions include:

1. Presenting forecasts in historical financial statement format.
2. Preparing the forecasts on a basis consistent with generally accepted

accounting principles that will likely be used in historical financial statements in the period forecasted.
3. Expressing forecasts ". . . in specific monetary amounts representing the single most probable forecasted result." This figure may be ". . . supplemented by ranges and probabilistic statements. . . ."
4. Disclosing important assumptions.

Sometimes CPAs are engaged to report on a forecast. The content of a report on forecasts should be responsive to Rule 201 of the AICPA *Code of Professional Ethics,* which does not permit the CPA's name ". . . to be used in conjunction with any forecast of future transactions in a manner which may lead to the belief that the member vouches for the achievability of the forecast." Further, *Interpretation 201–2* of the *Code of Professional Ethics* indicates that when an accountant is associated with a forecast, disclosure should be given of the: (1) source of the information utilized, (2) important assumptions used, (3) type of work done by the accountant, and (4) degree of responsibility the accountant is taking. (See Chapter 19.)

In 1980, the AICPA issued the *Guide for a Review of a Financial Forecast* (Guide). It covers situations in which a CPA has been engaged to independently review and then report on a financial forecast. The Guide was developed by the AICPA's Financial Forecasts and Projections Task Force.[5] It does not have the authority of an Auditing Standards Board pronouncement, but AICPA members may be called on to justify departures from it.

Objective of a Review.   The Guide states that the objective of a review of a financial forecast ". . . is to provide the accountant with a basis for reporting whether with respect to the forecast taken as a whole,

"•The forecast was properly prepared based on the stated assumptions, and the presentation conforms with the recommendations in *Statement of Position 75–4* . . . and

"•The underlying assumptions provide a reasonable basis for management's forecast."

The Review.   The Guide suggests the following guidelines for reviews and the resulting report.

1. The review should be performed by personnel with proper training and proficiency.
2. The reviewing accountant should be independent.
3. Due professional care needs to be used on the entire engagement.
4. "There should be adequate planning of the work ". . . and assistants, if any, should be properly supervised."

---

[5] The remainder of this section is based on *Guide for a Review of a Financial Forecast,* American Institute of Certified Public Accountants, 1980.

5. The accountant should understand the forecasting process so that the scope of the review can be determined.
6. The accountant's report should have proper support.
7. The report should note if the accountant believes the forecast ". . . is presented in conformity with applicable AICPA guidelines for presentation of a financial forecast and has been prepared using assumptions that provide a reasonable basis for management's forecast."

The Guide suggests that, in determining the scope of the review, the accountant should consider his or her knowledge of the client's business and forecasting process as well as the client's previous experience with forecasting and the length of the period forecast. Chapter 2 of the Guide contains details on the procedures to evaluate management's assumptions and the preparation and presentation of the forecast.

Accountant's Report on a Reviewed Financial Forecast. The Guide suggests that an accountant's report on a review of a forecast include:

1. An identification of the forecast information presented by management and a description of what it is intended to represent.
2. A statement that the review was made in accordance with applicable AICPA guidelines for a review of a financial forecast and a brief description of the nature of such a review.
3. A statement that the accountant assumes no responsibility to update the report for events and circumstances occurring after the date of the report.
4. A statement regarding whether the accountant believes that the financial forecast is presented in conformity with applicable AICPA guidelines for presentation of a financial forecast and whether the underlying assumptions provide a reasonable basis for management's forecast. . . .
5. A caveat regarding the ultimate attainment of the forecast results.

The Guide provides the following example of a standard review report:

The accompanying forecasted balance sheet, statements of income, retained earnings, and changes in financial position, and summary of significant forecast assumptions . . . of XYZ Company as of December 31, 19XX, and for the year then ending, is management's estimate of the most probable financial position, results of operations, and changes in financial position for the forecast period. Accordingly, the forecast reflects management's judgment, based on present circumstances, of the most likely set of conditions and its most likely course of action.

We have made a review of the financial forecast in accordance with applicable guidelines for a review of a financial forecast established by the American Institute of Certified Public Accountants. Our review included procedures to evaluate both the assumptions used by management and the preparation and presentation of the forecast. We have no responsibility to update this report for events and circumstances occurring after the date of this report.

Based on our review, we believe that the accompanying financial forecast is presented in conformity with applicable guidelines for presentation of a financial forecast established by the American Institute of Certified Public Accountants. We believe that the underlying assumptions provide a reasonable basis for management's forecast. However, some assumptions inevitably will not materialize and unanticipated events and circumstances may occur; therefore, the actual results achieved during the forecast period will vary from the forecast, and the variations may be material.

The report should be dated as of the date of the completion of the review procedures. The accountant's report also can include other information that is deemed relevant (e.g., statistical data).

The Guide suggests the following circumstances that may result in a departure from the standard report:

1. The accountant believes that the forecast departs from the presentation guidelines discussed in *Statement of Position 75–4.* . . .
2. The accountant believes one or more significant assumptions are unreasonable. . . .
3. The scope of the accountant's review is affected by conditions that preclude application of one or more procedures he considers necessary in the circumstances. . . .
4. The accountant is not independent. . . .
5. The accountant's evaluation is based in part on the report of another accountant. . . .
6. Historical financial information is presented for comparison to the forecast. . . .
7. The accountant wishes to emphasize a matter regarding the financial forecast. . . .

The Guide suggests that the use of a qualified report might cause confusion. Thus, ". . . when a departure from guidelines, an unreasonable assumption, or a limitation on the scope of the accountant's review has led him to conclude that he cannot issue an unqualified report, he should issue . . ." an adverse report or disclaim a conclusion.

Adverse Report.   An adverse report would be issued if the accountant believes either that there is a departure from the guidelines in *SOP 75–4* or that at least one significant assumption is not reasonable. The Guide gives the following example of an adverse report when the accountant concludes that a significant assumption is not reasonable:

(Explanatory Paragraph)

As discussed under the caption "Sales" in the summary of significant forecast assumptions, the forecasted sales include, among other things, revenue from the company's federal defense contracts continuing at the current level. The company's present federal defense contracts will expire in March 19XX. No new contracts have been signed and no negotiations are under way for new federal defense contracts. Furthermore, the federal government has entered into contracts with another company to supply the items being manufactured under the company's present contracts.

(Concluding Paragraph)

Based on our review, we believe that the accompanying financial forecast is not presented in conformity with applicable guidelines established by the American Institute of Certified Public Accountants because management's assumptions, as discussed in the preceding paragraph, do not provide a reasonable basis for management's forecast.

Disclaiming Conclusion. A scope limitation, whether client imposed or due to the circumstances of the forecast (e.g., the nature of the assumptions), may result in the accountant disclaiming a conclusion. When this becomes necessary, the report should indicate in an explanatory paragraph how the review did not comply with the Guide. The Guide gives the following example when the accountant was unable to evaluate a significant assumption:

(Second Paragraph)

We have made a review of the financial forecast. Except as explained in the following paragraph, our review was made in accordance with applicable guidelines for a review of a financial forecast established by the American Institute of Certified Public Accountants.

(Explanatory Paragraph)

As discussed under the caption "Income From Investee" in the summary of significant forecast assumptions, the forecast includes income from an equity investee constituting 23 percent of forecasted net income, based on the assumption that income from the investee will equal that of 19X1. The investee has not prepared a financial forecast for the year ending December 31, 19X2, and we were therefore unable to inspect suitable support for this assumption.

(Concluding Paragraph)

Since, as described in the preceding paragraph, we are unable to evaluate management's assumption regarding income from an equity investee and other assumptions that depend thereon, we express no conclusion with respect to the presentation of the accompanying financial forecast.

If there is both a scope limitation and a material departure from the guidelines of *SOP 75–4*, the departure also should be discussed in the report.

When the accountant reviewing the report is not independent, the accountant should note the lack of independence and no conclusion should be expressed. The following example is given by the Guide:

We are not independent with respect to XYZ Company, and the accompanying forecasted balance sheet as of December 31, 19XX, forecasted statements of income, retained earnings, and changes in financial position for the year then ending, and the summary of significant forecast assumptions were not reviewed by us in accordance with applicable guidelines for a review of a financial forecast established by the American Institute of Certified Public Accountants. Accordingly, we express no conclusion with respect to the accompanying financial forecast.

Other Accountants.   When the work of more than one accountant is used in a review of a forecast, the procedures used in the examination of historical statements should apply (see Chapter 16).

Comparative Statements.   When a forecast is compared to historical data, the report on the review should indicate what work the accountant did on the historical data and what responsibility the accountant is assuming for such data. The accountant also should refer to the source of the data and any previous accountant's report issued on such data.

Emphasizing a Matter.   The accountant may issue a report that is unqualified but may want to emphasize some matter relating to the forecast. Such information may be presented in a separate paragraph.

In 1982, the AICPA Task Force issued a *Statement of Position,* "Report on a Feasibility Study." This report supplements the *Guide for a Review of a Financial Forecast* and provides guidance for reporting on a financial feasibility study. Such a feasibility study normally includes a financial forecast.

UNAUDITED FINANCIAL STATEMENTS— PUBLIC ENTITIES[6]

Independent accountants often prepare or assist clients in the preparation of financial statements that are not audited. The nature of the accountant's involvement with unaudited statements of public entities is discussed in *SAS No. 26.* The nature of the accountant's involvement with unaudited financial statements or other unaudited financial information of a *nonpublic* entity is governed by the Accounting and Review Services Committee. Chapter 15 discussed the nature of the accountant's procedures related to unaudited financial statements of a nonpublic entity.

When an Accountant Is Associated with Financial Statements

SAS No. 26 (AU 504.03) specifies the conditions under which an accountant is considered to be associated with financial statements. It states that:

An accountant is associated with financial statements when he has consented to the use of his name in a report, document, or written communication contain-

---

[6] This section is based on *Statement on Auditing Standards No. 26,* "Association with Financial Statements," American Institute of Certified Public Accountants, 1979.

ing the statements. . . . Also, when an accountant submits to his client or others financial statements that he has prepared or assisted in preparing, he is deemed to be associated even though the accountant does not append his name to the statements. Although the accountant may participate in the preparation of financial statements, the statements are representations of management, and the fairness of their presentation . . . is management's responsibility.

SAS No. 26 (AU 504.04) recognizes that an accountant may be associated with either audited or unaudited financial statements and states:

Financial statements are audited if the accountant has applied auditing procedures sufficient to permit him to report on them as described in [*SAS No. 2*]. . . . The unaudited interim financial statements (or financial information) of a public entity are reviewed when the accountant has applied procedures sufficient to permit him to report on them as described in . . . [*SAS No. 36*].

Disclaimer of Opinion

If an independent accountant is associated with the financial statements of a public entity, but neither reviews nor audits the statements, *SAS No. 26* (AU 504.05) suggests the following form of report:

The accompanying balance sheet of X Company as of December 31, 19X1, and the related statements of income and retained earnings and changes in financial position for the year then ended were not audited by us and, accordingly, we do not express an opinion on them.

(Signature and date)

The independent accountant's report may be placed on the statements or it may accompany them. Each page of the financial statements should be labeled "unaudited."

Modified Disclaimer

Even though a CPA prepares the statements without an audit, it may be apparent that the statements are not in conformity with GAAP. *SAS No. 26* (AU 504.11) indicates that the CPA should ask the client to make the appropriate revisions. If the client does not comply, the CPA should explain the inadequacies in a disclaimer of opinion. Such an explanation should describe the departure and, if possible, its effect on the financial statements or include the information that will provide adequate disclosure. *SAS No. 26* (AU 504.12) notes that in some instances departures due to inadequate disclosure may be so substantial that it may not be practicable to include all omitted disclosures in the report. Then the accountant should describe this fact in the report (without including the actual disclosures). *SAS No. 26* (AU 504.13) also states that if the client will not revise the report or will not accept a modified disclaimer of opinion, the accountant should withdraw from the engagement.

UNAUDITED FINANCIAL STATEMENTS— NONPUBLIC ENTITIES[7]

Reporting Obligation

Statement on Standards for Accounting and Review Services (SSARS) No. 1 (AR 100.05) notes that an accountant who compiles or reviews statements for a nonpublic client should issue a report appropriate for the level of service performed. If more than one service is performed (e.g., a review and an audit) for a client, the accountant should issue a report applicable to the level of service that is highest.

SSARS No. 1 (AR 100.06) further indicates that an accountant should not allow his or her name to appear on any document that includes a nonpublic entity's unaudited financial statements unless (1) the accountant has either compiled or reviewed the statements and they are accompanied by a report or (2) there is an indication with the financial statements that the accountant has not done a compilation or review and is not assuming any responsibility. If the client uses the accountant's name improperly in a document (prepared by the client) containing unaudited financial statements, the accountant should (1) advise the client of the situation, and (2) consider taking other appropriate actions, including consulting an attorney.

SSARS No. 1 (AR 100.07) also points out that an ". . . accountant should not submit unaudited financial statements of a nonpublic entity to his client or others unless, as a minimum, he complies with the provisions of this statement applicable to a compilation engagement. This precludes the accountant from merely typing or reproducing financial statements as an accommodation to his client."

Compilation of Financial Statements

Each page of the financial statements should include a notation such as "See Accountant's Compilation Report." The date of the report should be the date the compilation procedures are completed.

---

[7] This section is based on *SSARS No. 1,* "Compilation and Review of Financial Statements," American Institute of Certified Public Accountants, 1978; *SSARS No. 2,* "Reporting on Comparative Financial Statements," American Institute of Certified Public Accountants, 1979; *SSARS No. 3,* "Compilation Reports on Financial Statements Included in Certain Prescribed Forms," American Institute of Certified Public Accountants, 1981; *SSARS No. 4,* "Communications Between Predecessor and Successor Accountants," American Institute of Certified Public Accountants, 1981; and *SSARS No. 5,* "Reporting on Compiled Financial Statements," American Institute of Certified Public Accountants, 1982.

SSARS No. 1 (as amended by SSARS No. 5) suggests the following form for a compilation report:

> I (we) have compiled the accompanying balance sheet of XYZ Company as of December 31, 19XX, and the related statements of income, retained earnings, and changes in financial position for the year then ended, in accordance with standards established by the American Institute of Certified Public Accountants.
>
> A compilation is limited to presenting in the form of financial statements information that is the representation of management (owners). I (we) have not audited or reviewed the accompanying financial statements and, accordingly, do not express an opinion or any other form of assurance on them.

disclaimer

SSARS No. 1 (AR 100.19) states that if the client asks the accountant to compile financial statements that ". . . omit substantially all of the disclosures required by generally accepted accounting principles," the accountant may compile the financial statements if (1) the fact that disclosures normally required are omitted is noted in the report and (2) omission of those disclosures is not, to the knowledge of the accountant, done to mislead financial statement users. SSARS No. 1 (as amended by SSARS No. 5) suggests the following report form for use in such a situation:

> I (we) have compiled the accompanying balance sheet of XYZ Company as of December 31, 19XX, and the related statements of income, retained earnings, and changes in financial position for the year then ended, in accordance with standards established by the American Institute of Certified Public Accountants.
>
> A compilation is limited to presenting in the form of financial statements information that is the representation of management (owners). I (we) have not audited or reviewed the accompanying financial statements and, accordingly, do not express an opinion or any other form of assurance on them.
>
> Management has elected to omit substantially all of the disclosures required by generally accepted accounting principles.[8] If the omitted disclosures were included in the financial statements, they might influence the user's conclusions about the company's financial position, results of operations, and changes in financial position. Accordingly, these financial statements are not designed for those who are not informed about such matters.

Finally, if an accountant is not independent, a report on his or her compilation may still be appropriate. In this situation, SSARS No. 1 (AR 100.22) suggests the following as the last paragraph of the report: "I am (we are) not independent with respect to XYZ Company."

---

[8] Authors' note: SSARS No. 1 states that "if the statement of changes in financial position is omitted, the first and third paragraphs of the report should be modified accordingly."

Review of Financial Statements

    SSARS No. 1 (AR 100.32–.34) notes that the financial statements should be accompanied by a report that is dated when the accountant completed his or her inquiry and analytical procedures. Each page of the financial statements should include a notation such as "See Accountant's Review Report." The following standard report is suggested by *SSARS No. 1* (AR 100.35).

> I (we) have reviewed the accompanying balance sheet of XYZ Company as of December 31, 19XX, and the related statements of income, retained earnings, and changes in financial position for the year then ended, in accordance with standards established by the American Institute of Certified Public Accountants. All information included in these financial statements is the representation of the management (owners) of XYZ Company.
>
> A review consists principally of inquiries of company personnel and analytical procedures applied to financial data. It is substantially less in scope than an examination in accordance with generally accepted auditing standards, the objective of which is the expression of an opinion regarding the financial statements taken as a whole. Accordingly, I (we) do not express such an opinion.
>
> Based on my (our) review, I am (we are) not aware of any material modifications that should be made to the accompanying financial statements in order for them to be in conformity with generally accepted accounting principles.

    If the accountant is not able to perform the procedures that are necessary for a proper review, a review report should not be issued. *SSARS No. 1* (AR 100.36) states that "in such a situation, the accountant should consider whether the circumstances resulting in an incomplete review also preclude him from issuing a compilation report on the entity's financial statements." (See *SSARS No. 1* for a further discussion of this point.) Further, the accountant should not issue a review report if he or she is not independent. However, *SSARS No. 1* (AR 100.38) states that "if the accountant is not independent, he may issue a compilation report provided he complies with compilation standards."

Departures from GAAP

    During a compilation or review, the accountant may become aware of material departures from GAAP (and related disclosure requirements) or the comprehensive basis of accounting used by the entity. Earlier we described when omission of substantially all disclosures in a compilation may be acceptable. In other circumstances, if the client does not make any recommended changes in the financial statements, a modified report may be needed. If a modified report is not adequate in the circumstances, the accountant should consider withdrawing from the engagement.

When a modified report is given, *SSARS No. 1* (AR 100.40) states that:

. . . the departure should be disclosed in a separate paragraph of [the] report, including disclosure of the effects of the departure on the financial statements if such effects have been determined by management or are known as the result of the accountant's procedures. The accountant is not required to determine the effects of a departure if management has not done so, provided the accountant states in his report that such determination has not been made.

SSARS No. 1 (as amended by *SSARS No. 5*) (AR 100.40) suggests the following examples of compilation and review reports that disclose departures from GAAP:

Compilation Report

I(we) have compiled the accompanying balance sheet of XYZ Company as of December 31, 19XX, and the related statements of income, retained earnings, and changes in financial position for the year then ended, in accordance with standards established by the American Institute of Certified Public Accountants.

A compilation is limited to presenting in the form of financial statements information that is the representation of management (owners). I (we) have not audited or reviewed the accompanying financial statements and, accordingly, do not express an opinion or any other form of assurance on them. However, I (we) did become aware of a departure (certain departures) from generally accepted accounting principles that is (are) described in the following paragraph(s).

(Separate Paragraph)

As disclosed in note X to the financial statements, generally accepted accounting principles require that land be stated at cost. Management has informed me (us) that the company has stated its land at appraised value and that, if generally accepted accounting principles had been followed, the land account and shareholders' equity would have decreased by $500,000.

or

A statement of changes in financial position for the year ended December 31, 19XX, has not been presented. Generally accepted accounting principles require that such a statement be presented when financial statements purport to present financial position and results of operations. . . . [Authors' note: A footnote in *SSARS No. 1* indicates that if the statement of changes in financial position is not present, the first paragraph needs to be appropriately modified.]

Review Report

I (we) have reviewed the accompanying balance sheet of XYZ Company as of December 31, 19XX, and the related statements of income, retained earnings, and changes in financial position for the year then ended, in accordance with standards established by the American Institute of Certified Public Accountants. All information included in these financial statements is the representation of the management (owners) of XYZ Company.

A review consists principally of inquiries of company personnel and analytical procedures applied to financial data. It is substantially less in scope than an examination in accordance with generally accepted auditing standards, the objective of which is the expression of an opinion regarding the financial statements taken as a whole. Accordingly, I (we) do not express such an opinion.

Based on my (our) review, with the exception of the matter(s) described in the following paragraph(s), I am (we are) not aware of any material modifications that should be made to the accompanying financial statements in order for them to be in conformity with generally accepted accounting principles.

(Separate Paragraph)

As disclosed in note X to the financial statements, generally accepted accounting principles require that inventory cost consist of material, labor, and overhead. Management has informed me (us) that the inventory of finished goods and work in process is stated in the accompanying financial statements at material and labor cost only, and that the effects of this departure from generally accepted accounting principles on financial position, results of operations, and changes in financial position have not been determined.

or

As disclosed in note X to the financial statements, the company has adopted (description of newly adopted method), whereas it previously used (description of previous method). Although the (description of newly adopted method) is in conformity with generally accepted accounting principles, the company does not appear to have reasonable justification for making a change as required by *Opinion No. 20* of the Accounting Principles Board.

Reporting on Comparative Statements

SSARS No. 2 establishes standards for the reports of nonpublic entities when the financial statements for more than one period are presented. Further, *SSARS No. 2* gives examples of reporting when different levels of services are performed on unaudited comparative financial statements. Guidance is also given for reporting when the current period's statements are compiled or reviewed and the prior period's were audited. *SSARS No. 2* indicates that when the current period's financial statements are audited and those of prior periods were compiled or reviewed, *SAS No. 26,* "Association with Financial Statements," should be referred to for guidance on reporting. The following are reports that can be used for comparative financial statements when the current period is unaudited but the accountant has performed different levels of service:[9]

Review in Current Period, Compilation in Prior Period

I (we) have reviewed the accompanying balance sheet of XYZ Company as of December 31, 19X2, and the related statements of income, retained earnings,

---

[9] These reports are taken from and/or based on *SSARS No. 2.*

and changes in financial position for the year then ended, in accordance with standards established by the American Institute of Certified Public Accountants. All information included in these financial statements is the representation of the management (owners) of XYZ Company.

A review consists principally of inquiries of company personnel and analytical procedures applied to financial data. It is substantially less in scope than an examination in accordance with generally accepted auditing standards, the objective of which is the expression of an opinion regarding the financial statements taken as a whole. Accordingly, I (we) do not express such an opinion.

Based on my (our) review, I am (we are) not aware of any material modifications that should be made to the 19X2 financial statements in order for them to be in conformity with generally accepted accounting principles.

The accompanying 19X1 financial statements of XYZ Company were compiled by me (us). A compilation is limited to presenting in the form of financial statements information that is the representation of management (owners). I (we) have not audited or reviewed the 19X1 financial statements and, accordingly, do not express an opinion or any other form of assurance on them.

March 1, 19x3

Compilation in Current Period, Review in Prior Period

I (we) have compiled the accompanying balance sheet of XYZ Company as of December 31, 19X2, and the related statements of income, retained earnings, and changes in financial position for the year then ended, in accordance with standards established by the American Institute of Certified Public Accountants.

A compilation is limited to presenting in the form of financial statements information that is the representation of management (owners). I (we) have not audited or reviewed the 19X2 financial statements and, accordingly, do not express an opinion or any form of assurance on them.

The accompanying 19X1 financial statements of XYZ Company were previously reviewed by me (us) and my (our) report dated March 1, 19X2, stated that I was (we were) not aware of any material modifications that should be made to those statements in order for them to be in conformity with generally accepted accounting principles. I (we) have not performed any procedures in connection with that review engagement after the date of my (our) report on the 19X1 financial statements.

Review in Current Period, Audit in Prior Period

I (we) have reviewed the accompanying balance sheet of XYZ Company as of December 31, 19X2, and the related statements of income, retained earnings, and changes in financial position for the year then ended, in accordance with standards established by the American Institute of Certified Public Accountants. All information included in these financial statements is the representation of the management (owners) of XYZ Company.

A review consists principally of inquiries of company personnel and analytical procedures applied to financial data. It is substantially less in scope than an examination in accordance with generally accepted auditing standards, the objective of which is the expression of an opinion regarding the financial statements taken as a whole. Accordingly, I (we) do not express such an opinion.

Based on my (our) review, I am (we are) not aware of any material modifications that should be made to the 19X2 financial statements in order for them to be in conformity with generally accepted accounting principles.

The financial statements for the year ended December 31, 19X1, were examined by us (other accountants) and we (they) expressed an unqualified opinion on them in our (their) report dated March 1, 19X2, but we (they) have not performed any auditing procedures since that date.

When reporting on comparative financial statements with different levels of service, each page of the financial statements should contain a notation such as, "See Accountants' Report."

Compilation Reports and Prescribed Forms

SSARS No. 3 notes that an accountant may be asked to compile financial statements in a prescribed form or format that is not in conformity with GAAP. Such prescribed forms are adapted or designed by the group (e.g., trade association, governmental agency) to which the form will be submitted. In those situations, *SSARS No. 3* (as amended by *SSARS No. 5*) suggests a specific form of accountant's report that is similar to the standard compilation report. See *SSARS No. 3* for further details. A departure from the prescribed form or the instructions related to such a form should be viewed by the accountant, for reporting purposes, as a departure from GAAP.

Communication between Accountants

SSARS No. 4 states that a successor accountant (an accountant who has been asked to make a proposal or has accepted an engagement) in either a compilation or a review engagement is not required to communicate with a predecessor accountant but has the option to do so. Examples of circumstances that may call for such contact include:

1. The client or prospective client has a history of frequently changing accountants.
2. The change of accountants takes place substantially after the end of the accounting period under consideration.
3. The successor accountant believes that more information is needed about the client or prospective client and/or its management.

As we have previously noted, a CPA must treat information regarding a client or former client as confidential. Consequently, the successor accountant should request the client to (1) permit contact with the predecessor accountant and (2) authorize the predecessor accountant to answer the successor accountant's inquiries. If a prospective client refuses to give such authorization, the accountant should take this into consideration in determining whether to accept the engagement.

QUESTIONS AND PROBLEMS

17–1. When are special reports appropriate?

17–2. If a client's financial statements are prepared in accordance with a comprehensive basis of accounting other than GAAP, in general, what should be included in an auditor's report?

17–3. What should an auditor include in a report on specific elements, accounts, or items?

17–4. If an accountant reviews a client's interim financial information, what should be included in the accountant's report?

17–5. When should a report on a review of interim financial information be dated?

17–6. If, while reviewing a client's interim financial information, an accountant notes a lack of consistency in applying accounting principles affecting the interim financial information, how will this affect the accountant's report?

17–7. What is a financial forecast? Is it part of the basic financial statements?

17–8. According to *Interpretation 201–2* of the *Code of Professional Ethics,* what disclosures should be made when an accountant is associated with a forecast?

17–9. What authority does the AICPA's *Guide for a Review of a Financial Forecast* have?

17–10. What is the objective of a review of a financial forecast?

17–11. When reviewing a financial forecast, what factors should an accountant consider in determining the scope of the review?

17–12. What should be included in an accountant's report on a review of a financial forecast?

17–13. What circumstances may cause an accountant to depart from the standard report when reviewing a financial forecast?

17–14. When might an accountant issue an adverse opinion on a financial forecast?

17–15. If an accountant reviewing a financial forecast is not independent, what kind of report should be issued?

17–16. If an accountant reviews a financial forecast and then the forecast is presented in comparison with historical data, what reference should be made to the historical data?

17–17. Select the best answer for each of the following items:

   a. The term *special report* may include all of the following *except* reports on financial statements:

(1) Of an organization that has limited the scope of the auditor's examination.

(2) Prepared for limited purposes such as a report that relates to only certain aspects of financial statements.

(3) Of a not-for-profit organization which follows accounting practices differing in some respects from those followed by business enterprises organized for profit.

(4) Prepared in accordance with a cash basis of accounting.

b. Whenever special reports, filed on a printed form designed by authorities, call upon the independent auditor to make an assertion that the auditor believes is *not* justified, the auditor should:

(1) Submit a standard audit report with explanations.

(2) Reword the form or attach a separate report.

(3) Submit the form with questionable items clearly omitted.

(4) Withdraw from the engagement.

c. When an independent CPA is associated with the financial statements of a publicly held entity, but has not audited or reviewed such statements, the appropriate form of report to be issued must include a(an):

(1) Negative assurance.

(2) Compilation opinion.

(3) Disclaimer of opinion.

(4) Explanatory paragraph.

d. Which of the following statements with respect to an auditor's report expressing an opinion on a specific item on a financial statement is correct?

(1) Materiality must be related to the specified item rather than to the financial statements taken as a whole.

(2) Such a report can only be expressed if the auditor is also engaged to audit the entire set of financial statements.

(3) The attention devoted to the specified item is usually less than it would be if the financial statements taken as a whole were being audited.

(4) The auditor who has issued an adverse opinion on the financial statements taken as a whole can never express an opinion on a specified item in these financial statements.

e. Which of the following would *not* be included in a CPA's report based upon a review of the financial statements of a nonpublic entity?

(1) A statement that the review was in accordance with generally accepted auditing standards.

(2) A statement that all information included in the financial statements are the representations of management.

(3) A statement describing the principal procedures performed.

(4) A statement describing the auditor's conclusions based upon the results of the review.

f. When asked to perform an examination in order to express an opinion on one or more specified elements, accounts, or items of a financial statement, the auditor:

(1) May *not* describe auditing procedures applied.

(2) Should advise the client that to issue such an opinion is not permitted by the profession.

(3) May assume that the first standard of reporting with respect to GAAP does not apply.

      (4)   Should comply with the request only if they constitute a major portion of the financial statements on which an auditor has disclaimed an opinion based on an audit.

  g. If the auditor believes that financial statements which are prepared on a comprehensive basis of accounting other than GAAP are *not* suitably titled, the auditor should:

      (1)   Modify the auditor's report to disclose any reservations.

      (2)   Consider the effects of the titles on the financial statements taken as a whole.

      (3)   Issue a disclaimer of opinion.

      (4)   Add a footnote to the financial statements which explains alternative terminology.

  h. A modification of the CPA's report on a review of the interim financial statements of a publicly held company would be necessitated by which of the following?

      (1)   An uncertainty.

      (2)   Lack of consistency.

      (3)   Reference to another accountant.

      (4)   Inadequate disclosure.

  i. An auditor's report would be designated as a special report when it is issued in connection with which of the following?

      (1)   Financial statements for an interim period which are subjected to a limited review.

      (2)   Financial statements which are prepared in accordance with a comprehensive basis of accounting other than GAAP.

      (3)   Financial statements which purport to be in accordance with GAAP but do not include a presentation of the statement of changes in financial position.

      (4)   Financial statements which are unaudited and are prepared from a client's accounting records.   (AICPA, adapted)

17–18. Rose & Company, CPAs, has satisfactorily completed the examination of the financial statements of Bale & Booster, a partnership, for the year ended December 31, 1986. The financial statements which were prepared on the entity's income tax (cash) basis include footnotes which indicate that the partnership was involved in continuing litigation of material amounts relating to alleged infringement of a competitor's patent. The amount of damages, if any, resulting from this litigation could not be determined at the time of completion of the engagement. The prior years' financial statements were not presented.

Required:

    Based upon the information presented, prepare an auditor's report which includes appropriate explanatory disclosure of significant facts.   (AICPA, adapted)

17–19. You were engaged to examine the financial statements of Barnes Corporation (a public entity) for the year just ended (December 31, 1985). The CPA firm previously engaged declined to make the examination because a son of one of the CPA firm's partners received a material amount of Barnes Corporation common stock in exchange for engineering services rendered to the corporation. The partner in the CPA firm advises his son in business affairs but does not own an interest in his son's engineering firm and had not participated in this examination in past years. Another of the CPA firm's 15 partners would have been in charge of the engagement.

This new client wants to receive three different reports from you. In the past the stockholders have considered and discussed the corporation's annual report containing the financial statements and the auditor's opinion at their annual meeting. Because of the shortage of time before the stockholders' meeting, corporation executives are willing to accept *(a)* your report containing unaudited statements to be used for the meeting and *(b)* your final report after your examination is complete. Thereafter, the client would like to receive *(c)* a report containing a forecast of the corporation's 1986–88 operations.

Required:

a. Should the CPA firm previously engaged by Barnes Corporation have declined the examination of the financial statements for the year just ended? Discuss the ethical issues involved.
b. Discuss the issues in the client's request that you render unaudited financial statements prior to rendering your final report. (AICPA, adapted)

17–20. CPA J is employed to compile the financial statements of the Reach Corporation for the year ended December 31, 1986. Each page of the financial statements includes the notation "Compilation." The compilation report prepared by J read as follows:

> The accompanying balance sheet of Reach Corporation as of December 31, 1986, and the related statement of income, retained earnings, and changes in financial position for the year then ended have been compiled by us. We have not audited the accompanying financial statements and accordingly do not express an opinion on them.

Required:

Cite any deficiencies that exist in CPA J's work.

17–21. CPA K submitted a review report for his client, Pear, Inc., (a non-public corporation) for the year ended December 31, 1987. You are to cite any deficiencies that exist in CPA K's work.

a. Each page of the financial statements is marked "Unaudited."
b. The report reads as follows:

> I have examined the accompanying balance sheet of Pear, Inc. as of December 31, 1987, and the related statements of income, retained earnings, and changes in financial position for the year then ended, in accordance with generally accepted review standards. All information included in the financial statements is the representation of the management of Pear, Inc.

> A review consists principally of inquiries of company personnel and audit procedures applied to financial data. It is substantially less in scope than an examination in accordance with generally accepted auditing standards, the objective of which is to compile financial statements. Accordingly, I do not express such an opinion.

> Based on my review, I am not aware of any material modifications that should be made to the accompanying financial statements in order for them to be in conformity with generally accepted auditing standards.

17–22. Arthur M. Proper, CPA is a partner in the CPA firm of Very and Proper. Proper has a tax client in the scrap business by the name of Scrap, Inc. (a nonpublic corporation). The business is small and the personnel consists of two sales people, a secretary, a controller, and the president. On the last day of the month, the president called Proper and said the secretary had just quit. The president requested that Proper's firm type on plain paper the monthly handwritten financial statements that had been prepared by the controller. The president said if Proper would have his firm do him the favor, he would sponsor Proper for membership in a club that Proper had been wanting to join. The president chairs the membership committee of the club. How should Proper respond?

REPORTS ON INTERNAL CONTROL AND MANAGEMENT LETTERS

During recent years, much public attention has been given to corporate accountability. There has been increasing pressure by the stock exchanges, Congress, and the SEC for corporate boards of directors and their audit committees to assume greater responsibility for corporate activities, especially for the maintenance of an adequate system of internal accounting control. The Foreign Corrupt Practices Act of 1977 requires, among other things, that publicly held companies devise and maintain a system of internal accounting control sufficient to provide reasonable assurance that transactions are properly authorized and recorded.

In earlier chapters, we described the importance of the auditor's evaluation of a client's system of internal accounting control in determining the nature, timing, and extent of auditing procedures needed in an audit. In some instances, a client may request that the auditor express an opinion on the system of internal accounting control in a separate report. In others, the auditor may be *required* to report findings relating to internal accounting control to the client. Or the auditor may voluntarily include comments relating to internal accounting and administrative controls as part of a report to the client known as a management letter.

A management letter is an important by-product of an audit. It is a written report by the auditor to the board of directors, audit committee, or management of a client, which contains suggestions for improving the company's internal controls, accounting systems, and administrative and operational procedures. The suggestions are based on matters observed by the auditor during the examination of the financial statements.

This chapter describes the guidelines and requirements in the Statements on Auditing Standards for reporting on a client's system of internal accounting control. Additionally, the chapter considers the importance of management letters to both the independent auditor and the client and presents some ideas for an auditor to consider in identifying comments for and preparing a management letter.

18

REPORTS ON INTERNAL CONTROL[1]

SAS No. 30 (AU 642.02) indicates that an independent accountant may be asked to issue a report on a client's system of internal accounting control. For example, the accountant may be asked to:

1. Express an opinion on the client's system of internal accounting control that is in effect as of a particular date or during a particular period of time.
2. Report on the system of internal accounting control based solely on the study of the system that was done as part of an audit. Such a report is for the restricted use of the client's management, a regulatory agency, or other specified third party.
3. Report on all or part of a client's system of internal accounting control strictly for the use of management or a regulatory agency, based on the preestablished criteria of the regulatory agency.
4. Issue special purpose reports on all or part of a client's system for restricted use of management or a particular third party.

Expressing an Opinion

In reports expressing an opinion on a client's system of internal accounting control, the auditor need not place any restriction on the report's usage. The nature of the study and evaluation necessary to issue such an opinion is described in *SAS No. 30* (AU 642.13–.36). Such an opinion can be expressed on any entity for which financial statements can be prepared that are in conformity with generally accepted accounting principles or such other crite-

---

[1] This section is based on *Statement on Auditing Standards No. 30,* "Reporting on Internal Accounting Control," American Institute of Certified Public Accountants, 1980.

ria that are applicable to the entity. *SAS No. 30* (AU 642.38) states that in such an engagement the accountant's report should contain:

a. A description of the scope of the engagement.

b. The date to which the opinion relates.

c. A statement that the establishment and maintenance of the system is the responsibility of management.

d. A brief explanation of the broad objectives and inherent limitations of internal accounting control.

e. The accountant's opinion on whether the system taken as a whole was sufficient to meet the broad objectives of internal accounting control insofar as those objectives pertain to the prevention or detection of errors or irregularities in amounts that would be material in relation to financial statements.

SAS No. 30 (AU 642.39) suggests the following report in expressing an unqualified opinion:

We have made a study and evaluation of the system of internal accounting control of XYZ Company and subsidiaries in effect at (date). Our study and evaluation was conducted in accordance with standards established by the American Institute of Certified Public Accountants.

The management of XYZ Company is responsible for establishing and maintaining a system of internal accounting control. In fulfilling this responsibility, estimates and judgments by management are required to assess the expected benefits and related costs of control procedures. The objectives of a system are to provide management with reasonable, but not absolute, assurance that assets are safeguarded against loss from unauthorized use or disposition, and that transactions are executed in accordance with management's authorization and recorded properly to permit the preparation of financial statements in accordance with generally accepted accounting principles.

Because of inherent limitations in any system of internal accounting control, errors or irregularities may occur and not be detected. Also, projection of any evaluation of the system to future periods is subject to the risk that procedures may become inadequate because of changes in conditions, or that the degree of compliance with the procedures may deteriorate.

In our opinion, the system of internal accounting control of XYZ Company and subsidiaries in effect at (date), taken as a whole, was sufficient to meet the objectives stated above insofar as those objectives pertain to the prevention or detection of errors or irregularities in amounts that would be material in relation to the consolidated financial statements.

SAS No. 20, "Required Communication of Material Weaknesses in Internal Accounting Control," (AU 323.01), as amended by *SAS No. 30*, defines a material weakness in internal accounting control as ". . . a condition in which the specific control procedures or the degree of compliance with them do not reduce to a relatively low level the risk that errors or irregularities in amounts that would be material in relation to the financial statements being audited may occur and not be detected within a timely period by employees in the normal course of performing their assigned functions."

If the auditor finds one or more material weaknesses, *SAS No. 30* (AU 642.40) suggests the following opinion paragraph:

> Our study and evaluation disclosed the following conditions in the system of internal accounting control of XYZ Company and subsidiaries in effect at (date), which, in our opinion, result in more than a relatively low risk that errors or irregularities in amounts that would be material in relation to the consolidated financial statements may occur and not be detected within a timely period.

SAS No. 30 goes on to state that:

> The report should describe the material weaknesses, state whether they result from the absence of control procedures or the degree of compliance with them, and describe the general nature of potential errors or irregularities that may occur as a result of the weaknesses.

The accountant can express an unqualified opinion on the system only if there have been no restrictions on the scope of the work. Scope restriction may necessitate a qualified opinion or a disclaimer of opinion.

Report Based on Audit Evaluation

An auditor may be asked to give a report on internal accounting control based solely on the study made during an audit. *SAS No. 30* (AU 642.48) states that such a report should indicate that it is solely for a particular party (e.g., management or a regulatory agency), describe the limited study, and disclaim an opinion on the system as a whole. However, the report may give negative assurance on the system of internal accounting control (i.e., no material weaknesses found). In those instances, *SAS No. 30* (AU 642.49) suggests the following form of written report:

> We have examined the financial statements of XYZ Company for the year ended December 31, 19X1, and have issued our report thereon dated February 23, 19X2. . . . As part of our examination, we made a study and evaluation of the Company's system of internal accounting control to the extent we considered necessary to evaluate the system as required by generally accepted auditing standards. The purpose of our study and evaluation was to determine the nature, timing, and extent of the auditing procedures necessary for expressing an opinion on the company's financial statements. Our study and evaluation was more limited than would be necessary to express an opinion on the system of internal accounting control taken as a whole.
>
> The management of XYZ Company is responsible for establishing and maintaining a system of internal accounting control. In fulfilling this responsibility,

estimates and judgments by management are required to assess the expected benefits and related costs of control procedures. The objectives of a system are to provide management with reasonable, but not absolute assurance that assets are safeguarded against loss from unauthorized use of disposition, and that transactions are executed in accordance with management's authorization and recorded properly to permit the preparation of financial statements in accordance with generally accepted accounting principles.

Because of inherent limitations in any system of internal accounting control, errors or irregularities may nevertheless occur and not be detected. Also, projection of any evaluation of the system to future periods is subject to the risk that procedures may become inadequate because of changes in conditions or that the degree of compliance with procedures may deteriorate.

Our study and evaluation made for the limited purpose described in the first paragraph would not necessarily disclose all material weaknesses in the system. Accordingly, we do not express an opinion on the system of internal accounting control of XYZ Company taken as a whole. However, our study and evaluation disclosed no condition that we believed to be a material weakness.

This report is intended solely for the use of management (or specified regulatory agency or other specified third party) and should not be used for any other purpose.

SAS No. 20 (AU 323.01) *requires* the auditor to ". . . communicate to senior management and the board of directors or its audit committee material weaknesses in internal accounting control that come to his attention during an examination of financial statements made in accordance with generally accepted auditing standards. . . ."

SAS No. 20 (AU 323.04) also states that it is preferable for the auditor's findings to be ". . . communicated in a written report to reduce the possibility of misunderstanding. If the auditor's findings are communicated orally, he should document the communication by appropriate notations in his audit working papers."

Further, *SAS No. 30* (AU 642.50) requires that in reporting a material weakness in internal control, the auditor state that the weakness was considered in determining the nature, timing, and extent of the tests applied in the audit. *SAS No. 30* (AU 642.49–.50) suggests the following opinion paragraph:

Our study and evaluation made for the limited purpose described in the first paragraph would not necessarily disclose all material weaknesses in the system. Accordingly, we do not express an opinion on the system of internal accounting control of XYZ Company taken as a whole. However, our study and evaluation disclosed the following conditions that we believe result in more than a relatively low risk that errors or irregularities in accounts that would be material in relation to the financial statements of XYZ Company may occur and not be detected within a timely period. (A description of the material weaknesses that have come to the auditor's attention would follow.)

These conditions were considered in determining the nature, timing, and extent of the audit tests to be applied in our examination of the 19X1 financial statements, and this report does not affect our report on these financial statements dated (date of report).

This report is intended solely for the use of management (or specified regulatory agency or other specified third party) and should not be used for any other purpose.

If the auditor wishes to report both material weaknesses and other weaknesses or problems (e.g., management letter comments), *SAS No. 30* (AU 642.51) indicates that comments on material weaknesses should be clearly distinguished from the others. The following transition paragraph may be appropriate:

In addition to the material weaknesses described above, we have the following suggestions for improvements in procedures and controls.

Reports Based on Criteria Established by Regulatory Agencies

Some regulatory agencies may require reports on internal accounting control of entities subject to their regulation. These agencies may set up criteria for evaluating the adequacy of internal accounting control and then require that the criteria be used as the basis for the report. *SAS No. 30* (AU 642.56) indicates that the auditor's report should cover the following:

1. Areas included in the study.
2. Whether the study included tests of compliance with the procedures covered by it.
3. ". . . objectives and limitations of internal accounting control and of accountants' evaluations of it. . . ."
4. Conclusions, ". . . based on the agency's criteria, concerning the adequacy of the procedures studied, with an exception regarding any material weaknesses. . . ."
5. An indication that the report is ". . . intended for use in connection with the grant or other purpose to which the report refers and that it should not be used for any other purpose. . . ."

Other Special-Purpose Reports

The auditor can issue special-purpose reports on all or part of a client's system for the restricted use of management or a particular third party. *SAS No. 30* (AU 642.61) indicates that the report should:

1. ". . . describe the scope and nature of the accountant's procedures. . . ."
2. ". . . disclaim an opinion on whether the system, taken as whole, meets the objectives of internal accounting control. . . ."

3. ". . . state the accountant's findings. . . ."
4. ". . . indicate that the report is intended solely for management or specified third parties. . . ."

SAS No. 44, "Special-Purpose Reports on Internal Accounting Control at Service Organizations," supplements *SAS No. 30* by providing guidance for the use by an independent auditor (user auditor) of a special-purpose report on internal accounting control of an organization that provides certain services (service organization) to the user auditor's client. *SAS No. 44* also provides guidance for the independent auditor who issues such a report (service auditor). The types of reports covered by *SAS No. 44* and their effect on a user auditor's evaluation of a client's accounting system are discussed in Chapter 5.

MANAGEMENT LETTERS

During an audit, an auditor acquires an understanding of the client's overall operations, which in turn provides a basis for suggesting various improvements. This understanding is the result of the audit integrating the areas of production, sales, finance, and administration. Through observation, interviews with key personnel, and audit procedures in each of these areas, the auditor is able to see how each area affects the overall operation and how the areas are interrelated—perhaps better than client personnel involved in day-to-day matters in particular areas. Further, auditors usually have a wide range of work experiences from which to draw ideas.

Thus, the auditor is in a unique position to recognize a client's needs and problems. To communicate such needs and problems, along with suggested improvements, benefits both the client and the auditor in the following ways:

1. An objective analysis of areas where the client's internal controls, accounting system, and administrative and operational procedures can be improved, can help safeguard the company's assets, promote efficiency, and increase profitability. It also helps the board of directors of the client in discharging its responsibilities.
2. Constructive suggestions for solving problems *(a)* demonstrate the auditor's interest in the client's operations beyond the audit; *(b)* reinforce the auditor's image as one who serves the client from a business perspective; and *(c)* increase the likelihood that the auditor will be asked to assist in solving these problems.
3. For some readers (e.g., audit committee members or other directors), the letter may be a major factor in comparing the auditor's capabilities with those of competitors. Thus, the letter could be influential in the selection or retention of auditors.

Identifying Management Letter Comments

Planning Considerations. While we referred to the management letter as a by-product of the audit, such a letter should not be considered as merely an afterthought. A management letter is most effective if it is considered as part of the initial audit planning process. As part of that process the auditor should:

1. Establish a timetable for the preparation of the letter and notify other personnel on the engagement of expectations regarding management letter comments. During audit planning meetings, discuss those areas which might lead to important management letter comments. Instruct audit personnel to document the problems and recommendations as field work is performed.
2. Allocate sufficient hours in the time budget to gather constructive comments, prepare an effective letter, and meet with management to discuss implementation of recommendations.
3. Involve tax and management services specialists where appropriate. A client may benefit from a tax specialist's review of such matters as tax planning objectives, documentation of compliance with tax laws, and tax administration practices. Similarly, constructive suggestions might be developed from a management services specialist's brief review of such areas as reporting and budgeting systems, production planning and inventory management, management information system, or organizational and long-range planning.

Topics for the Management Letter. Management letter comments may cover any subject within the auditor's expertise—accounting and auditing, tax, and management services. To convince management to act on the recommendations, the letter should address the client's specific needs, and the comments should be constructive. Many comments arise from the review and evaluation of internal control, but care should be taken to assure that the letter is not a mere list of defects in the accounting system. The auditor should make every reasonable effort to assure that the comments and recommendations are (1) practical, (2) relevant, and (3) free of insignificant items. Generally, only comments that are reasonably expected to improve the effectiveness and efficiency of operations, procedures, and controls should be included. If an auditor does not focus on important matters or make positive recommendations the letter may not receive adequate consideration. Topics that are often subjects in management letters are discussed and illustrated below.

Accounting Systems and Internal Controls. Besides the effectiveness of internal accounting control and adherence to management policies, the auditor might consider the efficiency and economy of information processing by reviewing the possibilities for eliminating unnecessary work or duplicated effort, and the use of work-saving devices. With respect to internal accounting control, particular attention should be given to physical deterrents against waste, pilferage, or misappropriation of assets by employees, customers, and vendors. For example, the auditor might consider controls over assets that are most susceptible to loss or misappropriation (e.g., cash, blank checks, negotiable securities, small tools, and inventories—especially small, high-value items and consumer goods).

Following are excerpts from management letters that illustrate comments that can be made regarding accounting systems and internal controls:

Accounts Receivable—Allowance for Doubtful Accounts

In 19X8, the Company established its allowance for doubtful accounts based only upon the formula prescribed by Corporate Standard Procedures. The same procedure also requires that operating companies review the aging for past-due accounts and provide an additional discretionary provision when there is an increase in past-due accounts in relation to total customer receivables; but that is not being done.

Account agings and trends are important tools in evaluation of collectibility of accounts. We recommend that a periodic review (i.e., at least quarterly) be made to determine the adequacy of the allowance for doubtful accounts. In evaluating the allowance, consideration also should be given to the impact of such factors as the economic environment, credit conditions, account mix, and change in credit practices.

Bank Reconciliations

Proper bank reconciliations are a key to maintaining adequate control over both cash receipts and disbursements. During much of the year, the operating bank account reconciliations contained unreconciled differences (over $1,000) and appear to be generally incomplete. The bank reconciliations should be reviewed for accuracy and completeness on a timely basis by the manager of accounting.

During the year, the operating bank account was reconciled by the accounts payable supervisor and the salaried and hourly payroll clerks reconciled each other's accounts. If bank reconciliations are to serve as an effective control over the cash accounts, the persons preparing the reconciliations should not have related cash receipts or disbursements duties. While the Company is in the midst of some relocation and personnel changes, reconciling duties should be assigned to employees with noncash functions as soon as possible.

EDP—Physical Security

The following are safeguards which might be taken to improve physical security in the computer center:

1. Doors to the computer center should be kept locked.
2. A formal security policy covering such items as visitors to the computer

center, housekeeping, neatness, and smoking should be developed and communicated to computer center personnel.

3. The installation of fire and smoke detection devices should be considered.
4. Specific procedures to be taken in an emergency (e.g., fire, blackout) should be in writing and posted so they are readily accessible to computer center personnel.
5. The installation of independent air conditioning equipment in the computer room should be considered. This equipment should be monitored by temperature and humidity controls located in the computer room.
6. The installation of voltage regulating or monitoring equipment should be considered to protect against electrical irregularity which may affect the accuracy of processing data.
7. A perpetual inventory control should be maintained for unused forms and computer supplies.
8. Forms and supplies expenses should be reviewed to determine that the quantities used are commensurate with the volume of operations.

Standardized Consolidating Financial Statements

To expedite the interim and year-end consolidation, the use of standardized consolidating statements should be considered. The statements should be prepared at the various accounting unit locations, subconsolidated at the appropriate locations, and then forwarded, together with consolidating details, to the Corporate office for inclusion in the consolidated financial statements.

Accounting for Warranty Costs

Presently, warranty costs are charged to expense as incurred. Because of the recent emphasis on consumer protection and the Company's increased sales of consumer products, management should establish a more systematic approach to estimating the reserve for future warranty costs. The amount of such a reserve should be based on detailed information compiled from claims. Such information should include:

1. Date the unit was sold.
2. Date of warranty service.
3. Model number of unit serviced.
4. Detail description of reason for service.
5. Whether the charge can be recovered from the vendor.

In addition, the chart of accounts should be appropriately revised so that warranty expenses are segregated from nonwarranty costs or allowances and classified in the necessary detail.

A well-devised system for collecting warranty claim information would not only assist in properly matching revenues and expenses but also could reduce costs and the claims themselves by identifying problems early enough to facilitate engineering or production changes.

Administrative and Operational Procedures.   Broad areas that may warrant comment in the management letter include the management information system, purchasing and inventory management, production control, order entry and shipping, and organizational controls. In addition, timely and meaningful financial information in the form of financial statements, statistical data, and operations analyses for subsidiaries, divisions, or other profit centers can help management monitor and improve operations. Where such information is incomplete or unavailable, a recommendation may be appropriate. In this area, the auditor should direct attention to important accounting-related elements of the client's management information system such as:

1. Long-range and short-range forecasts of revenues, costs and expenses, cash flow, and financial position.
2. Budgets for capital expenditures, annual cost allowances (e.g., for tooling, maintenance, or advertising), and variable expenses.
3. Analyses of return on investment.
4. Analyses of profitability for major products, product lines, territories, and customers.

In many instances, it is not practicable to review and comment on all important administrative and operational procedures each year. However, particular emphasis may be directed to a specific area each year so that all important areas will be reviewed over a period of several years. While an auditor should develop a general understanding of the important administrative and operational areas to the extent necessary to recognize the existence of significant weaknesses, the assistance of a management services specialist may be helpful to evaluate and comment on operational efficiency.

Following are excerpts from management letters that illustrate comments that can be made regarding administrative and operational procedures:

Accounting Organization

The Company's recent growth has been accompanied by increased responsibilities for most members of management. The distribution of additional responsibility generally has been accomplished informally on an "as available" basis. This approach may not have resulted in an optimum distribution of responsibilities.

We recommend that an organization chart and written descriptions of job responsibilities be prepared for all personnel in accounting and administrative functions. This would provide management with a basis for redistributing work loads, evaluating personnel requirements, and judging job performance.

As the Company and its accounting staff grow, efficient organization and effective controls may require that individuals in the accounting department become specialists in certain functions. We recommend that the accounting department policies and procedures be defined to maximize individual efficiency through specialization.

In addition, disruptions of established routines (such as that resulting from field assignments) should be minimized so that efficiency and accuracy will not suffer. Further, so that personnel turnover will have a minimum effect on the accounting department, department policies and procedures should be documented in manuals and memoranda.

Budgeting and Planning

Formal operating budgets are a valuable tool in the day-to-day control and measurement of Company activity. Consideration should be given to increased use of budgets. This would enable management to compare actual results with planned activity. It also would provide an indication of potential problems in their early stages when they can be most readily solved.

Formal budgets, when used with realistic sales and cash flow forecasting, provide a profit plan to show in advance the anticipated operating level for the coming year. This profit plan provides management not only with a preview of things to come but also an opportunity to make the changes required in order to maximize profitability. A short-range plan might cover the following areas:

Sales plan
Manufacturing plan
Expense budgets
Capital expenditure budgets
Cash flow forecast
Breakeven analysis

A long-range budget or operations plan should give consideration to:

Profit objectives
Marketing and sales objectives
Technological objectives
Financial resource objectives
Product planning

Cash Management

1. Effective cash management is becoming extremely critical. To improve the utilization of cash resources, the Company should consider implementation of a "lock-box" system of handling cash receipts for all divisions. Under this system, customer payments are mailed to the Company in care of a bank. The bank immediately credits the receipts to the Company account and forwards the details of the deposit. Use of this system (a) strengthens internal control by removing cash receipts from employees with access to accounting records until an independent listing has been prepared, (b) enables the Company to have receipts deposited at least one day earlier and, therefore, improves cash balances, and (c) eliminates duplications of accounting records by centralizing the cash receipts recording function.

2. The Company currently is financing accounts receivable at a local bank. Under the security agreement, all receivable collections must be applied directly against the outstanding debt. Since interest is charged on a daily basis, a lock box would eliminate the one or two day lag between receipt of the cash and subsequent deposit, with a resulting decrease in interest expense.

3. Periodically, one division is required to obtain short-term borrowings to meet immediate cash requirements while another division maintains invested funds. This condition may not produce the best economic utilization of the Company's available resources. Accordingly, we recommend that cash management be centralized under the direction of the corporate treasurer to assure optimum utilization of available cash funds.

4. The average monthly cash balance for the past year in the general account was in excess of $175,000, ranging in one instance to $452,000. Investment of these funds in short-term investments, assuming a 9 percent interest rate, could have produced annual earnings of $15,000.

Tax Matters. In addition to the normal review of the tax provision in an audit, a tax specialist might assist in preparing comments on such matters as:

1. Claiming the maximum investment tax credit or other credits.
2. Evaluating LIFO inventory and other tax-deferring elections.
3. Analyzing the tax implications of management compensation.
4. Maintaining adequate documentation for travel and entertainment expenses.
5. Analyzing the implications of liquidating subsidiaries.
6. Determining any advantage of changing the tax year.
7. Analyzing the tax implications of international operations.
8. Studying the effects of proposed tax legislation.

To assure that the client receives timely benefit from tax planning comments, it is desirable to obtain a tax specialist's assistance during an interim visit.

Following are excerpts from management letters that illustrate comments that can be made regarding tax matters:

Executive Compensation Plans

All salaried employees are currently included in the Company's basic compensation plans. Other specially treated compensation plans for certain key executives and directors are available under the current tax laws. Plans of this nature include, but are not limited to:

1. Nonqualified deferred compensation plans, whereby part of the executive's annual salary is deferred for a period of years and taxable when paid. The objective of this type of plan is to defer the taxation of income to periods when the executive's income is lower with corresponding lower effective tax rates. Unlike the existing qualified profit sharing plan, the Company is not allowed a tax deduction for this type of nonqualified deferred compensation until it is actually paid to the executive.

2. Deferred directors' fees plans, which are very similar to non-qualified deferred compensation plans for employees. The objective is to defer income representing directors' fees to a period in which there is lower total income and, therefore, lower effective tax rates.

3. Medical reimbursement plans, whereby the Company reimburses the exec-

utive for medical expenses and obtains an allowable deduction for tax purposes.

Executive Tax Planning

Many of the Company's executives have expressed an interest in personal and family tax planning considerations. Because of the interest expressed by our clients, we developed a special program on family financial planning. Normally presented to the executives as a group, this program's principal purpose is to motivate each executive to take necessary steps to arrange his financial affairs so as to better accomplish his personal objectives. Some of the topics covered in a typical program are:

1. Corporate-financed employee benefits:
    a. Group insurance.
    b. Pension plan.
    c. Stock option plans.
2. Federal estate tax.
3. Estate planning principles and considerations.
4. Trust arrangements:
    a. Short-term.
    b. Irrevocable.
    c. Revocable living.
5. Gift tax.
6. Personal financial and credit management.
7. Record retention.
8. Insurance.

International Tax Review

The Company's recent expansion in Europe and planned expansion in South America indicates that additional attention should be focused on international income taxes. At this time, a detailed analysis of the Company's current and planned international operations, as well as the related tax structure, would assure that available tax incentives are appropriately utilized, and that the Company has maximized the tax benefits from operating in countries having low tax rates. This type of review could be made by the Corporate Tax Manager.

We have developed a special service for our multi-national clients—the International Tax Review—which may be of assistance in completing the review in a timely manner. Our International Tax Review was designed specifically to meet the needs of a company operating overseas as well as one which is considering overseas expansion.

Tax Planning

Income tax planning is essential if the owners of the business and those charged with its management are to realize the full rewards of operational efficiency. The objectives of good tax planning include the following:

1. The structuring of business transactions so that the Company will be subject to the minimum amount of tax liability, yet will account for transactions in such a manner that sound business decisions can be made.

2. The documentation of transactions in a manner which minimizes unfavorable tax exposure.

3. The most favorable application of tax laws based upon all the facts of a particular transaction.

To effectively utilize the Company's $147,000 operating loss carryforward and $76,000 related to future tax deductions, we recommend the following:

1. Prior to the consummation of any significant transactions, the tax consequences should be reviewed.

2. Prior to the end of each taxable year, the Company should review its current and long-range tax planning in light of new developments or proposed tax legislation.

Current Developments. The client will expect the auditor to comment on the potential impact of changing conditions on accounting and administrative procedures and controls. Therefore, the auditor should consider the effects of the following:

1. New products or services.
2. New foreign operations.
3. Acquisition, liquidation, or sale of subsidiaries.
4. Technological changes.
5. Plans for "going public."
6. Regulatory environment.
7. Adverse changes in financial position (e.g., liquidity or capital adequacy).
8. Key personnel changes.
9. Adverse changes in level of employee turnover.
10. New computer installations.

A brief description of required changes in accounting systems or record-keeping requirements resulting from new accounting pronouncements often may be warranted. And if a new law affects the client, the auditor might suggest that management seek advice from legal counsel to evaluate the law's impact. In some cases, such as the Foreign Corrupt Practices Act, the auditor also might suggest a specific action plan and offer to assist the client.

Sources of Information

Besides observations made during normal audit procedures, there are several other important sources for comments:

1. *Internal management reports.* The contents of the client's internal audit reports, management studies, and outside consulting studies may identify areas which warrant further study. Of course, the auditor should not merely repeat recommendations made in those reports. However, the

auditor should evaluate whether there is a better solution than that already developed and discuss the available alternatives with management.

2. *Client conferences.*   One of the simplest ways to gain facts regarding problems that remain unsolved is to ask for them. It is important that the auditor let the client's personnel know that he or she is interested not only in the reliability of the accounting records but also in helping management improve administrative and operational procedures.

3. *Industry comparisons.*   Most organizations maintain comprehensive operating statistics. In some cases, by comparing the client's data with that for the industry or for competitors, the auditor may gain insight into adverse trends or changes that may warrant comments.

4. *Prior management letters.*   Although some of the auditor's comments contained in earlier management letters may be inappropriate later because of changed conditions, knowing how the client responded to them may improve current recommendations.

Generally, comments are based on specific audit findings or observations. However, in certain situations it may be appropriate for the auditor to comment on areas that have not been investigated thoroughly. For example, in a multilocation engagement where the auditor performs only limited audit procedures at certain locations, the auditor should be alert to symptoms of problems and opportunities to comment on areas requiring additional study. Similarly, a comment resulting from a tax or management consulting services specialist's brief review might identify a potential problem and suggest that management make a more extensive study.

Gathering Information

Throughout the examination the auditor should compile the following data in sufficient detail and in a form that allows efficient processing of the management letter:

1. Symptoms indicating need for corrective action.
2. Description of the problem in light of operations, procedures, and controls.
3. Possible corrective actions, including cost/benefit implications of possible solutions.
4. Recommended action to be taken.
5. Comments by the client's operating personnel regarding facts, implications, and proposed solutions.

Figure 18–1 is a sample working paper that may be used to accumulate information for the management letter.

FIGURE 18-1 Working Paper to Accumulate Management Letter Comments

	Name	Date
Prepared	_____	_____
Approved	_____	_____

Notes For Management Letter Comments

_____
Company/Division

_____
Audit Date

Description of problem (include specific examples) _____
_____
_____
_____
_____
_____
_____

How was problem noted (reference to working papers, if applicable)? _____
_____
_____
_____
_____

Suggestion for improvement _____
_____
_____
_____
_____
_____
_____

Benefit client should realize by adopting our suggestion _____
_____
_____

Comment discussed with _____
Client's comments _____
_____
_____
_____

Comment included in letter?   Yes ☐   No ☐
If not included, explain _____
_____
_____

Preparing the Management Letter

Timing of Issuance. A management letter is most effective if it is issued on a timely basis, in order to facilitate follow-up by management. Thus, the auditor should consider issuing more than one management letter each year. For example, where the auditor has comments for improving internal accounting control, it would be most helpful to issue the letter shortly after completing the interim work for the audit. Similarly, recommendations regarding any unique implementation problems related to a new accounting or reporting requirement should be communicated to management as soon as practicable rather than waiting until after year-end. When the audit is concluded, a second management letter may be issued to update interim comments and discuss additional items. This second letter should be issued as soon as possible so that the client will be able to address the issues early in the new fiscal year that already has begun.

Style and Format. The language of a management letter should demonstrate objectivity and regard for the client's main interests. It should also follow a logical format, i.e., the sequence of topics should reveal a clear understanding of what is most important for improving the client's procedures and controls. Following are some guidelines:

1. Include the most significant comments first. Group them according to problem area, location, or other logical basis (not simply by balance sheet categories). Use action-oriented headings and subheadings rather than balance sheet captions or audit areas (e.g., use "Safeguarding Securities" or "Control over Cash" rather than "Securities" or "Cash"). Consolidate less significant matters under a single caption such as "Other Observations," near the end of the letter.
2. Present comments uniformly. First, state the symptoms of the problem. Next, describe the problem and its magnitude. Then discuss the benefits of implementation of potential solutions (e.g., efficiencies that may be achieved) and/or the problem's implications in terms of what could go wrong (i.e., the type of error that might occur and not be detected) in operations, systems, or controls. Finally, recommend specific corrective action whenever possible.
3. Use amounts or percentages where applicable to quantify problems and to show the need for specific, measurable actions.
4. When client personnel indicate a planned course of action in response to the comment, describe their plans.

Consider the following points when writing the management letter:

Think of the client first. Organize and phrase comments to emphasize the client's actions. Where possible, stress the benefits of change rather than deficiencies in procedures.

Be positive. Express findings and recommendations in unbiased and even-tempered words which emphasize positive benefits rather than negative criticism. For example, write "The internal control weaknesses identified during the 19X8 audit indicate a need for more reviews" rather than "We unfortunately found, during the 19X8 audit, that poor internal controls remained undetected because of inadequate reviews."

Be specific. Eliminate wasted words such as "In our audit of . . . , we noted . . ." in favor of a concise description of the situation. Avoid generalizations.

Be brief. Include only what is essential to the reader's understanding.

Use technical language correctly. Demonstrate an understanding of terminology unique to the industry when necessary. However, do not overuse technical terms, buzz phrases, and jargon that appear to demonstrate expertise but actually impair the main objective of the letter—to communicate ideas effectively.

Avoid superlatives. Words such as "optimum," "best," "most effective," or "we assure you that . . ." promise more than can be delivered and convey a tone of absolute certainty that seldom, if ever, belongs in a management letter. Verbs such as "will occur" or "will be achieved" also are more certain and definite than is warranted in most situations. Use (but do not overuse) qualifiers such as "likely," "probably," "usually," "frequently," and "apparently," to help prevent misunderstandings and expectations that are not justified by the facts.

Consider sensitivities. Convince the reader of the value of observations and recommendations through tact and finesse. Avoid reference to specific individuals. Emphasize weaknesses in functions rather than in individuals.

Consider readers' backgrounds. Present observations and recommendations in a way that readers with various backgrounds will readily understand. A reader with an accounting background may agree with a suggestion to hire an internal auditor simply because it will "improve internal controls and procedures," but a nonaccounting executive or director will understand the substance of the recommendation only if it is stated in terms of the specific benefits that can be expected (e.g., "it will reduce the time spent by top management in developing new procedures and controls and provide excellent training for management positions").

Addressing the Letter to the Client. A management letter may be addressed to the board of directors, audit committee, chief executive officer, chief financial officer, or other executive as appropriate. Each letter should take into account the recipient's background, needs, and expectations.

Ordinarily, a letter longer than five or six pages (frequently needed for a multilocation audit) should be treated more as a formal report than as a letter. It might include an introductory letter that summarizes the most important comments, followed by a series of detailed comments. Also, for a multilocation audit, it may be appropriate to issue separate letters for the various locations and a compilation of the letters for corporate management.

In large, complex engagements, the varied backgrounds and needs of recipients also may require the auditor to prepare more than one letter. For example, detailed comments on accounting systems and procedures usually should be addressed to the individual directly responsible for that area (e.g., the corporate or a divisional controller). Similarly, detailed comments on tax matters usually should be addressed to the individual responsible for tax planning and administration. And a separate letter covering administrative and operational matters, as well as a summary of significant comments relating to accounting systems and tax matters, might be sent directly to the chief financial officer. Further, when reporting to the audit committee, the auditor should decide whether to send the entire management letter or instead a report that summarizes the comments in the management letter. This is a consideration that should be discussed with management or the audit committee.

Incorporating Management's Responses. Erroneous statements impair the effectiveness of the letter; thus, it is vital that the information supporting the recommendation be correct. After the information is accumulated by the auditor, it should be discussed with the client's personnel who are most affected by the recommendation. The client's personnel should be encouraged to suggest other possible solutions. Before issuing a management letter, the auditor should discuss the comments with appropriate members of management and obtain their responses. If the letter is issued to the board of directors or audit committee, it is advisable to briefly describe management's planned course of action regarding each recommendation. Including management's responses in the letter makes the comments more informative and constructive, and it facilitates the reader's review and follow-up.

To facilitate the timely compilation of client responses, especially for multilocation audits, the auditor should request management to inform appropriate personnel of the need to give prompt attention to each of the recommendations and provide written responses. Generally, they should provide their views on the following aspects of the comments:

Symptoms indicating a need for corrective action.

Practicality of implementing the recommendation.

Relative priority and expected timetable for implementation.

For example, management comments regarding a suggestion to improve segregation of duties for a particular area might be as follows:

> *Management's response.* After reviewing the various duties of available personnel, we agree that controls could be improved by reassigning the . . . duties to

the individual in charge of the . . . function. This improvement can be made without impairing efficiency, and we plan to implement the recommendation immediately.

Illustrative Example

Figure 18–2 is an example of a management letter. It is addressed to the client's audit committee and includes management's response to each comment. In addition, it provides negative assurance on the client's system of internal accounting control and refers to a more detailed letter that was sent to the treasurer of the client.

FIGURE 18-2 Example of a Management Letter—Addressed to an Audit Committee

---

Date

Audit Committee of the Board of Directors
of XYZ Company

We have examined the consolidated financial statements of XYZ Company and subsidiaries for the year ended December 31, 19X8, and have issued our report thereon dated February 23, 19X9. As part of our examination, we made a study and evaluation of the system of internal accounting control only to the extent we considered necessary to determine the nature, timing, and extent of our auditing procedures.

Our study and evaluation made for the limited purpose described above would not necessarily disclose all material weaknesses in the system. Accordingly, we do not express an opinion on the system of internal accounting control of XYZ Company and subsidiaries taken as a whole. However, our study and evaluation disclosed no condition that we believed to be a material weakness at December 31, 19X8.*

This report is intended solely for the use of management.*

We have submitted to Mr. Smart, Treasurer, a detailed report of our suggestions for improvements in procedures and controls for each of the divisions and subsidiaries. Our recommendations were discussed with personnel responsible for the various areas and many of them are currently being implemented. Summarized below are our suggestions of major importance which we believe warrant your attention.

Foreign Corrupt Practices Act

The Foreign Corrupt Practices Act of 1977 (the Act) prohibits domestic concerns, their officers, directors, employees, and shareholders from bribing foreign politicians and political parties. The Act also requires publicly held companies to maintain a system of internal controls designed to assure proper authorization and recording of transactions and to keep records which ''accurately and fairly'' reflect financial activities. Management should consider discussing the impact of the Act with legal counsel.

To assist in complying with the Act's accounting provisions, we have provided the Committee and management with a guide that describes a practical approach to documenting and evaluating systems of internal accounting control. The result of following this approach should lead to clear, easy to understand statements of how the company achieves the

---

* If the auditor does not provide negative assurance, the second and third paragraphs should be excluded and the next paragraph should begin as follows:

We have submitted to Mr. Smart, treasurer, a detailed report of our suggestions for improvements in procedures and controls for each of the divisions and subsidiaries, which resulted from our study and evaluation.

FIGURE 18-2 *(continued)*

objectives of the Act's accounting provisions. In addition, we have provided a suggested two-phase action plan for complying with the Act.

Management's response. We have contacted legal counsel to review and discuss our planned actions for compliance with the Act. A task force has been established to document and evaluate the Company's systems of internal accounting control using Ernst & Whinney's suggested approach. The initial phase of this project should be completed by the end of September 19X9.

Conflict of Interest Statement

In several cases, operating personnel were not aware of the existence of the Company's conflict of interest statement. This observation is included in our comments on the Machine Tool Division, Metal Division, Can Division, and Electronics Division. Operating personnel should be reminded of the established policy in this area and Group Staffs should follow-up to determine that all Divisions are in compliance.

Management's response. In March 19X9, we intend to discuss this departure at the quarterly meeting of Group Staffs. A review of compliance for 19X8 will be made by the Internal Audit Staff in April. In addition, our policy will be revised to require an annual declaration of compliance by operating personnel, and the Internal Audit Staff will monitor compliance annually.

Internal Audit EDP Reviews

In view of the rapid increase in the number of new computer installations and applications, the present staff of two EDP internal audit specialists may not be sufficient to provide adequate coverage. In addition, the control weaknesses related to the order entry and accounts receivable applications indicate a need for more internal audit EDP reviews. One of the most valuable results of these reviews is the examination and testing of controls of user department applications that affect the accounting and financial reporting systems. Management should consider expanding the EDP internal audit staff to perform more reviews and to make follow-up reviews where controls were previously found to be weak.

Management's response. We have reviewed the need for additional internal audit EDP specialists in light of existing and planned EDP facilities. We concur with this recommendation and have decided to add two specialists to the staff. Depending on the availability of qualified candidates, we expect to hire these specialists by the end of May 19X9 so additional reviews can be performed during the third and fourth quarters.

Obsolescence Reviews

Several departures from Corporate policies related to obsolescence were encountered. The Metal Division made a general review of obsolescence requirements but did not identify specific items included in the final provision. The Machine Tool Division did not review work in process and raw material for possible excess stock. Smith Switzerland AG made a provision based on incomplete information developed by a special data processing application. Because the approaches followed at these locations are very subjective, it was necessary for our staff and the internal auditors to expand audit procedures to satisfy ourselves as to the overall adequacy of the provisions for inventory obsolescence.

To provide adequate input to management for evaluating inventory levels or for isolating problem areas, the established Corporate policy should be consistently followed by all locations, and the results thereof should be documented.

Management's response. We have discussed with local personnel the circumstances underlying the departures from Corporate policy. We concur that the approach followed is very subjective and have instructed these locations to adhere to the Corporate policy. However, certain minor modifications to the Corporate policy are necessary to meet

FIGURE 18-2 *(concluded)*

the location's specific circumstances. These changes will be made by the end of March 19X9.

Electronics Division

Several departures from standard Corporate policy occurred. The most significant variance concerned the valuation of inventory. Adequate control of physical inventory tags was not maintained, shipping and receiving cutoffs were not accurate, and problems were encountered in inventory pricing. In addition, inaccuracies in costing procedures appear to be the principal cause for the Division's unusually large book-to-physical write-down. A high priority should be given to improvements in the inventory valuation procedures and in the cost accounting system.

The Division's accruals for payroll, property taxes, and several other liabilities were understated at year-end. These accruals should be reviewed periodically and adjusted as necessary.

Each of these problems was significant to the results of operations of the Electronics Division—although not significant to the consolidated results—and could affect negotiated expense rates on the government contracts.

Management's response. To improve the reliability of the financial information, we plan to hire an assistant controller by the end of May 19X9. This individual's principal responsibility will be to develop improved inventory valuation procedures. We also have asked Ernst & Whinney to assist in developing a standard cost system which should be implemented by October 31, 19X9.

In addition, until additional staff are available at the Division, the internal audit staff will review the Division's accruals quarterly to assure that they are adjusted as necessary.

Prior Year Comments

Early in 19X8, management developed a systematic approach to addressing the detailed comments contained in our letter following the 19X7 examination. Personnel at the various locations have made significant progress in responding to our comments as indicated in the following summary of changes in status during the period of five months ended December 31, 19X8.

	Status		
	July 31	Dec. 31	Net Change
Implementation or other action:			
Complete	27	62	35
In process	55	70	15
Pending	72	22	(50)

Management has adopted a similar approach for the comments included in our letter for the 19X8 audit. These comments are currently being considered and, in many cases, action has been taken. At our August meeting with the Audit Committee we will be prepared to discuss the current status of our recommendations.

*   *   *   *   *

We appreciate the opportunity to present these comments for your consideration and we are prepared to discuss them at your convenience.

Very truly yours,

Ernst & Whinney

QUESTIONS AND PROBLEMS

18–1. What should be contained in a report on a client's system of internal accounting control when an accountant has been engaged to express an opinion on such a system?

18–2. What should be contained in a report on a client's system of internal accounting control based solely on the study made during an audit?

18–3. Define a material weakness in internal accounting control.

18–4. What is the auditor's obligation if he or she discovers a material weakness during an examination of financial statements in accordance with generally accepted auditing standards?

18–5. What is a management letter?

18–6. Discuss how a management letter benefits both the client and the auditor.

18–7. List some general areas that may be the subject of management letters.

18–8. Besides observations made during normal audit procedures, what are some other important sources for comments in management letters?

18–9. What information should be gathered about a possible comment in a mangement letter?

18–10. "Management letters are only issued shortly after the conclusion of the year-end field work." Comment.

18–11. Describe the logical organization of a management letter.

18–12. You are giving some basic advice to an assistant concerning the elements of effective writing which should be used in writing management letters. What points should you include?

18–13. Is it true that in large, complex engagements several different management letters may have to be prepared? Explain.

18–14. Should management's responses regarding a recommendation be included in a mangement letter addressed to an audit committee? Explain.

18–15. The XYZ Corporation prepares sales forecasts in dollars only. Prepare a paragraph that might be included in a management letter stating that the forecasting should be in units, in dollars, and by product.

18–16. The Large Company's scrap reporting procedures do not include the cause of scrapping. Prepare a paragraph that might be included in a management letter stating that the cause should be included in the reporting.

18–17. The Small Company rarely uses purchase orders. Prices on purchases are only approved when the office manager checks the invoices. Prepare a paragraph that might be included in a management letter suggesting improvements.

18–18. During his audit of the Middle Company, J. Jones, CPA, is told by the treasurer that Middle Company has problems hiring and keeping production workers. The company is considering reviewing its compensation policies.

Required:

Prepare a paragraph on this situation that Mr. Jones might include in a management letter.

18–19. Read the following management letter which is to be issued to the partners of the law firm of Smart & Dumb. Discuss your specific comments on the following:

Is each topic presented effectively?

Is the letter organized effectively?

Could the writing be significantly improved?

Would you delete any topics?

What are the letter's strong points?

Do you believe you need more information to evaluate its effectiveness? If so, what information do you need and why is it necessary?

J. JONES. C.P.A.

April 12, 1987

The Partners of
Smart & Dumb

Gentlemen:

In connection with our examination of the balance sheet of Smart & Dumb as of December 31, 1986, we reviewed the accounting procedures and systems of internal control employed by the Partnership. We found no material weaknesses in internal accounting control. However, the attached comments and suggestions for improvements therein, are submitted for your consideration. They were derived from our examination of the records, general observations, and discussions with various partners and employees. We wish to express our appreciation for the cooperation and courtesy extended to us by your partners and employees. We would be pleased to discuss any of these matters with you further and to assist in their implementation if you so desire.

Very truly yours,
J. Jones. C.P.A.

Cash Receipts

Cash receipts are manually and separately posted to the cash receipts journal and detail accounts receivable ledger cards. Pending further evaluation as to the desirability of mechanizing the entire accounting system, we recommend that a pegboard system, which would eliminate this double posting, be implemented as an immediate time-saving device.

To facilitate the daily posting of cash receipts and avoid incorrect postings, we recommend that unidentified receipts be posted initially to a temporary (suspense) account. A listing of these unmatched receipts could be periodically circulated to the partners for proper identification. Requesting that clients return a copy of the invoice, or a detachable portion thereof, with their remittances would probably reduce the number of unidentified receipts.

Cash Disbursements

Approved invoices should be recorded by use of a pegboard system which would simultaneously prepare the checks.

Upon issuance of the checks, all supporting detail for the disbursement should be defaced to preclude the potential reuse thereof.

Signed checks should be mailed and bank accounts should be reconciled by individuals not connected with the preparation and recording of the respective disbursements.

Petty Cash

To improve internal control over petty cash, each disbursement should be evidenced by a prenumbered petty cash voucher. Applicable supporting detail should be attached thereto and, upon reimbursement, the voucher and supporting detail should be defaced to prevent potential reuse.

The petty cash custodian is frequently interrupted in performing her accounting duties to make change for the vending machines. Consideration should be given to maintaining a small change fund at the switchboard, possibly on an "honor" basis, for this purpose.

Accounts Receivable

Sixty-four accounts receivable confirmation requests were returned by the Post Office due to bad addresses, and 48 clients reported various differences in their account balances to us. These items were either satisfactorily resolved or were written off as uncollectible. Our review of the accounts and discussion thereof with the respective partners resulted in the write-off of accounts aggregating approximately $80,000 and the recording of allowances for additional doubtful accounts aggregating $40,000. We suggest that additional efforts be made to periodically furnish each partner with a listing of past-due accounts so that appropriate follow-up can be initiated on a timely basis.

A pegboard system which would provide simultaneous posting of the revenue journal and detail accounts receivable ledger cards should be instituted.

As a result of the additional effort expended, a reasonably accurate billing cutoff was achieved as of December 31, 1986. Similar efforts should be made at future fiscal year-ends and particularly at dates of admission, withdrawal, or retirement of partners, when cash payments are required to be calculated on the accrual basis net worth of the firm. However, accurate billing cutoffs are not essential at interim month ends; and to expedite the monthly closings, we suggest that the established twentieth of the following month cutoff date be strictly adhered to at these times.

Charges Reimbursable from Clients

Although it was impractical to make a complete reconcilement of this account as of December 31, 1986, our review of these charges resulted in a write-off of approximately $18,000 to adjust this account to a reasonable estimate of charges recoverable from clients as of December 31, 1986. To ensure that all items are billed or that approved write-offs are recorded for unbilled items, the detail of this account, which consists of various charge slips in the billing folders, should be periodically reconciled to the general ledger control account.

Luncheon Club Billings

A time savings may be achieved by requesting that the Luncheon Club bill each attorney separately or group charge slips by attorney. Each attorney's secretary could then segregate the charge slips and furnish the accounting department with the aggregate personal amount (to be deducted from the monthly dividend) and detail billing memos for amounts chargeable to clients.

Telephone Charges

Switchboard and accounting personnel spend approximately 40 hours each month checking telephone charges and investigating unidentified calls. Consideration should be given to charging unidentified calls, which we were informed were large in number but minor in aggregate amount, to office expense. This policy could be instituted after emphasizing to the staff the importance of placing toll calls through the switchboard, where detail charge slips would be prepared, or obtaining time and charges on calls made after office hours.

The telephone company could be requested to review the overall effectiveness of the present phone system.

Duties of Accounting Manager

The accounting manager presently spends approximately three hours each day performing duties that could apparently be handled by an office boy. These duties include (1) changing light bulbs; (2) making bank deposits; (3) ordering, checking, unpacking, and distributing supplies; (4) dealing with taxicab companies and the Highway Express Agency, Inc.; (5) post office errands; (6) personal errands; and (7) obtaining signatures on checks. An office boy (perhaps a college student on a part-time basis) could be hired at a much lower wage rate to handle these miscellaneous jobs, thereby enabling the accounting manager to devote full time to accounting matters.

Partners' Dividends

Cash receipts on the day of calculation are presently included in the computation of the partners' monthly dividends. To facilitate the orderly preparation of these dividends, consideration should be given to including cash receipts only through the previous day.

Mechanization of Accounting System

As previously mentioned, implementation of pegboard systems should provide immediate time savings in several areas at a nominal cost. However, we believe that further consideration could be given to the desirability of utilizing an accounting machine to further reduce clerical time and provide additional management information on a more timely basis.

Time and Billing Controls

We recommend that further consideration be given to improving and standardizing time control and billing procedures. Procedures could be established to:

1. Ensure that all chargeable time is billed.
2. Facilitate more timely billing.
3. Provide comparison of actual fees billed with fees at standard billing rates.
4. Provide an inventory of jobs in process including appropriate detail of unbilled charges.
5. Provide, if desired, a summary of time devoted to clients, administration, civic activities, professional societies, or other categories.
6. Provide a summary of billings by partner.
7. Ease the work load on attorneys' secretaries.

If it is decided to mechanize the accounting system, as mentioned in the preceding section, a time control and billing system would be an ideal application.

18–20. It has been quite a year for Delta Corporation, a September 30 audit client. For years the company was operated as a family business by R. Founder, who is now 68 years old, manufacturing a line of traditional toys in a single plant. Delta toys had been sold through department stores ever since Mr. Founder built the first one in his basement while working at the local supermarket. About two years ago a combination of factors caught up with the company in the form of declining sales and profits, which dipped below the toy industry average for the first time in many years.

On October 1, 1986, Bob Founder, Jr. became president and treasurer. In the six years since earning his MBA, Bob has worked in the sales, production, and accounting areas of the company and showed promise as a business executive. His first task as president was to analyze the market. After analyzing the market, Bob decided to phase out toy guns, a major product line, over the next three years and press development of more sophisticated and expensive battery-operated toys. He believed their profit potential was greater, but he recognized such high-fashion toys presented a greater risk of obsolescence as there was little demand for last year's best seller.

Three months later, at a meeting, Bob met Ray Builder, who owned Alliance, another family-owned toy company with capabilities in the sophisticated toy field and a progressive marketing group which uses the company's computer to analyze sales. His sales outlets included the larger hardgood discount chains. Delta acquired Alliance as a subsidiary on April 1, 1987, with a combination of cash and stock, and in doing so, incurred Delta's first bank loan in 30 years. Bob and Ray decided to work as a team with Ray managing Alliance's marketing and manufacturing operations at its two plants. All other activities will be handled at Delta's offices and key personnel from Alliance will transfer to Delta. They plan a secondary offering of part of the stock held by the two families after the audited financial statements are available for the year ended September 30, 1987.

You were the advanced staff accountant on the September 30, 1986, audit which was completed in late December as the books were not closed until December 7. You recall that the company's accounting department was doing a satisfactory job with relatively few people. The only significant problem was the length of time needed to close the books. Delta's chief accountant told you several times that the IRS had never made an adjustment to the company's returns and that "after I make my audit, you auditors have it clean as a whistle." Internal controls were generally very good. Last year's management letter discussed receipts from scrap sales, the high number of past-due customers' accounts at year end (almost all paid before the report was issued), and several matters of lesser importance.

The partner on the engagement recently had lunch with Bob Founder, who enthusiastically described the events of the last year. Since you will be the senior on the September 30, 1987, examination of Delta's consolidated financial statements, the partner suggested that you begin planning for the engagement now.

Required:

a. Describe the important events which have occurred since the last audit.
b. List the topics you plan to consider for possible management letter attention. Be as specific as possible.

PROFESSIONAL ETHICS AND ACCOUNTANTS' LIABILITY

In earlier chapters we discussed professional standards that govern the work of a CPA in public practice. Compliance with those standards demonstrates a CPA's competence as a professional. In addition, a CPA is bound by a code of ethics that includes provisions relating to the CPA's responsibility to society. Also, the CPA has an obligation under the law to exercise due professional care in the performance of his or her work. The obligation extends directly to clients and may extend indirectly to third parties. This chapter discusses both the accountant's ethical responsibilities and legal obligations under common law.

PROFESSIONAL ETHICS

The adoption of a code of ethics is important in the professionalization of any occupation. However, mere adoption of such a code is not enough. The individual members of the profession must let both the prescriptions and proscriptions of such a code actually guide their actions. By conscientiously following their code, the members earn the respect of others—both for themselves and their profession.

The AICPA and the state CPA societies and boards of accountancy have codes of professional ethics. In many instances, the state societies and boards of accountancy have adopted, or at least modeled their codes after, the *AICPA Code of Professional Ethics.* Consequently, this section is limited to a discussion of the *AICPA Code.*

THE AICPA CODE OF PROFESSIONAL ETHICS

The *AICPA Code* consists of Rules of Conduct (Rules) adopted by vote of the AICPA membership. The Rules are enforceable, and AICPA members

19

must abide by them. Further, a CPA is responsible for the conduct of any non-CPA who works under his or her supervision. The Rules are supplemented by a somewhat philosophical essay approved by the AICPA's Ethics Division, and the Interpretations of the Code and Rulings by the Ethics Division. The Rules and Interpretations are included as Appendices 19A and 19B, respectively.

The *Code* (ET 51.06) suggests that the Rules set only ". . . minimum levels of acceptable conduct, . . ." and that true ethical conduct should go beyond the minimum. The Code (ET 51.07–.08) identifies the following broad concepts or ethical principles, which provide a philosophical foundation for the Rules:

Independence, integrity and objectivity—A certified public accountant should maintain his integrity and objectivity and, when engaged in the practice of public accounting, be independent of those he serves.

General and technical standards—A certified public accountant should observe the profession's general and technical standards and strive continually to improve his competence and the quality of his services.

Responsibilities to clients—A certified public accountant should be fair and candid with his clients and serve them to the best of his ability, with professional concern for their best interests, consistent with his responsibilities to the public.

Responsibilities to colleagues—A certified public accountant should conduct himself in a manner which will promote cooperation and good relations among members of the profession.

Other responsibilities and practices—A certified public accountant should conduct himself in a manner which will enhance the stature of the profession and its ability to serve the public.

RULES OF CONDUCT

Independence, Integrity, and Objectivity

Independence (Rule 101). A CPA should issue an opinion on the fairness of presentation of financial statements only if he or she is independent of the client both in fact and in appearance. In other words, independence must be perceived by third parties. Unless CPAs are regarded as independent, their opinions will be looked upon as being of little, if any, consequence to financial statement users. For example, a CPA's independence would be considered to be impaired if, during the period of service, the CPA had a direct financial interest in the client.

Integrity and Objectivity (Rule 102). In the course of providing audit, tax, and management advisory services, a CPA should neither misrepresent facts nor subordinate his or her judgment to other individuals. In performing tax services, a CPA may resolve doubt in favor of the client if there is reasonable support for such a position.

General and Technical Standards

General Standards (Rule 201). There are five general standards that apply to all areas of public accounting. Under the Rule, a CPA is expected to:

1. Accept only those engagements which he or she ". . . can reasonably expect to complete with professional competence."
2. ". . . exercise due professional care in the performance of an engagement."
3. ". . . adequately plan and supervise an engagement."
4. ". . . obtain sufficient relevant data to afford a reasonable basis for conclusions or recommendations in relation to an engagement."
5. Not be associated with a forecast of future transactions so that it may be implied that the CPA ". . . vouches for the achievability of the forecast."

Auditing Standards (Rule 202). A CPA should not issue an opinion on the fairness of presentation of financial statements unless the audit examination was performed in accordance with the 10 generally accepted auditing standards discussed in Chapter 1. The Rule considers the *Statements on Auditing Standards* (*SAS*s) to be authoritative interpretations of the auditing standards and requires the CPA to follow them and justify any departures.

Accounting Principles (Rule 203). A CPA should not state that financial statements examined are in conformity with generally accepted accounting principles (GAAP) if the statements contain a material departure from an accounting principle established by the Financial Accounting Standards Board or its predecessors. A CPA may accept a departure from GAAP only if it clearly can be demonstrated that to follow GAAP in the circumstances would be misleading.

Other Technical Standards (Rule 204).   A CPA must comply with, and justify departures from, technical standards promulgated by appropriate bodies designated by the Council of the AICPA. The following groups have been designated by Council to establish the standards under Rule 204:

Group	Area of Responsibility
Financial Accounting Standards Board	Standards of disclosure of financial information outside the financial statements in financial reports that also contain statements (e.g., supplementary information on the effects of changing prices)
Auditing Standards Board	Responsibilities of CPAs with respect to standards of disclosure established by the FASB as described in the preceding item
Accounting and Review Services Committee	Unaudited financial statements and unaudited information for nonpublic entities
Management Advisory Service Executive Committee	Management services

In addition, the last three groups have been designated by Council ". . . to interpret the application of the general standards in Rule 201 to their respective areas of responsibility. . . ."[1]

Responsibilities to Clients

Confidential Information (Rule 301).   A CPA should not voluntarily reveal information that is confidential and obtained from a client without the client's consent. However, the Rule does not apply to:

1. The CPA's obligation to comply with generally accepted auditing standards and GAAP.
2. A requirement to release confidential information in a legal proceeding.
3. A review of the CPA's practices relating to professional matters authorized by the AICPA (e.g., peer review).
4. Any investigation of or disciplinary action against the CPA by the AICPA or a state board or society.

---

[1] *AICPA Professional Standards,* Vol. 2, ET Appendix E.

Contingent Fees (Rule 302).   A Certified Public Accountant's fees should not be based on variables or contingencies related to the findings or results of the services performed. Contingent fees could impair the CPA's independence. However, fees are not considered to be contingent if fixed by courts or other authorities.

Responsibilities to Colleagues

The *Code* emphasizes that CPAs should work in a spirit of cooperation. The *Code* (ET 55.01) states that "the public confidence and respect which a CPA enjoys is largely the result of cumulative accomplishments of all CPAs, past and present."

There are presently no Rules regarding "responsibilities to colleagues." Old Rules that have been deleted due to various pressures from the federal government are described below.

Competitive Bidding.   At one time, the *Code* prohibited competitive bidding by CPAs. Competitive bidding is now permitted and occurs regularly in public practice.

Offers of Employment.   Under an old Rule, a CPA firm could not make an offer of employment to an employee of another CPA firm without contacting the firm first. Because it was viewed as a possible violation of an employee's rights, the Rule was dropped from the *Code.*

Encroachment.   Formerly, the Rules stipulated that a CPA could not endeavor to serve another CPA's client unless the client requested him or her to do so. Specifically, a CPA could not accept an audit engagement if the prospective client was already the client of another CPA without first consulting the other CPA. In addition, a CPA who received a referral engagement from another practitioner was prohibited from providing additional services without first contacting the referring CPA. However, in 1979, the Institute's legal counsel advised that the Rule was a potential antitrust violation, and it was repealed.[2]

The issue of communication between a predecessor auditor and the successor auditor is covered in *SAS No. 7* (AU 315.04–.09).[3] Before accepting an engagement, the prospective successor auditor should ask the prospective client to authorize its predecessor auditor to respond to the successor auditor's inquiries. Under Rule 301, if the client does not give this permission, the

---

[2] See *Referendum: Background Information on Proposed Amendments to the Code of Ethics,* January 30, 1979, American Institute of Certified Public Accountants, 1979, p. 8.

[3] The remainder of this section is based on *Statement on Auditing Standards No. 7,* "Communications between Predecessor and Successor Auditors, "American Institute of Certified Public Accountants, 1975.

predecessor auditor may not respond. Failure of the prospective client to give permission should raise serious questions about whether the successor auditor should accept the engagement.

Once the client's permission is obtained, the prospective successor auditor should ask the predecessor about matters that may affect acceptance of the engagement. This includes: (1) the integrity of management, (2) disagreements with management on accounting or auditing matters, and (3) the reason for the proposed change in auditors. The predecessor should respond fully except when limited by an unusual circumstance (such as pending litigation). Either before or after accepting the engagement, the successor auditor should review the predecessor's working papers (after obtaining both the client's and the predecessor's permission) and make any other inquiries of the predecessor auditor that are needed to obtain evidence for an auditor's report.

Other Responsibilities and Practices

Discreditable Acts (Rule 501).   This Rule proscribes acts that are discreditable to the profession. The purpose of this Rule is to allow the AICPA a course of action against a member CPA who commits an undesirable act not specifically covered in the other sections of the *Code.*

Advertising and Other Forms of Solicitation (Rule 502).   A CPA should not employ ". . . false, misleading, or deceptive . . ." forms of advertising or solicitation in order to obtain clients. Solicitation using ". . . coercion, overreaching [fraud], or harassing conduct . . ." is proscribed.

The former Rule prohibited *all* forms of solicitation and advertising. However, in 1977 the AICPA began to consider a change in the *Code* to permit advertising, citing a number of reasons including the following:[4]

1. To completely prohibit advertising and solicitation is not consistent with the public's desire for information about CPAs and the services they perform.
2. To completely prohibit advertising and solicitation may violate antitrust laws.
3. Some forms of advertising and solicitation would enable CPAs to promote their services in areas where non-CPA competitors already advertise.
4. Some forms of advertising and solicitation might facilitate new CPAs making their services known to potential clients.

Thus, in 1978 the AICPA membership voted to permit advertising, but continued to prohibit direct uninvited solicitation. After further deliberation,

---

[4] Adapted from *Proposed Amendments to the Bylaws and Code of Professional Ethics: Referendum, January 30, 1978,* American Institute of Certified Public Accountants, 1978, pp. 13–14.

the membership dropped that prohibition in 1979, and the present Rule 502 is the ultimate result.

Interpretation 502–1 of Rule 502 (ET 502.02) indicates that informative and objective advertising is permitted. The following examples are adapted from Interpretation 502–1:

1. Name of firm, address, telephone number.
2. Number of partners, shareholders, or employees.
3. Office hours.
4. Date firm was established.
5. Proficiency in foreign languages.
6. Services offered and corresponding fees (both hourly rates and fixed fees).
7. Educational and professional attainments such as:
   a. Date and place of certifications.
   b. Schools attended and dates graduated.
   c. Degrees received.
   d. Memberships in professional groups.
8. Policy or position statements relating to public accounting or a subject of public interest.

Interpretation 502–1 indicates that media, frequency, or the artwork or style of advertising is not subject to restriction.

The following examples of false, misleading, or deceptive advertisements are adapted from Interpretation 502–2 (ET 502.03):

1. An activity that would create a false or unjustified expectation of favorable results.
2. An activity that implies the ability to influence any court, tribunal, regulatory agency, or similar body or official.
3. An activity that consists of self-laudatory statements that are not based on verifiable facts.
4. An activity in which unverifiable comparisons are made with other CPAs.
5. An activity that contains testimonials or endorsements.
6. An activity that contains representations of fees for current or future periods when the CPA is aware, but the potential client is not aware, that the fees likely will be substantially increased.
7. An activity that contains any other representations that would be likely to cause a reasonable person to misunderstand or be deceived.

Commissions (Rule 503). Commissions and fee splitting are not usually in the client's best interest. Fee splitting often raises the specter of conflict of interest. Also, such fees are often charged back to the client, either directly or indirectly. Consequently, the *Code* prohibits a CPA from paying a commission to another to obtain a client or accepting a commission for referring a client to another CPA.

Incompatible Occupations (Rule 504).   A practicing CPA should not at the same time be involved in another business or occupation that creates a conflict of interest with the practice of public accounting.

Form of Practice and Name (Rule 505).   A CPA may practice as either an owner or employee, in a proprietorship, partnership, or professional corporation. The name of the firm should not include any fictitious names or be misleading as to form of organization.

TAX PRACTICE

In addition to general applicability of the *Code* to a CPA's tax practice, the AICPA Federal Taxation Division issues *Statements on Responsibilities in Tax Practice* (*Statements*). These are a ". . . series of statements . . . intended to constitute a body of advisory opinion on what are good standards of tax practice, delineating the extent of a CPA's responsibility to his client, the public, the Government, and his profession" (TX 101.02). They ". . . are not intended to establish a separate code of conduct in tax practice, apart from the general ethical precepts of the Institute's Code of Professional Ethics" (TX 101.07).

To date, the AICPA has issued 10 *Statements*. However, the first two, which covered the CPA's responsibility to sign a tax return, were withdrawn in 1982 because the AICPA concluded that those Statements were more stringent than the Internal Revenue Code. The remaining eight are summarized below:[5]

> *No. 3.   Questions on returns.*   If the client does not provide answers to all of the questions on a tax return, the CPA must be satisfied that a reasonable effort was made to get them. The client should state the reasons why questions are left unanswered. If the client fails to comply, the CPA should decline to sign the return.
>
> *No. 4.   Recognition of an administrative proceeding from a prior year.*   In preparing a tax return, a CPA should consider only the facts and the rules existing in the current year, and should not be governed by the disposition of an item in an administrative proceeding for a prior year.
>
> *No. 5.   Using estimates.*   A CPA is permitted to prepare a tax return that involves the use of estimates if (*a*) their use is generally acceptable or (*b*) it is not practicable to obtain the actual data. Estimates should not be presented in a manner that implies greater accuracy than actually exists.
>
> *Nos. 6 and 7.   Knowledge of errors.*   Statement No. 6 suggests that if a CPA learns of an error in a client's previously filed tax return or of a client's

---

[5] This discussion is based in part on Walter C. Frank, "The CPA and Ethics in Tax Practice," *The Tax Adviser* (December 1973) pp. 716–22.

failure to file a return, the CPA should discuss the matter with the client and recommend what action should be taken. If the CPA is requested to prepare the current year's tax return and the client has not resolved an error in a prior return that resulted in, or might result in, a material understatement of a tax liability, the CPA should consider whether or not to prepare the return. If the CPA does prepare the return, he or she should make sure the error is not repeated. The CPA is, however, under *no* obligation to report this situation to the Internal Revenue Service (IRS). *Statement No. 7* also discusses the CPA's actions on finding an error in the course of representing a client in an administrative proceeding. The CPA should ask the client for permission to explain the error to the IRS. If the client does not agree, the CPA should consider withdrawing from the engagement.

No. 8. Advising clients. In giving tax advice to clients, the CPA should provide the client with high-quality service. The CPA may contact the client when subsequent developments relate to advice previously given. However, *Statement No. 8* (TX 181.03) notes that the CPA ". . . cannot be expected to have assumed responsibility for initiating such communications except while he is assisting a client in implementing procedures or plans associated with the advice provided. Of course, the CPA may undertake this obligation by specific agreement with his client."

No. 9. Various procedural aspects of return preparation. In most instances, a CPA is justified in relying on information supplied by the client. Where appropriate, the client should provide supporting data. The CPA should consider the implications of all information and make inquiries when it appears reasonable to do so. Finally, when signing a federal tax return, the CPA should not alter the preparer's declaration.

No. 10. Positions contrary to Treasury Department or IRS interpretations. While preparing a tax return, a CPA is allowed to take a position that is contrary to Treasury Department or IRS interpretations of the Internal Revenue Code without disclosing that this was done if there is reasonable support for the position. In rare instances, a CPA also may take a position contrary to a specific section of the Internal Revenue Code when there is reasonable support for the position. However, the CPA should disclose the treatment in the tax return.

MANAGEMENT SERVICES

During the past 25 years, CPAs have increased their management service activities substantially. CPA firms have performed many diverse services for clients in such areas as industrial engineering, systems analysis, and budgeting.

The performance of management services by CPAs raises several issues regarding accounting ethics. First, does the *Code* apply to the management services practitioner? The *Code* (ET 92.02) states that it does.

Another question is: Can a CPA perform management services for a client and still be regarded as independent in performing an audit examination? It is generally believed that as long as a CPA merely gives advice to the client and does not actually make the decisions, the CPA remains independent.

In 1978, an independent commission established by the AICPA considered management advisory services for audit clients and concluded:

> . . . There is little question that the provision of some other services to audit clients poses an obvious *potential* threat to the auditor's independence. . . .
>
> Public accounting firms have indicated that they make substantial effort to avoid conflicts of interest. Such statements recognize the undeniable fact that a potential for such conflict exists. However, this recognition and the efforts to avoid conflicts appears to have been successful.
>
> * * * * *
>
> . . . the relevant facts do not support a prohibition against any particular services that auditors are now permitted to offer.[6]

On the other hand, the original document establishing the SEC Practice Section of the AICPA division for CPA firms, which was approved by the AICPA's Council, placed some restrictions on the types of management advisory services that could be performed for audit clients who had securities registered with the SEC (e.g., public opinion polls, psychological testing, and executive recruiting were prohibited). The document indicated that the SEC Practice Section would continue to study this question.

At the request of the Executive Committee of the SEC Practice Section, its Public Oversight Board examined the question of management services and independence. In 1979, it issued a report that concluded that ". . . mandatory limitations on scope of services should be predicated only on the determination that certain services, or the role of the firm performing certain services, will impair a member's independence in rendering an opinion on the fairness of a client's financial statements or present a strong likelihood of doing so."[7] The report went on to say that ". . . at this time no rules should be imposed to prohibit specific services on the grounds that they are or may be incompatible with the profession of public accounting, might impair the image of the profession, or do not involve accounting or auditing related skills."[8] Thus, services such as executive recruiting are now permitted unless they impair the auditor's independence.

---

[6] The Commission on Auditors' Responsibilities: *Report, Conclusions, and Recommendations,* 1978, p. 102.

[7] *Public Oversight Board Report: Scope of Services by CPA Firms,* Public Oversight Board, SEC Practice Section, American Institute of Certified Public Accountants, 1979, pp. 4–5.

[8] Ibid., p. 5.

A third issue relates to competence. Rule 201 (ET 201.01A) states that "a member shall undertake only those engagements which he or his firm can reasonably expect to complete with professional competence." Thus, if a CPA does not have the necessary competence or is unable to acquire it, he or she should decline the job and refer the work to a practitioner who is competent in that particular area.

In December 1981, the AICPA's Management Advisory Services Executive Committee issued its first statement, "Definitions and Standards for MAS Practice." The statements are called Statements on Standards for Management Advisory Services (SSMAS). *SSMAS No. 1* presents a number of definitions and discusses MAS practice standards.

SSMAS No.1 defines management advisory services as ". . . providing advice and technical assistance where the primary purpose is to help the client improve the use of its capabilities and resources to achieve its objectives. . . ." However, "recommendations and comments prepared as a direct result of observations made while performing an audit, review, or compilation of financial statements or while providing tax services. . ." are not considered management services.

SSMAS No. 1 differentiates an *MAS engagement* from an *MAS consultation.* An MAS engagement is ". . . an analytical approach and process, applied in a study or project." It involves more than "incidental effort." An MAS consultation usually is given orally in a short time frame, and is based, for the most part, on ". . . existing personal knowledge about the client, the circumstances, the technical matters involved, and the mutual intent of the parties."

SSMAS No. 1 reiterates that the general standards in Rule 201 apply to MAS engagements and consultations. Further, *SSMAS No. 1* makes the following technical standards applicable to MAS engagements under Rule 204:

1. In an engagement the practitioner should not assume the role of management or take a position that would compromise his or her objectivity.
2. The practitioner and client should have a written or oral understanding on the nature, scope, and limitations of the engagement.
3. The practitioner should not guarantee results, and the limitations of results should be noted. Estimates should be clearly identified.
4. Results should be clearly communicated to the client either orally or in writing.

In 1982, *SSMAS No. 2* and *SSMAS No. 3* were issued to provide further guidance related to MAS engagements and consultations.

ENFORCEMENT OF THE CODE

The AICPA, the state societies, and the state boards of accountancy have the authority to enforce their individual codes of ethics. However, the nature of this authority varies. The AICPA and the state societies are voluntary, professional organizations, and can warn, censure, suspend, or expel a member. However, the right of a CPA to practice is not affected by these organizations. The real power to enforce the code of ethics lies with the state boards of accountancy, which issue, and thus have the power to suspend or revoke, a CPA's certificate or license to practice. A board also can warn or censure an individual at its discretion.

The disciplinary proceedings of both the professional organizations and state boards usually involve hearings for accused violators. They have the right to be present and usually to be represented by counsel. The findings of a professional organization sometimes may be appealed, and the findings of a state board often can be appealed in the courts.

ACCOUNTANTS' LIABILITY

Accountants' sources of possible liability include (1) civil liability under common law, (2) civil liability under statutory law (e.g., federal securities law), and (3) criminal liability.

This section discusses the independent accountant's civil liability (principally as an auditor) under various areas of common law and summarizes significant lawsuits that illustrate those areas. Chapter 20 discusses the accountant's legal liability under statutory law.

LIABILITY FOR ACTS OF OTHERS

Most CPA firms are organized as either partnerships or professional corporations. As such, the partners (or shareholders of a professional corporation) face possible civil liabilities for their work jointly—i.e., each partner is liable for the acts, errors, or omissions of all other partners. Further, under the laws of agency, the partners in a CPA firm may be liable for the work of others on whom they rely—for example, employees, other experts (e.g., lawyers, actuaries), or other CPAs.

A typical audit engagement is performed by several employees of the CPA firm, under the direction and control of a partner. If an employee commits errors or performs negligently, the partners in the firm may be ultimately liable for the employee's conduct.

Auditors must rely on their own professional judgment in expressing an opinion on whether financial statements are fairly presented. Because they cannot reasonably be expected to be experts in other areas, auditors may sometimes have to rely on the opinions of other experts. For example, the auditor may engage a lawyer to render an opinion on the potential impact of certain contracts, litigation, or other contingencies on a client's financial position. Or the auditor may consult with an actuary as to the adequacy of a client's pension liability or insurance reserves. The advice of these third parties may influence the auditor's judgment, but the auditor still could be held liable for his or her own actions.

Chapter 16 discusses reliance on other CPAs in greater detail, particularly with respect to whether and how the other CPA is mentioned in the audit report.

CONFIDENTIALITY OF AUDITOR-CLIENT RELATIONSHIP

Under the AICPA code of ethics, a confidential relationship exists between the auditor and the client. If the auditor voluntarily reveals confidential information to a third party which results in a loss to the client, the client may have a remedy against the auditor.

However, under common law there is *no privileged communication* between an auditor and a client. Thus, an auditor may be required to testify as a witness and release audit working papers in a court case. This would *not* constitute a breach of the normal confidential relationship between an auditor and a client. However, some state laws permit privileged communications between an auditor and a client, although certain states limit the scope of that privilege depending on either the intent of the parties at the time of the communication or the nature of the legal action involved. The privilege does not exist at the federal level.

LIABILITY TO CLIENTS

The relationship of an auditor to a client is that of an independent contractor. The rights and responsibilities of each party under contract law are established by the terms of the contract. The auditor may be liable to the client for a "breach of contract," i.e., failure to perform as required under the contract. However, failure of the auditor to perform due to a disability is not a breach of contract. In that case, the contract is invalidated.

The auditor also may be liable to the client for committing a "tort," i.e., a civil wrong (act, error, or omission) other than a breach of contract. Whether an auditor is subject to legal action for breach of contract, tortious conduct, or both, depends on the theory of law the plaintiff elects and the law of the jurisdiction where the lawsuit is pursued. The plaintiff's election can significantly affect factors such as the statute of limitations (which designates a certain time after which rights cannot be legally enforced), the available defenses (the methods and supporting facts used to protect the defendant against the plaintiff's action), and the remedy to which the plaintiff is entitled.

While the auditor's legal liability generally arises from the relationship with a *client,* in some cases the plaintiff will be a third party who had acquired the client's rights in the legal action through the process of "subrogation"—

acquiring by substitution rights belonging to another. For example, if an insurance company reimburses a client for losses attributable to an auditor's breach of contract or tortious conduct, the insurance company assumes any rights that the client had against the auditor.

Breach of Contract

The contract between an auditor and a client can be either a formal one with specific conditions or an informal one that is more general in nature. However, unless there are specific provisions to the contrary, the contract normally implies that the audit will be performed in accordance with generally accepted auditing standards. In addition, the client must not interfere with or prevent the auditor from performing the audit.

An important point to remember when considering the auditor's contractual relationship with a client is that normally the auditor does not have an obligation to discover fraud. Chapters 4 and 14 discuss the auditor's responsibility for detecting errors or irregularities and illegal acts, respectively.

If an auditor breaches a contract so that virtually no benefit is received by the client—for example, the auditor improperly fails to complete the examination or unjustifiably completes it beyond a critical date that was specified in the contract—the auditor may, in some juristictions, not be entitled to compensation. Further, a client who sustains a loss as a result of a breach may be entitled to other remedies. In an action for breach of contract, a plaintiff normally is not entitled to punitive damages.

To avoid ambiguities in the contractual relationship between auditor and client, the auditor should summarize the various aspects and details of their mutual agreement in an "engagement letter" to the client. The auditor should sign the letter and request that the client sign and return it. The engagement letter evidences their agreement and should be retained by the auditor. Figure 19–1 is an example of an audit engagement letter suggested in *International Auditing Guideline No. 2,* "Audit Engagement Letters," by the International Federation of Accountants (AU 8002.09).[9] While engagement letters are not required under generally accepted auditing standards, the following case illustrates their importance.

1136 Tenants' Corporation v. *Max Rothenberg & Co.*[10]   This case demonstrates the importance of defining each party's contractual obligation in an engage-

---

[9] As noted in the "Preface to International Auditing Guidelines of the International Federation of Accountants" (AU 8000.01) the International Federation of Accountants was formed in 1977 with the agreement by 63 accountancy bodies from 49 countries. The broad objectives of the Federation are to develop and enhance a coordinated worldwide profession with standards that are harmonized. International Auditing Guidelines are not binding on CPAs in the United States.

[10] *1136 Tenants' Corporation* v. *Max Rothenberg & Co.,* 277 N.Y.S. 2d 996 (1967), 319 N.Y.S. 2d 1007 (1971).

FIGURE 19–1   Example of an Audit Engagement Letter

To the Board of Directors (or the appropriate representative of senior management):

You have requested that we audit the balance sheet, statements of income, and changes in financial position of [client] as of and for the year ending _____. We are pleased to confirm our acceptance and our understanding of this engagement by means of this letter. Our audit will be made in accordance with generally accepted auditing standards with the objective of our expressing an opinion on the financial statements.

In forming our opinion on the financial statements, we will perform sufficient tests to obtain reasonable assurance as to whether the information contained in the underlying accounting records and other source data is reliable and sufficient as the basis for the preparation of the financial statements. We will also decide whether the information is properly communicated in the financial statements.

Because of the test nature and other inherent limitations of an audit, together with the inherent limitations of any system of internal control, there is an unavoidable risk that even some material misstatement may remain undiscovered.

In addition to our report on the financial statements, we expect to provide you with a separate letter concerning any material weaknesses in internal control which come to our attention.

May we remind you that the responsibility for the preparation of financial statements including adequate disclosure is that of the management of the company. This includes the maintenance of adequate accounting records and internal controls, the selection and application of accounting policies, and the safeguarding of the assets of the company. As part of our audit process, we will request from management written confirmation concerning representations made to us in connection with the audit.

We look forward to full cooperation with your staff and we trust that they will make available to us whatever records, documentation, and other information are requested in connection with our audit.

Our fees, which will be billed as work progresses, are based on the time required by the individuals assigned to the engagement plus direct out-of-pocket expenses. Individual hourly rates vary according to the degree of responsibility involved and the experience and skill required.

This letter will be effective for future years unless it is terminated, amended, or superseded.

Please sign and return the attached copy of this letter to indicate that it is in accordance with your understanding of the arrangements for our audit of the financial statements.

XYZ & Co.

I have read the letter and understand the arrangements for your audit.

Signed _____
(Client)

Source: Adapted from *AICPA Professional Standards, Vol. 2,* (AU 8002.09).

ment letter. During 1963, the managing agent of 1136 Tenants' Corporation (Tenants'), a cooperative apartment corporation, engaged a CPA firm (Rothenberg) to prepare financial statements and letters containing tax information for shareholders, under an oral agreement for a fee of $600 per year. Rothenberg performed the services until March 1965, when Tenants' discovered that an officer of its managing agent had not paid certain of Tenants' obligations that were supposed to have been paid, and instead had diverted the funds for his own use.[11]

Tenants' believed that Rothenberg should have performed an audit and detected the fraud, and sued Rothenberg. Rothenberg claimed that it had not agreed to perform an audit. However, Rothenberg's working papers indicated that the firm did examine some of Tenants' bank statements, invoices, and bills and made notations concerning "missing invoices."

In deciding the case, the court also considered the facts that the financial statements sent by Rothenberg each month contained a notation referring the reader to a letter of transmittal which said:

> Pursuant to our engagement, we have *reviewed* and summarized the statements of your managing agent and other data submitted to us by [the managing agent] . . . pertaining to 1136 Tenants' Corporation. . . . The following statements . . . were prepared from the books and records of the Corporation. No independent verifications were undertaken thereon. . . . [Emphasis added.][12]

The court concluded that, absent written evidence to the contrary (i.e., an engagement letter or contract), an audit had taken place. Further, had Rothenberg followed up on the missing invoices, the fraud would likely have been uncovered. Thus, it ruled that Rothenberg was liable to Tenants' for nearly $240,000.

Tort Liability

An auditor is obligated to exercise due professional care. In conducting an audit in accordance with generally accepted auditing standards, the auditor uses professional judgment in determining the nature and extent of the audit procedures to be used. If the auditor applies the degree of care and skill generally considered reasonable for the public accounting profession, he or she should not be considered negligent in committing an error in judgment. However, an auditor who acts improperly, commits significant errors, or omits an important step may be liable to the client for the torts of negligence, gross negligence, or fraud—which one is a question of judgment based on the facts and circumstances.

Negligence. An auditor is negligent if he or she fails to exercise *reasonable* care. If the negligence caused damage, the plaintiff may recover losses forseeable from such negligence. Some factors to consider in determining whether an auditor exercised reasonable care are compliance with generally accepted

---

[11] "AICPA-NYSSCPA Brief *Amicus Curiae* Submitted to the Court of Appeals of the State of New York," *The Journal of Accountancy* (November 1971) pp. 68–70.

[12] Ibid., pp. 68–69.

auditing standards and GAAP, specific conditions of the contract with the client, past court decisions in similar circumstances, and whether there was contributory negligence on the part of the client. The following cases illustrate application of the reasonable care criterion.

Flagg **v.** *Seng.*[13] A real estate syndicate maintained a policy of recognizing income on exchanges of land for land, and stock of the syndicate for land, though no cash was involved in the transactions. This violated GAAP. The auditors were not fully aware of the policy, and upon noting one such transaction, discussed it with the client's legal counsel. Counsel's responses dispelled their concern, and the transactions did not affect their opinion on the financial statements. Based on the audited financial statements, the board of directors declared an illegal dividend. The syndicate later was declared bankrupt and the trustee sued the auditors to recover the illegal dividend.

The court concluded that the accountants were not negligent, because in determining that the revenue recognition method was acceptable, they sought the advice of legal counsel regarding the transaction they discovered. Further, since the board knew about the syndicate's revenue recognition policy, it was not deceived by the audited financial statements when it declared the illegal dividend.

National Surety Corporation **v.** *Lybrand.*[14] A cashier misappropriated cash and covered the shortages through late deposits (lapping) and various bank transfers (kiting). In performing their audit procedures, the auditors did not check deposit slips against entries to accounts, nor did they perform the standard audit procedure of checking the balances in all banks as of the same day. The plaintiff charged that those procedures would likely have uncovered the fraud. In their defense, the auditors cited contributory negligence by the client in not discovering the fraud when preparing bank reconciliations.

The trial court concluded that the client was contributorily negligent and decided in favor of the defendant. However, the Appellate Division observed that the defendant failed to perform certain standard audit procedures and stated that contributory negligence ". . . is a defense only when it has contributed to the accountant's failure to perform his contract and to report the truth."[15] In this case, the client had not contributed to the auditor's negligence in excluding the procedures. Thus, the Appellate Division reversed the trial court's decision and ordered the case to be retried.[16] The

---

[13] *Flagg* v. *Seng,* 16 Cal. App. 2d 545, 60 P. 2d 1004 (1936).

[14] *National Surety Corporation* v. *Lybrand,* 256 App. Div. 226, 9. N.Y.S. 2d 554 (1st Dept. 1939).

[15] Ibid, p. 563.

[16] Ibid., p. 564.

case was not retried. If it had been retried, the original verdict probably would have been reversed.

Gross Negligence and Fraud.   An auditor may be liable for gross negligence if he or she engages in conduct that is an extreme departure from reasonable care. Gross negligence also is referred to as constructive fraud. Conversely, actual fraud is an intentional misrepresentation for the purpose of deceiving another party who is then injured by it. In some cases, the plaintiff also may be entitled to punitive damages as a result of gross negligence or fraud.

LIABILITY TO THIRD PARTIES

Primary Beneficiaries

A primary beneficiary is a third party for whose primary benefit an audit is performed. The client must identify a primary beneficiary for the auditor prior to the audit so that the auditor knows the audit report will affect the beneficiary's decisions. Examples of primary beneficiaries include banks and other creditors that require a special auditor's report regarding the client's compliance with debt covenants and landlords of commercial tenants that base the rental charge on a percentage of sales. The same degree of care is expected from an auditor by the primary beneficiary as by the client.

Unidentified Third Parties

Unidentified third parties who use audited financial statements do not have "privity" of contract with an auditor. Privity is the contractual relationship between the parties to a contract. The basic rule under common law is that the auditor is not liable for negligence to unknown third parties (e.g., potential investors or creditors). However, the auditor may be liable to them for gross negligence or fraud. The degree of auditor's liability to third parties has evolved through various court cases over the years and continues to do so. Some of those are summarized below.

Ultramares Corp.* v. *Touche.[17]   A creditor who relied on audited financial statements loaned money to a company that subsequently was declared bankrupt. The creditor sued the company's auditors, citing negligence and fraudulent misrepresentations.

The court eliminated the charge of negligence as a basis for suit because the third-party creditor was not a primary beneficiary of the audit. However, the court also concluded that the auditors were grossly negligent in not

---

[17] *Ultramares Corp.* v. *Touche,* 225 N.Y. 170, 174 N.E. 441 (1931).

discovering certain irregularities in the financial statements and that the plaintiff could recover from the auditor. This is considered a landmark case because it established that lack of privity is not a valid defense in cases of gross negligence or fraud, although lack of privity is a valid defense in the case of ordinary negligence.

More recently, some cases have expanded the auditor's liability for ordinary *negligence* to include all third parties which the auditor can *forsee* being injured. The following case illustrates this point.

Rusch Factors, Inc.* v. *Levin. [18]   The defendant audited the financial statements of a company, which in turn submitted them to Rusch Factors and received a loan. The financial statements portrayed the company as solvent, when in fact it was insolvent. The company was subsequently declared bankrupt, and Rusch Factors sued the auditors. The court concluded the following:

> . . . this court holds that an accountant should be *liable in negligence* for careless financial misrepresentations relied upon *by actually foreseen and limited classes of persons.* According to the plaintiff's complaint in the instant case, *the defendant knew that his certification was to be used for,* and had as its very aim and purpose, the *reliance of potential financiers* of the . . . corporation. . . . [Emphasis added.] [19]

CONCLUSION

Today's business environment is complex, and so are the problems associated with accounting and auditing in it. And in recent years our society has become more "litigation conscious." Particularly because recent cases have broadened the auditor's liability to third parties, the CPA today must be aware of the hazards he or she faces. Legal liability is not necessarily a negative factor. As a professional, the CPA should seek to maintain a standard of quality that reduces the risk of exposure to legal liability to a minimum.

In several of the cases summarized here, the auditors appeared to deviate to some extent from generally accepted auditing standards or correct application of GAAP. And in some cases, they did not appear to understand their client's business. The CPA has an obligation to exercise care in following the standards of the profession and to obtain a thorough understanding of a client's business environment (both internal and external) and the backgrounds of key members of management. It is also important to clearly define the contractual obligations of each party in an engagement letter. In addition to these preventive measures, it is advisable for the CPA to maintain adequate liability insurance.

---

[18] *Rusch Factors, Inc.* v. *Levin,* 284 F. Supp. 85 (D.C.R.I. 1968).

[19] Ibid., pp. 92–93.

APPENDIX 19A

A REPRODUCTION OF THE AICPA
RULES OF CONDUCT[20]

Definitions

The following definitions of terminology are applicable wherever such terminology is used in the Rules and Interpretations.

Client.   The person(s) or entity which retains a member or his firm, engaged in the practice of public accounting, for the performance of professional services.

Council.   The Council of the American Institute of Certified Public Accountants.

Enterprise.   Any person(s) or entity, whether organized for profit or not, for which a CPA provides services.

Financial statements.   Statements and footnotes related thereto that purport to show financial position which relates to a point in time or changes in financial position which relate to a period of time, and statements which use a cash or other incomplete basis of accounting. Balance sheets, statements of income, statements of retained earnings, statements of changes in financial position, and statements of changes in owners' equity are financial statements.

Incidental financial data included in management advisory services reports to support recommendations to a client and tax returns and supporting schedules do not, for this purpose, constitute financial statements; and the statement, affidavit, or signature of preparers required on tax returns neither constitutes an opinion on financial statements nor requires a disclaimer of such opinion.

Firm.   A proprietorship, partnership, or professional corporation or association engaged in the practice of public accounting, including individual partners of shareholders thereof.

Institute.   The American Institute of Certified Public Accountants.

Interpretations of Rules of Conduct.   Pronouncements issued by the division of professional ethics to provide guidelines concerning the scope and application of the Rules of Conduct.

Member.   A member, associate member, or international associate of the American Institute of Certified Public Accountants.

---

[20] Source: *AICPA Professional Standards,* Vol. 2.

Practice of public accounting.   Holding out to be a CPA or public accountant and at the same time performing for a client one or more types of services rendered by public accountants. The term shall not be limited by a more restrictive definition which might be found in the accountancy law under which a member practices.

Professional services.   One of more types of services performed in the practice of public accounting.

Applicability of Rules

The Institute's Code of Professional Ethics derives its authority from the bylaws of the Institute which provide that the Trial Board may, after a hearing, admonish, suspend, or expel a member who is found guilty of infringing any of the bylaws or any provisions of the Rules of Conduct.

The Rules of Conduct which follow apply to all services performed in the practice of public accounting including tax and management advisory services except (a) where the wording of the rule indicates otherwise and (b) that a member who is practicing outside the United States will not be subject to discipline for departing from any of the rules stated herein so long as his conduct is in accord with the rules of the organized accounting profession in the country in which he is practicing. However, where a member's name is associated with financial statements in such a manner as to imply that he is acting as an independent public accountant and under circumstances that would entitle the reader to assume that United States practices were followed, he must comply with the requirements of Rules 202 and 203.

A member may be held responsible for compliance with the Rules of Conduct by all persons associated with him in the practice of public accounting who are either under his supervision or are his partners or shareholders in the practice.

A member engaged in the practice of public accounting must observe all the Rules of Conduct. A member not engaged in the practice of public accounting must observe only Rules 102 and 501 since all other Rules of Conduct relate solely to the practice of public accounting.

A member shall not permit others to carry out on his behalf, either with or without compensation, acts which, if carried out by the member, would place him in violation of the Rules of Conduct.

Independence

Rule 101—Independence.   A member or a firm of which he is a partner or shareholder shall not express an opinion on financial statements of an enterprise unless he and his firm are independent with respect to such enterprise. Independence will be considered to be impaired if, for example:

A. During the period of his professional engagement, or at the time of expressing his opinion, he or his firm
   1. (a) Had or was committed to acquire any direct or material indirect financial interest in the enterprise; or
       (b) Was a trustee of any trust or executor or administrator of any estate if such trust or estate had or was committed to acquire any direct or material indirect financial interest in the enterprise; or
   2. Had any joint closely held business investment with the enterprise or any officer, director, or principal stockholder thereof which was material in relation to his or his firm's net worth; or
   3. Had any loan to or from the enterprise of any officer, director, or principal stockholder thereof. This latter proscription does not apply to the following loans from a financial institution when made under normal lending procedures, terms, and requirements:
       (a) Loans obtained by a member or his firm which are not material in relation to the net worth of such borrower.
       (b) Home mortgages.
       (c) Other secured loans, except loans guaranteed by a member's firm which are otherwise unsecured.
B. During the period covered by the financial statements, during the period of the professional engagement, or at the time of expressing an opinion, he or his firm
   1. Was connected with the enterprise as a promoter, underwriter or voting trustee, a director or officer or in any capacity equivalent to that of a member of management or of an employee; or
   2. Was a trustee for any pension or profit-sharing trust of the enterprise.

The above examples are not intended to be all-inclusive.

Integrity and Objectivity

Rule 102—Integrity and objectivity.   A member shall not knowingly misrepresent facts, and when engaged in the practice of public accounting, including the rendering of tax and management advisory services, shall not subordinate his judgment to others. In tax practice, a member may resolve doubt in favor of his client as long as there is reasonable support for his position.

General Standards

Rule 201—General standards.   A member shall comply with the following general standards as interpreted by bodies designated by Council, and must justify any departures therefrom.

A. Professional competence. A member shall undertake only those engagements which he or his firm can reasonably expect to complete with professional competence.

B. Due professional care. A member shall exercise due professional care in the performance of an engagement.

C. Planning and supervision. A member shall adequately plan and supervise an engagement.

D. Sufficient relevant data. A member shall obtain sufficient relevant data to afford a reasonable basis for conclusions or recommendations in relation to an engagement.

E. Forecasts. A member shall not permit his name to be used in conjunction with any forecast of future transactions in a manner which may lead to the belief that the member vouches for the achievability of the forecast.

Auditing Standards

Rule 202—Auditing standards. A member shall not permit his name to be associated with financial statements in such a manner as to imply that he is acting as an independent public accountant unless he has complied with the applicable generally accepted auditing standards promulgated by the Institute. Statements on Auditing Standards issued by the Institute's Auditing Standards Executive Committee[21] are, for purposes of this rule, considered to be interpretations of the generally accepted auditing standards, and departures from such statements must be justified by those who do not follow them.

Accounting Principles

Rule 203—Accounting principles. A member shall not express an opinion that financial statements are presented in conformity with generally accepted accounting principles if such statements contain any departure from an accounting principle promulgated by the body designated by Council to establish such principles which has a material effect on the statements taken as a whole, unless the member can demonstrate that due to unusual circumstances the financial statements would otherwise have been misleading. In such cases his report must describe the departure, the approximate effects thereof, if practicable, and the reasons why compliance with the principle would result in a misleading statement.

---

[21] *Authors' Note:* The Auditing Standards Executive Committee has been replaced by the Auditing Standards Board.

Other Technical Standards

Rule 204—Other technical standards. A member shall comply with other technical standards promulgated by bodies designated by Council to establish such standards, and departures therefrom must be justified by those who do not follow them.

Confidential Client Information

Rule 301—Confidential client information.   A member shall not disclose any confidential information obtained in the course of a professional engagement except with the consent of the client.

This rule shall not be construed (a) to relieve a member of his obligation under Rules 202 and 203, (b) to affect in any way his compliance with a validly issued subpoena or summons enforceable by order of a court, (c) to prohibit review of a member's professional practices as a part of voluntary quality review under Institute authorization or (d) to preclude a member from responding to any inquiry made by the ethics division or Trial Board of the Institute, by a duly constituted investigative or disciplinary body of a state CPA society, or under state statutes.

Members of the ethics division and Trial Board of the Institute and professional practice reviewers under Institute authorization shall not disclose any confidential client information which comes to their attention from members in disciplinary proceedings or otherwise in carrying out their official responsibilities. However, this prohibition shall not restrict the exchange of information with an aforementioned duly constituted investigative or disciplinary body.

Contingent Fees

Rule 302—Contingent fees. Professional services shall not be offered or rendered under an arrangement whereby no fee will be charged unless a specified finding or result is attained, or where the fee is otherwise contingent upon the findings or results of such services. However, a member's fees may vary depending, for example, on the complexity of the service rendered.

Fees are not regarded as being contingent if fixed by courts or other public authorities or, in tax matters, if determined based on the results of judicial proceedings or the findings of governmental agencies.

Acts Discreditable

Rule 501—Acts discreditable.   A member shall not commit an act discreditable to the profession.

Advertising and Other Forms of Solicitation

Rule 502—Advertising and other forms of solicitation. A member shall not seek to obtain clients by advertising or other forms of solicitation in a manner that is false, misleading, or deceptive. Solicitation by the use of coercion, overreaching or harassing conduct is prohibited.

Commission

Rule 503—Commission. A member shall not pay a commission to obtain a client, nor shall he accept a commission for a referral to a client of products or services of others. This rule shall not prohibit payments for the purchase of an accounting practice or retirement payments to individuals formerly engaged in the practice of public accounting or payments to their heirs or estates.

Incompatible Occupations

Rule 504—Incompatible occupations. A member who is engaged in the practice of public accounting shall not concurrently engage in any business or occupation which would create a conflict of interest in rendering professional services.

Form of Practice and Name

Rule 505—Form of practice and name. A member may practice public accounting, whether as an owner or employee, only in the form of a proprietorship, a partnership or a professional corporation whose characteristics conform to resolutions of Council.

A member shall not practice under a firm name which includes any fictitious name, indicates specialization or is misleading as to the type of organization (proprietorship, partnership or corporation). However, names of one or more past partners or shareholders may be included in the firm name of a successor partnership or corporation. Also, a partner surviving the death or withdrawal of all other partners may continue to practice under the partnership name for up to two years after becoming a sole practitioner.

A firm may not designate itself as "Members of the American Institute of Certified Public Accountants" unless all of its partners or shareholders are members of the Institute.

APPENDIX 19B

A REPRODUCTION OF AICPA
INTERPRETATIONS OF
THE RULES OF CONDUCT[22]

Interpretations under Rule 101—Independence

101–1—Honorary directorships and trusteeships. Members are often asked to lend the prestige of their names to not-for-profit organizations that limit their activities to those of a charitable, religious, civic or similar nature by being named as a director or a trustee. A member who permits his name to be used in this manner and who is associated with the financial statements of the organization would not be considered lacking in independence under Rule 101 so long as (1) his position is purely honorary, (2) it is identified as honorary in all letterheads and externally circulated materials in which he is named as a director or trustee, (3) he restricts his participation to the use of his name, and (4) he does not vote or otherwise participate in management functions.

It is presumed that organizations to which members lend only the prestige of their names will have sufficiently large boards of directors or trustees to clearly permit the member to limit his participation consistent with the foregoing restriction.

101–2—Retired partners and firm independence. A retired partner having a relationship of a type specified in Rule 101 with a client of his former firm would not be considered as impairing the firm's independence with respect to the client provided that he is no longer active in the firm, that the fees received from such client do not have a material effect on his retirement benefits and that he is not held out as being associated with his former partnership.

101–3—Accounting services. Members in public practice are sometimes asked to provide manual or automated bookkeeping or data processing services to clients who are of insufficient size to employ an adequate internal accounting staff. Computer systems design and programming assistance are also rendered by members either in conjunction with data processing services or as a separate engagement. Members who perform such services and who are engaged in the practice of public accounting are subject to the bylaws and Rules of Conduct.

On occasion members also rent "block time" on their computers to their clients but are not involved in the processing of transactions or maintaining the client's accounting records. In such cases the sale of block time constitutes a business rather than a professional relationship and must be considered

---

[22] *Source: AICPA Professional Standards,* Vol. 2.

together with all other relationships between the member and his client to determine if their aggregate impact is such as to impair the member's independence.

When a member performs manual or automated bookkeeping services, concern may arise whether the performance of such services would impair his audit independence—that the performance of such basic accounting services would cause his audit to be lacking in a review of mechanical accuracy or that the accounting judgments made by him in recording transactions may somehow be less reliable than if made by him in connection with the subsequent audit.

Members are skilled in, and well accustomed to, applying techniques to control mechanical accuracy, and the performance of the record-keeping function should have no effect on application of such techniques. With regard to accounting judgments, if third parties have confidence in a member's judgment in performing an audit, it is difficult to contend that they would have less confidence where the same judgment is applied in the process of preparing the underlying accounting records.

Nevertheless, a member performing accounting services for an audit client must meet the following requirements to retain the appearance that he is not virtually an employee and therefore lacking in independence in the eyes of a reasonable observer.

1. The CPA must not have any relationship or combination of relationships with the client or any conflict of interest which would impair his integrity and objectivity.

2. The client must accept the responsibility for the financial statements as his own. A small client may not have anyone in his employ to maintain accounting records and may rely on the CPA for this purpose. Nevertheless, the client must be sufficiently knowledgeable of the enterprise's activities and financial condition and the applicable accounting principles so that he can reasonably accept such responsibility, including, specifically, fairness of valuation and presentation and adequacy of disclosure. When necessary, the CPA must discuss accounting matters with the client to be sure that the client has the required degree of understanding.

3. The CPA must not assume the role of employee or of management conducting the operations of an enterprise. For example, the CPA shall not consummate transactions, have custody of assets or exercise authority on behalf of the client. The client must prepare the source documents on all transactions in sufficient detail to identify clearly the nature and amount of such transactions and maintain an accounting control over data processed by the CPA such as control totals and document counts. The CPA should not make changes in such basic data without the concurrence of the client.

4. The CPA, in making an examination of financial statements prepared from books and records which he has maintained completely or in part,

must conform to generally accepted auditing standards. The fact that he has processed or maintained certain records does not eliminate the need to make sufficient audit tests.

When a client's securities become subject to regulation by the Securities and Exchange Commission or other federal or state regulatory body, responsibility for maintenance of the accounting records, including accounting classification decisions, must be assumed by accounting personnel employed by the client. The assumption of this responsibility must commence with the first fiscal year after which the client's securities qualify for such regulation.

[101–4]—[Deleted]

101–5—Meaning of the term "normal lending procedures, terms and requirements." Rule 101(A)(3) prohibits loans to a member from his client except for certain specified kinds of loans from a client financial institution when made under "normal lending procedures, terms and requirements." The member would meet the criteria prescribed by this rule if the procedures, terms and requirements relating to his loan are reasonably comparable to those relating to other loans of a similar character committed to other borrowers during the period in which the loan to the member is committed. Accordingly, in making such comparison and in evaluating whether his loan was made under "normal lending procedures, terms and requirements," the member should consider all the circumstances under which the loan was granted including

1. The amount of the loan in relation to the value of the collateral pledged as security and the credit standing of the member or his firm.
2. Repayment terms.
3. Interest rate, including "points."
4. Requirement to pay closing costs in accordance with the lender's usual practice.
5. General availability of such loans to the public.

Related prohibitions (which may be more restrictive) are prescribed by certain state and federal agencies having regulatory authority over such financial institutions.

101–6—The effect of actual or threatened litigation on independence. Rule of Conduct 101 prohibits the expression of an opinion on financial statements of an enterprise unless a member and his firm are independent with respect to the enterprise. In some circumstances, independence may be considered to be impaired as a result of litigation or the expressed intention to commence litigation.

Litigation between client and auditor

In order for the auditor to fulfill his obligation to render an informed, objective opinion on the client company's financial statements, the relationship between the management of the client and the auditor must be characterized by complete candor and full disclosure regarding all aspects of the client's business operations. In addition, there must be an absence of bias on the part of the auditor so that he can exercise dispassionate professional judgment on the financial reporting decisions made by the management. When the present management of a client company commences, or expresses an intention to commence, legal action against the auditor, the auditor and the client management may be placed in adversary positions in which the management's willingness to make complete disclosures and the auditor's objectivity may be affected by self-interest.

For the reasons outlined above, independence may be impaired whenever the auditor and his client company or its management are in threatened or actual positions of material adverse interests by reason of actual or intended litigation. Because of the complexity and diversity of the situations of adverse interests which may arise, however, it is difficult to prescribe precise points at which independence may be impaired. The following criteria are offered as guidelines:

1. The commencement of litigation by the present management alleging deficiencies in audit work for the client would be considered to impair independence.

2. The commencement of litigation by the auditor against the present management alleging management fraud or deceit would be considered to impair independence.

3. An expressed intention by the present management to commence litigation against the auditor alleging deficiencies in audit work for the client is considered to impair independence if the auditor concludes that there is a strong possibility that such a claim will be filed.

4. Litigation not related to audit work for the client (whether threatened or actual) for an amount not material to the member's firm* or to the financial statements of the client company would not usually be considered to affect the relationship in such a way as to impair independence. Such claims may arise, for example, out of disputes as to billings for services, results of tax or management services advice or similar matters.

---

* Because of the complexities of litigation and the circumstances under which it may arise, it is not possible to prescribe meaningful criteria for measuring materiality; accordingly, the member should consider the nature of the controversy underlying the litigation and all other relevant factors in reaching a judgment.

Litigation by security holders

The auditor may also become involved in litigation ("primary litigation") in which he and the client company or its management are defendants. Such litigations may arise, for example, when one or more stockholders bring a stockholders' derivative action or a so-called "class action" against the client company or its management, its officers, directors, underwriters and auditors under the securities laws. Such primary litigation in itself would not alter fundamental relationships between the client company or its management and auditor and therefore should not be deemed to have an adverse impact on the auditor's independence. These situations should be examined carefully, however, since the potential for adverse interests may exist if cross-claims are filed against the auditor alleging that he is responsible for any deficiencies or if the auditor alleges fraud or deceit by the present management as a defense. In assessing the extent to which his independence may be impaired under these conditions, the auditor should consider the following additional guidelines:

1. The existence of cross-claims filed by the client, its management, or any of its directors to protect a right to legal redress in the event of a future adverse decision in the primary litigation (or, in lieu of cross-claims, agreements to extend the statute of limitations) would not normally affect the relationship between client management and auditor in such a way as to impair independence, unless there exists a significant risk that the cross-claim will result in a settlement or judgment in an amount material to the member's firm* or to the financial statements of the client.

2. The assertion of cross-claims against the auditor by underwriters would not usually impair independence if no such claims are asserted by the company or the present management.

3. If any of the persons who file cross-claims against the auditor are also officers or directors of other clients of the auditor, the auditor's independence with respect to such other clients would not usually be impaired.

Other third-party litigation

Another type of third-party litigation against the auditor may be commenced by a lending institution, other creditor, security holder or insurance company who alleges reliance on financial statements of the client examined by the auditor as a basis for extending credit or insurance coverage to the client. In some instances, an insurance company may commence litigation (under subrogation rights) against the auditor in the name of the client to recover losses reimbursed to the client. These types of litigation would not

---

* [Same as footnote on page 654].

normally affect the auditor's independence with respect to a client who is either not the plaintiff or is only the nominal plaintiff, since the relationship between the auditor and client management would not be affected. They should be examined carefully, however, since the potential for adverse interests may exist if the auditor alleges, in his defense, fraud, or deceit by the present management.

If the real party in interest in the litigation (e.g., the insurance company) is also a client of the auditor ("the plaintiff client"), the auditor's independence with respect to the plaintiff client may be impaired if the litigation involves a significant risk of a settlement or judgment in an amount which would be material to the member's firm* or to the financial statements of the plaintiff client. If the auditor concludes that such litigation is not material to the plaintiff client or his firm and thus his independence is not impaired, he should nevertheless ensure that professional personnel assigned to the audit of either of the two clients have no involvement with the audit of the other.

Effects of impairment of independence

If the auditor believes that the circumstances would lead a reasonable person having knowledge of the facts to conclude that the actual or intended litigation poses an unacceptable threat to the auditor's independence he should either (a) disengage himself to avoid the appearance that his self-interest would affect his objectivity, or (b) disclaim an opinion because of lack of independence. Such disengagement may take the form of resignation or cessation of any audit work then in progress pending resolution of the issue between the parties.

Termination of impairment

The conditions giving rise to a lack of independence are usually eliminated when a final resolution is reached and the matters at issue no longer affect the relationship between auditor and client. The auditor should carefully review the conditions of such resolution to determine that all impairments to his objectivity have been removed.

Actions permitted while independence is impaired

If the auditor was independent when his report was initially rendered, he may re-sign such report or consent to its use at a later date while his independence is impaired provided that no post-audit work is performed by such auditor during the period of impairment. The term "post-audit work," in this context, does not include inquiries of subsequent auditors, reading of subsequent financial statements, or such procedures as may be necessary to assess the effect of subsequently discovered facts on the financial statements covered by his previously issued report.

---

* [Same as footnote on page 654.]

[101–7]—[Deleted]

101–8—Effect on independence of financial interests in nonclients having investor or investee relationships with a member's client.

Introduction

Rule 101, Independence, provides in part that "A member or a firm of which he is a partner or shareholder shall not express an opinion on financial statements of an enterprise unless he and his firm are independent with respect to such enterprise. Independence will be considered to be impaired if for example, (A) . . . during the period of his professional engagement, or at the time of expressing his opinion, he or his firm . . . had or was committed to acquire any direct or material indirect financial interest in the enterprise . . . (B) during the period covered by the financial statements, during the period of the professional engagement, or at the time of expressing an opinion, he or his firm . . . was connected with the enterprise . . . in any capacity equivalent to that of a member of management . . ."

This interpretation deals with the effect on the appearance of independence of financial interests in nonclients that are related in various ways to a client. Some of the relationships discussed herein result in a financial interest in the client, while others would place the member in a capacity equivalent to that of a member of management.

Situations in which the nonclient investor is a partnership are not covered in this interpretation because the interests of the partnership are ascribed directly to the partners. A member holding a direct financial interest in a partnership that invests in his client has, as a result, a direct financial interest in the client, which impairs his independence.

Terminology

The following specially identified terms are used in this Interpretation as indicated:

1. *Client.* The enterprise with whose financial statements the member is associated.
2. *Member.* In this interpretation the term "member" means those individuals identified in the term "he and his firm" as defined in Interpretation 101–9.
3. *Investor.* In this Interpretation the term "investor" means (a) a parent or (b) another investor (including a natural person but not a partnership) that holds an interest in another company ("investee"), but only if the interest gives such other investor the ability to exercise significant influence over operating and financial policies of the investee. The criteria established in paragraph 17 of Accounting Principles Board Opinion Number 18 shall apply in determining the ability of an investor to exercise such influence.

4. *Investee.* In this Interpretation, the term "investee" means (a) a subsidiary or (b) an entity that is subject to significant influence from an investor. A limited partnership in which a client-investor holds a limited partnership interest would not be considered an "investee" subject to this interpretation unless the limited partner were in a position to exercise significant influence over operating and financial policies of the limited partnership.

5. *Material investee.* An investee is presumed to be material if:
   (a) the investor's aggregate carrying amount of investment in and advances to the investee exceeds 5% of the investor's consolidated total assets, or
   (b) the investee's equity in the investor's income from continuing operations before income taxes exceeds 5% of the investor's consolidated income from continuing operations before income taxes.

When the investor is a nonclient and its carrying amount of investments in and advances to the client investee is not readily available, the investor's proportionate share of the client investee's total assets may be used in the calculation described in (a) above.

If the income of an investor or investee from continuing operations before income taxes of the most recent year is clearly not indicative of the past or expected future amounts of such income, the reference point for materiality determinations should be the average of the incomes from continuing operations before income taxes of the preceding 3 years.

If a member has a financial interest in more than one nonclient investee of a client investor, the investments in and advances to such investees, and the equity in the income from continuing operations before income taxes of all such investees must be aggregated for purposes of determining whether such investees are material to the investor.

The 5% guidelines for identifying a material investee are to be applied to financial information available at the beginning of the engagement. A minor change in the percentage resulting from later financial information, which a member does not and could not be expected to anticipate at the beginning, may be ignored.

6. *Material financial interest.* A financial interest is presumed to be material to a member if it exceeds 5% of the member's net worth. If the member has financial interests in more than one investee of one investor, such interests must be aggregated for purposes of determining whether the member has a material financial interest as described in the preceding sentence.

Interpretation

Where a nonclient investee is material to a client investor, any direct or material indirect financial interest of a member in the nonclient investee would be considered to impair the member's independence with respect to the client. Likewise, where a client investee is material to a nonclient investor, any direct or material indirect financial interest of a member in the nonclient investor would be considered to impair the member's independence with respect to the client.

The remainder of this Interpretation discusses whether, in the other situations listed below, a member's financial interest in nonclient investor or nonclient investee of an audit client will impair the member's independence.

These situations are discussed in the following sections:

(1) Nonclient investee is not material to client investor.

(2) Client investee is not material to nonclient investor.

Other relationships, such as those involving brother-sister common control or client-nonclient joint ventures, may affect the appearance of independence. The member should make a reasonable inquiry to determine whether such relationships exist, and where they do, careful consideration should be given to whether the financial interests in question would lead a reasonable observer to conclude that the specified relationships pose an unacceptable threat to the member's independence.

In general, in brother-sister common control situations, an immaterial financial interest of a member in the nonclient investee would not impair the independence of a member with respect to the client investee provided the member could not significantly influence the nonclient investor. In like manner in a joint venture situation, an immaterial financial interest of a member in the nonclient investor would not impair the independence of the member with respect to the client investor provided that the member could not significantly influence the nonclient investor.

If a member does not and could not reasonably be expected to have knowledge of the financial interests or relationships described in this interpretation, such lack of knowledge would preclude an impairment of independence.

(1) NONCLIENT INVESTEE IS NOT MATERIAL
TO CLIENT INVESTOR

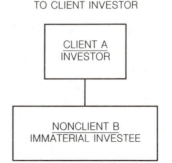

An immaterial financial interest of a member in Nonclient B (investee) would not be considered to impair the member's independence with respect to Client A (investor). A material financial interest of a member in Nonclient B would be considered to impair the member's independence with respect to Client A. The reason for this is that through its ability to influence Nonclient B, Client A could enhance or diminish the value of the member's financial interest in Nonclient B by an amount material to the member's net worth without a material effect on its own financial statements. As a result, the member would not appear to be independent when reporting on the financial statements of Client A.

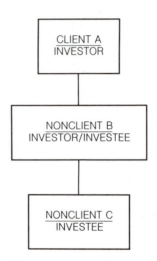

If Nonclient B (investee of Client A) had an investee, Nonclient C, the determination as to whether a financial interest in Nonclient C would be considered to impair the member's independence would be based on the same rules as above for Nonclient B, except that the materiality of Nonclient C is measured in relation to Client A, rather than to Nonclient B.

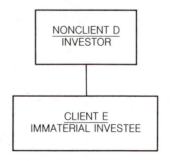

Except as indicated in the next paragraph, a financial interest of a member in Nonclient D (investor) would not be considered to impair the member's independence with respect to Client E (investee) even if the financial interest in Nonclient D were material to the member's net worth. The reason for this is that, since Client E is immaterial to Nonclient D, the member would not appear to be in a position to enhance his investment in Nonclient D.

If the member's financial interest in Nonclient D (investor) is sufficiently large to allow the member to significantly influence the actions of Nonclient D, the member's independence would be considered to be impaired. The reason for this is that a financial interest sufficient to allow the member to significantly influence the actions (operating and financial policies, intercompany transactions, etc.) of the investor could permit the member to exercise a degree of control over the client that would place the member in a capacity equivalent to that of a member of management. Such relationship would be considered to impair independence under Rule 101(b) (1).

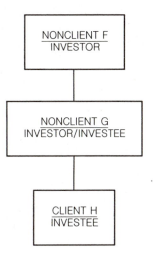

If Client H were an investee of nonclient G, who was an investee of another investor, Nonclient F, the determination as to whether a financial interest in Nonclient F would be considered to impair the member's independence would be based on the same rules as above for Nonclient G, except that the materiality of Client H is measured in relation to Nonclient F, rather than to Nonclient G.

101–9—The meaning of certain independence terminology and the effect of family relationships on independence.   This interpretation defines certain terms used in rule 101 and, in doing so, also explains how independence may be impaired through certain family relationships.

Terminology

He and his firm

For purposes of rule 101, "he and his firm" includes

1. An individual member performing professional services requiring independence.
2. The proprietor of, or all partners or shareholders in, a firm.
3. All full- and part-time professional employees* of a firm participating in the engagement.
4. All full- and part-time managerial employees* of a firm located in an office participating in a significant portion of the engagement.
5. Any entity (for example, partnership, corporation, trust, joint venture, pool, and so forth) whose operating, financial, or accounting policies can be "significantly influenced" (as discussed below) by one of the persons described in (1) through (4) or by two or more of such persons if they choose to act together.

For purposes of rule 101B, "he and his firm" does not include an individual solely because he was formerly associated with the client in any capacity described in rule 101B if such individual has disassociated himself from the client and does not participate in the engagement for the client covering any period of his association with the client.

Managerial employee

A managerial employee is a professional employee who either

1. Has a position generally similar to that of a partner, including an employee having the final authority to sign, or give final approval to the issuance of, reports in the firm's name or
2. Has a management position, in contrast with a nonmanagement position, with the firm.

The organizations of firms vary; therefore, whether an employee has a management position depends on his normal responsibilities and how he or the position itself is held out to clients and third parties. Some, but not necessarily all, of the responsibilities that suggest that an employee has a management position, are

1. Continuing responsibility for the overall planning and supervision of engagements for specified clients.
2. Authority for determining that an engagement is complete subject to final partner approval if required.

---

* Refers to employees irrespective of their functional classification (e.g., audit, tax, management advisory services).

3. Responsibility for client relationships (for example, negotiating and collecting fees for engagements, marketing the firm's services).
4. Responsibility for such administrative functions as assignment of personnel to engagements, hiring, and training of personnel.
5. Existence of profit-sharing as a significant feature of total compensation.

Significant influence

A person or entity can exercise significant influence over the operating, financial, or accounting policies of another entity if, for example, the person or entity

1. Is connected with the entity as a promoter, underwriter, or voting trustee.
2. Is connected with the entity in a policy making position related to the entity's primary operating, financial, or accounting policies, such as chief executive officer, chief operating officer, chief financial officer, chief accounting officer, and the key assistants who can influence their decisions.
3. Is connected with the entity in a capacity equivalent to that of a general partner.
4. Is connected with the entity as a director other than honorary.
5. Meets the criteria established in paragraph 17 of Accounting Principles Board Opinion no. 18, *The Equity Method of Accounting for Investments in Common Stock,* to determine the ability of an investor to exercise such influence.
6. Holds 20 percent or more of the limited partnership interests if the entity is a limited partnership.

The foregoing examples are not necessarily all-inclusive.

Effect of Family Relationships

Spouses and dependent persons

The term "he and his firm" includes spouses (whether or not dependent) and dependent persons (whether or not related) for all purposes of complying with rule 101 subject to the following exception:

The exception is that the independence of the member and his firm will not normally be impaired solely because of employment of a spouse or dependent person by a client if the employment is in a position that does not allow "significant influence" (as discussed above) over the client's operating, financial, or accounting policies. However, if such employment is in a position where the person's activities are "audit sensitive" (even though not a position of significant influence), the member should not participate in the engagement.

Generally, a person's activities would be considered audit sensitive if such activities are normally an element of or subject to significant internal accounting controls. For example, the following positions, which are not intended to be all-inclusive, would normally be considered audit sensitive (even though not positions of significant influence): cashier, internal auditor, general accounting clerk, purchasing agent, or inventory warehouse supervisor.

Nondependent close relatives

The term "he and his firm" excludes nondependent close relatives of the persons described in (1) through (4) of that definition. Nevertheless, in circumstances discussed below, the independence of a member or a firm can be impaired because of a nondependent close relative.

Close relatives are nondependent children, brothers, sisters, grandparents, parents, parents-in-law, and their respective spouses.

The independence of a member and his firm is impaired with respect to the enterprise if

1. A proprietor, partner, shareholder, or professional employee, any of whom are participating in the engagement, has a close relative who (a) can exercise significant influence over the operating, financial, or accounting policies of the client, (b) is otherwise employed in a position where the person's activities are "audit sensitive," or (c) has a financial interest in the client which is material to the close relative and of which the proprietor, partner, shareholder, or professional employee has knowledge.
2. A proprietor, partner, shareholder, or managerial employee, any of whom are located in an office participating in a significant portion of the engagement, has a close relative who can exercise significant influence over the operating, financial, or accounting policies of the client.

Other considerations

Members must be aware that it is impossible to enumerate all circumstances wherein the appearance of a member's independence might be questioned by third parties because of family or dependent person relationships. In situations involving assessment of the association of any relative or dependent person with a client, members must consider whether the strength of personal and business relationships between the member and the relative or dependent person, considered in conjunction with the specified association with the client, would lead a reasonable person aware of all the facts and taking into consideration normal strength of character and normal behavior under the circumstances to conclude that the situation poses an unacceptable threat to the member's objectivity and appearance of independence.

Interpretation under Rule 102—Integrity and Objectivity

102–1—Knowing misrepresentations in the preparation of financial statements or records. A member who knowingly makes, or permits or directs another to make, false and misleading entries in an entity's financial statements or records shall be considered to have knowingly misrepresented facts in violation of rule 102.

Interpretations under Rule 201—General Standards

201–1—Competence. A member who accepts a professional engagement implies that he has the necessary competence to complete the engagement according to professional standards, applying his knowledge and skill with reasonable care and diligence, but he does not assume a responsibility for infallibility of knowledge or judgment.

Competence in the practice of public accounting involves both the technical qualifications of the member and his staff and his ability to supervise and evaluate the quality of the work performed. Competence relates both to knowledge of the profession's standards, techniques and the technical subject matter involved, and to the capability to exercise sound judgment in applying such knowledge to each engagement.

The member may have the knowledge required to complete an engagement professionally before undertaking it. In many cases, however, additional research or consultation with others may be necessary during the course of the engagement. This does not ordinarily represent a lack of competence, but rather is a normal part of the professional conduct of an engagement.

However, if a CPA is unable to gain sufficient competence through these means, he should suggest, in fairness to his client and the public, the engagement of someone competent to perform the needed service, either independently or as an associate.

201–2—Forecasts. Rule 201 does not prohibit a member from preparing, or assisting a client in the preparation of, forecasts of the results of future transactions. When a member's name is associated with such forecasts, there shall be the presumption that such data may be used by parties other than the client. Therefore, full disclosure must be made of the sources of the information used and the major assumptions made in the preparation of the statements and analyses, the character of the work performed by the member, and the degree of the responsibility he is taking.

201–3—Shopping for Accounting or Auditing Standards. If a client of another public accountant who is retained to report on the client's financial statements requests a member to provide professional advice on accounting or auditing matters in connection with the financial statements of that client, the member before giving such advice must consult with the other accountant to ascertain that he is aware of all the available facts relevant to forming a professional judgment on the appropriate accounting or auditing standard to be applied. In deciding whether to provide such advice, the member should bear in mind that, among other things, the client and its public accountant may have disagreed about the facts, accounting or auditing standards, or similar significant matters.

Interpretation under Rule 202—Auditing Standards

202–1—Unaudited financial statements. Rule 202 does not preclude a member from associating himself with the unaudited financial statements of his clients. The Rule states in part that "A member shall not permit his name to be associated with financial statements in such a manner as to imply that he is acting as an independent public accountant unless he has complied with the *applicable* (Italics provided) generally accepted auditing standards promulgated by the Institute."

In applying this provision to situations in which a member's name is associated with unaudited financial statements, it is necessary to recognize that the standards were specifically written to apply to audited financial statements. The fourth reporting standard, however, was made sufficiently broad to be applicable to unaudited financial statements as well.

The fourth reporting standard states in part:

> ". . . In *all* cases where an auditor's name is associated with financial statements, the report should contain a clear-cut indication of the character of the auditor's examination, *if any,* and the degree of responsibility he is taking." (Italics provided)

Those sections of *Statements on Auditing Standards* and related guides which deal with unaudited financial statements provide guidance to members associated with such statements.

Interpretations under Rule 203—Accounting Principles

203–1—Departures from established accounting principles. Rule 203 was adopted to require compliance with accounting principles promulgated by the body designated by Council to establish such principles. There is a strong presumption that adherence to officially established accounting principles would in nearly all instances result in financial statements that are not misleading.

However, in the establishment of accounting principles it is difficult to anticipate all of the circumstances to which such principles might be applied. This rule therefore recognizes that upon occasion there may be unusual circumstances where the literal application of pronouncements on accounting principles would have the effect of rendering financial statements misleading. In such cases, the proper accounting treatment is that which will render the financial statements not misleading.

The question of what constitutes unusual circumstances as referred to in Rule 203 is a matter of professional judgment involving the ability to support the position that adherence to a promulgated principle would be regarded generally by reasonable men as producing a misleading result.

Examples of events which may justify departures from a principle are new legislation or the evolution of a new form of business transaction. An unusual degree of materiality or the existence of conflicting industry practices are examples of circumstances which would not ordinarily be regarded as unusual in the context of Rule 203.

203-2—Status of FASB interpretations.   Council is authorized under Rule 203 to designate a body to establish accounting principles and has designated the Financial Accounting Standards Board as such body. Council also has resolved that FASB Statements of Financial Accounting Standards, together with those Accounting Research Bulletins and APB Opinions which are not superseded by action of the FASB, constitute accounting principles as contemplated in Rule 203.

In determining the existence of a departure from an accounting principle established by a Statement of Financial Accounting Standards, Accounting Research Bulletin or APB Opinion encompassed by Rule 203, the division of professional ethics will construe such Statement, Bulletin or Opinion in the light of any interpretations thereof issued by the FASB.

203-3—FASB statements that establish standards for disclosure outside of the basic financial statements.   The Council resolution designating the Financial Accounting Standards Board as the body to establish accounting principles pursuant to Rule 203 through the issuance of Statements of Financial Accounting Standards relates solely to the provisions of Statements of Financial Accounting Standards (SFASs) which established accounting principles with respect to basic financial statements (balance sheets, statements of income, statements of changes in retained earnings, disclosures of changes in other categories of stockholder's equity, statements of changes in financial position, and descriptions of accounting policies and related notes).

SFASs which stipulate that certain information should be disclosed outside the basic financial statements are not covered by Rule 203.

Interpretation under Rule 301—Confidential Client Information

301-1—Confidential information and technical standards.   The prohibition against disclosure of confidential information obtained in the course of a professional engagement does not apply to disclosure of such information when required to properly discharge the member's responsibility according to the profession's standards. The prohibition would not apply, for example, to disclosure, as required by Section 561 of Statement on Auditing Standards No. 1, of subsequent discovery of facts existing at the date of the auditor's report which would have affected the auditor's report had he been aware of such facts.

Interpretations under Rule 501—Acts Discreditable

501–1—Client's records and accountant's workpapers. Retention of client records after a demand is made for them is an act discreditable to the profession in violation of Rule 501. The fact that the statutes of the state in which a member practices may specifically grant him a lien on all client records in his possession does not change the ethical standard that it would be a violation of the Code to retain the records to enforce payment.

A member's working papers are his property and need not be surrendered to the client. However, in some instances a member's working papers will contain data which should properly be reflected in the client's books and records but which for convenience have not been duplicated therein, with the result that the client's records are incomplete. In such instances, the portion of the working papers containing such data constitutes part of the client's records, and copies should be made available to the client upon request.

If a member is engaged to perform certain work for a client and the engagement is terminated prior to the completion of such work, the member is required to return or furnish copies of only those records originally given to the member by the client.

Examples of working papers that are considered to be client's records would include:

a. Worksheets in lieu of books of original entry (e.g., listings and distributions of cash receipts or cash disbursements on columnar working paper).

b. Worksheets in lieu of general ledger or subsidiary ledgers, such as accounts receivable, job cost and equipment ledgers or similar depreciation records.

c. All adjusting and closing journal entries and supporting details. (If the supporting details are not fully set forth in the explanation of the journal entry, but are contained in analyses of accounts in the accountant's working papers, then copies of such analyses must be furnished to the client.)

d. Consolidating or combining journal entries and worksheets and supporting detail used in arriving at final figures incorporated in an end product such as financial statements or tax returns.

Any working papers developed by the member incident to the performance of his engagement which do not result in changes to the clients' records or are not in themselves part of the records ordinarily maintained by such clients, are considered to be solely "accountant's working papers" and are not the property of the client, e.g.:

The member may make extensive analyses of inventory or other accounts as part of his selective audit procedures. Even if such analyses have been prepared by client personnel at the request of the member, they nevertheless are considered to be part of the accountant's working papers.

Only to the extent such analyses result in changes to the client's records would the member be required to furnish the details from his working papers in support of the journal entries recording such changes unless the journal entries themselves contain all necessary details.

Once the member has returned the client's records to him or furnished him with copies of such records and/or necessary supporting data, he has discharged his obligation in this regard and need not comply with any subsequent requests to again furnish such records.

If the member has retained in his files copies of a client's records already in possession of the client, the member is not required to return such copies to the client.

501–2—Discrimination in employment practices.   Discrimination based on race, color, religion, sex, age or national origin in hiring, promotion or salary practices is presumed to constitute an act discreditable to the profession in violation of Rule 501.

501–3—Failure to follow standards and/or procedures or other requirements in governmental audits.   Engagements for audits of government grants, government units or other recipients of government monies typically require that such audits be in compliance with government audit standards, guides, procedures, statutes, rules, and regulations, in addition to generally accepted auditing standards. If a member has accepted such an engagement and undertakes an obligation to follow specified government audit standards, guides, procedures, statutes, rules and regulations, in addition to generally accepted auditing standards, he is obligated to follow such requirements. Failure to do so is an act discreditable to the profession in violation of Rule 501, unless the member discloses in his report the fact that such requirements were not followed and the reasons therefor.

501–4—Negligence in the preparation of financial statements or records.   A member who, by virtue of his negligence, makes, or permits or directs another to make, false and misleading entries in the financial statements or records of an entity shall be considered to have committed an act discreditable to the profession in violation of rule 501.

Interpretations under Rule 502—Advertising and Other Forms of Solicitation

502–1—Informational advertising. Advertising that is informative and objective is permitted. Such advertising should be in good taste and be professionally dignified. There are no other restrictions, such as on the type of advertising media, frequency of placement, size, artwork, or type style. Some examples of informative and objective content are—

1. Information about the member and the member's firm, such as—
   a. Names, addresses, telephone numbers, number of partners, shareholders or employees, office hours, foreign language competence, and date the firm was established.
   b. Services offered and fees for such services, including hourly rates and fixed fees.
   c. Educational and professional attainments, including date and place of certifications, schools attended, dates of graduation, degrees received, and memberships in professional associations.
2. Statements of policy or position made by a member or a member's firm related to the practice of public accounting or addressed to a subject of public interest.

502–2—False, misleading, or deceptive acts. Advertising or other forms of solicitation that are false, misleading, or deceptive are not in the public interest and are prohibited. Such activities include those that—

1. Create false or unjustified expectations of favorable results.
2. Imply the ability to influence any court, tribunal, regulatory agency, or similar body or official.
3. Consist of self-laudatory statements that are not based on verifiable facts.
4. Make comparisons with other CPAs that are not based on verifiable facts.
5. Contain testimonials or endorsements.
6. Contain a representation that specific professional services in current or future periods will be performed for a stated fee, estimated fee or fee range when it was likely at the time of the representation that such fees would be substantially increased and the prospective client was not advised of that likelihood.
7. Contain any other representations that would be likely to cause a reasonable person to misunderstand or be deceived.

[502–3]—[Deleted]

[502–4]—[Deleted]

502–5—Engagements obtained through efforts of third parties.   Members are often asked to render professional services to clients or customers of third parties. Such third parties may have obtained such clients or customers as the result of their advertising and solicitation efforts.

Members are permitted to enter into such engagements. The member has the responsibility to ascertain that all promotional efforts are within the bounds of the Rules of Conduct. Such action is required because the members will receive the benefits of such efforts by third parties, and members must not do through others what they are prohibited from doing themselves by the Rules of Conduct.

Interpretation under Rule 503—Commission

503–1—Fees in payment for services.   Rule 503, which prohibits payment of a commission to obtain a client, was adopted to avoid a client's having to pay fees for which he did not receive commensurate services. However, payment of fees to a referring public accountant for professional services to the successor firm or to the client in connection with the engagement is not prohibited.

Interpretations under Rule 505—Form of Practice and Name

505–1—Investment in commercial accounting corporation.   A member in the practice of public accounting may have a financial interest in a commercial corporation which performs for the public services of a type performed by public accountants and whose characteristics do not conform to resolutions of Council, provided such interest is not material to the corporation's net worth, and the member's interest in and relation to the corporation is solely that of an investor.

505–2—Application of rules of conduct to members who operate a separate business.   Members in public practice who participate in the operation of a separate business that offers to clients one or more types of services rendered by public accountants will be considered to be in the practice of public accounting in the conduct of that business. In such a case, members will be required to observe all of the Rules of Conduct in the operation of the separate business.

In addition, members who are not otherwise in public practice must observe the Rules of Conduct in the operation of their business if they hold out to the public as being a CPA or public accountant and at the same time offer to clients one or more types of services rendered by public accountants.

QUESTIONS AND PROBLEMS

Professional Ethics

19–1. Is there a single code of ethics for the public accounting profession? Explain.

19–2. To what groups does the CPA have ethical responsibilities?

19–3. R. Jones, CPA, placed an ad in a charity program saying "Compliments of R. Jones, CPA." Is this ethical? Explain.

19–4. CPA J is called into federal district court. The government subpoenas his working papers for a particular client. J refuses to release them, claiming that he is a professional and therefore has "privileged communication" with that client. Is CPA J's position correct? Explain.

19–5. Steve Smith, CPA, is moving his office to a new building. He sends a notice to this effect to the local newspaper, which publishes it. Is his action correct? Explain.

19–6. The AICPA allows certain forms of advertising and other types of solicitation.
    a. Discuss the types of advertising and other solicitation in which CPAs are allowed to engage.
    b. What kinds of media may CPAs use to advertise?
    c. How often may a CPA advertise?
    d. What information may a CPA include in an advertisement?

19–7. List some kinds of advertising and other types of solicitation that, if engaged in by CPAs, would be considered false, misleading, or deceptive.

19–8. Does the *AICPA Code of Ethics* cover tax practice and management services? Explain.

19–9. Will suspension of a CPA from the AICPA prevent the individual from practicing as a CPA? Explain.

19–10. S. H. Smith, CPA, is building her own office building. She erects a sign on the building site which reads: "This is the future home of S. H. Smith, CPA." Comment on the CPA's action.

19–11. CPA R is retained by S. Jones, attorney-at-law, to serve as an expert witness in a fraud case. Jones represents the plaintiff and promises R a fee of 5 percent of any damages won in the case but nothing if the case is lost. Comment on this situation.
(AICPA, adapted)

19–12. CPA K has decided to add a systems analyst to her staff who specializes in developing computer systems. Must CPA K be able to perform all of the services that the specialist can perform to be able to supervise the systems analyst?
(AICPA, adapted)

19–13. The CPA firm of ABC acquires that portion of an insurance brokerage firm that performs actuarial and administrative services in connection with employee benefit plans. This new operation would be conducted as a separate partnership. Comment on this situation.
(AICPA, adapted)

19–14. CPA J places the following advertisement in the business section of the local newspaper:

> Having problems with your independent auditor?
>
> Call CPA J at 555-1834 to find out how inexpensive our unqualified opinions are. We have no dissatisfied clients.

Comment on this situation.

19–15. Select the best answer for each of the following items:

a. A CPA accepts an engagement for a professional service without violating the *AICPA Code of Professional Ethics* if the service involves:

(1) The preparation of cost projections for submission to a governmental agency as an application for a rate increase and the fee will be paid if there is a rate increase.

(2) Tax preparation and the fee will be based on whether the CPA signs the tax return prepared.

(3) A litigatory matter, and the fee is not known but is to be determined by a district court.

(4) Tax return preparation and the fee is to be based on the amount of taxes saved, if any.

b. Which of the following statements best describes why the public accounting profession has deemed it essential to promulgate a code of ethics and to establish a mechanism for enforcing observance of the code?

(1) A distinguishing mark of a profession is the acceptance of responsibility to the public.

(2) A prerequisite to success is the establishment of an ethical code that stresses primarily the professional's responsibility to clients and colleagues.

(3) A requirement of most state laws calls for the profession to establish a code of ethics.

(4) An essential means of self-protection for the profession is the establishment of flexible ethical standards by the profession.

c. The *AICPA Code of Professional Ethics* states, in part, that a CPA should maintain integrity and objectivity. Objectivity in the *Code* refers to a CPA's ability to:

(1) Maintain an impartial attitude on all matters which come under the CPA's review.

(2) Independently distinguish between accounting practices that are acceptable and those that are not.

(3) Be unyielding in all matters dealing with auditing procedures.

(4) Independently choose between alternate accounting principles and auditing standards.

d. A CPA who has given correct tax advice that is later affected by changes in the tax law is required to:

(1) Notify the client upon learning of any change.

(2) Notify the client only when the CPA is actively assisting with implementing the advice or is obliged to do so by specific agreement.

(3) Notify the Internal Revenue Service.

(4) Take no action if the client has already followed the advice unless the client asks the question again.

   e. A CPA's retention of client records as a means of enforcing payment of an overdue audit fee is an action that is:
   1. Considered acceptable by the *AICPA Code of Professional Ethics.*
   2. Ill-advised since it would impair the CPA's independence with respect to the client.
   3. Considered discreditable to the profession.
   4. A violation of generally accepted auditing standards.

   f. Upon discovering irregularities in a client's tax return that the client would not correct, a CPA withdraws from the engagement. How should the CPA respond if asked by the successor CPA why the relationship was terminated?
   1. "It was a misunderstanding."
   2. "I suggest you get the client's permission for us to discuss all matters freely."
   3. "I suggest you ask the client."
   4. "I found irregularities in the tax return which the client would not correct."

   (AICPA, adapted)

19–16. A prospective client asks H. T. Smith, CPA, to perform a management services engagement. Smith, realizing the engagement is beyond her abilities, refers the prospective client to R. Jones, CPA, who performs the engagement. R. Jones sends H. T. Smith 10 percent of the fee in payment for the referral. Comment.

19–17. E. E. Johne is a CPA. He is also an attorney. Johne lives in a small town that has very few CPAs and very few lawyers. To supply the community residents with full professional services, Johne decides to practice both as a CPA and as an attorney. Comment on this situation.

19–18. Sally Root, CPA, has a large practice that consists mostly of opinion audits. Being a sole practitioner, she is concerned that her working papers and reports do not receive as much review as they would in larger firms. Therefore, she asks the AICPA to periodically send in CPAs from other firms to review her working papers and reports to offer constructive criticisms. Is Root violating the rule on confidentiality?

19–19. Alan Room, CPA, a partner of Room & Room, CPAs, meets Alvin Staff, a senior accountant with another CPA firm, at a state society meeting. Room is very impressed with Staff and during their conversation offers Staff a job at a very high salary. Comment.

19–20. J. C. Conman, president of Marginal Corp., needs audited financial statements. He asks Mr. Honest, CPA, to estimate his fees for such an engagement. After a careful evaluation Honest gives Conman an estimate range. Conman says that the estimate is too high but says he would be happy to pay Honest 4 percent of net income for that year. Comment on this situation.

19–21. J. C. Wise, CPA, has a very large client, Future Inc., that needs a large bank loan. The bank, as part of the loan application, asks Future for a forecast of its operations for the next three years. The president of Future is very anxious to obtain the loan. He asks Wise to attest to the forecast. Comment.

19–22. I. M. Old, CPA, has a large practice and is approaching retirement. J. C. Young, CPA, is interested in purchasing Old's practice. To determine a fair purchase price for his practice, Old lets Young examine all of his records, working papers, and so on. Comment.

19–23. R. A. Sideline, CPA, decides to render an additional service for her clients by arranging for them to purchase office supplies from a particular company at a reduced price. The supplier gives Sideline one percent of all such sales. Comment.

(AICPA, adapted)

19–24. R. A. Bill, CPA, is asked by Small, Inc., a tax client, whether the corporation should file Form 8982 with its state income tax return. Form 8982 requires Small, Inc., to disclose the amount of inventory on hand. The state department of taxation always passes copies of Form 8982 on to the county property tax assessor. Since the penalty for not filing a Form 8982 is a $10 fine, Bill advises Small, Inc., not to file a form 8982. Comment on this advice.

19–25. An auditor's report was appended to the financial statements of Worthmore, Inc. The statements consisted of a balance sheet as of November 30, 1985, and statements of income, retained earnings, and changes in financial position for the year then ended. The first two paragraphs of the report contained the wording of the standard unqualified audit report, and a third paragraph read as follows:

> The wives of two partners of our firm owned a material investment in the outstanding common stock of Worthmore, Inc. during the fiscal year ending November 30, 1985. The aforementioned individuals disposed of their holdings of Worthmore, Inc., on December 3, 1985, in a transaction that did not result in a profit or a loss. This information is included in our report in order to comply with certain disclosure requirements of the *Code of Professional Ethics* of the American Institute of Certified Public Accountants.

Bell & Davis
Certified Public Accountants

Required:

a. Was the CPA firm of Bell & Davis independent with respect to the fiscal 1985 examination of Worthmore, Inc.'s financial statement? Explain.
b. Do you find Bell & Davis' auditor's report satisfactory? Explain.
c. Assume that no members of Bell & Davis or any members of their families held any financial interests in Worthmore, Inc. during 1985. For each of the following cases, indicate if independence would be lacking on the part of Bell & Davis, assuming that Worthmore, Inc. is a profit-seeking enterprise. In each case, explain your answer.
  (1) Two directors of Worthmore, Inc. became partners in the CPA firm of Bell & Davis on July 1, 1985, resigning their directorships on that date.
  (2) During 1985, the former controller of Worthmore, now a Bell & Davis partner, was frequently called on for assistance by Worthmore. He made decisions for Worthmore's management regarding fixed asset acquisitions and the company's product marketing mix. In addition, he conducted a computer feasibility study for Worthmore.   (AICPA, adapted)

19–26. *Part 1.* During 1985, your client, Big Corporation, requested that you conduct a feasibility study to advise management of the best way the corporation can utilize electronic data processing equipment and which computer, if any, best meets the corporation's requirements. You are technically competent in this area and accept the engagement. Upon completion of your study, the corporation accepts your suggestions and installs the computer and related equipment that you recommended.

Required:

a. Discuss the effect the acceptance of this management services engagement would have on your independence in expressing an opinion on Big Corporation's financial statements.

b. Instead of accepting the engagement, assume that you recommended Ike Mackey, of the CPA firm of Brown and Mackey, who is qualified in specialized services. Upon completion of the engagement, your client requests that Mackey's partner, John Brown, perform services in other areas. Should Brown accept the engagement? Discuss.

c. A local printer of data processing forms customarily offers a commission for recommending him as supplier. The client is aware of the commission offer and suggests that Mackey accept it. Would it be proper for Mackey to accept the commission with the client's approval? Discuss.

Part 2. Alex Pratt, a retired partner of your CPA firm, has just been appointed to the board of directors of Palmer Corporation, your firm's client. Pratt is also a member of your firm's income tax committee, which meets monthly to discuss income tax problems of the partnership's clients. The partnership pays Pratt $100 for each committee meeting he attends and a monthly retirement benefit of $1,000.

Required:

Discuss the effect of Pratt's appointment to the board of directors of Palmer Corporation on your partnership's independence in expressing an opinion on the Palmer Corporation's financial statements. (AICPA, adapted)

19–27. Independence traditionally has been associated with the CPA's function of auditing and expressing opinions on financial statements.

Required:

a. What is meant by "independence" as applied to the CPA's function of auditing and expressing opinions on financial statements? Discuss.

b. The Rocky Hill Corporation was formed on October 1, 1985, and its fiscal year will end on September 30, 1986. You audited the corporation's opening balance sheet and rendered an unqualified opinion on it.

A month after rendering your report, you are offered the position of secretary of the company because of the need for a complete set of officers and for convenience in signing various documents. You will have no financial interest in the company through stock ownership or otherwise, will receive no salary, will not keep the books, and will not have any influence on its financial matters other than occasional advice on income tax matters and similar advice normally given a client by a CPA.

Assume that you accept the offer but plan to resign the position before conducting your annual audit with the intention of again assuming the office after rendering an opinion on the statements. Can you render an independent opinion on the financial statements? Discuss. (AICPA, adapted)

19–28. Tom Jencks, CPA, conducts a public accounting practice. In 1985 Mr. Jencks and Harold Swann, a non-CPA, organized Electro-Data Corporation to specialize in computerized bookkeeping services. Mr. Jencks and Mr. Swann each supplied 50 percent of Electro-Data's capital, and each holds 50 percent of the capital stock. Mr. Swann is the salaried general manager of Electro-Data. Mr. Jencks is affiliated with the corporation only as a stockholder; he receives no salary and does not participate in day-to-day management. However, he has transferred all of his bookkeeping accounts to the corporation and recommends its services whenever possible.

Required:

Organizing your presentation around Mr. Jencks' involvement with Electro-Data Corporation, discuss the propriety of:

a. A CPA's participation in an enterprise offering computerized bookkeeping services.
b. The use of advertising by an enterprise in which a CPA holds an interest.
c. A CPA's transfer of bookkeeping accounts to a service company.
d. A CPA's recommendation of a particular bookkeeping service company.

(AICPA, adapted)

19–29. Judd Hanlon, CPA, was engaged to prepare the federal income tax return for the Guild Corporation for the year ended December 31, 1985. This is Mr. Hanlon's first engagement of any kind for the Guild Corporation.

In preparing the 1985 return, Mr. Hanlon finds an error on the 1984 return. The 1984 depreciation deduction was overstated significantly—accumulated depreciation brought forward from 1983 to 1984 was understated, and thus the 1984 base for declining balance depreciation was overstated.

Mr. Hanlon reported the error to Guild's controller, the officer responsible for tax returns. The controller stated; "Let the revenue agent find the error." He further instructed Mr. Hanlon to carry forward the material overstatement of the depreciable base to the 1985 depreciation computation. The controller noted that this error also has been made in the financial records for 1984 and 1985 and offered to furnish Mr. Hanlon with a letter assuming full responsibility for this treatment.

Required:

a. Evaluate Mr. Hanlon's handling of this situation.
b. Discuss the additional action that Mr. Hanlon should now undertake.

(AICPA, adapted)

Accountants' Liability

19–30. Is it true that a partner in a CPA firm can be held liable for acts of the other partners and of employees in the firm?

19–31. Is it true that an auditor may be held liable for his or her actions even though the advice of third-party experts was relied on in taking these actions?

19–32. Is the relationship between an auditor and the client a confidential relationship? Does the auditor have privileged communications; that is, can the CPA refuse to divulge information concerning a client in a courtroom when directed to do so?

19–33. Describe the auditor's liability to clients. Define subrogation.

19–34. Define what is meant by the term "privity." Of what significance is privity?

19–35. Describe the importance of having a clearly worded contract or engagement letter.

19–36. Distinguish between ordinary negligence, gross negligence, and fraud.

19–37. Is contributory negligence by a client a valid defense for the independent auditor whenever it can be proved? Comment.

19–38. Describe the auditor's liability to primary beneficiaries.

19–39. Describe the auditor's liability to unidentified third parties.

19–40. Select the *best* answer for each of the following questions:
  a. The traditional common law rules regarding accountants' liability to third parties for negligence:
  (1) Remain substantially unchanged since their inception.
  (2) Were more stringent than the rules currently applicable.
  (3) Are of relatively minor importance to the accountant.
  (4) Have been substantially changed at both the federal and state levels.
  b. The *1136 Tenants* case was chiefly important because of its emphasis upon the legal liability of the CPA when associated with:
  (1) A review of interim statements.
  (2) Unaudited financial statements.
  (3) An audit resulting in a disclaimer of opinion.
  (4) Letters for underwriters.
  c. You are a CPA retained by the manager of a cooperative retirement village to do "write-up work." You are expected to prepare unaudited financial statements with each page marked "unaudited" and accompanied by a disclaimer of opinion stating no audit was made. In performing the work you discover that there are no invoices to support $25,000 of the manager's claimed disbursements. The manager informs you that all the disbursements are proper. What should you do?
  (1) Submit the expected statements but omit the $25,000 of unsupported disbursements.
  (2) Include the unsupported disbursements in the statements since you are not expected to make an audit.
  (3) Obtain from the manager a written statement that you informed him of the missing invoices and his assurance that the disbursements are proper.
  (4) Notify the owners that some of the claimed disbursements are unsupported and withdraw if the situation is not satisfactorily resolved.
  d. Winslow Manufacturing, Inc., sought a $200,000 loan from National Lending Corporation. National Lending insisted that audited financial statements be submitted before it would extend credit. Winslow agreed to this and also agreed to pay the audit fee. An audit was performed by an independent CPA who submitted his report to Winslow to be used solely for the purpose of negotiating a loan from National. National, upon reviewing the audited financial statements, decided in good faith *not* to extend the credit desired. Certain ratios, which as a matter of policy were used by National in reaching its decision, were deemed too low. Winslow used copies of the audited financial statements to obtain credit elsewhere. It was subsequently learned that the CPA, despite the exercise of reasonable care, had failed to discover a sophisticated embezzlement scheme

by Winslow's chief accountant. Under these circumstances, what liability does the CPA have?

(1) The CPA is liable to third parties who extended credit.

(2) The CPA is liable to Winslow to repay the audit fee because credit was *not* extended by National.

(3) The CPA is liable to Winslow for any losses Winslow suffered as a result of failure to discover the embezzlement.

(4) The CPA is *not* liable to any of the parties.

e. Martinson is a licensed CPA. One of his clients is suing him for negligence alleging that he failed to meet generally accepted auditing standards in the current year's audit thereby failing to discover large thefts of inventory. Under the circumstances:

(1) Martinson is *not* bound by generally accepted auditing standards unless he is a member of the AICPA.

(2) Martinson's failure to meet generally accepted auditing standards would result in liability.

(3) Generally accepted auditing standards do not currently cover the procedures which must be used in verifying inventory for balance sheet purposes.

(4) If Martinson failed to meet generally accepted auditing standards, he would undoubtedly be found to have committed the tort of fraud.

f. DMO Enterprises, Inc., engaged the accounting firm of Martin, Seals & Anderson to perform its annual audit. The firm performed the audit, in a competent, non-negligent manner and billed DMO for $16,000, the agreed fee. Shortly after delivery of the audited financial statements, Hightower, the assistant controller, disappeared, taking with him $28,000 of DMO's funds. It was then discovered that Hightower had been engaged in a highly sophisticated, novel defalcation scheme during the past year. He had previously embezzled $35,000 of DMO funds. DMO has refused to pay the accounting firm's fee and is seeking to recover the $63,000 that was stolen by Hightower. Which of the following is correct?

(1) The accountants cannot recover their fee and are liable for $63,000.

(2) The accountants are entitled to collect their fee and are not liable for $63,000.

(3) DMO is entitled to rescind the audit contract and thus is not liable for the $16,000 fee, but it cannot recover damages.

(4) DMO is entitled to recover the $28,000 defalcation and is not liable for the $16,000 fee. (AICPA, adapted)

19–41. Jones, a CPA engaged in practice without any partners or associates, was retained by Abrams to audit his accounts and prepare a report including his professional opinion for submission to a prospective purchaser of Abrams' business. When the field work was about half completed Jones became seriously ill and was unable to complete the engagement. The prospective buyer lost interest and the sale of the business fell through. Abrams sues Jones for breach of his contract. Does he have a valid right of action for damages? Explain the legal principles involved.

(AICPA, adapted)

19–42. Abraham Jenkins, a CPA, performed an audit for Hiram Blanchard. Later, in a legal proceeding involving Blanchard as a party, Jenkins was subpoenaed as a witness.

He was asked to testify concerning Blanchard's financial affairs based on information he acquired during his audit. He refused to testify on the ground that such information is confidential and is privileged as between accountant and client.

a. The proceeding is a civil action for breach of contract in a state court. There is no applicable state statute with respect to privileged communications between accountants and their clients, and the common law prevails. Would Blanchard's refusal to testify be upheld? Explain.

b. Would your answer to "a" change if the proceeding is in a state where there is a statute relating to communications between accountants and clients?

(AICPA, adapted)

19–43. Meglow Corporation manufactured ladies' dresses and blouses. Because its cash position was deteriorating, Meglow sought a loan from Busch Factors. Busch had previously extended $25,000 credit to Meglow but refused to lend any additional money without obtaining copies of Meglow's audited financial statements.

Meglow contacted the CPA firm of Watkins, Winslow and Watkins to perform the audit. In arranging for the examination, Meglow clearly indicated that its purpose was to satisfy Busch Factors as to the Corporation's sound financial condition and thus to obtain an additional loan of $50,000. Watkins, Winslow & Watkins accepted the engagement, performed the examination in a negligent manner (ordinary negligence) and rendered an unqualified auditor's opinion. If an adequate examination had been performed, the financial statements would have been found to be materially misleading.

Meglow submitted the audited financial statements to Busch Factors and obtained an additional loan of $35,000. Busch refused to lend more than that amount. After several other factors also refused, Meglow finally was able to persuade Maxwell Department Stores, one of its customers, to lend the additional $15,000. Maxwell relied upon the financial statements examined by Watkins, Winslow & Watkins.

Meglow is now in bankruptcy and Busch seeks to collect from Watkins, Winslow & Watkins the $60,000 it loaned Meglow. Maxwell seeks to recover from Watkins, Winslow & Watkins the $15,000 it loaned Meglow.

Required:

a. Will Busch recover? Explain.

b. Will Maxwell recover? Explain. (AICPA, adapted)

19–44. The CPA firm of Winston & Mall was engaged by the Fast Cargo Company, a retailer, to examine its financial statements for the year ended August 31, 1986. Winston & Mall followed generally accepted auditing standards and examined transactions on a test basis. A sample of disbursements was used to test vouchers payable, cash disbursements, and receiving and purchasing procedures. An investigation of the sample disclosed several instances where purchases had been recorded and paid for without the required receiving report being included in the file of supporting documents. This was properly noted in the working papers by Martin, the junior who did the sampling. Mall, the partner in charge, called these facts to the attention of Harris, Fast Cargo's chief accountant, who told him not to worry about it, that he would make certain that these receiving reports were properly included in the voucher file. Mall accepted this and did nothing further to investigate or follow up on this situation.

Harris was engaged in a fraudulent scheme whereby he diverted the merchandise to a private warehouse where he leased space and sent the invoices to Fast Cargo for payment. The scheme was discovered later by a special investigation and a preliminary estimate indicates that the loss to Fast Cargo will be in excess of $20,000.

Required:

a. What is the liability, if any, of Winston & Mall in this situation? Discuss.
b. What additional steps, if any, should have been taken by Mall? Explain.

(AICPA, adapted)

19–45. Barton & Company have been engaged to examine the financial statements for Mirror Manufacturing Corporation for the year ended September 30, 1986. Mirror Manufacturing needed additional cash to continue its operations. To raise funds it agreed to sell its common stock investment in a subsidiary. The buyers insisted upon having the proceeds placed in escrow because of the possibility of a major contingent tax liability. Carter, president of Mirror, explained this to Barton, the partner in charge of the Mirror audit. He indicated that he wished to show the proceeds from the sale of the subsidiary as an unrestricted current account receivable. He stated that in his opinion the government's claim for additional taxes was groundless and that he needed an "uncluttered" balance sheet and a "clean" auditor's opinion to obtain additional working capital.

Barton issued an unqualified opinion on the financial statements, which did not refer to the contingent liability and did not properly describe the escrow arrangements.

The government's claim for additional taxes proved to be valid and, pursuant to the agreement with the buyers, the purchase price of the subsidiary was reduced by $450,000. This, coupled with other adverse developments, caused Mirror to become insolvent, with assets to cover only some of its liabilities. Barton & Company is being sued by several of Mirror's creditors who loaned money relying on the financial statements upon which it rendered an unqualified opinion.

Required:

What is the liability, if any, of Barton & Company to the creditors of Mirror Manufacturing? Explain.

(AICPA, adapted)

19–46. In conducting the examination of the financial statements of the Farber Corporation for the year ended September 30, 1986, Harper, a CPA, discovered that Nance, the president, who was also a significant (51 percent) shareholder, had borrowed substantial amounts of money from the Corporation. Nance indicated that the money would be promptly repaid, and that the financial statements were being prepared for internal use only. He requested that these loans not be accounted for separately in the financial statements, but be included in the other current accounts receivable. Harper acquiesced in this request. Nance subsequently became insolvent and was unable to repay the loans.

Required:

What is Harper's liability? Explain.

(AICPA, adapted)

19–47. Risk Capital Limited, a Delaware corporation, was considering the purchase of a substantial amount of the treasury stock held by Florida Sunshine Corporation, a closely held corporation. Initial discussions with the Florida Sunshine Corporation began late in 1986.

Wilson and Wyatt, Florida Sunshine's accountants, regularly prepared quarterly and annual unaudited financial statements. The most recently prepared financial statements were for the year ended September 30, 1987.

On November 15, 1987, after protracted negotiations, Risk Capital agreed to purchase 100,000 shares of no par, Class A capital stock of Florida Sunshine at $12.50 per share. However, Risk Capital insisted upon audited statements for calendar year 1987. The contract specifically provided:

Risk Capital shall have the right to rescind the purchase of said stock if the audited financial statements of Florida Sunshine for calendar year 1987 show a material adverse change in the financial condition of the Corporation.

Wilson and Wyatt were informed as to the specific use to be made of the audited financial statements but did not know the identity of the user.

The audited financial statements furnished to Florida Sunshine by Wilson and Wyatt showed no such material adverse change. Risk Capital relied upon the audited statements and purchased the treasury stock of Florida Sunshine. It was subsequently discovered that, as of the balance sheet date, the audited statements were incorrect and that in fact there had been a material adverse change in the financial condition of the Corporation. Florida Sunshine is insolvent and Risk Capital will lose virtually its entire investment.

Risk Capital seeks recovery against Wilson and Wyatt.

Required:

Assuming that only ordinary negligence is proved, would Risk Capital prevail under the more recent decisions, such as *Rusch Factors?* State yes or no and explain.
(AICPA, adapted)

19–48. Wells and White, the accountants for the Allie Corporation, provided various professional services for Allie over 15 years under annual retainer agreements. The services included tax return preparation, special cost analyses, and the preparation of the corporation's audited and unaudited financial statements.

The relationship had been quite harmonious until the retirement of Roberts, the president and founder of Allie Corporation. His successor, Strong, was a very aggressive, expansion-oriented individual who lacked the competence and personal attraction of his predecessor. Two years after Roberts' retirement, the unbroken record of increases in annual earnings was in jeopardy.

Strong realized that a decrease in earnings would have an unfavorable impact on his image and on his plans to merge with a well-known conglomerate. He called Wells, the senior partner of Wells and White, and demanded that the method of computing and reporting the current year's earnings be changed in a way that would preserve the upward trend.

Although the proposed method would be within the realm of GAAP, Wells subsequently told Strong that in its professional judgment, the firm could not agree to such a change. Strong promptly dismissed the firm and refused to pay the final billing of $10,000 for services rendered to the date of dismissal under its agreement with Wells and White.

Wells and White have brought suit against Allie Corporation for the $10,000. Allie Corporation responded by denying liability on the ground that the firm's refusal to cooperate constituted a breach of contract that precluded recovery. Allie also counterclaimed by demanding the return of all audit working papers, correspondence, and duplicate tax returns and supporting explanations pertaining to Allie Corporation. The counterclaim was denied since the working papers and duplicate tax returns are the property of the CPA firm (Wells and White).

Strong was unable to find other accountants who approved of the proposed change in the method of computing and reporting earnings, so he abandoned this demand and then engaged new accountants, Bar & Cross. Income continued to decrease in the next two quarters and Strong became convinced that the cause of this must be defalcations by some dishonest employee. Therefore, he engaged Bar & Cross to make a special study to discover the guilty person. After several months of intensive work, Bar & Cross were able to discover only minor defalcations of $950. Of this amount, $600 was stolen during the last two years while Wells and White were Allie Corporation's accountants.

Required:

a. Is the Wells and White account receivable valid and enforceable against the Allie Corporation? State "yes" or "no" and explain.

b. Can Allie Corporation recover the loss from Wells and White? State "yes" or "no" and explain.   (AICPA, adapted)

19–49. Millard & Hans, CPAs, has been engaged for several years by Happy Toys, Inc., to perform the "usual" examination of its financial statements and provide other accounting services. The understanding was oral, and the fee was based on an annual retainer.

Millard & Hans regularly prepared unaudited quarterly financial statements and examined and reported on Happy Toys' annual financial statements. During the current year's examination, Happy Toys decided to go public and requested that Millard & Hans assist in preparing all the necessary financial statements and other financial information and supply the independent auditor's reports as necessary for inclusion in a registration statement to be filed with the Securities and Exchange Commission (SEC). Millard & Hans is independent in accordance with SEC rules and regulations. Millard & Hans complied with Happy Toys' request and subsequently submitted a bill to Happy Toys for $15,000 for the additional work performed in connection with the SEC filing. Happy Toys refused to pay, claiming the additional work was a part of the "usual" engagement and was covered by the annual retainer.

Required:

a. If Millard & Hans sues Happy Toys for its $15,000 fee, who is likely to prevail? Explain.

b. Discuss how Millard & Hans can avoid similar problems in the future with Happy Toys and other clients.   (AICPA, adapted)

19–50. Jackson was a junior staff member of an accounting firm. She began the audit of the Bosco Corporation which manufactured and sold expensive watches. In the middle of the audit she quit. The accounting firm hired another person to continue the audit of Bosco. Due to the changeover and the time pressure to finish the audit, the firm violated certain generally accepted auditing standards when they did not follow adequate procedures with respect to the physical inventory. Had the proper procedures been used during the examination, they would have discovered that watches worth more than $20,000 were missing. The employee who was stealing the watches was able to steal an additional $30,000 worth before the thefts were discovered six months after the completion of the audit.

Required:

Discuss the legal problems of the accounting firm as a result of the above facts.

(AICPA, adapted)

19–51. CPA J has been asked to audit the financial statements of a publicly held company for the first time. All preliminary verbal discussions and inquiries have been completed between the CPA, the company, the predecessor auditor, and all other necessary parties. CPA J is now preparing an engagement letter.

Required:

List the items that should be included in the typical engagement letter.

(AICPA, adapted)

19–52. Marcall is a limited partner of Guarcross, a limited partnership, and is suing a CPA firm which was retained by the limited partnership to perform auditing and tax return preparation services. Guarcross was formed for the purpose of investing in a diversified portfolio of risk capital securities. The partnership agreement included the following provisions:

The initial capital contribution of each limited partner shall not be less than $250,000; no partner may withdraw any part of his interest in the partnership, except at the end of any fiscal year upon giving written notice of such intention not less than 30 days prior to the end of such year; the books and records of the partnership shall be audited as of the end of the fiscal year by a certified public accountant designated by the general partners; and proper and complete books of account shall be kept and shall be open to inspection by any of the partners or his or her accredited representative.

Marcall's claim of malpractice against the CPA firm centers on the firm's alleged failure to comment, in its audit report, on the withdrawal by the general partners of $2,000,000 of their $2,600,000 capital investment based on back-dated notices, and the lumping together of the $2,000,000 withdrawals with $49,000 in withdrawals by limited partners so that a reader of the financial statement would not be likely to realize that the two general partners had withdrawn a major portion of their investments.

The CPA firm's contention is that its contract was made with the limited partnership, not its partners. It further contends that since the CPA firm had no privity of contract with the third party limited partners, the limited partners have no right of action for negligence.

Required:

Discuss the various theories Marcall would rely upon in order to prevail in a lawsuit against the CPA firm. State reasons for your conclusions.

(AICPA, adapted)

19–53. Farr & Madison, CPAs, audited Glamour, Inc. Their audit was deficient in several respects:

1. They failed to verify properly certain receivables that later proved to be fictitious.

2. With respect to other receivables, although they made a cursory check, they did not detect many accounts that were long overdue and obviously uncollectible.

3. No physical inventory was taken of securities claimed to be in Glamour's possession, which in fact had been sold. Both the securities and cash received for the sales were listed on the balance sheet as assets.

There is no indication that Farr & Madison actually believed that the financial statements were false. Subsequent creditors, not known to Farr & Madison, are now suing the auditors, based upon the deficiencies in the audit described above. Farr and Madison moved to dismiss the lawsuit on the basis that the firm did not have actual knowledge of falsity and therefore did not commit fraud.

Required:

May the creditors recover without demonstrating Farr & Madison had actual knowledge of falsity? Give reasons for your conclusions. (AICPA, adapted)

THE SEC AND THE
INDEPENDENT AUDITOR

20

The two most significant federal statutes affecting the securities markets are the Securities Act of 1933 and the Securities Exchange Act of 1934. The 1933 act generally requires companies to register public offerings of securities, such as stocks, bonds, and limited partnership interests with the Securities and Exchange Commission (SEC, or Commission) before they are sold to the public. The 1934 act established the SEC with responsibility for administering the laws relating to the securities markets. The 1934 act requires companies that have securities registered with the SEC to file periodic reports.

This chapter provides an overview of the origin and organization of the SEC and discusses the securities laws and regulations that affect publicly held companies. Implications of the securities laws on the independent accountant's legal liability also are discussed.

ORIGIN OF THE SEC

Companies did not always provide the kind of information they do today. The stock exchanges, the predecessor of the American Institute of Certified Public Accountants (AICPA), and other interested parties worked together to require reports to shareholders and to improve their form, content, and dependability. By 1926, a company listed on the New York Stock Exchange (NYSE) had to provide its shareholders, at least 15 days before its annual meeting, with an annual report containing financial statements. However, the content of these reports still concerned many parties, and traded securities not listed on the NYSE were not subject to this requirement. Auditor involvement with financial statements was primarily intended to obtain loans or lines of credit. On April 27, 1933, nearly four years after the market crash of 1929, *The New York Times* (page 25L) stated:

> For several years the Exchange has been carrying on a campaign for better and more fully authenticated corporation reports. While this campaign has

obtained results, progress has been impeded at times by the absence of a suitable weapon to force reform upon companies whose securities have already been admitted to the list, according to officials of the Exchange.[1]

The weapon soon appeared in the form of federal regulation of security issues and trading. Congress enacted the Securities Act of 1933. The following year it passed the Securities Exchange Act of 1934, which created the SEC. Under these acts, all companies offering new issues of securities for interstate sale and all companies whose securities are traded publicly must register and file periodic reports with the SEC. Such registration statements and annual reports must contain financial statements audited by independent auditors. In many cases, a request for a security holder's vote must be accompanied by a proxy statement that includes financial statements prescribed by the SEC.

The origin of the independent auditor's role in SEC practice was described by the SEC as follows:

> The passage of the Securities Act . . . [was] an important landmark in the development of the concept of the responsibility of the independent accountant to the investor and the public. The original draft of the Securities Act did not require certification by independent accountants. A representative of the accounting profession appeared at the hearings on the bill before the Committee on Banking and Currency of the U.S. Senate to suggest revisions of the bill. . . . He pointed out that the bill as drafted imposed "highly technical responsibilities upon the Commission as to accounting principles, their proper application and their clear expression in financial statements," and suggested the bill be revised to require that "the accounts pertaining to such balance sheet, statement of income and surplus shall have been examined by an independent accountant and his report shall present his certificate wherein he shall express his opinion. . . ."

---

[1] Copyright © 1933 by The New York Times Company. Reprinted by permission.

The committee considered at length the value to investors and to the public of an audit by accountants not connected with the company or management and whether the additional expense to industry of an audit by independent accountants was justified by the expected benefits to the public. The committee also considered the advisability and feasibility of requiring the audit to be made by accountants on the staff of the agency administering the Act.

In the report on the bill the Senate committee stated that it was intended that those responsible for the administration and enforcement of the law should have full and adequate authority to procure whatever information might be necessary in carrying out the provisions of the bill, but it was deemed essential to refrain from placing upon any Federal agency the duty of passing judgment upon the soundness of any security. The proposal to require certification by independent public accountants was incorporated in the bill as passed.[2]

ORGANIZATION OF THE SEC

The SEC's principal responsibility is to administer the following federal laws governing the sale and trading of securities:

1. Securities Act of 1933
2. Securities Exchange Act of 1934
3. Public Utility Holding Company Act of 1935
4. Trust Indenture Act of 1939
5. Investment Company Act of 1940
6. Investment Advisers Act of 1940

These laws, as they relate to registration of securities and periodic reporting, are intended to provide the investor with information about the issuer of a security so an informed decision can be made on the merits of that security. The emphasis is on *disclosure;* therefore, the SEC usually does not prohibit the sale or trading of highly speculative securities if they are characterized as such in the filing. Of the above laws, this chapter is concerned with describing the provisions of only the 1933 act and 1934 act.

The Commission has five members, appointed to five-year terms by the President with the approval of the Senate. A maximum of three commissioners may be from the same political party. The Commission is assisted by a professional staff organized into divisions and offices. Figure 20–1 is an organization chart of the SEC. Independent auditors ordinarily work with the Division of Corporation Finance and the Office of the Chief Accountant.

The *Division of Corporation Finance* examines registration statements and applications (including financial statements), prospectuses, and annual and periodic reports. Filings are reviewed by 10 branches, each of which is assigned

---

[2] *Securities and Exchange Commission Accounting Series Release No. 81,* "Independence of Certifying Accountants—Compilation of Representative Administration Rulings in Cases Involving the Independence of Accountants," 1958.

FIGURE 20–1 Organization Chart of the SEC

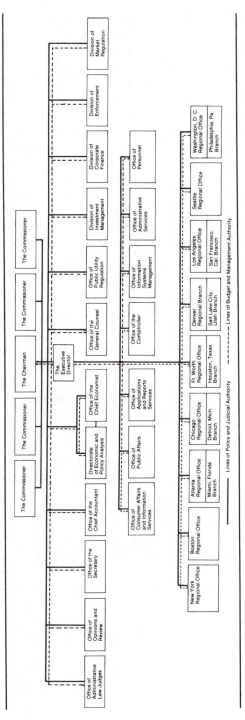

Source: Securities and Exchange Commission.

689

several industries. Typically, a branch is headed by a branch chief who is assisted by a professional staff. Generally, a company will have all of its work handled by one branch. The division has its own chief accountant.

The *Office of the Chief Accountant* advises the Commission on accounting and disclosure subjects. In its oversight function, the Office also monitors the organizations that establish accounting and auditing standards. The Office takes questions to the Commission and carries out the Commission's policies relating to accounting and auditing matters, and the composition of financial statements. It replies to inquiries on accounting and auditing matters from corporations and independent auditors. Its opinions on accounting questions that are of general interest are published by the SEC, as discussed in the "SEC Accounting and Reporting Releases" section later. The Office of the Chief Accountant participates in various proceedings involving accounting and disclosure matters and considers situations relating to the independence and fitness to practice of independent auditors.

MAJOR SECURITIES LAWS

The Securities Act of 1933

The 1933 act generally provides that public offerings of securities by companies (referred to as "registrants") must be registered with the Commission before they may be sold. Issues of less than $1,500,000 may be exempt from registration. Government securities and private sales (or private placements) also are exempt. A sale is considered a private placement if an entire issue is sold to a limited number of knowledgeable investors for their investment and the shares will not be resold to the public. Because the rules for exemption from registration involve important legal questions, potential issuers should obtain an attorney's opinion.

The 1933 act is a *selling* statute (as contrasted with the 1934 act, which is a *periodic reporting* statute). Its purpose is, as stated in the act, "to provide full and fair disclosure of the character of securities sold in interstate and foreign commerce and through the mails, and to prevent frauds in the sale thereof. . . ." The preparation of a registration statement is a complicated, technical process. The Commission's function is to see that registrants make full and accurate disclosure of all pertinent information, so that prospective investors may have a basis for deciding whether to purchase the securities.

The 1933 act provides for various registration statement forms, each for a particular class of issuer and security. Every registration statement includes a *prospectus*, which is the principal source of information for an investor about the securities to be offered for sale. The prospectus must be furnished to each person to whom the security is offered for sale. For example, a prospectus for a filing on Form S–1 must contain the terms of the offering, information about management, description of the business and properties, historical financial statements, and other information necessary for the prospective investor to make an informed investment decision.

The Securities Exchange Act of 1934

As stated in the act, the 1934 act, as amended in 1964, provides ". . . for the regulation of securities exchanges and of over-the-counter markets operating in interstate and foreign commerce and through the mails, to prevent inequitable and unfair practices. . . ." All companies registered under the 1934 act are subject to SEC rules on (1) annual and other periodic reporting, (2) proxies, and (3) insiders' trading. Since the 1964 amendments, all companies registering any securities under the 1933 act also are required to comply with the 1934 act reporting requirements.

Currently, companies must register their securities under the 1934 act when: (1) the securities are listed on a national exchange (with limited exceptions) or (2) the company is engaged in interstate commerce, has 500 or more shareholders, and has more than $3 million in total assets. The registration requirements are described in Section 12 of the 1934 act. The majority of the companies that are required to register initially under the 1934 act do so on *Form 10*.

Under the 1934 act, each company must file an annual report with the SEC on *Form 10–K* within 90 days after the end of its fiscal year. Special situations may require other forms. Assisting clients in preparing these annual reports to the SEC often provide auditors with their first experience with SEC filings. In addition, registered companies are required to file quarterly reports on *Form 10–Q* within 45 days after the end of each of the first three fiscal quarters.

The 1934 act requires every registered company to furnish *proxy information* when soliciting shareholders' votes. A *proxy* authorizes another person to cast the shareholder's vote.

The 1934 act also establishes margin requirements, which are regulated by the Federal Reserve Board, and prescribes rules that govern security trading by "insiders." The 1934 act requires that "short-swing" profits made by insiders be returned to the company. In recent years, the SEC has actively enforced its insider trading rules.

Generally, if the number of shareholders drops below 500 and assets in the last three years are less than $3 million *or* the number of shareholders drops below 300, a company may terminate its registration by notifying the SEC. After doing so, the company is no longer subject to SEC jurisdiction.

DECIDING WHAT REPORTS TO FILE

Whether a company must file an SEC report and, if so, on what form, are questions the company and its legal counsel should answer. Independent auditors do not make these decisions, although they can help the company determine if it fulfills the requirements to use a particular form.

More than 100 forms exist under the 1933 and 1934 acts. The following list of commonly used forms illustrates the diversity of filings.

The Securities Act of 1933 (Registration)

Form S–1   General form for registration of securities by first time registrants or companies with fewer than three years of 1934 act reporting and when no other form is authorized or prescribed.

Form S–2   For established companies that meet certain "registrant requirements" (the details of which are beyond the scope of this book).

Form S–3   For established companies that meet certain "registrant requirements," and for which the particular securities being registered meet certain "transaction requirements" (the details of which are beyond the scope of this book).

Form S–6   For unit investment trusts.

Form S–8   For securities and interests to be offered to employees under an employee benefit plan.

Form S–11 For certain real estate companies.

Form S–14 For securities issued in mergers, consolidations, and certain acquisitions requiring vote or consent of security holders.

Form S–15 Optional form for registration of securities to be offered in certain business combination transactions in which the company being acquired is substantially smaller than the company issuing the securities.

Form S–18 For the registration of small offerings (usually initial offerings).

The Securities Exchange Act of 1934 (Registration and periodic reports)

Form 8–A   Form for registering securities of companies that already file periodic reports.

Form 8–B   Used by an acquiring company (successor issuer) to notify the SEC that previously registered securities are to be under a new name.

Form 8–K   For current reports. Required to be filed when certain events have occurred (changes in control; acquisition or disposition of assets; bankruptcy or receivership; change in certifying accountant; and other important events).

Form 10 General form used by the majority of companies that are required to register initially under the 1934 act.

Form 10–K General form for annual reports.

Form 10–Q General form for quarterly reports.

DECIDING WHAT IS REQUIRED IN A FILING

An independent auditor's principal responsibility in any SEC filing is the report on the financial statements. The auditor does, however, read the entire filing to assure that nothing included elsewhere contradicts the audited financial statements. Although the auditor usually does not draft other sections of the filing and does not include them in the scope of the report, the auditor frequently may assist in compiling some of the financial data included in those sections. Accordingly, the independent auditor should be familiar with the requirements for financial statements and nonfinancial information in SEC filings.

SEC ACCOUNTING AND REPORTING RELEASES

Auditors involved in engagements that result in the filing of financial statements with the SEC should be thoroughly familiar with relevant Commission releases, such as the *Accounting Series Releases (ASRs), Financial Reporting Releases (FRRs), Accounting and Auditing Enforcement Releases (AAERs),* and *Staff Accounting Bulletins (SABs).* The purpose of ASRs was to cover accounting and financial matters; ASRs were used primarily by the SEC to issue: (1) all official regulations and changes in regulations affecting the accounting and reporting policies of registrants and the responsibilities of their independent public accountants; (2) information deemed appropriate by the SEC regarding administrative and enforcement proceedings involving independent public accountants and others; and (3) official opinions and interpretations of the SEC on financial and accounting matters.

In 1982, the SEC discontinued the *Accounting Series Releases* publications. Two new series of releases, *Financial Reporting Releases* (FRRs) and *Accounting and Auditing Enforcement Releases* (AAERs), have replaced the ASRs. *FRR No. 1* announced a codification of those ASRs that were still relevant for financial reporting. The Codification of Financial Reporting Policies (Codification) has been supplemented by FRRs that cover general accounting and auditing topics. ASRs relating to accounting and auditing matters that dealt with enforcement matters were not included in the Codification, since AAERs deal with those matters.

Over the years, the SEC had published 307 ASRs. However, a good deal of the content was no longer relevant. The SEC concluded that the relevant

ASRs should be summarized and presented in a logical format which would be easier to work with. Although the Codification now in effect does not refer to individual ASRs, at times we still refer to individual ASRs since they provide some historical perspective.

SABs describe some of the administrative accounting interpretations and practices followed by the SEC's Division of Corporate Finance and Office of the Chief Accountant. The SABs are not official rules of the Commission. However, because SABs represent staff policies, they should be viewed as authoritative references for SEC filings. The format of SABs is a series of questions and answers arranged under general topics with the surrounding facts, the question, and the staff's interpretation for each item.

INTEGRATION AND CONTINUOUS REPORTING

Before 1980, financial statement requirements were included in various registration and reporting forms. The rules covering financial statements and periods required often differed. These differences arose from the development of the separate reporting systems under the 1933 and 1934 acts and from attempts to tailor disclosure requirements to the particular circumstances of a form. Such differences in the requirements contributed to the complexity of the disclosure rules and frequently were a source of confusion for registrants.

Integrated Disclosure Programs

In 1980, the SEC issued *ASRs Nos. 279* through *281,* which represented a significant step toward establishing an integrated and simplified disclosure system. These releases provided for:

1. Amendments to Regulation S–X (discussed in the next section), to provide uniform financial statement requirements and to eliminate rules that duplicate GAAP.
2. A uniform package of disclosures required in annual reports to shareholders, Form 10–K, and other SEC filings.
3. Amendments to Regulation S–K (discussed in the next section), to provide uniform requirements for nonfinancial statement items such as selected financial data and management's discussion and analysis.

In *ASR No. 279,* the SEC stated that "there is a basic information package which most, if not all, investors expect to be furnished. Further, it has become apparent that this basic information package, which in the content of Form 10–K developed to support the current information requirements of an active trading market, is virtually identical to the similar information package independently developed in connection with the registration and sale of newly issued shares under the Securities Act." This basic information package includes:

Audited consolidated financial statements.

Summary of selected financial data appropriate for trend analysis.

Management's discussion and analysis of financial condition and results of operations.

Description of the registrant's business.

Common stock market prices and dividend information.

Because these disclosures are the same in both the annual shareholders report and Form 10–K, the registrant can incorporate by reference the information contained in its annual shareholders reports into its Form 10–K rather than include the same information in both reports. In addition, this same information satisfies many of the disclosure requirements for filings under the 1933 act.

Continuous Reporting

ASR No. 280 provided uniform instructions about the periods to be covered in most registration statements and reporting forms (e.g., Form 10–K), and in annual reports to shareholders furnished under the proxy rules. Practically speaking, periodic reporting updates the company's original registration statement. The diagram in Figure 20–2 illustrates the integration and continuous reporting concepts under the securities acts.

Financial Statement Requirements

Each form contains instructions as to the information required in the filing. These instructions refer to Regulation S–X for the form and content of, and requirements for, financial statements and to Regulation S–K for the content of most nonfinancial statement information.

Regulation S–X (together with the Codification and subsequent FRRs) describes the requirements for the certification, form, and content of financial statements. Regulation S–X also prescribes certain notes and schedules to be filed. Article 3 of Regulation S–X provides a centralized set of instructions for financial statements required in SEC filings.

Although the SEC has the power to prescribe the form and accounting methods used by public companies, it frequently relies on generally accepted accounting principles (GAAP) as established by the FASB and its predecessors. In fact, Rule 4–01 of Regulation S–X states:

> Financial statements filed with the Commission which are not prepared in accordance with generally accepted accounting principles will be presumed to be misleading or inaccurate. . . .

Thus, the SEC has incorporated GAAP into Regulation S–X.

Generally, Regulation S–X requires financial statement disclosures beyond

FIGURE 20–2 Integration and Continuous Reporting

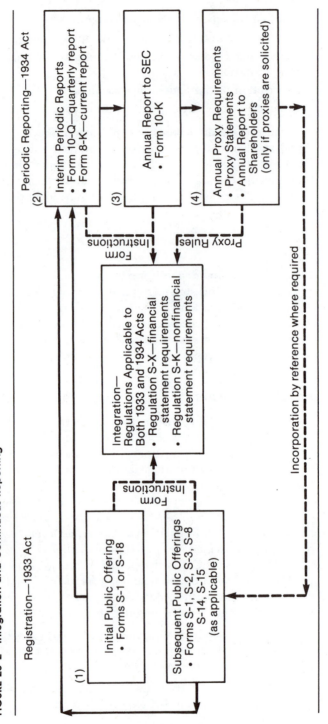

those required by GAAP. These may be required in footnotes, schedules, separate financial statements, or summarized financial information. The SEC considers these additional disclosures necessary for investors, security analysts, and other users of the financial statements.

To understand the instructions for financial statements in Regulation S–X, the independent auditor must know the precise meanings of the terms that are used. Thus, it often is necessary to refer to Rule 1–02 of Regulation S–X, Regulation C of the 1933 act, and to Regulation 12–B of the General Rules and Regulations under the 1934 act.

Regulation S–K (together with the general rules and regulations, interpretative releases, and forms under the 1933 and 1934 acts) describes the requirements for the content of nonfinancial statement portions of periodic reports and registration statements. Before Regulation S–K was adopted, the required content of nonfinancial statement disclosures in various filings was contained within the instructions to the related form.

MATERIALITY

The concept of materiality is as important in SEC matters as in other accounting matters. Rule 1–02 in Regulation S–X says, "The term 'material,' when used to qualify a requirement for the furnishing of information as to any subject, limits the information required to those matters about which an average prudent investor ought reasonably to be informed." In the BarChris case Judge McLean had the following comment:

> What are "matters as to which an average prudent investor ought reasonably to be informed?" It seems obvious that they are matters which such an investor needs to know before he can make an intelligent, informed decision whether or not to buy the security.

> * * * * *

> The average prudent investor is not concerned with minor inaccuracies or with errors as to matters which are of no interest to him. The facts which tend to deter him from purchasing a security are facts which have an important bearing upon the nature or condition of the issuing corporation or its business.

> * * * * *

> Since no one knows what moves or does not move the mythical "average prudent investor," it comes down to a question of judgment, to be exercised by the trier of the fact as best he can in the light of all the circumstances.[3]

Regulation S–X (Rule 5–04) provides that companies must file some schedules only if specified items exceed certain limits. For example, Schedule I, "Marketable Securities—Other Investments," is required if marketable securities or other security investments (at cost or market) exceed 10 percent

---

[3] *Escott* v. *BarChris Construction Corporation,* 283 F. Supp. 653, pp. 681–82 (S.D.N.Y. 1968).

of total assets, or if marketable securities plus other security investments exceed 15 percent of total assets, or if the total amount of securities of a single issuer included in either of the above captions exceeds 2 percent of total assets. Schedule V, "Property, Plant, and Equipment," must be filed if property, plant, and equipment (beginning or ending balance) exceed 25 percent of total assets. *However, Regulation S–X does not indicate materiality in matters of audit judgment.*

INDEPENDENCE

Accordingly, Rule 2–01(b) of Regulation S–X provides that:

The Commission will not recognize any certified public accountant or public accountant as independent who is not in fact independent. For example, an accountant will be considered not independent with respect to any person or any of its parents, its subsidiaries, or other affiliates (1) in which, during the period of his professional engagement to examine the financial statements being reported on or at the date of his report, *he or his firm or a member thereof had, or was committed to acquire, any direct financial interest or any material indirect financial interest, or (2) with which, during the period of his professional engagement to examine the financial statements being reported on, at the date of his report or during the period covered by the financial statements, he or his firm or a member thereof was connected as a promoter, underwriter, voting trustee, director, officer, or employee,* except that a firm will not be deemed not independent in regard to a particular person if a former officer or employee of such person is employed by the firm and such individual has completely disassociated himself from the person and its affiliates and does not participate in auditing financial statements of the person or its affiliates covering any period of his employment by the person. For the purposes of Rule 2–01 the term "member" means all partners in the firm and all professional employees participating in the audit or located in an office of the firm participating in a significant portion of the audit. [Emphasis added.]

AUDITORS' LIABILITY IN SEC FILINGS

The independent auditor should be familiar with the civil liabilities that may be imposed on parties involved in filing false or misleading information. The independent auditor's liability (like that of the underwriters, legal counsel, directors, and any persons signing a registration statement) in SEC filings is provided for by statute—namely, Section 11 of the 1933 act, Section 18 of the 1934 act, and Rule 10b–5 of the Rules and Regulations of the 1934 act.

1933 Act Liability Provisions

Section 11(a) focuses on the independent auditor:

In case any part of the registration statement, when such part became effective, contained an untrue statement of a material fact or omitted to state a material fact required to be stated therein or necessary to make the statements therein not misleading, any person acquiring such security . . . may . . . sue . . . every accountant . . . who has with his consent been named as having . . . certified any part of the registration statement . . . with respect to the statement in such registration . . . which purports to have been . . . certified by him; . . .

Section 11(b)(3) states what the independent auditor must prove to avoid liability:

. . . as regards any part of the registration statement purporting to be made upon his authority as an expert or purporting to be a copy of or extract from a report or valuation of himself as an expert, . . . he had, after reasonable investigation, reasonable ground to believe and did believe, at the time such part of the registration statement became effective, that the statements therein were true and that there was no omission to state a material fact required to be stated therein or necessary to make the statements therein not misleading. . . .

Thus auditors must prove three elements to establish defense under Section 11(b)(3): that they (1) had reasonable grounds to believe the financial statements they certified were true; (2) *in fact* did believe them to be true; and (3) based their beliefs on a "reasonable investigation." The *BarChris* case, which is discussed below, considered what is a "reasonable investigation" for purposes of Section 11(a) liability.

Saul Levy, in *Accountants' Legal Responsibility,* gives his interpretation of the practical effect of these sections on the CPA:

1. Any person acquiring securities described in the Registration Statement may sue the accountant, regardless of the fact that he is not the client of the accountant.
2. His claim may be based upon an alleged false statement or misleading omission in the financial statements, which constitutes his prima facie case. The plaintiff does not have the further burden of proving that the accountants were negligent or fraudulent in certifying to the financial statements involved.
3. The plaintiff does not have to prove that he relied upon the statement or that the loss which he suffered was the proximate result of the falsity or misleading character of the financial statement.
4. The accountant has thrust upon him the burden of establishing his freedom from negligence and fraud by proving that he had, after reasonable investigation, reasonable ground to believe and did believe that the financial statements to which he certified, were true not only as of the date of the financial statements, but beyond that, *as of the time when the Registration Statement became effective.* [Emphasis by Levy.]
5. The accountant has the burden of establishing by way of defense or in reduction of alleged damages, that the loss of the plaintiff resulted in whole or in part from causes other than the false statements or the misleading omissions in the financial statements. Under the common law it would have been part of the plaintiff's affirmative case to prove that the damages

which he claims he sustained were proximately caused by the negligence or fraud of the accountant.[4]

The BarChris Case

Few civil liability cases have had such a profound impact on the accounting, legal, and underwriting professions as the *BarChris* case. Some regard it as the first definitive judicial treatment of auditors' liability under the Securities Act of 1933. Purchasers of the subordinated debentures of BarChris Construction Corporation initiated the action under Section 11 of the Securities Act of 1933 against any persons signing the registration statement, the underwriters, and the auditors. They charged that the registration statement directly relating to the bond issue contained material false statements and material omissions.

The impact of this case, from a liability standpoint, revolved around the review of the registration statement. The court recognized that the review was not a complete audit. The auditors had prepared a written program for a review that the court found to be acceptable. This program included: (1) a review of various minutes of meetings, latest interim financial statements, the more important financial records; and (2) an inquiry into changes in material contracts, significant bad debts, and newly discovered liabilities as well as other investigations.

The auditors were unable to prove due diligence in performing their review. As a consequence, they were found liable.

The facts of the case and the judge's comments challenge all parties to reassess their approaches to SEC filings. To independent auditors, the findings stress again the importance of doing the best possible job of auditing and of maintaining an alert, skeptical attitude throughout the assignment. In his opinion, Judge McLean questioned the responsibilities of all parties for investigating the "nonexpertised" portions of the filing. Some of his comments included the following:

To BarChris' counsel (also a director);	"Much of this registration statement is a scissors and paste-pot job."[5]
To underwriters:	"In order to make the underwriters' participation in this enterprise of any value to the investors, the underwriters must make some reasonable attempt to verify the data submitted to them. They may not rely solely on the company's officers or on the company's counsel. A prudent man in the management of his own property would not rely on them."[6]

---

[4] Saul Levy, *Accountants' Legal Responsibility,* American Institute of Accountants, 1954, pp. 46–47.

[5] *Escott V. BarChris Construction Corporation,* 283 F. Supp. 643, p. 690 (S.D.N.Y. 1968).

[6] Ibid, p. 697.

To the independent   "He asked questions, he got answers which he consid-
auditor: ered satisfactory, and he did nothing to verify them.

                                         * * * * *

                         . . . As far as results were concerned, his S–1 review
                         was useless.
                         . . . He was too easily satisfied with glib answers
                         to his inquiries.
                         . . . It is not always sufficient merely to ask
                         questions."[7]

The *BarChris* case is important under the Securities Acts, since it clarifies
the due diligence responsibilities of attorneys, underwriters, and independent
auditors—especially as they relate to disclosure of events between the date
of the audit report and the effective date of a registration statement.

1934 Act Liability Provisions

Section 18 (as amended) of the 1934 act is reproduced below. There are
significant differences between it and the 1933 act provisions.

Section 18—Liability for Misleading Statements.

(a)   Any person who shall make or cause to be made any statement in any
      application, report, or document filed pursuant to this title or any rule
      or regulation thereunder or any undertaking contained in a registration
      statement as provided in subsection (d) of section 15 of this title, which
      statement was at the time and in the light of the circumstances under
      which it was made false or misleading with respect to any material fact,
      shall be liable to any person (not knowing that such statement was false
      or misleading) who, in reliance upon such statement, shall have purchased
      or sold a security at a price which was affected by such statement, for
      damages caused by such reliance, unless the person sued shall prove that
      he acted in good faith and had no knowledge that such statement was
      false or misleading. A person seeking to enforce such liability may sue
      at law or in equity in any court of competent jurisdiction. In any such
      suit the court may, in its discretion, require an undertaking for the pay-
      ment of the costs of such suit, and assess reasonable costs, including
      reasonable attorneys' fees against either party litigant.
(b)   Every person who becomes liable to make payment under this section
      may recover contribution as in cases of contract from any person who,
      if joined in the original suit, would have been liable to make the same
      payment.
(c)   No action shall be maintained to enforce any liability created under this
      section unless brought within one year after the discovery of the facts
      constituting the cause of action and within three years after such cause
      of action accrued.

---

[7] Ibid, pp. 702–03.

Under the 1933 act, the auditors are liable for events occurring up to the effective date of the registration statement. Section 18 of the 1934 act, on the other hand, holds the auditors liable "only" for statements that were false or misleading "at the time and in the light of the circumstance under which it was made." Saul Levy summarizes the more important points under Section 18:

1. There is no provision similar to the "effective date" requirement of a Registration Statement. . . . It would seem from this that the accountant is not obligated to extend his examination or inquiry beyond the completion of his audit work, even though the filing with the Securities and Exchange Commission may take place at some subsequent date. In the case of the 10–K report covering a calendar year, this is required to be filed on or before April 30 [now 90 days] following the close of the year. It usually includes financial statements, the audit work on which may have been completed . . . earlier. The accountant's report usually bears the date of the completion of his audit and it would seem that his responsibility would be limited to his compliance with generally accepted auditing standards applied down to the date of the completion of the audit. However, if the accountant has actual knowledge of the occurrence of subsequent events which are of material significance, it would be incumbent upon him to insist upon adequate disclosure in the report.

* * * * *

2. The plaintiff must prove his reliance upon the financial statement and prove damages that were caused by such reliance.
3. While the plaintiff does not have the burden of proving negligence or fraud on the part of the accountant, the accountant is given the statutory defense "that he acted in good faith and had no knowledge that such statement was false or misleading." This quoted language is consistent with freedom from fraud rather than freedom from negligence. It would seem, therefore, that . . . there would not be liability to third parties for mere negligence where the good faith of the accountant is established.[8]

Rule 10b–5

In recent years, many of the cases involving auditors' liability in SEC filings have been brought under Rule 10b–5 of the 1934 act which states that:

It shall be unlawful for any person, directly or indirectly, by the use of any means or instrumentality of interstate commerce, or of the mails, or of any facility of any national securities exchange,

(a) To employ any device, scheme, or artifice to defraud,
(b) To make any untrue statement of a material fact or to omit to state a material fact necessary to make the statements made, in the light of the circumstances under which they were made, not misleading, or

---

[8] Levy, pp. 49–50.

(c)   To engage in any act, practice, or course of business which operates or would operate as a fraud or deceit upon any person, in connection with the purchase or sale of any security.[9]

Rule 10b–5 may be described as a fraud rule (as opposed to a negligence rule). Under a fraud rule, liability requires specific intent—that is, the intent to defraud. Under a negligence rule, liability does not require a specific intent but merely a failure to satisfy an objective standard, such as the failure to exercise reasonable care. "Negligence" is not to be confused with "recklessness," which can be considered by a court as tantamount to the type of intent required to establish fraud.

Ernst & Ernst* v. *Hochfelder.   This case resulted from the accounting firm's audits of First Securities Company of Chicago, a small brokerage firm, during the period 1946 through 1967. The plaintiffs were customers of First Securities who invested in a fraudulent securities scheme perpetrated by the president of First Securities and owner of 92 percent of its stock. The president induced the plaintiffs to invest funds in "escrow" accounts that he represented would yield a high rate of return. Plaintiffs did so from 1942 through 1966. There were, in fact, no escrow accounts, as the president converted plaintiffs' funds to his own use immediately upon receipt. These transactions were not in the customary form of dealings between First Securities and its customers. The plaintiffs drew their personal checks payable to the president or a designated bank for his account. No such escrow accounts were reflected on the books and records of First Securities, nor were any shown by the company on its periodic accounting to plaintiffs in connection with their investments.

The fraud came to light in 1968 when the president committed suicide, leaving a note that described First Securities as bankrupt and the escrow accounts as "spurious." Plaintiffs subsequently sued the accounting firm to recover their losses, charging that the president's escrow scheme violated Section 10(b) of the 1934 act and Rule 10b–5, and that the firm had "aided and abetted" the president's violations by "failure" to conduct proper audits of First Securities and discover alleged internal control weaknesses. The principal such weakness, alleged by the plantiffs, was the president's rule that only he could open mail addressed to him at First Securities or addressed to First Securities to his attention, even if it arrived in his absence. The plaintiffs contended that if the accounting firm had conducted a proper audit, it would have discovered this "mail rule" and would have disclosed it in reports to the Midwest Stock Exchange and the SEC. Plaintiffs felt this would have led to an investigation of the president that would have uncovered the fraudulent scheme.

The accounting firm established in the U.S. District Court that there was

[9] Code of Federal Regulations. Title 17—*Commodity and Securities Exchanges* (Revised as of January 1, 1968), Section 240.10b–5.

no negligence. Hochfelder appealed the District Court decision in an attempt to gain another opportunity to prove negligence. When the case finally reached the U.S. Supreme Court, that Court put an end to any further efforts along these lines by Hochfelder with its conclusion that, even if negligence were proved, that would not be sufficient to establish liability under Rule 10b–5.

Rule 2(e) Proceedings

Under Rule 2(e) of the Commission's Rules of Practice, the SEC can limit the right to appear and practice before it. In several cases, the SEC has censured auditors, rather than withdraw their privilege to practice before the Commission. Besides censuring them, the SEC has required national CPA firms to:

1. Institute and maintain appropriate quality control procedures to prevent future violations.
2. Undergo peer reviews.
3. Accept firmwide restrictions on acquiring or otherwise merging with other accounting firms.
4. Suspend acceptance of new SEC engagements in one office and firmwide for specified periods.
5. Temporarily suspend partners from practicing before the SEC.

CONTINENTAL VENDING MACHINE CASE

SAS No. 37 (AU 711.04), "Filings Under Federal Securities Statutes," includes an ominous statement:

> This discussion of the independent accountant's responsibilities in connection with filings under the federal securities statutes is not intended to offer legal interpretations and is based on an understanding of the meaning of the statutes as they relate to accounting principles and auditing standards and procedures. *The discussion is subject to any judicial interpretations that may be issued.* [Emphasis added.]

This implies that in a court of law, the independent auditors who perform services in accordance with a SAS may nonetheless be subject to civil or criminal liabilities.

Consider the *Continental Vending Machine Corporation* case, under which two partners and a manager with an international accounting firm were criminally prosecuted. The case (which took place before *SAS No. 6,* "Related Party Transactions") involved disclosures about loans made to Continental's president and secured by Continental stock. Shortly after the 1962 annual report was mailed, Continental's stock declined significantly in value, and the company ultimately filed for bankruptcy. As a result, the collateral securing the loan became worthless. Continental's financial statements disclosed that a secured loan was made to the company's president but not that the security was Continental stock.

Although the defendants waived their right to a jury trial, the government insisted on one. After two months, the jury was deadlocked 11 to 1 for acquittal. The second trial resulted in conviction of the auditors on three counts of mail fraud and conspiracy.

The case made its way to the U.S. Supreme Court, with which the AICPA filed a brief that included the following:

Regarding generally accepted accounting principles:

> The trial court refused the defendants' request that the jury be instructed to test their professional work by the standards of their profession. Under the requested instructions, the jury would have been permitted to convict only if it found that Continental's balance sheet did not fairly present its financial position according to generally accepted accounting principles, and that the defendants knew that the presentation was not fair. Instead, the trial court charged that on the question whether the balance sheet was false or misleading the "critical test" was whether it "fairly presented" Continental's financial position but without reference to generally accepted accounting principles. . . . On the separate issue of intent, the jury was told that it could consider evidence that the balance sheet conformed to generally accepted accounting principles as "very persuasive" but "not necessarily conclusive" of defendants' good faith. . . .[10]

Regarding auditing standards:

> . . . It is fundamentally unfair to require a man to conform to an uncertain standard of conduct that is established by a jury after the fact, and that differs from and may well conflict with the standards of his profession. . . . This policy has special pertinence here, for the baneful effects of uncertainty are especially acute when professional men may not rely on the established standards of their profession but must, at the peril of well-nigh unbearable liability, conform to open-ended and essentially subjective standards established in retrospect by a lay jury.[11]

The Supreme Court refused to hear the case and the verdict stood.

The *Continental Vending* case is significant because it demonstrates that, in the context of criminal proceedings, GAAP and generally accepted auditing standards are subject to review in a court of law—and auditors may be judged by lay people using standards that go beyond generally accepted auditing standards and accounting principles.

LIABILITIES OF OTHER PARTIES

Liability under the 1933 and 1934 acts extends not only to the independent auditors but to others involved in the filing and reporting process—issuers,

---

[10] "AICPA Brief in Continental Vending," *The Journal of Accountancy*, (May, 1970), p. 70.
[11] Ibid, p. 73.

officers, directors, legal counsel, persons signing a registration statement, and underwriters.

The judge's opinion in the *BarChris* case says clearly that each party has a certain obligation to fulfill in any filing. By understanding the liability exposure of underwriters, officers, directors, and legal counsel, you can understand the reasons for their requests for assistance from independent auditors. The auditor must, of course, make the final decision on whether he or she can comply with these requests.

QUESTIONS AND PROBLEMS

20–1. List the various activities over which the SEC has jurisdiction.

20–2. What are Regulations S–X and S–K?

20–3. One of your fellow students says to you, "The underlying purpose of the federal laws governing the sale and trading of securities is to make recommendations to potential purchasers of these securities as to which one to buy." Comment.

20–4. With which two units of the SEC do independent accountants ordinarily deal?

20–5. What are the principal duties of the Chief Accountant of the SEC?

20–6. Briefly describe the purpose and significance of:
  a. The Securities Act of 1933.
  b. The Securities Exchange Act of 1934.

20–7. The sales of certain securities are exempted from the requirements of the Securities Act of 1933. Describe the characteristics that make these securities exempt.

20–8. Describe the accountant's civil (noncriminal) liability under the 1933 act.

20–9. Is it accurate to say that the 1933 act is concerned with the distribution of securities, while the 1934 act is concerned with the trading of securities?

20–10. Which companies are subject to the reporting requirements of the 1934 act?

20–11. Once a company is registered under the 1934 act, what events would permit the company to terminate its registration?

20–12. What is a 10–K report?

20–13. What is a 10–Q report?

20–14. What are some of the types of information that registered companies are required to report to the SEC on Form 8–K?

20–15. What acts are considered to be illegal acts under the SEC's Rule 10b–5?

20–16. What is "materiality" in SEC matters?

20–17. What is "independence" in SEC matters?

20–18. Select the best answer for each of the following items.
 a. A CPA is subject to criminal liability if the CPA:
   (1) Refuses to turn over the working papers to the client.
   (2) Performs an audit in a negligent manner.
   (3) Willfully omits a material fact required to be stated in a registration statement.
   (4) Willfully breaches the contract with the client.
 b. The most significant aspects of the *Continental Vending Machine* case was that it:
   (1) Created a more general awareness of the auditor's exposure to criminal prosecution.
   (2) Extended the auditor's responsibility for financial statements of subsidiaries.
   (3) Extended the auditor's responsibility for events after the end of the audit period.
   (4) Defined the auditor's common law responsibilities to third parties.
 c. A third-party purchaser of securities has brought suit based upon the Securities Act of 1933 against a CPA firm. The CPA firm will prevail in the suit brought by the third party even though the CPA firm issued an unqualified opinion on materially incorrect financial statements if:
   (1) The CPA firm was unaware of the defects.
   (2) The third-party plaintiff had no direct dealings with the CPA firm.
   (3) The CPA firm can show that the third-party plaintiff did not rely upon the audited financial statements.
   (4) The CPA firm can establish that it was not guilty of actual fraud.

(AICPA, adapted)

20–19. What is the integrated disclosure program?

20–20. What is the "basic information package?"

20–21. J. Kone, CPA, has been controller of Big Company for five years. Before that, she was a staff accountant for Little & Small, CPAs. The Big Company decides to hire Little & Small as auditors. Would the CPA firm meet the SEC's independence requirements?

20–22. Sam Adams, CPA, owns 10 shares of Tiny Company. Tiny has just hired Adams to be its independent auditor. Would the SEC consider Adams to be independent?

20–23. CPA J is a partner in the CPA firm of JKL & M, CPAs. CPA J is a member of the board of directors of Mill, Inc. CPA M (a partner of CPA J) makes an agreement with Mill, Inc., to do the annual audit. Since J is on the board, it is agreed that J will not participate in the audit. Would the SEC consider this arrangement to be independent?

20–24. The Chriswell Corporation decided to raise additional long-term capital by issuing $3 million of 8 percent subordinated debentures to the public. May, Clark & Company, CPAs, the company's auditors, were engaged to examine the June 30, 1986, financial statements which were included in the bond registration statement.

May, Clark & Company completed its examination and submitted an unqualified auditor's report dated July 15, 1986. The registration statement was filed and became effective on September 1, 1986. Two weeks prior to the effective date, one of the partners of May, Clark & Company called on Chriswell Corporation and had lunch with the financial vice president and the controller. He questioned both officials on the company's operations since June 30 and inquired whether there had been any material changes in the company's financial position since that date. Both officers assured him that everything had proceeded normally and that the financial condition of the company had not changed materially.

Unfortunately, the officers' representation was not true. On July 30, a substantial debtor of the company failed to pay $400,000 due on its account receivable and indicated to Chriswell that it would probably be forced into bankruptcy. This receivable was shown as a collateralized loan on the June 30 financial statements. It was secured by stock of the debtor corporation which had a value in excess of the loan at the time the financial statements were prepared but was virtually worthless at the effective date of the registration statement. This $400,000 account receivable was material to the financial condition of Chriswell Corporation, and the market price of the subordinated debentures decreased by nearly 50 percent after the foregoing facts were disclosed.

The debenture holders of Chriswell are seeking recovery of their loss against all parties connected with the debenture registration.

Required:

Is May, Clark & Company liable to the Chriswell debenture holders? Explain.
(AICPA, adapted)

20–25. Whitlow & Company is a brokerage firm registered under the Securities Exchange Act of 1934. The act requires such a brokerage firm to file audited financial statements with the SEC annually. Mitchell & Moss, Whitlow's CPAs, performed the annual audit for the year ended December 31, 1987, and rendered an unqualified opinion, which was filed with the SEC along with Whitlow's financial statements. During 1987, Charles, the president of Whitlow & Company, engaged in a huge embezzlement scheme that eventually bankrupted the firm. As a result, substantial losses were suffered by customers and shareholders of Whitlow & Company, including Thaxton, who had recently purchased several shares of stock of Whitlow & Company after reviewing the company's 1987 audit report. Mitchell & Moss' audit was deficient; if they had complied with generally accepted auditing standards, the embezzlement would have been discovered. However, Mitchell & Moss had no knowledge of the embezzlement, nor could their conduct be categorized as reckless.

Required:

Answer the following, setting forth reasons for any conclusions stated:
a. What liability to Thaxton, if any, does Mitchell & Moss have under the Securities Exchange Act of 1934?
b. What theory or theories of liability, if any, are available to Whitlow & Company's customers and shareholders under the common law? (AICPA, adapted)

20–26. Jackson is a sophisticated investor. As such, she was initially a member of a small group that was going to participate in a private placement of $1 million of common stock of Clarion Corporation. Numerous meetings were held among management and the investor group. Detailed financial and other information was supplied to the participants. Upon the eve of completion of the placement, it was aborted when one major investor withdrew. Clarion then decided to offer $2.5 million of Clarion common stock to the public pursuant to the registration requirements of the Securities Act of 1933. Jackson subscribed to $300,000 of the Clarion public stock offering. Nine months later, Clarion's earnings dropped significantly and, as a result, the stock dropped 20 percent beneath the offering price. In addition, the Dow Jones Industrial Average was down 10 percent from the time of the offering.

Jackson has sold her shares at a loss of $60,000 and seeks to hold all parties who participated in the public offering liable, including Allen, Dunn, and Rose, Clarion's CPA firm. Although the audit was performed in conformity with generally accepted auditing standards, there were some relatively minor irregularities. The financial statements of Clarion Corporation, which were part of the registration statement, contained minor misleading facts. It is believed by Clarion and by Allen, Dunn and Rose, that Jackson's asserted claim is without merit.

Required:

Answer the following, setting forth reasons for any conclusions stated:
a.   Assuming Jackson sues under the Securities Act of 1933, what will be the basis of her claim?
b.   What are the probable defenses that might be asserted by Allen, Dunn, and Rose in light of these facts?   (AICPA, adapted)

EXAMPLES OF ENVIRONMENTAL CONSIDERATIONS RELATED TO SPECIFIC CONTROL OBJECTIVES

The following lists may be helpful in relating environmental factors identified in the planning effort to specific control objectives. *The lists are not intended to be exhaustive; relevant factors will vary, depending on the unique circumstances and conditions of each client.* To determine the importance of the various factors identified, the auditor should assess their potential impact on accounts or transactions affected by each specific control objective. These factors may increase or decrease the likelihood of material error and lead the auditor to emphasize specific audit areas or help justify minimum audit effort.

In addition to the examples following, the auditor's prior experience with the client is an important input to the review of environmental factors. Equally important are changes in the environment from the prior year because they can result in increased or decreased risk.

In some cases, it may be appropriate to indicate on the risk analysis working paper the nature and extent of management attention to the activities associated with a specific control objective. And the competence of the employees involved may be relevant—especially where a high level of experience or expertise is required to deal with a complex area (e.g., cost accounting or income taxes).

SALES

S–1 Customer Orders Require Approval of Credit and Terms before Acceptance

S–2 Uncollectible Amounts Are Promptly Identified and Provided for

Factors to Consider

Nature of customers (e.g., few large customers or many small ones, blue-chip or less established concerns, domestic or foreign)

Extent of customer turnover

Effect of economic developments on customers

Customer dependence on company as source of supply

Extension of credit as part of marketing strategy

Salesmen's commissions computed as part of the billing or collection function, or adjusted for uncollectible accounts

Availability of credit information

Extent of management involvement in credit and collection

Philosophy on providing for doubtful accounts

Nature of recourse for factored receivables

Nature of product pricing (e.g., standard or contract)

Discount policy

S–3 Products Shipped or Services Rendered Are Billed

Factors to Consider

Nature of products (e.g., few high value items or many low value ones, custom or standard)

Methods of distribution (e.g., direct shipments, drop shipments, consignments)

Frequency of partial shipments and backorders

Nature of services

Basis for measuring services performed

Salesmen's commissions based on billing

S–4 Billings Are for the Correct Amount

S–5 Revenues Are Recorded Correctly as to Account, Amount, and Period

S–6 Recorded Billings Are for Valid Transactions

Factors to Consider

Complexity of billing or revenue recognition process (e.g., few products or many, standard or negotiated pricing, billing following contract terms, revenue recognized on percentage-of-completion basis, seasonal fluctuations in volume of billings)

Frequency of price changes

Regulatory control of pricing

Number of new products

Nature and extent of billing disputes

Extent of credits issued for billing errors

S–7 Customer Returns and Other Allowances Are Approved and Recorded Correctly as to Account, Amount, and Period

Factors to Consider

Nature of products (e.g., quality, perishability, damageability, custom or standard, new or established, difficulty of assuring product suitability for customer needs—high technology)

Number of new products

Economic developments (e.g., high interest rates and/or slowing economy may cause distributors to return goods to reduce inventories)

Quality control efforts

Philosophy on allowing returns and granting allowances

Rebates or quantity discounts offered

Frequency of price changes

Effect of seasonability on level of returns and allowances

PRODUCTION OR SERVICE/ADMINISTRATION

P–1, A–1 Goods or Services Are Purchased (Expenses Are Incurred) Only with Proper Authorization

P–2, A–2 Goods or Services Received (Expenses and Related Liabilities) Are Recorded Correctly as to Account, Amount, and Period

Factors to Consider

Principal types of goods or services purchased or expenses incurred

Number of principal suppliers

Method of purchase (e.g., blanket purchase order, contracts)

Centralized or decentralized purchasing function

Economic developments (e.g., anticipated material shortages leading to stockpiling or tight money leading to reduce expenditures)

Vendor billing practices (e.g., prepayment or deposit requirements)

Use of preestablished reorder points

P–3, A–3 Salary, Wage, and Benefit Expenses Are Incurred Only for Work Authorized and Performed

P–4, A–4 Salaries, Wages, and Benefits Are Calculated at the Proper Rate

P–5, A–5 Salaries, Wages, Benefits, and Related Liabilities Are Recorded Correctly as to Account (Department, Activity, Cost Center, etc.), Amount, and Period

Factors to Consider

Size and stability of work force

Use of different systems for executive, salaried, and hourly payrolls (or office and plant payrolls)

Location of work force (e.g., multiple plants, construction sites, field service)

Regulatory requirements (e.g., minimum wage requirements, workers' compensation)

Extent of unionization (e.g., wage rates pursuant to union contract)

Effect of strikes or other work interruptions

Complexity of wage rate calculations (e.g., effect of overtime, piecework, or other incentives, cost-of-living adjustments)

Nature of benefit plans (e.g., bonus, pension, profit sharing)

Terms of employment contracts

Expected relationship of labor costs to material processed or total production costs

P–6 Costs Are Assigned to Inventory in Accordance with the Stated Valuation Method

P–7 Usage and Movement of Inventory Is Recorded Correctly as to Account, Amount (Quantities and Dollars), and Period

Factors to Consider

Nature of product (e.g., high dollar and low quantity or low dollar and high quantity)

Inventory valuation method

Costing method for transfer between inventory accounts and to cost of sales (e.g., specific identification, standard cost, weighted (moving) average, percentage of completion)

Effect of complexity and number of manufacturing processes on related inventory cost determinations

Nature and frequency of revisions to standard costs (e.g., anticipated cost increases included in standards or standards revised quarterly, volatility of inventory component costs)

Number of new products

Relative significance of material, labor, and overhead inventory components

Plant capacity and current operating level

Timing of client's physical inventory

Number of plant locations and significance of inventory levels

Inventory processed at vendors

Inventory maintained on consignment or at warehouses

History of book-to-physical inventory adjustments (quantities or dollars)

Unit of measure for inventory quantities and conversion requirements for pricing

Transfer pricing and intercompany profit recognition

Background and training of cost accounting personnel

P–8 Physical Loss of Inventory Is Prevented or Promptly Detected

Factors to Consider

Nature of product (e.g., susceptibility to pilferage, marketability, likelihood of breakage, spoilage, or other damage)

Method of distribution

Cause of book-to-physical adjustments

Nature, quantity, and market value of scrap generated

Number and geographical dispersion of inventory locations

P–9 Obsolete, Slow-moving, and Overstock Inventory Is Prevented or Promptly Detected and Provided for

Factors to Consider

Nature of raw materials, work in process, and finished goods (e.g., standard items or customer order)

Customer demand

Technological innovation (by competitors or client)

Regulatory requirements

Marketing strategies

Stockpiling of items expected to be in short supply (e.g., fuel due to energy shortage or key material due to expected strike)

Handling of returned items

Timing of physical inventories

Use of formula write down for overstock inventory

P–10 Inventory Is Carried at the Lower of Cost or Market

Factors to Consider

Changes in customer demands (e.g., due to switches to competitor's state-of-the-art, energy-efficient, or more economical product; scarcity of related products, such as fuel for recreational vehicles; general increase or decrease in demand for industry's products; volatility of basic commodity prices)

Nature of normal margins (e.g., "narrow" or "wide")

P–11 Property, Plant, and Equipment Are Purchased Only with Proper Authorization

P–12 Property, Plant, and Equipment Purchases Are Recorded Correctly as to Account, Amount, and Period

Factors to Consider

Level of plant expansion or modernization

Nature and extent of leasing of facilities or equipment

Investment Tax Credit (ITC) election under 1982 Tax Act (i.e., 10 percent ITC with basis reduction for 50 percent of ITC, or 8 percent ITC with no basis reduction)

Extent of in-house construction

Loan covenant restrictions on property and equipment additions

P–13 Disposals, Retirements, Trade-ins, Idle Plant and Equipment and Other Losses Are Identified and Recorded Correctly as to Account, Amount, and Period

Factors to Consider

Frequency of equipment replacement

Frequency of trade-ins

Changes in demand or technology that may cause idle facilities

Extent of re-tooling required for changes in products or production process

Effect of foreign expropriation or nationalization

Regulatory requirements (e.g., EPA, OSHA)

P–14 Physical Loss of Property, Plant, and Equipment Is Prevented

Factors to Consider

Nature of equipment (e.g., susceptibility to theft or damage from fire, alternative uses)

Nature of preventative maintenance program

Extent of equipment held by customers (e.g., rentals) or used on their property (e.g., construction sites)

P–15 Depreciation Is Calcuated Using Proper Lives and Methods

Factors to Consider

Industry practices

Condition of property ledger/lapse schedules

Extent to which technological innovations or regulatory factors may affect useful lives

Differences in lives and methods for financial and tax reporting

Extent of property additions or disposals

FINANCE

F–1 Cash Receipts Are Recorded Correctly as to Account, Amount, and Period and Are Deposited

F–2 Cash Receipts Are Properly Applied to Customer Balances

Factors to Consider

Nature of receipts (e.g., mail receipts, cash sales, COD sales, wire transfers, lock box receipts, few large receipts or many small ones)

Extent of nonapplied cash receipts

F–3 Cash Disbursements Are for Goods or Services Authorized and Received

F–4 Cash Disbursements Are Recorded Correctly as to Account, Amount, and Period

Factors to Consider

Volume and frequency of disbursements

Number of bank accounts

Number of systems to process disbursements (e.g., computer prepared checks for scheduled payments and manual prepared checks for others)

Extent to which checks prepared and held prior to disbursement

F–5 Debt and Lease Obligations and Related Expenses Are Authorized and Recorded Correctly as to Account, Amount, and Period

Factors to Consider

Nature of debt and lease obligations

Significant terms of debt and lease obligations

Ability to meet debt service requirements and restrictive covenants, or obtain waivers

F–6 Equity Transactions Are Authorized and Recorded Correctly as to Account, Amount, and Period

Factors to Consider

Nature of stock ownership (closely held or publicly traded, number of shareholders)

Components of shareholders' equity

Nature of equity transactions (e.g., new issues for cash or business ac-

quisition, treasury stock purchases and sales, options exercised, dividends)

Nature of stock option or compensation plans

Regulatory or bylaw requirements

F–7 Investments in and Advances to/from Subsidiaries and Other Affiliates Are Authorized and Recorded Correctly as to Account, Amount, and Period

Factors to Consider

Nature of subsidiaries and affiliates (e.g., extent of ownership, type of business, domestic or foreign)

Nature and frequency of intercompany transactions

Availability and reliability of subsidiary and equity investee financial statements (e.g., timeliness, audited or unaudited, different year-ends)

Extent of client management involvement in business of equity investees

Foreign currency translation policies for foreign operations, subsidiaries, and equity investees (e.g., functional currencies, highly inflationary economies, hedging practices)

F–8 Investment Transactions Are Authorized and Recorded Correctly as to Account, Amount, and Period

F–9 Income Earned on Investments Is Recorded Correctly as to Account, Amount, and Period

Factors to Consider

Nature and extent of investment activities (e.g., types of investments, frequency and size of transactions)

Debt covenant or regulatory restrictions on type or amount of investment

F–10 Loss in Value of Investments Is Promptly Detected and Provided for

F–11 Physical Loss of Investments Is Prevented or Promptly Detected

Factors to Consider

Nature of investment (e.g., blue chip, speculative, income producing, bearer or registered)

Frequency of turnover in investment portfolio

Economic factors (e.g., effect of change in interest rate on marketable security prices)

ADMINISTRATION[1]

A–6 Amortization of Loss in Value of Intangibles Is Recorded Correctly as to Account, Amount, and Period

Factors to Consider

Nature of intangibles (e.g., type of asset, estimated period of future benefit, significance to total assets)

Risks associated with ongoing value (e.g., technological changes, loss of principal customers, new competitors)

A–7 Provisions for Income Taxes and Related Liabilities and Deferrals Are Recorded Correctly as to Account, Amount, and Period

Factors to Consider

Status of IRS, state, or local examinations

Potential tax audit issues

Emerging industry tax issues

Nature of significant permanent and timing differences

---

[1] For A–1 through A–5, see P–1 through P–5.

Recent tax rulings

Nature of significant expected tax credits (e.g., investment tax credits on new facilities or net operating loss carryforwards)

Investment Tax Credit (ITC) election under 1982 Tax Act (i.e., 10 percent ITC with basis reduction for 50 percent of ITC, or 8 percent ITC with no basis reduction)

Complexity of corporate structure

Background and training of company personnel who calculate tax provisions

Responsibility for preparation of federal, state, local, and foreign tax returns

Philosophy on tax matters (i.e., conservative or aggressive)

Policy for reinvestment of earnings of foreign subsidiaries

A–8 Commitments and Contingencies Are Identified, Monitored, and, if Appropriate, Recorded or Disclosed

Factors to Consider

Nature of commitments or contingencies (e.g., long-term purchase contracts, fixed price sales contracts, product warranties, asserted and unasserted claims)

Effect of regulatory agency reviews (e.g., OSHA)

REFERENCE LISTS FOR SYSTEM EVALUATION AND PRELIMINARY AUDIT APPROACH

The following material is organized according to the specific control objectives in each operating component. The information included may be summarized as:

1. *System attributes to consider.*   Internal control practices and procedures are listed; if present, these might contribute to achieving the specific control objective. These examples can be useful for thinking about the company's present internal accounting control. And they provide a practical reminder of ways in which the company can obtain reasonable assurance that control objectives are achieved. The various attributes may be functioning in a manual or computerized system.

2. *What can go wrong.*   Possible errors and irregularities if control objectives are not achieved are listed. These are not intended to be exhaustive lists but rather are included to encourage the auditor to consider the possibilities.

3. *Accounts affected.*   Accounts ordinarily affected by each specific control objective are listed to help in understanding how control objectives affect the financial statements and the audit program.

4. *Principal audit procedures to consider.*   These procedures are presented in two categories: (a) those to consider when the specific control objective is achieved, and (b) those to consider when the specific control objective is not achieved. *However, the preliminary audit approach should be based not only on the system evaluation but also on environmental considerations and observations from detail analytical review.*

The following is an index to the reference lists.

SALES

S–1—Customer Orders Require Approval of Credit and Terms before Acceptance Authorization

System Attributes to Consider

Customer purchase orders compared to approved schedules for prices, discounts, payment terms, and delivery terms

Special terms approved in advance in writing

Orders compared to list of approved customers

Quotes or price estimates independently approved

Credit worthiness reviewed independent of marketing and order entry

New customers screened and assigned credit limits; limits regularly reviewed, compared to balances outstanding

What Can Go Wrong

Errors

Orders accepted from poor credit risks (receivables stated above realizable value, bad debt allowance and expense understated)

Orders accepted at terms other than those established by management (e.g., excessive discounts and allowances granted)

Irregularities

Sales at terms other than those authorized, to facilitate "side deals" for benefit of management, employees, or third parties

Excessive and unwarranted granting of credit under kickback arrangement

Accounts Affected

Sales, service income

Discounts

Returns and allowances

Accounts receivable

Allowance for doubtful accounts/Bad debts expense

Principal Audit Procedures to Consider

If Objective Achieved

Test key authorization and/or approval attributes by examining a representative sample of transactions from sales orders, sales journal, or invoice file through an interim date. Also review for adherence to terms established or approved by management (e.g., prices, discounts, payment, delivery) and for compliance with special approval requirements.

Determine reasonableness of criteria used and adequacy of documentation required to establish customer credit limits.

Compare relationships of provision for bad debts to credit sales and of allowance for doubtful accounts to accounts receivable with prior periods.

Test adherence to credit limits for selected customers by comparison to outstanding balances for portion of period under audit.

Review collectibility of receivables at interim date on limited basis (e.g., significant past-due accounts).

If Objective Not Achieved

If client can collect from customers for previous errors, test an extensive number of sales transactions to detect and/or estimate amount of incorrect billings throughout entire period under audit.

Perform extensive review of collectibility of year-end receivables.

For large or unusual sales contracts uncompleted at year-end, request confirmation from customers as to pricing, discount, payment, and warranty terms.

Review evidence or obtain information concerning credit worthiness for large new accounts.

Compare relationships of provision for bad debts to credit sales and of allowance for doubtful accounts to accounts receivable with prior periods.

S–2 Uncollectible Amounts Are Promptly Identified and Provided for (Valuation)

System Attributes to Consider

Credit worthiness reviewed and approved independent of marketing and order entry

Accounts periodically aged and delinquent accounts followed up

Accuracy of accounts receivable aging independently checked

Identification of bad debts and approval of write-offs independent of marketing and credit review

Timely collection follow-up independent of accounts receivable and cash receipts

Management monitors trends in age of receivables

Formal policy for writing off receivable (e.g., automatic write-off after specified past due period)

What Can Go Wrong

Errors

Accounts receivable aging incorrectly compiled; potentially uncollectible amounts not recognized (understated allowance for doubtful accounts/ bad debts expense)

Irregularities

Excessive and unwarranted granting of credit under kickback arrangement

Accounts Affected

Accounts receivable

Allowance for doubtful accounts/bad debts expense

Principal Audit Procedures to Consider

If Objective Achieved

Examine evidence of key attributes for monitoring collectibility.

Determine reasonableness of criteria for judging an account uncollectible.

Compare aging, bad debts expense, and write-offs with prior periods. Evaluate trends in light of current economic conditions.

Test clerical accuracy of receivables aging on limited basis.

Review collectibility of receivables at interim date on limited basis (e.g., significant past-due accounts).

If Objective Not Achieved

Perform extensive review of clerical accuracy of receivables aging.

Review evidence or obtain information concerning credit worthiness for large new accounts.

Perform extensive review of collectibility of year-end receivables.

Compare aging, bad debts expense, and write-offs with prior periods. Evaluate trends in light of current economic conditions.

S–3 Products Shipped or Services Rendered Are Billed (Recording, Safeguarding)

System Attributes to Consider

Quantities shipped regularly reconciled to quantities billed

Payroll or other record of services rendered or service calls made regularly reconciled to amounts billed

Shipping documents issued in prenumbered order; sequence independently checked

Materials leaving premises checked for appropriate shipping documents

Billing performed independent of shipping and inventory control departments

Billing performed independent of scheduling services or dispatching service calls

Backlog information regularly reviewed

Progress billings on long-term projects regularly reviewed for compliance with contract terms

What Can Go Wrong

Errors

Unbilled deliveries (understated sales and receivables; if inventory is relieved and cost of sales charged based on billings, may result in overstated inventory and understated cost of sales)

Irregularities

Management, employees, or third parties receive products or services without being billed

Accounts Affected

Sales, service income

Accounts receivable

Inventory/cost of sales

Principal Audit Procedures to Consider

If Objective Achieved

Test key recording and safeguarding attributes by examining a representative sample of transactions from sales order file or shipping (service call) records through an interim date. Trace to subsequent recorded billings.

Observe shipments leaving premises with shipping documents.

Examine a representative sample of reconciliations of units shipped and billed.

Compare gross margins by product line and other operating relationships (e.g., both sales and cost of sales to units shipped) with prior periods.

Test shipping cutoff at interim physical inventory date on limited basis.

If Objective Not Achieved

Test an extensive number of sales transactions to detect errors and/or estimate amount of unbilled items throughout period under audit by tracing shipments to subsequent recorded billings.

Inquire about management, salesmen, or others receiving products without billings.

If inventory overstatement can result from unbilled deliveries, observe physical inventory at or near year-end. Arrange for heavy coverage of counts. Investigate inventory shortages.

Perform extensive test of shipping cutoff as of interim physical inventory date and year-end.

Review gross margins by product line; compare other operating relationships (e.g., both sales and cost of sales to units shipped) with prior periods.

S–4 Billings Are for the Correct Amount (Authorization)

System Attributes to Consider

Special prices approved in advance in writing

Billings independently checked for accuracy and agreement with approved price lists, discounts, written quotes, etc.

Amounts of progress billings on

long-term projects checked for agreement with contract terms

What Can Go Wrong

Errors

Customers billed at incorrect amounts

Irregularities

Management, employees, or third parties receive products or services at unauthorized reduced rates

Accounts Affected

Sales, service income

Discounts

Accounts receivable

Principal Audit Procedures to Consider

If Objective Achieved

Test key authorization attributes for a representative sample of sales invoices. Verify adherence to prices and discounts established or approved by management. Test clerical accuracy.

Circularize receivables at interim date on limited basis.

Review gross margins by product line.

If Objective Not Achieved

Examine an extensive number of sales transactions to detect errors and/or estimate amount of incorrect billings throughout entire period under audit (error estimation not appropriate if only understated billings are detected, unless client can bill customers for amounts of previous errors). Trace recorded prices and discounts to those approved by management and test clerical accuracy.

Perform extensive receivables circularization at or near year-end.

Review gross margins by product line.

S–5 Revenues Are Recorded Correctly as to Account, Amount, and Period (Recording)

System Attributes to Consider

Recordkeeping independent of billing, shipping, and cash receipts

Billings issued and recorded in pre-

numbered order; sequence independently checked

Unused and voided billing forms controlled

Prompt processing of billings

Accounts receivable postings reconciled to sales journal

Accounts receivable detail reconciled to control account

Revenues recognized on long-term project independently compared to contract term, engineering estimates of progess to date, and current estimates of costs to complete

What Can Go Wrong

Errors

Revenues misclassified or not recognized; accounts receivable not recorded*

Revenues recorded at wrong amounts*

Revenues recorded in wrong period*

Irregularities

Billings recorded at less than full amount; customers remit in full and difference misappropriated

Revenues recorded in wrong period to smooth earnings

Revenues suppressed to reduce taxes or rentals based on volume

Accounts Affected

Sales, service income

Accounts receivable

Inventory/cost of sales

Unearned income

Principal Audit Procedures to Consider

If Objective Achieved

Test key recording attributes by examining a representative sample of transactions from shipping documents or sales invoice file through an interim date. Trace sales invoices to customer accounts and to sales journal and trace journal postings to general ledger.

Circularize receivables at interim date on limited basis.

Review gross margins by product line.

Test shipping cutoff at interim physical inventory date on limited basis.

---

* If inventory relieved and cost of sales charged based on recorded billings, may result in misstated inventory and misstated cost of sales

Test propriety of timing and amount of revenue recognition by tracing significant amounts to long-term contracts, service agreements, etc. Review cost and progress estimation procedures.

Review rollforward of accounts receivable from date of circularization. Compare level of activity during rollforward period with prior periods.

Review year-end accounts receivable records for unusual changes in customer balances since date of circularization and consider need for additional circularization.

If Objective Not Achieved

Trace an extensive number of shipping documents or sales invoices to sales journal to detect errors and/or estimate amount of incorrectly recorded sales throughout entire period under audit. Trace shipping documents or sales invoices to sales journal and journal postings to general ledger.

Perform extensive receivables circularization at or near year-end.

If circularization procedures are applied at an interim date, perform tests of rollforward amounts and review detail of accounts receivable at year-end for unusual changes in customer balances since date of circularization. Consider need for additional circularization. Compare level of activity during rollforward period with prior periods.

If inventory overstatement can result from unrecorded billings, observe physical inventory at or near year-end. Arrange for heavy coverage of counts. Investigate inventory shortages.

Perform extensive test of shipping cutoff as of physical inventory date and year-end.

Perform extensive test of timing and amount of year-end revenue recognition by tracing to long-term contracts, service agreements, etc., to detect errors and/or estimate amount of incorrect revenue recorded. Review year-end cost and progress estimation procedures.

Review gross margins by product line.

S–6 Recorded Billings Are for Valid Transactions (Recording)

System Attributes to Consider

Billings issued and recorded in prenumbered order; sequence independently checked

Unused and voided billing forms controlled

Billings reconciled to shipping documents or approved sales orders

Monthly statements mailed to all (or delinquent) customers; complaints handled independent of cashier or accounts receivable bookkeeper

What Can Go Wrong

Errors

Billings recorded but goods not shipped or services not rendered at all or not until following period (overstated sales and receivables; if inventory relieved and cost of sales charged based on recorded billings, may result in understated inventory and overstated cost of sales)

Irregularities

Sales and receivables overstated to (1) improve performance picture, (2) meet sales forecast, or (3) increase commission, bonus, or profit sharing

Accounts Affected

Sales, service income

Accounts receivable

Inventory/cost of sales

Principal Audit Procedures to Consider

If Objective Achieved

Test key recording attributes by examining a representative sample of transactions from sales invoice file or sales register through an interim date. Trace to customer orders, shipping documents, and subsequent cash receipts.

Compare relationship of sales to units sold. Review trends in aging and days' sales in receivables.

Circularize receivables at interim date on limited basis. Omit or limit examination of remittance advices as part of alternative procedures.

Review rollforward of accounts receivable from date of circularization. Compare level of activity during rollforward period to prior periods.

Review detail accounts receivable records at year-end for unusual changes in customer balances since date of circularization and consider need for additional circularization.

Investigate significant credits to receivables detail other than cash receipts throughout period under audit.

If Objective Not Achieved

Test an extensive number of sales transactions selected from sales invoice file or sales register and trace to customer orders and shipping documents to detect errors and/or estimate amount of invalid sales throughout entire period under audit.

Reconcile billings with shipping documents for substantial portion of period.

Account for numerical sequence of billings for substantial portion of period.

Investigate significant credits to receivable detail other than cash receipts throughout period under audit.

Perform extensive receivables circularization at or near year-end; use positive requests.

If circularization procedures are applied at an interim date, perform tests of rollforward amounts and review detail of accounts receivable at year-end for unusual changes in customer balances since date of circularization. Consider need for additional circularization. Compare level of activity during rollforward period with prior periods.

Examine remittance advices and shipping documents as part of supporting year-end receivables balances.

S–7 Customer Returns and Other Allowances Are Approved and Recorded Correctly as to Account, Amount, and Period (Authorization, Recording)

System Attributes to Consider

Returns, allowances, discounts, and other credits approved before issuance

Customers required to obtain advance approval to return goods

Credit memos issued in prenumbered order; sequence independently checked

Credit memos compared to receiving/inspection report for returned goods or to other approval document

Prompt processing of credits

Employees responsible for approving or recording customer credits have no access to cash receipts or detail receivables records

Noncash credits to receivables periodically reviewed

Customer claims for repairs under guarantees/warranties checked for compliance with terms of sale

What Can Go Wrong

Errors

Returns or other allowances (including warranties) misclassified or not recorded (understated discounts, returns and allowances, warranty reserves/expense; overstated receivable accounts)

Credits issued for returns or allowances not earned or otherwise not according to company policy (overstated expense)

Irregularities

False credit memos issued and account receivable credited; customers remit in full and amount of credits misappropriated

Customers fail to pay within discount period and remit in full; payments recorded as if discount earned, amount of discounts misappropriated

Accounts Affected

Discounts

Sales returns and allowances

Accounts receivable

Inventory/cost of sales

Warranty reserves/expense

Accrual for unissued credits

Principal Audit Procedures to Consider

If Objective Achieved

Test key authorization and recording attributes by examining a representative sample of credit memos issued through an interim date. Also examine supporting documentation and trace to summaries and general ledger postings.

Compare discounts, returns, and allowances with prior periods (e.g., as a percentage of sales).

Determine time lag for credit issuance and review adequacy of accrual for unissued credits.

Circularize receivables at interim date on limited basis.

If Objective Not Achieved

Trace an extensive number of credit memos issued throughout entire period under audit to posting and supporting documentation to detect and/or estimate errors in issuing or posting. Include significant credit memos issued.

Investigate significant credits to receivables detail other than cash receipts throughout period under audit.

Check disposition of returned goods. Trace to terms and recording of original sale. Trace to addition to inventory and, for significant items, investigate whether usable or saleable.

Account for numerical sequence of credit memos issued throughout period under audit.

Determine adequacy of year-end accrual for unissued credits by examining credit memos issued and recorded subsequent to year-end.

Compare discounts, returns, and allowances with prior periods (e.g., as a percentage of sales).

Perform extensive receivables circularization at or near year-end; use positive requests.

PRODUCTION OR SERVICE—MATERIALS AND OVERHEAD

P-1 Goods or Services Are Purchased Only with Proper Authorization (Authorization)

Systems Attributes to Consider

Approval by specified personnel within specified dollar limits required for requisition and/or purchase orders

Purchasing performed by department or individual independent of receiving, accounts payable, and stores

Purchase orders compared to control list or file of approved vendors

Purchase orders issued in prenumbered order; sequence independently checked

Records of returned goods matched to vendor credit memos

Goods compared to purchase orders or other purchase authorization before acceptance

Unmatched receiving reports investigated; unauthorized items identified for return to vendor

Receipts under blanket purchase orders monitored; quantities exceeding authorized total returned to vendor

Competitive bids obtained when practicable; documentation maintained and periodically reviewed for compliance with company policy

Overhead expense budget approved by management

What Can Go Wrong

Errors

Unauthorized inventory purchases or overhead expenses incurred

Excess inventory or supplies purchased, which may become unusable or obsolete; unnecessary storage costs incurred

Irregularities

Management, employees, or third parties able to obtain items for personal use and charge to company

Purchases at other than most favorable terms to facilitate "side deals" for benefit of management, employees, or third parties

Accounts Affected

Purchases

Overhead accounts

Inventory

Prepaid expenses (e.g., prepaid insurance, prepaid taxes, prepaid rent)

Accounts payable, accrued liabilities

Principal Audit Procedures to Consider

If Objective Achieved

Test key authorization and/or approval attributes by examining a representative sample of inventory purchases and overhead expense items (concurrently with test of cash disbursements) incurred through an interim date.

Compare relationship of inventory purchases and level of production with prior periods. Compare relationship of major components of overhead expense to direct labor or level of production with prior periods. Compare major components of overhead expense with budget.

If Objective Not Achieved

Test an extensive number of inventory purchases and overhead expense items to estimate the effect of possible errors or irregularities. Include significant purchases throughout period under audit selected from those types for which objective is not achieved and test for approval and business purpose. Select purchases from different suppliers of the same inventory items and compare unit prices, terms, etc.

Compare relationship of inventory purchases and level of production with prior periods. Compare relationship of major components of overhead expense to direct labor or level of production with prior periods. Compare major components of overhead with budget.

P–2 Goods or Services Received Are Recorded Correctly as to Account, Amount, and Period (Recording)

System Attributes to Consider

Goods counted, inspected, and compared to packing slips before acceptance

Receiving reports issued by receiving/inspection department in prenumbered order; sequence independently checked or unused receiving reports otherwise controlled

Services received acknowledged in writing by responsible employee

Receiving documentation, purchase order, and invoice matched before recording liability

Invoice additions, extensions, pricing checked

Unmatched receiving reports and invoices investigated for inclusion in estimated liability at close of period

Invoices registered immediately upon receipt

Account distribution reviewed when recording liability or when signing check

Vendor statements regularly reconciled

What Can Go Wrong

Errors

Inventory, overhead purchases misclassified, recorded at wrong amounts, or not recorded

Inventory, overhead purchases not recorded in period incurred

Irregularities

Misclassification to conceal unauthorized purchases for benefit of management, employees, or third parties

Purchase discounts taken but not recorded; amount of discounts misappropriated

Accounts Affected

Purchases and related variances

Overhead accounts

Inventory

Prepaid expenses (e.g., prepaid insurance, prepaid taxes, prepaid rent)

Accounts payable, accrued liabilities

Principal Audit Procedures to Consider

If Objective Achieved

Test key recording attributes by examining a representative sample of purchases (concurrently with test of cash disbursements) incurred through an interim date. Also review for:

1. Correct account distribution
2. Recording in correct account
3. Agreement of recorded amount with invoice and/or purchase order
4. Recording in period received

Review gross margins and inventory turnover ratios. Compare relationship of overhead accounts and level of production with prior periods and budget.

Investigate significant price variance accounts.

Test receiving cutoff at physical inventory date on limited basis.

Limit accounts payable out-of-period search at inventory date and year-end. Use high minimum dollar amount for selecting subsequent disbursements and unmatched invoices and receiving reports to examine and limit reconciliation (or test of client's reconciliation) of statements from selected principal vendors.

If Objective Not Achieved

Test an extensive number of purchases to detect errors and/or estimate amounts incorrectly recorded. Include significant purchases incurred throughout period under audit selected from those types for which objective is not achieved.

Perform extensive test of receiving cutoff at inventory date and year-end.

Perform extensive accounts payable out-of-period search at inventory date and year-end. Request and reconcile (or test client's reconciliation of) statements from all principal vendors and use low minimum dollar amount for selecting subsequent disbursements and unmatched invoices and receiving reports to examine.

Review gross margins and inventory turnover ratios for periods prior and subsequent to physical inventory. Compare relationship of overhead accounts and level of production with prior periods and budget.

Investigate significant price variance accounts.

PRODUCTION OR SERVICE—LABOR/ADMINISTRATION

P–3, A–3   Salary, Wage, and Benefit Expenses Are Incurred Only for Work Authorized and Performed (Authorization)

System Attributes to Consider

Personnel records maintained independent of payroll and timekeeping departments

Changes to payroll (e.g., new hires, terminations, and transfers) not made unless personnel department sends approved notification direct to payroll department; notification not routed through timekeeping or employee's supervisor

Budgetary control over payroll expense, hours, and number of employees

Time clocks supervised

Terminated employees promptly removed from payroll

Time cards or reports approved by supervisor not responsible for paycheck distribution

Time paid reconciled to time worked

Overtime approved in writing

Sick leave, vacations, and holidays reviewed for compliance with company policy

Payroll details reviewed by responsible employee independent of paycheck distribution and unclaimed wages; individual gross amounts and overtime amounts over specified limits investigated

What Can Go Wrong

Errors

Work not authorized or not performed is accrued (overstated payroll expense and liability acocunts)

Accrual of benefits (e.g., sick leave, vacation, pension) not earned

Irregularities

Padded time cards or reports

Fictitious employees (e.g., terminated employees left on payroll)

Accounts Affected

Payroll expense

Labor and overhead components of inventory/cost of sales

Accrued payroll and related liabilities

Pension, profit sharing, and other benefit expenses and related liabilities

Principal Audit Procedures to Consider

If Objective Achieved

Test key authorization attributes by examining personnel records for a representative sample of employees selected from payroll records. Examine time cards or other records for required approvals. Also reconcile calculation of gross pay to time records.

Compare payroll expense with prior periods and budget. Compare relationships of payroll expense to cost of sales and sales with prior periods.

Compare vacation and sick leave accruals with prior periods and budget. Review for compliance with policies or labor contract provisions.

Review for approval and determine justification for retroactive pay increases, special bonuses, or other unusual compensation arrangements (e.g., tied to repayment of officers' loans or advances).

If Objective Not Achieved

Compare payroll expense to prior periods and budget (by department and in total); correlate with changes in number of employees. Compare relationships of payroll expense to cost of sales and sales with prior periods.

Recompute vacation and sick leave accruals. Review for compliance with policies or labor contract provisions.

Test to detect fictitious employees. Compare payroll records for an extensive number of employees selected throughout period under audit with personnel records. Trace new hires per payroll records to documentation of existence and approval to hire; trace terminations to deletion from payroll.

Observe payoff of selected employees. Reconcile calculation of gross pay to time records.

Determine reasons for employees receiving unusually large amounts of overtime pay.

Review for approval and determine justification for retroactive pay increases, special bonuses, or other unusual compensation arrangements (e.g., tied to repayment of officers' loans or advances).

P–4, A–4 Salaries, Wages, and Benefits Are Calculated at the Proper Rate (Authorization)

System Attributes to Consider

Pay rate and other personnel records maintained independent of payroll department

Pay rate or other payroll information not changed unless personnel department sends approved notification direct to payroll department; notification not routed through timekeeping or employee's supervisor

Overtime, bonuses, commissions, and other premiums reviewed for compliance with company policy

Clerical accuracy independently checked

Payroll details reviewed by responsible employee independent of paycheck distribution and unclaimed wages, individual gross amounts over specified limit investigated

Labor recorded at standard rates; labor variance accounts regularly reviewed

What Can Go Wrong

Errors

Employees' earnings over- or underaccrued due to improper rate or computation error

Irregularities

Intentional overaccrual under kickback arrangement

Accounts Affected

Payroll expense

Labor and overhead components of inventory/cost of sales

Accrued payroll and related liabilities

Pension, profit sharing, and other benefit expenses and related liabilities

Principal Audit Procedures to Consider

If Objective Achieved

Test key authorization attributes for a representative sample of employees selected from payroll records. Also compare the pay rate per personnel records or union contracts (including shift premiums, piecework, and other incentives of adjustments) with that used to calculate gross pay. Compare hours and production factors used to calculate gross pay to time records.

Review reasonableness of periodic payments to selected employees as reflected in year-to-date earnings records.

Compare relationships of payroll expense to sales, employee benefits to gross pay, and pension expense to covered employees with prior periods.

If Objective Not Achieved

Test gross pay calculations to detect errors and/or estimate amount of back pay that is recoverable or owed. For an extensive number of employees, compare pay rate per personnel records or union contracts (including shift premiums, piecework, and other incentives or adjustments) with that used to calculate gross pay. Compare hours and production factors used to calculate gross pay to time records.

Review reasonableness of periodic payments to selected employees as reflected in year-to-date earnings records.

Compare relationships of payroll expense to sales, employee benefits to gross pay, and pension expense to covered employees with prior periods.

P–5, A–5 Salaries, Wages, Benefits, and Related Liabilities Are Recorded Correctly as to Account (Department, Activity, Cost Center, etc.), Amount, and Period (Recording)

System Attributes to Consider

Distribution of hours (direct and indirect) to activity or departments reviewed and approved by supervisory personnel

Comparisons of actual payroll amounts to budgeted amounts regularly reviewed by management

Labor standards regularly compared to actual; variances analyzed

Labor charged to maintenance and construction-in-progress work orders regularly reviewed

What Can Go Wrong

Errors

Payroll cost or expense or liabilities misclassified

Payroll cost or expense or liabilities recorded at incorrect amounts

Payroll not recorded in period earned (e.g., recorded in subsequent period when paid)

Irregularities

Payroll deductions not recorded, amount of deductions misappropriated

Payroll details overfooted; inflated amount recorded and difference misappropriated

Payroll deductions transferred to credit of payroll clerk

Accounts Affected

Payroll expense

Labor and overhead components of inventory/cost of sales

Accrued payroll and related liabilities

Pension, profit sharing, and other benefit expenses and related liabilities

Principal Audit Procedures to Consider

If Objective Achieved

Test key recording attributes for a representative sample of employees selected from payroll records. Also compare expense account charged (department, activity, cost center, etc.) to position description. Trace selected payroll journal distribution summaries to general ledger.

Compare payroll expense with prior periods and budget. Compare relationship of payroll expense and number of employees with prior periods and labor variances to incurred amounts.

Review accrued payroll and related liability accounts for proper periodic clearance. Review year-end amounts for reasonableness.

If Objective Not Achieved

Test an extensive number of employees to detect and/or estimate amounts charged to incorrect financial statement classifications. Review the propriety of classification of individual employee payroll amounts selected throughout the period under audit. Consider possibility of errors in labor and overhead included in work in process and finished goods inventory.

Foot selected payroll journals; compare net payroll with transfer to payroll bank account. Trace payroll journal distribution summaries to general ledger.

Compare payroll tax reports with accrued tax liabilities.

Recompute year-end payroll accrual accounts and compare with subsequent payroll register.

Compare annual payroll expense with prior periods and budget. Compare relationship of payroll expense to number of employees and labor variances to incurred amounts.

PRODUCTION OR SERVICE— INVENTORY ACCOUNTABILITY AND PHYSICAL SAFEGUARDS

P–6 Costs Are Assigned to Inventory In Accordance with the Stated Valuation Method (Recording)

System Attributes to Consider

Cost accounting performed by department or individual independent of other accounting functions

Cost accounting subsidiary records regularly balanced to general ledger control accounts

Standard unit costs regularly compared to actual material prices, quantities used, labor rates and hours, overhead expenses, and proper absorption rate

Variances, including overhead, regularly analyzed and allocated to inventory; submitted to management for review

Written policies and procedures for performing LIFO computations, determining LIFO pools, adjusting LIFO layers; computations checked for compliance

Control procedures relating to the following cost accounting processes:

Materials costs charged to job orders

Production labor costs charged to job orders based on (or reconciled to) payroll records, job tickets, or production reports

Overhead charged to job orders based on measure of activity (e.g., direct labor hours or dollars)

Standard material quantities based on actual usage data or bills of materials developed by production engineers

Standard labor hours based on actual production records or time-and-motion studies

Departmental (or other work center) overhead rates established

Overhead rates based on accounting or engineering studies (e.g., standard hours based on practical capacity)

Labor and overhead associated with unusual or excess capacity excluded from inventory

What Can Go Wrong

Errors

Improper inventory classification

Improper cost allocation

Computation of LIFO inventory not in accordance with IRS Code and Regulations

Irregularities

Unauthorized adjustment of inventory records to conceal misappropriation of assets

Manipulation of inventory records by management to improve performance picture

Fictitious scrap reported to cover prior period inventory overstatement

Accounts Affected

Inventory/cost of sales

Principal Audit Procedures to Consider

If Objective Achieved

Determine date and method of most recent revision to cost records. Determine that cost buildups are supported by engineering studies and bills of material. Test clerical accuracy of selected cost buildups.

Test material prices by reference to vendor invoices. If LIFO is used, test replacement cost by review of last invoice price for significant items and/ or a representative sample of items.

Test standard material quantities in work in process and finished goods items by reference to bills of material and requisitions.

Compare unit prices for inventory items with those of prior periods and investigate significant changes and/or unusual trends in pricing.

Investigate significant variance accounts. Consider adjustment to inventory values.

Compare relationship of actual labor and overhead costs to materials put into production with same relationship in ending inventory and with prior periods. Review computation of labor and overhead rates and compare with actual rates in current and prior periods. Limit price tests of labor and overhead at inventory date to clerical accuracy and extension of assigned costs. Determine that costs used to compute overhead rates are properly inventoriable.

Test computation of LIFO inventory valuation and reserve. Consider effects of LIFO methodology and determine that it complies with IRS requirements.

If Objective Not Achieved

Test pricing for an extensive number of inventory items at or near year-end to estimate the effect of possible errors. Include significant and representative other inventory items, and perform the following:

1. Test material prices by reference to vendor invoices. If LIFO is used, test replacement cost by review of last invoice price.
2. Test standard material quantities in work in process and finished goods by reference to bills of material and requisitions.
3. Test labor rates by reference to payroll records or union contracts.
4. Test computation of overhead rates and compare with actual rates in current and prior periods. Determine that costs used to compute overhead rates are properly inventoriable.

Compare unit prices for inventory items with those of prior periods and investigate significant changes and/or unusual trends in pricing.

Investigate significant variance accounts. Consider adjustment to inventory values.

Compare relationship of actual labor and overhead costs to materials put into production with the same relationship in ending inventory. Compare with prior periods.

Test computations of LIFO inventory valuation and reserve. Consider effects of LIFO methodology and determine that it complies with IRS requirements.

P–7 Usage and Movement of Inventory Is Recorded Correctly as to Account, Amount (Quantities and Dollars), and Period (Recording)

System Attributes to Consider

Periodic comparisons of actual quantities to perpetual records for raw materials, purchased parts, work in process, subassemblies, finished goods

Documentation issued in prenumbered order for receiving, stores requisitions, production orders, and shipping (including partial shipments); sequence independently checked

Shipments of finished goods checked for appropriate shipping documents

Shipping, billing, and inventory records reconciled on a regular basis

Records maintained for inventory on consignment (in and out), held by vendors, or in outside warehouses; periodically reconciled to reports received from outsiders

Inventory accounts adjusted for results of periodic physical counts

Inventory adjustments documented and require management approval

Control procedures related to the following cost accounting processes:

Raw material receipts recorded from invoices, receiving reports, or physical counts

Raw material issues recorded from production orders or stores requisitions

Material costs charged to job order or material usage account

Production labor costs charged to job orders or departmental expense account based on payroll records, job tickets, or production reports

Overhead charged to job orders, departments, or work in process based on measure of activity (e.g., direct labor hours or dollars)

Work in process increased for raw materials placed in production

Work in process relieved and finished goods charged based on completed production orders, inspection reports, or finished goods receiving tickets

Finished goods relieved based on filled sales orders or storekeepers issue slip

Sale or recycling of scrap, returns to vendor, and inventory abandonments documented and recorded

What Can Go Wrong

Errors

Entries not properly reflected in general ledger inventory accounts for purchases, production, or sales transactions

Inventory properly stated in the aggregate, but significant book-to-physical adjustments required to report inventory properly by classification

Inaccuracies in detail perpetual inventory records result in unnecessary materials purchased or units produced, inventory overstock, and obsolescence

Irregularities

Unauthorized adjustment of inventory records to conceal misappropriation of assets

Manipulation of inventory records by management to improve performance picture

Accounts Affected

Inventory/cost of sales

Principal Audit Procedures to Consider

If Objective Achieved

Test key recording attributes for inventory quantities and amounts (concurrently with tests of payroll and material purchases) as of an interim date. Trace labor and raw materials to detail inventory records. Trace inventory flow to selected detail documents and records (e.g., raw material requisitions, production reports, finished goods inspection reports); note appropriate relief from/addition to inventory records and accounts.

Review gross margins and compare with prior periods. Summarize inventories by location and type; compare amounts and relationships of classifications with prior periods.

Observe client's physical inventory counts as of interim date. Make limited independent counts and list quantities, condition, classification, and stage of completion. Consider using inventory observation checklist.

Request confirmation of significant amounts of inventory on consignment or in outside warehouses.

Test inventory compilation on a limited basis.

Review entries adjusting inventories; examine documentation and required approvals. Summarize adjustments between book and physical inventories and obtain explanations. Review significance and frequency of adjustments.

Review inventory rollforward amounts for reasonableness. Compare level of activity in purchases, labor, overhead, and variance accounts from inventory date to year-end.

Test shipping and receiving cutoff at inventory date on limited basis.

If Objective Not Achieved

Observe physical inventory at or near year-end. Arrange for heavy coverage of counts. Make extensive listings of quantities, condition, classification, and stage of completion.

Physically observe or request confirmation of inventory on consignment or in outside warehouses.

Perform extensive tests of inventory compilation, including propriety of inventory classifications.

Perform extensive test of shipping and receiving cutoffs at inventory date and year-end.

Review entries adjusting inventories; examine documentation and required approvals. Summarize adjustments between book and physical inventories, and obtain explanations. Review significance and frequency of adjustments.

Review gross margins and compare with prior periods. Summarize inventories by location and class; compare amounts and relationships of classifications with prior periods.

If physical counts made at an interim date, perform tests of rollforward amounts. Compare levels of activity in purchases, labor, overhead, and variance accounts from inventory date to year-end.

P–8 Physical Loss of Inventory Is Prevented or Promptly Detected (Safeguarding, Reconciliation)

System Attributes to Consider

Responsibility for inventories assigned to specified storekeepers; written stores requisition or shipping order required for all inventory issues

Perpetual records regularly checked by cycle count or complete physical count

Where no perpetual records maintained, quantities regularly determined by physical count, costing, and comparison to inventory accounts

Inventory counts and recordkeeping independent of storekeepers

Written instructions for inventory counts; compliance checked

Formal policies for scrap gathering, measuring, recording, storing, and disposal/recycling; compliance periodically reviewed

Material standards anticipate scrap; variances measure excessive amounts

Cost of scrap, waste, and defective products regularly reviewed

Inventory adjustments documented and require management approval

Complete production reconciled to finished goods additions

Guards and/or alarm system used

Employees identified by badge, card, etc.

Employees bonded

Storage areas secured against unauthorized admission; protected against deterioration

Offsite inventories stored in bonded warehouses

Materials leaving premises checked for appropriate shipping documents

What Can Go Wrong

Errors

Undetected physical loss, deterioration of inventory (overstated inventory accounts, eventual book-to-physical adjustments)

Perpetual records overstate quantities on hand

Scrap not monitored, not properly reported (production inefficiencies result in excess waste)

Sale of scrap not reported (understated cash, other income accounts)

Materials double-counted (e.g., in work in process and raw materials)

Irregularities

Management, employees, or third parties able to obtain inventory items for personal use or sale

Nonexistent inventory items included in periodic physical inventory count (inventory overstated, cost of sales understated)

Inventory intentionally scrapped to facilitate misappropriation

Scrap or proceeds from sale of scrap misappropriated

Accounts Affected

Inventory/cost of sales

Scrap sales

Principal Audit Procedures to Consider

If Objective Achieved

Observe physical safeguards, housekeeping, and shipments leaving premises with shipping documents.

If perpetual records maintained, test count inventory items at interim date and reconcile to records. If perpetual records not maintained, observe client's physical inventory counts at interim date.

Request confirmation of significant amounts of inventory on consignment or in outside warehouses.

Review entries adjusting inventories; examine documentation and required approvals.

Test shipping and receiving cutoff at inventory date on limited basis.

Compare relationship of scrap cost with material put into production and the level of scrap sales with prior periods.

If Objective Not Achieved

Observe physical inventory at or near year-end. Arrange for heavy coverage of counts. Investigate inventory shortages.

Physically observe or request confirmation of inventory on consignment or in outside warehouses.

Inquire about management, salesmen, or others receiving products without billings. Observe inventory leaving premises with shipping documents.

Perform extensive tests of shipping and receiving cutoffs at inventory date.

Investigate scrap reports to identify any unauthorized disposition or misappropriation of scrap proceeds. Compare the relationship of scrap cost with material put into production and the level of scrap sales with prior periods.

Review entries adjusting inventories; examine documentation and required approvals.

P–9 Obsolete, Slow-moving, and Overstock Inventory Is Prevented or Promptly Detected and Provided for (Safeguarding, Valuation)

System Attributes to Consider

Perpetual records show date of last usage; stock levels and usability regularly reviewed

Physical storage methods regularly reviewed for sources of inventory deterioration

Purchase requisitions compared to preestabished reorder points and economic order quantities

Potential overstock identified by regularly comparing quantities on hand with historical usage

Production and existing stock levels related to forecasts of market and technological changes

Bill of materials and part number systems provide for identification of common parts and sub-assemblies; discontinued products reviewed for reusable components

Work in process periodically reviewed for "old" items

What Can Go Wrong

Errors

Continued purchase and/or production of items that cannot be used or sold (overstated inventory, understated cost of sales)

Irregularities

Inventory known to be obsolete, slow-moving, or overstock not written off

Accounts Affected

Inventory/cost of sales

Principal Audit Procedures to Consider

If Objective Achieved

Review procedures for monitoring obsolescence and overstock. Determine that such procedures result in adequate provision to cover losses that may be incurred in disposing of obsolete, slow-moving, and overstock items.

Inquire as to the existence of damaged, slow-moving, overstock, out-of-style, and obsolete inventories and of commitments for additional quantities of similar items. Make note of such items during:

1. Inventory observation
2. Review of perpetual records

3.   Price tests
4.   Review of gross margins

Compute inventory turnover and compare with prior periods and industry data.

If Objective Not Achieved

Inquire as to existence of damaged, slow-moving, overstock, out-of-style, and obsolete inventories and of commitments for additional quantities of similar items. Make note of such items during:

1.   Inventory observation
2.   Review of perpetual records
3.   Price tests
4.   Review of gross margins

Compare sales and usage with inventory quantities, considering backlog, sales forecasts, marketing plans, etc. Determine adequacy of provision to cover losses that may be incurred in disposing of obsolete, slow-moving, and overstock items.

Compute inventory turnover and compare with prior periods and with industry data.

P–10   Inventory Is Carried at the Lower of Cost or Market (Valuation)

System Attributes to Consider

Sales prices established in excess of cost

Carrying value periodically compared to net realizable value; adjustments recorded, if necessary

Product line income statements regularly prepared and reviewed

Valuation reserve in excess of LIFO reserve established at year-end (if necessary to reduce inventory to market, if lower than LIFO cost). Beginning of year valuation reserve reversed into income

What Can Go Wrong

Errors

Losses not provided for:

1.   Inventories priced above market
2.   Continued purchase or production of items being sold at loss
3.   Purchase commitments at prices above market

Irregularities

Unwarranted reduction of inventory value to facilitate bargain purchase by management, employees, or third parties

Accounts Affected

Inventory/cost of sales

Principal Audit Procedures to Consider

If Objective Achieved

Review product line operating statements and overall profitability to determine if costs are being recovered through selling prices.

Compare costs of inventory items with current *replacement costs* per vendor invoices, open purchase orders, current price lists, quotes, or published market prices. Consider the effect of lower current cost on materials and purchased parts content of inventory and on commitments for additional quantities of similar items. Consider necessity of valuation reserve in excess of LIFO reserve.

Compare costs of work in process and finished goods with *selling prices* as shown by recent sales invoices, current price lists (adjusted for discounts), and other sources to determine whether there is sufficient margin to cover costs to complete and dispose.

Inquire of management about adverse purchase or sales commitments and possible losses on completion of long-term contracts.

If Objective Not Achieved

Use procedures similar to those above, but generally increase audit effort to estimate the effect of aggregate inventory overpricing (e.g., expand comparison of costs with replacement costs and/or selling prices).

PRODUCTION OR SERVICE—PROPERTY, PLANT, AND EQUIPMENT

P–11 Property, Plant, and Equipment Are Purchased Only with Proper Authorization (Authorization)

System Attributes to Consider

Property acquisitions require authorization by specified employees or Board of Directors according to specified dollar limits

Purchase of major properties reviewed for capital budget compliance

In-house construction requires authorized work orders

Construction in progress regularly reviewed for adherence to budgeted amounts

Capital budget overages require authorization by specified employees or Board of Directors according to specified dollar limits

Purchasing, receiving, and recording of property acquisitions performed independently

Competitive bids obtained when practicable; documentation maintained and periodically reviewed for compliance with company policy

What Can Go Wrong

Errors

Unnecessary property acquired resulting in unused or idle capacity

Irregularities

Management, employees, or third parties able to obtain items for personal use and charge to company

Accounts Affected

Property, plant, and equipment

Accounts payable, accrued liabilities

Principal Audit Procedures to Consider

If Objective Achieved

Test key authorization and/or approval attributes by examining a representative sample of property acquisitions (concurrently with test of cash disbursements) through an interim date. Review unusual property acquisitions from interim date to year-end. Understand business purpose of acquisition.

Compare level of property acquisitions for year with prior period and capital budget. Compare repair and maintenance expense account balances with budget.

If Objective Not Achieved

Test documentation for an extensive number of property acquisitions to estimate the effect of errors and/or amounts requiring reclassification. Include significant acquisitions during the entire period under audit and test for approval and business purpose. Compare construction cost per square foot with prevailing level for similar construction in the area.

Compare level of property acquisitions for the year with prior period. Compare repair and maintenance expense account balances with budget.

P–12 Property, Plant, and Equipment Purchases Are Recorded Correctly as to Account, Amount, and Period (Recording)

System Attributes to Consider

Receiving documentation, purchase order or contract, and invoice matched before recording liability

Unmatched receiving reports and invoices investigated for inclusion in estimated liability at close of period

Invoices registered immediately upon receipt

Account distribution reviewed when recording liability or when signing check

Formal policy for distinguishing capital items from expense; invoices and account distribution reviewed for compliance

Property ledgers maintained and regularly reconciled to general ledger control accounts

Fixed asset I.D. tags issued in prenumbered order; sequence independently checked; issuances reconciled to property additions

Charges to construction in progress regularly reviewed for items to reclassify to expense

What Can Go Wrong

Errors

Property purchases recorded in wrong property account, expense accounts, or not recorded

Property purchases not recorded in detail records (out-of-balance with control accounts)

Irregularities

Misclassification to conceal unauthorized purchases for benefit of management, employees, or third parties

Accounts Affected

Property, plant, and equipment

Accounts payable, accrued liabilities

Repairs and maintenance expense

Principal Audit Procedures to Consider

If Objective Achieved

Test key recording attributes by examining a representative sample of property acquisitions (concurrently with test of cash disbursements) through an interim date. Also review for:

1. Correct account distribution
2. Recording in correct account
3. Agreement of recorded amount with invoice and contract or purchase order
4. Recording in correct period

Review any unusually large property acquisitions from interim date to year-end.

Trace in-house construction work orders to closing to correct account.

If Objective Not Achieved

Test an extensive number of property acquisitions (concurrently with test of cash disbursements) to detect and/or estimate amounts incorrectly recorded. Include significant property acquisitions throughout entire period under audit.

Analyze asset account balances and repair and maintenance expenses to identify classification errors.

Trace in-house construction work orders to closing to correct account.

P–13 Disposals, Retirements, Trade-ins, Idle Plant and Equipment, and Other Losses Are Identified and Recorded Correctly as to Account, Amount, and Period (Recording, Reconciliation)

System Attributes to Consider

Formal policy for reporting fixed asset disposals

Disposals identified with related gain or loss on sale amounts

Written authority required for removing assets from premises

Replaced assets and trade-ins removed from accounts as part of recording related acquisition

Property not used in business segregated in accounts

Property ledgers maintained and regularly reconciled to general ledger control accounts

Property ledgers regularly checked by partial or complete physical count

Ad valorem tax bills reconciled to property ledgers

What Can Go Wrong

Errors

Property remains on books after disposal (overstated property and allowance and expense accounts)

Idle property not identified, loss in value not provided

Undetected deterioration of property (overstated property or understated allowance and expense accounts)

Irregularities

Sale of property not recorded, proceeds misappropriated

Management, employees, or third parties misappropriate property, plant, or equipment

Accounts Affected

Property, plant, and equipment

Allowances for depreciation

Gain or loss on disposals

Principal Audit Procedures to Consider

If Objective Achieved

Review entries to record large reductions in carrying value and inquire as to important units of property not used (e.g., discuss with plant engineer or other nonaccounting personnel).

Scan miscellaneous cash receipts and investigate large or unusual amounts.

If Objective Not Achieved

Note: Use procedures similar to those above, but generally increase audit effort to identify possible unrecorded losses. Consider observation of selected significant property items and inquire of additional personnel as to idle facilities.

P–14 Physical Loss of Property, Plant, and Equipment Is Prevented (Safeguarding)

System Attributes to Consider

Guards and/or alarm system used

Employees identified by badge, card, etc.

Employees bonded

I.D. tags or serial numbers affixed to assets and periodically checked against property ledgers

Access to toolroom restricted

Property adequately secured, protected against deterioration

Keys signed out; locks changed regularly

Responsible employee regularly reviews adequacy of insurance coverage

What Can Go Wrong

Irregularities

Management, employees, or third parties misappropriate business property

Accounts Affected

Property, plant, and equipment

Allowances for depreciation

Expense

Principal Audit Procedures to Consider

If Objective Achieved

Observe physical safeguards.

If Objective Not Achieved

Physically observe significant property items selected from property records.

P–15   Depreciation Is Calculated Using Proper Lives and Methods (Valuation)

System Attributes to Consider

Assets lives and depreciation methods reviewed for compliance with company policies

Depreciation calculations independently checked for accuracy and overall reasonableness

Allowances for depreciation regularly reviewed for adequacy; useful lives and salvage values reviewed

What Can Go Wrong

Errors

Wrong lives assigned; miscalculation of depreciation

Accounts Affected

Allowances for depreciation

Depreciation expense

Principal Audit Procedures to Consider

If Objective Achieved

Review reasonableness of depreciation provision by reference to prior year provision and effect of acquisitions and disposals. Review useful lives assigned to significant additions for compliance with established policies.

Compare relationships of depreciation provision and related allowance account to asset balance. Review reasonableness of change in allowance accounts since prior year-end.

If Objective Not Achieved

Review reasonableness of depreciation provision by reference to prior year provision and effect of acquisitions and disposals.

Recalculate specific provisions on test basis. Determine reasonableness of useful lives assigned to significant property additions. Inquire of plant engineer as to factors (e.g., technological developments) affecting useful lives of significant items.

Compare relationships of depreciation provision and related allowance account to asset balance. Analyze change in allowance accounts since prior year-end.

FINANCE

F–1 Case Receipts Are Recorded Correctly as to Account, Amount, and Period and Are Deposited (Recording, Safeguarding)

System Attributes to Consider

Mail Receipts

Mail opened independent of cashier, accounts receivable bookkeeper, and other accounting employees who may initiate or post journal entries

Record of checks and cash received prepared by person opening the mail; list used as posting source and subsequently compared to daily deposit

Lock box used

Cash Sales

Independent check of prenumbered receipt and refund slips

Cash register tape totals compared with amount of cash in drawer

Clerks handling cash closely supervised

Cash refunds require approval

Receipts reconciled to stock sold

General

Employees handling receipts bonded

Cash receipts not handled or recorded by employees having access to accounts receivable records or general ledger

Cash receipts not handled by employees responsible for petty cash or other funds

Cash receipts remain with cashier until sent to bank

Each day's receipts deposited intact and without delay

Independent employees responsible for reconciling authenticated duplicate deposit slip, mail receipts listing, cash receipts book, bank statement

Cash funds (e.g., cash register, petty cash fund, non-client funds) each assigned to one individual, independent of other cash funds

Branch offices make deposits to home office account intact and without delay

Cash or checks not immediately deposited kept in fireproof vault or safe

Salesmen and/or drivers forbidden to accept or handle cash receipts

Miscellaneous receipts (scrap sales, rents, dividends) monitored to detect misappropriation

Bank accounts regularly reconciled independent of cash receipts, general ledger, or accounts receivable functions

Monthly statements sent to all (or delinquent) customers; complaints handled independent of cashier or accounts receivable bookkeeper

What Can Go Wrong

Errors

Cash or checks lost

Incorrect recording of cash receipts

Irregularities

Item sold for cash but no sale recorded or recorded at lesser amount; cash receipts misappropriated

Item sold for cash; cash refund documentation prepared and cash misappropriated

Checks received are deposited but not recorded; check written to employee for same amount also not recorded

Collections on account misappropriated, concealed by debits to other than cash accounts (e.g., expense accounts) or by improper issuance of credit memo

Salesmen or drivers misappropriate cash received

Accounts Affected

Cash

Accounts and notes receivable

Sales

Other income

Principal Audit Procedures to Consider

If Objective Achieved

Mail Receipts

Test key recording attributes and procedures by examining a representative sample of mail receipts through an interim date. Trace remittance from file of advices and/or deposit slip detail to recorded receipts. Test clerical accuracy of total and trace to bank statement.

Observe cash-handling procedures in mailroom. Compare prelisting of mail receipts or lock box report to bank statement deposits.

Circularize receivables at interim date on limited basis.

Cash Sales

Observe procedures for recording ongoing cash sales transactions and safeguarding receipts. Make cash counts, and reconcile to cash register tape or other control total. Reconcile daily control totals with amounts reported and deposited.

Compare volume of cash sales with corresponding days or periods of prior years. Review gross margins from cash sales and compare with prior periods.

Test cash refund transactions for compliance with approval requirements.

Investigate inventory shortages to detect possible unrecorded cash sales.

General

Verify one month's bank reconciliations, review remaining reconciliations for unusual reconciling items.

Review year-end bank reconciliations, cutoff bank statements; request confirmation of year-end balances.

Investigate significant or unusual reconciling items.

If Objective Not Achieved

Mail Receipts

Make listing of mail receipts at an interim date (consider performing at receivables circularization date), and trace to recorded receipts and bank statement deposits.

Trace recorded receipts to deposits per bank statement for significant portion of period under audit. Investigate receipts not deposited intact and unusual time delays from date of receipt to deposit.

Perform extensive receivables circularization at or near year-end.

Cash Sales

Use procedures similar to those for cash sales above, but generally increase audit effort to detect possible unrecorded cash sales. For example, consider arranging with client to "salt" cash sales with marked currency and intercept bank deposit to determine inclusion.

General

Verify year-end bank reconciliations by tracing to cutoff bank statements, bank advices, accounting entries; request confirmation of year-end balances.

Prepare proof of cash for a significant portion of period under audit to determine that cash receipts are recorded correctly and deposited.

F–2 Cash Receipts Are Properly Applied to Customer Balances (Recording)

System Attributes to Consider

Employees responsible for posting receivable accounts have no access to cash receipts

Employees responsible for initiating or approving customer credits (including writeoffs) have no access to cash receipts or detail receivable records

Cash receipts applied to specific invoices rather than to current balance

Postings to receivable accounts independently reconciled to total of cash received

Monthly statements sent to all (or delinquent) customers; complaints handled independent of cashier or accounts receivable bookkeeper

Delinquent accounts followed up independent of cashier

What Can Go Wrong

Errors

Receivables properly stated in the aggregate, but individual customer accounts misstated

Irregularities

Collectible accounts written off or otherwise credited; customer remittances misappropriated

Lapping (cash receipts misappropriated; shortages covered by delaying postings)

Accounts Affected

Cash

Accounts receivable

Notes receivable

Principal Audit Procedures to Consider

If Objective Achieved

Test key recording attributes by examining a representative sample of cash receipts through an interim date. Trace remittances from file of advices and/or deposit slip detail to receivable detail posting.

Circularize receivables at interim date on limited basis. Omit or limit examination of remittance advices as part of alternative procedures.

Review writeoffs of selected uncollectible accounts through an interim date for compliance with approval requirements.

Investigate significant noncash credits to receivable detail throughout period under audit.

If Objective Not Achieved

Perform extensive receivables circularization at or near year-end; use positive requests. Examine remittance advices as part of alternative procedures.

Examine details of writeoffs of uncollectible accounts; review with personnel who supervise those initiating the writeoffs. Request confirmation of accounts written off during the period.

Investigate noncash credits to receivable detail throughout period under audit.

F–3 Cash Disbursements Are for Goods or Services Authorized and Received (Authorization, Safeguarding)

System Attributes to Consider

Check prepared only when receipt and approval documented (e.g., goods—invoice matched with P.O. and receiver; services—receipt acknowledged by responsible employee)

Extensions, additions, discounts, and pricing checked

Supporting documents cancelled to prevent resubmission; referenced to check number

Imprest disbursement accounts used

Unissued checks locked up, numerically accounted for in log; access restricted to limited number of authorized personnel

Payroll

Payroll duties segregated as to approval (foremen, supervisors, etc.), payroll preparation, distribution, and handling unclaimed pay

Total net pay per payroll register compared to total of payroll checks issued

Check Signing

Check signers review supporting document before signing

Countersignature required over specified amount

Signing checks in advance prohibited

Check signing machine and signature plates locked; access restricted to limited number of authorized personnel

Checks signed by one or more individuals independent of employee initiating purchase, employee approving purchase, accounts payable clerk, employee preparing check, employee recording payment, and payroll department

Check signers do not maintain accounting or cash records

Signed checks not returned to preparer of accounts payable bookkeeper

What Can Go Wrong

Errors

Payment for goods or services not authorized or not received

Duplicate payments

Check made out to wrong payee

Check mailed or distributed to wrong vendor or employee

Irregularities

Company pays for goods or services received by management, employees,
or third parties

Company pays invoices a second time for goods not received, under kickback
arrangement

Vendor invoices altered and photocopied to conceal alteration; payment benefits management, employees, or third parties

Check signature(s) or endorsement forged

Questionable or illegal payments

Improper check requests submitted, funds misappropriated

Accounts Affected

Cash

Accounts payable and accrued liabilities

All other asset, liability, and expense accounts

Principal Audit Procedures to Consider

If Objective Achieved

Test key authorization and approval attributes by examining a representative
sample of cash disbursements (concurrently with test of purchases) made
through an interim date. Also review for:
    Documentation and approval according to policies (e.g., original vendor
    invoice with purchase order and receiver)
    Evidence of check of clerical accuracy
    Documentation marked "paid" or otherwise mutilated to prevent reuse
    Authorized check signature
    Proper endorsement

Foot disbursements journal for limited portion of period under audit and
compare totals with credits to cash account. Reconcile to total disbursements per bank statements.

If Objective Not Achieved

Test an extensive number of cash disbursements (concurrently with test of purchases) to detect and/or estimate the effect of possible errors or irregularities. Include significant disbursements made throughout period under audit selected from those types for which objective is not achieved. Test for documentation and approval of goods/services received and for propriety of check signature and endorsement. Challenge disbursements supported by photocopies of documents, vendor statements, or non-multi-lated invoices. Consider the possibility of questionable or illegal payments.

Foot disbursements journal for a significant portion of period under audit and compare totals with credits to cash account. Reconcile to total disbursements per bank statements.

Request statements of account from an extensive number of vendors and review file of disbursements to the same vendor to detect duplicate payments.

F–4 Cash Disbursements Are Recorded Correctly as to Account, Amount, and Period (Recording)

System Attributes to Consider

Checks issued and recorded in pre-numbered order; sequence accounted for when reconciling bank accounts

Voided checks defaced and retained

Unissued checks locked up; numerically accounted for in log; access restricted to limited number of authorized personnel

Imprest cash accounts

Petty cash funds regularly reimbursed and expense distributed

Both sides of transfers between banks reviewed for recording in same period

Bank statement and cancelled checks received and reconciled independent of check writing and recording

Paid checks compared to disbursements journal when reconciling bank accounts

Account distribution reviewed by check signer

What Can Go Wrong

Errors

Disbursements misclassified or not recorded

Disbursements recorded but checks held until following period

Checks mailed but disbursements not recorded until following period

Disbursements recorded at wrong amount

Irregularities

Checks issued for benefit of management, employees, or third parties; payees changed in cash disbursements journal

Cash disbursements journal overfooted; inflated amount recorded and difference misappropriated

Bank reconciliation changed to conceal misappropriation (e.g., offset against old outstanding checks)

"VOID" notation eradicated from signed check, cashed by management, employee, or third party

Kiting (use of "float" period to conceal shortage of cash in bank)

Accounts Affected

Cash

Accounts payable and accrued liabilities

All other asset, liability, and expense accounts

Principal Audit Procedures to Consider

If Objective Achieved

Test key recording attributes by examining a representative sample of cash disbursements (concurrently with tests of purchases and payroll) made through an interim date. Also review for:

    Agreement of recorded check number, amount, date, and payee with paid check

    Cancellation date within reasonable period after issuance

    Correct inclusion in or exclusion from month-end bank reconciliations

Review interim bank reconciliations for imprest accounts, noting proper periodic clearance of transactions.

Verify one month's bank reconciliations, review remaining reconciliations for unusual items.

Review year-end bank reconciliations, cutoff bank statements; request confirmation of year-end balances.

Investigate significant interbank transfers immediately before and after year-end.

Limit or omit vouching of documents supporting disbursement entries as part of related direct tests of balances.

If Objective Not Achieved

Test an extensive number of cash disbursements to detect errors and/or estimate amount of disbursements incorrectly recorded. Include significant disbursements made throughout period under audit and note agreement between cash disbursements journal and paid checks.

Prepare proof of cash for significant portion of period under audit. Examine checks returned with bank statements for cancellation date within reasonable period after issuance. Account for numerical sequence of checks. Not appropriate to support interim bank reconciliation.

Verify year-end bank reconciliations, including imprest accounts, by tracing to cutoff bank statements, bank advices, accounting entries; request confirmation of year-end balances.

Investigate interbank transfers immediately before and after year-end.

Vouch cash disbursements as part of direct tests of balances.

F–5 Debt and Lease Obligations and Related Expenses Are Authorized and Recorded Correctly as to Account, Amount, and Period (Authorization, Recording)

System Attributes to Consider

Debt and leases require authorization by Board of Directors according to specified dollar limits

Signatures of two or more specified officials required on notes payable, lease agreements, and renewals

Notes payable register maintained independent of check or note signing

Records maintained for restricted amounts of retained earnings; compliance with loan covenants and lease agreements monitored

Leases reviewed for classification as capital or operating

Interest expense regularly posted; fluctuations investigated by responsible official

What Can Go Wrong

Errors

Unrecorded debt

Company becomes obligated for debts not properly authorized or at unfavorable terms and/or interest rates

Misclassification of long- or short-term debt

Pledged assets not disclosed

Violation of restrictive covenants resulting in default

Capital leases not recorded; operating leases recorded

Interest expense misclassified, not recorded, recorded at wrong amount, recorded in wrong period

Miscalculation of contingent lease payments

Irregularities

Proceeds from notes payable, etc., used for other than business purposes

Obligations incurred for the benefit of management, employees or third parties (e.g., unauthorized lease of apartment)

Unauthorized pledging of assets

Management suppresses identification and disclosure of pledged assets

Accounts Affected

Cash

Long- and short-term debt

Accrued interest

Interest expense

Capital lease accounts

Principal Audit Procedures to Consider

If Objective Achieved

Review Board of Directors' and committee meetings minutes; trace obligations authorized therein to accounting records and appropriate financial statement classification and disclosure. Trace to recording of cash or other assets received and appropriate disclosure.

Review documentation supporting compliance with restrictive covenants. In case of noncompliance, review any waivers obtained and ascertain that debt is properly classified.

Request confirmation of the terms, including the nature and amount of collateral, liens, and security agreements, of significant notes payable and other obligations outstanding.

Review bank and other confirmations received for responses indicating unrecorded obligations.

Review leases for proper classification as capital or operating.

Review reasonableness of interest expense by relating average rates in effect to average debt outstanding.

If Objective Not Achieved

Use procedures similar to those above, but generally increase audit effort regarding notes payable, leases, etc. For example, consider the following additional audit procedures:

1. Examine support for recorded transactions affecting obligations.
2. Request confirmation of obligations paid off during the period.
3. Request listing of recorded security agreements filed under the Uniform Commercial Code.

4. Recompute interest expense.
5. Test propriety of classification of leases.

F–6 Equity Transactions Are Authorized and Recorded Correctly as to Account, Amount, and Period (Authorization, Recording)

System Attributes to Consider

Independent registrar used

Stock transfer agent used

Books of stock certificate stubs and unissued certificates in custody of specified official

Surrendered certificates cancelled and retained

Register of current shareholders and shares outstanding maintained; periodically reviewed for completeness

Dividends, treasury stock transactions, stock options approved by Board of Directors

Proposed dividends reviewed for compliance with statutory requirements and retained earnings restrictions

Independent dividend-paying agents used

Imprest account used to pay dividends

Returned or unclaimed dividend checks promptly redeposited and liability recorded

Treasury stock in custody of specified official

Treasury stock certificates regularly counted and reconciled to control account

Memo ledger maintained and regularly reviewed for stock options granted, exercisable, and expired

Stock options exercised reconciled to changes in shares outstanding and capital accounts

What Can Go Wrong

Errors

Sales of shares is unauthorized, violates legal requirements or loan covenants

Sale of shares not recorded, or recorded incorrectly

Stock options exercised which are unauthorized or not in accordance with terms of options granted

Dividend payments exceed legal limits or violate restrictive covenants

Dividends paid to wrong parties or at incorrect amounts

Irregularities

Proceeds from sale of shares used for other than business purpose

Improper dividend payments made to management, employees, or third parties

Unauthorized pledging of treasury stock

Accounts Affected

Cash

Dividends payable

Equity accounts

Compensation expense

Principal Audit Procedures to Consider

If Objective Achieved

Request confirmations from independent registrar, stock transfer agent.

Review Board of Directors' and committee meetings minutes; trace stock issuance, repurchases, retirements, dividends, or stock options authorized therein to accounting records.

Reconcile dividends paid with shares outstanding.

Support details of schedule of shares under option and dollar values by reference to Board of Directors' meetings minutes, provisions of stock option plan, market value quotations.

If Objective Not Achieved

Use procedures similar to those above, but generally increase audit effort regarding equity transactions. Consider the following additional audit procedures:

1. Reconcile number of shares outstanding with stock certificate stubs, certificates representing unissued, retired, or treasury shares.
2. Account for the numerical sequence of stock certificates and examine unissued shares. Request representation from corporate secretary as to shares issued and outstanding.
3. Examine cancelled dividend checks for agreement with records.

F–7 Investments in and Advances to/from Subsidiaries and Other Affiliates Are Authorized and Recorded Correctly as to Account, Amount, and Period (Authorization, Recording)

System Attributes to Consider

Formal policies for using consolidation, equity, or cost methods of accounting

Intercompany accounts balanced regularly

Current intercompany accounts zeroed out regularly

Intercompany profits eliminated

Investments regularly adjusted for share of earnings or losses, net of dividends

Investments and advances regularly reviewed for permanent impairment in value/collectibility

Currency translations of foreign affiliate financial statements checked for accuracy

What Can Go Wrong

Errors

Advances to/from subsidiaries and other affiliates misclassified, not recorded, or recorded in wrong period

Profit recognized prematurely on intercompany sales

Advances to subsidiaries and other affiliates are uncollectible, no provision is made and/or advances continue to be made which will not be recovered

Irregularities

Management conceals permanently impaired value of investment, uncollectibility of intercompany receivable

Improper accounting concealed by piecemeal recording of transactions on books of different entities

Unauthorized pledging of investments in subsidiaries and other affiliates

Accounts Affected

Investments in unconsolidated subsidiaries, corporate joint ventures, other investments of 50 percent or less of voting stock in which investor has ability to exercise significant influence

Advances to/from subsidiaries and other affiliates

Minority interest arising upon consolidation

Goodwill

Principal Audit Procedures to Consider

If Objective Achieved

Examine audited financial statements of subsidiaries and other affiliates as support of underlying equity. If unaudited, consider necessity of performing additional audit procedures to support underlying equity.

Examine stock certificates evidencing ownership.

Test the currency translation of foreign subsidiary financial statements.

Review consolidation entries. Test computation of intercompany profit eliminations.

Test intercompany transactions as part of tests of cash disbursements, sales, etc. Investigate intercompany transfers immediately before and after year-end; reconcile cutoff differences.

Review journal entries or other settlement of intercompany amounts.

Review reconciliation of intercompany accounts.

Consider whether share of losses exceeding initial investment are recorded to the extent of commitments for further investments or advances.

If Objective Not Achieved

Use procedures similar to those above, but generally increase audit effort to identify improperly handled transactions with subsidiaries and other affiliates.

F–8   Investment Transactions Are Authorized and Recorded Correctly as to Account, Amount, and Period (Authorization, Recording)

System Attributes to Consider

Investments reviewed for compliance with authorized objectives and dollar limits

Responsible official regularly reviews cash position and approves short-term investment of excess cash

Broker or trustee statements regularly reconciled with investment ledger

Investments periodically examined and reconciled with investment ledger

Investment ledger regularly reconciled with general ledger

Purchases, exchanges and sales of long-term investments approved in advance or ratified by specified officers, Board of Directors, investment committee of officers/directors, or independent investment advisor (appointed by officers/directors)

Calculations of gain or loss on sale of investments reviewed

What Can Go Wrong

Errors

Investments made which are not authorized

Unnecessary investment losses incurred, potential investment gains not realized

Irregularities

Investments are made or sold for benefit of management, employees, or third parties

Unauthorized pledging of investments in marketable securities

Accounts Affected

Gain or loss on sale

Dividend and interest income

Cash

Investments in marketable securities, real estate, etc.

Certificates of deposit, commercial paper

Principal Audit Procedures to Consider

If Objective Achieved

Test key authorization and/or approval attributes by examining a representative sample of investment transactions through an interim date. Review unusual transactions from interim date to year-end.

Review investment committee meetings minutes.

Note evidence of unusual investment transactions (e.g., churning or high-risk securities).

If Objective Not Achieved

Account for all security transactions during the period and examine underlying support.

F–9 Income Earned on Investments Is Recorded Correctly as to Account, Amount, and Period (Recording)

System Attributes to Consider

Income receivable detail regularly reconciled to general ledger control account

Calculations of interest income reviewed

Dividend income compared to published sources

Interest income regularly posted

Investment yield reports regularly prepared and fluctuations investigated by responsible official

What Can Go Wrong

Errors

Investment income misclassified, not recorded, or recorded in wrong period

Theft or other loss of investment instruments not reflected in accounting records

Irregularities

Investment income misappropriated

Accounts Affected

Dividend and interest income

Cash

Dividends and interest receivable

Investments in marketable securities, real estate, etc.

Principal Audit Procedures to Consider

If Objective Achieved

Review reasonableness of interest income by relating average rates to average investments.

Compare level of investment income and rate(s) of return with prior period.

Review supporting computations or documentation for selected entries accruing investment income, and trace to general ledger.

If Objective Not Achieved

Test computations or examine supporting documentation for accrual of investment income.

Recompute interest and other investment income. Compare dividend income to published sources.

Compare level of investment income and rate(s) of return with prior period.

F–10 Loss in Value of Investments Is Promptly Detected and Provided for (Safeguarding, Valuation)

System Attributes to Consider

Market values of investments regularly obtained and reviewed by management

Investments previously written off or for which a reserve has been created regularly reviewed for possible realization

What Can Go Wrong

Errors

Investment losses not monitored; not reflected in accounting records

Irregularities

Investments known to be worthless not written off

Accounts Affected

Gain or loss on sale

Investments in marketable securities, real estate, etc.

Dividend and interest income

Net unrealized loss of noncurrent marketable equity securities (equity account)

Principal Audit Procedures to Consider

If Objective Achieved

Compare carrying value of selected investments with fair market value. Determine management's intended holding period in the case of decline in value, distinguish permanent vs. temporary decline in value, and ascertain that investments are properly classified.

If Objective Not Achieved

Use procedures similar to those above, but generally increase audit effort to estimate aggregate amount of possible investment overstatement and to ascertain that investments are properly classified.

F–11 Physical Loss of Investments Is Prevented or Promptly Detected (Safeguarding, Reconciliation)

System Attributes to Consider

Investment instruments stored in bank safe deposit box, bank trust or safekeeping department, fireproof vault, safe, or with independent third party

Access to investment instruments denied to those authorizing or recording investments, handling cash, or maintaining general ledger

Presence of two or more officials required for access to investment instruments

Investments in name of company (or in nominee name if held by independent custodian)

Securities held for third parties or negotiable collateral safeguarded in same manner as company's own investments

Investment instruments regularly inspected and traced to investment ledger by internal auditors or specified officials

What Can Go Wrong

Errors

Investment instruments lost; loss not reflected in accounting records

Irregularities

Theft of investment instruments

Management, employees, or third parties able to obtain investments for personal use

Accounts Affected

Gain or loss on sale

Dividend and interest income

Investments in marketable securities

Certificates of deposit, commercial paper

Principal Audit Procedures to Consider

If Objective Achieved

Request confirmation of investments in the custody of third parties as of interim date.

If Objective Not Achieved

Physically count or observe count of securities at or near year-end.

Request confirmation of investments in the custody of third parties at or near year-end.

ADMINISTRATION

A–1   Expenses Are Incurred Only with Proper Authorization (Authorization)

System Attributes to Consider

Selling and administrative expense budgets approved by management

Purchase of selling and administrative expense items reviewed for budget compliance

Selling and administrative expense requisitions reviewed for proper authorization

Selling and administrative expenses reviewed for approval by designated personnel or Board of Directors within specified dollar limits

Purchasing performed by department or individual independent of receiving and accounts payable

Purchase orders compared to control list or file of approved vendors

Competitive bids obtained when practicable; documentation maintained and periodically reviewed for compliance with company policy

Formal policy for reimbursing expenses; compliance monitored

Expense reports and expense advance requests reviewed for compliance with company policy

Commissions reviewed by responsible employee for compliance with company policy

What Can Go Wrong

Errors

Unauthorized expenses incurred

Overpayment of expense reimbursement, commissions, etc. due to miscomputation

Irregularities

Management, employees, or third parties able to obtain items for personal use and charge to company

Unauthorized executive perquisites ("perks")

Purchases at other than most favorable terms to facilitate "side deals" for benefit of management, employees, or third parties

Questionable or illegal payments

Inflated expense reports

Management, employees, or third parties receive commissions not earned

Supplies, promotional items not inventoried, exposed to theft

Accounts Affected

Administrative expenses (e.g., supplies, officers' travel, legal and auditing, property taxes, insurance)

Selling expenses (e.g., freight, travel and entertainment, warranty, advertising, commissions)

Prepaid expenses (e.g., prepaid insurance, prepaid property taxes, prepaid rent)

Intangibles (e.g., deferred costs, patents, trademarks, copyrights)

Accounts payable and other accrued liabilities

Principal Audit Procedures to Consider

If Objective Achieved

Test key authorization and/or approval attributes by examining a representative sample of selling and administrative expense items (concurrently with test of cash disbursements) incurred through an interim date. Understand business purpose of each transaction.

Review overall reasonableness of selling and administrative expenses. Compare relationships of expenses and level of business with prior periods. Compare major components of expense with prior periods and budget.

Review officers' expense reports for compliance with client policy, propriety (business rather than personal expense), reasonableness, and adequacy of documentation of charges.

Review overall reasonableness of commissions paid or accrued during interim period by comparing expense to related sales.

Consider possibility of questionable or illegal payments.

If Objective Not Achieved

Test an extensive number of expense items to estimate the effect of possible errors or irregularities. Include significant expense items incurred throughout the period under audit selected from those types for which objective is not achieved. Review for approval and understand business purpose of transaction.

Consider possibility of questionable or illegal payments.

Review officers' and other expense reports for compliance with client policy, propriety (business rather than personal expense), reasonableness, and adequacy of documentation of charges. Review records of use of various corporate facilities by officers. Note proper accounting for personal use and consider possibility of hidden perks.

Test commissions paid or accrued during entire period under audit to determine if they relate to valid sales and were earned in period under audit. Examine supporting computations and required approvals, and trace to corresponding sale and collection of receivables.

Compare relationships of expenses and level of business with prior periods. Compare major components of expense with prior periods and budget.

A–2 Expenses and Related Liabilities Are Recorded Correctly as to Account, Amount, and Period (Recording)

System Attributes to Consider

Receiving documentation, purchase approval, and invoices matched before recording liability

Invoices registered immediately upon receipt; duplicate invoices identified

Selling and administrative expenses under budgetary control; budget vs. actual regularly reviewed by management

Unmatched receiving reports and invoices investigated for inclusion in estimated liability at close of period

Account distribution reviewed when recording liability or when signing check

Commissions reconciled to recorded sales

What Can Go Wrong

Errors

Expenses misclassified, recorded at wrong amounts, or not recorded

Expenses not recorded in period incurred

Irregularities

Misclassification to conceal unauthorized purchases for benefit of management, employees, or third parties

Executive perquisites not clearly identified in accounting records

Purchases recorded at amount greater than invoice amount; excess shared with vendor under kickback arrangement

Accounts Affected

Administrative expenses (e.g., supplies, officers' travel, legal and auditing, property taxes, insurance)

Selling expenses (e.g., freight, travel and entertainment, warranty, advertising, commissions)

Prepaid expenses (e.g., prepaid insurance, prepaid property taxes, prepaid rent)

Intangibles (e.g., deferred costs, patents, trademarks, copyrights)

Accounts payable and other accrued liabilities

Principal Audit Procedures to Consider

If Objective Achieved

Test key recording attributes by examining a representative sample of selling and administrative expense items (concurrently with test of cash disbursements) incurred through an interim date. Also review for:

1. Correct account distribution
2. Recording in correct account
3. Agreement of recorded amount with invoices and purchase order
4. Recording in correct period

Review overall reasonableness of selling and administrative expenses. Compare relationships of expenses and level of business with prior periods. Compare major components of expense with prior periods and budget.

Consider possibility of questionable or illegal payments and hidden "perks."

Review components of significant prepaid and accrual accounts for reasonableness. If not significant, compare prepaid expense and accrued liability balances with those of prior periods.

Limit accounts payable out-of-period search for selling and administrative expense items. Use high minimum dollar amount for selecting subsequent disbursements and unmatched invoices and receiving reports to examine and limit or omit requests for related vendor statements.

If Objective Not Achieved

Test an extensive number of selling and administrative expense items (concurrently with test of cash disbursements) to estimate the effect of possible errors or irregularities. Include significant expense items recorded throughout the period under audit.

Consider possibility of questionable or illegal payments and hidden "perks."

Trace sample of sales transactions to corresponding commissions (or other sales-related expenses) to detect and/or estimate amounts not recorded in period under audit.

Analyze and support components of significant prepaid expense and accrued liability accounts. If not significant, compare prepaid expense and liability balances with prior periods.

Perform extensive accounts payable out-of-period search for selling and administrative expense items. Request and reconcile (or test client's reconciliation of) statements from principal supply and service vendors and use low minimum dollar amounts for selecting subsequent disbursements and unmatched invoices and receiving reports to examine.

Compare relationships of expenses and level of business with prior periods. Compare major components of expense with prior periods and budget.

A–6 Amortization or Loss in Value of Intangibles Is Recorded Correctly as to Account, Amount, and Period (Recording, Valuation)

System Attributes to Consider

Formal policy for capitalization and amortization; compliance monitored

Periodic analysis of intangible assets; review for loss in value

Amortization calculations independently checked for accuracy and overall reasonableness

What Can Go Wrong

Errors

Goodwill, patents, other intangibles carried in excess of value

Amortization period exceeds period estimated to be benefited

Miscalculation of amortization

Intangibles remain on books after disposal or expiration

Irregularities

Sales of intangibles (e.g., patents) not recorded, proceeds misappropriated

Intangibles known to be worthless not written off

Accounts Affected

Deferred costs and expenses (e.g., pre-operating costs, deferred financing costs)

Patents, trademarks, copyrights, franchises, licenses, covenants not to compete

Goodwill

Amortization expense

Principal Audit Procedures to Consider

If Objective Achieved

Analyze changes in significant intangible asset accounts since prior year-end. If not significant, compare balances with prior periods.

Inquire as to continuing value of intangibles (e.g., goodwill—determine ongoing profitability of operation acquired at cost in excess of net assets). Consider necessity of write-off or adjustment of amortization period.

Review reasonableness of amortization expense.

If Objective Not Achieved

Use procedures similar to those above, but generally increase audit effort to substantiate significant changes in intangible assets and related amortization balances. For example:

Analyze and support significant changes in intangible asset accounts. Recompute amortization expense.

Obtain direct confirmation from attorneys or grantors of royalties, licenses, or trademarks.

A–7 Provisions for Income Taxes and Related Liabilities and Deferrals Are Recorded Correctly as to Account, Amount, and Period (Authorization, Recording)

System Attributes to Consider

Applicable taxing authorities identified

Calendar maintained, or other method used to assure all returns prepared, filed timely, and payments made

Formal policies for identifying, reporting permanent and timing differences

Reversal of timing differences monitored

Policy or written agreement for intercompany allocation of provision and settlement of tax liability among members of consolidated group

What Can Go Wrong

Errors

Required estimated payments not made

Tax liability/expense (including interest, penalties) not reflected in accounting records

Incorrect tax returns filed, subsequent audits by taxing authorities result in significant unrecorded liabilities

Irregularities

Tax evasion

Accounts Affected

Provisions for federal, state, local, and foreign income taxes—current and deferred

Income taxes payable—current and deferred

Refundable income taxes

Principal Audit Procedures to Consider

If Objective Achieved

Inquire of appropriate client personnel as to applicable taxing jurisdictions, filing requirements, and compliance therewith.

Reconcile taxable income as reported in the federal income tax return and in significant state and local returns to the tax provision for the prior year.

Recompute current and deferred provisions for federal and principal state and foreign income taxes. Review provisions for the other income taxes. Review reconciliation of book income to taxable income and consider proper tax treatment of the following (list is not exhaustive):

1. Non-taxable income
2. Valuation or other reserves (e.g., obsolescence "factor" or warranty reserve)
3. Other expenses not deductible or capitalizable
4. Deferred or capitalized amounts which are deductible
5. Investment credit on qualified property purchases and recapture on disposals
6. Other special deductions, limitations, credits, and exemptions (e.g., charitable contributions, percentage depletion, foreign tax credits, carryover items)
7. LIFO inventory computations
8. Revenue recognized under completed contract, installment, or other method for tax purposes different from books

Compare provisions for other taxes to prior periods. Compare relationships to pretax income and to total tax provisions with prior periods.

Review change in current and deferred liability accounts since prior year-end.

Determine effect of unsettled tax examinations or questionable items in returns open to examination.

If Objective Not Achieved

Use procedures similar to those above, but generally increase audit effort to identify timing differences and determine compliance with tax regulations. Consider the following additional audit procedures:

1. Analyze changes in current and deferred liability accounts since prior year-end. Support significant payments and other significant entries in income tax payable accounts.
2. Examine completed income tax returns prepared during period under audit to determine that returns have been filed with all appropriate taxing authorities.
3. Consider possibility of tax penalties, including those for underpayment of estimated tax or failure to file returns.

A-8 Commitments and Contingencies Are Identified, Monitored, and, if Appropriate, Recorded or Disclosed (Recording, Valuation)

System Attributes to Consider

Files of contracts, correspondence, legal judgments, etc. maintained and periodically reviewed

Legal and contractual matters always routed to in-house or outside counsel

Compliance with guarantee or warranty policies reviewed before incurring related costs

Records maintained of costs incurred under product warranties; reserves regularly reviewed for adequacy

Insurance coverage regularly reviewed

Specialists (e.g., actuaries) involved in analysis of historical data and current experience supporting computation of self-insurance reserves

Status of litigation regularly reviewed

Estimated costs to complete long-term contracts regularly reviewed; estimated loss provided

Reported claims reviewed by responsible official for appropriate consideration in determining accruals for losses (e.g., for self-insured damages, warranties)

Inventory purchase orders reviewed for commitments in excess of market

What Can Go Wrong

Errors

Provisions for losses which are probable and reasonably estimable are not recorded

Losses which are not probable or reasonably estimable are recorded

Product warranty costs not isolated in the accounts; no data base for estimating costs to be incurred under warranties currently in force

Losses due to inadequate insurance coverage

Irregularities

Unfavorable claims, judgments, commitments not disclosed; management suppresses identification

Reserve recorded or reversed to smooth earnings

Accounts Affected

Warranty reserves/expense

Cost of sales

Administrative expense

Accrued loss contingency/related expense

Self-insurance reserves

Principal Audit Procedures to Consider

If Objective Achieved

Request, through client, information on litigation, claims, assessments from principal legal counsel.

Review client's files regarding litigation, including attorneys' invoices received during period under audit.

Review components of significant accrued loss contingencies and related expense accounts. Compare levels of activity, operating relationships, and balances to prior periods. Determine adequacy of accruals in light of historical data and present conditions. Ascertain that current/non-current classification is appropriate.

Review for changes in warranty policy. Compare balance of warranty expense and reserve to prior periods and review relationship of expense to related sales or units shipped.

Review rationale and supporting data and computations for additions to estimated liability for self-insurance claims. Compare relationship of provision to claims made during the period. (Request this information, through client, from actuary or risk-management consultant, if applicable.)

Review bank and other confirmations received for responses indicating guarantees of indebtedness of others and any other commitments or contingencies.

Inquire as to material commitments to:

1. Complete sales contracts at a loss or which cannot be fulfilled.
2. Repurchase assets previously sold.

3. Purchase quantities in excess of requirements, or at prices in excess of prevailing market prices.
4. Construct or acquire property, plant, equipment, investments, intangibles, or other noncurrent assets.

Review cost and progress estimation procedures for long-term projects.

Obtain estimate of pension plan vested benefits and unfunded past service costs.

If Objective Not Achieved

Use procedures similar to those above, but generally increase audit effort to discover commitments or contingencies which client may not have identified as requiring loss provision or disclosure (e.g., inquire of additional officials as to material commitments).

EXAMPLES OF KEY DATA AND RATIOS RELATED TO SPECIFIC CONTROL OBJECTIVES

The following tabulation describes key data, ratios, and relationships that could be used in the detail analytical review for certain control objectives. Fluctuations in these relationships may indicate changes in operating policies, accounting methods, customer mix, or other conditions or circumstances (e.g., a change in gross margin may indicate different customer or product mix, changes in manufacturing, or changes in costs or selling prices). *The tabulation is not exhaustive, nor does it represent required procedures for all engagements. To avoid repetition, year-to-year (or other period) comparisons and comparisons to budget are not included in this list.*

Control Objective	Key Data/Ratios/Relationships
Sales	
S–1 Customer orders require approval of credit and terms before acceptance	Approximate number of customers and number of key customers
	Amount or percent of sales with key customers
	Allowance for doubtful accounts to accounts receivable or aging analysis
	Bad debt provisions to credit sales
S–2 Uncollectible amounts are promptly identified and provided for	Approximate number and dollar amount of accounts past due, over a specified dollar amount
	Average accounts receivable to net sales
	Bad debt write-offs to average accounts receivable
	Percent composition of accounts receivable aging
S–3 Products shipped or services rendered are billed	Approximate number of shipments per day
	Frequency of partial shipments
	Cost of sales to units shipped
	Sales to units shipped
	Gross margin
	Freight-out to units billed
S–4 Billings are for the correct amount	Average dollar amount per shipment
	Dollar amount of key shipments
	Approximate number of different items in each product line
	Gross margin
S–5 Revenues are recorded correctly as to account, amount, and period	Sales to units sold
	Cost of sales to units sold
S–7 Customer returns and other allowances are approved and recorded correctly as to account, amount, and period	Average number and dollar amount of credit memos issued per month
	Sales returns and allowances to sales
	Reserves for unissued credits to total credits

Control Objective	*Key Data/Ratios/Relationships*
Production or Service	
P–1 Goods or services are purchased only with proper authorization	Number of principal suppliers and average amount of business with each
	Labor costs to materials put into production
P–2 Goods or services received are recorded correctly as to account, amount, and period	Average number and dollar amount of purchases per month
	Material costs to direct labor
	Overhead costs to direct labor
	Material or overhead costs to cost of sales
	Units purchased to units sold
P–3 Salary, wage, and benefit expenses are incurred only for work authorized and performed	Approximate number of employees
	Direct labor cost to materials put into production
P–4 Salaries, wages, and benefits are calculated at the proper rate	Salaries of key employees
	Average wage rate for hourly employees
	Direct labor cost to cost of sales
P–5 Salaries, wages, benefits, and related liabilities are recorded correctly as to account, amount, and period	Benefits to direct labor cost, hours worked, or number of employees
	Average production per employee
	Average compensation per employee
P–6 Costs are assigned to inventory in accordance with the stated valuation method	Approximate number of different or key items (jobs) in current production
	Gross margin
	Direct labor and overhead to materials put into production
P–7 Usage and movement of inventory is recorded correctly as to account, amount, and period	Percent composition of inventory components
	Material costs to direct labor
	Overhead costs to direct labor
	Units purchased to units sold
P–8 Physical loss of inventory is prevented or promptly detected	Amounts or trends in book-to-physical adjustments
P–9 Obsolete, slow-moving, and overstock inventory is prevented or promptly detected and provided for	Inventory turnover
	Annual unit sales to ending finished inventory quantities
	Number of days of production in ending finished goods inventory
P–10 Inventory is carried at the lower of cost or market	Sales price to net realizable value
	Production or purchase cost to replacement cost
P–15 Depreciation is calculated using proper lives and methods	Depreciation to asset balance
	Allowances for depreciation to asset balance

	Control Objective	*Key Data/Ratios/Relationships*
Finance		
F–1	Cash receipts are recorded correctly as to account, amount, and period and are deposited	Approximate number and average dollar amount of receipts per day
F–2	Cash receipts are properly applied to customer balances	Approximate number and average dollar amount of receipts per day Approximate number of customers
F–3	Cash disbursements are for goods or services authorized and received	Average number of checks issued per month
F–4	Cash disbursements are recorded correctly as to account, amount, and period	Average number of checks issued per month
F–5	Debt and lease obligations and related expenses are authorized and recorded correctly as to account, amount, and period	Interest expense to average borrowing rates and outstanding debt
F–9	Income earned on investments is recorded correctly as to account, amount, and period	Investment income to average investments
Administration		
A–1	Expenses are incurred only with proper authorization	Number of principal suppliers and average dollar amount of business with each Administrative or selling expenses to sales
A–2	Expenses and related liabilities are recorded correctly as to account, amount, and period	Average number and dollar amount of purchases per month Specific expense items to sales
A–3	Salary, wage, and benefit expenses are incurred only for work authorized and performed	Approximate number of employees Administrative payroll to sales Administrative payroll to direct labor
A–4	Salaries, wages, and benefits are calculated at the proper rate	Salaries of key employees Average wage rate for hourly employees Employee benefits to administrative payroll Pension contribution to covered employees
A–5	Salaries, wages, benefits, and related liabilities are recorded correctly as to account, amount, and period	Payroll dollars to number of employees Payroll taxes to gross payroll
A–6	Amortization or loss in value of intangibles is recorded correctly as to account, amount, and period	Amortization to value of intangible Income produced to value of related intangible
A–7	Provisions for income taxes and related liabilities and deferrals are recorded correctly as to account, amount, and period	Income tax expense to pre-tax income Current tax provision to pre-tax income Deferred tax provision to tax expense or change in timing differences State tax provision to tax expense
A–8	Commitments and contingencies are identified, monitored, and if appropriate, recorded or disclosed	Warranty expense to cost of sales or units sold Self insurance reserve to claims paid

INDEX

This book has been set VideoComp System, in 10 and 9 point Palatino, leaded 2 points. Chapter numbers are 36 point Avant Garde Book and chapter titles are 24 point Avant Garde Book. The size of the type page is 35 by 47 picas.